THE IRWIN SERIES IN ECONOMICS

CONSULTING EDITOR

LLOYD G. REYNOLDS
YALE UNIVERSITY

BOOKS IN THE ERWIN SERIES IN ECONOMICS

COMPARATIVE ECONOMIC SYSTEMS

Models and Cases

COMPARATIVE ECONOMIC
SYSTEMS
Models and Cases

EDITED BY MORRIS BORNSTEIN

PROFESSOR OF ECONOMICS
THE UNIVERSITY OF MICHIGAN

1965
RICHARD D. IRWIN, INC.
HOMEWOOD, ILLINOIS

PREFACE

THIS BOOK is about the organization, operation, and performance of economic systems, both in theory and in practice. It deals with alternative methods of determining the bill of goods to be produced, the allocation of resources to produce it, and the distribution of the resulting income. These are some of the most vital questions of our time—urgent issues for all living economies, both non-Communist and Communist, both developed and underdeveloped. This book explores various alternative answers by analyzing different economic systems and comparing them with each other.

This collection of readings is primarily intended for use in college courses in comparative economic systems. It is somewhat unorthodox because it is specifically designed to serve either as collateral reading in conjunction with one of the textbooks in the field, or as the core around which a comparative economic systems course can be organized. With the latter purpose in mind, I have prepared editorial notes for each division, section, and article in the book which integrate the various parts and selections and which place them in an overall conceptual framework. With few exceptions, the selections are articles reprinted in their entirety, rather than isolated excerpts. As a result, they present the author's full argument and at the same time are of an appropriate length for student reading assignments.

The selections in this volume are the fruit of an extensive search of the literature over a number of years in connection with my courses in comparative economic systems at The University of Michigan. They include "classic" articles by the most distinguished figures in the field, as well as lesser known, often overlooked articles by other authors. In many cases, the articles are reprinted from out-of-print volumes or less accessible journals. All of them can be read with understanding and profit by students with a good grasp of the principles of economics. The book is designed for use in courses in comparative economic systems which require only a year's work in economics as a prerequisite. In a few instances, very technical passages, references to foreign language sources, or supplementary statistical tables have been omitted.

This book covers the principal topics included in most college courses in comparative economic systems, although it is impossible in a volume of reasonable size to include all of the topics treated by different instructors in a field as broadly defined as comparative economic systems. The book excludes certain topics which are covered by relatively few instructors, for example primitive economies, as well as other topics on which a considerable variety of material is readily available in inexpensive paperback form, such as the American economy and Marxism.

The various topics in this volume are presented in the order I have found most satisfactory in my courses in comparative economic systems at The University of Michigan. Part I provides a conceptual framework for the rest of the book by explaining the criteria by which the performance of an economy may be judged. Part II presents theoretical models of the three most important economic systems—capitalism, market socialism, and central planning. In Part III these models are illustrated by case studies, respectively, of France, Yugoslavia, and the Soviet Union. France, rather than the United States, was chosen to illustrate capitalism in order to acquaint students with another approach to regulated capitalism than the one with which they are familiar from their previous economics courses. The selections in Part IV compare different economic systems from several standpoints, including the role of money and banking, the nature of management, and the economic system as an instrument of economic development. The concluding selection, which summarizes some of the main points of the book, examines the proposition that Western market and Communist planned economies are becoming more alike.

Although the material is presented in this order, the articles are chosen and the book is constructed so that the selections can logically and conveniently be assigned in several different orders and combinations, to fit the particular instructor's approach to the subject. For example, each of the case studies in Part III can be assigned immediately after the theoretical model in Part II which it illustrates. Some instructors will prefer to discuss the intermediate case of market socialism after presenting the more extreme cases of capitalism and central planning. Others may find it desirable to use the selections on banking and management in different economic systems, in Part IV, in conjunction with the discussion of central planning in Parts II and III. Other suggestions for the use of this volume, in conjunction with existing textbooks or as a core book, are offered in the *Teacher's Manual* to accompany the book.

I wish to express my appreciation to the authors and publishers who kindly granted permission to reprint the selections included in this book. I am indebted to Professors Gregory Grossman and Shanti Tangri for their comments and suggestions about the content and organization of the book. Finally, I am grateful to my wife, Reva, for her encouragement and forbearance during its preparation.

MORRIS BORNSTEIN

ANN ARBOR, MICHIGAN
November, 1964

TABLE OF CONTENTS

PART IV.   SELECTED ASPECTS OF ECONOMIC SYSTEMS

Banking

Management

Economic Development

Convergence of Economic Systems?

PART I

Performance Criteria

An analytical framework for comparing economic systems is essential in the study of comparative economic systems—both economic models and living economies. The most common bases of comparison are (1) the ownership of the means of production and (2) the method of resource allocation. The means of production may be owned privately (individually), as in capitalism, or publicly (collectively), as in socialism. In turn, resources may be allocated by markets through the use of prices, as in a decentralized market economy, or by administrative commands expressed in real (physical) terms, as in a centrally planned economy. And there are various combinations of institutions and instruments; for example, market socialism combines public ownership with the use of markets and prices for decentralized resource allocation decisions. The nature and problems of capitalist and socialist, and market and centrally planned, economies are analyzed in detail in Parts II and III of this book.

In addition to studying similarities and differences in economic institutions and instruments, it is useful also to compare economic systems in terms of some common criteria which may be regarded as "performance" or "success" indicators. This is the approach of the two selections which follow. In the first, Bela A. Balassa offers an analytical framework for comparing economic systems in terms of success criteria and preference systems. In the second, Peter Wiles urges that one of these criteria, economic growth, be given great weight in the social preference system.

Bela A. Balassa

1. SUCCESS CRITERIA FOR ECONOMIC SYSTEMS*

How can the performance of economic systems —either models or actual cases—be compared? Balassa suggests that this can be done by (1) evaluating an economic system in terms of a number of criteria or "success indicators" and (2) combining the resulting "scores" according to a preference scale which expresses the relative importance of the various indicators. He distinguishes and analyzes five success indicators: static efficiency, dynamic efficiency, growth, consumer satisfaction, and income distribution. Some of these indicators are mutually supporting, while others are mutually conflicting. He compares a capitalist market economy and a socialist planned economy in regard to each indicator, showing the difficulty of reaching a clear-cut conclusion about the superiority of one economic blueprint over the other.

The relative importance of these success indicators, and thus the evaluation of an economic system, will, however, depend on whose preferences or scale of values are considered. For example, the preferences of households, expressed through consumer sovereignty in a market economy, are likely to be very different from those of a central planning authority. Balassa points out the shortcomings of both unlimited consumer sovereignty and authoritarian planning as preference systems. (In Selection No. 9, Jan Drewnowski argues that individual and state preferences can and must be combined into a "dual" preference system.)

* Reprinted, with permission, from *The Hungarian Experience in Economic Planning* (New Haven: Yale University Press, 1959), pp. 5–24. Bela A. Balassa is Associate Professor of Economics at Yale University.

Economists have long been concerned with the definition of an economic optimum and with the ways it can be achieved. In the first decade of this century V. Pareto defined an optimum (efficient) position by the requirement that there should not exist any possible reallocation of resources which could make anybody better off without making somebody worse off.[1] One of the conditions of a Pareto optimum is that there should be no possibility of increasing the production of one commodity without reducing the production of another. It has been pointed out that this Pareto optimum is not a single point, that there are many possible positions fulfilling the above criteria. All these optima are positions of general equilibrium.

Pareto optima indicate efficient allocation of resources among alternative uses. It can be shown that—within certain simplifying assumptions—efficient allocation of resources is achieved in pure competition, where the so-called marginal equivalences are fulfilled.[2] But the distribution of income resulting from pure competition may not be considered desirable. It is conventionally assumed that the distribution of income can be changed without impairing efficiency by so-called lump-sum redistributions.[3]

In a static system the fulfillment of the conditions for Pareto optima would supply us with a test of efficiency on the basis of which the performance of different economic systems could be evaluated. Since we do not live in a static world, such a test would not lead us very far. Whereas under static conditions the only variable considered is the efficient allocation of resources at a given point of time, in a dynamic world we have to consider more variables than mere static efficiency; next to it, the dynamic efficiency of the system, the growth rate, consumer satisfaction, and the distribution of income are those of basic importance.[4] Considering these variables as success indicators, the evaluation of different economic systems requires the following:

1. *Success Indicators.* We have to extend the meaning of "efficiency test," since efficiency (static and dynamic) does not exhaust the list of variables on the basis of which a conclusion with regard to different economic systems should be reached. We can assume that different values[5]

---

[1] *Manuel d'économie politique* (Paris, 1909), chap. 6.

[2] For a good exposition of the necessary marginal conditions for an optimum see K. E. Boulding's "Welfare Economics," in *A Survey of Contemporary Economics* (2 vols.; Homewood, Ill.: Richard D. Irwin, Inc., 1948–52), Vol. 2 (ed. B. F. Haley, 1952), pp. 14–23.

[3] Lump-sum redistribution means a system of taxes and subsidies which, not being anticipated, do not affect the individual's effort and risk-taking.

[4] These concepts will be defined and examined in the next section.

[5] By values we mean higher or lower levels of any success indicator, some of which are quantitatively measurable (for example, growth by the percentage rate of increase of national income). Some of these, on the other hand, are not measurable quantitatively (for example, static or dynamic efficiency); for them only ordinal ranking can be used.

of our success indicators can be achieved under conditions postulated in various economic systems. Some of the variables are partly cumulative, in the sense that an increase in A leads to an increase in B (for example, an improvement in dynamic efficiency leads to an increase of the growth rate); some are competitive in the sense that an increase in the value of C leads to a reduction in the value of D (for example, an equal distribution of income is likely to lead to less efficient resource allocation, or a higher growth rate requires restriction of present consumption). Naturally, even for partly cumulative variables there must be at least one other variable which serves as a restraint, that is, the reduction of which is needed for a further increase of the former variable. In technical terms, for any economic system there is a maximum value of any one variable attainable, given the values of the other variables. The maximum values of the success indicators obtained in this way show the performance of the system. For example, an economic system may achieve a higher degree of static efficiency and more equitable income distribution than another system with a higher degree of dynamic efficiency and a higher growth rate.

2. *Scale of Preferences.* There is only one case where there is no difficulty in choosing between two economic systems. That is when in system Z a higher value of all five success indicators can be achieved than in system W. If some of the success indicators show a higher value in one, some in another system, we need additional criteria in order to choose between the systems. One has to decide which success indicators are of greater importance, which have higher priority; in other words, a scale of preferences is needed. The choice between different economic systems should be made on the basis of their proficiency in the various fields enumerated above, given a certain scale of preferences with regard to the success indicators.

We face two questions here: Can we determine theoretically the workings of different economic systems with regard to our success indicators, and can we construct some kind of preference scale on the basis of which the importance of different values of the success indicators can be evaluated? Only if we are able to answer both questions in the affirmative is it possible to present the economist's case with regard to the choice between different systems. But even if this decision can be made, we face the further problem whether these systems can be realized in the real world in their theoretical purity.[6]

---

[6] In technical terms we have to devise a possibility function for the various economic systems, indicating the maximum achievable value of any success indicator given the values of the other variables. Furthermore, a social welfare function is needed to indicate the society's preferences for the various success indicators. That system would be judged to be superior the possibility function of which is tangent to the highest social welfare function.

THE SUCCESS INDICATORS

STATIC EFFICIENCY IN THE ALLOCATION OF RESOURCES

Static efficiency may be defined as production conforming to the preferences of the community[7] when there is no possibility of increasing the production of one commodity without reducing the production of another. It has been pointed out in the last section that static efficiency can be achieved in an economic system organized according to the rules of competition. Consequently, with regard to static efficiency, the real difference is not between a free enterprise and a socialist system but between, on the one hand, free enterprise and the socialist market solution, and on the other, centralized physical planning.

From the analytical point of view the workings of a purely competitive system and of the market solution for socialism, and the results they lead to, are essentially the same. Nevertheless, some analytical differences have already been noted; in addition, two more factors should be considered.

Socialist writers neglect the importance of the cost of information in the socialist market solution. Whereas in pure competition the information needed to reach equilibrium is possessed by the decision-making units, here it must be collected by the Planning Board, and its collection is time-consuming and costly. Although this disadvantage of the socialist market solution is not relevant in its Yugoslav form, the problem of incentives does arise there also. It can be argued that in a static world the profit motive as incentive leads to a more efficient allocation of resources in a free enterprise system than is possible in the competition of socialist firms.[8]

Centralized planning based on the physical allocation of resources dispenses with the price mechanism in resource allocation. Prices do not express relative scarcities in this system but serve only accounting purposes. Consequently, efficient allocation of resources cannot be achieved. On the other hand, the use of pricing in resource allocation would make centralized planning similar to the socialist market solution.

With regard to static efficiency pure competition appears to be superior to centralized planning on the physical level. Nevertheless, there are two

---

[7] "The preferences of the community" may mean either individual preferences or the authoritative decision of the Planning Board with regard to the final bill of goods (goods destined for ultimate consumption or investment). Efficiency as here defined corresponds to the concept of productive efficiency used by T. C. Koopmans, *Three Essays on the State of Economic Science* (New York: McGraw-Hill Book Co., Inc., 1957), p. 84.

[8] For some further problems concerning the operation of the socialist market solution see F. A. Hayek, "Socialist Calculation: The Competitive Solution," *Economica*, New Series, Vol. VII, No. 26 (May, 1940), pp. 125–49 [reprinted in this volume as Chapter 8, pp. 95–115].

types of "market failure"[9] which impair the efficiency of a competitive system: those existing in a static world with perfect information and foresight, and those connected with imperfect information and uncertain expectations.

The first type contains the following factors:

1. Under conditions of increasing returns competition will break down, partly because monopolies will be formed, partly because an optimum position may be reached only if enterprises producing under increasing returns minimize rather than maximize profit.[10]

2. Direct interaction between producers, between consumers, or between producers and consumers which is unaccounted for in market valuations, also impairs the efficiency of the system. A standard example for these external effects between producers is the apple-grower whose orchard blossoms provide food free of charge for the bees of the nearby beekeeper. Although the social productivity of apple-growing is therefore higher than its private productivity, the farmer's production decisions are based on the latter only; hence apple-growing stops short of the social optimum. A classic example of diseconomies in production is smoke nuisance.

3. Market valuation is no better guide in the case of collective goods either. Roads, education, and defense may be mentioned as examples. Proposed solutions are voting or decision by elected authoritative bodies.[11]

The second type of market failure comprises uncertainty and inconsistency of expectations, inertia and resistance to change, and imperfect information. These phenomena have dynamic implications; hence they will be dealt with in connection with dynamic efficiency, below. One further point needs mentioning here, however. Uncertainty and inconsistency of expectations will bring about fluctuations in the employment of resources. In other words, a purely competitive economy will work at least part of the time with less than full utilization of existing resources. Since static efficiency presupposes full resource use, this factor will result in inefficiencies. On the other hand, in a socialist system this form of unemployment may be avoided. Thus the shortcomings of a socialist system so far as static efficiency is concerned are (partly) counteracted by the full utilization of resources.

One final remark: in our discussion the hypothetical conditions of pure

---

[9] To use the convenient expression coined by F. M. Bator in "The Anatomy of Market Failure," *Quarterly Journal of Economics,* Vol. LXXII, No. 3 (August, 1958), pp. 351–88. It should be noted that Bator subsumes all factors belonging to the first type of market failure under the heading "externalities."

[10] See P. A. Samuelson, *Foundations of Economic Analysis* (Cambridge, Mass.: Harvard University Press, 1955), p. 232.

[11] For a solution based on individual preferences see P. A. Samuelson, "Public Expenditure: A Diagrammatic Exposition," *Review of Economics and Statistics,* Vol. XXXVII, No. 4 (November, 1955), pp. 350–56.

competition have been considered and we have disregarded monopolistic elements that impair static efficiency achievable in the blueprint of pure competition. Similarly, possible deviations of actual socialist systems from the theoretical blueprints have been left out of account.

DYNAMIC EFFICIENCY

Static efficiency is concerned with efficient resource allocation at a given point in time; an economic system may exhibit static efficiency even if production is unchanged from year to year. Dynamic efficiency, on the other hand, is concerned with the growth possibilities of an economy. Dynamic efficiency can be indicated by the hypothetical growth rate of national income achievable in different economic systems under identical resource use[12] and saving ratio.[13] (As with static efficiency, we do not require that production conform to individual preferences—it may as well correspond to the preferences of the planners.) The distinction between static and dynamic efficiency has been forcefully expressed in Schumpeter's classical words: "A system—any system, economic or other—that at *every* point of time fully utilizes its possibilities to the best advantage may yet in the long run be inferior to a system that does so at *no* given point of time, because the latter's failure to do so may be a condition for the level or speed of long-run performance."[14]

There is much disagreement on the question whether a free enterprise or a socialist economy is superior with regard to dynamic efficiency. According to Hayek, a higher growth rate could be secured in a free enterprise system "if we assumed that the same restriction of consumption, which has actually taken place [in Russia], had been caused by taxation, the proceeds of which had been lent to competitive industry for investment purposes."[15] The contrary conclusion is reached by, for example, Dobb[16] and Sweezy.[17] Bergson also inclines toward the latter view: "One may imagine that in a highly dynamic economy a Centralist allocation of investment might lead to fewer and smaller errors than a Competitive

---

[12] The term "identical resource use" is employed here as a shorthand expression for identical initial resources and the use of identical amounts of human labor.

[13] In technical terms, whereas static efficiency means that the economy operates on its production-possibility frontier, dynamic efficiency can be represented by the movement of this frontier in northeast direction. For a rigorous treatment of dynamic efficiency under the assumption of constant returns to scale, absence of technological change, and the knowledge of current rates of price changes on the side of the producers, see R. Dorfman, P. A. Samuelson, and R. M. Solow, *Linear Programming and Economic Analysis* (New York: McGraw-Hill Book Co., Inc., 1958), chap. 12.

[14] J. A. Schumpeter, *Capitalism, Socialism, and Democracy* (New York: Harper & Bros., 1942), p. 83. Italics in original.

[15] F. A. Hayek (ed.), *Collectivist Economic Planning* (London: Routledge and Kegan Paul, 1935), p. 205.

[16] Maurice Dobb, *On Economic Theory and Socialism* (New York: International Publishers, 1955), pp. 41–54.

[17] Paul M. Sweezy, *Socialism* (New York: McGraw-Hill Book Co., Inc., 1949), pp. 234–36.

allocation."[18] Although his remarks were addressed to the competitive (market) solution in a socialist economy, they may apply to free enterprise as well.

Some arguments of primary importance with regard to dynamic efficiency in a free enterprise system and in socialism are the following:

1. No conclusive argument can be offered as far as technical progress is concerned. It is widely held that a free enterprise system is more conductive to technical progress than a socialist economy, since both the endeavor to survive and the profit motive greatly contribute to the introduction of new production methods. On the other hand, it has been argued that under conditions of pure competition productive units are too small and the risk of introducing innovations of considerable importance is too great to permit revolutionary changes in technical methods.[19] If so, monopolistic market structures in a free enterprise economy or centralized direction of investments in a socialist system may achieve a higher rate of technical progress. However, a free enterprise economy with competing large production units could combine the advantages of the profit motive with possession of considerable means to finance innovating activity. Yet Schumpeter emphasizes that in large production units technological progress becomes automatic, "innovation itself being reduced to routine."[20] If this is true, the frequently used objection against the socialist system, that salaried employees are not interested in technical progress, loses much of its force.

Although technological change may come about sooner in a free enterprise economy than under socialism, technological progress can be smoother in a planned economy. Under free enterprise, when innovations are made by individual concerns, other firms may offer resistance; or secrecy, patents, etc. may delay the spreading of new production methods.

2. Primarily in underdeveloped countries a dynamic form of external effects is relevant. Investments in transportation facilities or public utilities are frequently unprofitable for the private producer although "profitable" from the viewpoint of social productivity. Investments of this sort, the so-called social overhead, facilitate the establishment of industrial enterprises. Here centralized decision-making has clear advantages. Nevertheless, one could object that central planning should be restricted to the provision for social overhead only and let private initiative do the rest.

---

[18] Abram Bergson, "Socialist Economics," *A Survey of Contemporary Economics*, Vol. 1 (ed. Howard S. Ellis) (Homewood, Ill.: Richard D. Irwin, Inc., 1948), p. 443.

[19] It should be added here that, according to William Fellner, in the absence of uncertainty and incomplete foresight and under the assumption of perfect rationality, technological progress would proceed in the same way under both pure competition and monopoly: "The Influence of Market Structure on Technological Progress," in *Readings in Industrial Organization and Public Policy* (Homewood, Ill.: Richard D. Irwin, Inc., 1958), p. 294.

[20] Schumpeter, *op. cit.*, p. 132.

3. Uncertainty and inconsistency of expectations in a free enterprise framework are frequently mentioned as a serious drag on dynamic efficiency.[21] Under competition, decisions to increase capacity are made separately by each firm, and these plans are coordinated *ex post facto* only, through the market mechanism. The lack of information on investment decisions of other entrepreneurs and the uncertainty of expectations may lead to a slowing down of investment activity because of excessive cautiousness. Furthermore, decisions with regard to the future are likely to clash, resulting in too much or too little investment in a particular field. It seems that the greater the dynamism of a free enterprise system, the higher the possible waste. On the other hand, the Planning Board (or the monopolist) has more information about investment decisions made, and can thereby avoid overlapping. Also, the planning authority may organize and co-ordinate investment activity well in advance. Nevertheless, this argument is not so conclusive as it seems. Thinking in terms of waste, people are liable to forget that waste may be a necessary corollary to progress. The path of growth may be smoother in a socialist economy, but a dynamic free enterprise system may achieve a higher rate of growth even at the expense of greater fluctuations. This is possible if the endeavor to survive and the profit motive overcompensate for the uncertainty and inconsistency of expectations. Moreover, the expectation that innovations will be made by others may act as a compelling rather than a restricting force.

These arguments and counterarguments suggest that the economist cannot make a conclusive judgment on the dynamic efficiency of the blueprints of different economic systems. It should be added that psychological and sociological factors and differences between the blueprint and its actual realization can also be of decisive importance.

GROWTH RATE OF NATIONAL INCOME

Distinction should be made between dynamic efficiency and the actual growth rate of national income.[22] It will be recalled that dynamic effi-

---

[21] Tibor Scitovsky, *Welfare and Competition* (Homewood, Ill.: Richard D. Irwin, Inc., 1951), pp. 233–41.

[22] Two difficulties should be mentioned here in regard to the estimation of the growth rate, although no attempt will be made to evaluate them. First, there is a conceptual problem: the definition of national income. Our results will be different depending on whether we use, for example, the Soviet concept of national income, which is equivalent to the value of material production, or a Western concept, which includes services. Second, there is the problem of measurement: no unequivocal measure of the growth rate can be found. Changes in the proportion of goods with decreasing costs, structural changes in production, new commodities, and quality changes—all make the measurement of the growth rate and the comparison of growth rates in different countries to a considerable degree inconclusive. For an extensive treatment of the problem of measurement see G. W. Nutter, "On Measuring Economic Growth," *Journal of Political Economy*, Vol. LXV, No. 1 (February, 1957), pp. 51–63. Also, "Comment" by H. S. Levine, "Reply" by Nutter, and "Rejoinder" by Levine, in the same journal, Vol. LXVI, No. 4 (August, 1958), pp. 357–63.

ciency was defined as the hypothetical growth rate of national income achievable in different economic systems under identical resource use and saving ratio. The actual growth rate is affected not only by the dynamic efficiency of the system but also by the central authority's action overruling individual preferences in regard to saving versus spending and work versus leisure. Despite dynamic inefficiencies, an economic system may achieve a higher growth rate through an increase in the saving ratio or through an involuntary increase in the amount of labor.

Recently more and more emphasis has been placed on the growth rate. One has the impression that in the eyes of many people the rate of growth is the *sole* success indicator. Much of the recent writing on economic growth as well as a host of political speeches convey the same impression. The dissenting voices—like that of J. K. Galbraith, who contends that "our concern for production is traditional and irrational"[23]—are comparatively few. It is not our concern here to appraise the importance of the growth rate as a success indicator. We shall rather restrict our discussion to the examination of various factors which affect the rate of growth.

In a free enterprise economy, saving is determined by the preferences of the individuals and by corporate saving. In a socialist economy, the central authorities decide what part of national income will be used for investment purposes. The possibility of enforcement of a higher saving ratio in a socialist state makes a higher rate of growth feasible. To quote Fellner: "A totalitarian government, if it could establish itself in a country such as the United States, might not find it difficult to operate the economy at a level of consumption 20 to 25 per cent lower than our present consumption level, and then let consumption rise slowly with the rise of aggregate output. By such a policy, the present American net capital formation could be *more than doubled*, and it is quite likely that the annual economic growth rate of the United States could be *almost* doubled."[24]

The disadvantage of a free enterprise system with regard to the proportion of national income invested can be offset by taxation, the proceeds of which could be lent to individuals for investment purposes, as envisaged by Hayek. But would Hayek really advocate such a policy; would he plead for encroachment upon the individual's freedom to consume or save at will? In view of his doctrine implying the undesirability of forced saving,[25] this is not very likely. But we should not forget that many representatives of "bourgeois" economics have regarded forced saving, brought about by having wage increases lag behind price rises, as a necessary condition for capitalist development.[26]

---

[23] J. K. Galbraith, *The Affluent Society* (Boston: Houghton Mifflin Co., 1958), p. 132.

[24] William Fellner, *Trends and Cycles in Economic Activity* (New York: Holt, Rinehart & Winston, Inc., 1956), p. 73. Italics in original.

[25] See his *Prices and Production* (London: Routledge and Kegan Paul, 1931).

[26] For example, J. M. Keynes, *A Treatise on Money* (2 vols.; New York: Harcourt, Brace & Co., 1930), Vol. 2, pp. 152–63.

We should deal here also with a frequent misunderstanding according to which an enforced increase in saving constitutes a sacrifice on the part of the present generation, the beneficiaries of which will be our descendants only. This is not necessarily true. It can be shown that under certain assumptions the centrally determined increase in saving will lead to an increase in the well-being of the present generation not accounted for in the individual saver's decision. Savings, if invested, may have a "complementarity effect" on wages that is not foreseen by the individual saver. Let us assume that there is sufficient technological change to counteract the fall of the interest rate that would result from an increase in the stock of capital under unchanged technology. Such being the case, the wage rate will rise (because of the increase in capital stock) with interest rate unchanged. Consequently, as soon as the addition to the capital stock has been completed, the savers will enjoy an additional—and at the time of saving unexpected—benefit in the form of wage increases. This complementarity effect appears as an argument for interference with the amount of saving based on individual preferences.

It is another question if we assume that the amounts invested will be used less productively in a centrally planned economy. Such a situation might arise from bureaucratic mismanagement or from the absence of a sufficient guide—in the form of the interest rate—for the comparison of investment alternatives. But even if this assumption is made, our problems would still not be solved. Let us assume the following hypothetical situation: in a socialist economy the saving ratio is 20 per cent, one-fourth of investment is "wasted" (because of the above-mentioned factors), and the growth rate is 6 per cent. Now in a free enterprise economy let us postulate a saving ratio of 10 per cent, no waste in investment, and a 4 per cent growth rate. How are we to decide the merits and demerits of these two hypothetical economies? We need some kind of "preference scale" to evaluate them, and Hayek's preference scale will surely differ from Dobb's.

The central authority may also overrule individual preferences in regard to work and leisure. It can enforce an increase in the amount of work performed: by forced labor, by an enforced extension of labor-hours, or by indirect pressure through the reduction of real wages to raise the number of workers per family. Such practices will lead to a higher growth rate at the expense of leisure.

Consumer Satisfaction

In discussing the three success indicators examined above, we have postulated that production should correspond to the preferences of the community, which may mean individual preferences as well as those of the planners. In other words, in evaluating these indicators no distinction has been made between a system based on consumer sovereignty and one based on autocratic decisions. We have disregarded the problem of *who* decides the goals of the economy and considered only *how* and *whether* these goals are attained. It can be said that the first three indicators are free from value judgments. Advancing consumer satisfaction as the fourth indicator, we introduce the possibility of making value judgments in evaluating the performance of various economic systems. It should be noted, however, that the above duality of the success indicators (individuals' or planners' preferences) can be further retained: although consumer satisfaction may serve as an indicator, the planners will assign zero value to it if they decide to disregard it completely. On the other hand, this indicator makes it possible to differentiate between the performance of economic systems based on consumer sovereignty and those based on autocratic decisions. If two economic systems achieve the same degree of static and dynamic efficiency and the same growth rate, the one based on consumer sovereignty will be judged as more desirable if consumer satisfaction is regarded as an objective. Three factors can be said to contribute to consumer satisfaction: (1) correspondence of production targets to individual preferences, (2) correspondence of the actual saving ratio to the saving ratio desired by individuals, and (3) correspondence of actual work performed to individuals' preferences for work versus leisure.

Consumer satisfaction in its last-mentioned two forms does not affect static and dynamic efficiency but can be regarded as a constraint to the growth rate. We have seen that, given the dynamic efficiency of an economy, the rate of growth can be increased only by overruling individual preferences with regard to saving versus spending and work versus leisure. Such a decision entails a diminution of consumer satisfaction. In other words, given dynamic efficiency, an increase in the growth rate of national income requires loss of satisfaction on the part of the individuals. In the von Neumann model maximization of the growth rate presupposes that the population is being held on the subsistence level: the portion of national income above the amount necessary for subsistence is reinvested.[27] In this study we consider the direct or indirect pressure on the part of the central authority to increase the work performed as a further factor that increases the growth rate and reduces consumer satisfaction.

The level of consumer satisfaction reached can be indicated by the living standards of the population. In appraising this we have to take into account whether the goods produced are those desired by individuals, and also have to consider leisure. For a longer period, the temporal change in living standards should be considered. In this connection it should be noted that over a period sufficiently long to enable the population to enjoy the results of investment activity, a high growth rate may raise future consumption. Yet this is not necessarily so: if, for example, the planners regard the increase of military capacity as their primary objective, a high growth rate will be accompanied by a permanent restriction in consumption.

---

[27] See Dorfman et al., op. cit., p. 296.

DISTRIBUTION OF INCOME

In the works of economists following Pareto, income distribution has been said not to affect efficiency. It is assumed that once an efficient allocation of resources has been reached, income distribution can be changed at will, without impairing efficiency, by the use of lump-sum redistribution. But this is far from being true. Lump-sum redistribution is not only impractical; in a dynamic economy even lump-sum measures will affect efficiency. Lump-sum taxes and subsidies altering income distribution in one period will affect the amount of work supplied and risk-taking in the succeeding periods, which, in turn, will affect the dynamic efficiency of the economy.

Consequently, income distribution in its impact on effort and risk-taking has considerable effect on the other success indicators and primarily on the efficiency of the system. It can rightly be assumed that if risk-taking and superior performance are not properly rewarded, the efficiency of the economic system will suffer. On the other hand, income distribution is not only one of the factors affecting other success indicators but a success indicator in itself. The distinguishing characteristic of this indicator is that we need a value judgment in determining what kind of income distribution is desirable and how different distributions are valued. A may prefer an equal distribution of income, B may give priority to distribution on the basis of productivity, the problem of unearned incomes enters the picture, natural scarcities complicate the issue, etc.[28] The economist can hardly do more than state the fact that income distribution is one of the success indicators which influence the other variables in the economic system, when evaluation of the desirability of different income distributions cannot be made without invoking value judgments.

WHOSE PREFERENCES?

We have now examined the five success indicators which would provide a way to measure the performance of different economic systems. Let us assume for the moment that the values and relationships of these variables for various economic systems are known. As has been seen, we then face the problem of devising some kind of preference scale on the basis of which the values of the success indicators can be rated. The question arises, whose preferences should be relied upon? Two extreme cases may be mentioned: we may say that the decisions of individuals should be considered, or we may rely on a paternalistic authority whose decisions overrule consumers' preferences.

---

[28] For conflicting interpretations of the concept "just distribution" cf. T. J. B. Hoff, *Economic Calculation in the Socialist Society* (London: Hodge, 1949), pp. 34 ff.

The Case for and against Consumer Sovereignty

Consumer sovereignty may mean two things: (*a*) Consumers are free to choose among the commodities available, or (*b*) Consumers are able to guide production decisions via their demand for consumer goods. The first alternative must be rejected, since it is compatible with central determination of quantities produced of various consumer goods; here the consumer market is only a rationing device to distribute the given amount of goods among consumers. On the other hand, the second alternative means that consumer decisions should regulate the allocation of resources among alternative uses.

If we unconditionally accept consumer sovereignty as the guiding rule, there is no problem of evaluating the various success indicators, since a free enterprise economy with no government intervention would result in such values of these variables that correspond to the individuals' wishes. But are consumers' preferences a reliable guide? Consumer sovereignty has been exalted by many exponents of free enterprise as a measure of freedom. Nevertheless, free consumers' choice can be ensured in a socialist economy as well; the proponents of the market solution also favor consumer sovereignty and reject the authoritative decision-making of the Planning Board with regard to consumer goods.[29]

The doctrine of consumer sovereignty is based on two assumptions. First, it is maintained that it is morally right that the consumer decide what should be produced and what proportion of national income should be saved, and the consumer's decision is realized on the market by "voting," where money serves as a "ballot"; second, it is assumed that there is no interaction in consumption, and consumer demand is determined by factors independent of production. The following qualifications are intended to show the inadequacies in these assumptions and the limitations of the doctrine of consumer sovereignty.[30]

1. It has been pointed out by many that the existing distribution of wealth and income cannot be regarded as desirable. The "ballots" in the possession of the individuals are only partly the result of one's own productive activity. In Knut Wicksell's words: "There is one inequality from which we can never abstract, without making a serious mistake, namely social differences and the unequal distribution of property."[31] If this is so, state intervention is needed to change the quantity of "ballots" in the hands of some individuals.

[29] Cf. A. P. Lerner, "Economic Theory and Socialist Economy," *Review of Economic Studies,* Vol. II, No. 1 (October, 1934), pp. 53–54; Oskar Lange, "On the Economic Theory of Socialism," in Benjamin E. Lippincott (ed.), *On the Economic Theory of Socialism* (Minneapolis: University of Minnesota Press, 1938), pp. 93–95.

[30] Market imperfections on the production side have already been dealt with above.

[31] Knut Wicksell, *Lectures on Political Economy* (2 vols.; London: Routledge and Kegan Paul, 1934), Vol. I, p. 77.

2. Against the assumption that consumer wants are independent of production, the social determination of individual tastes and wants has been argued. To quote Samuelson: "Individual tastes and wants are socially conditioned by advertising and custom so that they can hardly be said to belong to him in any ultimate sense."[32] Galbraith uses the analogy of the squirrel wheel: the squirrel (production) moves upward but the wheel turns—that is, individuals, acquiring new tastes, consume the newly produced goods.[33]

Consumption being, in part, socially determined (either by advertising or by the consumption of others), it cannot be said that consumer demand is an independent factor; one can even argue that state intervention may be needed to correct socially conditioned consumer wants.

3. Collective consumption presents similar problems. It has been noted before that a considerable part of national income is spent on goods which are consumed not individually but by the society. Education, road construction, defense, and internal security are the most conspicuous examples. The market mechanism cannot be used to determine the quantity of goods collectively consumed. Galbraith remarks that there is a tendency in the present-day United States to belittle the importance of collective consumption, which is partly due to the conditioning of demand for private goods by advertising.[34] The need for a proper balance between private and collective goods has been emphasized by James Tobin: "Government dollars spent for such things as fire and police protection, education, postal service, highways, parks, hospitals, libraries, sanitation and flood control, need have no inferiority complex with respect to private dollars spent for steaks, television, freezers, alcohol, horse racing, gasoline, comic books, and golf."[35] The need for collective consumption arises from indivisibilities; another form of interpersonal relations appears in the external effects of consumption. One person's consumption may increase the satisfaction of another person (an increase in the telephone network is a good example), or may reduce someone else's well-being (for example, boisterous behavior caused by excessive drinking).

4. Another qualification is connected with the problem of time horizon. Forming their plans, individuals consider time periods of differing lengths for which plans are made. The implications of the clash of individual decisions on time horizon and on investments have been explored by Jan Graaf, who maintains that "these are not decisions which households, acting separately, are equipped to make . . . Politics—or paternalism—is involved."[36]

---

[32] Samuelson, *op. cit.*, p. 224.

[33] Galbraith, *op. cit.*, p. 156.

[34] *Ibid.*, chap. 18.

[35] James Tobin, "The Eisenhower Economy and National Security: Two Views. I. Defense, Dollars and Doctrine," *Yale Review*, Vol. 47 (1958), p. 329.

[36] Jan Graaf, *Theoretical Welfare Economics* (Cambridge, Eng.: Cambridge University Press, 1957), chap. 6.

5. A. C. Pigou contends that preference for present goods does not imply that the utility of present consumption is greater than the utility of future consumption. In his opinion mankind's "telescopic faculty" is perverted in the sense that, apart from the fact that we do not attach sufficient importance to the welfare of future generations, we are unable to size up our future satisfactions from future goods. In Pigou's words: "the aggregate amount of economic satisfaction which people in fact enjoy is much less than it would be if their telescopic faculty were not perverted, but equal (certain) satisfactions were desired with equal intensity whatever the period at which they are destined to emerge."[37] Consequently Pigou advocates state intervention in saving, since "economic welfare could be increased by some rightly chosen degree of differentiation *in favour* of saving."[38] The idea of man's telescopic faculty crops up also in the writings of some socialist authors, for example in the works of Dobb.[39] Reference should also be made to the previously mentioned complementarity effect, which is independent of man's telescopic faculty.

6. Another argument is that we are inconsiderately using up coal and other scarce natural resources; hence state intervention is needed to preserve such resources. This argument certainly has importance, for example in the case of forests. In other cases it appears to be somewhat overrated: Jevons' fears about the exhaustion of coal reserves have not been realized, because of the substitution of other sources of energy for coal.

On the basis of all these arguments one comes to the conclusion that consumer sovereignty in its pure form cannot serve as a guiding rule in evaluating different economic systems. We turn now to its very opposite: the paternalistic solution.

The Paternalistic Solution

The unconditional acceptance of consumer sovereignty lurks behind advocacy of complete freedom from state intervention. At the other extreme, it is asserted that the planning authority knows the individuals' and the community's needs better than the individuals themselves. The central authority appears, according to this view, to be omniscient and omnipotent. A typical expression of this view can be found in the *History of the Communist Party of the Soviet Union:* "The power of the Marxist-Leninist theory lies in the fact that it enables the party to find the orientation in any situation, to understand the inner connection of current events, to foresee their course and to perceive not only how and in what

---

[37] A. C. Pigou, *The Economics of Welfare* (London: Macmillan, 1932), p. 26.

[38] *Ibid.,* p. 29. Italics in original.

[39] Maurice Dobb, *Political Economy and Capitalism* (New York: International Publishers, 1945), p. 309.

direction they are developing in the present, but how and in what direction they are bound to develop in the future."[40]

If this is so, why do we need individual preferences? Can't we leave everything to be determined by the infallible authority—the Party? Some Western socialists adhering to the centralist solution put the manner more mildly, calling authoritarian decisionmaking "a diet prescribed by a doctor to a patient."[41] On the other hand, for those who rightly reject totalitarian schemes and the idea of the infallible central authority assistance is furnished by proponents of the socialist market solution. Lange writes, on the abrogation of consumer sovereignty: "Mr. Lerner has sufficiently shown the undemocratic character of such a system and its incompatibility with the ideals of the socialist movement. Such a system would scarcely be tolerated by any civilized people."[42]

A COMPROMISE?

We have attempted to find criteria on the basis of which the relative importance of our success indicators could be evaluated and the merits and demerits of different economic systems judged. We have seen that this evaluation can be made either by unconditionally accepting consumer sovereignty or by letting a central authority decide the issues. In the first case the market would automatically supply the answer; in the second case a central authority would make the decision. But these extreme cases do not stand up to searching criticism. It may be suggested that in some form or other we should rank and weigh individual preferences in regard to the success indicators. A may think that the efficient allocation of resources is the measure of success for an economic system, B may give priority to the growth rate, C may favor an equal distribution of income; but is it possible to strike an average of supposedly widely differing opinions? Can we construct a preference scale for the whole community based on individual preferences? The answer is in the negative. It would require a "superman" to compare and rank the preferences of individuals; hence the community's preference scale in regard to the success indicators cannot be devised.

CONCLUSION

We can conclude, then, that economic arguments are not sufficient to make a choice between economic systems—in the present case between the blueprints of a free enterprise and of a socialist system. Two reasons have

---

[40] (New York: International Publishers, 1939), p. 355. This book was officially ascribed to Stalin and until recently was regarded as one of the holy books in the Communist orbit.

[41] Dobb, *Political Economy and Capitalism, op. cit.,* pp. 307–14.

[42] Lange, *op. cit.,* p. 95. Cf. Lerner, *op. cit.,* pp. 51–61.

been established: we cannot determine the performance of the various blueprints with regard to the five success indicators, and we are unable to construct a scale of preferences which would give the ranking of different values of the success criteria. Moreover, even if the relative merits and demerits of the blueprints of various economic systems could be judged, their actual realization shows substantial deviations from the theoretical construction. Also as a result of sociological and psychological factors, a free enterprise blueprint may work better in one and worse in another country. Similar considerations are relevant with regard to a socialist blueprint.

Not only do noneconomic factors influence the workings of an economic system, but noneconomic objectives may also modify any results reached by the use of our success indicators. The planners may set targets that are in no way connected with the economic performance of a system. A dictator may be interested exclusively in increasing his power and may disregard economic considerations. Political objectives may exclude the use of efficiency prices if the central authorities do not want to disseminate information on the relative valuation of military and consumer goods. Furthermore, the objective of centralization in decision-making for fear of sabotage on lower levels may hinder the decentralization of production decisions. In all these cases, noneconomic "success indicators" would appear on the scene. Nevertheless, we do not include these indicators in our model, since they are not amenable to evaluation by economic tools and would bring a considerable degree of vagueness into the discussion.

Although our success indicators do not give much help in evaluating the blueprints of various economic systems, they can be useful in appraising the performance of real-world economies. In the examination of any economy two questions can be raised: How does the actual working of the economy differ from the blueprint? How does the economy under consideration "score" in terms of our success indicators?

Peter Wiles[1]

2. GROWTH VERSUS CHOICE*

*Analyzing the conflict between the success in-
dicators of "growth" and "choice," Wiles argues
that the former should be given much more
weight than it is usually accorded. Rapid growth
of per capita output, he asserts, is more important
than "choice" in the sense of consumer sovereignty or in the sense of efficiency in resource
allocation. Rapid growth can provide consumer
satisfaction without consumer sovereignty, and
it can compensate for misallocation of resources.*

POLITICAL INTRODUCTION

ECONOMIC growth is beginning to reoccupy a central position in economics—in theory though not yet in practice—that it has not had since
Adam Smith. This re-instatement is very right, since growth is obviously
the "best" thing that can happen in economics—better than Free Trade or
the attainment of the optimum allocation of resources between competing
ends or even full employment. This can be very simply shown: the prime
end of economic man is material plenty, he wants to have as much of
everything as possible. But in order that this state of affairs should be
achieved the economy must grow, *i.e.*, production per head must be
increased. Growth is then, by definition, the *sine qua non* for the attainment of the supreme end, and therefore itself supreme. It is, and should be,
a cuckoo in the nest of economic topics. This article will survey its
relation to one other topic only: that of choice or scarcity economics.

We must inquire first as to the optimum rate of growth. At the present
time, in the cold war, the purposes of propaganda, foreign policy and
military strategy require that the rate of economic growth in NATO

---

[1] Parts of this article were read as a paper to the British Association in September,
1954. I am indebted for criticisms and corrections to Miss P. Ady and Messrs. N. H.
Leyland and G. B. Richardson.

* Reprinted, with the permission of the author and the Royal Economic Society,
from *Economic Journal*, Vol. LXVI, No. 262 (June, 1956), pp. 244–55. Peter Wiles is
Professor of Economics at Brandeis University.

countries should not fall below that in the Communist countries: say 5% per annum in the real net national income. Actually Soviet growth is at 6% per annum,[2] but doubtless Chinese is slower than that, and it would suffice to double the 2½ characteristic of a healthy average non-Communist economy. Are such hardships really necessary, it may be asked? Is not our present economic superiority enough? Out of our superfluity we are to-day in fact spending more than the Communists on re-armament, and investing much more than they in the neutralist backward areas. But although we can beat the Communists at that today, they are growing twice as fast as we and will be able to beat us tomorrow. The cold war will last a very long time. Only by outgrowing the enemy can we keep on winning it. Nor does it suffice that backward areas only should achieve such rates of growth. For so long as they remain free they can only grow by importing capital, and the capital required is so enormous that the advanced countries cannot provide it without themselves growing, especially as they must be able *easily* to provide it, in the face of Communist competition to do so. Moreover, to argue only in terms of backward-area growth is to forget the need for superiority in armaments.

INDEFINITE GROWTH

So much for politics. On pure welfare grounds, however, the question is much more complicated, and we shall not discuss it here, except to stress that the *maximization* of growth would be very unpleasant indeed for the generation then alive. The ideal rate is less than that,[3] though there is little reason on the demand side to suppose that growth should begin to fall off in any foreseeable future. That is to say, we need not here consider the possibility of an "exhaustion of consumption opportunities," of a near approach to what the Communists call full Communism. This is when productivity is so great that all consumer needs can be satisfied, even if not clothed in effective demand. Leisure increases to almost intolerable proportions, money falls out of use, and we all go and help ourselves in the shops. Choice and scarcity cease to be a problem, and economics to be a worthwhile study. Such a state of affairs, if possible at all, is obviously very far off indeed. We deal here with the intervening period.

---

[2] The pre-war rate (1928–37). Cf. Grossman in *Soviet Economic Growth* (ed. A. Bergson), pp. 5–12. In 1948–50 the rate of growth was much greater: Jasny, *Social Research*, Spring 1954, pp. 37–38. The current United States rate (1948/49 to 1952/53) is a mere 3% per annum. The British rate is about 2%. All these figures are, of course, lower if taken per head: by 1% in Britain, 1.5% in the U.S.S.R. and the United States. Such a comparison, relating to economies in entirely different states of maturity, is not, of course, to be taken as ranging them in any order of merit. For that purpose it would be necessary so far as possible to compare the three economic systems at the same stage of maturity. This I have done very briefly in *Foreign Affairs*, July 1953. In fact, the same order of merit emerges. In its youth the Soviet economy has grown faster than any other young economy recorded; must we not suppose, then, the same of its middle age?

[3] Cf. F. P. Ramsey, *Economic Journal*, 1928.

In dismissing this interesting problem as beyond our purview, and in insisting that mature capitalist economies can and must grow as fast as immature Communist ones, I imply that on the supply side economic growth curves are not S-shaped but exponential or at any rate linear. Population growth curves may—and do—have almost any shape. Growth should, however, be defined for most purposes as growth in productivity. This in turn depends, so long as there is unemployment of any sort, on capital widening (which increases production per head, of course, but not per worker); and on technical progress (the lowering of the real cost of output), whether or not there is unemployment. Now so long as mere capital widening can take up unemployed or under-employed workers— for instance the flow of Soviet peasants into an ill-organized and inefficient industry during the first Five Year Plan—or so long as there remains great technical leeway to make up, growth can be very rapid indeed. These initial advantages of immaturity exhausted, the rate falls, as it now depends solely on new technical progress. But the fall occurs once for all, and there is no reason at all why the new moderate rate of growth should further taper off. This is not only evident from the actual history of growth in mature countries (neglecting periods of war and slump), but also from the nature of technical progress. For in so far as "inventions" or "innovations" can be made into statistically comparable units, research shows that their growth curve is exponential.[4] Whether this will always be so, whether the sum of economically applicable scientific knowledge hitherto undiscovered is finite, is another question. Enough that there is no sign whatsoever of this.[5] *A priori*, it is difficult to see why an exponential curve in the acquisition of cost-reducing or product-innovating knowledge should lead to an S-shaped curve in the rise of productivity. Yet in a mature economy productivity depends in the long run almost solely on knowledge.

GROWTH AND INVESTMENT

Another proposition must also be laid down at the start: *the prime cause of growth of output per head is investment.* This is not obvious and may not be, as it so often is, simply assumed. Clearly of course capital widen-ing—the mere accumulation[6] of durable assets similar to those already in existence—is by definition an increase in the quantity of resources available

---

[4] Ogburn and Nimkoff, *Handbook of Sociology*, p. 525. Compare Ffrangcon Roberts, *The Cost of Health*, pp. 55–56.

[5] I am also unable to say *a priori* whether finiteness is more probable than infinity here. It is difficult to see how to begin to reason on such a question.

[6] How much more revealing, incidentally, is the Communist phrase, "capital accumulation," than the Keynesian "investment"—which is to be sure, more general. "Investment" connotes getting rid of surplus savings, keeping up full employment somehow or other. It leads one to think of the allocation of income, and of the short run generally. It deflects one's attention from the ensuing increase in productivity and/or production. "Capital accumulation" has none of these associations. It simply connotes growth.

for production; it is like the discovery of new land. Its usefulness is severely limited, as we have seen, by the quantity of the labor force—not, of course, by that of the total consuming population. There is no use— quite the reverse, indeed—in capital widening if there are no un- or under-employed to man the new machines. So when the labor force is fully used, growth of output per head is very largely due to the discovery *and application* of new techniques, new minerals, new plants, etc.

Now some writers[7] set technical progress over against, not only capital widening in particular, but investment in general, as a superior cause of growth. Superior maybe, but not separate. For investment is the ugly but indispensable handmaiden of nearly all technical progress. First both the discovery and the application of new techniques and materials require a great deal of money, *i.e.*, of savings. In other words, though quite different from the multiplication, improvement or renewal of capital assets, research is investment.[8] And as research goes on we find that all the easiest discoveries have already been made. Though the remaining field of knowledge is surely infinite, and for all we know that of economically useful knowledge too (see above), new discoveries become more costly. More and more equipment, and ever less intelligent assistants with ever longer and more specialized training, are drawn in.

Technical education is a too often forgotten corollary of research; forgotten, no doubt, in part because it is foolishly entered as consumption in the national income accounts. Whatever we may think of elementary education and of arts degrees, which benefit citizenship and culture quite as much as productivity, technical education is surely a kind of investment. The fragmentation of knowledge, as we have seen, demands ever longer courses from more and more, and therefore less intelligent, students.[9] Research and technical education, then, will surely claim an ever larger share of the national income.[10]

Thirdly, there is always an immense lag in the application of new techniques between the best and the worst firms. This is not to be cured by a once for all spurt in investment, since a backward firm changes its technique not only later but also less often than a progressive one. The more technical progress there is, the more obsolescence there is. This, too, increases the need for capital.

---

[7] Principally Professor Cairncross, in his important "The Place of Capital in Economic Progress" (*International Social Science Bulletin*, UNESCO, 2/1954; this number also contains an admirable bibliography on economic growth).

[8] In 1947–52 in the United States 0.8% of the G.N.P. was spent on research, or from 6 to 8% of business expenditure on new plant (National Science Foundation, *Federal Funds for Research and Development 1952* (Washington, 1953)).

[9] Cf. Ffrangcon Roberts, *op. cit.*, pp. 71–74.

[10] Neglecting, as we must for lack of adequate research, questions of quality, we must note that Britain lags behind many advanced countries in the number of her technical students. And these in turn, as is so depressingly usual, lag behind the Communist countries (Benjamin Fine, *New York Times*, November 7, 1954).

Even the mere rationalization of an industry or the re-deployment of labor within a factory requires some saving to finance it. There are, perhaps, only two serious causes of economic growth that are free of investment costs. The first is the supposed capital-saving trend of modern, as opposed to Victorian, technical progress. Taking years of full employment only, the ratio of national capital to income in the United States has fallen by about 40% since the all-time high of 1911–14.[11] But we have no good ground for extrapolating the course of this ratio in any particular direction. Moreover, the fall is exaggerated by, and may even wholly result from, the omission of consumers' durables from the national capital. Finally, comparable figures for Britain show no such trend.[12]

The second possible cause of growth without capital costs is an increase in the worker's will to work or the adoption by the manager of the American attitude to costs, innovation and output, both so constantly recommended by the Anglo-American productivity teams. But this is clearly the least hopeful of all solutions to the whole problem, since it cannot be applied administratively at all, but is purely a matter of sociology and propaganda—the cost of which would also be an investment! It is fair to claim that investment solutions are quicker and easier. We must therefore increase the *absolute total* of investment, though not necessarily, perhaps, its proportion to the national income for very long.

Naturally all solutions must be applied together. A country that applies both the sociological and the investment solutions (U.S.S.R.) will outgrow one that applies only the sociological (United States), just as that country will outgrow us, who apply neither.[13]

We shall not broach here the question of the direction of investment: should it be, for instance, in industry, where owing to the low capital coefficient a little investment leads to much growth, or in public utilities, where the capital coefficient is high and growth correspondingly slow? Or, more significant, should it be in capital goods making consumer goods (*e.g.*, looms) or in capital goods making capital goods (*e.g.*, machine tools)? The latter naturally leads to far higher rates of growth; indeed, without it no sustained growth is possible at all. We use here the word "investment" as a catch-all, neglecting this extremely important distinction. It is no part of my argument, then, that investment is the sole determinant of growth or that its rate stands in any definite relationship to

---

[11] Domar, source as for Cairncross.

[12] Phelps-Brown, *Economic Journal*, 1953. Mr. Redfern's figures for Britain do show a slight downward trend, but they, too, omit technical education and consumers' durables (*Economist*, January 22, 1955).

[13] *Saving* (defined to cover productive net investment, armaments and the personal consumption of the armed forces, but not depreciation) was the following percentages of net national income at factor cost: U.K., 18% in 1948, 21% in 1951; U.S.A., 20% in 1950; U.S.S.R., 31% in 1937, 41% in 1948. Cf. A. Bergson and H. Heymann, *Soviet National Income and Product, 1940–1948*, pp. 24–25, 70–71. The Soviet figures are exceedingly speculative and controversial.

the rate of growth. Enough merely that, if defined to include expenditure on the acquisition of knowledge, it is a—indeed the only—necessary condition of growth: that it is also sometimes a sufficient condition, and that in any case the more investment there is, the more growth there is.

SCARCITY ECONOMICS AND HESITANCY

In this and the following sections we discuss the effect of growth-consciousness upon scarity economics. Too delicate a comprehension of "scarity" problems, a determination never to violate Professor Lerner's welfare equations for however short a period or in however unimportant a connection, slows up the rate of growth. For it leads to hesitation, whether on the part of the government or of the individual entrepreneur, before investing, even sometimes before beginning current production. It creates an atmosphere hostile to rationalization, standardization and mass production, and thus interferes with the technical efficiency of whatever is, despite all hesitation, produced.

This applies more especially to underdeveloped countries. Thus Professor Nurkse has emphasized the need for balanced growth:[14]

> . . . the difficulty caused by the small size of the market relates to individual investment incentives in any single line of production taken by itself. At least in principle, the difficulty vanishes in the case of a more or less synchronized application of capital to a wide range of different industries. Here is an escape from the deadlock; here the result is an overall enlargement of the market. . . . Experience has certainly shown that large-scale public investment plans, in their practical execution if not in their conception, often have a tendency to develop a marked lack of balance.

True, but balance means investing at the pace of the slowest: either of the slowest entrepreneur, which means a snail's pace, or of the slowest-spending government department, which is not quick enough. The balance problem is but a special case of the scarcity problem,[15] and we have here again the dichotomy: good resource allocation versus rapid growth. There can be too much worry about balance. Moderate inflation would tide over many of these temporary difficulties.

All this has been hinted at by Professor Kindleberger,[16] who complains that colonial developers tend to compare their client country with a fully developed one, and noting all the differences "subtract the former from the latter. The difference is a program." The desire for balanced development bogs them down in all sorts of pettifogging detail. It also bogs down

---

[14] *Problems of Capital Formation in Underdeveloped Countries*, pp. 11–17.

[15] It is not, as presented by Professor Nurkse, a matter of physical bottlenecks, which would be more serious (if there were no foreign exchange), but of markets, *i.e.*, of choice.

[16] *Review of Economics and Statistics*, November 1952, p. 391.

the execution of the program. The conclusion is clearly that Soviet development technique is more effective: choose a few "leading branches" and concentrate on them. The details and the secondary industries can catch up later. The fact that such a program is unbalanced and violates "scarcity" rules matters less than its superior speed.

SCARCITY ECONOMICS AND THE MEASUREMENT OF GROWTH

All this is by no means to say that we must not consider "scarcity" when investing in new projects or undertaking technical research, for without *some* consideration of the due proportion between one article and another growth may not be growth at all. Thus in a starving community a 10% per annum rise in industrial production combined with a 1% fall in agricultural production—the two being of roughly equal value to start with—may truly be called on grounds of "scarcity" not growth at all but diminution. That is, the Laspeyres index of production, which weights industrial and agricultural products by the scarcity relationships of the initial year, is wholly misleading, and for welfare purposes only the Paasche index applies; and with a suitable choice of the present-year weights this index can easily be arranged to show a fall. This indeed is what might fairly be claimed on welfare grounds for the planned economy in Stalin's life-time, although on strategic grounds we have only too good a reason to know that Laspeyres' index, which gives a heavy weight to the increase in military production, is correct enough.

GROWTH AND CONSUMER SOVEREIGNTY

"Scarcity," however, is not the same thing as consumer sovereignty. Wherever "the man in Whitehall (or the Kremlin) knows best" consumer sovereignty is, of course, in abeyance, although resources continue to be scarce *vis-à-vis* competing ends—the manifold, even when properly co-ordinated, ends of Whitehall. There is, of course, no reason why the man in Whitehall should not on occasion know best, and it is mere dema-goguery to suggest the opposite. In particular, the voluntary decision of the consumer to save, without which there can under *laissez faire* be neither investment to promote economic growth nor personal security for the individual, is by any reasonable standards always too low in the modern world; except of course when decisions to invest are even lower, causing unemployment. But the talk should always be of under-investment, not over-saving. The latter phrase has the most harmful anti-growth connota-tions. The "expansionary way out," beloved of Keynesians, is not at all to save less but to invest more. Even when there is deflation, savings are still in an important sense too small: they are smaller than the volume of investment that there ought to be. Though this is not, of course, to deny that in such circumstances an attempt to save less would actually increase investment, up to the level of full employment.

To this irrationality must be added one which follows from competition among consumers, or among producers. This is that the technical specifications laid down by the uncoordinated purchasers of final or intermediate goods, each thinking only of himself, usually pay too little attention to the economies of rationalization and standardization; while the producers, engaged in a struggle for goodwill under imperfect competition, may be aware of these economies but cannot individually enforce them. Here too, then, the man in Whitehall—or the promoter of the merger—knows best. Only by excluding this latter aspect of consumer sovereignty is it possible to satisfy the consumer to the fullest extent out of any given quantity of resources. Only, perhaps, by forced saving can resources be increased, to the consumer's still greater ultimate good. For it is consumer *satisfaction* not sovereignty that is the essence of welfare economics. The substitution of the word sovereignty for "satisfaction" is a piece of unconscious political bias. The sovereignty must in the above cases be violated in order to achieve the satisfaction.

Perfect competition, again, as every undergraduate knows, is the organization of industry that best ensures consumer sovereignty. Hence many lyrical passages in the text-books, ending in an almost theological *O Altitudo*. And the accepted case against monopoly is that it restricts output below the competitive level. Now empirically this case is quite unproven since the Managerial Revolution. And even if it were proven it would be unimportant, since it would be only a violation of the welfare equations. The real criterion for judging the organization of an industry is whether it promotes investment and technical progress: and the Managerial Revolution has clearly brought monopoly from the lowest place in this order of merit to the highest—which it shares, let us hasten to add, with any oligopoly of sufficiently large firms.

It is useless to protest that perfect competition is supposed to be the most efficient form. For in this context the word efficient takes on an entirely new and indeed bogus meaning: "responsive to changes in consumer demand" (not necessarily to changes in long-run scarcity relationships—a monopoly might perceive these better). This has little to do with technical progress or with growth, nay even directly hinders them. Extreme responsiveness of this kind is a disadvantage, leading to low investment and low profitability, and therefore stifling technical research. Also it can hardly exist in conjunction with large scale, which is, of course, a condition of efficiency *proprement dit*. Efficiency—meaning low real cost—is the microeconomic duty of man; given that, growth follows, either spontaneously or through planning that uses up the resources set free. It is characteristic of our growth-blind economics that we blur this vital concept by making the word do duty in the field of "scarcity" too.

THE RELATIVE IMPORTANCE OF GROWTH AND CHOICE

Growth conflicts, then, at certain points with consumers' sovereignty and even with "scarcity" itself.[17] It is quite wrong to throw either wholly overboard, however. The advantages of each must as far as possible be quantified, and a balance struck. Thus to correct an important and permanent misallocation of resources is in itself economic growth; for unwanted production is not production at all. The industry/agriculture case quoted above is a good instance. On the other hand, the violation of the welfare equations is not an absolute, unconditional crime; it depends how long and how great the violation is. On any common-sense view of inter-personal or inter-temporal utility comparisons a certain increase in growth is worth any amount of minor allocation errors. Rapid growth diminishes the harm done by violation not only of consumer sovereignty but also of rational allocation in general. There are two main reasons for this.

First there is the "hair brushes and nail brushes" argument. As I have said elsewhere

. . . in the Soviet economy there are, as it were, always too few hair brushes and too many nail brushes in view of the resources available, while in "capitalist" economy this proportion is always more nearly right. But the production of both these articles is growing at about 10% per annum in the U.S.S.R. and at about 2% per annum in "capitalist" countries. In the end the Soviet citizen will be supplied better even with hair brushes.[18]

The mere fact of growth then floats off even a *permanent* misallocation of resources.

But, secondly, the misallocation need not be permanent. "Scarcity" need not be violated always in the same direction. Those who object to planning, monopolies, cartels, imperfect competition, etc., on "scarcity" grounds, implicitly assume that these things always exert their malign influence on resource allocation in the same place in the economy; but if monopoly, planning, etc., crop up in different places as time passes—and they do do so—then in the long run the relative quantity of hair brushes and nail brushes will vary about the "scarcity" optimum. If stocks in the hands of the users are large relative to current purchases no great harm at all will be done by these fluctuations, and even if they are not, the right proportion must often be hit as the pendulum of planning, monopoly, etc., swings from one side to the other.

"SCARCITY" AND A FORCED INVESTMENT PROGRAM

These considerations are particularly important when we weigh the pros and cons of forced saving and forced investment. Both are, as we have

---

[17] This conflict is quite separate, be it noted, from the possibility that one day economic growth will have gone so far that resources will cease to be scarce at all. This is the question of "full Communism," dismissed as irrelevant in Section 2.

[18] Wiles, *Oxford Economic Papers*, October 1953, pp. 315–16.

seen, clearly inevitable if the actual rate of growth is to exceed the "natural," "warranted" or *laissez faire* rate of growth in the immediate future, whether in undeveloped areas proper or in mature backward areas like Great Britain. This is very far from saying, to repeat, that forced saving and forced investment are the only desideratum for such growth, but they do raise interesting "scarcity" problems that other expansionary measures do not. Suppose that the institutional solution least disruptive of our present political, social and economic structure is adopted in order to effect this program of forced investment. Current production is sold on a free market, or at least on a market as free as that which we now have. Much greater funds than now are made available for investment by a large Budget surplus above the line. A central committee is set up which in any year must allocate the investment funds that private enterprise has not spontaneously taken up. In practice it will almost certainly do this "irrationally." Ideally, of course, this need not be so. But, in fact, what with human fallibility, the haste with which decisions must be taken, political influence and corruption, the direction of these investment resources will be irrational. Then within twelve months the errors that have been made will be sufficiently clear. In the first instance private enterprise will step in to enlarge the bottlenecks and correct the disproportions created by the planners' previous errors, and these latter will invest the new year's surplus funds in such a manner as to create bottlenecks and disportions elsewhere. Making *different* errors every year, they will make no serious errors at all.[19]

Again, precisely because of economic growth, really serious overinvestment in any particular branch of the economy is unlikely to occur. Provided that a project is technically feasible—that it is not a groundnuts scheme[20]—aggregate demand, growing through additional investment in other directions than this, will after an interval float off a particular mistake and render it an *ex post facto* necessity.

Thirdly, even absolute waste—and of this there must be some—is merely a necessary by-product of the superior prosperity that the system brings. Conceive, that is, a project that will become useful neither when completed nor at a later date, but never, no matter how much growth there is. This might be either because it is a technical failure (a groundnuts scheme) or something simply not demanded. Now a fashion house must buy some clothes that turn out to be unsaleable. Champagne manu-

---

[19] The Soviet Five Year Plans have undoubtedly made serious and permanent "scarity" errors. This is because the *pricing* system, as well as the *allocation* system, has been irrational. Had it not been for this, the very weak but still real influence of the Soviet consumer would have eventually corrected the investment program. For the extent of this influence compare Wiles, *op. cit.*, pp. 314–15.

[20] This was a technical failure, not a failure to predict demand or an error in the estimation of "scarcity" relationships. It is assumed in the text that gross technical errors of this kind will not be made. ["Groundnuts scheme" refers to an unsuccessful British development program in Africa.—Editor.]

facturers must make some bottles which explode.[21] If they knew which clothes or which bottles they would, of course, be able to lower their costs. But they do not sit down and produce nothing at all because they do not know; they write off this loss as a cost of production. So the growing economy may write off the irremediable errors of its program of forced investment as a cost of growth. Suppose a purely numerical example, entirely without empirical warrant: owing to the program 30% of the national income is invested, instead of 15%, and wasted projects instead of being 2% of the old investment are 6% of the new. Then something like an extra 1½% of the national income will be wasted every year. But the rate of growth rises, let us say, from 2 to 3% compound—we suppose rather sharply diminishing returns to the new investment; and already in two years the national income is greater than it would otherwise have been. Thereafter, of course, the excess becomes very great indeed, though consumption takes a good deal longer to catch up.[22]

Fourthly, it is not true that this sort of planning requires an impossibly long view of the future structure of demand. Such foresight, it is objected, is more than is vouchsafed to the wisest of us. Statistical exercises, whether governmental or private, in demand prediction are often simply bogus.[23] Now while this is perfectly true it does not affect the case for investment planning here put forward. The planner is not asked to estimate future demand for a longer period than the life of the particular capital asset he is at any moment considering. If it happens to be very durable he must, of course, just like a private entrepreneur, make a long-term estimate; if not, not. No new problem of forecasting has arisen. Indeed, one problem has fallen away, and actually *less*, not more, forecasting is required. For since the economy is growing more quickly than before, the likelihood of an absolute decline in any branch of production is smaller than before. Now when there is the possibility of an absolute decline, not only extensive investment (expanding capacity at present costs) but also intensive investment (reducing costs at present capacity) becomes a doubtful proposition.

---

[21] F. H. Knight, *Risk, Uncertainty and Profit*, p. 213.

[22] Let P be the present and F_n the future national income as now expected. Then $P(1.02)_n = F$, where n is any number of years. Under the new dispensation we start with 0.98 P, owing to the wasted investment projects, and $0.98\ P\ (1.03)^n = F'$, the new terminal national income. Then $F' = F$ when $n = \dfrac{\log\ 0.98}{\log 1.02 - \log 1.03}$. Consumption, as opposed to income, takes very much longer to recover. Thus it is not until the twenty-third year that it equals what it would have been in the same year under the old dispensation, and not until the eighth year that it regains the level obtaining when the change was introduced (always supposing we continue to invest 30% of the national income; naturally if we invest less after a while we can easily consume more than we should have been able to under the old dispensation). In the dreary length of these periods lies the explanation of much recent Soviet economic history.

[23] That they are indeed bogus is amply demonstrated by Professor Devons, in *Lloyds Bank Review*, July 1954, pp. 30–35.

We must forecast demand to know if it will really be profitable. Only intra-marginal firms should make such expenditure, and it is a matter of prediction to know just how many—and which—*are* intra-marginal. All this problem is much reduced by greater growth, so that we may fairly claim that investment planning of the type proposed actually reduces the amount of crystal-gazing required.

The amount of misallocation can be exaggerated in yet another way. When investing we make an allocation not only of all the ordinary scarce resources but also of "capital," *i.e.*, of "waiting." A program of forced investment need involve the misallocation of "waiting" only. For there is always at any moment an enormous number of profitable schemes that ought to be undertaken one day, "when the capital is available." There is no need to undertake unprofitable schemes: the more modest proposal suffices that all the profitable schemes be put in hand at once. Just as an investment cut, imposed by the Government, means merely that schemes are postponed, so an increase means merely that they are accelerated. The direction of investment is still determined by the market, or by direct welfare considerations: the amount only is increased over what would naturally have occurred.

There is a certain tendency for welfare economists, when contemplating the rate of interest, to say: "here is this list of possible schemes; the rate of interest tells us in which order, and, indeed whether, they should be undertaken." This is too static a view: there is no finite list of schemes, nor need there by any such thing as the exhaustion of capital opportunities. Investment causes growth. Therefore, *capital expenditure increases the number of capital opportunities*, making some schemes more desirable than before, others desirable for the first time, and some of both classes technically possible for the first time.

Extra funds for investment should then be fearlessly extracted from the consumer and splashed about. "Scarcity" will not suffer greatly—as Stalin said so very rightly:

Some comrades conclude from this that the law of the planned development of the national economy, the planning of the national economy, destroys the principle of profitability. This is quite wrong and quite the contrary is true. If one considers profitability not from the point of view of individual enterprises or branches of production, and not within the span of one year, but from the point of view of the whole national economy and within the span of, say, ten to fifteen years—which would be the only correct approach—then the temporary and unstable profitability of individual enterprises or branches of production cannot even bear comparison with that higher, stable form of profitability, which the operation of the law of the planned development of the national economy and the planning of the national economy give us, saving us from periodic economic crises which destroy the national economy and inflict colossal material damage on society, and securing for us the uninterrupted growth of the national economy with its high tempos.[24]

_____
[24] "Economic Problems of Communism," *Bol'shevik*, 18/1952.

GROWTH AND THE CLIMATE OF ECONOMIC THOUGHT

"Plenty, not scarcity, is the essence of economics." There is a sense in which this phrase is the cheapest of unscholarly rabble-rousing. But it contains a great truth. For while an emphasis on choice and scarcity is logically compatible with due insistence on growth, it is not psychologically so. Its implications are all wrong, and economists who are interested in choice are not in fact interested in growth, as Mr. Colin Clark taught us long ago in his brusque but salutary dismissal of the classical economics.[25] Mr. Clark is, of course, as he would be the first to admit, theoretically unsound, but how much healthier than the spectacle of Professor Robbins wringing his hands:

> The time at our disposal is limited. There are only twenty-four hours in the day. We have to choose between the different uses to which they may be put. The services which others put at our disposal are limited. The material means of achieving ends are limited. We have been turned out of Paradise.[26]

For Communists paradise lies ahead, and we may fairly reply with Karl Marx: "The philosophers have only *interpreted* the world, in various ways; the point, however, is to *change* it."[27] This means, of course, that economists should make value judgments. But Professor Robbins is most explicitly in favor of that activity, denying to it only the name of economics. His error is merely one of misplaced emphasis, and this article has no other object than to shift that emphasis. It contains, so far as its writer is aware, no concrete innovation. "Scarcity," then, is an effective reply to the redistributive, democratic socialist of the West, whose one idea is to squeeze a quart out of a pint pot. But the totalitarian, growth-conscious socialist of the East has a shattering rejoinder: "Why aren't you making a quart pot, like me?" Over and above all our micro-choices there hangs, as the logicians would say, a meta-choice. The satisfaction of the welfare equations is itself a competing end. We must choose, to some extent, between choice and growth.

---

[25] *Conditions of Economic Progress,* preface to the first edition. The withdrawal of these strictures in the second edition seems a shade premature: that funds are now available for the study of the national income brings us only a very short way towards an economics of plenty.

[26] *The Nature and Significance of Economic Science,* 2d ed. p. 15.

[27] *Theses on Feuerbach.*

PART II

Models of Economic Systems

Models of economic systems offer blueprints of schemes of economic organization and control intended to answer the fundamental questions of what, how much, how, and for whom to produce. These models are, necessarily and desirably, simplified abstractions from the complex reality of actual national economies. For that very reason, models enable us to distinguish and compare the basic characteristics and problems of different economic systems. They illuminate in sharp relief alternative answers to the fundamental questions of economic organization, and they provide essential tools for the analysis of living economies, such as the three cases studied in Part III of this book.

There are various possible classifications of theoretical economic systems, of which the most basic are capitalist versus socialist economies, and decentralized market versus centrally planned economies. The most common combinations, from these two schemes, are (1) the capitalist decentralized market model and (2) the socialist central planning model. However, other important combinations are (3) market socialism and (4) the detailed central planning within a formally capitalist framework that characterizes fascism. Finally, it is possible, in theoretical models as in actual cases, to find "mixed" economies combining, for example, public and private ownership or centralized and decentralized allocation of resources. It is noteworthy that virtually all the following selections do in fact envision some such combinations, that is, some sort of "mixed" economy. This feature reflects the intention of theory to elucidate reality, not to escape it.

The selections that follow analyze in turn (1) the capitalist market model, (2) market socialism, and (3) central planning in a capitalist as well as a socialist institutional framework. The case studies in Part III then provide examples of living economies which approximate each of the theoretical models.

Capitalism

The basic characteristics of a capitalist economic system are (1) private ownership of, and private enterprise with, the means of production; (2) the predominance of economic gain as the guiding force in production decisions; and (3) reliance on markets and prices to allocate resources and distribute income.

Two types of capitalism may be distinguished. In "laissez faire" capitalism, government intervention in the economy is absent or negligible. In "regulated" or "mixed" capitalism, there is a substantial amount of government intervention—intended for the most part to improve or bolster the private enterprise market system, rather than to curtail or replace it. There are few advocates of a 100 percent laissez faire economic system with no government intervention, and none exists today, except perhaps in very primitive economies. Rather, the issue, for both theory and policy, is the nature, extent, and success of government intervention in the regulated capitalist economy.

The following selections examine the nature, strengths, and weaknesses of a capitalist economy. The first shows how the decentralized price system ideally accomplishes the allocation of resources and distribution of income in a capitalist market economy. The second selection asserts the superiority of such a system over the alternative of central planning on the ground that it makes better use of economic knowledge. The third analyzes the shortcomings of the private enterprise market economy and explains the efforts of government to correct them in a regulated capitalist economy.

Bela A. Balassa

3. THE WORKING OF A PRICE SYSTEM*

> *Balassa shows how the price system, under conditions of pure competition, allocates resources to maximize consumer satisfaction and thus achieve "static efficiency."*

A DEMONSTRATION of how the price mechanism brings about an efficient allocation of resources is given here. Efficient resource allocation (static efficiency) has been defined as a situation where the output of any commodity can be increased only by reducing the output of another commodity, with production conforming to the community's preferences. We now turn to the conditions of efficient resource allocation.

By "cost of production" the layman usually means money expenses or expenses in physical units, such as labor hours, land use, etc. But from the economic point of view, cost is the loss of possible alternatives (alternative or opportunity cost). Costs are opportunities foregone by using productive resources for the production of commodity *A* instead of commodity *B*. In an economy where only two goods, for example beer and bread, are produced, the cost of an additional pound of bread is expressed in terms of gallons of beer, since by increasing the production of bread by one pound we forego the use of resources for manufacturing, say, two gallons of beer. In a money economy we shun the cumbersome usage of expressing the cost of a given good in terms of all the other goods and express cost in money terms instead. Nevertheless, the essence of cost measurement remains the same: cost is alternative (opportunity) cost; it expresses opportunities foregone.

Let us examine a simple case of money economy where land and labor are the only factors of production (inputs) and bread and beer are the only commodities produced (outputs). Our model will be presented as follows.

---

* Reprinted, with permission, from *The Hungarian Experience in Economic Planning* (New Haven: Yale University Press, 1959), pp. 239–43.

THE PARTICIPANTS OF THE ECONOMIC PROCESS

Resource-holders supply the factors of production inelastically—that is, a change in the price for services of land and labor will not result in an alternation of the quantity of factors of production brought on the market. The number of resource-holders is sufficiently large to ensure that the quantity of factors supplied by any one of them does not affect the market price of land and labor, and they take the market price as given.

Producers manufacture two commodities: beer and bread. Any producer may engage in the production of one or both commodities. The production possibilities for any producer can be expressed in the form of a production (transformation) function. The production function expresses the transformation possibilities of inputs into outputs, and the possibility of substitution between factors and between products.

It is assumed that the proportions of land and labor are not the same in the production of the two commodities. For example, bread requires relatively more land and less labor: it is land-intensive, while beer is labor-intensive. The technological coefficients in production (the quantities of land and labor used for producing any of the commodities) are variable. For example, if there is an increase in the number of laborers, labor will become cheaper and there will be a tendency to substitute labor for land in the production of both commodities. In other words, the technological coefficients are partly determined by the availability and price of the productive factors.

The number of producers is sufficiently large to ensure that a single producer cannot affect the market prices of the inputs and outputs; he regards these prices as given.

Consumers are the resource-holders who consume their income obtained by selling the services of land and labor. The consumers desire to consume our two commodities, bread and beer. The demand functions (schedules) of consumers indicate the quantity of particular products demanded at different prices. The demand functions of individual consumers summed up give the demand functions of the society for our two commodities. Perfect certainty and absence of market failures are assumed throughout.

BEHAVIORAL ASSUMPTIONS

Producers aim at profit maximization—that is, they endeavor to maximize the difference between total revenue from the sale of the commodities and total cost incurred in producing them. In view of our assumption that the individual producer cannot affect market prices, and assuming that there is a rise in the additional cost due to an additional unit of output, profit maximization is achieved at the point where the price of an additional unit of output equals the cost of production of this additional unit *and* for further units of output the price would not cover additional costs. This is the famous "price equals marginal cost" rule. To give an example: If the cost of the first ton of bread is $300, of the second $310, of the third $320, and of the fourth $330, and the price of a ton of bread is $320, our producer will produce no more than 3 tons of bread, since he would lose $10 on the fourth ton. At this point his profits are maximized in the amount of $30.

Under the above assumptions the "price equals marginal cost" rule can also be expressed as follows: an additional unit of input will be used up to the point where the revenue obtained from the increase in value of output due to the last unit of this input still covers the remuneration paid to the factor of production.

Investments are made in the production of the commodity bringing profit, and producers withdraw if they incur losses. Thereby investments tend to have an equilibrating effect.

Consumers aim at maximizing satisfaction out of given income. They reshuffle their consumption expenditure until they reach the point where nothing can be gained from further exchange. At this point the last dollar spent gives the same satisfaction in the consumption of both commodities.

EQUILIBRIUM AND EFFICIENCY

Equilibrium is reached when there is no incentive to reshuffle production or consumption any more. At this point, resources are allocated efficiently, since if any factor could be used more profitably in producing another commodity, the profit motive would induce the entrepreneur to change his production plan. Similarly, if any two consumers could gain from further exchange, commodities would be exchanged between them. In (general) equilibrium, production corresponds to consumers' demand, and it is no longer possible to increase the production of any commodity without reducing the production of another. The price system and the behavioral assumptions of our model lead, through a continuous reshuffling of production and consumption, to an efficient position. The resulting prices are so-called scarcity prices, which means that (1) the prices of the factors of production reflect the scarcity of resources in view of consumer demand for commodities for whose production the resources are used; and (2) the prices of the commodities reflect consumer demand, resource scarcities, and transformation possibilities, and express the alternative cost of producing one commodity instead of another.

Under the assumption of given resources the pricing of the factors of production can be regarded as a process of "imputation." Consumer demand determining quantities of consumption goods to be produced constitutes the indirect demand for productive factors. Given the indirect demand for the factors of production and their quantity, factor prices are determined at the point where the quantity demanded equals the quantity supplied.

Our results are essentially unchanged if we introduce more commodities, more factors of production, and intermediate products (for example, grain), and if we assume that the supply of the factors of production reacts to changes in their prices. In this generalized case our system will consist of the following components:

1. The demand functions of consumers, indicating the quantity of particular commodities demanded at various prices.

2. The transformation functions of producers, expressing transformation possibilities from resources into intermediate products (from land and labor to grain) and from intermediate products into final commodities (from grain to bread) and, furthermore, indicating the possibilities for substitution between factors, between intermediate products, and between final commodities.

3. Supply functions of the factors of production, indicating the quantity of particular factors supplied at various prices.

These functions can be regarded as part of a mathematical equation system, the equations being solved by the market through a reshuffling of production and consumption until equilibrium is reached where resources are allocated efficiently. Besides achieving static efficiency, our model of pure competition is also conducive to progress, since every producer will attempt to cut costs by introducing innovations and thereby increasing profit. Hence profit maximization is not only a powerful means to accomplishing efficient resource allocation in a static situation but also a dynamic force.

In our model the efficient allocation of resources was achieved with the assistance of the price system and the profit motive in harmony with consumer preferences. But the price system and the profit motive can help in allocating scarce resources efficiently among *any given ends*. It is conceivable that a central authority will decide the final bill of goods, distribute them among consumers (for example, by rationing), and demand the production of these goods on the market. The individual producers, confronted with this demand, will bid for the contracts, will organize production with a view to maximizing profits, and will thereby achieve an efficient allocation of resources among given ends. Factor prices are still scarcity prices, but now they reflect resource scarcities in regard to the final bill of goods determined by the central authority rather than by consumer sovereignty. This situation may be approximated in a free enterprise economy in wartime if military production is organized along the lines of private enterprise and consumer goods are allocated by some form of rationing.

Friedrich A. Hayek

4. THE PRICE SYSTEM AS A MECHANISM FOR USING KNOWLEDGE*

Efficiency in resource allocation requires full use of knowledge of the opportunities of supply and demand in the economy. Hayek argues that decentralized decisions in response to prices determined by market forces can utilize this knowledge much better than central planning, which is unable to assemble all the detailed information needed for sound decisions. Market prices can serve as proper guides to economic decisions because they are "rates of equivalence" which embody the whole end-means structure of the economic system. At the same time, the price system achieves "economy of knowledge" by concentrating in simple and unambiguous signals for action the information relevant for each participant in the economic process. On the basis of these price signals, decentralized decisions can be made that are consistent with the activity of the economic system as a whole.

I

WHAT IS the problem we wish to solve when we try to construct a rational economic order?

On certain familiar assumptions the answer is simple enough. *If* we possess all the relevant information, *if* we can start out from a given sys-

* Reprinted, with the permission of the author and the American Economic Association, from *American Economic Review*, Vol. XXXV, No. 4 (September, 1945), pp. 519–30. Originally published under the title, "The Use of Knowledge in Society." Friedrich A. Hayek, who formerly taught at the University of London and the University of Chicago, is now Professor of Economics at the University of Freiburg, Germany.

tem of preferences and *if* we command complete knowledge of available means, the problem which remains is purely one of logic. That is, the answer to the question of what is the best use of the available means is implicit in our assumptions. The conditions which the solution of this optimum problem must satisfy have been fully worked out and can be stated best in mathematical form: put at their briefest, they are that the marginal rates of substitution between any two commodities or factors must be the same in all their different uses.

This, however, is emphatically *not* the economic problem which society faces. And the economic calculus which we have developed to solve this logical problem, though an important step toward the solution of the economic problem of society, does not yet provide an answer to it. The reason for this is that the "data" from which the economic calculus starts are never for the whole society "given" to a single mind which could work out the implications, and can never be so given.

The peculiar character of the problem of a rational economic order is determined precisely by the fact that the knowledge of the circumstances of which we must make use never exists in concentrated or integrated form, but solely as the dispersed bits of incomplete and frequently contradictory knowledge which all the separate individuals possess. The economic problem of society is thus not merely a problem of how to allocate "given" resources—if "given" is taken to mean given to a single mind which deliberately solves the problem set by these "data." It is rather a problem of how to secure the best use of resources known to any of the members of society, for ends whose relative importance only these individuals know. Or, to put it briefly, it is a problem of the utilization of knowledge not given to anyone in its totality.

This character of the fundamental problem has, I am afraid, been rather obscured than illuminated by many of the recent refinements of economic theory, particularly by many of the uses made of mathematics. Though the problem with which I want primarily to deal in this paper is the problem of a rational economic organization, I shall in its course be led again and again to point to its close connections with certain methodological questions. Many of the points I wish to make are indeed conclusions toward which diverse paths of reasoning have unexpectedly converged. But as I now see these problems, this is no accident. It seems to me that many of the current disputes with regard to both economic theory and economic policy have their common origin in a misconception about the nature of the economic problem of society. This misconception in turn is due to an erroneous transfer to social phenomena of the habits of thought we have developed in dealing with the phenomena of nature.

II

In ordinary language we describe by the word "planning" the complex of interrelated decisions about the allocation of our available resources. All economic activity is in this sense planning; and in any society in which many people collaborate, this planning, whoever does it, will in some measure have to be based on knowledge which, in the first instance, is not given to the planner but to somebody else, which somehow will have to be conveyed to the planner. The various ways in which the knowledge on which people base their plans is communicated to them is the crucial problem for any theory explaining the economic process. And the problem of what is the best way of utilizing knowledge initially dispersed among all the people is at least one of the main problems of economic policy—or of designing an efficient economic system.

The answer to this question is closely connected with that other question which arises here, that of *who* is to do the planning. It is about this question that all the dispute about "economic planning" centers. This is not a dispute about whether planning is to be done or not. It is a dispute as to whether planning is to be done centrally, by one authority for the whole economic system, or is to be divided among many individuals. Planning in the specific sense in which the term is used in contemporary controversy necessarily means central planning—direction of the whole economic system according to one unified plan. Competition, on the other hand, means decentralized planning by many separate persons. The half-way house between the two, about which many people talk but which few like when they see it, is the delegation of planning to organized industries, or, in other words, monopoly.

Which of these systems is likely to be more efficient depends mainly on the question under which of them we can expect that fuller use will be made of the existing knowledge. And this, in turn, depends on whether we are more likely to succeed in putting at the disposal of a single central authority all the knowledge which ought to be used but which is initially dispersed among many different individuals, or in conveying to the individuals such additional knowledge as they need in order to enable them to fit their plans in with those of others.

III

It will at once be evident that on this point the position will be different with respect to different kinds of knowledge; and the answer to our question will therefore largely turn on the relative importance of the different kinds of knowledge; those more likely to be at the disposal of particular individuals and those which we should with greater confidence expect to find in the possession of an authority made up of suitably chosen experts. If it is today so widely assumed that the latter will be in a better position, this is because one kind of knowledge, namely, scientific knowledge, occupies now so prominent a place in public imagination that we tend to forget that it is not the only kind that is relevant. It may be admitted that, so far as scientific knowledge is concerned, a body of suitably chosen experts may be in the best position to command all the best knowledge available—though this is of course merely shifting the difficulty to the problem of selecting the experts. What I wish to point out is that, even assuming that this problem can be readily solved, it is only a small part of the wider problem.

Today it is almost heresy to suggest that scientific knowledge is not the sum of all knowledge. But a little reflection will show that there is beyond question a body of very important but unorganized knowledge which cannot possibly be called scientific in the sense of knowledge of general rules: the knowledge of the particular circumstances of time and place. It is with respect to this that practically every individual has some advantage over all others in that he possesses unique information of which beneficial use might be made, but of which use can be made only if the decisions depending on it are left to him or are made with his active coöperation. We need to remember only how much we have to learn in any occupation after we have completed our theoretical training, how big a part of our working life we spend learning particular jobs, and how valuable an asset in all walks of life is knowledge of people, of local conditions, and special circumstances. To know of and put to use a machine not fully employed, or somebody's skill which could be better utilized, or to be aware of a surplus stock which can be drawn upon during an interruption of supplies, is socially quite as useful as the knowledge of better alternative techniques. And the shipper who earns his living from using otherwise empty or half-filled journeys of tramp-steamers, or the estate agent whose whole knowledge is almost exclusively one of temporary opportunities, or the *arbitrageur* who gains from local differences of commodity prices, are all performing eminently useful functions based on special knowledge of circumstances of the fleeting moment not known to others.

It is a curious fact that this sort of knowledge should today be generally regarded with a kind of contempt, and that anyone who by such knowledge gains an advantage over somebody better equipped with theoretical or technical knowledge is thought to have acted almost disreputably. To gain an advantage from better knowledge of facilities of communication or transport is sometimes regarded as almost dishonest, although it is quite as important that society make use of the best opportunities in this respect as in using the latest scientific discoveries. This prejudice has in a considerable measure affected the attitude toward commerce in general compared with that toward production. Even economists who regard themselves as definitely above the crude materialist fallacies of the past constantly commit the same mistake where activities directed toward the acquisition of such practical knowledge are concerned—apparently because in their scheme of things all such knowledge is supposed to be "given." The common idea now seems to be that all such knowledge should as a matter of course be readily at the command of everybody, and the reproach of irrationality leveled against the existing economic order is frequently based on the fact that it is not so available. This view disregards the fact that the method by which such knowledge can be made as widely available as possible is precisely the problem to which we have to find an answer.

IV

If it is fashionable today to minimize the importance of the knowledge of the particular circumstances of time and place, this is closely connected with the smaller importance which is now attached to change as such. Indeed, there are few points on which the assumptions made (usually only implicitly) by the "planners" differ from those of their opponents as much as with regard to the significance and frequency of changes which will make substantial alterations of production plans necessary. Of course, if detailed economic plans could be laid down for fairly long periods in advance and then closely adhered to, so that no further economic decisions of importance would be required, the task of drawing up a comprehensive plan governing all economic activity would appear much less formidable.

It is, perhaps, worth stressing that economic problems arise always and only in consequence of change. So long as things continue as before, or at least as they were expected to, there arise no new problems requiring a decision, no need to form a new plan. The belief that changes, or at least day-to-day adjustments, have become less important in modern times implies the contention that economic problems also have become less important. This belief in the decreasing importance of change is, for that reason, usually held by the same people who argue that the importance of economic considerations has been driven into the background by the growing importance of technological knowledge.

Is it true that, with the elaborate apparatus of modern production, economic decisions are required only at long intervals, as when a new factory is to be erected or a new process to be introduced? Is it true that, once a plant has been built, the rest is all more or less mechanical, determined by the character of the plant, and leaving little to be changed in adapting to the ever-changing circumstances of the moment?

The fairly widespread belief in the affirmative is not, so far as I can ascertain, borne out by the practical experience of the business man. In a competitive industry at any rate—and such an industry alone can serve as a test—the task of keeping cost from rising requires constant struggle, absorbing a great part of the energy of the manager. How easy it is for an inefficient manager to dissipate the differentials on which profitability rests, and that it is possible, with the same technical facilities, to produce with a great variety of costs, are among the commonplaces of business experience which do not seem to be equally familiar in the study of the economist. The very strength of the desire, constantly voiced by producers and engineers, to be able to proceed untrammeled by considerations of money costs, is eloquent testimony to the extent to which these factors enter into their daily work.

One reason why economists are increasingly apt to forget about the constant small changes which make up the whole economic picture is probably their growing preoccupation with statistical aggregates, which show a very much greater stability than the movements of the detail. The comparative stability of the aggregates cannot, however, be accounted for—as the statisticians seem occasionally to be inclined to do—by the "law of large numbers" or the mutual compensation of random changes. The number of elements with which we have to deal is not large enough for such accidental forces to produce stability. The continuous flow of goods and services is maintained by constant deliberate adjustments, by new dispositions made every day in the light of circumstances not known the day before, by B stepping in at once when A fails to deliver. Even the large and highly mechanized plant keeps going largely because of an environment upon which it can draw for all sorts of unexpected needs; tiles for its roof, stationery for its forms, and all the thousand and one kinds of equipment in which it cannot be self-contained and which the plans for the operation of the plant require to be readily available in the market.

This is, perhaps, also the point where I should briefly mention the fact that the sort of knowledge with which I have been concerned is knowledge of the kind which by its nature cannot enter into statistics and therefore cannot be conveyed to any central authority in statistical form. The statistics which such a central authority would have to use would have to be arrived at precisely by abstracting from minor differences between the things, by lumping together, as resources of one kind, items which differ as regards location, quality, and other particulars, in a way which may be very significant for the specific decision. It follows from this that central planning based on statistical information by its nature cannot take direct account of these circumstances of time and place, and that the central planner will have to find some way or other in which the decisions depending on them can be left to the "man on the spot."

V

If we can agree that the economic problem of society is mainly one of rapid adaptation to changes in the particular circumstances of time and place, it would seem to follow that the ultimate decisions must be left to the people who are familiar with these circumstances, who know directly of the relevant changes and of the resources immediately available to meet them. We cannot expect that this problem will be solved by first communicating all this knowledge to a central board which, after integrating *all* knowledge, issues its orders. We must solve it by some form of decentralization. But this answers only part of our problem. We need decentralization because only thus can we ensure that the knowledge of the particular circumstances of time and place will be promptly used. But the "man on the spot" cannot decide solely on the basis of his limited but intimate knowledge of the facts of his immediate surroundings. There still remains the problem of communicating to him such further information as he needs to fit his decisions into the whole pattern of changes of the larger economic system.

How much knowledge does he need to do so successfully? Which of the events which happen beyond the horizon of his immediate knowledge are of relevance to his immediate decision, and how much of them need he know?

There is hardly anything that happens anywhere in the world that *might* not have an effect on the decision he ought to make. But he need not know of these events as such, nor of *all* their effects. It does not matter for him *why* at the particular moment more screws of one size than of another are wanted, *why* paper bags are more readily available than canvas bags, or *why* skilled labor, or particular machine tools, have for the moment become more difficult to acquire. All that is significant for him is *how much more or less* difficult to procure they have become compared with other things with which he is also concerned, or how much more or less urgently wanted are the alternative things he produces or uses. It is always a question of the relative importance of the particular things with which he is concerned, and the causes which alter their relative importance are of no interest to him beyond the effect on those concrete things of his own environment.

It is in this connection that what I have called the economic calculus proper helps us, at least by analogy, to see how this problem can be solved, and in fact is being solved, by the price system. Even the single controlling mind, in possession of all the data for some small, self-contained economic system, would not—every time some small adjustment in the allocation of resources had to be made—go explicitly through all the relations between ends and means which might possibly be affected. It is indeed the great contribution of the pure logic of choice that it has demonstrated conclusively that even such a single mind could solve this kind of problem only by constructing and constantly using rates of equivalence (or "values," or "marginal rates of substitution"), *i.e.*, by attaching to each kind of scarce resource a numerical index which cannot be derived from any property possessed by that particular thing, but which reflects, or in which is condensed, its significance in view of the whole means-end structure. In any small change he will have to consider only these quantitative indices (or "values") in which all the relevant information is concentrated; and by adjusting the quantities one by one, he can appropriately rearrange his dispositions without having to solve the whole puzzle *ab initio*, or without needing at any stage to survey it at once in all its ramifications.

Fundamentally, in a system where the knowledge of the relevant facts is dispersed among many people, prices can act to coördinate the separate actions of different people in the same way as subjective values help the individual to coördinate the parts of his plan. It is worth contemplating for a moment a very simple and commonplace instance of the action of the price system to see what precisely it accomplishes. Assume that somewhere in the world a new opportunity for the use of some raw material, say tin, has arisen, or that one of the sources of supply of tin has been eliminated. It does not matter for our purpose—and it is very significant that it does not matter—which of these two causes has made tin more scarce. All that the users of tin need to know is that some of the tin they used to consume is now more profitably employed elsewhere, and that in consequence they must economize tin. There is no need for the great majority of them even to know where the more urgent need has arisen, or in favor of what other needs they ought to husband the supply. If only some of them know directly of the new demand, and switch resources over to it, and if the people who are aware of the new gap thus created in turn fill it from still other sources, the effect will rapidly spread throughout the whole economic system and influence not only all the uses of tin, but also those of its substitutes and the substitutes of these substitutes, the supply of all the things made of tin, and their substitutes, and so on; and all this without the great majority of those instrumental in bringing about these substitutions knowing anything at all about the original cause of these changes. The whole acts as one market, not because any of its members survey the whole field, but because their limited individual fields of vision sufficiently overlap so that through many intermediaries the relevant information is communicated to all. The mere fact that there is one price for any commodity—or rather that local prices are connected in a manner determined by the cost of transport, etc.—brings about the solution which (it is just conceptually possible) might have been arrived at by one single mind possessing all the information which is in fact dispersed among all the people involved in the process.

VI

We must look at the price system as such a mechanism for communicating information if we want to understand its real function—a function which, of course, it fulfills less perfectly as prices grow more rigid. (Even when quoted prices have become quite rigid, however, the forces which would operate through changes in price still operate to a considerable extent through changes in the other terms of the contract.) The most significant fact about this system is the economy of knowledge with which it operates, or how little the individual participants need to know in order to be able to take the right action. In abbreviated form, by a kind of symbol, only the most essential information is passed on, and passed on only to those concerned. It is more than a metaphor to describe the price system as a kind of machinery for registering change, or a system of telecommunications which enables individual producers to watch merely the movement of a few pointers, as an engineer might watch the hands of a few dials, in order to adjust their activities to changes of which they may never know more than is reflected in the price movement.

Of course, these adjustments are probably never "perfect" in the sense in which the economist conceives of them in his equilibrium analysis. But I fear that our theoretical habits of approaching the problem with the assumption of more or less perfect knowledge on the part of almost everyone has made us somewhat blind to the true function of the price mechanism and led us to apply rather misleading standards in judging its efficiency. The marvel is that in a case like that of a scarcity of one raw material, without an order being issued, without more than perhaps a handful of people knowing the cause, tens of thousands of people whose identity could not be ascertained by months of investigation, are made to use the material or its products more sparingly; i.e., they move in the right direction. This is enough of a marvel even if, in a constantly changing world, not all will hit it off so perfectly that their profit rates will always be maintained at the same constant or "normal" level.

I have deliberately used the word "marvel" to shock the reader out of the complacency with which we often take the working of this mechanism for granted. I am convinced that if it were the result of deliberate human design, and if the people guided by the price changes understood that their decisions have significance far beyond their immediate aim, this mechanism would have been acclaimed as one of the greatest triumphs of the human mind. Its misfortune is the double one that it is not the product of human design and that the people guided by it usually do not know why they are made to do what they do. But those who clamor for "conscious direction"—and who cannot believe that anything which has evolved without design (and even without our understanding it) should solve problems which we should not be able to solve consciously—should remember this: The problem is precisely how to extend the span of our utilization of resources beyond the span of the control of any one mind; and, therefore, how to dispense with the need of conscious control and how to provide inducements which will make the individuals do the desirable things without anyone having to tell them what to do.

The problem which we meet here is by no means peculiar to economics but arises in connection with nearly all truly social phenomena, with language and most of our cultural inheritance, and constitutes really the central theoretical problem of all social science. As Alfred Whitehead has said in another connection, "It is a profoundly erroneous truism, repeated by all copy-books and by eminent people when they are making speeches, that we should cultivate the habit of thinking what we are doing. The precise opposite is the case. Civilization advances by extending the number of important operations which we can perform without thinking about them." This is of profound significance in the social field. We make constant use of formulas, symbols and rules whose meaning we do not understand and through the use of which we avail ourselves of the assistance of knowledge which individually we do not possess. We have developed these practices and institutions by building upon habits and institutions which have proved successful in their own sphere and which have in turn become the foundation of the civilization we have built up.

The price system is just one of those formations which man has learned to use (though he is still very far from having learned to make the best use of it) after he had stumbled upon it without understanding it. Through it not only a division of labor but also a coördinated utilization of resources based on an equally divided knowledge has become possible. The people who like to deride any suggestion that this may be so usually distort the argument by insinuating that it asserts that by some miracle just that sort of system has spontaneously grown up which is best suited to modern civilization. It is the other way round: man has been able to develop that division of labor on which our civilization is based because he happened to stumble upon a method which made it possible. Had he not done so he might still have developed some other, altogether different, type of civilization, something like the "state" of the termite ants, or some other altogther unimaginable type. All that we can say is that nobody has yet succeeded in designing an alternative system in which certain features of the existing one can be preserved which are dear even to those who most violently assail it—such as particularly the extent to which the individual can choose his pursuits and consequently freely use his own knowledge and skill.

VII

It is in many ways fortunate that the dispute about the indispensability of the price system for any rational calculation in a complex society is now no longer conducted entirely between camps holding different political views. The thesis that without the price system we could not preserve a society based on such extensive division of labor as ours was greeted with a howl of derision when it was first advanced by von Mises twenty-five years ago. Today the difficulties which some still find in accepting it are no longer mainly political, and this makes for an atmosphere much more conducive to reasonable discussion. When we find Leon Trotsky arguing that "economic accounting is unthinkable without market relations"; when Professor Oscar Lange promises Professor von Mises a statue in the marble halls of the future Central Planning Board; and when Professor Abba P. Lerner rediscovers Adam Smith and emphasizes that the essential utility of the price system consists in inducing the individual, while seeking his own interest, to do what is in the general interest, the differences can indeed no longer be ascribed to political prejudice. The remaining dissent seems clearly to be due to purely intellectual, and more particularly methodological, differences.

A recent statement by Professor Joseph Schumpeter in his *Capitalism*,

Socialism, and Democracy provides a clear illustration of one of the methodological differences which I have in mind. Its author is preeminent among those economists who approach economic phenomena in the light of a certain branch of positivism. To him these phenomena accordingly appear as objectively given quantities of commodities impinging directly upon each other, almost, it would seem, without any intervention of human minds. Only against this background can I account for the following (to me startling) pronouncement. Professor Schumpeter argues that the possibility of a rational calculation in the absence of markets for the factors of production follows for the theorist "from the elementary proposition that consumers in evaluating ('demanding') consumers' goods *ipso facto* also evaluate the means of production which enter into the production of these goods."[1]

Taken literally, this statement is simply untrue. The consumers do nothing of the kind. What Professor Schumpeter's "*ipso facto*" presumably means is that the valuation of the factors of production is implied in, or follows necessarily from, the valuation of consumers' goods. But this, too, is not correct. Implication is a logical relationship which can be meaningfully asserted only of propositions simultaneously present to one and the same mind. It is evident, however, that the values of the factors of production do not depend solely on the valuation of the consumers' goods but also on the conditions of supply of the various factors of production. Only to a mind to which all these facts were simultaneously known would the answer necessarily follow from the facts given to it. The practical problem, however, arises precisely because these facts are never so given to a single mind, and because, in consequence, it is necessary that in the solution of the problem knowledge should be used that is dispersed among many people.

The problem is thus in no way solved if we can show that all the facts, *if* they were known to a single mind (as we hypothetically assume them to be given to the observing economist), would uniquely determine the solution; instead we must show how a solution is produced by the interactions of people each of whom possesses only partial knowledge. To assume all the knowledge to be given to a single mind in the same manner

---

[1] J. Schumpeter, *Capitalism, Socialism, and Democracy* (New York, Harper & Bros., 1942), p. 175. Professor Schumpeter is, I believe, also the original author of the myth that Pareto and Barone have "solved" the problem of socialist calculation. What they, and many others, did was merely to state the conditions which a rational allocation of resources would have to satisfy, and to point out that these were essentially the same as the conditions of equilibrium of a competitive market. This is something altogether different from showing how the allocation of resources satisfying these conditions can be found in practice. Pareto himself (from whom Barone has taken practically everything he has to say), far from claiming to have solved the practical problem, in fact explicitly denies that it can be solved without the help of the market. See his *Manuel d'économie pure* (2d ed., 1927), pp. 233–34. The relevant passage is quoted in an English translation at the beginning of my article on "Socialist Calculation: The Competitive 'Solution,'" in *Economica*, New Series, Vol. VII, No. 26 (May, 1940), pp. 125–49 [reprinted in this volume as Chapter 8, pp. 95–115].

in which we assume it to be given to us as the explaining economists is to assume the problem away and to disregard everything that is important and significant in the real world.

That an economist of Professor Schumpeter's standing should thus have fallen into a trap which the ambiguity of the term "datum" sets to the unwary can hardly be explained as a simple error. It suggests rather than there is something fundamentally wrong with an approach which habitually disregards an essential part of the pehnomena with which we have to deal: the unavoidable imperfection of man's knowledge and the consequent need for a process by which knowledge is constantly communicated and acquired. Any approach, such as that of much of mathematical economics with its simultaneous equations, which in effect starts from the assumption that people's *knowledge* corresponds with the objective *facts* of the situation, systematically leaves out what is our main task to explain. I am far from denying that in our system equilibrium analysis has a useful function to perform. But when it comes to the point where it misleads some of our leading thinkers into believing that the situation which it describes has direct relevance to the solution of practical problems, it is time that we remember that it does not deal with the social process at all and that it is no more than a useful preliminary to the study of the main problem.

Procter Thomson

5. GOVERNMENT AND THE MARKET*

What is the proper role of government in a capitalist market economy? Procter Thomson distinguishes two necessary types of government intervention in economic life, both of which are intended to assist, improve, and supplement the private enterprise market economy. Through its "framework activities" the government affects the environment in which the private economy operates. The government's "allocative activities," on the other hand, involve the use of resources for public purposes, modify the distribution of income, or influence the level and rate of growth of economic activity. In contrast to these desirable forms of government activity, there are more questionable types of government intervention which interfere with, or displace, the private market economy, such as price-fixing and public enterprise.

THE DIVISION OF LABOR BETWEEN GOVERNMENT AND THE MARKET

MOST OF the great problems of social policy in this century involve the division of labor between government and the market. The conditions of freedom and equity, of order, efficiency, and progress depend upon our answer to the question: What things should be done by group decision operating through the political process, and what things should be done by individual decisions mediated by the mechanism of the market? The line which divides these processes is neither intuitively obvious nor eternally

* Reprinted, with permission, from *Federal Expenditure Policy for Economic Growth and Stability* (Papers Submitted by Panelists Appearing before the Subcommittee on Fiscal Policy, Joint Economic Committee, 85th Cong., 1st sess.) (Washington, D.C.: U.S. Government Printing Office, 1957), pp. 130–52. Procter Thomson is John C. Lincoln Professor of Economics and Administration at Claremont Men's College.

51

fixed; it must be decided by free discussion among the responsible citizens of a free society; it changes according to the circumstances of the times, the understanding of the citizenry, and the capabilities of the Government. Nevertheless, there are some general principles which can, or should, guide rational discussion of this great problem.[1]

What are the peculiar characteristics of these two processes? What ends do they seek? How can they work together to achieve these ends?

THE POLITICAL PROCESS

In any society, the political process is concerned with the allocation of power. In a democratic society that process is designed to secure a group consensus on specific issues of social policy. The consensus is always subject to discussion and modification, but, while it remains in effect, the rules of the game compel individual dissent to be subordinated to group decision. An importer of Swiss watches, for example, may doubt the wisdom of protective tariffs, but, so long as these duties stand on the schedules, he foots the bill and harbors his questions till the next election.

If we take a broad and cursory view of the political process, we find that the scene is occupied by the following groups of actors:[2] First, the electorate, the citizens, who exercise the franchise in the light of their values, their information, and their interests; second, the political parties, who propose issues to the electorate; third, the legislature or parliament, who are selected by the electorate, from the parties, to represent their interests and to transplant the general consensus into specific laws; fourth, the executive, who translates both the laws of the legislature and the consensus of the body politic into specific acts of policy; fifth, the permanent bureaucracy, who carry out the details of executive policy and perform the routine tasks of government; sixth, the judiciary, who interpret the law and adjudicate disputes.

The role-structure of the political process is extraordinarily complex. Equally complex are the functions carried on within this structure. For, in

---

[1] For background, see Frank H. Knight, "The Ethics of Competition," *The Ethics of Competition and Other Essays* (reprint ed., London: George Allen & Unwin, 1936), especially pp. 49–58. Classical discussion of the problem can be found in Adam Smith, *Wealth of Nations*, book V, ch. i, "Of the Expenses of the Sovereign or Commonwealth," and John Stuart Mill, *Principles of Political Economy*, book V, ch. i, "Of the Functions of Government"; ch. xi, "Of the Grounds and Limits of the Laissez-Faire or Non-Interference Principle."

For a summary of current economic thought, see Fritz Machlup, "The Division of Labor Between Government and Private Enterprise," *American Economic Review*, XXXIII (March 1943), pp. 87–104. For a sociological treatment, see Max Weber, *The Theory of Social and Economic Organization*, trans. by A. M. Henderson and Talcott Parsons (New York: Oxford University Press, 1947), ch. ii. Also consult Henry C. Simons, *A Positive Program for Laissez-Faire: Economic Policy for a Free Society* (Chicago: The University of Chicago Press, 1948).

[2] This is an expanded version of the list given in Ernest Barker, *The Parliamentary System of Government, Essays on Government* (2d ed.; Oxford: The Clarendon Press, 1951).

all its variety and complexity, the political process represents the most characteristic activity of organized society; namely, problem solving according to specified rules, under given conditions, in an environment of uncertainty. Despite the humbug and chicanery, the oratory and ideologies which lend color and interest to the process, political choice in a democratic society is the solution of common problems through group discussion. Discussion is the essence of democracy. And since the solution of the problem cannot be known before hand, the outcome of the process is indeterminant; it cannot be predicted from given conditions. In this respect it differs radically from the market process in which the given conditions of consumer preferences, industrial technology, and available resources dictate the outcome within tolerable limits of accuracy.

Another outstanding feature of decisions made through political discussion is their uniformity. They must be, so to speak, the same for everyone—everyone, that is, whose circumstances are similar. By contrast with the market mechanism, individual differences are not taken into account save through the ad hoc device of administrative discretion. For example, if the political process determined the disposition of goods among consumers, every household might have an annual dividend of 4 pairs of shoes and 5 quarts of whisky, even though a barefoot teetotaler would find these goods superfluous. On distribution day he would truck them to the public square and barter them for something else, a costly and annoying expedient which the price system renders unnecessary.

Despite the indeterminancy of the political process in general, the roles of some of the actors can be identified and tentative predictions ventured. The individual citizen, in his capacity as a voter, a lobbyist, and a political persuader, acts to maximize the satisfactions he receives from his government. Representatives act to maximize their terms of office. Political parties act to maximize the power they command which, under democratic conditions, is equivalent to maximizing the votes they receive.[3] In this connection, political parties act as entrepreneurs and innovators. Just as entrepreneurs in the market economy design and offer for sale the commodities among which consumers choose, so political parties package the issues on which elections are decided. But the range of choices is much narrower for the American voter than for the American consumer. The voter, therefore, is confronted with a "tie-in purchase." To buy a box of apples, he must take a peck of leeks. To get a labor and taxation policy he likes, he may have to swallow a foreign policy he abominates.

The differences between voting and purchasing also call for brief comment. In democratic societies, the rule is, "One citizen, one vote"— except for juveniles, prisoners, and migrants across political boundaries unable to establish legal residence before the election. In the market, the

---

[3] Anthony Downs, *An Economic Theory of Democracy* (New York: Harper & Bros., 1957).

rule is "Purchases are made with money, and money income is distributed among people in accord with inheritance, effort, and the chances of life." Though public policy must ultimately be ratified by votes, voting is by no means the crucial nexus of the political process, and the formal equality of the ballot box is countervailed a hundred times over by inequalities of power and ability which made themselves felt in the strategy of decision. Given its initial inequality in the distribution of wealth and income, the democracy of the market consists in the fact that one man's dollar is the equal of another man's dollar. Neither race, religion, nor prejudice can stay these instruments from their appointed ends—to guide production and govern the allocation of resources. Finally, the voting mechanism accomplishes its results indirectly and by remote control, as it were; the vote does not immediately call forth that which was voted for. Purchasing, on the other hand, both indicates a preference and accomplishes possession of the thing preferred.[4]

Problem solving through the political process is a necessary consequence of the existence of uncertainty. The degree of uncertainty faced by the society exercises a profound influence on the structure and function of its institutions: The greater the degree of uncertainty, the higher is the cost of acquiring information on issues of public policy. The ordinary citizen being unwilling to bear the costs of acquainting himself with the issues, society specializes the function of detailed policy decisions in a small group of elected representatives. But, again, the greater the uncertainty, the greater the likelihood of error. Thus, the necessity of checks and balances to hold legislative folly within tolerable limits. Political parties are another byproduct of uncertainty; they specify the issues to which voters react, and conduct exploratory expeditions to sample the consensus of the body politic. The normal administrative work of the bureaucracy represents still another aspect of society's unending struggle to routinize the unexpected.

If uncertainty were to vanish, by far the greater part of the apparatus of government would be altogether superfluous. No uncertainty, no problems; no problems, no politics. For in a world without uncertainty the costs of acquiring information about the future are reduced from infinity to zero; the consensus of the body politic is formulated and made known without doubt or delay. Therefore "representative" government and political parties would be obsolescent. Administrative decisions would be reduced to repetitive routine so that the executive arm of the Government would consist of tax collectors and producers of public services. Given perfect certainty, both the verdict of justice and the balance sheet of power are intuitively obvious so that neither adjudication nor a trial of strength are necessary. Order follows inevitably. For disorder arises ei-

---

[4] For further comment, see James M. Buchanan, "Social Choice, Democracy, and Free Markets," *Journal of Political Economy*, Vol. LXII (April 1954), pp. 114–23.

ther from fraud or from an appeal to force; the first is impossible when concealment is impossible and the second is superfluous when the outcome is inevitable. In this event a society which shared a common pattern of values and which was not plagued with fundamental conflicts of interest has no use for a central authority to maintain order. A society divided into contending interest groups but united by a common standard of justice would decide differences by rational compromise in order to establish equity and preserve stability. In both cases the reserves of force are impounded in a common bank and need never pass into active circulation. (Only the uncertain society needs a central authority to collect and, on occasion, spend these reserves of force.) But a divided society without common standards of justice would impose order in the interests of the strongest.[5]

THE MARKET MECHANISM

The market mechanism is concerned with the allocation of resources. It is designed to answer the questions: (1) What things shall be produced? (2) How shall they be produced? (3) How shall the output be distributed among the agents who, jointly, produce it? (4) How shall society provide for maintenance and progress?

In an individualistic social order characterized by free exchange, private property, and personal responsibility these decisions are initiated by individual consumers and individual producers; but the market is a device for making these multitudes of choices mutually consistent, for translating individual decisions about bread, houses, and automobiles into social decisions about prices and outputs. For the buyer, prices are costs which provide both a signal and an incentive to cut back on his use of things that are dear and push forward on his use of things that are cheap. For the seller, prices are returns which provide both signal and incentive to make more of the things that are expensive and less of those that are cheap. For the system as a whole, prices settle at the level which clears the market. The prices of productive services, together with the pattern of ownership of resources, determine the distribution of income among persons and families; and the income of resource owners represents the costs of producers, while the expenditures of resource owners—as consumers of goods and services—represents the income of producers.

The broad and general case for the free market is simply this: Left to their own devices owners of resources will be guided by the signals of the market to put scarce agencies to the most productive uses. Given freedom of maneuver plus reasonable knowledge of the facts, resources will be channeled into the areas where demand is brisk and returns are high and diverted from the uses where demand is slack and returns are low. And the

---

[5] In the uncertain society, as Thomas Hobbes argued in his *Leviathan* (1651), preservation of order is the elementary task of civilized government. But whatever the degree of uncertainty, order without equity is tyranny.

attempt of each economic agent to maximize his net returns leads, under free competition, to equal returns at the margin for agents of equal capacity. Finally, equal returns at the margin means maximum returns for the community as a whole.

But even if the system of the market worked with perfect efficiency, the ends it secures are no better and no worse than the initial distribution of resource ownership on which it is based. Allocative efficiency does not mean distributive justice. Further, the sovereign consumer whom the market serves may command it to perform services which are, at best, frivolous and, at worst, subversive of higher esthetic and moral values.[6] Consumer sovereignty is no guaranty of individual integrity.

These, however, are evils easier indicted than remedied. For, in addition to the democratic presumption of individual responsibility which forbids arbitrary interference with the means he commands and the ends he chooses, we encounter the political dilemma that public intervention can scarcely be expected to rise above the private standards of the citizens who sanction it. It would be a rare thing, indeed, if citizens displayed more wisdom at the polls than in the market.

Still further, one of the notorious facts of economic and social life is that not all individuals have effective power to exercise their formal freedoms. Freedom without power is illusory. The faith, the presumption, or the hope that the individual is the best judge of his own interests is altogether untrue if his abilities are limited or his understanding corrupted. Here again, however, democracy faces one of its critical dilemmas: How do we detect significant aberrations from rational self-interest and how do we intervene to correct them? Above and beyond the limits of individual ability are the subtle barriers to formal freedoms erected by prejudice, by custom, and by overt coalitions that narrow his range of effective action.

The market, like the political process, is powerfully affected by the degree of uncertainty which the society faces. Economic knowledge is a scarce commodity; and actual adjustments of the market are bound to diverge from the ideal because of the intrusion of the unexpected into the affairs of both producers and consumers. Chance creates both windfall gains and losses in the lifetime income stream of the individual. Uncertainty also takes its toll on the income stream of the society in the form of periodic fluctuations in income, employment, and prices. The market creates an elaborate series of adjustments to handle the problem of uncertainty. The major adjustment consists of a division of labor between those who receive relatively fixed returns (sellers of labor and renters of capital) and those who receive fluctuating returns (stockholders or owners) based on the fortunes of the enterprise. In this picture, the business entrepreneur bundles together the risks which a specific firm is designed to exploit and sells pieces of these chances to owners (or to himself) who pledge their capital to the firm.

---

[6] Frank H. Knight, *The Ethics of Competition.*

In the absence of uncertainty, most of economic life would be reduced to repetitive routine. Entrepreneurship would vanish; administration and decisionmaking would become unnecessary. The business cycle would cease to trouble us. The economic problems remaining would be the age old ones of scarcity and poverty in—I might add—an environment of unrelieved monotony.

FRAMEWORK ACTIVITIES OF GOVERNMENT

In discussing the various grounds on which government participates in economic activity, I have divided the normative role of the state into two broad categories. The first covers the "framework" or regulatory activities of government, the second the "allocative" activities. Framework activities establish the structure within which the market functions. They alter or help to establish the "given conditions"—the tastes, resources, and technology—which govern the equilibrium of market forces. Though framework activities involve some use of resources, this aspect of the problem is relatively trivial; the chief issue is the substantive content of the rules and orders which government establishes. Allocative activities, on the other hand, involve substantial use of resources, or modify the distribution of income, or affect the level of economic activity. As we shall see presently, there is some overlap in these categories.

In this and the section following I have attempted to say what government should do; i.e., to extract from the existing body of doctrine in political economy some normative criteria for the economic role of the state. But Leviathan has an insatiable appetite; in the effort to satisfy the political temper of the times, parties often propose and enact measures of doubtful—doubtful, I say, not negative—economic value. These dubious expedients are briefly treated under the catchall heading of "Price Fixing and Government Enterprise."

RULES OF THE GAME

In democratic societies, standards of behavior can be regarded as a series of overlapping circles: The circle of broadest compass is the mores, values, and norms of the society. Inside this is the domain of the common law, based on judicial recognition of social mores. Inside this is basic or constitutional law plus judicial interpretation of constitutional provisions. Still narrower in scope but more detailed in form is statutory law. At the final and smallest of the circles we find administrative law and administrative custom.[7]

Government, then, codifies and administers the common rules of the market as part of this set of overlapping sanctions. It does in two different ways.

---

[7] The breadth of the circles does not indicate legal priority. Constitutions and statutes can, to be sure, set aside the common law, and the evolution of judicial decisions which modify the common law need not parallel the evolution of the mores. I am indebted to my colleague Prof. Winston M. Fick for this formulation.

1. Standards and norms: The State is the agency which standardizes practices. The great body of doctrine which defines the "law of contract," establishes the meaning of "private property," or implements "the rule of reason" represents the standardizing activities of government as the articulate instrument of custom. This body of rules governs the legal qualities of money, the procedures for buying and selling, the liabilities of partners and stockholders, the means for collecting debts, and the paths to be followed in going into bankruptcy. Law and administrative decisions also guide the process of taking out a trademark, of conducting collective bargaining, of selling stocks and bonds, and of passing on an inheritance.

These positive rules implement order and stability in commercial interchange. In economic terms, they are part of the definition of "resources." For an agent of production is not just a technological datum, for example, so many acres of land or man-hours of labor; it is that plus an invisible penumbra of rights and duties embodied in the law of contract and other parts of the framework.[8]

2. Prevention of force and fraud: Government exercises a monopoly of force in order to prevent fraud and forestall the use of force by private parties. Private force must be held in check, because its use is subversive of both public order and justice. So far as the market is concerned, the reservoir of force at the disposal of the State is employed to uphold contracts and prevent "taxation" of one private citizen by another.

Though illegal use of force almost always involves fraud or concealment, prevention of fraud per se rests on different grounds than does prevention of force. In the long run the fraudulent merchant, the vendor of stocks in nonexistent oil wells, or the manufacturer of tainted foods would be forced into bankruptcy by a free and informed market. But in the meantime the costs of detecting fraud through trial and error involve extraordinary burdens on those who are short-changed, fleeced, or poisoned. It is cheaper all around, therefore, to rule these practices illegal and provide the machinery for enforcing these rules. At the Federal level the Pure Food and Drug Act or the activities of the Securities and Exchange Commission are notable examples of this practice.

Defining the Group Whose Welfare Is to Be Maximized

Part of the exercise of national sovereignty consists in defining the limits of the social body whose welfare is to be maximized. In practice this ordinarily means the ethnic and racial groups who occupy the territory of the state. This object is implemented by a simple but enormously important device—the restriction of immigration.

The broad outlines of social policy on immigration are very largely a closed issue in most nations of the Western World, though they may be

---

[8] The "institution of the contract" is discussed in Émile Durkheim, *On the Division of Labor in Society*, translated by G. Simpson (New York: The Macmillan Co., 1933).

reopened for review by changes in the balance of power or by shifts in population structure. Barriers to migration raise the income of labor competitive to potential immigrants and lower the earnings of specialized resources that are complementary to poetential migrants. If no restraints are imposed on exports of capital or imports of commodities, neither the rate of interest nor the relative price of internationally traded goods will be much affected by these barriers.

FREEDOM OF ENTRY

Given a framework of rules and a definition of the group to be served, the case for freedom of entry is overwhelming on both economic and political grounds. Freedom of access is both an implication of political democracy and a necessary condition for economic efficiency.

So far as economic efficiency is concerned, barriers to entry result in the production of less of the restricted commodities and more of all other things than the economy either wants or could have if the barriers were broken down. How do these restrictions arise and how should the State move to demolish them? In the absence of public intervention, the degree of restraint on the free movement of resources would be established by the balance of two contrary tendencies: On the one hand, there is a clear and obvious gain from combining to restrict competition and raise prices—as, for example, a coalition of bakers or of housebuilders in a particular locality or a cartel of metal fabricators or a syndicate of truckdrivers in the country at large. (These gains are greater the smaller the possibility of securing substitutes for the commodity or service the coalition controls.)[9] On the other hand the costs of coordinating the coalition plus the restless forces of competition act to erode these gains away.

The State should, and in some cases does, aid the market in restraining the growth of coalitions. As a minimum it ought not to countenance nor encourage these barriers by law and administrative decisions that create a favorable climate for suspending competition. At the maximum it ought to seek out and break up trusts, combines, and syndicates. This is no easy matter as the complex history of law and court procedures under antitrust clearly demonstrates. However the existence of the Sherman and Clayton Acts plus the activities of the Federal Trade Commission have exercised a profound influence on our economic structure and have helped to prevent the growth of cartelized inefficiency on the European model.

Restrictive practices by trade unions represent still another example of barriers to free entry. The union need not ration entry to the trade or occupation by direct controls such as membership quotas, elaborate ap-

---

[9] For discussion of the underlying economic issues see Alfred Marshall, *Principles of Economics* (8th ed.; London: Macmillan & Co., 1920), book V, ch. vi; as modified by J. R. Hicks, *The Theory of Wages* (reprint ed.; New York: Peter Smith, 1948), pp. 241–47. Further see George J. Stigler, *The Theory of Price* (rev. ed.; New York: The Macmillan Co., 1952), p. 208.

prenticeship requirements, or high membership dues. The same result can be accomplished indirectly by persuading the buyer of labor services not to offer employment below some stipulated wage. The wage rations entry. Unlike producer coalitions, unions have very low overhead costs and can proliferate indefinitely without running into diseconomies of scale.

REGULATION OF NATURAL MONOPOLY

Natural monopoly is an obvious candidate for public regulation. Monopoly creates economic inefficiency by distorting the pattern of production. The price of monopolized articles is higher, the output lower, and the output of all other things is greater than would be the case if monopoly were conducted in the public interest.[10]

Natural monopoly ordinarily arises when the advantages of large-scale production plus the conditions of demand are such that one producer engrosses the entire market for a commodity. And competition in the industry will be imperfect if production and demand conditions are such that a small number of firms dominate the scene. For either pure monopoly or "competition among the few," the individual producer occupies a large enough share of the market so that variations in his output exert an appreciable influence on the price of the goods. In the effort to maximize returns producers will jack up prices above the incremental costs of production.

Given the definition of "the commodity," the degree of monopoly power depends on the extent of substitution in both production and consumption. Everyone has a bit of a monopoly on something: The unctuous manners of a neighborhood grocery-store proprietor may earn him a preferred position over his quarrelsome competitors, but if he attempts to capitalize this dividend into his prices he will merely increase the business of the chainstore down the block. A rutabaga monopoly would be of small avail so long as potatoes, lima beans, and squash could readily be had. A monopoly on gas or electric power in a particular town is a somewhat more serious matter, however, because of the unavailability of close substitutes. Most State and local regulation of monopoly lies in the field of public utilities, and the Federal Power Commission exercises jurisdiction over interstate movements of natural gas and hydroelectric power. A monopoly over a factor of production such as aluminum would also raise questions of public policy even though a host of other metals compete with it for its various purposes.

Now given the economic indictment of monopoly, regulation ought to be designed to encourage efficient use of resources; that is, to force the monopoly to price at its incremental cost of production. But this criterion

---

[10] Melvin W. Reder, *Studies in the Theory of Welfare Economics* (New York: Columbia University Press, 1947), ch. iv, "An Obstacle to the Attainment of Maximum Welfare: Monopoly."

raises a host of technical issues which it is inappropriate to pursue here.[11]

In some instances the public may elect to take over and run the monopoly. In principle, both regulation and operation should arrive at the same end, but since the latter involves government ownership and allocation of resources it will be briefly treated under another heading.

EXTERNAL ECONOMIES AND DISECONOMIES

In allocating resources by the market, private welfare is synonymous with public welfare so long as prices reflect the full costs or the full benefits of economic activity. But this reflection is often imperfect, and some of these imperfections raise important issues of policy. A famous illustrative example concerns the manufacture of a commodity which creates smoke or noxious vapors that pollute the surrounding air. The "private cost" to the manufacturer is the expense of labor, raw materials, wear and tear on the plant, et cetera, incurred in producing the article. The "social cost" is that plus the inconvenience and danger which pollution creates for the inhabitants roundabout.[12] For an inhabitant of southern California this is no trivial example, I might add. (In the long run with free choice of places of residence no one would put up with the nuisance unless he felt that other advantages of the locale compensated for it; and thus the place affected would have to offer lower rents or a higher dividend of conveniences in order to be of equal attractiveness with other places. Thus, the long-run cost of the nuisance would be the distortion it created in regard to choice of residence.)

This case illustrates an external diseconomy—external because it operates outside the price system and diseconomy because it creates a cost for someone. In general an external economy (or diseconomy) is created whenever the consumption or production of some commodity or service by one agent creates benefits (or costs) for other persons not covered in the price. There are four categories of these external effects: (1) between consumers, (2) between producers, (3) from producers to consumers, and (4) from consumers to producers.[13] In order to push forward on the production and consumption of things which create external economies and to cut back on those that create diseconomies, public intervention in the interests of economic efficiency is required if the effects are important enough to be worth bothering about. In some instances laws and regulation alone will suffice; in others—to be discussed under the second of our major headings—public resources must be expended.

---

[11] For a summary of these issues see Nancy Ruggles, "The Welfare Basis of the Marginal Cost Pricing Principle and Recent Developments in the Theory of Marginal Cost Pricing," *Review of Economic Studies*, Vol. XVII (1949–50), pp. 29–46, 107–26.

[12] A.C. Pigou, *The Economics of Welfare* (4th ed.; London: Macmillan & Co., 1932). pt. II, ch. ix.

[13] Tibor Scitovsky, "Two Concepts of External Economies," *Journal of Political Economy*, Vol. LXII (April 1954), pp. 143–51.

For the smoke nuisance case, as an example, zoning regulations and requirements concerning manufacturing processes, private incinerators, and perhaps automobile exhausts seem the appropriate remedy, though—as the Los Angeles case again demonstrates—considerable research, financed by public money, will be needed before precise correctives are discovered.

Most of the important cases where regulation is appropriate involve external diseconomies between producers, or between producers and consumers. Many of these instances also involve the conservation of resources.

An important instance where intervention can improve allocation is presented by external diseconomies between lumbering and farming. Cutting timber increases the rate at which water drains off the surface and exposes farmlands downhill or downstream to the likelihood of flood and erosion. Various remedies have been proposed: one is a requirement that lumber companies replant as they cut (some of them find this profitable to do on their own); another is that they modify the cutting pattern so as to leave undergrowth and small trees standing.

External diseconomies between producers in the same industry are exemplified by the extraction of crude oil from a particular deposit or pool. If drilling rights are owned by a variety of operators, each will seek to pump the deposit as rapidly as possible with the result that pressure of natural gas inside the dome will fall and cut down the yield of the pool. Each producer creates external diseconomies for the others. But production could be maximized if ownership were unified so that external burdens would be transformed into internal costs. If one producer cannot buy out the others—because it is too troublesome or requires more capital than he can lay his hands on—unified extraction can be achieved by public regulation, providing the rules are enforceable and technologically feasible.[14]

The fisheries case is another instance of producer diseconomies, with one additional complication—the economic opportunity, the fishing ground, cannot be owned. Given certain biological variables, which are but imperfectly known at present, the annual rate of take will exert an influence on the total population of certain species of ocean fish. But the individual fisherman does not consider changes in the underlying stock of resources when he voyages out to make his catch. Each one, consequently, creates diseconomies for the others; rational management of the fish population goes by default and is left to chance.[15] The remedy would appear to include some sort of international licensing organization.

Still another aspect of producer diseconomies is found in activities whose unregulated pursuit would clutter up the city streets or create

[14] Clair Wilcox, *Public Policies toward Business* (Homewood, Ill.: Richard D. Irwin, Inc., 1955), pp. 363–66.

[15] Anthony Scott. "The Fishery: The Objectives of Sole Ownership," *Journal of Political Economy*, Vol. LXIII (April 1955), pp. 116–24.

chaos through unlimited exploitation of limited facilities. An interesting, but somewhat trivial, example is taxicabs in metropolitan areas. In the interests of holding down the burden on other forms of traffic, the number of licenses granted to cabdrivers is limited, the number being decided by a rough estimate of the advantages of service to the consumer versus the disadvantages of cabs to other drivers. Taverns and liquor stores are similarly limited on the presumption, no doubt, that a plethora of such facilities would lower the character and quality of the region. A much more important example is Federal licensing of radio and TV broadcasting in order to prevent dual exploitation of a single channel. Now, whatever the grounds on which such limits are fixed, the license to exploit the facility represents a partial patent of monopoly. Public authority may place hedges on the license; for example, the Federal Communications Commission in granting TV licenses seeks to disperse control over the channels of mass communication. But other things the same, it is surely contrary to either policy or economy to give these prerequisites away. They should be sold on the open market to the highest bidder—providing the applicant meets the other conditions which policy imposes. This criterion most certainly applies to radio and television franchises.

ECONOMIES IN PURSUING INTERESTS AND ACQUIRING KNOWLEDGE

The case for the free market presumes that the individual knows his own interests and is aware of economic alternatives. Common observation suggests that departures in practice from these conditions are as pervasive as they are regrettable. Individual conduct shows many instances of obstinate attachment to "irrational" objectives; the costs of acquiring knowledge of the market are frequently so high that, in the absence of outside help, the sensible man decides that it is more efficient to remain ignorant.

Now the paternalistic role of the state in democratic societies, intervention to improve behavior or combat ignorance, is capable of infinite abuse and must be severely limited. The following represent some of the steps that may be taken on this ground.

Some transactions are restricted or altogether prohibited—e. g., sale of habit-forming drugs, gambling, and the practice of the world's oldest profession. While dope addiction and other aberrations work some hardships on persons outside the transaction, i. e., create external diseconomies, the primary reason for their prohibition is that they do violence to the self.

On a somewhat different level, the state requires the individual to maintain ownership in himself; he may offer his services for rent but cannot sell himself in bondage. Nor can individual citizens sell their electoral franchise. Clearly, however, these actions are prohibited because of their adverse external effects since, if widely practiced, they would subvert the whole climate of freedom.

An intrusion of the state which is widely accepted in practice but still debated in principle is compulsory saving under the Social Security Act. Although the actuarial value of the pension exceeds the accumulated worth of the contributions, the compulsory portion of old-age and survivors insurance is founded on the theory that the ordinary worker shortchanges his future, i. e., discounts future income at a higher rate of interest than he ought rationally to employ.

A still different set of interventions, directed, I think, against the effects of ignorance of market alternatives is licensing of professional practitioners such as doctors, lawyers, and pharmacists. A free market with exact knowledge makes licensing unnecessary, for the self-interest of the buyer rewards the seller according to his worth, and the incompetent can find no customers. But in the absence of exact knowledge the license testifies, when properly administered, to some minimum level of competence and saves the time and cost of determining whether the practitioner deserves his title. For law or medicine these costs would be high. I doubt whether the same is true, however, for barbers, beauticians, and others who need a public certificate to set up shop.

ALLOCATIVE ACTIVITIES OF GOVERNMENT

"Allocative" activities of Government employ resources, influence the distribution of income, or affect the level of national output. Despite their great variety and complexity and despite the even greater complexity of that incredible document, the Federal Budget, which authorizes them, the grounds or reasons for undertaking them are relatively few in number.

INDIVISIBLE SERVICES

Among its other functions, market price is a rationing device which governs the volume of goods or services at the disposal of the user. No price, no service. But many activities that are "in the highest degree necessary" cannot be rationed by price and must be available to everyone if they are available to anyone. An example which conveys the essence of the case: lighthouses.[16]

In some cases an indivisible activity could easily be carried on by a voluntary agency which supported itself by fees charged to the user. Shipowners, conceivably, might band together in an association to build lighthouses, or the residents of a river valley might embark on a joint operation to control floods—another indivisible activity which Government ordinarily performs—but the difficulties of promoting and administering the agency, the trouble involved in collecting fees from unwilling beneficiaries, etc., would render the prospect of such associations dubious. In this connection, however, Government may be regarded as a holding company for a group of associations rendering a variety of indivisible

---

[16] J. S. Mill, *Principles*, Book V, ch. xi, sec. 15.

services to the citizenry.[17] While Government can more readily promote and finance such associations, the holding company is likely to be somewhat larger than optimum size (and not always responsive to the needs of its customers).

Headed by national defense, the dominant function of central governments under existing conditions, the major indivisible services may be listed as follows:

1. National defense and related functions.
2. Police protection.
3. Foreign aid and development.
4. Public health.
5. Pure research.
6. Navigational aids and flood control.
7. Streets and highways—with exceptions as noted below.
8. Wildlife preservation.
9. Public monuments, buildings, and parks—with exceptions.

Comments on selected items:

(2) Individuals can and do hire private watchmen and carry arms to fend off marauders but prevention, detection, and punishment of crime are public offices.

(3) Foreign aid is a function of political and military policy, but long range economic development probably depends on exports of private capital.

(4) Pure research is undertaken both by government and by private nonprofit agencies, such as universities and foundations.

(6) Navigational aids and flood control on inland waterways are often conducted jointly with power production and irrigation which can be rationed by prices.

(7) Save for limited access roads and bridges, highways are indivisible services in the first instance but can be financed by taxes on cars and gasoline in joint demand with highways. These taxes represent user charges whose yield provides a clue to the optimum size of the highway network.

(9) Imposing public edifices and parks, to the extent they have esthetic value, are an indivisible service for the public in general. But visiting a national park, hunting on a game preserve, and using a public recreation facility should, if practicable, be rationed by admission charges or licences in order to prevent overcrowding and cover the costs of operation.[18]

How should indivisible services be produced? Both economic efficiency and political liberty require that Government use the signals and incentives of the price system in acquiring and combining the resources which

---

[17] Paul A. Samuelson, "The Pure Theory of Public Expenditures," *Review of Economics and Statistics*, Vol. XXXVI (November 1954), pp. 387–89.

[18] Procter Thomson, "Prices versus Taxes in the Allocation of Public Resources," Proceedings of the 48th Annual Conference of the National Tax Association (Sacramento, Calif.: National Tax Association, 1956), pp. 140–57.

supply these services. The market for indivisibles is blind on the demand side, but the supply side should use prices to the fullest extent possible. This clearly implies (1) that Government should pay market prices for the resources it hires, (2) that, whenever possible, Government should contract with private producers to perform services instead of supplying them directly. For, to amplify the second of these criteria, the optimum size of government from the standpoint of political policy may exceed the optimum for purposes of managerial efficiency. If public bodies can contract out or delegate the task of management to private enterprise, they may both reduce the costs and improve the quality of operations.

To exemplify: Highways, public buildings, and dams can. be, and normally are, built by private contractors rather than by public employees. The complex weapons and devices needed for military preparedness in the postatomic age are manufactured by private concerns rather than by Government arsenals. The thousands of different items used in the daily operation of government are ordinarily purchased from private dealers. To these statements there are some exceptions. Highway departments sometimes build their own roads; the Military Establishment does manufacture some of its own weapons; and Government agencies sometimes fabricate their own supplies. These exceptions ought to be rigorously and carefully scrutinized. In all too many cases the waste and malfeasance which there occurs would be incompatible with survival under private auspices. But the details of this topic belong elsewhere.

Requisition of military manpower represents one important area where Government ignores the signals of the price system though, to be sure, the ground rules for the draft vary from time to time and coercion is sweetened by persuasion. As a result, it is impossible to ascertain the real costs of defense, i. e., the costs in terms of the value of manpower in other uses. Cheap military manpower secured via the draft is, moreover, an expensive bargain in the long run. In an age where the soldier must command a formidable arsenal of technical weapons, these reluctant defenders are scarcely the equal of a seasoned cadre of professionals recruited by voluntary inducements. At a time, moreover, where potential annihilation lurks in the dark of night for those who stay at home as well as those who go to war, no great premium would be necessary to hire all the permanent staff of our forces or to pay, if need be, for short periods of duty followed by transfer to the Reserves. In a mature and responsible society, finally, a mercenary army of professional soldiers poses no great threat to our democratic freedoms.

EXTERNAL ECONOMIES AND DISECONOMIES

As was argued above, prices sometimes fail to reflect the full costs and benefits of particular activities, with the result that the private market produces too few of the things that create external economies and too many of those that create diseconomies. In many cases these departures from optimum can be handled by public regulation and involve no direct use of resources. Particularly is this true of external diseconomies, e. g., the smoke-nuisance case and the oil-well case. But where the activity creates benefits for persons other than the producer or customer, a subsidy is needed to stimulate its production. From the standpoint of public resources, education represents by far the most important example of this principle.

The education of individual A produces, of course, a direct and immediate benefit to A himself; and self-interest alone would induce him, or his parents acting for him, to build up his capital of ability. But A's education also confers advantages on B, and C, and D. For in a democratic society with a universal franchise, education is a necessary condition for wise and responsible exercise of political freedoms. A, if uninstructed and ignorant, could not exercise his franchise wisely and an illiterate electorate would imperil the whole future of democracy. Further, cultural interchange and all the amenities of civilized society demand individual sensitivity to values, ideas, and the world about us. But if left to its own devices, family A might not purchase as much schooling as B, C, and D would like to see them buy. This important instance of external economies in consumption justifies public subsidy for education.

The school government, in this context, is a corporation that implements the interest of each in the education of others. For, to be sure, B's concern for A (and A's for B, etc.) could be implemented by a series of private gifts. But these interests would be better served by a mutual compact among families A, B, C, and D stipulating that each would match—or meet in some agreed ratio—the contributions of the other. A community referendum on school taxes and expenditures assumes precisely this sort of mutual compact. Because of external economies, families A, B, C, and D would elect to expend a greater amount per child than would have resulted from individual purchases plus private philanthropy.

Public subsidies for schools could be expended in a number of ways. Government could subsidize private schools; it could dispense certificates to the family, who could spend the certificate at an accredited school of their choice; or it could operate schools as a department of government. For political and other reasons, current practice favors the latter alternative.

External economies are a pervasive feature of human life but most of them are too trivial to be worth bothering about as subjects of public intervention. Examples are the householder whose well-kept lawn beautifies the neighborhood, or the merchant whose store windows gladden the eye of passing pedestrians.

An analytical curiosity which puzzles and intrigues economists but may or may not be of great practical importance is the possibility of "increasing returns to scale" for a particular industry. In this form of external economy, expansion of production by the firm lowers costs for the industry because optimum size for the exploitation of some common facility has not yet been achieved.[19] These cases, when identified, are appropriate candidates for subsidy. But possibilities for such economies appear to be rather limited, and, in any event, no one seems able to identify these curiosities in practice.[20]

OPERATION OF NATURAL MONOPOLIES

Monopoly, as already argued, represents an obvious threat to efficiency. The case for controlling it by public intervention is equally obvious. The choice between regulation or public operation turns upon some difficult issues of politics, economics, and administration whose solution varies according to circumstances. Regulation may tempt an alert and aggressive monopoly to befuddle or bribe the regulators. Operation involves the possibility of aggravated bureaucratic waste.

Monopolies in power, water, gas, and transport are often operated by municipalities. The Post Office Department is a monopoly operated by the Federal Government. How should these monopolies be conducted? On the one hand, optimum efficiency is achieved when the price of the service covers the cost of producing the last unit of that service. On the other hand optimum efficiency requires that total sales receipts cover total costs of producing the service; for taxes to finance subsidies inevitably warp the pattern of economic alternatives; moreover equity (equal treatment of equals) is violated when nonusers subsidize users—except in special cases where nonusers receive benefits that are not reflected in the structure of prices. These criteria conflict when the demand schedule for the service intersects the schedule of incremental (or marginal) costs at a point which lies below the schedule of average costs.[21]

If pricing on the basis of incremental costs involves subsidizing the monopoly from the Public Treasury, the governing authority has a number of strings to its bow which it can employ in important special cases. It can vary the quality of the product. By reducing the cost and quality of its services it can eventually come to rest at a point where demand price, incremental cost, and average cost coincide, and where incremental pricing, therefore, just covers total expenses.[22]

---

[19] Allyn Young, "Increasing Returns and Economic Progress," *Economic Journal*, Vol. XXXVIII (December 1928), pp. 527–42.

[20] Scitovsky, *op. cit.*

[21] For background and further exposition see the articles of Nancy Ruggles cited in footnote 11. Roughly, however, when average cost (total cost divided by number of units) falls as output rises, because of economies of scale, the expenses of producing the last increment of the service are bound to be lower than the average cost of the entire range of output. (For instance if a batter who is hitting .250 before a particular game, pulls his average down, his "incremental" performance that day was less than 1 out of 4.) It follows as a matter of simple arithmetic that incremental cost times number of units sold falls short of total cost.

[22] The existence of an equilibrium at this intersection can be shown as follows: Given an enterprise where incremental cost and demand schedules intersect at any

For the post office, a Federal monopoly which chronically runs at a substantial deficit, these technical considerations are relevant and important.[23] Under existing practices and rates, the postal deficit subsidizes advertisers, book publishers, magazines, other departments of government, and inhabitants of rural areas. (Due to the vagaries of Government accounting, the post office does not bear the full cost of contributions to pensions for employees; on the other hand it is, or was, used as a vehicle for delivering handsome subsidies to private transport agencies such as airlines.) Subsidy in general is justified by the presence of a substantial degree of external economies. In the remote past subventions to publishers might have been justified as a contribution to literacy and education. Surely this presumption is of negligible worth at the present juncture. Surely, also, the diseconomies of high taxes render the postal deficit, and the additional taxation thereto attached, an enterprise devoutly to be liquidated.

Through what steps can the postal service be induced to balance its budget? First, put it on notice that it must balance its accounts. Second, unscramble the records so that it bears the full costs, but no more than the full costs, of its operation; this implies payment by other departments for use of postal buildings and delivery of Government mail and payment of overhead and retirement costs by the post office. Third, and most important, let it set its own rates and establish a defensible system of mail classification. Under this dispensation the postal service would be a quasi-independent corporation free to use the methods of the market, save for the stipulation that (having no stockholders) surpluses, if any, must be plowed into additional facilities. Deficits, when they occurred, would be financed by postal bonds sold to the private market.

If these three steps were taken, might it not be possible to contemplate a fourth and more radical proposal, namely opening the postal business to private enterprise? The quaint and antiquated devices by which, it is

---

point, each increase (or decrease) in quality will raise (or lower) the cost schedules and raise (or lower) the demand schedule. Given diminishing returns to investment in quality of service, each rise in quality will raise the demand price (for a given output) by less than the cost price; each fall in quality will lower the demand price by less than the cost price. Eventually the average cost schedule can be made to overtake the demand schedule where the former crosses the schedule of incremental costs.

By similar reasoning, a monopoly that earns a surplus in the first instance is in the happy position of being able to achieve balance by raising its level of service.

If, now, increasing returns to investment in quality prevail over the relevant range, a public monopoly that incurs a deficit in the first instance should raise rather than lower the quality of its service.

What do variations in "quality" entail? For a city transport system obviously, or for the Federal Post Office (as argued below) many such variations in convenience, promptness, and comfort can be undertaken. For municipal gas, water, and electricity, technical possibilities of variation are much more limited. Installing and repairing facilities, and billing customers would appear to exhaust the range.

[23] Jane Kennedy, "Structure and Policy in Postal Rates," *Journal of Political Economy*, Vol. LXV (June 1957), pp. 185–208.

sometimes alleged, the post office conducts operations would be put to the test of the market, while prospects of private monopoly would be counteracted by public competition.

EQUALITY

A free and open market tends to pay productive agents the value of what they produce. The income of individuals depends on the unit price of productive services times the number of units which they own—including both capital goods and their own labor power. The number of units of productive services which they own, or have embodied in them, depends on inheritance, effort, and luck. For reasons too obvious to enumerate, the benefits of inheritance, effort, and luck are not equally distributed in the existing social order and are not likely to be so distributed in any conceivable scheme of social organization.

But inevitability does not justify inequality. More accurately speaking, inequality of wealth and income can be modified by social policy; and a democratic social order is powerfully determined to undertake that policy. Equality, or mitigation of gross inequalities, is both an end value of the democratic community and a means to other ends.

In this context the happiest exercise of the power of the state is to promote equality by removing the barriers which restrict opportunity; barriers founded on caste or prejudice, barriers heightened by the presence of ignorance, and barriers which the market itself would sweep away if given scope to do so—all this is a necessary exercise of democratic public power.[24]

The state also intervenes to purchase equality, or mitigate inequity, through the tax-expenditure mechanism. Depending on the schedule of taxes and the imputation of benefits to individuals, the balance of benefits bestowed minus taxes collected is generally positive for the lower income groups and negative for higher income groups.[25] Despite opportunities for evasion, the sawtooth monster embodied in present income and inheritance tax schedules has cut down significantly on the relative share of upper income groups in the national dividend over the past quarter century.[26] Approach toward equality, then, is both a valid aim and a real accomplishment of our democratic fiscal system.

Given the conditions of economic life, a tax-expenditure system which promotes equality conflicts, after a certain point, with other end values of the community. Specifically it conflicts, after some specified point, with

---

[24] Allan G. B. Fisher, "Alternative Techniques for Promoting Equality in a Capitalist Society," *American Economic Review*, Vol. XL (May 1950), pp. 356–68.

[25] James M. Buchanan, "The Pure Theory of Government Finance: A Suggested Approach," *Journal of Political Economy*, Vol. LVII (December 1949), pp. 496–505, refers to this balance—with the sign reversed, however—as the "fiscal residuum."

[26] Simon Kuznets, *Shares of Upper Income Groups in Income and Savings* (New York: National Bureau of Economic Research, 1952).

productivity. In full perspective, the relation between equality and productivity doubtless runs as follows: If wealth and income were very unequally distributed, there is a range over which the community could probably achieve both higher output and more equality by redistributing resources from rich to poor. If redistribution continued, a point of maximum productivity and moderate equality would be reached. Thereafter, additional degrees of equality could be purchased only at the expense of some sacrifice of productivity. These sacrifices would be small at first, but would increase steadily till, at the limit, complete equality—the same income for everyone—would be reached only by a very considerable sacrifice of total output.

Now why must equality and productivity be competitive values beyond a certain point? Answer No. 1 is to be found in the adverse incentive effect of progressive taxation on initiative, risk taking, and enterprise. Answer No. 2 rests on the adverse incentive effect of receiving income without expending effort. (Up to a point, of course, the latter effect would be counterbalanced by improvements in ability and standard of living created by subsidies to low-income families.)

To continue: So long as society can get more of both values, both more equality and more income (from a given body of resources), it would be wasteful not to do so. But the problem of choice arises when the two values cannot increase simultaneously, when, that is, additional equality can be purchased only by some sacrifice of productivity and progress. Because we are, or may be, faced with this kind of choice is, of course, no reason for adjuring additional equality. We may judge it worth the price. But in so judging we must take account of the terms of trade between equality and productivity. Here, in brief, is a central problem of democratic government—how much more (or less) equality do we want in terms of the sacrifice (or gain) in productivity involved in moving toward it.

Finally, equality is not achieved by any one activity of government. It is a byproduct and an end product of the whole system of government finance.

Humanitarianism

The market is an impersonal agency. It takes no account of need unless signalized by price and recognizes virtues only when they are marketable. In larger perspective, however, "no man is an island," or, in the language of economics rather than literature, one man's utility function may contain a term for the welfare of another. Humanitarian activities are thus an important special case of external effects between consumers.

Humanitarian objectives can be undertaken by voluntary nonprofit agencies to which individuals contribute in accord with their means and desires. (In the division of labor between government and the market these institutions share some of the elements of both.) Citizen X, however, might be more willing to support some humanitarian activity if assured that Y and Z would follow suit. Accordingly he makes a compact with them under which each is to vote on the amount that all will contribute. Before voting, they decide that the total will be allocated between them in accord with their means. In this way each dollar that X contributes will be accompanied by, say, half a dollar from Y and two from Z. When the vote is taken, therefore, the tax each levies on himself exceeds the amount he would have contributed on his own. Government philanthropy, then, can be regarded as a device to administer such a compact for the community as a whole, voting, of course, being conducted by representatives rather than by the entire electorate.

Humanitarian activities of government include a series of transfer payments for assistance to dependent children, aid to the aged, compensation of the unemployed, and general relief for the indigent and unfortunate.

ECONOMIC STABILITY

An economic environment of individual decisions, mutual interdependence, and uncertain prospects is inevitably subject to fluctuations in income, employment, and prices. While these erratic movements are, in some sense, a concomitant of progress, the business cycle generates a train of evils which no responsible society will passively endure. (1) Uncertainty itself creates costs; elaborate and expensive adjustments must be undertaken by individuals in order to cope with it. (2) Both inflation and depression generate diseconomies in the form of overexpansion of certain sectors of the economy during a runaway boom and underutilization of resources during a slump. (3) The incidence of the cycle is inequitably distributed between individuals. (4) Aggravated uncertainty of the system plus waste and inequity generate political pressures which threaten the stability of democracy.

From the individual point of view the cycle appears as a capital levy of arbitrary amount, levied without announcement or compensation. If the cycle cannot be tamed but must be accepted as an act of providence, social policy, as a bare minimum, ought to share its burdens more equitably.

Under modern conditions, the cycle can, or some of its components can, be mitigated, though not completely controlled, by fiscal and monetary policy. Government can stabilize certain elements of the budget and these in turn can exert a tranquillizing effect upon the market; it can stabilize the level of expenditures over the cycle; it can fix the rates, though not the yield, of the tax system; it can stabilize the quantity of money but not, of course, the number of times that money circulates during the period.

Government can also intervene to stabilize several important variables for the market as a whole. It can, if needed, fix the price of particular things though not the quality and quantity of goods exchanged at this price; it can fix the rate of interest; it can stabilize the general level of prices; and it can stabilize the level of employment.

Under modern conditions, however, the chief problems of fiscal policy are conflict among objectives and inadequacy of means. Regarding conflict, the Government may not be able simultaneously to stabilize the level of prices and the volume of employment. Full employment at forced draft spells inflation, although the terms of trade between more inflation and more employment vary erratically over the course of the cycle. Regarding means, stabilizing either employment or prices or some selected combination of the two can be attempted either through automatic devices or through forecasting and administrative action. Automatic devices or built-in stabilizers take time to operate; forecasting is subject to error, and administrative action may involve both error and delay.

In any event economists know appallingly little about the cure of the cycle and still less about its causes. The situation counsels humility, caution—and more resources for basic research.

MISCELLANEOUS ACTIVITIES: PRICE FIXING AND GOVERNMENT ENTERPRISE

PRICE FIXING

On an ad hoc basis, the Central Government intervenes to regulate the prices of particular goods and services. In most instances save the control of prices during wartime, these interventions establish minimum prices and redound to the advantage of particular producers.

Primary instances of these activities are farm price supports, tariffs, transportation prices, and minimum wage legislation.

In the short run, parity prices and production quotas on basic agricultural commodities sold in the private market represent an income subsidy to wealthy farmers financed by a sales tax on low income city consumers. For the rise in price is equivalent to a levy on consumption; the larger the farmer's output (or acreage) the greater is the extent of the subsidy which this rise in prices (or soil bank payments) confers upon him; and the wheat, cotton, corn, and tobacco which this program covers are staples of the city worker's budget. (The portion of the crop sequestered in storage by the Commodity Credit Corporation and its equivalents is paid for from general revenues, though a portion of the cost may be recovered if the commodity is later sold or dumped abroad.)

In the long run, the portion of the subsidy that finds its way into income of farm labor tends to retard the migration of workers to the city and slow down the rate of urban economic development. The portion imputed to land bids up the price of farms.[27] In addition to the income

---

[27] For general discussion see T. W. Schultz, *Agriculture in an Unstable Economy* (New York: McGraw-Hill Book Co., Inc., 1945).

subsidy, the stability of agricultural prices which the program administers enables farmers to employ resources more effectively.[28]

Tariffs and import quotas subsidize producers at the expense of consumers in the short run, while in the long run they draw more resources into the protected trades than would otherwise be the case and lower the national dividend by cutting us off from the advantages of international specialization. In addition, tariff hampers exports, fosters domestic monopoly, and creates political pressures for subsidies to foreign governments. Tariff, however, prevents deterioration in the economic position of workers and investors who are threatened by foreign competition and who can raise enough leverage to secure protection.

The legal minimum wage raises the price but reduces the volume of employment for workers in the trades it protects. For no tendency in economics is more certain or definite than the principle that states: the higher the price of something, other things the same, the less the volume of purchases. This principle, unfortunately, applies to the hiring of unskilled workers in sweated industries. An effective floor on wages which raises costs of production will diminish employment because, first, employers substitute capital for labor and, second, consumers substitute other goods for those produced by the protected trades. If demand for unskilled labor is elastic the minimum wage also reduces the total wages bill and purchasing power placed in the hands of the protected workers.

Benefits of minimum wages are secured by those who gain employment under its provisions. Costs are borne, first, by the workers whom it prices out of the market, second, by consumers who buy the products of protected industries, and third, by resources which are complementary to unskilled labor.

GOVERNMENT ENTERPRISES

In addition to operating natural monopolies which sell to the general public, Government also produces a great variety of supplies and services; for many, but not all of these, Government itself is the sole customer. The Defense Department operates a galaxy of establishments which manufacture arms, build ships, and produce supplies. The Government operates a railroad in Alaska and in Panama; it has turned its hand to the production of rum and molasses in the Virgin Islands; it lends money to farmers (the Farmers' Home Administration), to small-business men (the Small Business Administration), and to importers and exporters (the Export-Import Bank). It builds and owns ships which are leased to private concerns. Finally, Government is the landlord of 400 millions of acres within the 48 States.

What issues of principle and practice are raised by these activities? In

---

[28] D. Gale Johnson, *Forward Prices for Agriculture* (Chicago: The University of Chicago Press, 1947).

general, as suggested above, Government is a most indifferent manager of enterprises. Why? Because Government employees are stupid and lazy? Not at all; here, as elsewhere, the servant is worthy of his hire. Because the civil service, while an admirable device for preventing corruption, tends to protect mediocrity and inhibit initiative? Perhaps; but too much cannot be made of this argument. Because Government is immune from the discipline of the competitive market? In part, yes, but large sections of corporate bureaucracy also enjoy some relative immunity. The ineffectiveness of Government management arises from its diseconomies of scale. Government is too large for maximum efficiency. Or, put a bit more carefully, Government may be no larger than necessary in order to discharge the functions which it alone must command, but if some activity which the market could have performed is added to its structure, that activity will, in general, be conducted less effectively than it could have been conducted by the market. Not only that; but the addition of this activity will dilute the managerial capacity of the top echelon, and existing activities will suffer in consequence.

Now, of course, this general presumption must be modified in particular cases. Many old-line Government bureaus (such as the Forestry Service) and many quasi-public corporations (such as the TVA) have great dedication and initiative with high esprit de corps amongst their staff and are fully the equal of comparable sectors of private enterprise. But the general presumption against Government enterprise should not lightly be cast aside. Government ought not be duplicate the efforts of the market and when it has done so, because of some temporary expediency, it should withdraw as gracefully and rapidly as possible. Exceptions require very strong proof indeed.

Unfortunately, once Government is embroiled in one of these ventures, the cost of disentanglement is high. In some cases no private firms are willing to take the thing off the Government's hands save at bargain-basement prices. Or—as in the case of loans to farmers and small-business men—the activity involves a concealed subsidy which the political power of the beneficiaries is mobilized to retain. Or an arsenal, a manufacturing plant, and an insurance agency become symbols of empire and all the massive power and artful devices of entrenched bureaucracy are arrayed in their defense.

RATIONAL CHOICE IN BUDGETARY POLICY

Given the grounds which sanction Government activities, how should we decide how much of our resources to devote to public purposes? Since the market cannot register the demand for these services, the political process must answer this question for us.

To economize on the labor of decision-making, elected representatives review policy and decide the details of public expenditure. In this, however, they do but reflect the ultimate consensus of the body politic so far as it lies within their power to determine it. Let us inquire, therefore, how the rational society would determine expenditures if the people themselves, after due investigation and debate, held a mass referendum on budgetary policy.

The decision could be made in two separate stages. The first order of business would be determination of the system of taxes, i. e., the array of rates for collecting any given amount of revenue from various income groups. To simplify exposition let us suppose that the revenue is to be collected by a universal tax on personal income. For each amount of revenue some sets of rates promise more equality, and some less; some would exact a smaller sacrifice in productivity, others a greater sacrifice. Indeed each set of rates would yield a specific combination of equality and productivity. The rational voter would select the rates that corresponded to his preferences as a citizen and his interests as a producer.

The society as a whole, let us say, decides to accept some rough average of the systems of rates for which its members voted. This being decided, the taxes levied upon members of each income class for each different amount of revenue are ascertained and announced.

Our citizen-taxpayers repair to the polls again to vote for the level of expenditures. Let us suppose that they are to cast a separate vote for each of the major categories: national defense, health and welfare, conservation, and so forth. How does the rational taxpayer cast his vote? He is aware that, say, expenditures of $10 billion of the community entail $100 in personal taxes, $15 billions, $150 and so on. Given his income and the structure of taxes, each extra dollar levied on him is accompanied by an additional $100 million from the community at large. (These accompanying amounts, of course, vary from one income group to another and from one expenditure level to another.) As a rational citizen-taxpayer he assesses the technical results of these expenditures and evaluates the personal satisfactions they create for him. For each class of activities, he votes for the level of public expenditures where the satisfactions created through Government by the outlay which necessarily accompanies the last dollar in personal taxes equal the satisfactions he would have secured from a dollar of private expenditure. He equalizes at the margin the satisfactions secured from alternative avenues of expenditure.

Depending on their income, their preferences, and the structure of the tax system, each individual selects some different level of expenditures in each category of the budget. The community, let us suppose, balances off these votes by compromising at the median, by taking, that is, the level which slices the votes in half; 50 percent voted for some higher level, 50 percent for some lower amount.

The result, inevitably, satisfies no one perfectly and dissatisfies some exceedingly. First, the tax system appears arbitrary when viewed by citizens who hold different preferences for the terms of trade between equality and productivity. Second, the degree of freedom the voter exercises depends on the number of expenditure categories arrayed for his decision. Third, the optimum for which he votes is surrounded by a margin of doubt. For his choice on "national defense" is bound to be affected by public expenditures and personal taxes for "conservation." But he votes for each in ignorance of the amount the community will determine for the other. Fourth, the community—under the median rule or any other rule—is not likely to satisfy his preferences precisely (unless, by accident, he was the median voter). If, for instance, the community chooses $10 billion, those who wanted more will feel shortchanged, while those who selected less may fancy themselves abused.

What role does representative government play in rational budgetary policy? The variety and complexity of government are beyond the scope of the ordinary citizen, nor would it be at all sensible for him to spend any large fraction of his time and his fortune in public business. That task is entrusted to elected agents who both accumulate knowledge of public affairs and serve as middlemen between the body politic and its government. Even the most dedicated of these agents can form no more than a rough estimate of the issues at stake, and can collect only the most cursory of samples of the true state of public opinion. But given their limits and their commitments, the role of the legislator is to vote as the citizens would have voted if they knew as much as he knows.

Market Socialism

Market socialism (sometimes called "democratic" or "liberal" socialism) seeks to combine the socialist principles of (1) public ownership and (2) limited inequality in income distribution with (3) the use of markets and prices to allocate resources and goods. (In contrast, authoritarian socialism combines public ownership with central planning and allocation by administrative orders.)

In the market socialist model, households have freedom of choice of occupation, as differential wages in the labor market allocate the labor force among jobs. The resulting income differences are reduced by a social dividend paid on a uniform basis unrelated to occupation or wages. Households also have consumer choice in the expenditure of income, as well as a large measure of consumer sovereignty. The latter, however, is abridged but not superceded by the intervention of the Central Planning Board (CPB) in the economy to affect the rate of investment in order to achieve stability and growth.

Two principal solutions to the problem of pricing and resource allocation in market socialism have been suggested. In the solution advocated by Fred M. Taylor and Oskar Lange, the CPB attempts by trial and error to fix market-clearing prices which equate supply and demand. Given these "parametric" prices and some very broad rules for managerial behavior, individual enterprise managers determine the level and composition of their output and their use of inputs. An alternative solution, advanced by Abba Lerner and others, proposes that the prices themselves be determined by the interplay of the supply and demand of socialist firms and households in the market.

These blueprints for market socialism originated in response to the argument of various prominent economists in the 1920s that rational economic calculation and efficient allocation of resources were in principle impossible in a socialist economy. The most famous member of this school is Ludwig von Mises, whose views are summarized in the first of the following three selections. To refute this conclusion, Oskar Lange developed the model of market socialism presented in the next selection. Lange's solution to the problem, in turn, has been challenged by Hayek (in the last selection) on the ground that, while perhaps conceivable in theory, it cannot be successfully applied in practice. (Selection No. 14, in Part III, explains how a number of the problems identified by Hayek have been met in the Yugoslav variant of market socialism.)

Ludwig von Mises

6. ECONOMIC CALCULATION IN SOCIALISM*

*Mises denies the possibility of economic calcula-
tion and rational resource allocation in socialism.
He argues that economic calculation can take
place only by means of money prices established
in a market for producer goods resting on private
ownership of the means of production. Because
such markets cannot, by definition, exist in socialism, he concludes that a socialist economy
cannot achieve efficient allocation of resources.
"Artificial" markets in socialism cannot successfully replace the true markets of capitalism in
pricing producer goods so as to use them most
effectively.*

WITHOUT calculation, economic activity is impossible. Since under Socialism economic calculation is impossible, under Socialism there can be no
economic activity in our sense of the word. In small and insignificant
things rational action might still persist. But, for the most part, it would no
longer be possible to speak of rational production. In the absence of
criteria of rationality, production could not be consciously economical.

For some time possibly the accumulated tradition of thousands of years
of economic freedom would preserve the art of economic administration
from complete disintegration. Men would preserve the old processes not
because they were rational, but because they were sanctified by tradition.
In the meantime, however, changing conditions would make them irrational. They would become uneconomical as the result of changes brought
about by the general decline of economic thought. It is true that production would no longer be "anarchical." The command of a supreme au-

*Reprinted, with permission, from *Socialism: An Economic and Sociological
Analysis* (New Haven: Yale University Press, 1951), pp. 119–22, 137–42. This volume
is an expanded translation of *Die Gemeinwirtschaft*, originally published in 1922.
Ludwig von Mises was Professor of Economics at the University of Vienna.

thority would govern the business of supply. Instead of the economy of "anarchical" production the senseless order of an irrational machine would be supreme. The wheels would go round, but to no effect.

Let us try to imagine the position of a socialist community. There will be hundreds and thousands of establishments in which work is going on. A minority of these will produce goods ready for use. The majority will produce capital goods and semi-manufactures. All these establishments will be closely connected. Each commodity produced will pass through a whole series of such establishments before it is ready for consumption. Yet in the incessant press of all these processes the economic administration will have no real sense of direction. It will have no means of ascertaining whether a given piece of work is really necessary, whether labor and material are not being wasted in completing it. How would it discover which of two processes was the more satisfactory? At best, it could compare the quantity of ultimate products. But only rarely could it compare the expenditure incurred in their production. It would know exactly—or it would imagine it knew—what it wanted to produce. It ought therefore to set about obtaining the desired results with the smallest possible expenditure. But to do this it would have to be able to make calculations. And such calculations must be calculations of value. They could not be merely "technical," they could not be calculations of the objective use-value of goods and services. This is so obvious that it needs no further demonstration.

Under a system based upon private ownership in the means of production, the scale of values is the outcome of the actions of every independent member of society. Everyone plays a two-fold part in its establishment first as a consumer, secondly as producer. As consumer, he establishes the valuation of goods ready for consumption. As producer, he guides production-goods into those uses in which they yield the highest product. In this way all goods of higher orders also are graded in the way appropriate to them under the existing conditions of production and the demands of society. The interplay of these two processes ensures that the economic principle is observed in both consumption and production. And, in this way, arises the exactly graded system of prices which enables everyone to frame his demand on economic lines.

Under Socialism, all this must necessarily be lacking. The economic administration may indeed know exactly what commodities are needed most urgently. But this is only half the problem. The other half, the valuation of the means of production, it cannot solve. It can ascertain the value of the totality of such instruments. That is obviously equal to the value of the satisfactions they afford. If it calculates the loss that would be incurred by withdrawing them, it can also ascertain the value of single instruments of production. But it cannot assimilate them to a common price denominator, as can be done under a system of economic freedom and money prices.

It is not necessary that Socialism should dispense altogether with money. It is possible to conceive arrangements permitting the use of money for the exchange of consumers goods. But since the prices of the various factors of production (including labor) could not be expressed in money, money could play no part in economic calculations.

Suppose, for instance, that the socialist commonwealth was contemplating a new railway line. Would a new railway line be a good thing? If so, which of many possible routes should it cover? Under a system of private ownership we could use money calculations to decide these questions. The new line would cheapen the transportation of certain articles, and, on this basis, we could estimate whether the reduction in transport charges would be great enough to counterweigh the expenditure which the building and running of the line would involve. Such a calculation could be made only in money. We could not do it by comparing various classes of expenditure and savings in kind. If it is out of the question to reduce to a common unit the quantities of various kinds of skilled and unskilled labor, iron, coal, building materials of different kinds, machinery and the other things which the building and upkeep of railways necessitate, then it is impossible to make them the subject of economic calculation. We can make systematic economic plans only when all the commodities which we have to take into account can be assimilated to money. True, money calculations are incomplete. True, they have profound deficiencies. But we have nothing better to put in their place. And under sound monetary conditions they suffice for practical purposes. If we abandon them, economic calculation becomes absolutely impossible.

This is not to say that the socialist community would be entirely at a loss. It would decide for or against the proposed undertaking and issue an edict. But, at best, such a decision would be based on vague valuations. It could not be based on exact calculations of value.

A stationary society could, indeed, dispense with these calculations. For there, economic operations merely repeat themselves. So that, if we assume that the socialist system of production were based upon the last state of the system of economic freedom which it superseded, and that no changes were to take place in the future, we could indeed conceive a rational and economic Socialism. But only in theory. A stationary economic system can never exist. Things are continually changing, and the stationary state, although necessary as an aid to speculation, is a theoretical assumption to which there is no counterpart in reality. And, quite apart from this, the maintenance of such a connection with the last state of the exchange economy would be out of the question, since the transition to Socialism with its equalization of incomes would necessarily transform the whole "set" of consumption and production. And then we have a socialist community which must cross the whole ocean of possible and imaginable economic permutations without the compass of economic calculation.

All economic change, therefore, would involve operations the value of which could neither be predicted beforehand nor ascertained after they had taken place. Everything would be a leap in the dark. Socialism is the renunciation of rational economy.

*   *   *   *

Some of the younger socialists believe that the socialist community could solve the problem of economic calculation by the creation of an artificial market for the means of production. They admit that it was an error on the part of the older socialists to have sought to realize Socialism through the suspension of the market and the abolition of pricing for goods of higher orders[1]; they hold that it was an error to have seen in the suppression of the market and of the price system the essence of the socialistic ideal. And they contend that if it is not to degenerate into a meaningless chaos in which the whole of our civilization would disappear, the socialist community equally with the capitalistic community, must create a market in which all goods and services may be priced. On the basis of such arrangements, they think, the socialist community will be able to make its calculations as easily as the capitalist entrepreneurs.

Unfortunately the supporters of such proposals do not see (or perhaps *will* not see) that it is not possible to divorce the market and its functions in regard to the formation of prices from the working of a society which is based on private property in the means of production and in which, subject to the rules of such a society, the landlords, capitalists, and entrepreneurs can dispose of their property as they think fit. For the motive force of the whole process which gives rise to market prices for the factors of production is the ceaseless search on the part of the capitalists and the entrepreneurs to maximize their profits by serving the consumers' wishes. Without the striving of the entrepreneurs (including the shareholders) for profit, of the landlords for rent, of the capitalists for interest and the laborers for wages, the successful functioning of the whole mechanism is not to be thought of. It is only the prospect of profit which directs production into those channels in which the demands of the consumer are best satisfied at least cost. If the prospect of profit disappears the mechanism of the market loses its mainspring, for it is only this prospect which sets it in motion and maintains it in operation. The market is thus the focal point of the capitalist order of society; it is the essence of Capitalism. Only under Capitalism, therefore, is it possible; it cannot be "artificially" imitated under Socialism.

The advocates of the artificial market, however, are of the opinion that an artificial market can be created by instructing the controllers of the different industrial units to act *as if* they were entrepreneurs in a capitalistic state. They argue that even under Capitalism the managers of joint stock companies work not for themselves but for the companies, that is to say, for the shareholders. Under Socialism, therefore, it would be possible

---

[1][Producers' goods.—EDITOR.]

for them to act in exactly the same way as before, with the same circumspection and devotion to duty. The only difference would be that under Socialism the product of the manager's labors would go to the community rather than to the shareholders. In such a way, in contrast to all socialists who have written on the subject hitherto, especially the Marxians, they think it would be possible to construct a decentralized, as opposed to a centralized, Socialism.

In order to judge properly such proposals, it is necessary in the first place to realize that these controllers of individual industrial units would have to be appointed. Under Capitalism the managers of the joint stock companies are appointed either directly or indirectly by the shareholders. In so far as the shareholders give to the managers power to produce by the means of the company's (i.e. the stockholders') stock they are risking their own property or a part of their own property. The speculation (for it is necessarily a speculation) may succeed and bring profit; it may, however, misfire and bring about the loss of the whole or a part of the capital concerned. This committing of one's own capital to a business whose outcome is uncertain and to men whose future ability is still a matter of conjecture whatever one may know of their past, is the essence of joint stock company enterprise.

Now it is a complete fallacy to suppose that the problem of economic calculation in a socialist community relates solely to matters which fall into the sphere of the daily business routine of managers of joint stock companies. It is clear that such a belief can only arise from exclusive concentration on the idea of a stationary economic system—a conception which no doubt is useful for the solution of many theoretical problems but which has no counterpart in fact and which, if exclusively regarded, can even be positively misleading. It is clear that under stationary conditions the problem of economic calculation does not really arise. When we think of the stationary society, we think of an economy in which all the factors of production are already used in such a way as, under the given conditions, to provide the maximum of the things which are demanded by consumers. That is to say, under stationary conditions there no longer exists a problem for economic calculation to solve. The essential function of economic calculation has *by hypothesis* already been performed. There is no need for an apparatus of calculation. To use a popular but not altogether satisfactory terminology we can say that the problem of economic calculation is of economic dynamics: it is no problem of economic statics.

The problem of economic calculation is a problem which arises in an economy which is perpetually subject to change, an economy which every day is confronted with new problems which have to be solved. Now in order to solve such problems it is above all necessary that capital should be withdrawn from particular lines of production, from particular undertakings and concerns and should be applied in other lines of production, in other undertakings and concerns. This is not a matter for the managers of joint stock companies, it is essentially a matter for the capitalists—the capitalists who buy and sell stocks and shares, who make loans and recover them, who make deposits in the banks and draw them out of the banks again, who speculate in all kinds of commodities. It is these operations of speculative capitalists which create those conditions of the money market, the stock exchanges and the wholesale markets which have to be taken for granted by the manager of the joint stock company, who, according to the socialist writers we are considering, is to be conceived as nothing but the reliable and conscientious servant of the company. It is the speculative capitalists who create the data to which he has to adjust his business and which therefore gives direction to his trading operations.

It follows therefore that it is a fundamental deficiency of all these socialistic constructions which invoke the "artificial market" and artificial competition as a way out of the problem of economic calculation, that they rest on the belief that the market for factors of production is affected only by producers buying and selling commodities. It is not possible to eliminate from such markets the influence of the supply of capital from the capitalists and the demand for capital by the entrepreneurs, without destroying the mechanism itself.

Faced with this difficulty, the socialist is likely to propose that the socialist state as owner of all capital and all means of production should simply direct capital to those undertakings which promise the highest return. The available capital, he will contend, should go to those undertakings which offer the highest rate of profit. But such a state of affairs would simply mean that those managers who were less cautious and more optimistic would receive capital to enlarge their undertakings while more cautious and more sceptical managers would go away empty-handed. Under Capitalism, the capitalist decides to whom he will entrust *his own* capital. The beliefs of the managers of joint stock companies regarding the future prospects of their undertakings and the hopes of project-makers regarding the profitability of their plans are not in any way decisive. The mechanism of the money market and the capital market decides. This indeed is its main task: to serve the economic system as a whole, to judge the profitability of alternative openings and not blindly to follow what the managers of particular concerns, limited by the narrow horizon of their own undertakings, are tempted to propose.

To understand this completely, it is essential to realize that the capitalist does not just invest his capital in those undertakings which offer high interest or high profit; he attempts rather to strike a balance between his desire for profit and his estimate of the risk of loss. He must exercise foresight. If he does not do so then he suffers losses—losses that bring it about that his disposition over the factors of production is transferred to the hands of others who know better how to weigh the risks and the prospects of business speculation.

Now if it is to remain socialistic, the socialist State cannot leave to other hands that disposition over capital which permits the enlargement of existing undertakings, the contraction of others and the bringing into being of undertakings that are completely new. And it is scarcely to be assumed that socialists of whatever persuasion would seriously propose that this function should be made over to some group of people who would "simply" have the business of doing what capitalists and speculators do under capitalistic conditions, the only difference being that the product of their foresight should not belong to them but to the community. Proposals of this sort may well be made concerning the managers of joint stock companies. They can never be extended to capitalists and speculators, for no socialist would dispute that the function which capitalists and speculators perform under Capitalism, namely directing the use of capital goods into that direction in which they best serve the demands of the consumer, is only performed because they are under the incentive to preserve their property and to make profits which increase it or at least allow them to live without diminishing their capital.

It follows therefore that the socialist community can do nothing but place the disposition over capital in the hands of the State or to be exact in the hands of the men who, as the governing authority, carry out the business of the State. And that signifies elimination of the market, which indeed is the fundamental aim of Socialism, for the guidance of economic activity by the market implies organization of production and a distribution of the product according to that disposition of the spending power of individual members of society which makes itself felt on the market; that is to say, it implies precisely that which it is the goal of Socialism to eliminate.

If the socialists attempt to belittle the significance of the problem of economic calculation in the Socialist community, on the ground that the forces of the market do not lead to ethically justifiable arrangements, they simply show that they do not understand the real nature of the problem. It is not a question of whether there shall be produced cannons or clothes, dwelling houses or churches, luxuries or subsistence. In any social order, even under Socialism, it can very easily be decided which kind and what number of consumption goods should be produced. No one has ever denied that. But once this decision has been made, there still remains the problem of ascertaining how the existing means of production can be used most effectively to produce these goods in question. In order to solve this problem it is necessary that there should be economic calculation. And economic calculation can only take place by means of money prices established in the market for production goods in a society resting on private property in the means of production. That is to say, there must exist money prices of land, raw materials, semi-manufactures; that is to say, there must be money wages and interest rates.

Thus the alternative is still *either* Socialism or a market economy.

Oskar Lange

7. ON THE ECONOMIC THEORY
OF SOCIALISM*

*In Lange's model of market socialism, house-
holds, the Central Planning Board (CPB), and
socialist managers share in the decisions which
guide the economy. Consumer preferences, expressed in a market for consumer goods, decide
the goods to be produced. The CPB, by trial and
error, sets the prices of consumer and producer
goods so as to equate the supply and demand for
each good. Given these "parametric" prices, the
managers of socialist enterprises and industries
determine their inputs and outputs according to
two broad rules. First, they must combine factors
of production so as to minimize the average cost
of production for any output. Second, they must
fix output at the level where marginal cost equals
the price set by the CPB. In combination, these
two rules secure the most economical production
of the optimum output.*

*The CPB distributes a social dividend to
households which reduces the inequality of income resulting from market-determined wages.
It also decides the rate of investment and then
sets an interest rate on capital which equates the
demand for capital, on the part of socialist managers, to the amount available.*

IN ORDER to discuss the method of allocating resources in a socialist
economy we have to state what kind of socialist society we have in mind.
The fact of public ownership of the means of production does not in itself

* From *On the Economic Theory of Socialism*, by Oskar Lange and Fred M.
Taylor, ed. Benjamin E. Lippincott (Minneapolis: University of Minnesota Press,

determine the system of distributing consumers' goods and of allocating people to various occupations, nor the principles guiding the production of commodities. Let us now assume that freedom of choice in consumption and freedom of choice of occupation are maintained and that the preferences of consumers, as expressed by their demand prices, are the guiding criteria in production and in the allocation of resources. . . .

In the socialist system as described we have a genuine market (in the institutional sense of the word) for consumers' goods and for the services of labor. But there is no market for capital goods and productive resources outside of labor.[1] The prices of capital goods and productive resources outside of labor are thus prices in the generalized sense, i.e., mere indices of alternatives available, fixed for accounting purposes. Let us see how economic equilibrium is determined in such a system. Just as in a competitive individualist regime, the determination of equilibrium consists of two parts. (*A*) On the basis of *given* indices of alternatives (which are market prices in the case of consumers' goods and the services of labor and accounting prices in all other cases) both the individuals participating in the economic system as consumers and as owners of the services of labor and the managers of production and of the ultimate resources outside of labor (i.e., of capital and of natural resources) make decisions according to certain principles. These managers are assumed to be public officials. (*B*) The prices (whether market or accounting) are determined by the condition that the quantity of each commodity demanded is equal to the quantity supplied. The conditions determining the decisions under *A* form the *subjective*, while that under *B* is the *objective*, equilibrium condition. Finally, we have also a condition *C*, expressing the social organization of the economic system. As the productive resources outside of labor are public property, the incomes of the consumers are divorced from the ownership of those resources and the form of condition *C* (social organization) is determined by the *principles of income formation adopted.*

The possibility of determining condition *C* in different ways gives to a socialist society considerable freedom in matters of distribution of income. But the necessity of maintaining freedom in the choice of occupation limits the arbitrary use of this freedom, for there must be some connection between the income of a consumer and the services of labor performed by him. It seems, therefore, convenient to regard the income of consumers as composed of two parts: one part being the receipts for the labor services

1938), pp. 72–86. Originally published in *Review of Economic Studies*, Vol. IV, No. 1 (October, 1936), pp. 60–66. Reprinted with the permission of the *Review of Economic Studies* and the University of Minnesota Press. Oskar Lange, formerly Professor of Economics at the University of Chicago, is now Deputy Chairman of the Council of State of Poland and Professor of Political Economy at Warsaw University.

[1] To simplify the problem we assume that all means of production are public property. Needless to say, in any actual socialist community there must be a large number of means of production privately owned (e.g., by farmers, artisans, and small-scale entrepreneurs). But this does not introduce any new theoretical problem.

performed and the other part being a social dividend constituting the individual's share in the income derived from the capital and the natural resources owned by society. We assume that the distribution of the social dividend is based on certain principles, reserving the content of those principles for later discussion. Thus condition C is determinate and determines the incomes of the consumers in terms of prices of the services of labor and social dividend, which, in turn, may be regarded as determined by the total yield of capital and of the natural resources and by the principles adopted in distributing this yield.[2]

A. Let us consider the subjective equilibrium condition in a socialist economy:

1. Freedom of choice in consumption being assumed,[3] this part of the subjective equilibrium condition of a competitive market applies also to the market for consumers' goods in a socialist economy. The incomes of the consumers and the prices of consumers' goods being given, the demand for consumers' goods is determined.

2. The decisions of the managers of production are no longer guided by the aim of maximizing profit. Instead, certain rules are imposed on them by the Central Planning Board which aim at satisfying consumers' preferences in the best way possible. These rules determine the combination of factors of production and the scale of output.

One rule must impose the choice of the combination of factors which minimizes the average cost of production. This rule leads to the factors being combined in such proportion that the marginal productivity of that amount of each factor which is worth a unit of money is the same for all factors. This rule is addressed to whoever makes decisions involving the problem of the optimum combination of factors, i.e., to managers responsible for running existing plants and to those engaged in building new plants. A second rule determines the scale of output by stating that output has to be fixed so that marginal cost is equal to the price of the product. This rule is addressed to two kinds of persons. First of all, it is addressed to the managers of plants and thus determines the scale of output of each plant and, together with the first rule, its demand for factors of production. The first rule, to whomever addressed, and the second rule when addressed to the managers of plants perform the same function that in a

---

[2] In formulating condition C capital accumulation has to be taken into account. Capital accumulation may be done either "corporately" by deducting a certain part of the national income before the social dividend is distributed, or it may be left to the savings of individuals, or both methods may be combined. But "corporate" accumulation must certainly be the dominant form of capital formation in a socialist economy.

[3] Of course there may be also a sector of socialized consumption the cost of which is met by taxation. Such a sector exists also in capitalist society and comprises the provision not only of collective wants, in Cassel's sense, but also of other wants whose social importance is too great to be left to the free choice of individuals (for instance, free hospital service and free education). But this problem does not represent any theoretical difficulty and we may disregard it.

competitive system is carried out by the private producer's aiming to maximize his profit, when the prices of factors and of the product are independent of the amount of each factor used by him and of his scale of output.

The total output of an industry has yet to be determined. This is done by addressing the second rule also to the managers of a whole industry (e.g., to the directors of the National Coal Trust) as a principle to guide them in deciding whether an industry ought to be expanded (by building new plants or enlarging old ones) or contracted (by not replacing plants which are wearing out). Thus each industry has to produce exactly as much of a commodity as can be sold or "accounted for" to other industries at a price which equals the marginal cost incurred *by the industry* in producing this amount. The marginal cost incurred by an industry is the cost to that industry (not to a particular plant) of doing whatever is necessary to produce an additional unit of output, the optimum combination of factors being used. This may include the cost of building new plants or enlarging old ones.[4]

Addressed to the managers of an industry, the second rule performs the function which under free competition is carried out by the free entry of firms into an industry or their exodus from it: i.e., it determines the output of an industry.[5] The second rule, however, has to be carried out irrespective of whether average cost is covered or not, even if it should involve plants or whole industries in losses.

Both rules can be put in the form of the simple request to use always the method of production (i.e., combination of factors) which minimizes average cost and to produce as much of each service or commodity as will equalize marginal cost and the price of the product, this request being

---

[4] Since in practice such marginal cost is not a continuous function of output we have to compare the cost of each additional *indivisible input* with the receipts expected from the additional output thus secured. For instance, in a railway system as long as there are unused carriages the cost of putting them into use has to be compared with the additional receipts which may be obtained by doing so. When all the carriages available are used up to capacity, the cost of building and running additional carriages (and locomotives) has to be compared with the additional receipts expected to arise from such action. Finally, the question of building new tracks is decided upon the same principle. Cf. A. P. Lerner, "Statics and Dynamics in Socialist Economics," *Economic Journal*, Vol. XLVII (June, 1937), pp. 263–67.

[5] The result, however, of following this rule coincides with the result obtained under free competition only in the case of constant returns to the industry (i.e., a homogeneous production function of the first degree). In this case marginal cost incurred by the industry equals average cost. In all other cases the results diverge, for under free competition the output of an industry is such that average cost equals the price of the product, while according to our rule it is marginal cost (incurred by the industry) that ought to be equal to the price. This difference results in profits being made by the industries whose marginal cost exceeds average cost, whereas the industries in which the opposite is the case incur losses. These profits and losses correspond to the taxes and bounties proposed by Professor Pigou in order to bring about under free competition the equality of private and social marginal net product. See A. C. Pigou, *The Economics of Welfare* (3d ed., London, 1929), pp. 223–27.

addressed to whoever is responsible for the particular decision to be taken. Thus the output of each plant and industry and the total demand for factors of production by each industry are determined. To enable the managers of production to follow these rules the prices of the factors and of the products must, of course, be given. In the case of consumers' goods and services of labor they are determined on a market; in all other cases they are fixed by the Central Planning Board. Those prices being given, the supply of products and the demand for factors are determined.

The reasons for adopting the two rules mentioned are obvious. Since prices are indices of terms on which alternatives are offered, that method of production which will minimize average cost will also minimize the alternatives sacrificed. Thus the first rule means simply that each commodity must be produced with a minimum sacrifice of alternatives. The second rule is a necessary consequence of following consumers' preferences. It means that the marginal significance of each preference which is satisfied has to be equal to the marginal significance of the alternative preferences the satisfaction of which is sacrificed. If the second rule was not observed certain lower preferences would be satisfied while preferences higher up on the scale would be left unsatisfied.

3. Freedom of choice of occupation being assumed, laborers offer their services to the industry or occupation paying the highest wages. For the publicly owned captial and natural resources a price has to be fixed by the Central Planning Board with the provision that these resources can be directed only to industries which are able to "pay," or rather to "account for," this price. This is a consequence of following the consumers' preferences. The prices of the services of the ultimate productive resources being given, their distribution between the different industries is also determined.

B. The subjective equilibrium condition can be carried out only when prices are *given*. This is also true of the decisions of the managers of production and of the productive resources in public ownership. Only when prices are given can the combination of factors which minimizes average cost, the output which equalizes marginal cost and the price of the product, and the best allocation of the ultimate productive resources be determined. But if there is no market (in the institutional sense of the word) for capital goods or for the ultimate productive resources outside of labor, can their prices be determined objectively? Must not the prices fixed by the Central Planning Board necessarily be quite arbitrary? If so, their arbitrary character would deprive them of any economic significance as indices of the terms on which alternatives are offered. This is, indeed, the opinion of Professor Mises.[6] And the view is shared by Mr. Cole, who says: "A planless economy, in which each entrepreneur takes

---

[6] "Economic Calculation in the Socialist Commonwealth," reprinted in F. A. Hayek (ed.), *Collectivist Economic Planning* (London, 1935), p. 112.

his decisions apart from the rest, obviously confronts each entrepreneur with a broadly given structure of costs, represented by the current level of wages, rent, and interest. . . . In a planned socialist economy there can be no objective structure of costs. Costs can be imputed to any desired extent. . . . But these imputed costs are not objective, but *fiat* costs determined by the public policy of the State."[7] This view, however, is easily refuted by recalling the very elements of price theory.

Why is there an objective price structure in a competitive market? Because, as a result of the parametric function of prices, there is generally only *one* set of prices which satisfies the objective equilibrium condition, i.e., equalizes demand and supply of each commodity. The same objective price structure can be obtained in a socialist economy if the *parametric function of prices* is retained. On a competitive market the parametric function of prices results from the number of competing individuals being too large to enable any one to influence prices by his own action. In a socialist economy, production and ownership of the productive resources outside of labor being centralized, the managers certainly can and do influence prices by their decisions. Therefore, the parametric function of prices must be imposed on them by the Central Planning Board as an *accounting rule*. All accounting has to be done *as if* prices were independent of the decisions taken. For purposes of accounting, prices must be treated as constant, as they are treated by entrepreneurs on a competitive market.

The technique of attaining this end is very simple: the Central Planning Board has to fix prices and see to it that all managers of plants, industries, and resources do their accounting on the basis of the prices fixed by the Central Planning Board, and not tolerate any use of other accounting. Once the parametric function of prices is adopted as an accounting rule, the price structure is established by the objective equilibrium condition. For each set of prices and consumers' incomes a definite amount of each commodity is supplied and demanded. Condition C determines the incomes of the consumers by the prices of the services of ultimate productive resources and the principles adopted for the distribution of the social dividend. With those principles given, prices alone are the variables determining the demand and supply of commodities.

The condition that the quantity demanded and supplied has to be equal for each commodity serves to select the equilibrium prices which alone assure the compatibility of all decisions taken. *Any price different from the equilibrium price would show at the end of the accounting period a surplus or a shortage of the commodity in question.* Thus the accounting prices in a socialist economy, far from being arbitrary, have quite the same objective character as the market prices in a regime of competition. Any mistake made by the Central Planning Board in fixing prices would an-

---

[7] G. D. H. Cole, *Economic Planning* (New York, 1935), pp. 183–84.

nounce itself in a very objective way—by a physical shortage or surplus of
the quantity of the commodity or resources in question—and would have
to be corrected in order to keep production running smoothly. As there is
generally only one set of prices which satisfies the objective equilibrium
condition, both the prices of products and costs[8] are uniquely determined.[9]

Our study of the determination of equilibrium prices in a socialist
economy has shown that the process of price determination is quite
analogous to that in a competitive market. The Central Planning Board
performs the functions of the market. It establishes the rules for combining factors of production and choosing the scale of output of a plant,
for determining the output of an industry, for the allocation of resources,
and for the parametric use of prices in accounting. Finally, it fixes the
prices so as to balance the quantity supplied and demanded of each
commodity. It follows that a substitution of planning for the functions of
the market is quite possible and workable.

Two problems deserve some special attention. The first relates to the
determination of the best distribution of the social dividend. Freedom of
choice of occupation assumed, the distribution of the social dividend may
affect the amount of services of labor offered to different industries. If
certain occupations received a larger social dividend than others, labor
would be diverted into the occupations receiving a larger dividend.
Therefore, the distribution of the social dividend must be such as not to
interfere with the optimum distribution of labor services between
the different industries and occupations. The optimum distribution is that
which makes the differences of the value of the marginal product of the
services of labor in different industries and occupations equal to the
differences in the marginal disutility[10] of working in those industries or

---

[8] Hayek maintains that it would be impossible to determine the value of durable
instruments of production because, in consequence of changes, "the value of most of
the more durable instruments of production has little or no connection with the costs
which have been incurred in their production" (*Collectivist Economic Planning*,
p. 227). It is quite true that the value of such durable instruments is essentially a
capitalized quasi-rent and therefore can be determined only after the price which will
be obtained for the product is known (cf. *ibid.*, p. 228). But there is no reason why
the price of the product should be any less determinate in a socialist economy than
on a competitive market. The managers of the industrial plant in question have simply to take the price fixed by the Central Planning Board as the basis of their calculation. The Central Planning Board would fix this price so as to satisfy the objective
equilibrium condition, just as a competitive market does.

[9] However, in certain cases there may be a multiple solution.

[10] It is only the *relative* disutility of different occupations that counts. The absolute
disutility may be zero or even negative. By putting leisure, safety, agreeableness of
work, etc., into the preference scales, all labor costs may be expressed as opportunity costs. If such a device is adopted each industry or occupation may be regarded
as producing a joint product: the commodity or service in question *and* leisure,
safety, agreeableness of work, etc. The services of labor have to be allocated so that
the value of this marginal *joint* product is the same in all industries and occupations.

occupations.[11] This distribution of the services of labor arises automatically whenever wages are the only source of income. *Therefore, the social dividend must be distributed so as to have no influence whatever on the choice of occupation.* The social dividend paid to an individual must be entirely independent of his choice of occupation. For instance, it can be divided equally per head of population, or distributed according to age or size of family or any other principle which does not affect the choice of occupation.

The other problem is the determination of the rate of interest. We have to distinguish between a short-period and a long-period solution of the problem. For the former the amount of capital is regarded as constant, and the rate of interest is simply determined by the condition that the demand for capital is equal to the amount available. When the rate of interest is set too low the socialized banking system would be unable to meet the demand of industries for capital; when the interest rate is set too high there would be a surplus of capital available for investment. However, in the long period the amount of capital can be increased by accumulation. If the accumulation of capital is performed "corporately" before distributing the social dividend to the individuals, the rate of accumulation can be determined by the Central Planning Board *arbitrarily*. The Central Planning Board will probably aim at accumulating enough to make the marginal *net* productivity of capital zero,[12] this aim being never attained because of technical progress (new labor-saving devices), increase of population, the discovery of new natural resources, and, possibly, because of the shift of demand toward commodities produced by more capital-intensive methods.[13] But the rate, i.e., the *speed*, at which accumulation progresses is arbitrary.

The arbitrariness of the rate of capital accumulation "corporately" performed means simply that the decision regarding the rate of accumulation reflects how the Central Planning Board, and not the consumers, evaluate the optimum time-shape of the income stream. One may argue, of course, that this involves a diminution of consumers' welfare. This difficulty could be overcome only by leaving all accumulation to the saving of

---

[11] If the total amount of labor performed is not limited by legislation or custom regulating the hours of work, etc., the value of the marginal product of the services of labor in each occupation has to be *equal* to the marginal disutility. If any limitational factors are used, it is the marginal *net* product of the services of labor (obtained by deducting from the marginal product the marginal expenditure for the limitational factors) which has to satisfy the condition in the text.

[12] Cf. Knut Wicksell, "Professor Cassel's System of Economics," reprinted in his *Lectures on Political Economy* (L. Robbins, ed., 2 vols., London, 1934), Vol. I, p. 241.

[13] These changes, however, if very frequent, may act also in the opposite direction and diminish the marginal *net* productivity of capital because of the risk of obsolescence due to them. This is pointed out by A. P. Lerner in "A Note on Socialist Economics." *Review of Economic Studies*, October, 1936, p. 72.

individuals.[14] But this is scarcely compatible with the organization of a socialist society.[15] . . .

Having treated the theoretical determination of economic equilibrium in a socialist society, let us see how equilibrium can be determined by a method of *trial and error* similar to that in a competitive market. This method of trial and error is based on the *parametric function of prices*. Let the Central Planning Board start with a given set of prices chosen *at random*. All decisions of the managers of production and of the productive resources in public ownership and also all decisions of individuals as consumers and as suppliers of labor are made on the basis of these prices. As a result of these decisions the quantity demanded and supplied of each commodity is determined. If the quantity demanded of a commodity is not equal to the quantity supplied, the price of that commodity has to be changed. It has to be raised if demand exceeds supply and lowered if the reverse is the case. Thus the Central Planning Board fixes a new set of prices which serves as a basis for new decisions, and which results in a new set of quantities demanded and supplied. Through this process of trial and error equilibrium prices are finally determined. Actually the process of trial and error would, of course, proceed on the basis of the prices *historically given*. Relatively small adjustments of those prices would constantly be made, and there would be no necessity of building up an entirely new price system.

----

[14] This method has been advocated by Barone in "The Ministry of Production in the Collectivist State," *Collectivist Economic Planning*, pp. 278–79.

[15] Of course, the consumers remain free to save as much as they want out of the income which is actually paid out to them, and the socialized banks could pay interest on savings. As a matter of fact, in order to prevent hoarding they would have to do so. But *this* rate of interest would not have any necessary connection with the marginal *net* productivity of capital. It would be quite arbitrary.

Friedrich A. Hayek

8. SOCIALIST CALCULATION: THE COMPETITIVE "SOLUTION"*

In this article, Hayek criticizes weaknesses and omissions in the market socialist blueprints of Oskar Lange and H. D. Dickinson. For several reasons, Hayek doubts that the "parametric" prices set by the Central Planning Board can in fact be market-clearing prices which equalize supply and demand. He questions whether managers will be able to apply the rules for input and output decisions set forth by Lange. And he points out problems of managerial responsibility, initiative, and incentives not resolved in the market socialist blueprints. Hayek concludes that much more detailed central planning and control would be involved in market socialism than its advocates acknowledge. As a result, the difference between market socialism and authoritarian socialism, and the superiority of the former over the latter, is much less than market socialists claim.

I

Two CHAPTERS in the discussion of the economics of socialism may now be regarded as closed. The first deals with the belief that socialism will dispense entirely with calculation in terms of value and will replace it with some sort of calculation *in natura* based on units of energy or of some other physical magnitude. Although this view is not yet extinct and is still held by some scientists and engineers, it has been definitely abandoned by

* Reprinted, with the permission of the author and publisher, from *Economica*, New Series, Vol. VII, No. 26 (May, 1940), pp. 125–49.

economists. The second closed chapter deals with the proposal that values, instead of being left to be determined by competition, should be found by a process of calculations carried out by the planning authority which would use the technique of mathematical economics. With regard to this suggestion, V. Pareto (who, curiously enough, is sometimes quoted as holding this view) has already said what probably will remain the final word. After showing how a system of simultaneous equations can be used to explain what determines prices on a market he adds:

> It may be mentioned here that this determination has by no means the purpose to arrive at a numerical calculation of prices. Let us make the most favorable assumption for such a calculation, let us assume that we have triumphed over all the difficulties of finding the data of the problem and that we know the *ophélimités* of all the different commodities for each individual, and all the conditions of production of all the commodities, etc. This is already an absurd hypothesis to make. Yet it is not sufficient to make the solution of the problem possible. We have seen that in the case of 100 persons and 700 commodities there will be 70,699 conditions (actually a great number of circumstances which we have so far neglected will still increase that number); we shall therefore have to solve a system of 70,699 equations. This exceeds practically the power of algebraic analysis, and this is even more true if one contemplates the fabulous number of equations which one obtains for a population of forty millions and several thousand commodities. In this case the rôles would be changed: it would not be mathematics which would assist political economy, but political economy would assist mathematics. In other words, if one really could know all these equations, the only means to solve them which is available to human powers is to observe the practical solution given by the market.[1]

In the present article we shall be mainly concerned with a third stage in this discussion, for which the issue has now been clearly defined by the elaboration of proposals for a competitive socialism by Professor Lange and Dr. Dickinson.[2] Since, however, the significance of the result of the past discussions is not infrequently represented in a way which comes very near to an inversion of the truth, and as at least one of the two books to be discussed is not quite free from this tendency, a few further remarks on the real significance of the past development seem not unnecessary.

The first point is connected with the nature of the original criticism directed against the more primitive conceptions of the working of a socialist economy which were current up to about 1920. The idea then current (and still advocated, e.g. by Dr. O. Neurath) is well expressed by F. Engels in his *Anti-Dühring*, when he says that the social plan of production "will be settled very simply, without the intervention of the

---

[1] V. Pareto, *Manuel d'économie politique* (2nd ed., 1927), pp. 233–34.

[2] The two recent books with which this article is mainly concerned, Oskar Lange and Fred M. Taylor, *On the Economic Theory of Socialism*, edited by B. E. Lippincott (Minneapolis, 1938), and H. D. Dickinson, *Economics of Socialism* (Oxford, 1939), will be referred to throughout this article as LT (Lange-Taylor) and D (Dickinson) respectively.

famous 'value'." It was against this generally held belief that N. G. Pierson, L. v. Mises, and others pointed out that if the socialist community wanted to act rationally its calculation would have to be guided by the same *formal* laws which applied to a capitalist society. It seems necessary especially to underline the fact that this was a point made by the critics of the socialist plans, since Professor Lange and particularly his editor[3] now seem inclined to suggest that the demonstration that the formal principles of economic theory apply to a socialist economy provides an answer to these critics. The fact is that it has never been denied by anybody, except socialists, that these formal principles *ought* to apply to a socialist society, and the question raised by Professor Mises and others was not whether they ought to apply but whether they could in practice be applied in the absence of a market. It is therefore entirely beside the point when Professor Lange and others quote Pareto and Barone as having shown that values in a socialist society would depend on essentially the same factors as in a competitive society. This of course had been shown long before, particularly by Wieser. But none of these authors has made an attempt to show how these values, which a socialist society ought to use if it wanted to act rationally, could be found, and Pareto, as we have seen, expressly denied that they could be determined by calculation.

It seems then that, on this point, the criticisms of the earlier socialist schemes have been so successful that the defenders, with few exceptions,[4] have felt compelled to appropriate the argument of their critics, and have been forced to construct entirely new schemes of which nobody thought before. While against the older ideas that it was possible to plan rationally without calculation in terms of value it could be justly argued that they were logically impossible, the newer proposals designed to determine values by some process other than competition based on private property raise a problem of a different sort. But it is surely unfair to say, as Professor Lange does, that the critics, because they deal in a new way with the new schemes evolved to meet the original criticism, "have given up the essential point" and "retreated to a second line of defence" (LT 63). Is this not rather a case of covering up their own retreat by creating confusion about the issue?

There is a second point on which Professor Lange's presentation of the present state of the debate is seriously misleading. The reader of his study can hardly avoid the impression that the idea that values should and could be determined by using the technique of mathematical economics, i.e. by solving millions of equations, is a malicious invention of the critics, intended to throw ridicule on the efforts of modern socialist writers. The fact, which cannot be unknown to Professor Lange, is of course that this

---

[3] See B. E. Lippincott in LT, p. 7.

[4] The most notable exception is Dr. M. Dobb. See his *Political Economy and Capitalism* (1937), ch. viii, and his review of Professor Lange's book in the *Modern Quarterly*, 1939.

procedure has more than once been seriously suggested by socialist writers as a solution of the difficulty—among others by Dr. Dickinson, who now, however, expressly withdraws this earlier suggestion.[5]

II

A third stage in the debate has now been reached with the proposal to solve the problems of determining values by the re-introduction of competition. When five years ago the present author tried to appraise the significance of these attempts[6] it was necessary to rely on what could be gathered from oral discussion among socialist economists, since no systematic exposition of the theoretical bases of competitive socialism was then available. This gap has now been filled by the two books here to be discussed. The first contains a reprint of an essay by Professor Lange, originally published in 1936 and 1937, together with an older article by the late Professor Taylor (dating from 1928) and an introduction by the editor, Professor B. E. Lippincott, which in addition to a quite unnecessary restatement of Professor Lange's argument in cruder terms, does much by the unmeasured praise he bestows on this argument and the extravagant claims he advances for it,[7] to prejudice the reader against the essentially scholarly piece of work that follows. Although written in a lively style and confining itself to the outlines of the subject, it does seriously grapple with some of the main difficulties in the field.

Dr. H. D. Dickinson's more recent book is a far more comprehensive survey of the field, proposing essentially the same solution.[8] It is unquestionably a book of great distinction, well organised, lucid and concise, and should rapidly establish itself as the standard work on its subject. To the economist, the reading of the book provides indeed the rare pleasure of feeling that recent advances of economic theory have not been in vain and have even helped to reduce political differences to points which can be rationally discussed. Dr. Dickinson himself would probably agree that he shares all his economics with—and indeed has learnt most of it from—non-socialist economists, and that in his essential conclusions on the desirable economic policy of a socialist community he differs much more from most of his socialist colleagues than from "orthodox" economists. This, together with the open-mindedness with which the author takes up and considers the arguments advanced by his opponents, makes discussion of his views a real pleasure. If the socialists, like the economists, are ready to accept his

---

[5] D, p. 104, and K. Tisch, *Wirtschaftsrechnung und Verteilung im zentralistisch organisierten sozialistischen Gemeinwesen* (1932).

[6] In *Collectivist Economic Planning* (London, 1935), essay on "The Present State of the Debate."

[7] Dr. Lange's essay is described as the "first writing to mark an advance on Barone's contribution" and to show by "irrefutable" argument the "evident feasibility and superiority" of a socialist system (LT, pp. 13, 24, 37).

[8] It is a curious fact that Dr. Dickinson nowhere in his book (except in the bibliography) refers to Professor Lange's work.

book, as the most up-to-date general treatment of the economics of socialism from the socialist point of view, it should provide the basis for much fruitful further discussion.

As has already been mentioned, the main outlines of the solution offered by the two authors are essentially the same. They both rely to some extent on the competitive mechanism for the determination of relative prices. But they both refuse to let prices be determined directly in the market and propose instead a system of price-fixing by a central authority, where the state of the market of a particular commodity, i.e. the relation of demand to supply, merely serves as an indication to the authority whether the prescribed prices ought to be raised or lowered. Neither of the two authors explains why he refuses to go the whole hog and to restore the price mechanism in full. But as I happen to agree (although probably for different reasons) that this would be impracticable in a socialist community, we can leave this question aside for the moment and shall take it for granted that in such a society competition cannot play quite the same rôle as it does in a society based on private property, and that, in particular, the rates at which commodities will be exchanged by the parties in the market will have to be decreed by the authority.

We shall leave the details of the proposed organization for later consideration and first consider the general significance of this solution under three aspects. We shall ask firstly how far this kind of socialist system still conforms to the hopes that were placed on the substitution of a planned socialist system for the chaos of competition; secondly, how far the proposed procedure is an answer to the main difficulty, and, finally, how far it is applicable.

The first and most general point can be dealt with fairly briefly, although it is not unimportant if one wants to see these new proposals in their proper light. It is merely a reminder of how much of the original claim for the superiority of planning over competition is abandoned if the planned society is now to rely for the direction of its industries to a large extent on competition. Until quite recently, at least, planning and competition used to be regarded as opposites, and this is unquestionably still true of nearly all planners except a few economists among them. I fear that the schemes of Professor Lange and Dr. Dickinson will bitterly disappoint all those scientific planners who, in the recent words of Professor B. M. S. Blackett, believe that "the object of planning is largely to overcome the results of competition."[9] This would be even more true if it were really possible to reduce the arbitrary elements in a competitive socialist system as much as is believed by Dr. Dickinson, who hopes that his "libertarian socialism" "may establish, for the first time in human history, an effective individualism" (D 26). Unfortunately, as we shall see, this is not likely to be the case.

---

[9] See Sir Daniel Hall and others, *The Frustration of Science* (London, 1935), p. 142.

III

The second general question we must consider is how far the proposed method of centralized price fixing, while leaving it to individual firms and consumers to adjust demand and supply to the given prices, is likely to solve the problem which admittedly cannot be solved by mathematical calculation. Here, I am afraid, I find it exceedingly difficult to understand the grounds on which such a claim is made. Professor Lange (LT 70, 86) as well as Dr. Dickinson (D 103 and 113) assert that even if the initial system of prices were chosen entirely at random, it would be possible by such a process of trial and error gradually to approach to the appropriate system. This seems to be much the same thing as if it were suggested that a system of equations which was too complex to be solved by calculation within reasonable time and whose values were constantly changing could be effectively tackled by arbitrarily inserting tentative values and then trying about till the proper solution was found. Or, to change the metaphor, the difference between such a system of regimented prices and a system of prices determined by the market seems to be about the same as that between an attacking army where every unit and every man could only move by special command and by the exact distance ordered by headquarters and an army where every unit and every man can take advantage of every opportunity offered to them. There is of course no *logical impossibility* of conceiving a directing organ of the collective economy which is not only "omnipresent and omniscient" as Dr. Dickinson conceives it (D 191), but also omnipotent and which therefore would be in a position to change without delay every price by just the amount that is required. When, however, one proceeds to consider the actual apparatus by which this sort of adjustment is to be brought about one begins to wonder whether anyone should really be prepared to suggest that, within the domain of practical possibility, such a system will ever even distantly approach the efficiency of a system where the required changes are brought about by the spontaneous action of the persons immediately concerned.

We shall later, when we consider the proposed institutional setting, come back to the question how this sort of mechanism is likely to function in practice. In so far as the general question is concerned, however, it is difficult to suppress the suspicion that this particular proposal has been born out of an excessive pre-occupation with problems of the pure theory of stationary equilibrium. If in the real world we had to deal with approximately constant data, that is, if the problem were, to find a price system which then could be left more or less unchanged for long periods, then the proposal under consideration would not be so entirely unreasonable. With given and constant data such a state of equilibrium could indeed be approached by the method of trial and error. But this is far from being the situation in the real world, where constant change is the rule. Whether and how far anything approaching the desirable equilibrium is ever reached depends entirely on the speed with which the adjustments can be made. The practical problem is not whether a particular method would eventually lead to a hypothetical equilibrium, but which method will secure the more rapid and complete adjustment to the daily changing conditions in different places and different industries. How great the difference in this respect would be between a method where prices are currently agreed upon by the parties of the market and a method where these prices are decreed from above is of course a matter of practical judgment. But I find it difficult to believe that anybody should doubt that in this respect the inferiority of the second method would be very great indeed.

The third general point is also one where I believe that preoccupation with concepts of pure economic theory has seriously misled both our authors. In this case it is the concept of perfect competition which apparently has made them overlook a very important field to which their method appears to be simply inapplicable. Wherever we have a market for a fairly standardized commodity it is at least conceivable that all prices should be decreed in advance from above for a certain period. The situation is however very different with respect to commodities which cannot be standardized, and particularly for those which to-day are produced on individual orders, perhaps after invitation for tenders. A large part of the product of the "heavy industries," which of course would be the first to be socialized, belongs to this category. Much machinery, most buildings and ships and many parts of other products are hardly ever produced for a market, but only on special contract. This does not mean that there may not be intense competition in the market for the products of these industries, although it may not be "perfect competition" in the sense of pure theory; the fact is simply that identical products are rarely produced twice in short intervals; and the circle of producers who will compete for the services of a particular plant will differ from week to week. What basis is there in all these cases for fixing prices of the product so as "to equalize demand and supply"? If prices are here to be fixed by the central authority, they will have to be fixed in every individual case and on the basis of an examination by that authority of the calculations of all potential suppliers and all potential purchasers. It is hardly necessary to point out the various complications that will arise according as the prices are fixed before or after the prospective buyer has decided on the particular piece of machinery or building which he wants. Presumably it will be the estimates of the producer which, before they are submitted to the prospective customer, will have to be approved by the authority. Is it not clear that in all these cases, unless the authority in effect takes all the functions of the entrepreneur on itself (i.e. unless the proposed system is abandoned and one of complete central direction substituted), the process of price fixing would either become exceedingly cumbersome and the cause of infinite delay, or a pure formality?

IV

All these considerations appear to be relevant whatever particular form of organization is chosen. Before we go further, however, it becomes necessary to consider somewhat more in detail the concrete apparatus of industrial control which the two authors propose. The sketches they provide of the organization are fairly similar, although in this respect Professor Lange gives us somewhat more information than Dr. Dickinson, who, for most of the problems of economic organization, refers us to the works of Mr. and Mrs. Webb and Mr. G. D. H. Cole (D 30).

Both authors contemplate a socialist system in which the choice of occupation would be free and regulated mainly by the price mechanism (i.e. by the wage system) and in which the consumers also would be free to spend their incomes as they chose. Apparently both authors also want prices of consumers' goods to be fixed by the ordinary market processes (although Dr. Dickinson does not seem to be quite decided on this point) (LT 78, D 60), and also to leave the determination of wages to the bargaining between the parties concerned (LT 78, D 126). Both also agree that for various reasons not the whole of industry should be socialized, but that, besides the socialized there should also remain a private sector, consisting of small enterprises run on essentially capitalistic lines. I find it difficult to agree with their belief that the existence of such a private sector parallel with the socialized sector creates no special difficulties. But as it would be difficult within the space of this article to deal adequately with this problem, we shall, for the purposes of this discussion, disregard the existence of the private sector and assume that the whole of industry is socialized.

The determination of all prices, other than those of consumers' goods and of wages, is the main task of the central economic authority, Professor Lange's Central Planning Board or Dr. Dickinson's Supreme Economic Council. (We shall, following Dr. Dickinson, henceforth refer to this body as the S.E.C.) As regards the technique of how particular prices are announced and changed we get more information, although by no means enough, from Professor Lange, while Dr. Dickinson goes more fully into the question by what considerations the S.E.C. should be guided in the fixing of prices. Both questions have a special importance and they must be considered separately.

According to Professor Lange, the S.E.C would from time to time issue what, following Professor Taylor, he calls "factor valuation tables," that is, comprehensive lists of prices of all means of production (except labor) (LT 46, 52). These prices would have to serve as the sole basis for all transactions between different enterprises and the whole calculation of all the industries and plants during the period of their validity and the managers must treat these prices as constant (LT 81). What we are not told, however, either by Professor Lange or by Dr. Dickinson, is for what period these prices are to be fixed. This is one of the more serious obscurities in the exposition of both authors, a gap in their exposition which makes one almost doubt whether they have made a real effort to visualize their system at work. Are prices to be fixed for a definite period in advance, or are they to be changed whenever it seems desirable? F. M. Taylor seemed to suggest the former alternative when he wrote that the appropriateness of particular prices would show itself at the end of the "productive period" (LT 53); and Professor Lange, on at least one occasion, gives the same impression when he says that "any price different from the equilibrium price would show at the end of the accounting period a surplus or shortage of the commodity in question" (LT 82). But on another occasion he says that "adjustments of those prices would be constantly made" (LT 86), while Dr. Dickinson confines himself to stating that after, "by a process of successive approximation," "a set of prices can ultimately be established in consonance with the principles of scarcity and substitution," "small adjustments will be sufficient to keep the system in equilibrium except in the case of major technical innovations or of big changes in consumers' tastes" (D 100, 102, 103). Could the failure to understand the true function of the price mechanism, caused by the modern preoccupation with stationary equilibrium, be better illustrated?

While Dr. Dickinson is very uninformative on the mechanism of bringing price changes into effect, he goes much more fully than Professor Lange into the considerations on which the S.E.C. would have to base their decisions. Unlike Professor Lange, Dr. Dickinson is not satisfied with the S.E.C. merely watching the market and adjusting prices when an excess of demand or supply appears, and then trying to find by experimentation a new equilibrium level. He rather wants the S.E.C. to use statistically established demand and supply schedules as a guide to determine the equilibrium prices. This is evidently a residue of his earlier belief in the possibility of solving the whole problem by the method of simultaneous equations. But although he has now abandoned this idea (not because he regards it as impossible, since he still believes it could be done by solving merely "two or three thousand simultaneous equations" (D 104), but because he realizes that "the data themselves, which would have to be fed into the equation-machine, are continually changing"), he still believes that the statistical determination of demand schedules would be useful as an aid to, if not as a substitute for, the method of trial and error, and that it would be well worth while to try and establish the numerical values of the constants (sic) in the Walrasian system of equilibrium.

V

Whatever the method by which the S.E.C. fixes prices, and particularly whatever the periods at which and for which prices are announced, there are two points about which there can be little question: the changes will occur later than they would if prices were determined by the market parties, and there will be less differentiation between prices of commodities according to differences of quality and the circumstances of time and place. While with real competition price changes occur when the parties immediately concerned know that conditions have changed, the S.E.C. will be able to act only after the parties have reported, the reports have been verified, contradictions cleared up, etc.; and the new prices will become effective only after all the parties concerned have been notified, that is, either a date will have to be fixed in advance at which the new prices will become effective, or the accounting will have to include an elaborate system by which every manager of production is constantly notified of the new prices upon which he has to base his calculations. Since in fact every manager would have to be informed constantly on many more prices than those of the commodities which he is actually using (at least of those of all possible substitutes), some sort of periodic publication of complete lists of all prices would be necessary. It is clear that while economic efficiency demands that prices should be changed as promptly as possible, practicability would confine actual changes to intervals of fair length.

That the price fixing process will be confined to establishing uniform prices for classes of goods and that therefore distinctions based on the special circumstances of time, place and quality will find no expression in prices is probably obvious. Without some such simplification the number of different commodities for which separate prices would have to be fixed would be practically infinite. This means, however, that the managers of production will have no inducement and even no real possibility to make use of special opportunities, special bargains and all the little advantages offered by their special local conditions, since all these things could not enter into their calculations. It would also mean, to give only one other instance of the consequences, that it would never be practicable to incur extra costs to remedy a sudden scarcity quickly, since a local or temporary scarcity could not affect prices until the official machinery had acted.

For both these reasons, because prices would have to be fixed for periods and because they would have to be fixed generically for categories of goods, a great many prices would be at most times in such a system substantially different from what they would be in a free system. This is very important for the functioning of the system. Professor Lange makes great play with the fact that prices act merely as "indices of terms on which alternatives are offered" (LT 78) and that this "parametric function of prices" (LT 70, 86) by which prices are guiding the action of individual managers without being directly determined by them, will be fully preserved under such a system where prices are fixed. As he himself points out, "the determinateness of the accounting prices holds, however, only if all discrepancies between demand and supply of a commodity are met by an appropriate change of price," and for this reason "rationing has to be excluded" and "the rule to produce at the minimum average cost has no significance unless prices represent the relative scarcity of the factors of production" (LT 93/94). In other words, prices will provide a basis for rational accounting only if they are such that at the ruling prices anyone can always sell as much or buy as much as he wishes, or that anyone should be free to buy as cheaply or to sell as dearly as is made possible by the existence of a willing partner. If I cannot buy more of a factor so long as it is worth more to me than the price, and if I cannot sell a thing as soon as it is worth less to me than the price which somebody else would be willing to pay for it, prices are no longer indices of alternative opportunities.

We shall see the significance of this more clearly when we consider the action of the managers of the socialist industries. But before we can consider their action we must see who these people are and with what functions they are invested.

<h1 style="text-align:center">VI</h1>

The nature of the industrial unit under separate management and the factors which determine its size and the selection of its management are other points on which both our authors are deplorably vague. Professor Lange seems to contemplate the organization of the different industries in the form of national trusts, although this important point is only just touched upon once when the National Coal Trust is mentioned as an example (LT 78). The very important and relevant question of what is *one* industry is nowhere discussed, but he apparently assumes that the various "managers of production" will have monopolistic control of the particular commodities with which they are concerned. In general Professor Lange uses the term "managers of production" exceedingly vaguely (LT 75, 79, 86), leaving it obscure whether the directors of a whole "industry" or of a single unit are meant; but at critical points (LT 76, 82 note) a distinction between the managers of plant and the managers of a whole industry appears without any clear limitation of their function. Dr. Dickinson is even more vague when he speaks of economic activities being "decentralized and carried on by a large number of separate organs of collective economy" which will have "their own nominal capital and their own profit and loss account and will be managed very much as separate enterprises under capitalism" (D 213).

Whoever these managers of production are, their main function would appear to be to decide how much and how to produce on the basis of the prices fixed by the S.E.C. (and the prices of consumers' goods and the wages determined by the market). They would be instructed by the S.E.C. to produce at the lowest possible average costs (LT 75) and to expand production of the individual plants till marginal costs are equal to price

(LT 76, D 107). According to Professor Lange the directors of the industries (as distinguished from the managers of individual plants) would have also the further task of seeing that the amount of equipment in the industry as a whole is so adjusted that "the marginal cost incurred by the industry" in producing an output which "can be sold or 'accounted for' at a price which equals marginal cost" is the lowest possible (LT 77).

In this connection a special problem arises which unfortunately cannot be discussed here as it raises questions of such difficulty and complexity that a separate article would be required. It concerns the case of decreasing marginal costs where, according to both our authors, the socialist industries would act differently from capitalist industry by expanding production till prices are equal, not to average, but to marginal costs. Although the argument employed possesses a certain specious plausibility it can hardly be said even that the problem is adequately stated in either of the two books, still less that the conclusions drawn are convincing. Within the space available on this occasion however we can do no more than seriously question Dr. Dickinson's assertion that "under modern technical conditions, diminishing costs are far commoner than increasing costs"—a statement which in the context in which it occurs clearly refers to marginal costs (D 108).

Here we shall confine ourselves to considering one question arising out of this part of the proposal, the question how the S.E.C. will ensure that the principle that prices are equalized to the lowest marginal cost at which the quantity concerned can be produced, is actually put into force. The question which arises here is not "merely" one of the loyalty or capacity of the socialist managers. For the purpose of this argument it may be granted that they will be as capable and as anxious to produce as cheaply as the average capitalist entrepreneur. The problem arises because one of the most important forces which in a truly competitive economy brings about the reduction of costs to the minimum discoverable will be absent, namely, price competition. In the discussion of this sort of problem, as in the discussion of so much of economic theory at the present time, the question is frequently treated as if the cost curves were objectively given facts. What is forgotten here is that the method which under given conditions is the cheapest is a thing which has to be discovered, and to be discovered anew sometimes almost from day to day, by the entrepreneur, and that, in spite of the strong inducement, it is by no means regularly the established entrepreneur, the man in charge of the existing plant, who will discover what is the best method. The force which in a competitive society brings about the reduction of price to the lowest cost at which the quantity saleable at that cost can be produced is the opportunity for anybody who knows a cheaper method to come in at his own risk and to attract customers by underbidding the other producers. But if prices are fixed by the authority this method is excluded. Any improvement, any adjustment of the technique of production to changed conditions will be dependent on convincing the S.E.C. that the commodity in question can be produced cheaper and that therefore the price ought to be lowered. Since the man with the new idea will have no possibility of establishing himself by undercutting, the new idea cannot be proved by experiment till he has convinced the S.E.C. that his way of producing the thing is cheaper. Or, in other words, every calculation by an outsider who believes that he can do better will have to be examined and approved by the authority, which in this connection will have to take over all the functions of the entrepreneur.

VII

Let us briefly consider a few of the problems arising out of the relations between the "socialist managers of production" (whether of a plant or an industry) and the S.E.C. The manager's task is, as we have seen, to order production in such a way that his marginal costs are as low as possible and equal to price. How is he to do this and how is the fact of his success to be verified? He has to take prices as given. This turns him into what has recently been called a pure "quantity adjuster," i.e. his decision is confined to the quantities of factors of production and the combination in which he uses them. But as he has no means of inducing his suppliers to offer more, or to induce his purchasers to buy more, than they want to at the prescribed price, he will frequently be simply unable to carry out his instructions; or at least, if he cannot get more of a material required at the prescribed price, the only way for him, e.g., to expand production so as to make his cost equal to price, would be to use inferior substitutes or to employ other uneconomic methods; and when he cannot sell at the prescribed price and until the price is lowered by decree, he will have to stop production where under true competition he would have lowered his prices.

Another great difficulty arising out of the periodic price changes by decree is the problem of anticipations of future price movements. Professor Lange, somewhat too bravely, cuts this Gordian knot by prescribing that "for purposes of accounting, prices must be treated as constant, as they are treated by entrepreneurs on a competitive market" (!). Does that mean that the managers, although they know for certain that a particular price will have to be raised or lowered, must act as if they did not know? Clearly this won't do. But if they are free to meet expected price movements by anticipatory action, are they to be allowed to take advantage of the administrative delays in making price changes effective? And who is to be responsible for losses caused by wrongly timed or wrongly directed price changes?

Closely connected with this problem is another one, to which we also get no answer. Both our authors speak about "marginal costs" as if they were independent of the period for which the manager can plan. Clearly actual costs depend in many instances as much as on anything on buying at the right time. And in no sense can costs during any period be said to depend solely on prices during that period. They depend as much on whether these prices have been correctly foreseen as on the views that are held about future prices. Even in the very short run costs will depend on the effects which current decisions will have on future productivity. Whether it is economical to run a machine hard or to economize in lubricants, whether to make major adjustments to a given change in demand or to carry on as well as possible with the existing organization, in fact almost every decision on how to produce now depends at least in part on the views held about the future. But while the manager clearly must hold some views on these questions, he can hardly be held responsible for anticipating future changes correctly if these changes depend entirely on the decision of the authority.

Not only, however, will the success of the individual manager depend to a large extent on the action of the planning authority. He will also have to satisfy the same authority that he has done as well as was possible. Either beforehand, or more likely retrospectively, all his calculations will have to be examined and approved by the authority. This will not be a perfunctory auditing directed to find out whether his costs have actually been what he says they have been. It will have to establish whether they have been the lowest possible ones. This means that the control will have to consider not only what he actually did but also what he might have done and ought to have done. And from the point of view of the manager it will be much more important that he should always be able to prove that in the light of the knowledge which he possessed the decision actually taken was the right one than that he should prove to be right in the end. If this must not lead to the worst forms of bureaucracy I do not know what would.

This brings us to the general question of the responsibility of the managers. Dr. Dickinson clearly sees that "responsibility means in practice financial responsibility" and that unless the manager "bears responsibility for losses as well as for profits he will be tempted to embark upon all sorts of risky experiments on the bare chance that one of them will turn out successful" (D 214). This is a difficult problem with managers who have no property of their own. Dr. Dickinson hopes to solve it by a system of bonuses. This may indeed be sufficient to prevent managers from taking too great risks. But is not the real problem the opposite one, that managers will be afraid of taking risks if, when the venture does not come off, it will be somebody else who will afterwards decide whether they have been justified in embarking on it? As Dr. Dickinson himself points out, the principle would be that "although the making of profits is not necessarily a sign of success, the making of losses is a sign of failure" (D 219). Need one say more about the effects of such a system on all activities involving risk? It is difficult to conceive that under these circumstances any of the necessary speculative activities involving risk-bearing could be left to managerial initiative. But the alternative is to fall back for them on that system of strict central planning to avoid which the whole system has been evolved.

VIII

All this is even more true when we turn to the whole problem of new investments, that is, to all the questions which involve changes in the size (i.e. the capital) of the managerial units, whether they involve net changes in the total supply of capital or not. Up to a point it is possible to divide this problem into two parts, the decisions about the distribution of the available capital supply and the decisions about the rate at which capital is to be accumulated, although it is dangerous to carry this division too far, since the decision about how much is to be saved is necessarily also a decision about which needs for capital are to be satisfied and which are not. Both our authors agree that, as regards the problem of the distribution of capital between industries and plants, the interest mechanism should as far as possible be retained, but that the decision of how much to save and invest would necessarily have to be arbitrary (LT 85, D 80, 205).

Now however strong the desire may be to rely on the interest mechanism for the distribution of capital, it is fairly obvious that the market for capital can in no sense be a free market. And while for Professor Lange the rate of interest is also "simply determined by the condition that the demand for capital is equal to the amount available" (LT 84), Dr. Dickinson takes great pains to show how the S.E.C. will, on the basis of the alternative plans of activity drawn up by the different undertakings, construct an aggregate demand schedule for capital which will enable it to determine that rate of interest at which the demand for capital will equal supply. The ingenuity and the astounding trust in the practicability of even the most complicated constructions which he displays in this connection may be illustrated by his statement that in a certain case "it will be necessary to establish a provisional rate of interest, then to allow the different organs of collective economy to re-contract with each other on the basis of this provisional rate, and so to draw up their final demand schedule for capital" (D 83n).

All this, however, does not meet the main difficulty. If indeed it were possible to accept at their face value the statements of all the individual managers and would-be managers about how much capital they could with advantage use at various rates of interest, some such scheme as such might appear feasible. It cannot be too often repeated, however, that the planning authority cannot be conceived "simply as a kind of super-bank which lends the available funds to the highest bidder. It would lend to persons who have no property of their own. It would therefore bear all the risk and would have no claim for a definite amount of money as a bank has. It would simply have rights of ownership over all real resources. Nor can its decisions be confined to the redistribution of free capital in the form of money, and perhaps of land. It would have to decide whether a particular plant or piece of machinery should be left further to the entrepreneur who has used it in the past, at his valuation, or whether it should be transferred to another who promises a higher return for it."

These sentences are taken from the essay where the present author discussed five years ago the "possibility of real competition under socialism."[10] At that time such systems had only been vaguely discussed and one could hope to find an answer when systematic expositions of the new ideas should become available. But it is most disappointing to find no answer whatever to these problems in the two books now under discussion. While throughout the two works claims are made about how beneficial the control of investment activity would be in many respects, no indication is given of how this control is to be exercised and of how the responsibilities are to be divided between the planning authorities and the managers of the "competing" industrial units. Such statements as we find, as for instance that "because the managers of socialist industry will be governed in some choices by the direction laid down by the planning authority, it does not follow that they will have no choice at all" (D 217), are singularly unhelpful. All that seems to be fairly clear is that the planning authority will be able to exercise its function of controlling and directing investment only if it is in a position to check and repeat all the calculations of the entrepreneur.

It seems that here the two writers are unconsciously led to fall back on the earlier beliefs in the superiority of a centrally directed system over a competitive system and to console themselves with the hope that the "omnipresent, omniscient organ of the collective economy" (D 191) will possess at least as much knowledge as the individual entrepreneurs and will therefore be in as good if not in a better position to make the decisions as the entrepreneurs are. As I have tried to show on another occasion, it is the main merit of real competition that through it use is made of knowledge divided between many persons which, if it were to be used in a centrally directed economy, would have all to enter the single plan.[11] To assume that all this knowledge would be automatically in the possession of the planning authority seems to me to be to miss the main point. It is not quite clear whether Professor Lange means to assert that the planning authority will have all this information when he says that "the administrators of a socialist economy will have exactly the same knowledge, or lack of knowledge, of the production functions as the capitalist entrepreneurs have" (LT 61). If the "administrators of a socialist economy" here means merely all the managers of the units as well as of the central organization taken together, the statement can of course be readily ac-

---

[10] *Collectivist Economic Planning*, 1935, pp. 232–37.

[11] See the article on "Economics and Knowledge," *Economica*, February, 1937.

cepted, but does in no way solve the problem. But if it is intended to convey that all this knowledge can be effectively used by the planning authority in drawing up the plan, it is merely begging the whole question and seems to be based on the "fallacy of composition."[12]

On this whole all-important question of the direction of new investment and all that it involves, the two studies do not really give any new information. The problem remains where it was five years ago and I can confine myself on this point to repeating what I said then: "The decision about the amount of capital to be given to an individual entrepreneur and the decisions thereby involved concerning the size of the individual firm under a single control are in effect decisions about the most appropriate combination of resources. It will rest with the central authority to decide whether one plant located at one place should expand rather than another plant situated elsewhere. All this involves planning on the part of the central authority on much the same scale as if it were actually running the enterprise. And while the individual entrepreneur would in all probability be given some definite contractual tenure for managing the plant entrusted to him, all new investments will be necessarily centrally directed. This division in the disposition over the resources would then simply have the effect that neither the entrepreneur nor the central authority would be really in a position to plan, and that it would be impossible to assess the responsibility for mistakes. To assume that it is possible to create conditions of full competition without making those who are responsible for the decisions pay for their mistakes seems to be pure illusion. It will be at best a system of quasi-competition where the persons really responsible will not be the entrepreneur but the official who approves his decisions and where in consequence all the difficulties will arise in connection with freedom of initiative and the assessment of responsibility which are usually associated with bureaucracy."[13]

IX

The question how far a socialist system can avoid extensive central direction of economic activity is of great importance quite apart from its relation to economic efficiency: it is crucial for the question of how much personal and political freedom can be preserved in such a system. Both authors show a reassuring awareness of the dangers to personal freedom which a centrally planned system would involve and seem to have evolved

---

[12] Another and even worse instance of this fallacy occurs in Professor Lippincott's introduction to the essays of Professors Lange and Taylor, when he argues that "there can be no doubt that the Central Planning Board would exercise great power, but would it be any greater than that exercised collectively by private boards of directors? Because the decisions of private boards are made here and there, this does not mean that the consumer does not feel their collective impact, even though it may take a depression to make him aware of it."

[13] *Collectivist Economic Planning*, p. 237.

their competitive socialism partly in order to meet this danger. Dr. Dickinson even goes so far as to say that "capitalist planning can exist only on the basis of fascism" and that in the hands of an irresponsible controller even socialist planning "*could* be made the greatest tyranny the world has ever seen" (D 22, 227). But he and Professor Lange believe that their competitive socialism will avoid this danger.

Now if competitive socialism could really rely for the direction of production largely on the effects of consumers' choice as reflected in the price system and if the cases where the authority will have to decide what is to be produced and how were made the exception rather than the rule, this claim would be to a large extent substantiated. How far is this really the case? We have already seen that with the retention of the control over investment the central authority wields most extensive powers over the direction of production, much more extensive indeed than is easily possible to show without making this discussion unduly long. To this have yet to be added however a further number of arbitrary elements of which Dr. Dickinson himself gives a quite substantial although by no means complete list (D 205). There is in the first instance the "allocation of resources between present and future consumption" which, as we have already seen, always involves a decision about what particular needs will be satisfied and which needs will not be satisfied. There is, secondly, the need for arbitrary decision in respect to the "allocation of resources between communal and individual consumption" which, in view of the great extension of the "division of communal consumption" which he envisages means that another very large part of the resources of the society is put outside the control of the price mechanism and subject to purely authoritarian decision. Dr. Dickinson expressly adds to this only "the choice between work and leisure" and the "geographical planning and the pricing of land," but at other points of his exposition further questions emerge on which he wants effective planning in order to correct the results of the market. But although he (and still more so Professor Lange) frequently hint at the possibilities of "correcting" the results of the price mechanism by judicious interference, this part of the program is nowhere clearly worked out.

What our authors here have in mind perhaps comes out clearest in Dr. Dickinson's attitude towards the problem of wage changes: "If wages are too low in any one industry, it is the duty of the planning organ to adjust prices and quantities produced, so as to yield equal wages to work of equal skill, responsibility, and difficulty in every industry" (D 21). Apparently here the price mechanism and the free choice of occupation are not to be relied upon. Later we learn that although "unemployment in any particular job affords a prima facie case for lowering the standard wage" (D 127), a lowering of wages is objectionable "on social grounds, because a lowering in wages . . . causes discontent; on economic grounds, because it perpetuates an uneconomic allocation of labor to different occupations."

(How?) Therefore, "as invention and improved organization make less labor necessary to satisfy human wants, society should set itself to discover new wants to satisfy" (D 131). "The powerful engine of propaganda and advertisement, employed by public organs of education and enlightenment instead of by the hucksters and panders of private profit-making industry, could divert demand into socially desirable directions while preserving the subjective impression (*sic*) of free choice" (D 32).

When we add to this and many other similar points where Dr. Dickinson wants his S.E.C. to exercise a paternalistic control,[14] the fact that it will be necessary to co-ordinate national production "with a general plan of exports and imports" (D 169), since free trade "is inconsistent with the principles of collectivism" (D 176), it becomes fairly evident that there will be precious little economic activity which will not be more or less immediately guided by arbitrary decisions. In fact, Dr. Dickinson expressly contemplates a situation where "the state, through a definite planning organ, makes itself responsible for the consideration of economic activity as a whole" and even adds that this destroys the "illusion" maintained in a capitalist society "that the division of the product is governed by forces as impersonal and inevitable as those which govern the weather" (D 21). This can only mean that, with most other planners, he himself thinks of production in his system as one which is largely directed by conscious and arbitrary decisions. Yet in spite of this extensive rôle which arbitrary decisions are to play in his system, he is confident (and the same applies to Professor Lange) that his system will not degenerate into an authoritarian despotism.

Dr. Dickinson just mentions the argument that "even if a socialist planner wished to realize freedom he could not do so and remain a planner," yet the answer he gives makes one doubt whether he has quite seen on what considerations this argument is based. His answer is merely that "a plan can always be changed" (D 227/228). But this is not the point. The difficulty is that, in order to plan at all on an extensive scale, a much more extensive agreement among the members of the society about the relative importance of the various needs is required than will normally exist, and that in consequence this agreement will have to be brought about and a common scale of values will have to be imposed by force and propaganda. I have developed this argument at length elsewhere and I have not space here to restate it.[15] And the thesis I have developed there, that socialism is bound to become totalitarian, now seems to receive support from the most unexpected quarters. This at least appears to be the meaning when Mr. Max Eastman, in a recent book on Russia, states that "Stalinism

---

[14] Cf. for instance the passage (D 52) where Dr. Dickinson speaks about the "people who will not pay voluntarily beforehand for what they are only too glad to have once they have it."

[15] See *Freedom and the Economic System* (Public Policy Pamphlet, No. 29), (University of Chicago Press, 1939).

is socialism, in the sense of being an inevitable, although unforeseen, political and cultural accompaniment."[16]

In fact, although he does not seem to see it, Dr. Dickinson himself, in the concluding passages of his book, makes a statement which comes very much to the same thing. "In a socialist society," he says, "the distinction, always artificial, between economics and politics will break down; the economic and the political machinery of society will fuse into one" (D 235). This is of course precisely the authoritarian doctrine preached by Nazis and Fascists. The distinction breaks down because in a planned system all economic questions become political questions, because it is no longer a question of reconciling as far as possible individual views and desires, but one of imposing a single scale of values, the "social goal" of which socialists ever since the time of Saint-Simon have been dreaming. In this respect it seems that the schemes of an authoritarian socialist, from those of Professor Hogben and Mr. Lewis Mumford, whom Dr. Dickinson mentions as an example (D 25), to those of Stalin and Hitler, are much more realistic and consistent than the beautiful and idyllic picture of the "libertarian socialism" in which Dr. Dickinson believes.

X

There can be no better testimony of the intellectual quality of the two books under discussion than that after having written about them at such length one is conscious of having only just scratched on the surface of the problems raised by them. But an examination in greater detail would clearly exceed the scope of an article; and since many of the doubts which are left with the reader concern points which are not answered in the two books, an adequate treatment of the subject would require another book even longer than those discussed. There are however also important problems which are discussed at some length, particularly in Dr. Dickinson's book, which we have scarcely been able to mention. This applies not only to the difficult problem of the combination of a private sector with the socialized sector, which both authors propose, but also to such important problems as the international relations of a socialist community and to the problems of monetary policy, to which Dr. Dickinson devotes a very brief, and on the whole the least satisfactory, section.

A fuller discussion would also have to point out various passages in the argument of both authors where apparently residues of earlier beliefs or views which are purely matters of political creed creep in and strike one as curiously inconsistent with the plane of the rest of the discussion. This applies for instance to Dr. Dickinson's repeated references to class-conflict and exploitation or his gibes at the wastes of competition (D 22, 94), and

---

[16] Max Eastman, *Stalin's Russia and the Crisis in Socialism* (New York, 1940). As the book is not yet available in this country, the quotation is taken from a review that appeared in the American press.

to much of Professor Lange's interesting section on the "economist's case for socialism," where he seems to employ arguments of somewhat questionable validity.

These, however, are minor points. On the whole the books are so thoroughly unorthodox from a socialist point of view that one rather wonders whether their authors have not retained too little of the traditional trappings of socialist argument to make their proposals acceptable to socialists who are not economists. As courageous attempts to face the real difficulties and completely to remold socialist doctrine to meet them they deserve our gratitude and respect. Whether the solution offered will appear particularly practicable, even to socialists, may perhaps be doubted. To those who, with Dr. Dickinson, wish to create "for the first time in human history, an effective individualism" (D 26), a different path will probably appear more promising.

Central Planning

Central planning may take place in a capitalist or a socialist institutional framework. In a capitalist economy in wartime, there is likely to be a large amount of central planning, as the government mobilizes and deploys the nation's resources for the war effort. Fascism preserves the outward forms of the capitalist institutions of private property and enterprise, but it subjects them to comprehensive regulation in the interests of the state as defined by the supreme leader at the head of the totalitarian government. Authoritarian socialism combines central planning with public owner-ship.

Whatever the ownership of the means of production, central planning has two main features. (1) There is comprehensive and detailed planning and control of almost all phases of economic life, in response to planners', rather than consumers', sovereignty. (2) Resources are allocated primarily by administrative "commands" in real (physical) terms—such as production targets, allocation orders, and rationing—rather than chiefly by markets and prices.

The selections that follow analyze the characteristics and problems of central planning in various institutional contexts. In the first, Jan Drewnowski considers different combinations of planners' and consumers' sovereignty which are possible in a centrally planned economy. In the second article, Gregory Grossman examines the nature and implications of the "command" principle which is the basis of central planning and control of the economy. In the next, Walter Eucken analyzes the centrally administered economy in operation, as illustrated by fascist Germany, comparing it with the market economy. In the last article, Oskar Lange, acknowledging the disadvantages of excessive centralization, proposes a combination of central planning and the market mechanism to guide the economy.

Jan Drewnowski[1]

9. THE ECONOMIC THEORY OF SOCIALISM: A SUGGESTION FOR RECONSIDERATION*

Drewnowski points out that Lange's model of decentralized market socialism, in which consumer sovereignty is largely preserved, is not applicable to the centralized socialist economies of the Communist countries, in which planners' sovereignty predominates. Drewnowski undertakes to formulate a model of socialism relevant to these countries by analyzing how state and individual preferences can combine to guide the economy.

In socialism (and also in capitalism), two systems of preferences must be distinguished: the multiple system of individual preference functions of consumers, and the single state preference function. The latter embodies the state's economic policy, as formulated by the government and as revealed by its economic activities. In contemporary centrally planned socialist economies, state preferences determine the distribution of resources among consumption, military programs, and investment, as well as the compo-

[1] When this was written I was a guest of the Center for International Studies, Massachusetts Institute of Technology, as a Ford Foundation exchange professor. I wish, therefore, to express my thanks to the Foundation, which made my work possible, and to all those economists in Cambridge, Massachusetts, with whom I had the opportunity to discuss many problems relevant to the subject of this paper. As it is impossible to give all their names here, I shall only say that my greatest debt is to Professor Paul N. Rosenstein-Rodan, from whom I received constant help and encouragement during my stay at M.I.T.

* Reprinted from *Journal of Political Economy*, Vol. LXIX, No. 4 (August, 1961), pp. 341–54, by permission of The University of Chicago Press. Copyright 1961 by The University of Chicago. Jan Drewnowski is a member of the Polish Planning Commission and a professor at the Central School of Planning and Statistics in Warsaw.

*sition of military and investment output. How-
ever, a dual preference system exists in the sphere
of consumer goods production, where state and
individual preferences jointly decide the allocation of resources and distribution of goods.*

*Drewnowski distinguishes three possible com-
binations of state (planners') and individual (consumers') preferences, with increasing degrees of
influence for the latter. In the "first-degree market economy," households possess only consumer
choice in the purchase of consumer goods, the
quantities of which are fixed by the planners. In
the "second-degree market economy," consumer
preferences also influence which goods are to be
produced, with the resources allocated by the
planners, by the existing plants producing consumer goods. In the "third-degree market economy," the pattern of new investments in plants
producing consumer goods also responds to consumer demand. Even in the last case, however,
planners' preferences determine the overall magnitude of consumption (its share in national product) and the amount of investment devoted to
consumer goods industries. As Drewnowski
notes, most of the Communist countries are now
in transition from a "first-degree market economy" to a "second-degree market economy," extending the sphere of influence of individual
preferences somewhat.*

I. INTRODUCTION: PRESENT STATE OF THE DEBATE

THERE are queer traits in what is recognized today as the economic theory
of socialism. Not only has it remained for a number of years in a stationary
state which contrasts strangely with the dynamic growth in the number of
descriptive works on socialist and particularly soviet economies, but also it
takes an approach that is far from realistic and might even be termed
utopian.[2] Incredible as it may seem, the convictions of the authors, rather
than the realities of socialist economics, are taken as the basis for theories.

---

[2] A theory may be termed utopian if it can be shown not only that it is normative
but that the system it regards as ideal cannot possibly work in practice. I believe it
could be proved that the recognized theory of socialism is utopian, but I do not
propose to prove it here. The fact that the theory is explicitly normative and remote
from reality is a sufficient ground for criticism.

It can, of course, easily be explained why the economic theory of socialism started that way. When Pareto and, later, Barone discussed the working of the socialist state, no such state existed.[3] They solved a theoretical problem and that was all they could do. Mises, as everybody agrees now, was wrong in his main contention that economic calculation under socialism is theoretically impossible, but he may be forgiven for not taking into account the realities of socialist economics, as he certainly could not have possessed sufficient data at that time about the actual economic problems of the Soviet Union and how they were being solved in practice.[4]

But strangely enough when the discussion of the problem was resumed in the thirties it continued along the same lines. In replying to the arguments of Hayek and Robbins concerning the practical impossibility of economic calculation in socialism, Lange put forward his celebrated proposal for the application of the trial and error procedure in socialist economics.[5] This is a "decentralized decisions" approach which is an alternative to the "centralized decisions" approach of Pareto and Barone. Lange's solution was intended as an answer to criticism based on practical considerations, but in fact it had nothing to do with practice, that is, with the conditions that existed in the only place where socialism in practice could be found at that time—the Soviet Union. Lange's theory was a considerable intellectual achievement, but it did not explain any reality because its premises were never based on existing conditions.

A similar explicitly normative approach characterizes the next important work on the theory of socialism, Lerner's *Economics of Control.*[6] In the Introduction to his book Lerner explicitly states that he is concerned with the principles of a system that does not exist but that can "reap the benefits of both capitalist economy and collectivist economy." He calls his system a controlled economy "*to contrast it with the actual world.*"[7]

Lerner's analysis, though much more elaborate, does not differ essentially from Lange's. Consequently, this approach to the economic theory of socialism has come to be known as the Lange-Lerner approach. After all

---

[3] V. Pareto, *Cours d'économie politique*, Vol. II (Lausanne: F. Rouge; Paris: Pichou, 1897), pp. 91 f, 364 ff.; and his *Manuel d'économie politique* (Paris: V. Giard & Brière, 1909), pp. 362 ff.; E. Barone, "Il ministero della produzione nello stato collettivista," *Giornale degli economisti*, 1908; English trans. in F. A. Hayek (ed.), *Collectivist Economic Planning* (London: G. Routledge & Sons, 1935), pp. 245–90.

[4] L. Mises, "Die Wirtschaftsrechnung im sozialistischen Gemeinwesen," *Archiv für Sozialwissenschaften*, Vol. XLVII (1920); English trans., pp. 87–130 in Hayek (ed.), *op. cit.*

[5] F. A. Hayek, "The Present State of the Debate," pp. 201–43 in Hayek (ed.), *op. cit.*; L. Robbins, *The Great Depression* (London: Macmillan & Co., 1934), p. 151; O. Lange, *On the Economic Theory of Socialism*, ed. B. E. Lippincott (Minneapolis: University of Minnesota Press, 1938), pp. 57–142.

[6] A. P. Lerner, *The Economics of Control* (New York: Macmillan Co., 1944).

[7] *Ibid.*, p. 2 (italics mine).

the years that have passed since the works were published, the Lange-Lerner theory still enjoys the status of a recognized theory of the socialist economy.

There is no doubt that the time is ripe for some attempt at reconsideration. A theory of socialism should start from an analysis of the existing socialist systems.[8] It should, of course, be a positive theory, free from normative judgments. These are evident and even commonplace conditions, but they are not easy to fulfil. I shall try to keep as close as possible to the realities of socialist economies and not to indulge in building castles in the air. A strictly positive theory can be constructed, however, only when the rational core of the real system under consideration can be discovered. This rational element is not always easy to detect. In such cases the theory must acquire some normative features and suggest solutions compatible with the general rational pattern of the system. Thus, though I shall try hard to be "positive," I shall often be moving on the boundary between "positive" and "normative," trespassing now and then into the "normative."

It is my conviction that the analysis of socialist economies must lead to an economic theory of socialism very much different from the theory of capitalism as it exists at present. The differences between the institutional frameworks of the two systems are very great indeed, though they are sometimes obscured by a terminology which calls socialist institutions by their old capitalist names. As a result of these institutional differences, the systems must work in different ways. The forces leading toward equilibrium are different and the equilibrium positions must be different.

This approach is in striking contrast to that which employs a mock-perfect competition equilibrium as a model for a socialist economy's equilibrium. When confronted with reality, such an approach must seem very strange indeed to an observer not aware of the history of the problem.

II. THE FOUNDATIONS OF THE THEORY OF SOCIALISM

All modern societies have a common characteristic of which little account is taken in economic theory. It can be stated as follows: the population has two ways of achieving its economic ends, the direct and the indirect way, or the individual and the collective way. The individual way consists of actions undertaken by individuals within the framework of existing restraints resulting from institutional, technological, and market

---

[8] The term "socialism" is used throughout this article in the sense in which Pareto, Mises, and Lange used it. It means a system in which all the means of production are owned by the state. It is perhaps useful to state this explicitly because in the discussion of practical problems the socialist economies have come to be known as "centrally planned" or "soviet type." But we shall retain the old term which, besides being shorter, has the merit of being diametrically opposite to "capitalism." This will help us now and again to show the contrasts that exist between capitalism and socialism.

conditions. The simplest pattern of those actions is made up of actions directed at acquiring income and actions directed toward spending that income to acquire goods that satisfy wants. The collective way consists of inducing the state authority to take actions that will satisfy the wants of the population.

Not all the economic objectives of individuals can be realized by the individuals' actions. The economic objectives a person has as an earner of income and as a consumer may, in most cases, be achieved in a direct way. He will base his choices on his preference function and act on the market by selling his labor and buying consumer goods. But the economic objectives a person has as a member of a nation, class, party, or group connected with some sort of activity (peasant, scientist, etc.) and also a number of long term consumers' objectives can be achieved only by the indirect way.

If an individual wants the economy to grow at a faster rate, he may not be able to achieve this objective by saving more out of his income; the result may even be the opposite of his desire. If an individual wants the advancement of science, better working conditions, or cheaper public utilities, he cannot achieve these by individual action. He cannot vote for these objectives with his dollars but has to vote at the election to bring to power a government that would have this sort of policy. If he wants more butter and fewer guns, he can achieve this, not by spending more on butter, but only by overthrowing the government that is sponsoring armaments.

The influence the population may have on the state is exerted through political channels by various means through which public opinion makes itself heard—by elections and, in some circumstances, by revolution. The degree of sensitiveness of the state to the interests and aspirations of the population may be taken as a measure of the degree of democracy in the political system. But we must not fall into the error of believing that the population ever transmits to the state detailed prescriptions as to the activities the latter has to undertake. From what we know of political programs, election platforms, and revolutionary slogans, we must infer that only broad lines of economic policy are explicitly transmitted from the population to the state. The state authority, being aware of the needs and wishes of the population, determines the particular objectives of its economic activity and makes appropriate decisions.[9]

---

[9] An interesting and apparently similar classification of social choices is made in K. J. Arrow's *Social Choice and Individual Values* (New York: John Wiley & Sons, 1951), chap. i. Arrow divides the decisions into political (expressed by voting) and economic (making use of the market mechanism). He aims to construct "a procedure for passing from a set of known individual tastes to a pattern of social decision making" (p. 2); but in the sphere of political decision this endeavor is frustrated from the outset by the well-known "paradox of voting." He then proceeds to discuss the impact of individual decisions on social choice under the familiar assumptions of welfare economics. This approach is very different from that made in the present

When people use the direct way to achieve their economic ends, they make their own decisions and act accordingly. Those decisions reveal their scales of values, which can be represented by individual preference functions.

The same is true of the state. If it makes decisions, it must have some implicit scale of values, and these can be represented by a "state preference function."[10] As was explained above, the state preference function emanates in a very general way from the wishes of individuals, but it is determined by the state and is not any sort of total of individual preferences.

In the national economy there exist, therefore, two systems of valuation: the multiple system of individual preference functions and the single state preference function.

The important point to bear in mind is that these two systems of valuation are not mere theoretical models but do exist in actual fact. They exist in the sense that the decisions based on each of them are a reality. The preference functions may not be consciously plotted by the subjects that "have them," but they can be "revealed" by analysis of the decisions based on them.

Preference functions upon which actual decisions and actions are based may be called "effective preference functions." Only effective functions can be revealed, and only such functions can be recognized as legitimate instruments of economic analysis.

Therefore, it is meaningless to have objectives that can be achieved only by the state as variables of individual preference functions. They are certainly not weighed by the individual against other objectives, and *there is no way of revealing his preferences concerning them.* It is illegitimate to say that they are part of an individual preference function. They belong to

---

paper, where the political decision is assumed to consist in electing the kind of government that would correspond to individuals' general ideas but where the detailed aims of state policy are formulated by the government itself. How those state aims (we shall call them state preferences) are arrived at (brain trusts, committee bargaining, lobbying, etc.) is not for economists to investigate, just as we always ignore the problem of why the consumers' preferences are what they are.

[10] I used the concept of a state preference function in an article on the theory of economic planning published in 1937 ("Próba ogólnej teorii gospodarki planowej," *Ekonomista*, 1937, No. 4; 1938, No. 1). The concept as used now differs in many important respects from the old one.

A line of approach that may be considered similar to this concept may be found in an earlier article by H. Zassenhaus, "Über Die Ökonomische Theorie der Planwirtschaft," *Zeitschrift für National Ökonomie*, Vol. V, No. 4 (1934); English trans. "On the Theory of Economic Planning," in *International Economic Papers*, No. 6 (1956). Brilliant as it was, the contribution of Dr. Zassenhaus never got the recognition it deserved, and in a few years the Lange-Lerner approach prevailed as the recognized theory.

An even earlier, but probably better-remembered, article by M. Dobb, "Economic Theory and the Problems of Socialist Economy" (*Economic Journal,* Vol. XLIII [December, 1933], pp. 588–98), can be looked upon as a plea for recognition that a state preference function exists, though the author never used that term. Again, this article has not had much influence on the subsequent development of the theory of socialism.

the state preference function; they enter the state's scale of values as their significance is weighed by the state against other objectives of the same kind. They can be revealed as part of the state preference function.

All this is true of any system, capitalist or socialist. It may be noted here that, though the concept of a dual preference system has not been developed in theory,[11] in the discussion of the practical economic problems of capitalism it is being increasingly taken for granted that the targets of economic policy do not result from the signals of the market but are determined by the government's pursuing economic aims adopted with a view toward the future.[12] If we speak of a "big-push" or the conditions for a "take-off," or of an "implanted economic development," we admit this fact and urge a policy which would bring real benefits to consumers but would ignore consumers' sovereignty.[13] It is not the "invisible hand" of the market mechanism but the more and more prominent hand of the state that guides the economy under contemporary capitalism.[14] The significance of the dual-preference approach for the theory of a capitalist economy will not be elaborated here.

While it has been possible (though more and more inadequate) to base the economic theory of capitalism on one preference system only and to take account of the state activities but occasionally, this sort of approach is inadmissible for socialism. There the state plays too important a role to be ignored.

The theory of a socialist economy must be built upon the concept of

---

[11] It must be noted, however, that such a system was mentioned by O. Lange in a short passage on p. 96 of his *Economic Theory* (*op. cit.*); but he dismissed it as "not very probable."

[12] An emphatic statement of the independence of state investment decisions from consumers' preferences may be found in P. N. Rosenstein-Rodan, "Programming in Theory and in Italian Practice," in *Investment Criteria and Economic Growth* (Cambridge, Mass.: Center for International Studies, Massachusetts Institute of Technology, 1955), p. 24.

[13] P. N. Rosenstein-Rodan, "Notes on the Theory of the 'Big Push,'" (Cambridge, Mass.: Center for International Studies, Massachusetts Institute of Technology, 1957); W. W. Rostow, "The Take-off into Self-sustained Growth," *Economic Journal*, 1956; A. Bonné, *Studies in Economic Development* (London: Routledge & Kegan Paul Ltd., 1957), chaps. xi, xii.

[14] An early recognition of the existence of economic aims of the state can be found, naturally enough, in writings on public finance (see E. Lindahl; *Die Gerechtigkeit der Besteuerung* [Lund: Gleerup, 1919]; and also Mauro Fasiani, "Der gegenwärtige Stand der reinen Theorie der Finanzwissenschaft in Italien," *Zeitschrift für Nationalökonomie*, Vol. III [1931/32], 652–91; Vol. IV [1932/33], 79–107, 357–88).

A more recent and very explicit recognition of the important role played by the capitalist state today may be found in J. Tinbergen, *Economic Policy: Principles and Design* (Amsterdam: North-Holland Publishing Co., 1956), particularly chap. i.

Another interesting contribution to the problem of state preferences under capitalism is found in a mimeographed memorandum by Ragnar Frisch, "Numerical Determination of a Quadratic Preference Function for Use in Macroeconomic Programming" (Oslo: Universitet Socialøkonomiske Institut, 1957). Frisch suggests a method of plotting preference functions from data collected by interviewing prominent politicians about the policies to be pursued by the state.

the dual valuation system—on the state preference function and on the system of individual preference functions.[15] In a socialist economy it is necessary, therefore, to analyze two sets of decisions, those of the state and those of the individuals.

To determine the sphere of influence of state decisions as against that of individual decisions is the central institutional problem of a socialist state. But it is a problem which exists also under capitalism. In fact, the difference in the location of the boundary between those two spheres may serve as a definition of capitalism as against some intermediate system. In what follows we will, however, be concerned exclusively with socialism.

III. SOME RELATED CONCEPTS OF WELFARE ECONOMICS

Before we proceed any further, it may be useful to make a few remarks about some concepts used in welfare economics that bear some resemblance to our state preference function but, in fact, differ from it in many important respects.

The greatest affinity can be discovered between the state preference function and the welfare function defined in the most general way.[16] The state preference function may be considered to be a special case of the general welfare function. But the interest of welfare economics has moved in a different direction. No concept of the state preference function, as it is understood here, has been developed. The most generally used form of a welfare function is one in which the utilities of different persons are ordered according to some not specifically defined ethical criteria.[17] As variables of the welfare function we have individual utilities, which, in fact, are not known (unless fragments of them are revealed ex post facto by consumers' market behavior), and the shape of the function is determined by ethical convictions held by the observer or attributed by the observer to somebody else. This sort of function is very far removed from

---

[15] We therefore dismiss as not realistic a "dictatorial model" of a socialist economy where only the valuations of the state are valid, as mentioned, for example, by Lange (*op. cit.*, p. 90). This approach to the economics of socialism cannot be described as a generally recognized theory but has found its way into a number of textbooks, probably on account of its simplicity. The "dictatorial model" may be looked upon as a limiting special case in a theory of socialism conceived in a more general way.

[16] See A. Bergson, "A Reformulation of Certain Aspects of Welfare Economics," *Quarterly Journal of Economics*, Vol. LII (1938), p. 312. In P. A. Samuelson's *Foundations of Economic Analysis* (Cambridge, Mass.: Harvard University Press, 1958), the welfare function is given the form $W = W(Z_1, Z_2, \ldots)$, "where the Z's represent all possible variables," and the function characterizes "some ethical belief, that of a benevolent despot or a complete egotist or of all men of good will, the misanthrope, the state, race or group mind, God, etc." (p. 221).

[17] Such a function would take the form
$$W = F(U^1, U^2, U^3, \ldots),$$
as in A. Bergson's "Socialist Economics," in *A Survey of Contemporary Economics*, Vol. I, ed. Howard S. Ellis (Homewood, Ill.: Richard D. Irwin, Inc., 1948), p. 418 . . .

any reality; it cannot be revealed by anyone's activities and will be of no use in our analysis of the socialist economy.

Nor can much virtue be found, for the purposes of a theory of socialist economics, in the otherwise very interesting attempt to derive "community" or "social" indifference curves from the individual preference curves.[18] This sort of summing-up process is never performed in practice and can be conceived only under unrealistic assumptions. It is essentially utopian. This is, in fact, admitted by many, if not by all, of those examining this concept.[19]

The state preference function contains the scale of values of the state and so can be considered a special case of the general welfare function. But, first, this scale of values is the scale of the state, which actually has authority over the economy; it is not just any ethically derived scale. Second, it is concerned not with individual utilities but with measurable quantities existing in the national economy. Third, it is observable and can be "revealed" by the actions of the state. In brief, it is an effective function.

The state preference function is not deduced from individual preference functions. To someone accustomed to the traditional way of thinking in terms of consumers' sovereignty this may seem improper. But, as explained above, in some special (but not at all irrelevant) way the state preference function represents the wishes of consumers. What is most important, it is a fact: it exists and manifests itself in observable economic actions.

IV. THE STATE PREFERENCE FUNCTION

A satisfactory theory of the socialist economy must be able to explain how a socialist economy actually works. Such a theory is, of course, the ultimate aim, but what is attempted in this paper is the much more limited objective of making the main elements of the socialist economy subject to the tools of econoimc analysis. I shall, therefore, state the problems rather than solve them; I shall remain on a high level of abstraction and be concerned only with the most crucial problems. The first concept we must tackle is that of the state preference function. This concept is significant in either system but is fundamental to the theory of socialism;

---

[18] The earliest use of this technique is in T. Scitovsky, "A Reconsideration of the Theory of Tariffs," *Review of Economic Studies*, Vol. IX (1941/42), pp. 89–110. The most important contribution to this problem is P. A. Samuelson's "Social Indifference Curves," *Quarterly Journal of Economics*, Vol. LXX, No. 1 (1956), pp. 1–22.

[19] See, for example, Samuelson, "Social Indifference Curves," p. 15.

Tinbergen "doubts the relevance of the question whether social welfare functions can or cannot be derived from individual ones. . . . For the time being . . . the theory of economic policy would be better to take the policy-maker's welfare function as its starting point. But, no doubt, this has to be a temporary attitude only" (*op. cit.*, pp. 14–15). While I am in full agreement with the main line of Tinbergen's argument, I, of course, strongly disagree with the last sentence in the quotation.

and it ought to be expressed in such a way as to make possible the substitution of numerical data for its variables. Second, a framework must be provided for analyzing the interrelation between the state and individual preference functions. All the more detailed analysis (for which, it is hoped, the approach presented here will provide a basis) is left to some future studies.

The preference function of the state has the same formal features as does the individual preference function. Its independent variables represent the means by which the state achieves its aims. They must be expressed in some measurable way.[20] The simplest solution would be to express those variables in quantities of final goods or services available in the national economy for consumption, investment, or export. The variables so expressed we may call the "goods" of the state preference function. These "goods" will usually be aggregates, such as food, clothing, rolling stock, etc. This implies a further problem of disaggregating the totals into particular goods, which may be a rather intricate process but which for the time being we shall ignore.

The value of the function which the state maximizes may be taken to represent some sort of "state utility"; but it may also have another significance which I shall explain later.

The function may be represented by an indifference map, the curves of which will be convex to the origin (decreasing marginal rate of substitution). This is a familiar property of a preference function, which can be accepted as a property of the state function without raising any serious problems; but it is not a very illuminating property. The important problem is the shape of the function. Even a fragment of it would suffice, but no state so far has published a white or blue book containing its preference function. The preference function is implicit in the state's activities, but it is never stated explicitly. However, neither is the consumer's preference function, and that has not prevented economists from making it the basic concept of economic theory.

The consumer's preference function has to be revealed,[21] and so has the state preference function. The consumer's preference function is revealed through the consumer's market behavior. This is not an ideal way of discovering the preference function, but we have no better device. Its main defect is that the consumer's preference function is revealed only after he has acted on the market. The manifestation of the consumer's preferences in the form of demand is an "ex post" phenomenon.

With the state preference function we are in a better position. We have not only ex post facto manifestations of the function in the form of

---

[20] If, therefore, we consider such a state aim as "education," we have to make it measurable by expressing it by the number of classrooms in use or, better still, by the number of classroom-hours per month or year.

[21] P. A. Samuelson, "Consumption Theory in Terms of Revealed Preference," *Economica*, 1948, pp. 243–51.

actually executed policies of the state but also what we may call "declared targets of policy," which are "ex ante." In a socialist state these targets are officially determined and published as a national economic plan.

A published plan is, of course, a "co-ordinated" one (a term from the parlance of planning commissions), and that means not only that the plan is feasible in terms of resources and techniques but also that all the resources and technical possibilities are to be used fully. A plan determines the "ex ante" equilibrium of the system.

If this is the case, the point of equilibrium must be on the production-possibility curve. The shape of the production-possibility curve, at least in the range where production is practical, must be assumed to be known. Consequently, if we have a point on the production-possibility curve, we have also the transformation rate at this point and in its immediate vicinity.

But a "co-ordinated" and approved plan implies also that the targets of the plan correspond to what the state considers most desirable. Therefore, the co-ordinates representing the targets determine a point which is not only on the production possibility curve but also at the point on the curve that the state considers best. In other words, that point is a point of equilibrium determined by the production possibilities and the preferences of the state. A state indifference curve can be drawn through that point. Its slope would, of course, be equal to the slope of the production-possibility curve.

The segment of the state preference function directly adjoining the equilibrium point would therefore be revealed. It is, of course, only a small segment of the function, but it gives us important information: the rate of substitution between or relative valuation of the two state "goods" in the neighborhood of the equilibrium point.

The procedure may be generalized and applied to many goods, in which case a whole system of rates of substitution will be revealed. These rates will be equal to the slopes of the indifference curves of the state preference function near the equilibrium points. They may also be looked upon as relative shadow prices implicit in the state's decisions about quantities. We may call these prices "state preference prices." They constitute a price system connected to and consistent with the plan targets expressed in physical quantities. In its policies the state should maintain this link between quantities and prices as a condition of consistency. In other words, state preference prices ought to be included in the state plan as an important supplementary chapter to the chapter containing quantities.[22]

---

[22] As things happen now in socialist states, the prices are not part of the national plans. And it may be taken for granted that, if the state-preference-price criteria were applied, some inconsistencies in the plans would be discovered. This is exactly one of the points at which we have to introduce some normative element into our analysis.

The state preference prices are relative prices, but there is nothing to prevent us from making them absolute by expressing them in any arbitrary unit we may choose. Once we do that, the sum total of values of all products (which is being maximized by the state) ceases to be some "state utility"—an ordinal concept—and becomes a value of national product expressed in whatever units we choose—a quantity measurable in cardinal numerals. To distinguish it from the national product as understood in the ordinary way, we may call it the "state-preference national product."

There is really nothing new or surprising in this. The state-preference national product is a purely conventional concept, and a similar measure could be constructed for any preference function. It is only when there are numerous individual preference functions with utilities having no common measure that this concept cannot be applied. With a single state preference function the state-preference national product is merely one way of evaluating the real national income. A problem that is insoluble if we look at it from the point of view of many individual preference functions is, of course, simple if we start from one function only.[23] And again this simplified approach, which is of no use under individualistic assumptions, may be useful for our analysis of a socialist society.

What we have done is to show how the state preference function is revealed by the data that are declared by the state. This is a realistic approach, because in practice the socialist state determines plan targets in physical quantities, and the rates of substitution which indicate the shape of its preference function are implicit and have to be revealed. But this is not the only procedure that could be used. Contrary to what is possible with consumers' preferences, the state might very well declare not the production targets but the shape of the function itself. By confronting the preference function with production possibilities, the planners might then determine the production targets. To a theoretical economist, such a procedure presumably is simpler and states the issues more clearly. But what the opinion of the practical planner would be is an open question. What is really important is to have target quantities of "goods" consistent with transformation rates and state preference prices, both elements being equally valid parts of the national plan. This alone would be a great improvement on the present system because it would require an internally consistent model of the whole interdependent national economy and, consequently, would necessitate concentration on the determinateness of the system. This is important because overdeterminateness is the curse of socialist economies. And note that it is not an overdeterminateness of the theoretical model, which can trouble only the armchair economist counting his equations, but an overdeterminateness in practice which leads to uninvited and mostly unpredictable consequences.[24]

---

[23] P. A. Samuelson, "Evaluation of Real National Income," *Oxford Economic Papers*, Vol. II, No. 1 (1950), pp. 1–21.

[24] By "overdeterminateness in practice" I mean the overdeterminateness of the system of decisions taken by the state. These decisions determine the "ex ante"

This has been, of course, a very simplified presentation of the problem. For practical planning purposes we must make much more elaborate assumptions. What is intended here is only to show the lines along which this sort of problem can be attacked.

V. THE ZONES OF INFLUENCE IN SOCIALIST ECONOMY

So far I have concentrated on the state preference function. But the crucial problem of an economic theory of socialism is the interaction of the state and individual preferences.

If we take a short-term view, we may abstract from the influence the individual has on the state preference function through political channels and consider the state and individual preference functions to be independent of each other.

There may be areas in which state and individual preferences do not meet, that is, areas in which each unit is confronted with possibilities depending only on natural or technical conditions. But where they meet they constitute restraints for each other. Each of them (or, rather, the activities resulting from each of them) becomes a part of the environment restraining the actions resulting from the other's preferences. We must try, therefore, to determine the zone in which state preferences are supreme (the zone of state influence), the zone in which individual preferences are supreme (the zone of individual influence), and the zone in which state and individual preferences meet (the zone of dual influence). To determine which part of the national economy belongs to which zone means to define the nature of the economic system in question.

Capitalism once was, or was, at least, considered, a system in which the whole national economy belonged to the individual zone. But in present-day capitalism there is usually some state zone and a quite significant dual-influence zone.

At this point one more important difference between the two systems must be stated: Capitalism is a system in which the boundary lines between the zones as defined above are fairly stable. The reason is, of course, the greater rigidity of economic institutions under capitalism. The most important single cause of this rigidity is the link that exists in capitalism between private property and production. This link is in fact a basic feature of capitalism. When there is private property in production, the organization of the system cannot easily be changed without affecting private property rights. Indeed, any encroachments by the state on the economic life of the country are difficult. Capitalism has certainly changed

---

equilibrium which, in socialism, is an emphatically practical phenomenon, since the state's decisions lead to real actions. The socialist system, like any system, cannot be either overdetermined or underdetermined "ex post," but, if it is overdetermined "ex ante," it determines itself "ex post" in a way not desired or expected by the planners.

in the last hundred years—the state- and dual-influence zones have expanded, and the individual zone has contracted. But the change has been slow and painful; the economic theory of capitalism tacitly recognizes this fact by taking the institutional framework of capitalism for granted and not bothering much about examining the consequences of its changes.

Socialism may be defined as a system in which the national economy is divided between the state-and the dual-influence zones. No individual zone exists under full socialism. The boundary between the state- and the dual-influence zone, however, may be anywhere in the range between the limiting case in which the whole national economy is in the state zone and that in which the state zone is not much more extensive than in capitalism. This makes socialism a system of which many different variants may exist and in which the change from one variant to the other can be made fairly easily and promptly by nothing more than a governmental decision, since many institutional rigidities characteristic of capitalism do not exist under socialism.

In socialism institutional changes are a part of the operation of the system. Changes in the position of the boundary between state- and dual-influence zones may occur at any time and may sometimes be instantaneous. Institutional changes inside each zone are even easier;[25] institutional change may often take less time than changes in capital equipment. The theory must take account of this and look upon institutional changes as a particular class of available alternatives.

This sort of approach would permit an economic theory more general in nature than the traditional theory of capitalism. In such a theory capitalism would be considered as a small range of special cases in which the zone of state influence is fairly limited and the institutional setting is fairly rigid. Socialism would be represented by a much wider range of special cases at the opposite end of the scale where no zone of individual influence is allowed but where one case can easily be transformed into another. Intermediate systems, such as "the welfare state," or "people's democracies on the way to socialism," can be defined in a similar way.

I must now attempt a more detailed analysis of the zones of state, dual, and individual influence, and try to determine the nature of the boundary line between those zones. This will require a theoretical model, which must be a simplification of reality, but I shall try to keep it as close as possible to what happens in socialist economies.

The state zone is the part of the national economy in which the scales of values are the preferences of the state. No consumers' preferences enter into the picture. In socialism this situation exists as a rule in the investment-goods industries, where resources, capital equipment, and products are all owned by the state.

---

[25] For example, changes in the sizes of enterprises, which are of considerable importance but cannot be discussed here because of limited space.

In all branches producing consumer goods there is the possibility of a dual-influence zone, with the boundary of the state zone being drawn differently in different cases.

Let us start with the limiting case and assume that all the national economy belongs to the state zone; consumers' preferences have no significance. The only restraints are then natural resources and techniques. This is the familiar theoretical dictatorship model. It corresponds roughly to "war communism," a system that existed in Soviet Russia for a short time during the civil war, 1918–20.

The quantities of all goods produced and the distribution of them among the members of the population are determined by the state. In other words, there is a full rationing system. This sort of model is not realistic in present circumstances and of little use except as a limiting theoretical case of the institutional alternatives. We may describe this case as a case of "no market economy."

The next alternative would be a system in which consumer goods are sold in the market. In this market the state is the only supplier and determines all the quantities brought for sale. The consumers (as buyers) are free to buy as much or as little as they want. The state, being anxious to sell what is produced, will adjust the prices to consumer demand so as to have no unsold stocks. It may, therefore, be said that quantities are fixed by the state, but prices are determined by the consumer demand according to consumers' tastes.

The difference between this case and the previous one is that the distribution of consumer goods has been transferred from the state zone to the dual-influence zone or, preferably, that the boundary between the zones has been moved so as to leave the distribution of consumer goods in the dual-influence zone and permit a market for consumer goods to be established.

On that market, it must be noted, consumers' preferences (strictly, consumers' demands) influence prices and the distribution of goods only. The quantities of particular goods are *not* affected, nor are the resources used in their production, nor the distribution of resources among particular producing plants.

This is a very typical situation in present-day socialist economies—an equilibrium between supply and demand on the market for consumer goods is maintained by adjusting prices, whereas quantities produced are not affected by demand at all and are governed by the central plan. We may call this case a "first-degree market economy."[26]

The "second-degree market economy" exists when the next adjoining

---

[26] It might be possible to conceive a *first-degree market economy* in which prices are fixed by the state and quantities determined by consumers' preferences. This possibility of applying alternative instruments of economic policy seems to be of considerable theoretical interest. It is probable that it could be applied to higher degree market economies. In the present article only the simplest case is presented.

range of economic variables is transferred from the state- to the dual-influence zone. In other words, these variables are made to depend not only on state but also on consumers' preferences. This "adjoining range" includes the quantities produced of particular consumer goods, the quantities of resources (excluding new investments) used in their production, and the distribution of resources among particular plants.

This would leave unaffected by the change the aggregate quantity of consumer goods, the aggregate quantity of resources used in producing consumer goods, and the capital equipment employed in industries producing consumer goods. The second (unaffected) set of quantities being kept constant, the first set of quantities will be determined by adjusting production to consumers' demands and maximizing profits in the whole consumer-goods sector. The principle of maximization of profits would assure rational distribution of resources and the production of rational quantities of particular goods.

The second-degree market economy corresponds roughly to the system aimed at by the "decentralization reforms" and "model reconsiderations" which are at present taking place in the people's democracies.

The "third-degree market economy" exists when the determination of the pattern of new investments in plants producing consumer goods depends on the consumers' demands for finished products. This means that decisions concerning what sorts of investment are to be made and to which plants they should be assigned are transferred from the state- to the dual-influence zone. The aggregate quantities of produced consumer goods, of resources used, and of new investments remain in the state zone.

This simple classificatory system may be made more complicated in many ways; for example, the consumer-goods sector may be divided into a number of subsectors. But our aim here is simply to demonstrate how the interaction of state and consumers' preferences and their differing spheres of influence can be taken into account.

One more important observation might be added: As a result of the dual influence of the state and the consumers, the socialist economy will have two independent sets of prices, one coming from the state preference function and one from the consumers' preference functions. Both systems of prices are rational and "correct" in their particular way. The "state" prices will be applied to all dealings between state enterprises and will be used in all national accounting calculations. The "consumers'" prices will apply to sales by state enterprises to consumers. The coexistence of these two sets of prices must be a characteristic of a rationally managed socialist economy.[27]

---

[27] This opinion has a normative element in it. The necessity of two simultaneous systems of prices is not generally recognized. No clear, uniform principle for determining prices has so far been accepted in socialist countries.

VI. CONCLUSIONS

The aim of this article has been to lay a basis for a realistic theory of a socialist economy. It started from the fact that there are two sets of preference functions that are effective in a national economy: the preference functions of the population, which manifest themselves in purchases and sales in the market, and the state preference function, which is expressed by the economic plans and policies of the state. Both are necessary to express the economic interests and aspirations of the population. The population influences the state preference function through political channels. A perfect democracy might be defined as a system in which the state's preferences represent people's interests in an accurate way. The examination of the working of these political channels is, however, outside the scope of economics and must be left to political science. What the economist has to do is to take account of the observable fact that two systems of preference exist and are sources of decisions in every economy and to try to understand the results of their interaction. The existence of dual preference systems ought to be comprised in the economic theory of any system, but it is basic to the development of a theory of the socialist system. From these assumptions some fundamental propositions for the economic theory of socialism were derived.

The preferences of the state were examined in some detail. It was found that in a contemporary socialist state they exist in an implicit form but may be "revealed" by the declarations and activities of the state.

A method was suggested for attaching numerical values to the state preference system. It could be used to make the socialist system internally consistent and not overdetermined.

Once the concept of the state preference function was defined, its interaction with individual preference functions had to be explained. The possibility of various institutional arrangements was discussed and the principles of interaction stated. It was suggested that this might lead to a more general theory that would embrace both the theory of capitalism and the theory of socialism as special cases. To explain the interaction of state and individual preferences, the device of zoning the national economy was introduced, the zone of dual influence being the crucial one. It was noted that some sorts of market exist in that zone. Their properties differ considerably from those of capitalist markets.

All this has been a suggestion for a new approach to the economic theory of socialism. The theory itself still remains to be worked out.

It is possible to list some fundamental problems that ought to be examined first. The working of the markets under "zoning" conditions is, perhaps, the most important problem. Particular attention should be paid to the labor market, which also falls under the "zoning" system but was not discussed here. Then comes the problem of the socialist state enterprise, which has to take decentralized decisions consistent with the preferences of the state. Collective consumption, a feature of socialism, should be examined along with the problem of the markets. Then, of course, an analysis of growth must be initiated, since growth problems are crucial in every socialist system. The investigation of monetary problems may be considered less urgent, but would present ample scope for concepts differing widely from those used in capitalism.

Very much remains to be done. It is hoped that the approach suggested in this article will be of use in that work.

Gregory Grossman[1]

10. NOTES FOR A THEORY OF THE COMMAND ECONOMY*

Grossman compares the market mechanism and the command principle as alternative methods of directing the economy. He points out that the bulk of the "planning" effort in a centrally administered economy is devoted to striving for physical balance between the sources and uses for the many different resources and goods. Because of the enormity and difficulty of performing this task administratively, rather than through the market, the command economy is more concerned with coordination than with efficiency or optimality in resource allocation. Although centralization of economic decision making has various advantages, its disadvantages are serious enough to require the central planners to seek some compromise between the command and market mechanisms, by using money and prices as instruments of decentralization. However, Grossman shows, such compromises tend to be both unsatisfactory and unstable.

THERE are many criteria for distinguishing between "economic systems" and the undogmatic will refuse to be committed to any one of them. These notes focus on one such criterion, the nature of the relation between the

[1] This is a somewhat revised version of a paper read in October 1962 before the Joint Faculty Seminar on the Communist World, University of California (Berkeley), and subsequently also at a few other universities in the USA. Many of the points discussed herein are treated extensively in Peter Wiles' imaginative and stimulating *The Political Economy of Communism* (Blackwell and Harvard, 1962), which unfortunately reached me too late to be fully taken into account in this paper. I am grateful for comments to several friends and colleagues, especially Professors Robert W. Campbell and Benjamin Ward.

* Reprinted from *Soviet Studies*, Vol. XV, No. 2 (October, 1963), pp. 101–23, with the permission of the author, the editors of *Soviet Studies*, and the publisher, Basil Blackwell & Mott, Ltd. Gregory Grossman is Professor of Economics at the University of California (Berkeley).

135

individual production unit and the rest of the economy and the attendant forms of information and communication. A closed economy is assumed. The discussion that follows draws primarily on the author's reading of Soviet reality.

I

A prime imperative of a social economy—i.e., an economy with significant division of labor and exchange among production units—is *micro-balance*. By micro-balance (hereafter, "balance" for short) we mean that minimal degree of coordination of the activities of the separate units (firms) which assures a tolerably good correspondence between the supply of individual producer and consumer goods and the effective demand for them. We speak of "balance" rather than "equilibrium" in order to escape semantic association with an equilibrating market mechanism, since we do not take such a mechanism for granted. Thus, particular equilibrium in a market or simulated market is one form of balance.[2] Efficiency in the economist's sense, whether static or dynamic, is a far less pressing social imperative than balance. Without balance a social economy could not carry on for long, but many actual economies function quite adequately at rather low levels of efficiency.

These elementary propositions are perhaps worth restating because of the Western economist's tendency to take balance for granted and to focus his attention on efficiency and growth. If the problem of balance is trivial to the Western economist, or at best remote, it is because he generally takes the existence of the market as a datum, and, whatever its faults on other scores, the market mechanism assures balance almost without fail at *some* level of economic activity. (Let us recall that we defined balance in relation to *effective* demand. As we know, the market mechanism need not automatically achieve satisfactory growth or economic stability (*macro*-balance)). But the same cannot be taken for granted if the context is shifted to non-market economies. Thus, serious imbalance, i.e., lack of micro-balance, is a chronic hazard in the contemporary Soviet economy and the other economies of the Soviet type. At another time in its history, during so-called War Communism with substantially different institutions of a non-market character, the Soviet economy in fact went over that brink and its wheels virtually ground to a halt.

The ambiguity introduced into the above definition of balance by the word "tolerable" is deliberate. While obviously no social economy will function if its internal coordination is so low as to cause its wheels literally to stop turning, in most cases there will be clamor for remedial institutional measures long before paralysis is reached. Balance and imbalance are

---

[2] Cf. the use of the word "balance" by Tjalling C. Koopmans, *Three Essays on the State of Economic Science* (New York, 1957), p. 45.

relative notions; they come in degrees. At what point the effects of imbalance will cease to be tolerable would necessarily vary from society to society, depending on its past experience, its values, the urgency of its social goals, its political mechanism for the venting of discontent and the carrying out of reforms, and so forth. One might guess that American business with its present attitudes would not tolerate the kind of chronic and ubiquitous undependability of supply that is and has long been the norm for Soviet producers, although American business has shown considerable tolerance for *macro*-imbalance in recent decades.

Generally speaking, there are three institutional arrangements whereby a social economy, or any set of producers within it, can maintain balance: by means of a market mechanism, by virtue of directives from above (the "command principle"), or by force of tradition. Economies in which each of these predominates as the coordinating principle we call, respectively, the market economy, the command economy, and the traditional economy. More on the first two presently, but let us first dispose of the traditional ecnomy, which we can do rather quickly. The effect of tradition is to constrain the scope of action, to eliminate options, or even to prescribe mandatory acts. It may be implicit or explicit, unwritten or elaborately documented, suggestive or mandatory. It may be the dominant principle of organizing economic exchange, as in fairly primitive societies guided, often ritually, by reciprocity and redistribution,[3] or in the medieval manor. Or, the force of tradition may exercise a secondary, though significant, function in economies organized predominantly on other principles. In our own setting, examples range from racial discrimination, which eliminates options, through featherbedding practices, to the giving of Christmas presents. And even the contemporary Soviet economy—true, not as iconoclastic as in its younger days—has examples to offer.

This much is well known. Another moment's reflection also suggests that tradition is unlikely to be the *main* exchange-organizing principle in a modern industrial economy, if only because industrialism has not been around long enough to create its own traditional pattern to this effect (though Schumpeter held it was "marching" in that direction at a brisk pace). We are therefore left with the market mechanism and the command principle as the two chief alternative coordinating principles in industrial economies.[4] The two may of course successfully co-exist in any given society, as they may in turn co-exist with the force of tradition—although, as we shall presently see, there are certain probable conditions and limits to the co-existence.

---

[3] For examples of exchange through reciprocity and redistribution, see the essay on this subject by Walter C. Neale in Karl Polanyi et al., *Trade and Market in Early Empires* (Glencoe, Ill., 1957).

[4] In the Dahl and Lindblom fourfold classification of "central socio-political processes" the "price system" and "hierarchy" stand roughly for what we call the market mechanism and the command principle (*Politics, Economics, and Welfare*, Harper, 1953). Note that their definition of command (p. 106) differs from ours.

II

Let us agree that the *market mechanism* operates when (a) individual economic units (households, firms, etc.) decide the levels of their economic activities and enter into exchange with their environment with significant reference to the terms of exchange (prices) facing them and do so with the general aim of benefiting their net economic positions;[5] and (b) prices respond to the interaction of demand and supply, however imperfectly and sluggishly and by whatever institutional means. (To anticipate queries regarding price control, let us agree that when *effective* prices are truly fixed over a long period of time, and when there is hence the likelihood of significant disequilibrium, we may consider the price mechanism not to be *fully* operative.) As we have already said, a market economy is one in which the market mechanism performs the chief task of coordinating the activities of individual economic units.

Note that this definition says nothing at all about the structure of the markets (competition, oligopoly, monopoly, etc.), the size of the autonomous units, the static or dynamic efficiency of resource use, the goals of economic activity or the allocation of the national product, the level of the economy's development, or its rate of growth. Nor does it say anything about the legal ownership of productive assets; it admits of private market economies, socialist market economies, and perhaps other types as well. It does, however, imply the substantial *autonomy* of the firm in deciding what, how much, and when to produce or consume—to be sure, an autonomy that may well be circumscribed by innumerable legal, institutional, and traditional constraints. Moreover, the firm's decisions may be "guided" ("steered") by a central authority by changing various parameters of the unit's choice (taxes, customs duties, subsidies, interest rates), by manipulating (e.g., rationing) the availabilities of credit or foreign exchange or certain producer goods, or by means of direct constraints (e.g., zoning, prohibition of child labor)—but not by means of direct, positive production commands. Yet a certain significant autonomy of the firm, a certain significant range of choice, is fundamental to the concept of the market economy as we understand it here. This is another way of saying that the market economy is, by definition, a significantly *decentralized* economic system.[6]

Turning now to the command economy, and leaving the household

---

[5] I.e., we do not assume profit maximization in the strict sense. Something like Lerner's Rule—output at the point where marginal cost equals price—is subsumed.

[6] In his suggestive recent article, "The Economic Theory of Socialism: A Suggestion for Reconsideration" (*Journal of Political Economy*, Vol. LXIX, No. 4 [August, 1961], pp. 341–54) the Polish economist Jan Drewnowski stresses that in the socialist case, which he considers, the market mechanism need not apply to the production sector as well as to the household sector, nor to long-term decisions as well as to short-term ones. Consequently, he distinguishes between three "degrees" of the socialist market economy. "First-degree market economy" is one with free

sector aside for the moment, we define it as one in which the individual firms produce and employ resources primarily by virtue of specific directives (commands, targets) from some higher authorities. The firm's (management's) principal behavioral rule is therefore to execute the commands—in Soviet parlance, to fulfil the plan. The firms in a command system are therefore sometimes aptly called "executants." Since the higher (or "central") authorities are doubtless concerned with maintaining a minimal degree of balance within their purview, they "plan" to this end and try to formulate the directives accordingly, i.e., they aim at *consistency*. The planning and the directives may also aim at relatively *efficient* or even *optimal* resource use, which might be done by the planners "playing at" markets or simulating markets with the aid of electronic computers. This, however, is incidental for present purposes. It would not disqualify the system from being a command economy so long as the firms are assigned, and are expected to fulfil, specific producion and input-utilization targets. In other words, our definition is in terms of the managers' behavior rules, not in terms of the method of determining the targets.

Thus, in a command economy the firms have little autonomy, and the system as a whole is relatively little decentralized, or relatively centralized, compared to the market economy. Yet even within a command economy structure there may be varying degrees of centralization and varying degrees of autonomy for the firms; hence the qualifying word "primarily" in the first sentence of the preceding paragraph. Except in the extreme (and unrealistic) case, some decisions are taken by the executants themselves—whence stem many of the interesting problems of the command economy, to some of which most of the remainder of this paper is devoted.

But first let us complete our definitional efforts. Returning to the extreme and unlikely case where the executants have no range of choice whatever, we label it the "absolute command economy." Here, the central authorities prescribe everything and in the minutest detail to the production unit, if this is imaginable. We may evoke an even starker picture by bringing in the household sector: an absolute command economy without any "household choice" (i.e., consumer choice or choice of job), in which

---

buyer's choice in consumer goods markets and roughly equilibrium consumer goods prices, though the quantities of their output are decided on non-market principles. In the "second-degree market economy" the *producers* of consumer goods are also guided by the market mechanism, but only with regard to current decisions. In the "third-degree market economy," investment decisions in the consumer goods industry are also "dependent on consumers' demand," i.e., are also in some sense subject to market determination. However, in all three cases the magnitude of overall consumption is left to central decision.

A weakness in his approach is that he regards the household as a purchaser of goods but not as a seller of labor, and accordingly he does not concern himself with the labor market, which detracts from the completeness and symmetry of his analysis. He may have so limited his treatment because it is not proper in Eastern Europe to regard labor as being sold in a socialist economy or to regard the labor market as a market.

consumer needs are satisfied through physical doling out and labor is assigned. Forbidding as it may seem, the system has something of a historical counterpart in Soviet War Communism, or at least the non-peasant segment thereof.

A *less-than-absolute* command economy (which we henceforth call simply a command economy) with relatively free household choice is of course the normal situation in the USSR and other Soviet-type countries. Organizationally, it is a hierarchy; not despite some decentralization but because of it, for, as Herbert Simon has correctly pointed out, a hierarchical organization in itself signifies some delegation of authority and hence some decentralization. Its political context is almost certainly authoritarian. Perhaps one might conceive of a whole national economy organized on the command principle in a politically democratic milieu. But the very high accentuation of national goals which provide its social rationale, the destruction of autonomous economic powers that its creation entails, and the enforcement of obedience to directives that its operation supposes, all strongly suggest an authoritarian rather than a libertarian setting.

It is often said that a Weberian ideal-type bureaucracy is the most efficient method of carrying on social processes, of which the economic process is of course one. By implication, a command economy is superior to a market system. However, in the case of the economy taken as a whole the superiority of a Weberian bureaucracy is less obvious, owing to three specific features of the economic process: (1) a degree of interdependence of separate decisions that is much higher than in other social spheres, requiring in turn a much higher degree of internal coordination of dispersed activities; (2) a very much greater quantifiability of the variables than in other social spheres; and (3) the possibility of focusing on a single dominant (if not exclusive) and quantifiable social objective, such as the level of total national income. Because of (1), a very heavy burden of coordinative planning, let alone optimization, is thrown on the bureaucracy; while because of (2) and (3), the function of coordination (and, under certain conditions, optimization) can be turned over almost entirely to the market mechanism, thus doing away with an economy-wide bureaucracy altogether, insofar as the production sector is concerned. Naturally, this is not to say that a Weberian bureaucracy may not be the most efficient form of organization *within* production units, up to a certain size, or for other economic tasks, e.g. fiscal administration. In both of these instances the task of internal coordination is very much smaller than for a hierarchical structure embracing all or most of the economy.

III

Obviously, command economies do not arise spontaneously; they are imposed. In modern times there have been three main instances of such imposition: in the USSR in the early years of the Plan Era, in Nazi Germany after the mid-thirties, and in those countries which went communist after World War II. There are also two instances of the abandonment of command economy: Yugoslavia after 1948, and West Germany after the Nazi defeat; as well as two cases of transformation of a commond economy of the Nazi type into one of the Soviet variety: East Germany and the Czech lands. There is also the interesting case of something like a command economy advocated by the American Technocrats, especially in the thirties, but we shall not dwell on it here.

In both the Nazi and the Soviet instances,[7] an anti-market and anti-capitalist ideological bias was no doubt of considerable import. But one cannot escape the feeling that in both instances the actual adoption of a command economy was, if not purely accidental, largely unplanned. It was, so to say, pushed by the logic of events, with the transformation lubricated rather than propelled by ideological tenets. By contrast, in the case of the USSR's satellites the transformation was quite deliberate.

The Nazis apparently slid into a command economy thanks to a conjunction of pressing national goals, flagging entrepreneurial incentives, and a weakening of the market mechanism, the last two largely brought about by the 1936 *Preisstop*. Eucken[8] cites this as an example of a general process of the inevitable rise of authoritarian economics in the wake of a full employment policy, the latter being the villain. His argument is rather simple: full employment policies produce inflationary pressures; to avoid inflation, price controls are imposed; these undermine incentives and the market, and thus lead to authoritarianism. As a general proposition, Eucken's argument seems overdrawn, but it may be applicable to the Nazi paradigm, where the authoritarianism was already present.

It would take us too far afield to discuss the historical circumstances of the adoption of a command economy by the Soviet Union in the early thirties. A simple explanation would probably not do. Numerous factors would have to be considered in this regard in addition to ideological biases and Stalin's dictatorial tendencies—factors such as the enormous pressure on resources imposed by the first five-year plan, the need to move resources rapidly,[9] the extremely rapid technological transformation and vast changes in relative scarcities, the stark priorities, the shortage of managerial personnel, the waning of willing responsibility owing to the mounting terror, and the rapidly growing inflation. As with collectivization of agriculture, the eventual adoption of a non-market economy ("planned economy" in Soviet parlance) was doubtless also a matter of

---

[7] We are thinking of the transition from the socialist market economy of the NEP to the command economy at the end of the twenties and the beginning of the thirties.

[8] Walter Eucken, *This Unsuccessful Age* (Edinburgh, 1951).

[9] The advantage in moving resources rapidly and on a large scale is regarded by W. Arthur Lewis as the chief advantage of "planning by direction" as compared with "planning by inducement" (*The Principles of Economic Planning*, 1951, ch. VI).

fundamental ideological commitment; but in both regards the ideological commitment is inadequate to explain the particular timing and circumstances of institutional transformation.

IV

The chief persistent systemic problem of a command economy is the finding of the optimal degree of centralization (or decentralization)[10] under given conditions and with reference to given social goals. On this more later. But its chief daily task and chore is the maintenance of balance with regard to each economic good over the short term. It is *this* task that in fact constitutes by far the largest part of the so-called planning in the command economy, *not* what we in the West usually understand by this term, namely, the delineation of economic goals and the selection of strategies and instruments for their realization. In other words, the bulk of the so-called planning effort in a command economy is devoted to an arduous activity that substitutes for the most elementary accomplishment of the market mechanism. (We leave aside here the question whether it does so less or more expensively in terms of real resources than does the market.) We may call this *coordinative planning*, as against developmental planning, optimization planning, or financial planning, all of which are or should also be of concern to Soviet authorities. Coordinative planning as it is conducted in the Soviet Union does little by way of consciously steering the economy's development or finding efficient patterns of resource allocation. Its overwhelming concern is simply to equate both sides of each "material balance" by whatever procedure seems to be most expeditious. It is apparently conducted with little reference to systematic, rational rules of choice or definite notions of efficiency. The concepts of economic calculation,[11] efficiency, and optimality have been virtually absent from Soviet economics until recently. In any case, rational rules of choice would have been difficult to incorporate into the primitive, "manual" procedure of adjusting the thousands of material balances simultaneously.

To appreciate the full gravity of the balancing problem we should remember that the command economy is rooted in the logic of haste. The imposition of the command economy, that is to say, the extreme centralization of socio-economic processes that it represents, is in response to the pressing contrast between urgent political goals and available resources.[12]

---

[10] Cf. in this connection the suggestive article by A. K. Cairncross, "Programmes as Instruments of Co-ordination," *Scottish Journal of Political Economy*, Vol. VIII (June, 1961), pp. 85–101.

[11] As distinct from engineering calculation or administrative fiat.

[12] While Gerschenkron does not discuss the command economy as such, his analysis of the "tension" generated by a state of economic backwardness, and of the ideological and institutional responses thereto, is highly relevant here. Cf. Alexander Gerschenkron, *Economic Backwardness in Historical Perspective* (Harvard, 1963), the first essay and elsewhere.

The short-run effectiveness of the resources may have already been impaired by nationalization, collectivization, price control, and even the initial centralizing organizational measures themselves; hence, a cumulatively mounting urgency to centralize. Operationally, the contrast between goals and resources manifests itself in the command system in the ambitiousness of targets and in a dearth of *usable* stocks[13]—which naturally renders coordinative planning particularly difficult. But, the more arduous the attainment of balance, the greater the attention to this task at the expense of any search for allocative efficiency. We may therefore add that, paradoxically, a bias against allocative efficiency is also built into the command economy via the underlying logic of haste.

In Soviet economic reality, the gravity of the balancing problem manifests itself in the chronic supply shortages or the so-called sellers' market. (We are here thinking primarily of producer goods.) But while ambitious targeting ultimately underlies the sellers' market, other proximate causes may be at work: easy credit policy (itself a child of the logic of haste), the ever-present planning mistakes, bad incentives, an inefficient distribution system, a faulty price structure, and the various reactions to the sellers' market itself, such as the hoarding of supplies.

To state the tendency of the command economy toward ambitious targeting is of course not to exhaust the question. There are degrees of ambitiousness or "tautness" in planning, and as one proceeds up the scale one encounters both functional and dysfunctional effects. The dysfunctional effects include supply shortages with their numerous harmful consequences, neglect of allocative efficiency, and possibly the spread of corruption and cynicism. The positive effects of more ambitious targets are, at least up to a point, on the resource-mobilizing, psychological, educative, political, and—for the planners—information-yielding planes. These are not to be dismissed, especially in a relatively backward country. Hence, there may exist, so to say, plans of optimum tautness.[14]

V

The crucial importance of balancing is the reason that planning in a command economy must be chiefly *physical planning*. The financial plans apart—their chief purpose is the prevention of inflation—Soviet plans are almost entirely either in physical units or in crypto-physical units, the so-called constant prices. To attain and preserve balance a command

---

[13] It should be noted that inventories in Soviet-type economies are larger, not smaller, than in comparable market economies, because of faulty distribution and hoarding. But they are of little help because they tend to be, for good systemic reasons, of the wrong things and in the wrong places (in the hands of users rather than producers or distributors).

[14] The phrase is Holland Hunter's, who has inquired into the problem; see his "Optimum Tautness in Developmental Planning," *Economic Development and Cultural Change*, Vol. IX, No. 4 (July 1961), Part I, pp. 561–72.

economy must collate the physical availabilities and requirements of very many commodities, and this in turn necessitates physical targets for production and input utilization for the executants.

The maintenance of balance in a complex economy such as the Soviet requires the drawing up of many thousands of material balances at all levels. For the 1963 plan, 18,000 material balances were prepared at the *Gosplan USSR level alone;* at the lower levels the number is much larger. Since each of these represents commodity distribution over the plan period, the number of commodities subject to production directives and to materials allocation, in physical terms, must be about as great. The number of input-output norms (technical coefficients) is roughly proportional to the square of the number of "planned" commodities.

Physical targets carry a certain appeal at first glance. Isn't the real stuff of economic life physical rather than monetary and financial? As Marxists would put it, physical planning is free of those irrationalities that "value categories" cast over social relations among men in an exchange economy. Or, in the words of that hoary false dilemma, doesn't physical planning concern itself with production for use and not for profit? And yet, the whole Soviet experience bears eloquent testimony to the fact that planning—especially short-term planning—in physical terms leads to enormous waste and inefficiency, to production for waste as much as for use. Today, no one is better aware or more critical of it than the Soviet economists themselves. (Let us remind ourselves that we are still talking only of such elementary desiderata as balance and avoidance of obvious waste, not of economic efficiency or optimality.) A full explanation would call for an extended treatise on the Soviet economy, and so we shall merely try to present the argument briefly under three captions.

(1) *Grossness.* A physical production target refers to the firm's product, not to its net contribution to national income. The firm is induced and exhorted to maximize the former, not the latter. Actually, it should be maximizing its net contribution. The argument is not changed if the production plan is expressed in value terms at constant prices rather than in physical units. The concentration on the firm's gross product rather than on its net contribution may be particularly harmful when the good is an intermediate commodity or service. For example, foundries pour as much metal into castings as they can get away with, the metal only to be machined away at the next stage; or truckers run up as many ton-miles as possible, like the dishonest taxi with a meter in any country. Is an increase in ton-miles carried or in the weight of castings an indication of more production or more waste?

Among other things, the grossness of production targets has led to a preference for material-intensive products on the executants' part, thus leading to imbalances, much waste of materials, and that peculiarly Soviet phenomenon—upward-sloping demand curves for producer goods. To avoid such perverse effects, in certain industries with a low proportion of value added—e.g., the needle trades and food canning—for several years now targets have been set in terms of standard value added per unit of product. Though apparently an improvement over the old method, it does not seem to have worked out well either, judging from the Soviet literature.

(2) *Aggregation.* However detailed they may seem to the outside observer, physical targets are rarely detailed enough in the sense of pertaining to every type and sub-type of the commodity. They always refer to some level of aggregation. Or, alternatively, we may say that they refer to commodities but not to sub-commodities, the mix of sub-commodities being left to the firm's discretion. But in determining this mix the firm shows little sensitivity to demand; rather, it suits its own gain and convenience. As a result, supply and demand of the sub-commodities are out of balance, even if for the aggregate commodity category they are in balance, of whatever significance that may be. Steel pipe in general may be in balance, but each kind of pipe is either in short or in excess supply. If this is remedied by rendering the classification finer and the targets more detailed—by promoting the sub-commodities to commodity status, so to say—a greater burden is thrown on the central authorities and the various evils of over-centralization proliferate.

We may regard amounts of the given commodity produced within individual sub-periods of the plan period as sub-commodities, and the same argument follows with regard to the time pattern of production.

(3) *Unit of Measure.* Physical planning takes place in terms of definite physical units of measure. For the sake of convenience, a single unit of measure should attach to a given commodity and it should not be changed too often. But every commodity has several, sometimes many, physical dimensions. Therefore, the particular unit of measure that is specified in the directives is partly arbitrary, and is inevitably inconvenient or even unsuitable for some purposes. Moreover, the specification of a unit of measure is not neutral with regard to production, because the firms will so manipulate the character and quality of the commodity as to obtain the largest output in the specified unit from their production possibilities. If paper is specified in tons, as happens to be the case in the USSR, then the firms will tend to produce heavy kinds of paper and to shun thin kinds. Such examples can be cited *ad infinitum* from Soviet practice.[15]

Note that there are two general classes of physical units of measure in this respect: "use-oriented" and "input-oriented" units. The former relate

---

[15] This of course is a property of physical indicators in any setting, and not a specific feature of the Soviet scene. For example, at one time the US Army Dental Corps introduced quasi-physical success indicators ("points") to evaluate the performance of dental officers, who were assigned minimum daily quotas in "points." This led to such misdirected and inferior work that the scheme had to be abandoned. Col. George F. Jeffcott, *United States Army Dental Service in World War II*, Department of the Army, Office of the Surgeon General (Washington, D.C., 1955), p. 223.

to some dimension of importance to the commodity's user or consumer (power of motors, area of leather, length of pre-stressed concrete beam). The latter are of less interest to the user but are the same in which the principal material input is measured (tons of steel in the case of the motor, of hides in the case of leather, and of cement in the case of the beam). More often than not the latter is a unit of weight. While maximization of output in terms of a use-oriented specified unit of measure may (though need not always) be of advantage to the commodity's users, and hence to the economy as a whole, maximization of output in terms of the input-oriented unit is rarely of such benefit. And yet, paradoxically, there is a strong tendency for the specified units of measure to be input-oriented; witness such absurdities as rolling equipment or chemical equipment expressed in tons. The reason is simple: the difficult job of drawing up the material balance for the *input* is simplified in each case if the product is in the same unit of measure as the input. It is relatively easy to estimate how much steel will be required for the equipment if the latter is also expressed in tons. Needless to say, this leads to the production of excessively heavy equipment, the wrong kind of equipment, and so forth—a phenomenon that is only too common in Soviet practice.[16]

VI

The advantages of *decentralization* within a command economy are the familiar ones that apply to all economic organizations, except that the sheer size of the organization in this instance tends to multiply their urgency manyfold. These advantages of decentralization and of the consequently shorter lines of communication are: greater speed and fidelity of transmission of information, lesser volume and cost of information processing, faster and better adaptation to changing conditions (demand, technology, resource position), resolution of conflicts at lower levels (hence, a lesser politicization of economic conflicts), and larger chance for the realization of dispersed initiative for improvement and innovation. The advantages that decentralization brings *within* the command economy are essentially identical with the advantages of the more decentralized socioeconomic process, the market mechanism, in comparison with the more centralized one, and administrative hierarchy operating on the command principle.

The advantages of centralization are perhaps less commonly appreciated. (Is this because of our society's ideological bias in favor of decentralization? Local and states' rights are issues with us, but never federal rights!) We may begin with the irrational reasons for centralizing—irrational, that is, from the point of view of society or the regime if not from that of certain individuals—such as the ubiquitous tendencies toward "em-

---

[16] More on the effects of the unit of measure may be found in my *Soviet Statistics of Physical Output of Industrial Commodities* (NBER—Princeton, 1960), pp. 69 ff.

pire building" and "power grabbing" at the upper levels and "buck passing" from below. These tendencies seem to be quite well developed in the Soviet Union. But there are also perfectly rational grounds for centralization of economic decision-making; for instance:

(1) *Enforcement of the Regime's Values.* Clearly, the official values and priorities are not completely shared thoughout the economy or society; often they are challenged and opposed, albeit covertly. The lifting of certain decisions to higher levels may protect the priorities and values from being undermined. Among the more important official values that tend to be subverted at lower levels are the full mobilization of resources, their full use on the given job, and the introduction of innovations—all clearly high on the Soviet regime's priority list. The economist will recognize here an inadequacy of economic signals and of behavior rules and incentives. But whether prices, rules and incentives could be so restructured as to eliminate the likelihood of serious infringement of the regime's priorities seems to be a moot point. It is of course the regime itself which is the judge of whether the infringement is "serious" or not.

(2) *Resource Mobility on a Large Scale, Especially in Emergency Situations.* The broader the range of resources under single command and the greater the power over their deployment and commitment, the wider the possibilities for massive manoeuvre with them. This is especially important in the USSR where intermediate goals are often shifted and "crash programs" ("campaigns") are endemic, but where there is little slack, and where, further, "departmentalism" (*vedomstvennost*) and "localism" (*mestnichestvo*) thwart resource mobility at intermediate and lower levels. When a particularly vast emergency campaign is mounted, as, for example, the *mettre en valeur* of the Virgin Lands, it is significantly the Party and the Komsomol that are given the chief mobilizing and redeploying function, their local secretaries being, so to say, the vicars of the top authorities throughout the land.

(3) *Concentrating Scarce Skills and Talents at the Top.* This reason is often cited in support of centralization, though its advantages do not appear to be unambiguous. Being concentrated at the top the best specialists may indeed have more scope for the exercise of their abilities than otherwise, but they may also dispose of faulty, insufficient, or tardy information, and too much of their time may be absorbed by "paperwork" (a common Soviet complaint).

(4) *Maintaining Balance.* In the absence of the proper signals (prices) and behavior rules to produce corrective responses at the executants' level, the balancing function is best performed by those who have the broadest view of the economy, i.e., the most complete pertinent information. As one descends in the hierachy, the hazard of a "failure of overview" (Dahl-Lindblom) increases, the *Übersehbarkeit* (in the apposite German expression) declines. The chronic threat to balance with regard to individual goods is thus a continuous argument for the (re)centralization of

planning and materials allocation. The Soviet economy is constantly subject to "creeping re-centralization" on this account. For the same reason, a
partial decentralization of planning and management in a command economy may do more harm than good; it may impair balance without
yielding sufficient benefit from the shortening of the lines of communication. A virtually complete decentralization, in the sense of a virtually full
devolution of the major production decisions to the firm level, would be
disastrous from the standpoint of balance, unless the price structure were
simultaneously altered to provide proper signals to firms *and* suitable
behavior rules were prescribed, i.e., unless a market mechanism were
introduced. Without these conditions there would indeed result a Mises-
like socialist chaos, though one hardly need be like Mises and hold that
these necessary conditions of decentralization could not possible be established under socialism.[17]

We have been arguing so far as though centralization-decentralization
were a simple unidimensional matter, a question of the effective decision-
making level along the vertical lines of a single hierarchy. This is gross
oversimplification. In reality there are many dimensions of decision-
making and control in the Soviet-type economy: coordinative planning,
materials allocation, day-to-day management, investment planning,
finance, price setting, and, last but not least, the Party which performs
many managerial functions *de facto*. Vertical shifts along one of these
dimensions may be accompanied by either opposite or like shifts along
other dimensions, depending on the needs for preserving or strengthening
surveillance, control, and balance. For instance, the delegation of managerial functions to lower levels (though not necessarily to the firm) is
likely to be accompanied by a parallel delegation of economic duties
within the Party structure so as to strengthen lateral surveillance at the
lower level, and possibly at the same time by a re-centralization of price
setting and financial functions in order to "firm up" the parameters with
which the newly delegated powers are to deal.

VII

The place and role of *money* in the command economy can now be
viewed from the standpoint of the system's partial decentralization. But
first we must distinguish its different classic roles. Money can serve as a
standard of value and as a unit of account without also serving as a medium
of exchange. Examples abound: the "imaginary money" of the middle
ages, various more-or-less stable units of account during modern hyper-

---

[17] Michael Polanyi holds an interesting variant of the Mises position. Like Mises,
he maintains that "direct planning" is impossible, but explains the ability of the Soviet
economy to function by its being in fact, if not in name and theory, a market
economy. The last is dubious. See his "Theory of Conspicuous Production," *Survey*,
No. 34 (October–December, 1960), and comments thereon.

inflations, the standards of value implicit in the "accounting prices" and "shadow prices" used by planners, those implicit in the Soviet constant prices (such as those of "1926/27")—*Messwerte* in East Germany, the *trudoden*—the intra-kolkhoz unit of value and account, and so forth. What the unit is and what it is called is irrelevant. So long as it serves as the common denominator of value for a sufficiently wide range of goods it is a monetary unit for our purposes. Thus, the Bolshevik "labor unit" of the early post-revolutionary years and the Technocrats' "energy unit" are monetary units, professions of their originators to the contrary notwithstanding.

The converse—money serving as a medium of exchange but not as a standard of value—is however not admissible simply because any exchange presupposes at least an implicit price, and hence a standard of value. (But note that the classic function of money as a store of value is derivative from its function as a medium of exchange and arises from the introduction of the time dimension into the exchange of goods for which money serves as the medium.)

So long as it limits itself to balancing and does not strive for allocative efficiency, the extreme notional case of an absolute command economy *cum* doling out of consumer goods requires no unit of account or medium of exchange, i.e., no money. All its accounting can be done in *ad hoc* physical units. Should the absolute command economy become concerned with allocative efficiency, it will require money as a unit of account and calculation, though *not* as a medium of exchange. Money as a medium of exchange and a store of value becomes necessary only with the introduction of some decision-making autonomy. If, in the present example, households are transferred from the dole in kind to a certain amount of freedom of consumer choice (possibly even with ration cards)—in other words, are given autonomy—money becomes almost necessary for the effective operation of the distribution system. (Conceivably, households could be paid in kind and allowed to barter among themselves, but this would be inconvenient. On the other hand, scrip would be money in our sense.) Hence prices for consumer goods to indicate the terms on which alternatives are offered to consumers; hence money as a medium of exchange to allow the choices to be realized; and hence also money as a store of value, i.e., as a means of imposing a budget constraint on the amount of society's resources that the household can claim in a given period. A most important by-product is the use of money wages for incentive purposes, though here, too, graduated payments in kind are conceivable. But all this does not yet signify the use of money as a medium of exchange in the *production* sector.

Money enters the production sector in its three major functions if some appreciable decision-making power is granted to the individual production unit, i.e., if the command economy is not absolute. In this instance, money's function is precisely the same as in the case of the household that is taken off the dole *in natura:* to permit the establishment of terms for alternative resource uses (i.e., prices) and to impose a budget constraint on the total claim on resources by the individual firm. In the Soviet case, the role of money as a unit of account to facilitate proper choice of inputs by the firm has been subsidiary to the enforcement of the budget constraint over the firms. In sum, money as a standard of value or unit of account derives from the need to economize at whatever level the decisions are taken. But money as a medium of exchange derives from the need to economize with some devolution of decision-making to the lowest economic units, households and firms. In both cases the need for money derives from the fact of scarcity.

Since a considerable degree of freedom of household choice is desirable for psychological and administrative reasons, and since some measure of decentralization of decisions in the production sector is unavoidable, money has a most important place in a command economy, including of course money as a medium of exchange and store of value, i.e., not merely as a unit of calculation and account but money that can be spent. But so long as money is money, any amount of it in someone's hands is also a certain amount of power that lies outside the effective control of the central authorities, power that may be used contrary to the authorities' values and system of priorities. To curb it—by limiting individual money balances of households and of "socialist" firms, and by erecting obstacles and limits to their use—is also in some measure to sacrifice the advantages of whatever decentralization there may be in the system. And conversely, making fuller use of these advantages requires more freedom of disposition or holding of money funds and hence runs the risk of accumulations of power outside the control of the regime.

The use of money just described accords with the Soviet system of *khozraschet*. This term, which is often translated as "economic accounting," is perhaps best rendered into English by the phrase "businesslike management." It is essentially a set of behavior rules that is supposed to govern the actions of Soviet managers beyond their primary responsibility, the fulfilment of output targets. Khozraschet calls for (1) keeping cost accounts, (2) maximizing profits (which—with rigid production plans—in effect amounts to minimizing production outlays, though production targets may in fact be subverted in the quest for profits), and (3) solvency (unless losses are planned and made up by the Treasury). It is important to note that the Soviet manager has very little scope for substitution among inputs because most of the important ones are rationed to him; therefore, cost minimization means essentially the minimization of the consumption of each input taken singly. Thus, khozraschet amounts to a rule that directs managers to maximize technical efficiency, i.e., minimize avoidable waste, and be subject to an overall budget constraint in claiming society's resources for productive use. The budget constraint is often further tightened by the earmarking of funds and various other forms of financial control from above. So understood, khozraschet is a system that is well devised to control the behavior of managers in a command economy where a certain minimal amount of devolution of power to them is inevitable, and where, further, the managers' goals and values do not necessarily coincide with the official ones. If it has worked far from satisfactorily—it has not been able to prevent enormous waste, for example—the fault is not so much in its design but in that it was overpowered by the zealous and jealous application of the command principle to the firm.

Another important Soviet institutional arrangement for the exercise of decentralized powers in the command economy is the system of inter-firm contracts. At first blush it seems to be superflous, at least for that predominant range of goods that is subject to production targets and central allocation. And indeed, in our notional absolute command economy it *would* be superfluous. But in a partly decentralized system inter-firm contract performs two vital functions: (1) it formally communicates to the two parties the specifications for the product and the conditions and timing of its delivery, and (2) it establishes a formal commitment, enforceable at law, on both sides. The specifications and the commitments are derivative from the plans and directives to which both sides are subject, which is a prolific source of complications, especially because the plans are often revised. In our terminology, the chief rationale of the contracts is to define the flow of sub-commodities rather than of commodities, and thus to relieve coordinative planning from a certain amount of detail. If the contract system has not been able to assure the smooth flow of (sub)commodities, it is for the same basic reason that khozraschet has been only a partial success. In both cases, the fault at bottom perhaps lies with the great difficulty of dovetailing any decentralizing institutional arrangement with a command principle that is consistently and compulsively applied.

At the root of this difficulty is the conflict between the will, purposes, incentives, and priorities of the higher authorities and those of the lower levels, particularly of the firms and their managements. Even if managers follow quite faithfully the behavior rules laid down for them and adhere closely to the innumerable regulations and proscriptions—which is assuming quite a lot—there is no reason to believe that these rules and regulations will, in conjunction with the signals (prices) available to managers, lead to decentralized decisions that generally coincide with those that the higher authorities would take in the given instances. (For simplicity we speak of the higher authorities as though they were all of one mind, which is of course a fiction.) To complicate matters, the rules and regulations are often ambiguous or mutually inconsistent, and in any case may be violated for selfish or enlightened reasons. In this conflict between central will and the tendencies of dispersed decision-makers the latter often prevail—witness the classic cases of the unresponsiveness of agriculture to central control and of the remarkable resistance of industrial managers to innovation. The most powerful weapon at the disposal of the central authorities is centralized materials allocation (*materialno-tekhni-cheskoye snabzheniye*), not the police or the Party apparatus. This is why the just-cited cases of defiance of central will (agriculture and innovation) are relatively widespread and successful; in both instances control over material inputs cannot do much to force a positive response on the executants' part. . . .

VIII

These considerations would seem to preclude a major role for the market mechanism in a command economy, especially if the rationing (allocation) of producer goods is maintained. Such rationing, however, is likely to exist because of the pressure on resources that—as we have argued—constitutes the *raison d'être* of a command economy. More than that, the admission of the market mechanism on a substantial scale into a command economy may in itself prompt the maintenance of producer-goods rationing in order to afford to the central authorities a direct instrument of control over the market. Under such conditions co-existence between the command principle and the market mechanism would seem to be unstable and ephemeral. Since the two are apt to be continuously in conflict, the command principle, aided by the club of materials rationing, will inevitably push back and eventually eliminate the market mechanism—unless of course a full-fledged market economy be deliberately adopted, as in Yugoslavia.

In other words, it would seem that there is no half-way house between a market economy and a command economy. Peter Wiles writes: "Those who wish to de-Stalinize their economies *must* create a free market, as the Yugoslavs discovered; those who dislike the laws of supply and demand *must* Stalinize their economies. There is no third way."[18] In large measure Wiles is right; but it seems to us that the matter is somewhat more complicated than this.

Let us take a closer look. First, the command principle functions and even thrives in certain compartments of what otherwise are market economies—for instance, *within* many a large western firm (whether private or nationalized) and within the sphere of government *sensu stricto*. Secondly, because of the intrusion of uncertainty and for socio-political reasons, a good deal of long-term investment in a market economy, both private and governmental, is undertaken with only limited reference to information generated by markets. But the question that concerns us here is somewhat different: can an industry or sector, call it (M), be successfully tied by means of the market mechanism to the rest of the economy (C) which is organized according to the command principle? To answer it

---

[18] Wiles, *op.cit.*, p. 19; italics in the original.

let us see what would constitute failure in the eyes of the central authorities.

There may be three reasons for failure: (1) Unpredictability of the flow of goods between M and C, in detail as well as in the aggregate, owing to difficulty of guiding or controlling the behavior of M. This would render physical planning for and plan-fulfilment in C difficult, especially if C depends on M for significant inputs. Hence, the more C depends on M the less successfully can the latter be "separated out," and the higher the priority that attaches to the corresponding production in C the less will the unpredictability of M's behavior be tolerated. Buffer stocks would help, but, as we have seen, they are not easy to establish in the right places in a command economy. (2) Production in M tends to violate the regime's values and priorities, and is not susceptible to corrective measures in this regard (short of abolishing the market nexus). (3) M fails to mobilize its production resources fully. (We are assuming that the regime continues to abhor slack and to set ambitious targets.)

On the other hand, the regime may reap the following benefits from separating an industry or sector from the command pyramid and tying it to the rest of the economy by the market mechanism: (*a*) shortening of lines of communication, and hence faster and better response to changing conditions in M; (*b*) reduction in the over-all burden of coordinative planning (especially important if production in M is not of a routine and repetitive nature); (*c*) possibility of tying incentives more closely to results; (*d*) higher morale and initiative in M thanks to a greater feeling of freedom by the human agents, and (*e*) shifting certain costs and risks to the latter as a corollary (or partial price for) the freedom. Thus, theoretically, a rational decision whether to separate M out of the command pyramid would involve balancing considerations (*a*)–(*e*) against (1)–(3), and, one might add, against certain political factors as well.

Several examples of M are to be found in Soviet-type economies. First, the household sector is typically outside the command pyramid and is tied to the latter *via* a market nexus that follows what we have called the freedom of household choice. Generally speaking, consumer goods are offered to the public (insofar as offered at all) in quantities predetermined by the planners but at posted prices and on a take-it-or-leave-it basis, and jobs are similarly offered to workers. To be sure, an able-bodied individual is under severe social pressure to do *some* socially-approved work, but he or she is not, as a rule, assigned to a given job.[19] Also to be sure, the freedom of choice of job is limited in many ways, but so it is in other economic systems in some ways or other. The advantage of

---

[19] There are of course some well-known exceptions to this generalization: forced labor, assignment of graduates of higher educational institutions to their first jobs, "volunteer" work of various kinds, etc. However, at present, as in the thirties though on a smaller scale, excessive turnover of labor is a major problem in the Soviet economy.

so "separating out" the household sector with regard to both consumer goods distribution and the furnishing of labor services could be discussed in terms of (1)–(3) and (a)–(e). We forgo it here for lack of space, except to point out that (b), (c), and (d) would seem to be particularly important in this instance.

Another case in point is Polish agriculture after 1956, which has not only been separated out of the command pyramid but has also been re-privatized (de-collectivized). At its present technical level, Polish agriculture takes relatively few inputs from the rest of the economy, and, what is equally important, these inputs (fertilizer, building materials, equipment, even fuel) do not bear a rigid relation to agricultural output, which affords some freedom of action to those who plan and manage industrial production. At the same time, while agriculture produces some vital goods for the rest of the economy (food, fibers, foreign exchange), considered as inputs they generally do not bear a rigid relation in *detail* to production processes in other sectors. On the other hand, all of the listed advantages, (a) through (e), seem to hold.

As for Soviet (and Czech, East German, etc.) agriculture, the situation is in part similar with regard to the private sector, which in the USSR was still contributing close to 40% of gross agricultural output in the later fifties. However, it is much more complicated than in Polish agriculture because the Soviet private sector is in uneasy symbiosis with collectivized agriculture and tends to detract labor and other inputs from the latter. As for the collective farms themselves, it is perhaps appropriate to regard them as being substantially within the command pyramid, especially since March 1962.[20] The attempt in 1955 to steer agricultural (kolkhoz) production at least in part by means of market instruments, while of course retaining large compulsory delivery quotas, was never really put into practice. The reasons for this are many and mostly fall outside the scope of the present essay. The one conclusion that we may draw here (apart from the general ineffectiveness of market instruments in a command environment) is that the more inadequate the incentives, and the less directly they are related to effort, the harder it is to introduce elements of the market mechanism, especially where the producers (individual peasants or collective farms) have the alternative of consuming the produce (above compulsory deliveries) rather than selling it. If it is too expensive to bribe the kolkhozy to produce and market they will be commanded to do so—which, as we know, is not too effective either. Thus, only the private sector of Soviet agriculture is still left—grudgingly—to respond to market stimuli.

Certain minor peripheral or interstitial activities are also separated out of the command pyramid in the Soviet economy; for instance: the services of "uncooperated artisans" (e.g., tailors, seamstresses, some repairmen),

---

[20] [When the administration of Soviet agriculture was reorganized.—EDITOR.]

the production of consumer goods out of waste materials by state-owned enterprises, or the activities of individual mining prospectors (*starateli*). Each of these cases can be easily explained with reference to (1)–(3) and (*a*)–(*e*). There are of course also large and far-reaching black markets in all economies of the Soviet type, but this is someting else again.

In sum, the household sector and private farming apart, the prospects for a successful separation of an industry or sector from the command pyramid are quite limited even on economic grounds. The peripheral and interstitial areas we mentioned are the exceptions that "prove the rule." These prospects shrink if ideological and political considerations are also brought to bear. Planning (*à la russe*) is, after all, "one of the main achievements of the October Revolution"; the market mechanism is capitalist and (worse) revisionist. Moreover, those sectors in which production is or could well be carried on in units of small size (e.g., retail trade, some services, agriculture) cannot be easily turned over to the market mechanism without raising the specter of legalized or clandestine private enterprise. The prospects shrink much further when we think of the enormous vested bureaucratic interests in the present system of planning and materials allocation. It required a political upheaval of the magnitude of the purging of the "anti-party group" to make possible the mere "territorialization" of the command structure, i.e., the replacement of economic ministries by sovnarkhozy.[21] In Poland, it took the "Polish October" to decollectivize (and "marketize") agriculture—something that would be much harder to accomplish within the USSR itself.

What adds poignancy to the problem is that its dimensions are far from static. The growth and modernization of an economy that is already organized on the command principle render the maintenance of balance progressively more difficult, and therefore militate for strengthening of this principle, particularly in the form of further centralization.[22] In this sense, the experience of the USSR during 1958–1963, an experience of progressive re-centralization on virtually all economic fronts, is as instructive as it is *zakonomerno*.[23] As time goes on, the dilemma of either fullblown Stalinist economics or a comprehensive Titoist economic reform indeed becomes starker and starker.

But this assumes a more or less constant political factor, a more or less constant degree of tension between imperatives and aspirations on the one hand and resources on the other. Might not time wear down this tension? Specifically, might not a significant détente in relations with the West

---

[21] [Regional economic councils.—EDITOR.]

[22] Unless greater regional autarky be permitted or tolerated. Autarky shortens lines of communication and facilitates the maintenance of balance within each region, but at considerable economic and political cost. I have discussed this point in "The Structure and Organization of the Soviet Economy," *Slavic Review*, Vol. XXI, No. 2 (June 1962), pp. 209–20.

[23] "In conformance with law or principle."

(but China!), a greater sense of security and comfort thanks to material progress, a reduction in defense expenditures for one or both of these reasons, the waning of the ideological *élan* (which greatly worries the leaders as these lines are written), the change of generations, the *embourgeoisement* of the population, the growing expertise and self-confidence of professionals, and so forth—might not these developments lead to a more relaxed attitude toward resource mobilization and the enforcement of priorities? They might also incidentally permit the accumulation of inventories in the right places. If so, certain sectors might be separated out of the command pyramid and "marketized"; for example, agriculture (albeit still largely socialized) and construction (or some parts thereof). But then such a hybrid structure might prove to be only a transitional stage, for the same political developments would probably make it more difficult to resist the lure of a thoroughgoing socialist market economy *à la yougoslave*. But we are now on very "iffy" ground.

Walter Eucken

11. ON THE THEORY OF THE CENTRALLY ADMINISTERED ECONOMY: AN ANALYSIS OF THE GERMAN EXPERIMENT*

In this comprehensive article, Eucken analyzes in detail the problems and weaknesses of a centrally planned economy, as illustrated by the operation of the Nazi German economy. Almost all of his analysis, however, applies as well to centrally planned socialist economies, like that of the Soviet Union, as the selections on the Soviet economy in Part III show.

Eucken explains how plans for the production and distribution of goods are made in the centrally administered economy. He stresses the many serious problems caused by the movement from economic calculation in value terms to planning and allocation in physical terms. In this connection, he points out how the central authorities relied for the fulfillment of their plans on the illegal activity and unreported inventories of individual firms. Eucken shows the essential differences between market economies and centrally administered economies in investment decisions, economic fluctuations, the distribution of income, and international trade. Thus, he concludes, any use of markets and prices to direct the economy necessarily curtails the power of the central administration to control it.

* Reprinted, with the permission of the author's executor and the publisher, from *Economica*, New Series, Vol. XV, No. 58 (May, 1948), pp. 79–100, and No. 59 (August, 1948), pp. 173–93. The article was translated from the German by T. W. Hutchinson. Walter Eucken was Professor of Economics at the University of Freiburg, Germany.

INTRODUCTION

1. AFTER 1936 the German economy came more and more under central
direction and administration. This was not the result of a conscious effort
of policy to create a new form of economic organization. It was rather a
result produced accidentally. It was the full-employment policy which
started the movement, and it was the implementation of this policy which
led step by step towards a centrally administered economy ("Zentral-
verwaltungswirtschaft").

In 1932–33 the full-employment policy began with public works, expansion of credit, a cheap money policy, and a pegging of the exchange
rate. As this policy threatened to bring a sharp rise in prices, a general
price-freeze was ordered in 1936. Germany—like many other countries
since then—entered upon a period of "repressed inflation." Prices ceased to
give expression to the scarcity of goods and services on the markets. This
state of affairs gave rise to the creation of a central administrative apparatus to direct the economy, to supervise foreign trade, to allocate the most
important raw materials such as coal, iron and cement, to weigh up
priorities, distribute licences and so on. This was the beginning. With the
growing danger of war, and with its actual outbreak, the measures of
central administration and direction played an increasingly important role
in the economy. It was necessary to concentrate productive resources on
armaments and to force up the rate of investment. There was the growing
pressure of an expanded but immobilized supply of money. So more and
more branches of production, and even the distribution of labor supplies
and consumers' goods, came under the orders of the central planning
authorities.

It was not that the *whole* everyday economic life of the country was
controlled by the central administration through the direction of labor,
production orders, compulsory deliveries, rationing and so on. On the
contrary, important markets remained free for a long time. Only in recent
years did barter develop on a large scale, when the German people not
only got their rations of bread, potatoes, or meat, from the central authorities, but tried to obtain food and other consumers' goods by barter, or
grew vegetables and potatoes for themselves. Then different forms of
economic organization were combined together. But since 1938 it was *one*
of these forms which dominated, that of the centrally administered economy.

The following pages are concerned almost exclusively with this element
in the German economic system ("Wirtschaftsordnung"), and not with
the very important problems of money and barter which arose in the
course of this interesting episode. An economic order in reality is always
made up of a combination of different pure forms. We are only concerned

here with one of these. A centrally administered economy is not to be confused with one where all property is collectively owned. Certainly, central administration and direction of an economy can be combined with collective ownership of property, as, for example, in Russia since 1928. But this combination is not necessary. The interesting point is that in Germany the means of production remained predominantly in private ownership, and farms and factories alike continued to belong mainly to private individuals and companies. But the private owners could only dispose over their means of production to a limited extent. There was widespread requisitioning of industrial stocks, which were only released for definite purposes consistent with the central plan. We can say, in fact, that for the economic process as a whole, it was not the plans and actions of individual businesses and households that were decisive, but the plans and orders of the central authorities.

2. What questions do we want to put about the German experiment? In our case, a question which has been much discussed, and which has shown itself to be a fruitful one: are the same economic "laws" valid in the centrally administered economy as in the exchange economy?

Economists have given two fundamentally different answers to this question. J. S. Mill spoke of "the very different laws" which held for the competitive as compared with the collectivist economy. Similarly also Dietzel.[1] In contrast with these "dualists," the "monists" hold that the economic processes of an exchange and of a collectivist economy—two concepts usually not at all precisely defined—are essentially similar. This was the view of Wieser, Pareto, and especially Barone. The point of view of these writers has been widely accepted, and on the whole the monists predominate.

Who is right? Is the fundamental logic of economic action really the same in the commercial as in the socialist society, as Schumpeter has recently held?[2] Or, are these two quite different worlds? This is much more than a purely academic question. In the economic life of this century both methods of direction are being applied, that of the exchange economy and that of the centrally administered economy. The history of our time offers for our analysis, as to our forefathers it did not, many experiments in the central administration of economic life. We are dealing with this one experiment. Can we understand the economic phenomena of the twentieth century if we approach them with a single unified theoretical apparatus created for the analysis of the exchange economy? Or is it necessary to work out a special theory of the centrally administered economy to do justice to economic reality?

---

[1] J. S. Mill, *Logic*, Book 6, chap. 10, para. 3; H. Dietzel, *Theoretische Sozialökonomik* (1895), p. 85 ff.

[2] Barone, in *Giornale degli Economisti*, 1908; Pareto, *Manuel*, p. 362 ff.; and Schumpeter, *Capitalism, Socialism, and Democracy* (1942), chap. 16.

Wieser and Barone had no knowledge of such definite examples as we have. Of course, historical cases of a predominantly centrally administered economic order are numerous, for example those of Egypt or of the Incas. But economic processes in our modern industrial age are so much more complex and comprehensive, and the tasks of direction so much more difficult, that these older examples are of secondary interest. Economists today have material before them quite unknown to their predecessors.

Our analysis of the German experiment was undertaken just at the moment when this experiment was coming to its close. The direction of the economy by central administration broke down in 1946–47. Procedures and forms pertaining to monetary and barter economies, and to an economy of self-sufficient household units, began to spread. But this investigation is not a historical one; nor is it an obituary notice. Our aim rather is to get a grasp of the general principles which German experiences can teach. It is agreed that the direction of economic life by a central administration came about in Germany mainly for purposes of war. Frequently improvisations had to suffice, instead of the long-term planning possible in peace. What is simply a peculiarity of war conditions must not be attributed to the centrally administered economy.

I. THE ECONOMIC PROCESS AS A WHOLE

1. How a Central Administration Works

The study of the organization of an exchange economy begins with the procedures of individual firms or households, let us say, in a leather factory. It is ascertained that the firm bases its plans on price and cost calculations, that is, on the relation of the prices of the products to the prices of the factors of production. This is what is decisive in guiding production. In this way each firm controls, in its own sphere, a fraction of the economic process, and the process as a whole is controlled by means of prices.

The study of a firm in a centrally administered economic order—for example during the German experiment—leads to quite another conclusion. Our leather factory produces on the orders of the Leather Control Office. This "Control Office," "Department" or "Planning Branch" ("Fachabteilung" or "Planstelle") allocates raw hides and auxiliary materials. It gives the firm its instructions to produce, and disposes of the leather it produces. For knowledge as to how the plans are formed by which the economy is guided in a centrally administered system, we must go to these control offices. There were "Controls" for textiles, clothing, glass, pottery, iron and so on. How did this central direction work out?

In four stages:—

First, there was the collection of statistical material for which the

Controller would have at his disposal a Statistical Section. This primary importance of statistics is a characteristic of the centrally administered economy. The statisticians tried to assemble for the planning authorities all the important data necessary: thus, for example, equipment, storage capacity, the need for storage space, the needs for coal and electricity, the production and import of raw materials, the production and uses of, for example, leather, textiles or other raw materials and other products. From this statistical material a quantitative balance-sheet was obtained which put the supplies against the consumption for the preceding year, half year, or quarter.

The statistics had to follow precise orders with regard both to their collection and treatment. They formed the foundation for the planning itself which was the *second* stage of the process. This consisted of drawing up programs for requirements and supplies, and for the means by which the two were to be balanced.

It is an essential point that the figures planned for requirements had their source only partially in the demands of the higher authorities, who would be requiring for purposes of armaments, or investment in general, particular quantities of iron, machinery, leather, etc. Another part originated with other users ("Bedarfsträger"), that is, mostly other control offices. Thus for example, leather would be ordered by the Shoe Control, or the Machinery Control, while the Leather Control ordered tanning materials, oils, fats, coal and so forth from the control offices responsible. Requirements always came in to the particular planning branch or control office collectively, or in aggregates ("gebündelt"). It is important that at this very early stage in drawing up the plan, standardization of goods became a necessity. Determining the leather requirements, for example, of the Shoe Control was all the more difficult the greater the variety of types of shoe in production. Central planning requires standardization.

After the centrally administered economy had been working some time, the planning offices often used the figures for earlier planning periods, which could be ascertained with precision. The figures were intended for the *future* planned quantities, but were taken over without further scrutiny from previous plans. There was a danger here that the necessary consistency with the facts of the present position might be lacking. For this reason the central authorities higher up, for example in the Ministry of Economics, often had occasion to warn against the exuberance of the statisticians. For example, it was on one occasion explained that: "However much planning may require a statistical basis, it must never be forgotten that statistics can only relate to the past. The outward form which planning assumes, that is, balances of figures, is not the essence of planning, which is rather an active shaping of the future." Incidentally, the calculating of needs per head of the population was held of small significance, as it took no account of local and occupational differences.

With regard to supplies, the principal item apart from imports and drawing on stocks, was, of course, production. Here the principle was laid down that production had to be estimated on the basis of the narrowest bottleneck. For instance, equipment and raw materials might be ample, but if it was coal or labor that was in short supply, it was in accordance with *these* that plans had to be drawn up. As bottlenecks were constantly shifting, the basis of the plan had constantly to be altered. The real art of this sort of central planning lay in recognizing promptly where the bottleneck was to be expected next.

Over the balancing of requirements against supplies, long battles were necessary, and we shall be dealing with these repeatedly later on. The many single control offices fought for allocations of more coal, or transport, or labor. On the other side, the requirements of each "consuming" party, every one trying to get hold of as much leather, textiles or petrol as possible, had to be cut down. The attempt would be made first at the level of the individual Control Office, by lengthy negotiations, to get the different "consumers" to moderate their demands. But the higher authorities took a hand from the start. They did so, in the *first* place, by fixing grades of priority, and *secondly*, by giving the decision in cases of conflict.

As an instance for the fixing of priority rankings, the petrol arrangements may be taken. First, in November, 1941, it was ordered that petrol was to be used only for war purposes in the strict sense. Allocations were to be made on the basis of the following priorities:

1. For providing the population with food and fuel.
2. For clearing railway stations and docks.
3. For maintaining agricultural production.
4. For sanitary organization and the police.
5. For firms on important war work and for the building plans of the Plenipotentiary Authority for Special Problems of Chemical Production.
6. For providing for the armaments and other production decisive to the war effort.
7. For providing for the building plans of other industries decisive for the war effort.

For the valuing and directing of the stream of goods the grading of needs in this way was essential, and the individual control offices had to proceed accordingly. If no agreement was arrived at, let us say, as to how much coal the Leather Control should get, the Minister of Economics himself had to decide.

The results of this procedure were set down in a Budget or Balance Sheet ("Mengenbilanz"), for a quarter or half a year, or for a whole year, according to the peculiarities of each process of production. Here is an outline of one of these Budgets:

Outline Budget

Supplies	Consumption
1. Home production	1. Home consumption (arranged according to uses)
2. Additions from occupied territories	
3. Imports	2. Needs of occupied territories
	3. Exports

1—3 Total of current supplies	1—3 Current consumption
4. From stocks	4. Additions to stocks

1—4 Total supplies	1—4 Total consumption

Under heading 1 on the right (home consumption), it would be set out in detail how much, say, leather, had been fixed for the armed forces, for agriculture, for machinery, for shoes, and so on.

That is what the plans of the centrally administered economy looked like. They consisted of a long series of interlocking budgets of one control authority after the other. The controls for coal, iron, electricity, petrol, leather, textiles, and so on, set out their budgets which together made up the plan as a whole. But the fitting together of the detailed programs was brought about through the general directions (e.g., priority rankings) of the higher authorities, and through their actual intervention in many particular cases. Thus, although the control officers carried out and worked out the programs, they were dependent on, and subordinate to, the ministeries and other central offices. That was how the planning process was unified.

The *third* stage was the issuing of production orders to individual firms. The production of the firms was fixed in terms of quantities for particular periods of time, and with regard to varieties and qualities. Requisitioned raw materials were released to the individual factories for their production, and orders for the disposal of the resulting product were issued. The very difficult task of working out production orders for individual firms was often carried out through industrial organizations like the "Reichsgruppe Industrie," cartels, associations, etc. Experts had to be used who were at the same time highly interested parties, and, similarly, organizations which were private pressure-groups. We shall be returning, also, to this subject.

Fourthly, and finally, there was the check-up on results. Firms were obliged continuously, either quarterly, monthly, or even daily, to report their stocks and production, and the control offices had continually to be checking that the actual figures and the "programmed" figures agreed. Shortfalls might be traceable either to particular firms, or to the non-arrival of allotted raw materials, or through labor being drawn off by other control offices, and so forth.

In any case, the heads of the control offices had to intervene. So the carrying out of the plans was accompanied by continual negotiations and running battles. In the end another factor would intervene in this checking up on the plans. The plans were naturally often being carried through months, or even a year, after their original working out. Meanwhile the data had altered, for instance, with regard to coal supplies. It was then necessary to revise the plans and production orders.

This was how the four interconnected stages proceeded and were continually repeated. Other centrally administered economies might proceed in a similar way or in a different way. What is the economic significance of this procedure?

2. THE DIRECTING MECHANISM

Let us consider for a moment a small, closed, self-sufficient, household economy ("Eigenwirtschaft"), a community of thirty people, who produce for themselves everything they consume, and are under the authority of a single individual. The task of directing such an economy would be as follows: the director day by day has to decide how the factors of production shall be combined, where each worker is to work, who on the potato field, who in the forest, and what tools each shall have at his disposal. At the same time he has to decide as to the use of the land, buildings, livestock, and transport. He has to decide also the time-structure of production, that is, as to investment and savings. This is only possible if the director is clear the whole time as to the importance of different requirements, and how much each unit of the factors of production can contribute, in each different use, to satisfy the community's needs. All these valuations are interdependent. If, for example, the director decides to build a bridge, that is, to invest, then *all* values are altered. Each unit of the means of production, an hour's work on the potato field, or in the forest or the stables, gets a different relative significance and a general shifting may prove necessary.

Economic calculations run in three directions. The planner constantly examines how far the factors of production in their previous use and occupation have actually met the needs of the community. These cost calculations relating to the *past* are the basis of the plans for the *future*. Plans for the future are tentatively built up from past experience, the task being to meet *existing* scarcities, or those expected in the near or distant future. Economic calculation, therefore, is made up out of examination of the past and projection into the future, with attention to the present. Each individual unit of consumers' goods and means of production is allotted its niche in the economic cosmos by the plans of the directing authority.

With division of labor, and an economy of many millions of people, there is a corresponding task. But in this case the direction will not be set by calculations by the individual. Rather, the task will be to find *the form of organization for economic life best suited to a satisfactory direction of the economic process from the point of view of the needs of the community.*

The particular solution to the problem of direction which the centrally administered economy in Germany arrived at, had two essential characteristics. (1) Planning and direction were based on round aggregate valuations without individual values or calculations of marginal cost. (2) As economic calculation had no compelling force behind it, this method of direction was able to survive for a long time.

(1) (*a*) To take the first of these two points: the offices of the central administration worked with aggregate valuations derived from the calculations of the statisticians.

Who made these valuations? In the first place they were proposed by the sectional control offices. In our example, the Leather Control proposed to distribute leather among different users (e.g., the armed forces, footwear, industrial purposes), according to the users' own valuations. After negotiations with the "consumers," alterations would be made; that is, an attempt would be made to bring the valuations of the Leather Control into equilibrium with those of the "consuming" control offices. The dealings were always in mass quantities. Values were not given to single units but were calculated for total quantities, perhaps for five or eight thousand tons at a time. These aggregate valuations, and thereby the direction by the control office of the factors of production and of consumers' goods, were supported by the fixing of priority gradings by the higher central authorities which we have just referred to. But these priority grades were always ineffective. They were too crude, and the individual grades were made up of too many different kinds of needs. (For example, Grade three, "petrol for maintaining agricultural production.") Secondly, these gradings took insufficient account of the decreasing importance of particular types of need as they came to be satisfied. Finally, they took no account of the supply position with regard to complementary goods. A decree of the Central Planning Office of December, 1944, deals with this very clearly: "The problems of directing production by the crude process of priority grades become more and more difficult as scarcities increase. Unimportant production must not merely be slowed down, but stopped altogether. To fix an order of priority for important production in accordance simply with the nature of the product must lead to serious mistakes and misdirection, if the supply position of the consumer is not taken into account. The provision of single screws, which may be all that is needed to complete some agricultural machinery, may be much more important than supplying the same screws to a tank factory, which has a much higher priority, but which will need the screws only some months ahead. The various levels of need, in conditions of general shortage, cannot be dealt with by priority orders. Particularly with the present strain on all the means of production, all offices responsible for directing production must maintain a close scrutiny, to ensure that each item as it is produced is directed to the right destination. I lay it down that the time has come to enforce the principle: 'Planning instead of Priorities.' I decree that with effect from January 1st, 1945, all priority rankings lapse."

If particular sectional controls were unable to agree about aggregate values, the decision had to be made higher up by central authorities. This is clearly shown in a decree of 1942: "Every effort is to be made by the sectional controls, in agreement with the consuming organization, to fit requirements to productive possibilities. Only in exceptional cases, when a decision of this kind is not possible, may it be referred to the Ministry concerned. If the planning office and the consuming organization are not under the authority of the same Ministry, the decision must be made by a common superior authority."

No values could be reckoned in individual detailed quantities. Decisions had to be made daily about single tons of iron or copper, or about individual workers. Where and for what purpose were these factors to be used? What value had they in each of the many various possible uses? Where and how were they to be used for the maximum satisfaction of needs? These questions could not be answered by such round aggregate valuations. If there were 1,000 cbm. of wood to be disposed of, this would be distributed in round quantities for fuel, mining, artificial silk and so on, without any full consideration being possible with regard to particular qualities.

(b) Some sort of cost calculation did find a place in the set up. But this cost accounting was also of a "round" aggregate kind. When the Petrol or Leather Control made allocations to the different "consuming" parties or sectional controls, they were continually comparing the services and foregone services which petrol and leather in general rendered in different uses. Also, in cases of conflict, when the responsible Ministry was asked for a decision, say, as to how much leather was to go for shoes and how much for machinery, the decision was made on a general cost comparison. Costs were made after general considerations as to the aims of the economic system. It would be considered whether these general aims would be better served by using leather for workers' shoes or for machinery. The services rendered in one direction to the overall plan were weighed against those foregone in another direction. Thus, however generally and imprecisely, there was some consideration of cost questions.

Certainly any calculation of marginal costs was impossible: for example, in one province in 1945 there were 1,000 tons of iron to distribute. Iron was needed by all sorts of branches of the economy, by handworkers, engineering, textiles, railways, repair works and so on. How many tons should each particular branch of industry and each firm receive? Should the textile industry get 80 tons? Or more? Or less? A choice had to be made. Here also cost considerations were weighed up. The services iron could render in this use and that were compared. But the value of *single tons* used in one way or another could not be calculated. So values were reckoned in round aggregates, and distribution followed according to general estimates of this kind.

(c) As has been explained, a comparison of realized and planned figures would be made in order to compare actual production with that planned.

But there was no real economic accounting. The quantities set out in the plans were compared with the quantities actually used or produced by the firms. But whether the factors of production were used economically, whether, that is, the planned cost figures were rightly worked out or in need of amendment, could not be deduced by comparing the planned and the actually realized figures. A tile works for example would be allotted far more coal than it needed, and this would be corrected only many months later. If the figures of actual production agreed with those planned, then there were no grounds for any correction. This comparison of planned and actual figures afforded no possibility of approaching an optimum combination of factors by trial and error. And the control offices realized this.

(2) (*a*) *The compelling force of economic calculation:* The price system in an exchange economy is not merely a measure of scarcity or a calculating apparatus (the efficiency of which, incidentally, we are not concerned to judge here). The price system, rather, is a controlling mechanism of compelling force. If costs exceed returns, the discrepancy forces the firm in the long run to make a change or to close down. To put it in another way, if price relationships are such that the prices of the factors of production necessary for producing a good are higher than the price obtainable for this good, then there must be a change.

But in the centrally administered economy, valuations—themselves arrived at in a different way—play a different role. For example: during the war a silk-weaving factory was built at C. (Hanover). Even from rough "aggregate" valuations it was clear that this location was unsuitable, and that the Crefeld silk-weaving factories could produce much more cheaply. The consumption of iron, cement, machinery and labor for the new factory in C. was unnecessary and a wrong investment. This could have been ascertained even by a rough aggregate value-cost comparison. The factors of production could have served the needs of the plan better in a different use. Nevertheless the decision to build was carried out. Personal considerations turned the balance. In the exchange economy, the factory in C. would have been condemned as a failure. In the centrally administered economy, where there is no automatic process of selection, it could be built and kept working. For these overall valuations have no compelling force behind them. Economic science should pay more attention to this peculiarity of economic calculation in a centrally administered economy, for it exercises a significant influence on the way in which the economic process works out.

(*b*) How are these facts to be explained? How is it that in the centrally administered economy economic calculation exerts no decisive force? The purpose in calculating costs in a perfectly competitive system is well known from the textbooks. Costs show what values the factors of production could realize in an alternative use. All sorts of needs, effectively backed by the purchasing power of income-receivers, struggle for the versatile factors, and the decision is made by price-cost calculations, in which costs represent foregone utilities. Production *must* meet needs backed by purchasing power. This is the compelling *"must"* of economic calculation. Through the agency of cost calculation, it is effective needs which control the productive process. Certainly, in monopolistic or oligopolistic markets the directing power of the consumers is essentially prejudiced and weakened.

In the centrally administered economy, there is quite another relationship between needs and supplies. The tension between the two finds no effective expression in the markets. Demand and supply for iron, coal, and all other goods do not originate with different independent economic individuals, each with his own plans. Rather, the fixing of needs and the direction of production are in a single hand. The planning authorities consequently proceed by first fixing the requirements for coal, bread, houses, and so on, and then adjusting the productive process to these needs by their aggregate valuations and production orders. But they do not have to proceed like this. They can also proceed subsequently by altering the consumption side of the equation, which is then adjusted to the production side. Allocations of textile goods can suddenly be cut or the construction of a new factory halted. Consumers cannot control the central administration. All economic power is concentrated in the central administration, which is thus itself subject to no controlling mechanism.

Perhaps this may be regarded as a weak point in the centrally administered economy. In fact, it is only a weak point if the maximum satisfaction of needs is regarded as the purpose of production. The absence of any compelling force in value and cost estimates is at the same time a source of strength, for it makes full employment comparatively simple to bring about. We shall return later to this point at greater length. Furthermore, the political authority is able, in the centrally administered economy, to shape developments in economic life in accordance with its political objectives, regardless of cost calculations.

3. The Role of Prices

We shall study this question also from two points of view: (1) What role did prices play in Germany? and (2) What general lessons are to be derived from German experience?

(1) German economic policy was concerned as far as possible to control the economic process by indirect methods. Here, for example, is what an important decree had to say: "All planning must have the aim of exercising the maximum directive effective effect on the economy with the minimum of interference. Interventions are unnecessary so long as individual firms voluntarily cooperate in the policy laid down by the State, or where, from considerations of purely private self-interest, their actions correspond with the requirements of the nation." On this principle, an attempt was made to avoid all direct control over intermediate stages of

the productive porcess. The central control of weaving, for instance, made possible indirectly the control of spinning.

From the efforts of the central authorities to control the economic process indirectly, rather than by direct order, it was a short step to attempting the use of prices, and this attempt was actually made.

A. In order to be able to use prices as an instrument for controlling economic life, the Ministry of Economics and the Price Commissioner endeavored to unify and improve accounting and the calculations of their profits by private firms. Particularly as deliveries for the armed forces gained in importance, very precise instructions as to cost accounting were issued. The economic calculation of many German firms was markedly improved and unified at this time. At certain points too, prices were used with success to achieve a combination of the factors of production somewhat nearer to the optimum, for instance with regard to the production of munitions for which no former prices existed.

At first, in these cases, the costs of production of the individual firms were calculated, and prices fixed accordingly for each individual firm on the basis of its costs. Consequently, the firms had no interest in working economically, for profits were a percentage of costs, and were greater if costs were high than if they were low. Therefore, in 1940, to induce firms to produce economically, another system of calculating prices was introduced: on the delivery of the munitions a uniform price was paid, reckoned in accordance with the costs of an average enterprise. A stimulus was thus given to improved production methods in order to make profits. This procedure was later much refined.

Particular achievements of this kind do not alter the fact that the prices, as they existed, were inadequate for controlling economic life as a whole. The current prices expressed the scarcity relationships of the autumn of 1936. Any change had been prevented by the price freeze. If the plans of the central authorities had envisaged meeting a requirement equal approximately to the earlier demand, then the prices and price relationships would have remained serviceable longer. But the opposite was the case: public works, and investment for armaments purposes, brought about big discrepancies between the centrally planned needs and the earlier demand curves. The prices fixed for iron, coal, tiles and so forth, no longer expressed the relationship between needs and supplies as these were laid down in the plans of the central authorities. Calculations based on these prices for products and for the means of production could not command the factors of production to meet the needs of the plan; and profit and loss calculations and budgets gave no information as to whether the factors of production were being combined in the optimum way for the production of the goods as planned by the central authorities.

No improvement in the methods of calculation could get round this fact. The prices which the firms reckoned with in their books failed as an expression of scarcities, and so lost their controlling function.

B. This made a second question all the more important: would it not have been possible to fix prices afresh? The prices of 1936 were useless for the purpose of reducing the aggregate valuations of the central authorities to prices for particular quantities. But would it perhaps have been not impossible to do this by new prices? The existing prices represented a long obsolete system of data. Couldn't new prices be fixed which would have given the maximum support to the plans of the central administration?

Two methods were discussed in connection with this problem: (1) was it perhaps possible for higher authorities themselves to fix important prices afresh? Or (2), if this was not possible, could not the prices be refixed by a temporary application of the market mechanism?

To take a particular example in Germany, namely that of the price and use of copper-beechwood. Almost throughout the whole of the nineteenth century beechwood had been used only for fuel and charcoal. Owing to a series of discoveries in the last 50 years it found many new uses and gained considerably in importance. There was the discovery that the soaking of the wood with tar would turn beech logs into railway sleepers of high quality. The discovery of artificial drying and steaming methods led to beech being used on a wide scale for furniture and woodwork of many kinds. Many discoveries in the plywood industry again considerably extended the range of uses. Finally, there was the discovery which made beechwood a basic material for the production of cellulose and opened up a further field of consumption.

What would constitute a reasonable distribution of the continual supplies of beechwood between these almost unlimited uses if an optimum utilization was to be obtained? Without doubt, the pegged price of beechwood as compared with other timber prices, and with most other prices, was much too low. It had been kept at the same level since 1932. Would it not have been reasonable, by raising the price of beechwood, to ensure an efficient use of particular qualities and quantities?

The forestry authorities had several times examined the question as to whether a new and higher price for beechwood should be fixed, but the right price could not be discovered. The central forestry administration only knew that the current price for beechwood was too low. It was able to get a rough conception of the new value of beechwood and thus could make a rough aggregate valuation. But from this aggregate valuation no exact price per unit could be discovered. The new data and prices were far too imprecisely known to venture on such an experiment. A distinguished forestry specialist said at the time: "We do not know the value of beechwood; we only know that it is relatively high. How high, the market must decide later."

It may well be asked whether the market could not have decided then and there. That would have been to adopt our *second* method: to have left the prices of wood free for a time. Wouldn't then the right price for beechwood have resulted? But the prices of all the products of the consuming industries, of furniture, plywood, cellulose, mining, railways, and so on, were fixed. So were the prices of all the substitutes for beechwood. Thus, the prices of all the various products which made use of wood as a raw material gave no expression to the relationship between needs and supplies in the market for wood. In short, the partial freeing of the prices of a single group of goods would have been pointless. The interdependence of *all* markets and of the economic process as a whole, would have necessitated the freeing of *all* prices and the determining of the scarcities of *all* goods, in order thereby to establish them in the single case of beechwood.

Here we reach a more fundamental question. Why were not all prices free? *Wouldn't it then have been possible to determine relative scarcities by new price relationships, and thus reduce the new round aggregate valuations of the central authorities to individual prices?* Such a step, alone for reasons of monetary policy, was ruled out by the German government. The general freeing of prices would not merely have led to the development of new price relationships. The existing inflationary pressure would have led to a sharp rise in the general level of prices, to an appreciable fall in the value of money, to irrefutable wage claims, to obvious losses for savers, and to a rise in the cost of armaments. The tight hold on prices at their previous level, and the repression of inflation by pegging prices, became a dogmatically held principle of economic policy, as it has since become in other countries.

This negative answer in the German case does not dispose of the whole problem. Let it be supposed that there was no inflationary pressure, and that the arguments on monetary grounds against freeing prices had not held. Could not freely formed prices have replaced the aggregate valuations of the central authorities? For example: an armament firm receives 10 millions on account of deliveries, and pays 5 millions of this to its workers. If the workers had been allowed with this purchasing power to express freely their demands for consumption goods, for bread, meat, clothing, housing, and so on, they would of course have expressed their own valuations for consumption goods and not those of the central authorities. Prices would have expressed the valuations of the mass of consumers, not those of the central administration. The prices of bread, houses, clothing, and of all the factors of production responsible for these goods, would have conflicted with the carrying through of the plans of the central authorities. Prices would have expressed the plans of consumers and not the plans of the central administration. Above all, goods would have been drawn into consumption rather than investment uses, and a conflict would have arisen between the central plans and those of individual households and firms. Here we reach the basic question.

(2) Would it not perhaps have been possible to graft prices on to the controlling mechanism of the centrally administered economy in the following way? The central administration would have distributed con-

sumption goods by rationing, as well as fixing prices. With regard to consumption goods, demand and supply would have been equated by rationing. But with regard to the factors of production, there would have been no rationing. Entrepreneurs would have applied for these to the state authorities. The factors would have been priced, and then these prices adjusted according to the extent of demand. By this adjustment of prices would not demand and supply have been brought into equilibrium and would not thus exact cost calculations have been possible? In this way, the German authorities would have been proceeding in accordance with proposals outlined by, for example, O. Lange. Wouldn't it have been possible to follow out this proposal?

The position was that a constant struggle was taking place for the factors of production between the different control offices, planning departments, and ultimate users. To stick to our example, the representatives of agriculture fought to get leather for harness, those of industry for machinery, of the workers for shoes. Or iron was wanted for small craftsmen, for machinery, for transport and so forth. The quantities available were generally too small and didn't meet the demands of all the sectional controls and departments. The proposal we are discussing would have had these battles fought out through a pricing system. The distribution of suitable supplies of leather between individual uses would have been effected by prices.

This method of control was out of the question for the central administration, for it would have meant to some extent letting the control of the means of production—in this case leather or iron—out of its hands. When fixing prices and rations for food and also for manufactured goods, and in its investment program, the central administration could not know the amount of leather or iron that would be wanted by the different control authorities or the other requirements for such materials. These demands only appeared subsequently. If the allocation of the means of production had been left to the decision of the price-bids of the businesses and departments, then the results might have contradicted the plans of the central administration. For example, it might have happened that a relatively large quantity of leather would have been used for agricultural purposes, or for workers' shoes, which would have brought about an acute shortage of, say, driving belts for machinery, and thus jeopardized the production program of the central administration in other branches of industry. Therefore, the central administration cannot leave the direction, in any important respects, of such means of production to be decided through pricing, but must reserve the direction for itself, which was what happened in Germany.

As soon as the firms, or sectional controls, had been left free to determine their own demand independently, with the central administration confining itself to fixing prices in relation to scarcities, conflicts would have arisen between the plans of the central administration and the plans of the firms and controls. Such conflicts would have been resolved by orders from the central authorities, that is, by abandoning the price mechanism. This proposal, therefore, cannot be carried through in practice, even under the assumption of a suitable monetary policy. *Competition can be used to improve efficiency, but as a mechanism of direction for an important section of the economy it cannot be applied without the abdication of the central authority.*

4. SOME CONSEQUENCES

It is possible to understand the economic process in the centrally administered economy, now we have seen the place in this process of the central factors: these are, the plans and production orders of the central authorities arrived at by calculations of physical quantities to which "overall" aggregate valuations are assigned. The following features at once arrest the attention:

1. Central planning presupposes standardization and the fixing of norms and types for production. It is impossible for the planning authorities to take full account of the countless changing individual needs of consumers, to provide variety in clothes or shoes, to get these goods to those who want them most, and to adapt their plan to changing wants. Central orders are the easier to give, the more schematized are production and consumption.

The needs of *consumers* can easily be reduced to norms by rationing and allocations, and the influence of the infinite variety of individual preferences eliminated. "The experiences of the last seven years clearly demonstrate," wrote a textile expert in 1946, "that it was not only the deployment of industry for war purposes, but rather, the increasingly dominating role of the planning authorities that constantly tended to reduce the number of goods (raw materials or finished products) which the plans envisaged." Simplifying the *production* side was more difficult. The multitude of small and middle-sized firms in Germany had each their own different variety of demand for machines, spare parts, materials and so on, which it was very difficult for the planning authorities to weigh up and decide upon. In every way the small and middle-sized firms in their infinite variety are difficult to fit into central plans. Planning authorities can best carry out their tasks of valuation and direction with respect to mass-produced goods, which use a few standardized materials and a small number of processes. The comparatively standardized character of agricultural production explains why agriculture is easier to plan than industry.

Central administration of the economy has led not only to standardization but to a general preference for the largest scale for production when new factories are being built. The Volkswagen factory in Fallersleben is an example. The significant point here is that it is not only the size of the plant which affects the economic order. Much has been written about this in the literature of the subject, and it has been argued that the growing size of the plant must result either in monopoly or in a centralized economy. Sometimes this development has in fact taken place. But the causal connection runs also in the reverse direction. *According to the type of economic system, different optimum sizes of plants will be aimed at.* For example, in the centrally administered economy, a particularly large scale will be preferred or created such as would never have come into being otherwise. This is what happened in Germany. The preference for particularly large-scale units results from the special form which planning takes in the centrally administered economy. Over a period of years, under a centrally administered economic regime, the German economy took on quite another shape: the trend was all to standardization and large-scale units. But where this could not develop quickly enough—which of course was apt to happen—difficulties and disturbances were inevitable. For example, as a consequence of the numerous different types of motor car, it was very difficult for the central administration to keep the armed forces supplied with spare parts.

2. As we have seen, the programs were drawn up by the sectional controls. Each control was out to produce as much as possible, for each held its own line of production to be specially important. So the Leather Control would try to get hold of as much coal and transport as possible in order to step up leather production. Coal and transport facilities were needed by all the other sectional controls. The resulting struggle between the controls for the factors of production, and particularly for labor supplies, had, as we have seen, to be decided by orders from the center. But much time went by before the ministry or political authority responsible could be called in and give its decision. Meanwhile, each control would be using every means it could to procure factors of production or labor supplies. This collision between sectional controls was a characteristic of the centrally administered economy. A sort of group anarchy seemed to be inherent in the system. In spite of the intervention of the higher authorities, this "anarchic" tendency must be recognized if the apparatus of control is to be understood.

3. The centralized method of control also results in the leadership responsible for directing the economic process passing into quite other hands than those which wield it in a competitive economy. The business man disappears with the rise of a centrally administered economy, because his main function, that is, the meeting of consumers' needs and the discovery of possibilities for supplying them at a profit, disappears also. In his place, the technician moves into the key position both in the firms and in the planning offices. Friction in firms between the technical and the business side is a well-known phenomenon. In the centrally administered economy in Germany it was the technician who gained the supremacy. But along with the privileged technician the statistician took on an important role in the direction of planning, for the entire planning process was

based on statistics from the first proposals to the working out of budgets, and to the comparison of planned and actual figures.

This change in the nature of the leadership was no accident, but a direct result of the special method of control in the centrally administered economy, in which the tendency is increasingly to replace economic considerations by technical.

4. Finally we must ask whether any equilibrium emerges in the centrally administered economy.

Those of the planners who pondered this question were inclined to answer in the affirmative. They understood by "equilibrium" the balancing of the budget of physical quantities in their section of the economy, and they were concerned that this should finally be completely achieved. Extensive negotiations among the sectional controls, and finally decisions by the central authorities higher up, could, they thought, bring it about that, for example, the quantity of coal which the Leather Control used came to the same figure both in the balance sheet of the Coal Control and in that of the Leather Control: or that the quantities of leather goods, shoes, harness, and so on, which appeared in the balance sheets of different sections of industry and agriculture, corresponded with the quantities in the budget of the Leather Control. The plans then were held to "balance," and a quantitative equilibrium was held to have been attained.

Certainly this equilibrium, when it actually existed, was not an equilibrium in the economic sense. The question thus remains open whether an *economic* equilibrium can be said to emerge in the centrally administered economy, or whether any tendency to such an equilibrium exists.

This question is difficult to answer, because the concept of equilibrium in an exchange economy is not immediately applicable to a centrally administered economy. In the exchange economy, three different levels of equilibrium can be distinguished.

First, there is equilibrium for the individual household or firm. In the centrally administered economy, equilibrium for the household is not possible nor is it aimed at. Rather, it is a characteristic of the centrally administered economy that the household cannot actively press its demands, but is simply the passive recipient of quantities fixed in the aggregate "overall" allocations from the center. Hence the case can occur in a household of a scarcity of bread with a superfluity of tobacco. Thus the balancing of satisfactions or marginal utilities in accordance with Gossen's second law does not take place. This brings it about that households try to approach nearer to maximum satisfaction by means of exchange, that is by other procedures than those of the centrally administered economy. (Barone and many of his followers come to a different conclusion because they work with a model which is not that of a centrally administered economy. They assume that the individual income receiver gets a particular sum of money from the central authority which he can freely dispose of. Here the principle of Gossen's second law and of the equilibrium of the household would actually be fulfilled. But then the State would be surrendering the directing of the economy to consumers and would cease to direct it from the center.)

Partial equilibrium for the *individual firm* is also impossible in the centrally administered economy. It is impossible to speak of the marginal returns to capital for each kind of factor of production being equal, or of there being any "law" of, or even tendency to, equimarginal returns. For the individual firm only makes subsidiary decisions and has to fit in with the allocations of factors that come from the planning authorities.

Similarly, the concept of *partial equilibrium of individual markets* is not applicable in the centrally administered economy. With regard, for example, to accommodation in a town, if this is distributed not by demand and supply in the market, but by allocation, there can be no equilibrium in the sense of the commercial economy. There is no equating of two independent quantities, demand and supply, but the distribution of a supply fixed to correspond with the planned requirements of the central authorities.

If these two conceptions of equilibrium fail to apply to the centrally administered economy, must this also be so with regard to the *third* conception, that of *general* economic equilibrium? The question arises whether in the centralized economy the productive processes for all goods, that is, the proportions in which labor and the means of production are applied in each case, can be so fitted in with one another as to represent an optimum fulfillment of the requirements of the plan. In the centralized economy in Germany, these proportions were not realized. One bottleneck followed another. Often they accumulated simultaneously, and there was no mechanism for guiding the processes of production in the direction of equilibrium proportions. Aggregate valuations and calculations, which could not be essentially improved on by the grafting on of a price mechanism, did not suffice to bring about these adjustments. This fact, as remains to be shown, was of particular importance with regard to investment.

5. Supplementary Remarks

1. It was shown at the start that the study of an economic system predominantly of the centrally administered type, as in Germany, must turn away from the private households and firms and be focused rather on the planning authorities. That is where the mechanism of direction is to be found. But if one subsequently turns back to the firms and households it will be noticed that what goes on there does not correspond with the account given by the planners. This discrepancy was of essential importance for economic life in Germany—and indeed not only in Germany. Certainly the procedure in private firms was completely overshadowed by the plans of the central administration. But the firms had their own

subsidiary plans, and to understand German economic life in this period it is necessary to take account of this subsidiary private planning.

A shoe factory gets allocations of leather, coal and electric power, and in accordance with its orders, produces shoes of a particular quality. Often, particular materials would be lacking, say, spare parts for machines, or chemicals; or allocations of these would arrive late. In one way or another, there would be "disequilibrium." The firm helped itself by resorting to its own "black" stocks, or by purchase or exchange. Otherwise, production would have been impossible. The central plans often related only to the so-called "key" materials, while the others would be obtained privately. The planning authorities often reckoned with the firms helping themselves, or with their possessing their own unreported stocks, or with their making their own deals. In this way, the private plans of the firms supported and supplemented the centrally administered economy.

It is not correct that the black market always hindered the attainment of the central administration's targets. On the contrary: in modern industrial production, firms require too many different kinds of auxiliary materials and parts for the central authority to keep track of them all, in spite of the most far-reaching standardization. A factory making machinery, for example, had completed certain machines punctually as ordered. But they couldn't be dispatched because there were no nails for nailing down the cases. It actually happened that a manager waited for months with delivery until the nails were allocated. Other managers would not. Fearing the consequences of late delivery, they got themselves the nails by exchange. Such "illegal" actions were of daily occurrence, but in spite of their illegality they were an essential aid to the fulfillment of the "legal" plans. In other cases, such transgressions certainly were harmful.

2. We reach here an important general question: can such complicated processes of production as those of a modern industrial economy be directed alone by the methods of a central administration? If, conceivably, all exchange deals and all black markets were completely suppressed by the confiscation of all stocks, could a central administration direct the economy at all? In modern factories, dozens, even hundreds, of materials are used daily in changing quantities. Is it conceivable that all these raw materials, goods, spare parts, chemicals and so on could be allocated by the central authorities in the right qualities and at the right time? Wouldn't an attempt of this kind at a *total* direction of the central administration throughout the economic system be suicidal? Would the disproportionalities be kept within tolerable limits?

This question cannot be precisely answered on the basis of German experience. For in Germany the procuring of many materials, and even of labor supplies outside the official channels of the central administration, played an important role. Certainly from what could be observed, the conclusion followed that without the procurement of black supplies of the means of production and of labor, the productive process would have suffered severe disturbances in many of its branches and for considerable periods of time. What is unique about this phenomenon is not that one pure form of economic order—that of the centrally-administered economy—has to be supplemented by other forms. This is also the case with regard to other economic orders of society. The subsistence economies of small family groups directed by the head of the family are not usually found in their pure form. Usually certain goods, say, salt, or metals, are got by exchange, so that here too, though for quite other reasons, there is a mixture of different pure forms of economic order. In contrast to other mixed economies, supplementary arrangements outside the central plan are explicitly forbidden by the planning authorities and the State. This is not the case in other mixed economies. It is a peculiarity with widespread consequences. The functioning of a centrally administered economy and its methods of control presuppose—at any rate they did in Germany— private exchanges which were often undertaken against the special orders of the central authorities.

3. The following definite conclusions can be drawn. The economic planning of a central administration consists of the balancing of the physical budgets of the sectional controls, and out of that balance a certain statistical "equilibrium" emerges. But because aggregate economic calculations permit of only the roughest cost estimates, the central administration has no means of bringing about any sort of general economic equilibrium. Firms and households, within the framework of the central plans, attempt by exchange to realize as far as possible the principle of equimarginal returns and of individual equilibrium. Thus, by these subsidiary and independent plans and actions, firms and households approach more nearly an equilibrium than is possible by the methods of direction of the centrally administered economy alone.

II. THE ECONOMIC PROCESS IN ITS SEPARATE BRANCHES

1. INVESTMENT AND SAVING

1. The student of history will remark that where an economy is predominantly under the direction of a central administration, it is usual for an exceptionally large amount of investment to be undertaken. This was the case in Germany after 1936, in Russia after 1928, and in quite other societies, such as those of the Incas in 1500 and of ancient Egypt, and in many other examples. How is this historical fact to be explained?

One decisive element responsible cannot be dealt with by economic theory, since it lies quite beyond its range. This is the sociological fact that the leadership in such a community builds towns and roads, factories, railways, power stations, and so on, in order to strengthen its political power. The methods of centrally administered control may be introduced for the specific purpose of speeding up investment. This consideration played an important part in Germany in the thirties. A central administration is less concerned with the production of consumers' goods. It is particularly those branches of industry—like the iron and steel industry—which go to produce investment goods, which will be expanded. If this investment is successful in increasing political power, its effects on consumption will be disregarded. Political and economic authorities may not always be in the grip of this sort of striving, but it always plays a certain role.

The economist cannot explain why the central administration *wants* to force up the rate of investment, but he *can* answer the equally important question as to *how* it can enforce its will, since this depends on economic factors. In this respect, the apparatus of a centrally administered economy is of particular interest.

2. What are the differences in the processes of investment in a commercial economy and a centrally administered economy?

(*a*) A machine tool factory is being expanded. If this happens in the commercial economy, it is the plan of the entrepreneur which decides whether and how this project will be carried out. His plan will be based on existing and expected prices, that is, on the costs of the new construction and equipment, and on the expected prices for raw materials and the finished product. Here the length of the prospective period of amortization for the new equipment is decisive. With the data constantly changing as they do today, investments may often not be undertaken if the amortization is reckoned to take longer than three to five years.[3] In any case, economic calculation acts as something of a brake, by enforcing a definite selection between different projects, and it is a factor of some influence with regard to every investment or the purchase of every machine.

It is quite otherwise in the centrally administered economy, with its indecisive aggregate valuations. Whether a machinery factory was to be built or not was decided in Germany by the Ministry of Economics (later by the Ministry of Armaments Production). The Ministry examined and estimated whether a factory as a whole was useful to the total plan. But the Ministry could not compare the values invested in the new construction with the values this new construction would yield. The amortization period and the rate of interest were not taken into account. Neither acted as a brake. So huge investment projects were undertaken, stretching ahead for very long periods into the future. Only round aggregate comparisons were made of the uses rendered by the labor and other factors employed in this and competing directions. The checks on investment, effective in the commercial economy, are lacking in the centrally administered economy.

If a project was approved, the necessary labor supplies, cement, steel, and so on, were released and allocated by the Ministry, via the departmental "Controls," and the investment began. The banks were left with a

---

[3] Cf. F. Lutz, "The Interest Rate and Investment in a Dynamic Economy," *American Economic Review*, Vol. XXXV, No. 5 (1945), p. 811.

quite subsidiary role, for it was not their granting of credit, but the central administration, which decided about the investment. Of necessity, the banks will have an insignificant place in a centrally administered economy. The fact that the banks later provided intermediate credits, and that it was through their agency that the machinery factory met its obligations, was of no essential importance, except for subsequent accounting. It was not the granting of credits that directed the labor supplies and means of production, but the orders of the central authorities. The purchase of securities, and saving out of incomes, were only of secondary significance (in so far as they represented a restriction on spending). The control of investment was not influenced by them. In short, the process of investment was very simple, and could not fail because of insufficient liquidity, or the state of the security market, or the threat of price changes.

(*b*) To understand the problem rightly, we must look more closely at the economic process as a whole.

A very simple example will show what investment implies. A peasant has harvested twenty units of wheat. Part of the wheat will go via the mill and the bakery to the final consumer, and part will be used for fodder or seed. This second part is "put back" (zurückversetzt), that is, it does not go by the shortest route to the consumer from its point in the productive process, but is used as a means of production in another process further removed from final consumption. This "keeping back" of goods is what is meant by capital investment.

Let us survey a whole economy—for example the Germany economy in 1939—and look at all the land, mines, railways, stocks of raw materials and labor supplies as they were at that moment. How should the economic process then have been directed *with regard to time?* Labor supplies and the physical means of production could have been directed to the greatest possible extent to new construction, expanding railways, roads, to the more intensive cultivation of the land, *away from* supplying goods for present consumption. Then goods would have been "put back," or there would have been investment on the maximum scale. Or the opposite could have occurred. Labor supplies and the means of production could have been concentrated as completely as possible for consumption in the present or in the immediate future, and machines, livestock, and so on consumed without replacement. The temporal direction of the economic process is decisive with regard to the supply of consumption goods and the extent of productive equipment. In reality, some course will be followed between the two extremes we have described.

How the decision is made will differ according to the structure of the economic order. If income receivers or consumers command the system, then the inter-temporal direction of the economy will depend on them and on their inter-temporal dispositions, including, that is, their savings. With perfect competition and an appropriate monetary system, voluntary restriction of consumption precedes investment.

If, however, the money supply may be expanded by credit creation, or under monopolistic conditions, investment can be planned ahead of saving and the restriction of consumption is forced upon certain groups of income receivers subsequently. To that extent, entrepreneurs and banks, rather than the consumers, decide the amount of investment. Even under these conditions the voice of the consumer can still make itself heard through the medium of voluntary savings, and prices and price expectations.

In the centrally administered economy, the consumer is dethroned. He cannot control the economic process. He can no longer, through the instrument of price changes, attract the factors of production or decide how much of them shall be set aside for investment. The central administration distributes consumers' goods, and it directs the factors to the production-goods industries, or rather, it decides the quantity of factors to be "put back" for these industries. Consumers cannot foil the administration in its plans, for it can do what is not possible in any form of exchange economy, that is, exclude *any* influence from the side of consumers on the economy, and thereby on the level of investment.

The special characteristics of the investment process in a centrally administered economy may now be distinguished and explained more precisely. They consist, *first*, in the ability to concentrate to the maximum on investment, labor supplies and the means of production; *secondly*, special difficulties arise with regard to the *proportions* of investments.

3. *How is a central administration able to concentrate labor supplies and means of production to such a high degree on investment?* How did this happen after 1938 with regard to the German armaments industry, and after 1945 in the Eastern Zone for reparations investment? Two facts were and are decisive:

(*a*) Without interference from consumers, factors of production can be directed to investment purposes in the manner described. Instead of producing textile goods for consumers, foodstuffs, or housing, they can be *ordered* to build roads, blast-furnaces, airplane factories, etc.

What are the limits to this re-direction, or to the quantity of investment? In the subsistence levels of the different categories of the population. If all the supplies of labor and the factors of production were used for building, machinery, and on production-goods—(that is, if all were "put back")—no consumption goods at all would be produced, the people would starve, and the investment plans could obviously never be completed. Evidently, the central administration cannot go so far. So particular quantities of the factors are devoted to producing food, clothing, etc., in order to keep in being the labor supplies necessary for reaching the investment targets.

This concept of the Subsistence Minimum is of great practical importance for the centrally administered economy, and is indispensable for understanding it theoretically. The Subsistence Minimum consists of the quantity of goods that must be distributed to the different categories of labor in order to preserve their efficiency. It differs according to the branch of production—(the lumberjack needs more pairs of shoes than the metal-worker)—and in accordance with the region, climate, and habits of the population. But the planning authorities much always take account of the Subsistence Minimum. If the miners are not getting this minimum, as detailed investigations in Germany have shown, coal production falls off.

It might be that this Subsistence Minimum is only of a temporary significance? It might be argued that this rate of investment would surely make possible in the future an improved supply of consumers' goods? This does not follow. So long as the chief aim of the central plans is the maximum expansion of investment, then the earlier investments in iron and steel works, power stations and the other production goods industries, serve principally to produce goods which are again applied to further investment. Strong historical forces work in this direction.

(b) There is a second reason for the rapid expansion of investment by the methods of a centrally administered economy.

The central administration can take over supplies of goods without giving anything equivalent in exchange. For example, the stocks of spinning or weaving firms, or of metals, can be requisitioned without compensation. This often happened in Germany. Certainly the firms were paid in money, but they could get no goods for this money. In this way, means of production were "saved" for investment. Often these firms used the vast balances of money in their possession for lending to the government. This procedure shows very plainly how the centrally administered economy is based not on exchange but on allocations.

Side by side with investment in some fields went a disinvestment or capital consumption in others. This consumption of capital was an essential aid to investment in other branches. German industry took on a curiously schizoid appearance. On the one side, there were firms with stocks falling and machinery deteriorating, and on the other new construction and the expansion of equipment. Even within the same firm these processes, partially of capital consumption and partially of increased investment, could be observed. In any case, by these methods the central administration was able to get more factors released for investment than would have been possible by the methods of an exchange economy. The essential point is not simply this re-direction of the means of production from consumption goods industries to investment, but that this re-direction took place uncompensated.

4. This is one aspect of the investment process in a centrally administered economy: its facility in rapid concentration of labor and means of production on particular investment programs. Now for another equally important aspect:

Every investment requires complementary investment. If, for example, in a small closed economy it is decided that a new cattle-shed be built, attention will be given to proportional increases in cattle, carts, fodder, etc. Otherwise the new cattle-shed will not be fully used, and the investment will be of no, or only a small, use. Even in this small closed economy there are difficult problems of valuation and planning in bringing about an expansion of the number of cattle, the fodder, and sheds, so that the different investments fit in and synchronize with one another.

In a modern economy with its complex organization and extensive division of labor, made up of millions of firms, the task is incomparably more difficult. This was apparent even in Germany. As we are aware, the centrally administered economy with its round aggregate valuations and statistical calculations, commands no mechanism of direction by which the proportions of goods produced are harmonized. Thus, for example, the investments in motor-roads in the middle thirties were much too large and in no suitable proportion to the expansion of petroleum production. On the other hand, investment in railways was neglected for a long period, and corresponded in no way with the increased transport requirements resulting from other investments.

It was clear that the central administration was in no position to bring about a balanced investment program.

5. In this respect, too, there are contradictory tendencies in the centrally administered economy.

Its peculiar propensity to invest can easily be asserted through its ability to limit the claims of current consumption, and to undertake extensive investment programs regardless of risk. At the same time it is characterized by one-sided disproportionate investments, with some branches of industry excessively expanded while others are unduly contracted.

These contradictory tendencies derive from the fact that a central administration can certainly step up investment quantitatively but cannot satisfactorily plan it qualitatively. If its complementary investments are lacking, the economic value of a single investment project is correspondingly reduced—for example, with regard to the cattle-shed in the private economy for which no complementary investments were undertaken. The economic value of the huge road construction was small. The economic quantity of investment, that is its value, depends on a balancing of investment projects or on their proportions.

For these reasons it is difficult to compare quantities of saving with quantities of investment. What is the quantity of investment? Economically, it can only be expressed through prices. Its level depends on the single investments being physically and temporally co-ordinated. The amount of labor and means of production used is not decisive, but rather the directions and proportions of the individual investments. The volume and value of investments are not identical—as the example of the motor roads demonstrates. Economically, estimates of savings and investments can only be estimates of values.

2. Fluctuations and Employment

1. Full employment can be brought about comparatively easily in the centrally administered economy, and there are no depressions and dismissals of workers. Why this should be so follows readily from what we have said above.

First, it is because investment on a relatively large scale is always taking place in the centrally administered economy. In the different types of exchange economy, as is well known, the cycle of depression and recovery is usually connected with fluctuations in investment. By avoiding any falling off in investment, depressions can be avoided also. In the centrally administered economy, one long process of investment follows another.

Secondly, there need be no unemployment because every worker can be taken on regardless of costs. In an exchange economy, workers are dismissed because there exists a measure of scarcity with regard to single units, that is with regard to efficiency units of labor, *and* because this measure of scarcity has a compelling force behind it. Workers are dismissed if the return resulting from their employment does not cover the costs. The central administration with its methods of round aggregate valuations cannot determine whether an individual worker at road-building is thereby producing goods of a value to cover the costs. Furthermore, even if it is estimated that the costs of employing several thousand workers on road constructions are not covered, the central administration does not have to cut the work short. In these conditions full employment is always attainable.

2. But this is only one side of the problem. The absence of depressions and unemployment and of checks to the expansion of investment, does not alter the fact that the economic process in a centrally administered economy can have no equilibrium. For this would have to mean that investments, for example, in mining, railway construction, or in the steel or shoe industries, would have to be co-ordinated in the right proportions. It is just this which is not possible. Because an acute coal shortage threatened coal production would be increased. But with more coal would come a shortage of railway wagons. This would be because there was insufficient investment in rolling-stock factories and because the repair shops were insufficient. Consequently, while there was more coal produced, its value would be relatively low, because the complementary goods would be lacking. One-sided expansion of particular lines of investment by the directing authorities at the center was constantly finding expression in such disproportionalities.

This lack of an equilibrium positon made itself felt in firms, or branches of industry, through sudden shortages of spare parts, raw materials, particular chemicals, or means of transport. The apparatus of production would be unduly expanded in some directions and unduly contracted in others. Finally, the efficiency of the apparatus in producing either capital or consumption goods would suffer.

3. Modern trade cycle theory must be extended to take account of these facts.

Economists have been concerned to describe and explain the upward and downward swings of boom and slump in exchange economies, and the sequence of events in the various markets for the factors of production and for consumption goods, capital, labor, and so forth. When we turn to economic societies of a predominantly centrally administered type, it is apparent that the cyclical phenomena just described are absent or else have a different significance: price fluctuations signify little or nothing, capital markets either do not exist or play a minor role; saving has another meaning, and interest almost none at all. There are none of the fluctuations of boom and depression so often described for the exchange economy.

Economists must not withdraw at this point, but widen the field of their investigations. If, in the past, they have studied the disproportionalities in economic development as these arise in a predominantly exchange economy, now they have to do the same for the type of economy dominated by a central administration. That is, not simply disequilibrating tendencies in the American economy of 1948 have to be investigated, but also the other kinds of disequilibria such as arise in the Russian economy. England's difficulties in 1947, which are those of an economy of a centrally administered type, must be studied just as much as the depression of 1929-32.

Certainly these disproportionalities are of quite another character, just because the processes of different types of economic system develop very differently. The theory of fluctuations becomes a theory of disproportionalities, or of divergencies from equilibrium, which may occur in the processes of different kinds of economic systems.

3. PRODUCTION AND DISTRIBUTION

1. The distribution of the social product proceeds fundamentally differently in a centrally administered economy from the way in which it proceeds in a competitive economy. In the competitive economy, incomes are fixed mechanically. Prices for the factors of production are formed as part of the process of combining together capital, labor and the means of production. Production and distribution are bound up together as one procedure. It is the same fact seen from two different angles.

In the centrally administered economy, distribution and the fixing of incomes are in the hands of the central authorities. It is not the productive contribution as automatically worked out by the calculating mechanism of prices that is decisive, but the plans of the central authorities.

How do they decide?

Centralized economic plans, as we have seen, usually aim at a maximum of investment. This determines, pretty well of necessity, the distribution of income. Income receivers get neither so *little* that the maximum possible investment cannot be reached because of a falling off in the efficiency of labor, nor so *much* that it is more than will maintain efficiency. Either of these alternatives would mean withdrawing labor supplies and means of production for consumption purposes away from investment. So the various categories of labor get Subsistence Minima for food, clothing and housing. (In order to avoid confusion with the concept in Ricardo's chapter five, it should be emphasized that the Subsistence Minimum consists of the quantity of consumers' goods which the different types of labor must get in order to carry out a particular task.)

2. The Subsistence Minimum naturally cannot be fixed individually for each worker—an impossible task for the central administration relying on its round aggregate valuations. How many consumers' goods the particular individual needs to maintain a certain efficiency at his job cannot be determined by the planning authorities. So instead of individual decisions round allocations are decreed. Ration cards for food are graded by groups ("normal consumers," "heavy workers," "specially heavy workers").

In Germany attempts have also been made to raise productivity by bonuses for good performance, but this hardly alters the fundamental principle of distribution and the provision of consumers' goods. Such bonuses are simply a means of raising efficiency as far as possible within the framework of the fixed Subsistence Minima. No comparison of value is, or could be, made between the additional production resulting and the additional consumers' goods allocated. Competition, here also, is adopted by the centrally administered economy simply as a means of increasing production, not of deciding its direction.

This is how the workers, employees, and managers fare. It might be asked how the incomes of the leaders at the narrow apex of the pyramid are formed. The answer would have to be that the allocation of goods to this class was regarded as of the same importance as investment.

3. Barone and his followers have put forward the view on the relation between distribution and production that these can be separated by the central authority. The fixing of incomes does not have to follow the economic principles of the competitive economy, with shares fixed by an anonymous procedure. Men are to be freed from the economic mechanism, and the authorities can distribute shares according to other than economic principles, e.g., according to some ethical rule. First the distribution of consumers' goods, then production, would be adjusted to the right and just income levels.

The accuracy of this statement can be judged from the foregoing account.

(*a*) It is true that the process of distribution in the centrally administered economy is quite different from that under competition, because it is decided by central authorities and not by the price mechanism.

(*b*) It is true also that the level of income, for example, in return for eight hours' work, is not dependent on the productive contribution of the worker. This is the way in which production and distribution are made independent of one another. (Whether this independence is socially desirable is a serious issue of social policy.)

(c) But the relation between production and consumption is quite different, and this is what Barone and his followers fail to see. They assume that a central aim of the economic planners is to bring about as large and as fair a distribution of consumers' goods to the entire people as possible. They therefore assume that a fair distribution is decided on *first*, and *then* production is adjusted accordingly.

Whether this could be a central aim of policy need not be argued. Perhaps it could. But economic science has to investigate reality, and in reality the leadership of a centrally administered economy has as a main objective the forcing through of a maximum of investment. That was the case in Germany and in Russia too. The facts are that the total supplies of consumers' goods, and their distribution to individuals, are mainly determined by the investment programs. It is not what is considered the ethically right distributive shares which determine the direction of production. It is not incomes allotted in just proportions which govern production. On the contrary, the centrally determined production programs govern distribution, and these programs are determined by the striving after a maximum of investment.

It is not correct that the distribution of the social product can be completely separated from its production. Distribution is fitted into the production programs so as to promote maximum output. In consequence the processes of distribution in a centrally administered economy can be analyzed theoretically. In all cases where, as in Germany, production plans were directed at a maximum level of investment, distribution proceeded according to certain principles.

4. Monopoly and the Centrally Administered Economy

1. The transition to a centrally administered economy, under the impetus of the full employment policy, was made much easier in Germany by industrial concentration in combines and syndicates. Where, for example, firmly established syndicates existed, as in coal mining, and in the iron and steel, cement, and potash industries, the administration of the syndicates simply had to be changed into branches of the central authority. The syndicates took on legally the status of public bodies, and became compulsory. The pig-iron syndicate, for example, now *allocated* what previously it had sold centrally. The officials of the syndicates and their internal organization remained essentially the same. The combines also, as in the steel and chemical industries, proved to be easily adaptable to the structure of a centrally administered economy. The administrative apparatus of I.G. Farben was used as it stood, as the controlling instrument for parts of the chemical industry. Not that it had been originally designed

for that purpose, but it now fulfilled it admirably. Wherever syndicates and combines did not exist, as in the many sections of the engineering or paper industries, it was more difficult to build up the apparatus of the centrally administered economy. The central organization had first to be created, and the officials necessary were lacking.

The relationship between the combines and the central administration was still closer. The great partially monopolistic combine in the cigarette industry sold its cigarettes as branded goods at fixed prices to the final purchaser, and had made the whole trade completely dependent on it. It is only a short step from this partially monopolistic control of the market to the rationed allocations of cigarettes by the central administration, with the fixing of a margin for the distributor. In the centrally administered economy, not only does the influence of consumers disappear, but traders lose their independent directing function in the economic process. Here too, the combines and syndicates prepared the way. Moreover, it can be shown that the processes of economic calculation by the combines show similarities with those of the centrally administered economy. Already in combines difficulties arise over satisfactory cost accounting, and statistics play a more important part in economic calculation. The centrally administered economy is like a single huge combine comprising the whole economic life of the country.

This connection between private business and the central administration is even closer than we have so far described. Private pressure groups are not merely the pace-makers for the centrally administered economy. In the course of the experiment in Germany the private bodies and central administrative offices were closely interlocked. Power in the central administration lay partly with the heads of the combines and syndicates. This union of the central administration of the economy with private property was of key importance. It encouraged that tendency to "group anarchy" to which we referred.

The centrally administered economy has in this connection considerably increased industrial concentration, not merely with regard to the size of the technical unit as has already been mentioned. Industrial concentration does not consist so much in the growth of the size of the productive unit, but in the combining together of many units under unified leadership in trusts and syndicates. In the centrally administered economy these combinations were encouraged and furthered. In Germany many compulsory cartels and marketing agreements were organized, as, for example, in the milling industry as early as 1933. These associations and cartels were needed to control the industry. An important order of 1942 explains: "To carry through planning simply and efficiently, it is nearly always necessary to take over the individual organizations, the cartels, distributing agencies, rings and committees as well as the regional offices from which the individual firms get their orders." They became organs of the central planning authority. Moreover, it was simpler for the central authorities to negotiate with a few large units than with many small ones. For these reasons, private organizations exercised a powerful influence, while small competitors were at a disadvantage. The private and public bodies which wielded economic power were fused together.

2. Should then the centrally administered economy be correctly regarded as a case of monopoly, or of a conglomeration of monopolies?

This question is given an affirmative answer by some theoretical economists. If they were right, the German and Russian economic systems of, say, 1942, would be systems in which monopoly was predominant and the monopolies which existed for each branch of production were united in a total monopoly. The analysis of monopoly would thus "swallow up" the theory of the centrally administered economy.

Certainly, theoretical analysis revealed similarities in the two cases in their economic processes, as, for example, in fixing wages. Under conditions of monopsony the wage can of course be forced down well below the marginal productivity as when a single spinning mill provides the one demand for workers who offer their labor competitively. In a centrally administered economy, also, the workers are dependent not on the private owner of a spinning mill but on the central administration—in either case on a monopoly.

3. However, the essential difference between monopoly and the centrally administered economy is clear from this example. The position of the management of the spinning mill in the cases of monopsony is certainly very powerful, and the workers are dependent on it. But there is no obligation or compulsory national service as in the centrally administered economy, and consumers' goods are not allocated but can be bought on the market.

To summarize, there are no demand or supply and no markets in a centrally administered economy; nor is there exchange. This is replaced by allocations. In the centrally administered economy, there are no independent agents, with their own plans, meeting for economic exchange.

In the exchange economy, there are always at least two such units, even in the case of bilateral monopoly, as when the railway authority as monopsonist purchases carriages from the rolling-stock combine as monopolist. But as soon as rolling-stock production was taken under the direction of the central administration, the combine was no longer an independent agent with its own plan, but an instrument of the central administration which controlled also the state railways. Steel, labor and so on were allocated from the center for rolling-stock. The volume of production was not determined by markets or prices. There was certainly a plan for rolling-stock, but this plan was only partial and dependent.

Monopoly and the centrally administered economy are similar at many points, but they are two domains in which the economic process develops very differently. The characteristic of the centrally administered economy is that demand is decided by the same central authorities which direct production.

5. INTERNATIONAL TRADE

1. In the exchange economy the decision as to which goods are to be traded internationally, on what terms and in what quantities, and how the flow of capital is to be directed, is made through the mechanism of the price systems of the countries concerned and the rates of exchange which purport to bring these systems of prices into equilibrium. In detail the procedure differs greatly in accordance with the form of the markets and the monetary systems. When monopolies, partial monopolies, or oligopolies are predominant, foreign trade is dependent on their strategy with regard to demand or supply, while this strategy will be absent under perfect competition. How does international trade proceed with regard to countries whose economies are directed by a central administration?

2. This single question contains a whole complex of others. For there are many different possible cases to be investigated. It might be that the central administration in country A is negotiating with the central administration of country B or with a single private monopoly organization, or with partial monopolies or oligopolies in B, or that competition ruled in B's markets. Foreign trade would proceed differently in each case, and differently also in accordance with the place of foreign trade in the total plan of A. The central administration may build its plans for foreign trade into the total plan from the start, or it may be concerned rather to plan on the basis of autarchy, with foreign trade only having the role of smoothing out disproportionalities as they occur. All these issues are of importance, and German experience has something to contribute to their answer.

Here we shall discuss one example which in fact seldom occurs, but which is of special interest for the analysis of the centrally administered economy, because it is an extreme case. In 1945 the territory of the German economy was split up into four zones, and within each of these zones into a number of "Länder," each with its own government, and each constituting a separate centrally administered economy. Out of one comprehensive economy there were now some dozen and a half. Orders previously valid for the whole of Germany ceased. Instead, trade between the zones began, that is, trade between a number of centrally administered economies. For example, a machinery works in South Baden was no longer allotted steel by a Reich authority, but the central government of South Baden had to get it in exchange from the central authorities of the British or American zone, for tobacco, sewing cotton, or carbide.

These exchanges differed from those usual in international trade, in that the partners to the exchange not only used the same currency, the mark, but that the same prices had been fixed for all goods and services. So that if "Land" A exchanged steel goods for potatoes with "Land" B, it would be on the basis of the same officially fixed prices for potatoes and steel, and certainly these prices played a peculiar role in the transaction.

3. What was the result of this experiment?

(*a*) Central administration of the economy necessarily requires a central direction of foreign trade. If merchants and industrialists in Land B had exchanged freely tobacco and textile goods, for steel or leather, on the basis of contracts with merchants in Land A, then both A and B would have had to give up the centralized planning of their internal economies. For steel, leather and textile goods would have been put outside the control of the central plans by this sort of foreign trade. Freedom of foreign trade and central administration of the economy cannot be reconciled. All attempts failed—even on the part of the Control Commission authorities—to bring about a greater freedom of exchange inside Germany without giving up the central administration of the economy.

(*b*) The central authorities with their round valuations tended to trade in quantities of standardized goods—coal, timber, or electricity. Even those Länder which would have been interested in exchanging more highly finished goods with other Länder, cut down this sort of trade while keeping up deliveries of standardized goods or even increasing them. A central administration is not in the position to distribute to consumers by means of exchange a variety of more highly finished industrial products; the adaptability and quick decisions necessary to exploit the fleeting opportunities of the market are lacking.

(*c*) What and how much was exported and imported did not depend on precise calculations, nor could the cost principle be given any precise validity. For example: Land A would be offered typewriters by Land B to a total price of forty thousand marks, and would ask for sewing cotton in exchange from B. The responsible authorities in B would now have to solve the valuation problem, *in spite of* the official fixed prices for both typewriters and thread being the same in the two Länder. For these prices no longer gave expression to the relative shortages of the goods. The officials in B would have to refuse to exchange the quantity of thread which cost forty thousand marks at these prices, for the one hundred and fifty typewriters at forty thousand marks. To correspond with the far higher value of thread, ten thousand marks worth only would be offered, and the balance of thirty thousand marks in paper money of little practical value. To arrive at precise valuations it would have been necessary to compare the uses of smaller quantities of the two goods. But the data were not available to determine exactly the value of one hundred and fifty or one hundred and forty typewriters as against that foregone in delivering each kilo of thread. The exchange was proposed on the basis of a rough estimate. The values of other goods would also have had to be estimated if the exchange was to be properly calculated; and it would have been necessary to work out whether exactly this quantity of thread should have been offered, or whether it would not have been better to have imported not typewriters but potatoes or wheat in exchange for the last fifty kilos, and if so in what quantities? Or, wouldn't it have been better to offer, at least in part, other goods and not thread, say, tobacco, medical instruments, or wine, also produced in this Land? The foreign trade authorities in B would have had to have known the values of all other goods, and of individual units of all other goods, to trade to the full advantage.

Those who have taken part in such negotiations must have sometimes wished that theoretical economists could have been present who believed that the problem was solved if a number of equations could be set out equal to the number of unknowns—equations which represent in the abstract the general interdependence of economic quantities but tell us nothing concrete. In such cases as we have been discussing the only possible course was to import or export certain goods on the basis of round aggregate estimates.

(d) To back up these estimates and the resulting transactions, the central authorities resorted to statistics. They tried to estimate statistically consumption per head of potatoes, butter, or coal, and then work out the necessary imports and the quantities available for export. But the figures showed only what quantities had been consumed *previously*, and were only of any use if the data had not changed. Since this often was the case, the statistical calculations were of little help.

(e) Owing to the great difficulties the central administrative authorities had in carrying through exchanges with other Länder, they sought the advice of expert circles in industry, agriculture, trade, etc. These experts were always interested parties, who in that way came to exercise political and economic power. So in this field also, economic pressure groups furthered their interests through the central administration.

4. Exchange between two Länder is not the same as in the case of bilateral monopoly.

In the case of bilateral monopoly, as is well known, there is no equilibrium though there are certain limiting factors, as Carl Menger in 1871 and Edgeworth, more precisely, in 1881, showed.[4] It might be assumed that the theoretical proposition that exchange relationships are not precisely determinate in the case of bilateral monopoly, though they can be brought within a determinable range, could be applied to exchange between two Länder with centrally administered economies. If, in fact, as in our case, Land A is a monopolist with regard to the supply of typewriters and B of thread, the requisite assumptions seem to be given for applying the theory of bilateral monopoly.

Such an application would be incorrect. The theory of bilateral monopoly starts from the assumption that the two monopolists know the value of their individual products and also the costs at which they are

---

[4] Cf. C. Menger, *Grundsätze der Volkswirtschaftslehre* (1871), p. 175 ff; Edgeworth, *Mathematical Physics* (1881). On the development of the theory of bilateral monopoly, see Stackelberg, *Marktform v. Gleichgewicht* (1934), p. 89 ff.

producing them. The central authorities do *not* know these values, and there are no determinable limits given within which the exchanges between two central administrations have to take place.

If an isolated autarchic economy A buys a certain quantity of barley from another such economy B and pays in wool, then the range for the price of barley in terms of wool is fixed by the valuations put upon these two goods by the authorities in A and B, who can fix them with precision. The foreign trade department of a centrally administered economy cannot. They are not in a position, relying on round aggregate valuations and statistical data, to value and compare precisely individual units of the two goods which depend on the data and values of individual units of all other goods in the economy. There is no precisely limited range for exchange relationships or "prices" in transactions between centrally administered economies, and there is no equilibrium of exchange.

III. CONCLUSION

1. SOME COMPARISONS

It is now possible to return to our original question. In spite of great variations in the details, does the economic process in the centrally administered economy proceed in essentially the same way as in the exchange economy? Is the basic logic in the two cases the same?

1. In either case the aim is to provide for certain needs by combining means of production and labor supplies for productive purposes as in any form of economy.

Does the similarity hold at least with regard to the task the economic process has daily to solve?

The answer is no, only in appearances. In the exchange economy individuals are face to face, day in, day out, with the scarcities in food, clothing, etc., which they have to overcome by acting in one way or another. As they produce little for their own consumption, there are division of labor and exchange between a number of individual households and firms. No one is surveying the process as a whole. The requirements even of bread are expressed simply by, and for, each individual according to his purchasing power. It is the meeting of the scarcities as felt by the individual person or household which is the objective of the economic process in an economy controlled by competitive prices.

It is different in the centrally administered economy. Economizing there does not find its origin and purpose in the scarcities felt by the individual, since these never effectively assert themselves. The central administration and the planning authorities fix a total requirement for bread, meat, steel, etc., for a particular period of time, and in doing this leave out of account individual needs, valuations, and plans, on which individuals base their actions in the exchange economy. Individuals may strongly prefer their bread to be of wheat rather than of rye, but the central administration can simply substitute rye bread; similarly, individuals may voluntarily save very little, but centrally planned investment may be put much higher. The planned requirements of the central administration are what is decisive. If the central plans in the centrally administered economy are completely and successfully carried through, then the economic process has reached its objective, even if the needs of individuals are satisfied to a far smaller extent than they might be.

Scarcity means two quite different things in the centrally administered economy as compared with the exchange economy. The basic purpose of economizing is quite different.

2. Inevitably, the method by which the economy is controlled must be equally different.

In the exchange economy, it is the exchange relationships—that is the prices—which have to regulate the economic process, because it is with a view to exchange that firms and households make their plans. In the centrally administered economy, the plans of firms and households have lost their independent power. Therefore there can be no exchange, no markets, no direction by prices, even when prices are calculated. Prices can only have a completely subsidiary role. Instead of *exchanges*, there are *allocations* of raw materials, machinery, etc., to the firms, of jobs to workers, of consumers' goods to consumers. No such question ever can arise, for example, as to whether for an individual worker there is any correspondence to him between his particular work in a machinery works, and the rations of consumers' goods he receives, and whether these goods represent the same value as his productive contribution.

With exchange replaced by allocations, all other economic institutions and procedures change their character, even though they do not change their names. Cartels, co-operatives and trade unions become instruments of control, and no longer represent groups in the market. Labor exchanges are no longer intermediaries between demand and supply, but are the authorities for the central direction of labor supplies.

To believe in the possibility of grafting prices on to the mechanism of control in a centrally administered economy is to believe in a squaring of the circle. Either the central administration is directing labor and means of production by its allocation, or the multitude of households and firms are decisive in the economy, in which case prices are formed. If control is left to the price mechanism, the central administration abdicates economically, while if the central administration takes over control, prices lose their directing function.

3. The analysis of the German experiment shows the full extent of the differences arising from this fundamental contrast. In the centrally administered economy, saving, investment, distribution, international trade, etc., are quite different processes.

The centrally administered economy embodies the maximum possible concentration of economic power. The opposite is a system of complete competition in all markets, where the individual has virtually no power, apart from each man's infinitesimal influence on the economic process. An exchange economy, with monopolies, partial monopolies, or oligopolies, stands with regard to the distribution of economic power between these two extremes.

4. In economic orders of society where the method of centrally administered control predominates, the center of gravity shifts. Consumers and entrepreneurs are no longer in control, but the central administration. *First*, the meeting of individual consumers' needs recedes into the background, for the central administration is unable to find out what they are, and to weigh them up. It has to fix consumers' needs "overall" or "totally." *Secondly*, there are no exact cost calculations according to which production can be organized. *Finally*, such economies are as a rule dominated by the objective of a maximum of investment, and therefore aim at cutting consumption to the Subsistence Minimum. In fact, such an economy is not one directed to meeting consumers' needs. The basic principle of control is quite different.

Therefore, a special and different theory of the centrally administered economy is required and is possible.

2. CRITICISMS OF SOME HYPOTHESES

1. How did it come about that many economists failed to see the fundamental differences between the centrally administered economy and the exchange economy and therefore misconceived the nature of an essential part of economic reality? They believed that in both cases there was the same economic scarcity to be overcome. As perfect competition gave the optimum solution, the Ministry of Production in the centrally administered economy had to act as though perfect competition ruled. Only with regard to the distribution of the social product would there be a deviation from "economic" principles. The same economic categories—so Barone believed—such as price, wages, interest, profit, saving, would emerge, even though under other names. The principle of costs in both cases would control the economic process.

In fact, neither is the same thing, neither scarcity, nor the method of control, which works not through prices but through round aggregate valuations. The principle of cost cannot operate with regard to individual units, and has no compelling force behind it.

In economic orders of society in which the methods of control are those of a central administration, in contrast with the views of Barone and his followers, the same terminology may be in use as in the exchange economy ("price," "interest," etc.), *but these words mean something entirely different.* The terminology is being applied to categories of quite another form. In both types of economy, there are "farmers," "traders" and "banks" but their economic significance is fundamentally different, since they are instruments for carrying out central plans rather than themselves independent planning agents.

It would be scientifically convenient to have a single simple theoretical apparatus of universal applicability, irrespective of whether the British economy of 1900, the German economy of 1939 or that of Russia in 1948 is under discussion. But that is not practicable. The variety of forms realized in practice has to be taken into account, for they are decisive for the way in which the economic process works itself out.

2. Barone tried to show that for the collectivist economy also as many independent equations could be set out as are necessary mathematically to determine the unknowns. He believed that the solution of the equilibrium equations would in fact be possible, without himself showing how it could be done. The work of Taylor, Lange, Lerner and others followed this up. They asked how the indices of significance for the different individual goods could be determined under "socialism," and they believe they have found a simple effective method, that of trial and error. The calculating process of perfect competition was to be applied in a socialist order of society—"socialist" in the sense that property was to be collectively owned.

We have shown above that this possibility does not exist, partly for monetary reasons (because of the excess money) and partly for a more important reason, namely, that any use of the price mechanism for controlling the economic process sets a limit to the power of the central administration. There is a simple "either-or" alternative. *Either* the control is through prices, and therefore on the basis of the plans of households and firms, *or* it is based on the plans and valuations of a central authority. The two methods of control exclude one another.

It is no accident that even in contemporary economic orders of the centrally administered type—as, for example, in Germany—experiments on Barone's principles are not in fact attempted. Such theoretical analysis is not based on deduction from economic reality. Perhaps economists have been induced to formulate the problem in this unrealistic way because of their interest in politico-economic controversies. Our analysis here is not concerned with issues of economic policy. (At the same time it might be pointed out that the problem has its peculiarities even from the point of view of policy. Can an efficient and just competitive mechanism be created with collective ownership of the means of production? With regard to this question it might be remarked that the concentration of economic power brought about by collective ownership of the means of production renders it highly improbable that the all-powerful collective property owners would undertake the experiment of leaving the control of the economic process to competition, and that they would not rather themselves control the economy by central orders, that is through a central administration. From the point of view of the history of ideas it is of interest that the socialist movement which started from a criticism of competition at the beginning of the last century, is today itself proposing to establish a competitive mechanism.)

4. How can the theoretical problem be formulated to correspond with reality?

Modern theory deviates from reality in two directions. Often models are constructed *a priori* with no reference to economic reality, and the question is then asked as to how economic activity would proceed in such an *a priori* model. Such attempts are dangerous, because the builders of these models think that a question about reality is being answered, while the very form of the question, as they put it, excludes reality.

On the other hand, the analysis may start from crude imprecise concepts like "capitalism," "*laisser-faire*," or "socialism." Such terms as these fail to describe actual economic systems. We must beware of proceeding like the chemists in earlier centuries who made experiments without specifying precisely the conditions under which they were making them. Theoretical deductions are of little service when the conditions postulated are not clearly set out. "In the excitement of perfecting our instruments of analysis, we have tended to neglect a study of the framework which they assume" (L. C. Robbins). Models constructed *a priori* and imprecise "blanket" concepts like "capitalism," "socialism" and the like can be of little help in the investigation of economic reality.

How can we come by a more precise understanding of the forms in which the economic process really develops? By penetrating and investigating real businesses, households or planning authorities, and by examining each form of economy as it occurs. We shall then discover that in economic reality in the past and in the present, in spite of its variety, a limited series of pure forms has occurred and does occur, and that these are mixed together in different ways and different combinations. It is apparent that actual economic orders always represent some particular combination of pure forms. In Russia, for example, in the fourth decade of this century, the economy is by no means exclusively dominated by the central administration and its plans. Though this method predominates, side by side there exist elements of an exchange economy, there is also barter, and there are self-sufficient rural economies. All these forms of organization should be taken account of in a scientific analysis of the every-day economic process in Russia.

An analysis of the forms of economic reality should precede theoretical analysis. The actual forms of economic organization must be derived from economic reality, and these will then provide a basis for theoretical analysis. In this way it becomes possible to explain individual cases and bring out their significance for a knowledge of general principles—for example, the case of the German experiment from 1936 to 1947.

Oskar Lange

12. THE ROLE OF PLANNING IN SOCIALIST ECONOMY*

In this article, Oskar Lange discusses a centrally planned socialist economy, in contrast to the decentralized market socialist economy depicted in Selection No. 7 above. He believes that comprehensive planning and detailed control of the economy are justified in order to mobilize the economy to achieve important goals—such as a war effort, the elimination of traces of capitalism in the early days of socialism, and rapid industrialization. But, he contends, as a socialist economy develops and matures, it becomes both possible and necessary to introduce a large area of decentralized decision making into the economy.

Lange proposes that the central authorities continue to determine the basic proportions and directions of the economy, but give up detailed, day-to-day management of the economy by administrative orders. Instead, he envisions the central authorities achieving the results they desire by "economic means"—financial mechanisms and incentives which induce, rather than command, managers and households to do what the plan requires. Such "economic means" include market prices which equalize supply and demand and supplant administrative distribution of producer goods. In this way, Lange hopes to combine central control of the main features of economic development with a high degree of decentralization of detailed decision making.[1]

* Reprinted from *The Political Economy of Socialism* (Publications on Social Change, Institute of Social Studies, No. 16) (The Hague: Van Keulen, 1958), pp. 16–28, by permission of the author, the Institute for Social Studies, and the publisher.

[1] Lange's proposal has not, however, been adopted in Poland, for a number of

198

ECONOMIC planning, or, more precisely, the planning of economic development, is an essential feature of socialism. It expresses the fact that socialist economy does not develop in an elemental way but that its development is guided and directed by the conscious will of organized society. Planning is the means of subjecting the operation of economic laws and the economic development of society to the direction of human will.

The experience of the construction of socialism in various countries indicates that the establishment of planned economy is one of the first achievements of the socialist revolution. It precedes the full development of socialist relations of production, though it requires a certain minimum of such relations. In the transitional period, when non-socialist modes of production still play an important role, the economy becomes already subject to planned direction of its development. This is made possible by the existence in the economy of a large socialist sector which controls, as one frequently says, the "commanding outposts" of economic life. This is the minimum requirement of establishing planned economy.

Economic planning starts with the direct intervention of the state in economic relations. This intervention has for its objectives the liquidation of capitalist relations of production and the control of the non-socialist sectors of economy which still remain. The basis which makes control of the non-socialist sectors possible is the existence of a socialist sector, particularly that part of the socialist sector which is nationalized, and which controls the commanding outposts of the economy.

In this first, transitional phase the new revolutionary state is not neutral with regard to the various sectors of the economy. It consciously utilizes the nationalized socialist sector as an instrument of controlling the development of the whole economy. The means it utilizes consist of economic instruments which result from the existence of the nationalized sector comprising the decisive controlling part of the economy, and also of intervention by political force, i.e., non-economic force. In the first revolutionary period, intervention into economic processes by political force plays a decisive role.

In the first period of development of a socialist economy, both the planning of economic development and the day-to-day management of the socialist sector are highly centralized.

There may be some doubts of how far this represents a universal necessity. For instance, in Poland, we had some discussions whether such a period of highly centralized planning and management was a historical necessity or a great political mistake. Personally, I hold the view that it was a historical necessity.

complex political and economic reasons. These are lucidly discussed in John Michael Montias, *Central Planning in Poland* (New Haven: Yale University Press, 1962), chaps. 9, 10.

It seems to me that, first, the very process of the social revolution which liquidates one social system and establishes another requires centralized disposal of resources by the new revolutionary state, and consequently centralized management and planning. This holds, in my opinion, for any socialist revolution.

In under-developed countries, there is a further consideration. Socialist industrialization, and particularly very rapid industrialization, which was necessary in the first socialist countries, particularly in the Soviet Union, as a political requirement of national defense and of the solution of all kinds of political and social problems, due to backwardness, requires centralized disposal of resources. Thus, the very process of transformation of the social system and in addition, in under-developed countries, the need of rapid industrialization, impose the necessity of high centralization of planning and management.

The process of rapid industrialization requires such centralized disposal of resources for two reasons. First, it is necessary to concentrate all resources on certain objectives and avoid dissipation of resources on other objectives which would divert resources from the purpose of rapid industrialization. This is one of the reasons which leads to highly centralized planning and management and also to the allocation of resources by means of administrative establishment of priorities. The second reason why rapid industrialization demands centralized planning and management is the lack and weakness of industrial cadres. With the rapid growth of industry the cadres are new and inexperienced. Such old cadres which had some experience in management of industry and other economic activities are frequently politically alien to the socialist objectives. In consequence high centralization of managerial decisions becomes necessary.

Thus, the first period of planning and management in a socialist economy, at least according to our present experience, has always been characterized by administrative management and administrative allocation of resources on the basis of priorities centrally established. Economic incentives are in this period replaced by moral and political appeals to the workers, by appeals to their patriotism and socialist consciousness. This is, so to speak, a highly politicized economy, both with regard to the means of planning and management and with regard to the incentives it utilizes.

I think that, essentially, it can be described as a *sui generis* war economy. Such methods of war economy are not peculiar to socialism because they are also used in capitalist countries in wartime. They were developed in the first and the second world wars. In capitalist countries, similar methods were used during the war, namely, concentration of all resources on one basic purpose, which is the production of war material, centralization of disposal of resources in order to avoid leakages of resources to what was considered non-essential utilization (everything which was not connected with the prosecution of the war). Allocation of resources by administrative decision according to administratively established priorities and wide scale use of political incentives to maintain the productivity and discipline of labor through patriotic appeals were characteristic of war economy. This was the case in all capitalist countries during the war.

It shows clearly that such methods of centralized planning and management are not peculiar to socialism, that they are rather certain techniques of war economy. The difficulty starts when these methods of war economy are identified with the essence of socialism and considered as being essential to socialism.

One of the methods of war economy, which most of the socialist countries used at one stage or another, was compulsory deliveries by peasants of part of their produce. Many comrades in my country feel rather upset by the present program of our government of abolishing such deliveries. They fear that this implies giving up some socialist principle. I usually answer them by asking whether they remember who in Poland first introduced compulsory deliveries by peasants. Such deliveries were first introduced during the first world war by the occupation army of Kaiser Wilhelm the Second, whom I do not think anybody regards as a champion of socialism. These methods cannot be considered as an essential aspect of socialism; they are simply methods of war economy necessary in a revolutionary period of transition.

The fate and history of these methods is a classical example of the dialectical character of the development of socialist society. Methods which are necessary and useful in the period of social revolution and of intensive industrialization become an obstacle to further economic progress when they are perpetuated beyond their historic justification. They become obstacles because they are characterized by lack of flexibility. They are rigid; they lead, therefore, to waste of resources resulting from this inflexibility; they require a wasteful bureaucratic apparatus and make it difficult to adjust production to the needs of the population. However, it seems that the greatest obstacle to further progress results from the lack of proper economic incentives in this bureaucratic centralistic type of management. This hampers proper economic utilization of resources, encourages waste, and also hinders technical progress.

Therefore, when the socialist society starts to overcome these centralistic, bureaucratic methods of administrative planning and management, it indicates, so to speak, that it is maturing. I would not want to make this a final definition of the period of transition. But I might say that substituting for the methods of administrative and centralized management new methods based on the utilization of economic laws indicates the end of the period of transition and the beginning of the functioning of an established socialist economy. I would not say that this is the only aspect of the problem of the period of transition, but it is certainly an important aspect of it.

The period of centralized planning and management, as I said, is the result partly of the necessities of the revolutionary transformation of society and, in under-developed countries, also of the needs of rapid industrialization. In studying this period, a certain important sociological factor has to be taken into account, which is the weakness of the working class in an under-developed country. It seems to me that it is on the basis of this weakness, under conditions of under-development, that the bureaucratic state machine gains great importance, and phenomena like the "cult of personality" develop. It, so to speak, in a way substitutes for the spontaneous activity of the working class.

But here again, the dialectics of the processes of construction of socialism becomes apparent. The centralistic methods are successful in achieving rapid industrialization and, as a consequence, cause a rapid growth of the working class. The working class grows in numbers as well as in consciousness and political maturity. Next to the growth of the working class, another important sociological element appears. This is the growth of a new socialist intelligentsia which largely comes from the ranks of the workers and peasants. When it becomes clear that the highly centralized administrative and bureaucratic methods of management create obstacles to further progress, a part of the political and state apparatus becomes convinced that a change of methods of administration and management is needed. Thus, new social forces mature which require and also make possible a change of these methods.

This precisely is the basic difference between the development of a socialist society and a society which is based on antagonistic class relations. There is no ruling class which may oppose these changes. There may be certain strata or groups which have a vested interest in the old methods and create obstacles, but these obstacles can never become of such importance as to make impossible the changes required by new historical circumstances.

This is very clear if you take, for instance, the experience of Poland, where the industrialization by means of centralized administrative planning and management has led to a great increase of the working class. Our working class is now more than three times what it was before the war. The working class has got experience in large industrial establishments. It was at first to a large extent of peasant origin and that, of course, weighed on its psychology. But that was only a transitional phase. Industrialization and the social revolution have created a new intelligentsia—largely coming from workers and peasants. All that led to a maturing of the forces of the new socialist society. In consequence, we got such a phenomenon as the great movement of workers' councils demanding self-government of workers in industry—the general demand to change the methods of management of the national economy. The party has accepted these demands of the people and given them organized expression.

Changes in the methods of planning and the management of the economy are taking place today in practically all socialist countries. Forms and contents are different, but all these changes imply a certain decentralization or deconcentration of management. I do not want to enter into a description of what is happening in the various socialist countries. I shall rather present to you what I personally believe is the proper formulation of the role and methods of planning in a socialist economy.

First, it must be stated that in a socialist society, planning of the economy is active planning. Some of the economists in Poland use the term "directive planning," but this term is ambiguous; therefore, I shall rather use the term "active planning." By this, I mean that planning does not consist only of coordination of the activities of various branches of the economy. It is something more: namely, it is an active determination of the main lines of development of the national economy. Otherwise, if planning were mere coordination, the development of socialist economy would be elemental; it would not really be directed by the will of organized society. If economic development is not to be elemental but is to be directed by organized society, then planning must be active economic planning.

Two problems arise with regard to active economic planning. First, what is its scope; what activities in the economy have to be planned? And second, what are the methods of securing the realization of the plan?

The active character of planning does not require that it go into each detail of economic life. We actually had a period in the socialist countries (perhaps with the exception of China, which started at a later level and profited by the experience of other socialist countries) when the output of even the least important commodity was planned. There was the famous joke in Poland—really, it was not a joke, but it was true—that the production of pickled cucumbers was in the national-economic plan. Another case, which again was not a joke but a fact, was that the State Planning Commission made a plan of the number of hares which were to be shot during the year by hunters. At the same time, you could not get, for instance, buttons or hairpins for ladies, simply because they had been forgotten in the plan.

Active planning and effective direction of the development of the economy are quite possible without planning such details. Even more, planning such details hampers really effective direction of the economy. Actually, I think it may be said that controlling such details had nothing to do with planning. It was a part of the high centralization of day-to-day management of the economy by means of administrative measures. This is a different thing than planning.

However, the plan which is to determine the development of the economy must include at least two things: first, the division of national income between accumulation and consumption; second, the distribution of investments among the different branches of the economy. The first determines the general rate of economic growth; the second determines the direction of the development.

Unless these two things are in the plan, there is no active guidance of

the development of the economy. This is, therefore, the minimum requirement of the plan. In addition, it may or may not include the targets for the
production of certain basic commodities, like basic raw materials, basic
means of production, and so on. These are technical problems, not fundamental problems.

These are the fundamental aspects of the plan which determine the pace
and the direction of development of the economy. In addition, economic
planning must be concerned with coordination of the activities of the
various branches of the economy—first of all, with coordination of the
financial aspects of the plan and of its real aspects, in particular coordination of the total purchasing power at the disposal of the population and
the amounts of consumer goods which are provided for distribution to
individuals. The plan must also in some way and by some means be
interested in the coordination of the output of the various branches of the
national economy. Otherwise, the determination of the directions of development established by the plan may not be realized. If there is no
proper coordination between the output of the various branches, investments may not be realized because the necessary investment goods
are not produced. All kinds of bottlenecks appear and cause difficulties
which may make it impossible to carry out the investment plan. So much
for the content of the plan.

The second problem is that of the methods of securing the realization of
the plan. Here, we have basically two possible methods. One consists of
administrative orders and administrative allocation of resources. The various units in the socialist economy are ordered to do certain things—for
instance, to produce so much of something. The resources which are
necessary for that purpose, both material and financial, are allocated in an
administrative way. This was the traditional method of realizing the plan
in the past period. The second method consists in the use of what we call
"economic means," namely, of setting up a system of incentives which
induces people to do exactly the things which are required by the plan. It
seems to me that in effective planning, both methods have to be used,
though in different proportions.

Preference should be given to the use of economic means. Administrative methods should be limited to those fields where, for some reason or
other, economic means are ineffective. Such situations, where economic
means are not effective, always do exist. They exist, of course, particularly
in periods of very great changes, because economic means are rather subtle
instruments responding to "normal" changes in the situation and frequently breaking down when very fundamental or revolutionary changes
are needed. In such cases the use of administrative means must be accepted.
Even in a capitalist country, in situations of profound change, the state
uses measures of administrative control, because the normal kind of economic means is not sufficient to provoke the responses which are necessary.

The fundamental decisions of the plan—the division of national income between accumulation and consumption and the basic direction of investments—are really of a political character, and the means of implementation must be partly administrative. The decision of the plan concerning the rate of accumulation is basically realized by administrative measures. Part of the national income produced is not paid out in the form of individual incomes; part of the profits of the socialist enterprises are held back by the state, and this is an administrative measure. So also are all forms of taxation of enterprises and individuals. The basic directions of investments—for instance, the decision to build an electric power plant—are usually not made as a reaction to market situations, but are made as basic decisions of economic policy, though in this case the realization of the decisions may make use of all kinds of economic instruments.

We may ask in what sense the economic plans must take account of economic laws. Even when the realization of the plan is achieved by administrative measures, the plan must observe the general economic laws concerning the proportions necessary in the process of production and reproduction. For instance, if the plan provides for an increase of the production of steel, it must provide for a certain additional output of coal which is needed to produce the additional steel. *Any* kind of planning has to take care of such objective kinds of relationships.

There are also other economic laws which must be observed by the plan. These are the laws which result from the operation of economic incentives under the circumstances created by the plan. The process of realization of the plan sets into motion definite economic incentives to which the people react in a certain way which can be calculated. Even in the period of administrative planning, certain economic incentives were operative, and their consequences had to be taken into account. In this period, however, economic means were only subsidiary in relation to administrative means. I would say that now the situation has to change in the sense that the economic means are the rule and administrative means become subsidiary to the economic means. Thus, the plan has to observe the laws of production and reproduction; and insofar as the realization is based on the use of economic means, i.e., the operation of economic laws, it also has to consider these laws.

By utilizing economic means, planning makes use of the automatic character of people's responses to given incentives. Thus, certain automatic processes in the economy are established. However, these automatic processes are not elemental. These two things should be distinguished. The difference is that in a socialist society, where the automatic processes are part of the method of realization of the plan, the conditions establishing incentives are set up by economic policy; whereas in capitalist society, these conditions develop in an elemental way. There is a basic difference: In one case (capitalism), the incentives develop in an elemental way and are not subject to conscious control of society; in the other case (socialism), they are consciously established by organized society in such a way as to produce the desired results. As Engels said: "The social causes set into motion will produce to an ever-increasing extent the results desired by man."

I shall illustrate this by an analogy. The capitalist economy may be compared to an old-fashioned balloon which is moved by the currents of the air in the direction in which the wind pushes it. Man has no control whatever over the direction in which the balloon is moving. The socialist economy in the period of realization of its plan by administrative measures can be compared to an old-fashioned airplane, in which the pilot with his hands moves the steering gear. By always attending to the steering gear, the pilot directs the plane in the direction he chooses; whenever the current of the air changes, he moves the gear in such a way as to keep in his chosen direction. Planning in which the realization is based on economic means I would compare to a modern plane which has an automatic steering mechanism. The pilot sets the mechanism in the direction in which he wants the plane to go, and the automatic mechanism keeps the plane in the desired direction. The pilot can read a book or a newspaper in the meantime, and the plane by itself keeps the desired direction. But it is not the direction where the wind pushes the plane, but the direction which the pilot has chosen—consciously chosen. It is the pilot who determines the direction of the plane; if he wishes, he can change the direction by re-setting the automatic mechanism.

If I were to carry the analogy to the end, I would say that the pilot must, of course, from time to time determine whether the automatic steering mechanism is working. As a rule, experience shows that when the wind is very strong, the automatic mechanism does not work, and the pilot has to take the steering gear in his hand and steer himself. When the wind again becomes quiet, he can once more let the automatic mechanism work. In sudden upsetting situations, administrative measures have to be used in managing a socialist economy.

The next problem is to what extent the decisions implied in the plan, (not their realization, but the decisions themselves) can be centralized, or can or even must be decentralized. The need for centralized decisions obviously results from the need for coordination. Such decisions as the basic direction of investments, since they also must be coordinated through the coordination of various branches of economy, must be centrally planned. Each plan must have centralistic elements. I would say that the basic decisions of the plan must be made centrally. In addition to that, the plan may have as subsidiary parts certain decentralized subsidiary plans, in order to secure the proper flexibility. There are two criteria which determine the decentralization which economic planning can or must have. One determines the possibility of decentralization and the other the necessity of decentralization.

Economic planning should be decentralized so far as it is possible to set up economic incentives such that the decisions of the decentralized units are the same as the decisions which would be made centrally. Second, economic planning *must* be decentralized in all cases where the central decision responds to a situation too late, because in such cases, unless there is decentralization, central planning becomes fictitious. What actually is obtained is an elemental development. It is important to notice that in all socialist countries, in the period of highly centralized planning and management, there were many elemental processes of this type.

For instance, in Poland in a certain period the elemental processes were so common that one could have asked whether a planned economy still existed. On the one hand, there was a plan; but on the other, the economy produced results in a very elemental way. The elemental character of this process was the result of two facts. One was the over-centralization of the plan. Before processes that took place in various branches of the economy came to the attention of the central authority, and before the central authority took action, irreversible things had already happened. The result was purely elemental. The other fact was the existence of "wrong" economic incentives. When the old moral and political incentives stopped working (they can only work for a certain period), it was discovered that all kinds of incentives were implicit in the plan of which the central authority was not aware and which hampered the realization of the plan.

Thus, it is a practical and important question to know how many of the decisions are made in the central economic plan, and how many decisions are delegated to lower economic units, e.g., enterprises or organizations of enterprises in the industry, etc. This is particularly important with regard to the investment plans. In Poland, for instance, we are now developing a scheme which provides central planning of what we call fundamental investments, for instance, building a new plant or substantially enlarging an existing plant. We give the enterprises the right to undertake the subsidiary investments autonomously, without asking anybody for approval.

The latter has proved to be necessary in order to assure greater flexibility of investment decisions. For instance, if the enterprise needs to put up funds for unforeseen repairs, or if it wants to buy machines to increase output quickly, or to make some technical improvement, it must have the power to do so. Our experience was that before it got the approval of the central authority to make the necessary investments, the whole situation was already different. Thus, the situation was utterly inflexible. The financial resources for such subsidiary investment would consist of a part of the amortization fund of the enterprise and of bank credits it could take up for the purpose of such investments. Investments of small enterprises are to be entirely financed by bank credits without appearing at all in the central economic plan.

Now, of course, one thing should be kept in mind. The fact that a part of that investment is financed by bank credits does subject them in an indirect way to central planning, because obviously the bank can refuse to give the credit. The bank acts on the basis of a certain general economic policy in deciding how much credit it is going to give, for what purpose it is going to give it, and on what conditions it will give it. These are indirect ways by which the central authority influences the subsidiary investments.

A similar economic problem, and a more acute one, exists with regard to the planning of production. In the former period, even the smallest product had to be in the central economic plan. Now, however, only the basic production of enterprises is in it. The enterprise has the right to undertake what is called subsidiary production, which is not in the plan. There is quite a discussion among Polish economists as to whether production should be in the economic plan. There are a few economists who think that production should not be in the economic plan at all, but that it should respond only to the economic incentives of the market. The practical solution which will probably be adopted in Poland will be to put in the central economic plan the output of certain basic commodities, like coal, steel, raw materials, certain means of production, and textiles of mass production, i.e., commodities of a particular significance for the national economy. As to the rest, the enterprises will have a plan of output in terms of its total net value without prescribing the detailed assortment. A shoe factory, for instance, will have a total value plan of output but be able to produce any assortment of men's shoes, ladies' shoes, and children's shoes, according to its own decision.

All these are problems of technique and not of principle. I think that the one essential thing in the socialist economy is that the plan has to be an active one which determines the pace and the direction of development of the national economy. The other things are really questions of technique, which may change under different conditions. There is, however, one more problem which I want to mention in this connection. This is an essential and not a technical thing—the plan must be based on correct economic accounting. Correct accounting of economic costs and economic benefits, and consequently a correct price system, are indispensable.

In a socialist economy, prices have two purposes: One is as a means of distribution, and the other as a means of economic accounting. Therefore, there are two principles which must be taken into account in the formation of prices. This requires a calculation, at least as we see it now in our work in Poland, of two kinds of prices, namely, market prices and accounting prices.

Unless distribution of consumers' goods is done by rationing, the market price must obviously be such as to establish equilibrium on the market, to equalize demand and supply. The same holds also for prices of the means of production when administrative allocation is removed and enterprises freely buy and sell their products. Market conditions determine the equilibrium prices which equalize demand and supply. The principle of determining the market prices is very simple. They simply must equalize demand and supply.

However, market prices are not sufficient. In addition, there must be calculated accounting prices, which reflect the social cost of production of the various products. The accounting prices, of course, may strongly differ from the market prices. In Poland, we propose now to calculate what we call the initial or normal prices, which would be the cost of production plus a profit, which serves to cover accumulation and the collective consumption of society. To these normal prices, we propose to add a (positive or negative) markup in order to obtain the market prices which equalize demand and supply. Then the (positive or negative) differences between the market prices and the normal prices would be an indicator for economic planning.

The indication for the next plan would be to increase output (by making the necessary investments) where the market price is high above the normal price, and to stop expansion or even diminish output where the market prices does not cover the normal price.

The great controversy at this moment among Polish economists is what cost should be included in the normal price: whether it should be average cost of the enterprises in a given industry or marginal cost. The majority of economists take the view that it should be marginal cost. Those who are in favor of average cost really consist of two groups: one is in principle in favor of average cost, and the other is in principle in favor of marginal cost but believes that this would in practice be a very difficult system of calculation and so takes average cost simply because the other solution, though theoretically better, is very difficult to realize in practice.

The proponents of marginal cost, of course, propose to use a practical approximation to marginal cost. The cost on the basis of which the normal price is to be calculated is the average variable cost of the group of enterprises which have the highest cost in the industry. The method proposed is to classify the enterprises in several groups (not too many, because it has to be practically easy), and then to take the group of enterprises which have the highest cost as the pilot group. It serves as the indicator. There is a reason for using average variable cost of the group. If we take just one enterprise, we may get a very unrepresentative figure. We want to have something which represents the real cost structure of the industry. Therefore, we take the average variable cost of the enterprises in that last group.

The argument in favor of marginal cost and of this procedure of practical interpretation of marginal cost is this: We have, for instance, electric power plants. Each plant produces at a different cost. Suppose we can save electric power. What is the diminution of cost to society? Obviously, when we save electric power, we still stop or diminish production not in the plants which have the lowest cost, but in the plants which have the highest cost. The cost in the latter plants represents the resources we save; it represents the saving to society. If we have to expand the output of electricity, the cost to society is the cost of operation of electric power plants which produce at the highest cost. Consequently, if changes in the use of electric power take place, the effect on the cost to society is determined in the most costly plants, and that change is marginal cost. We consider only variable cost in the highest cost plants, because the fixed cost is given and does not change in consequence of a change of utilization of electricity.

This is basically the system which a majority of Polish economists propose. To the marginal cost, there must be added something to cover all the fixed costs in the industry. This may be zero, because the larger profits of the enterprises which produce at lower cost may be sufficient for this purpose. If not, we must add something to marginal cost. Such additions would have everywhere to be proportional to the marginal cost so that the normal prices would be proportional to the marginal costs of the various products and cover the fixed cost.

The indicator for the plan would be whether the market price is higher or lower than this normal price, i.e., whether it socially pays to expand or reduce the output of a product. I have to add that this normal cost would also have to include a surcharge to cover capital accumulation and collective consumption, e.g., non-productive expenses of the state, etc. Such additions would have to be in the same proportion in all branches of the economy so as not to affect the proportions between the normal prices and marginal costs.

So much on this subject. It is clear that good and effective economic planning requires a development of economic science and that it must be based on scientific economic analysis. This is one of the basic differences between a socialist and a capitalist economy. In a capitalist economy, the economic processes are elemental; whereas under socialism, they can be directed on the basis of scientific knowledge of the needs and possibilities of the whole national economy.

PART III

Case Studies of Economic Systems

The case studies of the French, Yugoslav, and Soviet economic systems which follow are living illustrations, respectively, of the theoretical models of capitalism, market socialism, and central planning analyzed in Part II of this book. These case studies show how the models' abstract principles of economic organization and control are applied in real economies. They reveal the compromises and adaptations required by cultural, historical, and geographical factors. And they demonstrate that actual economies are hybrids or mixtures of theoretical economic systems, rather than pure examples of them.

It is striking to note that all three of these working economies combine—though in different proportions—private and public ownership of the means of production, consumers' and planners' sovereignty, and the decentralized market and central planning in resource allocation. The selections that follow explain and appraise the nature of, and reasons for, the specific combination of seeming alternatives which each of these living economies has chosen.

France: Regulated Capitalism

The French variant of regulated, mixed capitalism differs significantly from the American one. In addition to indirect guidance of the economy by monetary and fiscal measures, the French Government attempts to steer the private economy by aggregative "indicative planning."

Using input-output tables and national economic accounts, the Government, in collaboration with representatives of business, agriculture, and trade unions, draws up an agreed plan for the future development of the economy. This plan, however, is only "indicative," not "imperative." It is essentially a forecast, not a directive, and it is prepared only at the branch level, not covering individual private firms. Nevertheless, by coordinating the production and investment programs of the different branches of the economy, the plan reduces uncertainty and risk for individual firms and promises them a "balanced market" in which to acquire factors of production and sell output. Firms still make their own decisions freely in the market. But they do so with the benefit of knowledge, provided by the plan, about the intentions of the rest of the economy and the Government's credit, tax, and price policies. In this way, the French economy endeavors to combine a limited amount of overall government planning with decentralized private decision making.

The French approach to economic planning is explained further in the following selection.

Pierre Massé

13. FRENCH METHODS OF PLANNING*

> *In this article, Pierre Massé, head of the French plan organization, explains the evolution of the French "indicative" plan, its logic and objectives, and the methods of preparing and implementing it. He concludes with a discussion of the probable future directions of government planning in France.*

I. THE PLAN'S ORIGINS AND MOTIVES

FRENCH experience in planning is now sixteen years old. Its origin goes back to the decision taken by the provisional government of the Republic, presided over by General de Gaulle, to initiate a "modernization and equipment plan" and to put in charge a newly conceived government agency, the Commissariat Général du Plan.

Between the difficulties caused by the dramatic shortages of the immediate post-war years and the problems set today by the Common Market and by decolonization, there is hardly any analogy. Yet the French experiment has followed its course and has even been enlarged. Several thousand people are associated in drawing up the Fourth Plan which is to cover the 1962–65 period.

The experience and lessons of the last sixteen years as well as the evolution of the problems to be solved have enriched our reflections, altered our methods, rendered our procedures more flexible. It is possible, however, to measure how much has already been done, the fairly remarkable continuity of the task, and the means used to achieve it.

While the idea of *planification* was the subject, not so long ago, of heated doctrinal debates, one cannot help being struck by the fact that in France *practical* planning preceded the *theory* by a long time. I underline this point: the method as a whole which forms the basis of French

* Reprinted, with the permission of the author and publisher, from *Journal of Industrial Economics*, Vol. XI, No. 1 (November, 1962), pp. 1–17. Pierre Massé is General Commissioner of the French Plan for Economic and Social Development.

213

planning is not the result of a preconceived doctrine, the product of a school of thought, the privileged instrument of a political majority. In France in 1945 the planning of economic activity was desired by different circles. The wind of reform which swept over France brought with the idea of nationalizing key sectors, the idea of substituting the Plan for certain market mechanisms which had failed before the war to remedy the social and economic aftermath of the great 1930 depression. In those days the political origin of the ministers in office reflected that dominating tendency.

Even more than ideology, a realistic appreciation of the country's situation pleaded in favor of "planning," that is to say for defining and setting up an organization likely to obtain from limited means of production the maximization of national income. France in 1945 had not only to build from the ruins of the war and repair the damages of the occupation. She also had to catch up with the advance taken by other great industrial nations during the 1930–40 decade. "Modernization" or "decadence" were the alternatives which faced the authors of the First Plan.

The shortages (in equipment, manpower, hard currency, raw materials) were such that very rigorous choices had to be made. The choices actually favored basic sectors (energy, steel, transport, tractors, cement, fertilizers) and were not understood by everybody. The First Plan for instance was blamed for having overlooked housing and textile problems. Experience showed, however, that the concentration of our limited means on those sectors permitted a decisive development of the national potential.

The government then in office faced the fact that France in the days of the Liberation temporarily needed external aid. In setting up an economic recovery plan the government strengthened the hand of the negotiators who were being sent to the United States, and also showed how the hard currencies requested and their equivalent in francs would be allocated to supply our Equipment Fund.

Political situation, acute shortages, foreign aid, such were the facts which governed the French experiment at its outset. They alone cannot explain why the experiment is being continued. If the conjunction of similar circumstances led other countries to adopt recovery programs, most experiments were not followed up.

The success of the French attempt, meaning in the first place the length of time it has already lasted, can be better explained by the methods of work adopted from the outset and maintained later on under Jean Monnet's influence. M. Monnet had understood that despite the political situation (a majority leaning towards socialism) and despite the economic situation (the "dirigiste" state having all powers) the French Plan would only work if it was a collective enterprise and if people directly or indirectly concerned in its execution were associated in drawing it up. The report of the First Plan explicitly referred to the notion of *pre-concerted economy* (agreed on after being freely discussed).

The tool created by Jean Monnet to realize these ideas was also quite an original novelty as far as French Public Services were concerned. It can be characterized by the small number of people involved in contrast to the large area on which it impinged.

Originally officials of the Commissariat Général du Plan numbered 30 to 40. Including drivers, office boys and secretaries the total staff came up to 100 people. If the staff numbers 140 today it is only due to the fact that the department of the former Commissariat Général for Productivity and the Plan were merged. Officials in charge of planning in the real sense of the word have not increased in number despite the very large extension of the field they have to cover. It is one of the very few exceptions to Parkinson's law.

The small number of "chargés de mission" (specially appointed people usually drawn from other government departments) could not—and still cannot—cope with all the work involved in planning. They must receive outside help. Thus the risks of being faced with conflicts of competence, an administrative calamity, are reduced from the outset. The varied background of the Commissariat's collaborators (engineers, "Inspecteurs des Finances," university scholars, agronomists) and the fact that some of them are merely detached from their original department provide, on this point, an additional safeguard. The Plan is not the citadel of a clan or a group, but a meeting place where all people are welcome.

Compelled because of its small staff to work with other public departments, the Commissariat Général could not compensate this apparent weakness by the extent of its powers. Inside the administrative and governmental machinery it plays a part consisting only of conceiving, advising or estimating. It takes part in procedures and prepares decisions, but holds no power of its own and manages no funds for economic intervention. No department, no ministry can reasonably fear an encroachment on its field. On the other hand it can provide the administration as a whole with the opportunity of collating its schemes and settling disagreements on neutral ground.

Limited in material means, the Plan owes part of its strength to its position in the administrative machine. During the first years it was a department of the Prime Minister's office. The complex characters of political coalitions in France meant that the Minister of Finance had not the same extended powers as, say the British Chancellor of the Exchequer. Experience showed nevertheless the necessity of bringing the Plan closer to the whole system governing Finances and Economic Affairs. But by putting the Commissariat Général under the direct authority of the Minister of Finance and Economic Affairs to whom the Prime Minister delegates his powers, one has not gone as far as to reduce it to a simple ministerial department. A more subtle solution has prevailed, which combines links of personal allegiance with a talent for intellectual independence. The Commissaire Général is able to play the role of a conciliator often necessary because each department tends to consider things from a different point of view, according to its own particular responsibility.

But the Commissariat Général does not owe its success merely to its weakness. It also owes it to the fact that it is a permanent meeting place in which to exchange information and discuss schemes set up by the administration or by the business world. In Jean Monnet's mind the main agent for that cooperation was to be the "Modernization Commissions" which still play an essential role in our organization.

A Modernization Commission includes 30 to 40 people, seldom more, who are not paid for their work in helping draw up the Plan. Its members are appointed by the government on the "Commissaire Général's proposals." They belong essentially to three big categories: heads of firms and leaders of employer's associations; workers (all four big unions have representatives in the commissions); civil servants of the departments involved. Experts, mostly with an academic background, and users' representatives, as appropriate, make up the rest of the Commission. No exact proportion is stipulated for the composition of a commission and this adds to the flexibility of the organization. The spirit counts more than the letter. Commissions seek agreement and not majority votes.

Their goal is not to referee between winners and losers but to piece together a picture of future economic and social activity in connection with national development. In deciding that such commissions should meet M. Jean Monnet hoped to achieve a real mobilization of talents, all the more necessary since available statistics did not provide sufficient material for a small team of specialists to draw up the plan. Furthermore, he was convinced that by working together on the Plan those who would have to carry it out would spontaneously see that it was carried out. In this way the government's intervention during the execution of the Plan would not need to be too heavy. Experience confirmed that he was right.

The improvement of our statistical material and the development of national accounts would now make it possible, up to a certain point, to reduce the importance of the commissions' technical contribution. But it still remains true that they facilitate the airing of different points of view and favor convergence in action. The usefulness of such contacts has kept growing and the number of commissions has increased at the very demand of those (public services or businesses) which did not previously benefit from their existence. Possibly such demands may partly rest on the hope that the Plan may act as a mediator with the Ministry of Finance. But they also partly indicate a broader acknowledgement of the merits of such contacts. In all, 25 commissions exist today: 20 related to branches of economic or social activity, 5 concerned with the main problems of all branches (financing, manpower, research, productivity, regional planning). The total number of members in commissions and working groups was around a thousand during the First Plan. It is now approximately 3,500.

An open organization, favoring the rapprochement of points of view and concerted action on strategic points—thus could have been defined the machinery set up for the First Plan. It still can be defined today in the same way. Methods used have become more detailed, the field of action covers more ground, the goal is always the same.

II. A GLANCE AT THE FIRST THREE PLANS

The First Modernization and Equipment Plan was a plan for economic recovery. One had to decide between a modest development in all sectors, and substantial progress in sectors having a driving influence whilst providing resources for all the rest. A bold choice was made in favor of the latter. Six basic sectors were given consideration: coal, electricity, steel, cement, agricultural machinery and transport. I remember the shock we received at Electricité de France, where I had just been appointed director of the equipment department, when we heard that the target had been set at 39.5 billions of kilowatts compared with 21 billion kilowatts at the most consumed in the best pre-war year. Success was the reward of this act of faith since the consumption of electric power in France is today double the figure set in the initial objective.

The difficulties which we met were none the less considerable and I must admit that Marshall Aid arrived at the right moment to support our own efforts. It also led to a short extension of the period covered by the Plan and it was finally decided it would end in 1952/53. At the same time fuels and nitrogen were added to the sectors which were given priority.

At the end of the Plan, these objectives had approximately been attained: slightly less than 100 per cent for coal, electricity and steel, a little over 100 per cent for cement and fuels. Compared with 1946, production increases were over 15 per cent for coal, 75 per cent for electricity, 140 per cent for steel, 150 per cent for cement.

The Second Plan's length was to be four years, a rule which has since been observed, and which we do not intend to change. The four years of the Second Plan extended from 1954 to 1957 inclusive.

An important innovation was the extension of the plan to all productive activities, mainly agriculture, manufacturing industries, housing and overseas development. Priority to key industries was no longer a major concern and a harmonized growth in all sectors became the main preoccupation. Improvements in national accounts, giving a better overall view of the economy, supplied at the right time the necessary instrument to deal with problems of coherence. This is a logical necessity but it is also—and I stress this point because it was brought up during our discussions—a psychological requirement. Every sector of activity insists on knowing what part it is due to play in connection with the development as a whole.

Moreover, the goal of the Second Plan was not merely to produce more. It was essentially to produce better, meaning that quality and price conditions were to be competitive. Undoubtedly this came as a result of the trend towards trade liberalization, and of the feeling that French economy had to prepare to compete in a world of open frontiers. About the same time, and in view of the same problems, the Commissariat Général for Productivity was created which later on merged with the Commissariat Général du Plan. Finally the Second Plan emphasized the more or less long-run possibilities, to reduce costs, to develop scientific and technical research, to step up the specialization of firms, the training of labor, the organization of markets.

In this new perspective, and thanks to the measuring instrument supplied by National Economic Accounts, it became possible for the first time to draw up objectives in aggregate terms. Thus the national product was to increase in index numbers from 100 to 125 and industrial production from 100 to 130.

On the whole, results were higher than the objectives set by the Second Plan. In 1957 national product reached index 130 (instead of 125) and industrial production, excluding housing, index 146 (instead of 130). Electricity, motor-cars, and chemicals achieved particularly brilliant results.

However remarkable these achievements there is another side to the picture. The super-development of productive activities was obtained at the cost of the basic equilibria of the economy. Need for imports increased massively while labor shortages, causing a notable increase of wage incomes, contributed to the pressure of domestic demand and to slow the export drive. Thus the high rate of progress affected the structural development by accelerating it and throwing it out of balance. We learned the lesson of these events and henceforth gave more importance to adjustment to cyclic factors.

It is in these circumstances that the Third Plan (1958–61) sought to achieve a significant economic expansion, increasing national production by 20 per cent in four years, while maintaining monetary stability and balancing foreign payments. At the same time it was meant to adapt a rather isolated economy to Common Market conditions, to develop relationships between Metropolitan France and African French-speaking people, as well as to secure full employment for the numerous youths due to reach working age towards 1963/64.

A first set of measures to restore a balance were decided in the autumn of 1957. Nevertheless the decisive turning point only came at the end of

1958, when an adequately planned devaluation took place at the right moment. It is true on the other hand that national product only increased by 2.5 per cent during both 1958 and 1959. But with the success of the devaluation and the improvement in the financial situation, the conditions for a fresh economic drive were fulfilled. To signalize a new start a document called "interim plan" was published in the spring of 1960. It provided for an advance in the national product of 11 per cent during the second half of the Third Plan (1960–61). It can be said that in the course of the Third Plan the economy found its balance, renounced foreign aid, resumed its march forward and achieved the investment planned in key sectors, but it fell half a year behind schedule so far as general production goals were concerned.

What stands out from this quick glance at French post-war economic history?

In my opinion the most remarkable feature seems to be that with a stable working population (18.86 millions in 1949 and 18.84 in 1959) while the total population increased by almost 10 per cent (41.4 in 1949 and 45.1 in 1959), France managed despite several contingencies of which the most important was the currency crisis of 1957/58 to increase its national production at an average rate higher than 4.5 per cent per year. The apparent disorder of spiraling prices and exchange rates had masked the real and deep improvement shown by the fact that industrial production doubled in ten years.

III. THE LOGIC OF THE PLAN

The modern economy requires considerable investment and the return can be greatly affected by developments in the environment. Such developments occur fast and are difficult to forecast. Without going as far as Keynes in saying that information available to investors "amounts to little, sometimes to nothing," it must be admitted that isolated firms have no serious basis for calculations. No "generalized markets" in which orders can be placed for several years ahead and according to future circumstances, and at fixed prices for food, clothes, raw materials, manufactured goods, etc., no such markets exist. This gap can only be bridged by market surveys. All companies resort to such studies when they want to establish their manufacturing and investment programs. The metallurgist will secure his supplies of ore and coke, study opportunities in different branches—mechanical engineering, energy, and housing. He will inform himself about the plans of his competitors. He makes his decisions only after having carefully examined his industrial environment. But he may overlook other fields of activity which seem far apart from his own but which are, however, likely to react on his own situation. The evolution of farmers' incomes, for instance, can have effects transmitted, step by step, to the whole economy. The production of tractors can influence the sales of steel.

The directing idea of indicative planning consists in integrating all these interdependent effects and extending to a nation-wide scale the behavior of the metallurgist in connection with his supplies and market opportunities. "Forecasts and long-term programs drawn up on a nation-wide scale in Western countries basically amount to nothing more than the transposition and generalization of the technique of commercial conventions in statute law" (R. Marjolin and Duquesne de la Vinelle).

The tool for these forecasts and programs is really François Quesnay's economic table, described by Mirabeau as "the great discovery which glorifies our century and will yield posterity its fruits." Posterity was kept waiting a long time, until Leontief gave economic tables their modern form and, in France, when M. Gruson developed National Economic Accounts.

An economic table is initially a description of material flows moving between the main sectors. But once assured that technological coefficients remain invariable, it becomes an instrument of forecast. If the production of the various sectors and the imports are known, one can directly obtain, by subtracting intermediate consumptions, the amount of goods and services available for general consumption, investment and export. Inversely one can take as a starting point consumption, considered as the true end of programming, and by means of reasonable assumptions concerning investment and foreign trade deduce the total production required. Inversely is the right word since mathematical computations consist of "inversing a matrix." This is how a first outline of the Plan is sketched.

The plan thus plays the part of a "generalized market." It is, however, drawn up at branch-activity—and socio-professional-category—level and does not deal with firms or individuals. This difference in scale, added to an urge for individual liberty and free choice of action, is a practical reason in favor of the French Plan being indicative and not imperative.

In this aggregative, and therefore approximative form, a general program is drawn up. Every branch of activity is promised the possibility of acquiring its production factors and selling its goods on a balanced market. The promise, however, is only kept if everybody plays the game. The promise acts merely as an incentive. It is not binding on anybody. Firms are not dispensed from working out their valuations and choosing their own attitude concerning risks. But they can do so in a better informed manner.

Partial adjustments remain necessary while the plan is being carried out, under the influence of the market, operating in a frame which allows it to work more smoothly. Thus the economy retains its flexibility and every participant a feeling of liberty.

Some people may think that this substitute role is rather modest. But one should not forget it is the real model of an unattainable mechanism. In so far as it attempts to bridge gaps and correct faults related to the spontaneous evolution of the economy it bears evidence of a will. Here we come across a basic problem which goes beyond the logic of the Plan and which concerns its ends. I shall deal with that in the last section of this paper.

IV. THE METHOD ADOPTED IN DRAWING UP THE PLAN

The method used in drawing up the Plan includes several stages which I can illustrate by describing our work on the Fourth Plan. In the first phase preliminary outlines are drawn up by the Commissariat du Plan in connection with the Department of Economic and Financial Studies of the Finance Ministry. The starting point of each of them, for the last year of the Plan, consists in a structure of final consumption accompanied by a hypothesis concerning foreign trade and the investment required to carry on expansion in the following plan. From such data, it is possible to set up an economic table for the last year, providing for each sector its purchases and sales to other sectors. According to a more or less detailed analysis, the overall economy is broken down in 17 or 28 sectors.

It is possible to work from production back to employment, and also, from investment expressed in physical terms to the needs for finance expressed in terms of value.

Without going into details one can state that the best sketch-plan is the one which allows for the maximum growth rate of the economy while taking into account basic equilibria: full employment, investment equal to savings, balance of public finance and of foreign payments. For instance, the sketches drawn up at the beginning of 1960 corresponded to three yearly growth rates of national production: 3, 4.5, and 6 per cent. The 6 per cent variable quickly appeared a little too ambitious because it led to a vulnerable balance of foreign payments with practically no safety margin.

Anyhow, before deciding, the government consulted the Investment and Planning Section of the Economic and Social Council, an Assembly of representatives of all active forces of the nation. This is new. It reinforces economic democracy and provides those who are often unfairly called technocrats with the possibility of broad contacts. The council drafted two valuable reports. One favored a high rate of growth. The other stressed the structure of final consumption emphasizing the necessity of developing collective investment in education, research, health, housing and culture.

After considering the various sketches and reports, the government gave the Commissariat, in June 1960, its directives to enable it to carry on the work. The directives said: "The goal of the Fourth Plan is to develop

France's economic means . . . to make France a great industrial metropolis capable of carrying out the nation's task and of improving the standard of life of the population."

Thus the country has been given two important targets. First, France must combine both her defense obligations and her commitments resulting from her inclusion in a network of particular alliances, in Europe and in Africa, with the broader tasks which confront all the Western nations. The second great target is the improvement of the living conditions of the French people. This expression does not only refer to increasing real purchasing power. The improvement of living conditions implies qualitative requirements. The limitations of industrial civilization are the counterparts of its benefits: long journeys between homes and offices, traffic jams, noises, smog, lack of social facilities and of green spaces. The long-term problem is one with which I shall deal in the last part of this paper.

The governmental directives ended the first stage of the Plan. We then entered the second stage and started working with the Modernization Commissions.

The Modernization Commissions, are of two different types "vertical" and "horizontal." The vertical commissions correspond to the various sectors of activity: agriculture, energy, chemistry, manufacturing industries, housing, education, social and health equipment, etc. These commissions provide the Plan's technical backbone. They enable the planners to move a step forward from the overall sketch to the more detailed programs for each sector. They determine the evolution of technological coefficients and the development of productivity. They select production techniques corresponding to the minimum total cost necessary to achieve their objectives.

Horizontal commissions work at maintaining basic equilibria. The Labor Commission deals with employment by qualification and by region. The Commission for General Economy and Financing adjusts investments and savings, public receipts and expenditure, currency movements. The Commission for Regional Plans tries to reduce imbalances which the spontaneous economic evolution may have caused between different areas.

The work of the Modernization Commissions which started last summer has just materialized in the shape of a first provisional synthesis. It shows that, provided certain appropriate measures are taken, there is no major obstacle to prevent our achieving a growth rate of 5 per cent which was the hypothesis chosen as a working basis. This growth rate can even be slightly improved on. What is possible links up here with what is desirable, meaning full employment of a working population which will grow by a million men and women between 1960 and 1965 while productivity gains tend to reduce, all things being equal, the demand for manpower. Thus the planned expansion will be compatible with an important reduction of active farming population and will only cause a moderate increase of the active industrial population. Major increases will affect people employed in housing, transport, trade, liberal professions, education.

Naturally the work of Modernization Commissions never tallies perfectly. One can roughly say that compared to the stage of preliminary outline, the Commissions bring more realism and less coherence. Any contradictions and antagonisms have to be overcome. To this effect views are exchanged between commission chairmen and officials. Sometimes common working groups are set up.

In this way, the Commissions in due course hand the Commissaire Général reports which one may hope will have ironed out most divergencies. The final synthesis of the plan then follows. A plenary session of the Economic and Social Council will be called to advise, and Parliament may debate the subject in time for final approval to be obtained before the plan is due to start.

V. MEANS OF EXECUTION

I must return here to the distinction between decisions to be made by the government and estimates related to probable economic evolution.

As far as decisions are concerned, nothing could be simpler. By approving the Plan, the government is morally obliged to set the example, which means that its budgetary, credit, taxation and price policies must fit into the framework of the planned development. The government's attitude, however, during the four years over which the Plan extends, is often influenced by short-term considerations or by outside economic factors. It can be said that day-by-day economic action is the result of compromises between the short and the long-term points of view. To overlook the first would be to ignore the demands of life. The Commissaire Général, while the Plan is being carried out, must be both very understanding and very firm.

On the side of psychology, two facts must be remembered. First, agreement achieved while the Plan was being drawn up tends spontaneously to extend itself when it comes to implementing the Plan. If the real forces of the country have been associated in the scheme, they are more likely to stand together in action.

A second reason for the Plan's success is its coherence, the fact that it foreshadows, if everybody plays the game, a situation in which inputs and outputs of different branches will be exchanged on balanced markets. For electricity, steel, cement, the Plan's valuations are relatively sound because they are concerned with factors affecting a great number of outputs and therefore errors tend to compensate each other. It is fortunate this should be so because the corresponding investments are so slow to materialize that alterations to the initial programs would be difficult and costly.

The field of ordinary goods is much more fluid. It is almost impossible to assess four years ahead which new gadget will be the public's craze. But here the situation is regulated by easy transformations and relatively quick-yielding investment.

There are cases which fall half way and are more difficult, such as that of the motor-car industry.

After the psychological effects let us take a look at the practical mechanisms.

There is, in the first place, state-controlled investment, government agencies' equipment, programs of nationalized enterprises, housing in which private initiative is largely dependent on state aid. Each of these sectors has an influence on other sectors upstream. For instance the SNCF (the nationalized railways) and Electricité de France have an influence on electrical equipment industries. It is no exaggeration to state that directly or indirectly the state controls or is the driving influence behind half the total national investment.

Finally—last but not least—the government has at its disposal incentives to facilitate the execution of programs which conform with the Plan's targets. These incentives are granted after separate examination of each case. Some consist in tax reduction affecting real estate taxes and increases in capital assets as well as a liberal interpretation of the rules applying to mother-companies and their subsidiaries. Other incentives amount to credit facilities and, exceptionally, may include cuts in interest rates. In case of success refundable subsidies can be granted for research purposes. Special agreements can help start new production. Finally, equipment premia depending on the amount invested and the number of new jobs created can be granted, in accordance with the spirit of the Rome Treaty,[1] in certain areas subject to difficulties.

VI. PROGRESS LEFT TO BE MADE

Certain criticisms have been voiced concerning our methods. I have even read that: "French plans are too often drawn up in vague and elliptical terms."[2]

It is true that we have up to now been reluctant to formulate completely the models underlying our plans. Three reasons explain our hesitation: the fact that any mistake in initial information or any improper approximation in drawing up our model may yield misleading results; the contrast between the elaborate and accurate algebra of the programming methods and the blurred picture of what remains uncertain, which has, however, to be taken into account; the difference between orientation

---

[1] [Establishing the European Common Market.—EDITOR.]

[2] S. Wellisz, "Economic Planning in the Netherlands, France, and Italy," *Journal of Political Economy*, Vol. LXVIII, No. 3 (June, 1960), pp. 252–83.

prices implicit in every model and the actual prices which may reflect irrational past development. I can add that the econometric theory of the optimum is based on the actualization method which amounts to admitting that all investments are financed through loans while in this respect firms cannot borrow beyond certain limits. In short we are faced here with a conflict between rationality and realism and have to discover, as Ragnar Frisch said, "the art of producing realistic models."

I speak all the more freely of this difficulty since I came across it myself and think I have solved it, in an important sector of activity, that of electric power, where goods are manufactured according to alternative techniques. Linear programming with about 200 unknowns enables one to draw up coherent, optimal and sufficiently realistic plans. But Electricité de France was successful only after several setbacks.

That period of my life will always remind me of the sweet taste of the "optimum." I plainly realize, however, the enormous difference between aggregate and sectorial optimums, especially when the sector involved has vast economic and statistical information available. Moreover, I have noticed that the Dutch Plan described by Mr. Wellisz as "the most explicit in its objectives and rigorous in its methods" only provides for partial optimization because, Mr. Wellisz claims, "the problem of long-term plannning practically amounts to choosing a level of imports calculated in order to maximize the *per capita* income." In particular, "no factor substitution is possible." I understand that our Dutch friends have now got beyond that stage.

I, myself, think it would be desirable to "replace in practice the Leontief model by a frame of thought taking into account the multiplicity of techniques" (Malinvaud). Practical reasons prevent us from going into great detail. But there could be, in each sector, the alternative "national production versus imports" or the alternative "a strongly capitalistic activity versus a moderately capitalistic activity." This would amount to an "extension of the input-output theory using optimization principles borrowed from programming" (Chenery and Kretschmer).

Progress on these lines which would not have been imagined possible ten years ago, is today within our power thanks to the computing power of electronic machines. It assumes the development of the economic education of responsible people and the existence of an "information plan" providing the programmer with the indispensable statistical material. It also requires an intellectual exploration which we have decided to undertake and which will be the task of a small team subsidized by the National Fund for Scientific and Technical Research. This involves a comparative test of the cost and the usefulness of the anticipated progress.

We already accomplish a first optimalization of an overall character by choosing the highest growth rate which a cautious estimate gives as compatible with the basic equilibria of the economy. One can wonder with J. K. Galbraith if we have thus achieved the essential, in other words, if full employment of production factors is not comparatively much more important than the best way of employing them. Personally I tend to think that both are of great importance and that is why I pin great hopes on the research I have just been speaking of.

It seems to me to be essential, using modern methods and machines to increase the variety of alternative programs and replace the exploration of a large range of possibilities by the thorough exploration of fewer possibilities in order to avoid being caught unprepared to meet future hazards. This should not raise any fundamental objection if you bear in mind that the plan is merely a frame meant to guide action and not a detailed, accurate picture of what the economy may become in four years' time.

The paths of progress I have just indicated have an internal link with the character of our organization. There is another path for progress which I shall refer to briefly. It is the extension of planning on a national scale to planning on a multinational scale.

I know quite well that in the Western world "Planning" is not a very good label. But it has acquired in France a significance which would make it difficult for us to give it up.

Anyhow if one tries to face facts rather than be contented with words, the problem our countries will have to face is that of preconcerted development programs on a multinational scale. If I may give my personal opinion, it seems to me that the reasons which have been found good at nation-wide scale also apply to a group of nations. The question could have been evaded so long as the European area was partitioned by a protective system of quotas and tariffs. It is bound to come up inside large economic zones now being formed such as the Common Market, whatever form these zones will take. One may even ask if some of the apprehensions which are voiced in certain quarters would not be swept away by preconcerted development programs. In such a delicate matter it is best, however, to advance cautiously and every step forward should be preceded by proper exploration. Before speaking of programs, preconcerted development studies could be drawn up. To begin with these would be limited to essential points. The first which comes to the mind is to try to obtain agreement on the growth rate desirable, taking into account the special conditions prevailing in each country. It looks as if open frontiers must be accompanied by expansion policies which do not present striking differences between one another, if the desired equilibrium of exchanges is to be attained at a high level. If agreement were reached on this point, the next step would be, following the empirical approach of the Monnet plan, to collate development programs in basic activities and key-sectors, in order to avoid the kinds of overcapacity which seem to arise in certain branches. Naturally every country may think it is going to win the race. But it ought to consider that the other nations think precisely the same. I certainly admit the merit of competition as a stimulant but one must recognize the boundary between incentive and wastage, especially when costly investment is concerned.

President Kennedy's words concerning political antagonism seem to me to apply particularly well to economic competition: "We should not negotiate out of fear, but we should never be afraid to negotiate."

VII. THE PLAN'S GOALS

The problem of the long-term goal of the Plan has not really been brought up until recently. Immediate demands were too pressing for a serene reflection on the future. To rebuild the ruins of the war, to equip and modernize basic activities, to render production competitive, to restore basic equilibria, to promote economic expansion while maintaining monetary stability, were clear and simple targets.

But as development progresses, several choices begin to appear. Unimportant when related to a single plan they may, over a generation, alter living conditions. The problem thus looming ahead is none other than that of basic orientations in a modern society.

A certain number of choices have been taken into account in the Fourth Plan. But to be truthful, only on a timid scale. Significant choices, however, will be made.

The first choice provided for, in accordance with a recommendation made by the Economic and Social Council related to the desirable final demand structure, stresses the need for collective investment services rather than increases in consumers's goods for households. Such collective investment covers essential or, so far, insufficiently developed sectors: scientific and technical research, health, culture, education, housing and urbanization equipment. In particular the Fourth Plan will pay more attention to the growth of towns, which affect the development of the tertiary sector.

The second choice is related to social action in aid of the less favored sections of the population: families, aged people, wage-earners with small pay packets, agricultural laborers and students.

The third choice refers to regional action to lessen disequilibria between different areas. Disparity is a natural phenomenon. Paris and Lyon are crossroads. Marseilles, Bordeaux, Nantes, Le Havre have developed around sheltered harbors or estuaries. Other towns have prospered because they were next to the mineral resources of the north, the center or the east. However, new centers of interest have appeared. Signs of aging and saturation are becoming visible. He who grew old first will age first. All these factors amount on the present economic and social map of France to disparities in population, in dynamism, in employment, and in income.

The economic theory of optimal localization is less advanced than that of the optimal allocation of resources. One must therefore be contented, as far as regional action is concerned, with relatively rough criteria. If we distinguish—a rather improper simplification—dynamic and stagnant regions, one can say that the Fourth Plan provides for a supporting policy in dynamic areas and a driving policy in certain well-selected points of the stagnant areas.

Finally we must also mention a negative choice, in one way symmetrical to the previous positive choices. To enable a rapid expansion, creating employment for the numerous youths who will soon reach working age, to facilitate the important collective investment I have just mentioned, and contribute through higher incomes to the elimination of certain shocking situations, we have dropped the idea of reducing working hours. Extended leisure, which remains a valid economic long-term policy, cannot be envisaged until the Fourth Plan has been a success.

These rather limited modifications affect, however, certain essential options. What contents will men give the Affluent Society which Galbraith heralds? Will it be power, consumption, creation, or leisure? More precisely in what proportion will complementary objectives have to be combined? Taking a prospective view on development is a different function from that of setting up plans and programs. The planner, according to the French conception, has to prepare, with very limited means, a stage of coherent development on the lines suggested by the preferences of the nation. He may have, as a citizen, his personal preferences. But he is no judge.

The judge of his preferences is the nation itself through its political institutions. The verdict is not at all evident, if it is true, as Valery once wrote, that: "nothing can be more difficult than to determine the true interests of a nation, which should not be confused with its wishes." The choice must at least be made openly. It is the role of forward thinking and perhaps too, on a different level, that of the programmer submitting to the government and public opinion a few alternative variables to the plan. A first modest attempt has been made in this direction during the period of preliminary outlining of the Fourth Plan. We shall try to do better in the future, as we remain faithful to the initial inspiration which considers that the Plan's success depends on the largest possible convergence of minds and the active enlistment of all goodwill.

Yugoslavia: Market Socialism

Yugoslavia is the only true example of a market socialist economy which combines public ownership with decentralized resource allocation through markets and prices. As a result, the organization, operation, and performance of the Yugoslav economy are of great interest not only to economic theorists and students of comparative economic systems, but also to policy makers both inside and outside the Communist orbit. The Yugoslav experience has been followed closely in many newly independent, less developed countries committed to government ownership and entrepreneurship but aware of the enormous difficulties of comprehensive, detailed central planning. To these countries, the Yugoslav economy has appeared to offer a promising model which could be adapted to their own economic and cultural circumstances.

The contemporary Yugoslav economy both resembles and differs from the theoretical model of market socialism described in Part II above. Its similarities include (1) public ownership; (2) a combination of consumers' and planners' sovereignty; and (3) decentralized decision making by enterprises in response to market forces, instead of detailed planning and administrative orders in physical terms by the central authorities. At the same time, the Yugoslav economy differs from the Lange model of market socialism in several important respects: (1) Prices, with some exceptions, are determined by market forces, rather than set centrally. (2) Enterprises do not follow the Lange rules for choosing outputs and inputs but instead attempt to maximize profits. (3) Investment funds are not rationed by an equilibrium interest rate. (4) Workers councils play a major role in enterprise management.

Yugoslavia has devised its own answers to the problems, such as imperfect competition and managerial incentives, raised by the critics of the theoretical model of market socialism. It has also had to deal with problems of foreign trade and agricultural organization not considered in the theoretical writings on market socialism. The Yugoslav economy thus offers a unique and original example of market socialism, adapted to Yugoslavia's particular economic, political, and cultural conditions. The following article offers a comprehensive survey of the Yugoslav economic system.

J. Marcus Fleming and Viktor R. Sertic

14. THE YUGOSLAV ECONOMIC
SYSTEM*

This article analyzes the main characteristics and problems of the Yugoslav market socialist economy. The authors explain the nature and operation of the socialist enterprise, the role of the workers council, and the formation of prices and wages. They describe the private agricultural sector which exists alongside the socialist economy. They show how the central authorities exert control over autonomous socialist enterprises through monetary and fiscal measures, financing of investment, and regulation of foreign trade.

YUGOSLAVIA is a federal state in which there are four levels of government: Federation, Republics, Districts, and Communes. In this political organism, the main economic functions are exercised by the Federation and by the Communes.

The Yugoslav economic system has many features that differentiate it both from the collectivist economies of the Soviet pattern and from the more or less capitalistic economies of the West, with their varying combinations of private and public initiative in the economic sphere. In the early part of the postwar period, Yugoslavia ran its economic affairs on the Soviet model, with public ownership and state management in industry and trade, with collective farms and compulsory deliveries in agriculture, with prices of all sorts fixed by authority, and with detailed central planning not only of investment but also of the current operation of enterprises. Since 1950, a transition has been taking place toward a much freer type of economy which, while it retains public ownership of all but the smallest enterprises in industry and trade, affords a greatly increased

* Reprinted, with permission, from *International Monetary Fund Staff Papers*, Vol. IX, No. 2 (July, 1962), pp. 202–23. The authors are economists of the International Monetary Fund.

scope for the initiative of consumers, farmers, and enterprises, whose activities are increasingly coordinated through the market mechanism.

By now, central economic planning, operating mainly through measures of fiscal and credit policy—including long-term investment credits—and decreasingly through direct intervention, is largely confined to determining or influencing (1) the allocation of national resources between saving and consumption, (2) the geographical and sectoral distribution of new investment, (3) the degree of participation in world markets, and (4) the distribution of national income between different groups in the population and different public authorities. The scale and composition of current output are, as a rule, decided in the prodution units themselves, in response to the economic incentives provided by markets that are increasingly free from price control. In certain cases, however, local governments influence the decisions of the production units on the basis of noneconomic considerations.

While many of the economic functions performed by the State in Yugoslavia are also the responsibility of the State in other noncollectivist countries, there are important differences between Yugoslavia and these countries, both in the organizational structure of the economy and in the scope of state intervention. As mentioned above, all enterprises employing more than a few persons are in public ownership. More important, the operation of each enterprise in the socialized sector is largely controlled by the employees of that enterprise; and the workers are paid, not by a wage representing in some sense a market price of labor, but rather by a share in the gross profits of the enterprise after deduction of cost of materials, depreciation, and various taxes.

An important feature of the system is the high level of taxation which, when supplemented by substantial savings on the part of enterprises, provides the means to finance an exceptionally high level of investment and is largely responsible for the rapid pace of economic growth and industrialization. Since a substantial proportion of national investment is financed out of funds directly controlled by the central authorities, and since long-term lending between enterprises has not been allowed until recently, the authorities are in a position to ensure that the distribution of investment between the different branches of activity conforms fairly closely to pre-established investment plans. In addition to the savings put at the direct disposal of the central authorities, there are a variety of general and special purpose investment funds accumulated, partly out of taxation, by enterprises, public institutions, and local authorities. The use of such funds is subject to various restrictions and regulations imposed from time to time. The National Bank, which now firmly controls the banking system, has not only, as in other countries, the function of regulating the supply of short-term and medium-term credit and controlling the supply of money in the light of the general degree of demand pressure prevailing in the country, but also the function of recording

the transactions of enterprises and institutions and controlling the fulfillment of legal obligations.[1]

THE INDIVIDUAL ENTERPRISE IN YUGOSLAVIA

Private enterprises in Yugoslavia are confined by law to small-scale
production and trade (employing no more than five people, plus the
owner's family) and to farms not normally exceeding ten hectares in size.
Socialized enterprises and institutions account for much the greater part of
the employment and output in the country outside agriculture and handicrafts, where private enterprise still predominates.

The individual enterprise in the socialized sector enjoys a relatively
high degree of freedom from state control. Within a framework of laws
and general regulations, its management is legally in the hands of its own
workers, whose incomes are dependent on its profitability.

New enterprises may, in principle, be established by public authorities,
associations, enterprises, or individuals; but since the founder of an enterprise has to guarantee any loans raised to finance the initial capital stock,
while having no right, as founder, to control or draw income from the
new enterprise, it is not surprising that in practice most enterprises are set
up by public authorities, particularly the Communes.

Once an enterprise is established and its working force recruited, it is
put under the control of a Workers Council representing all its workers.
An Executive Board (elected by the Council) and a Director, the legal
representative of the enterprise (appointed by agreement between the
Workers Council and the Commune), are responsible for the implementation of the Council's decisions and for day-to-day management.

The enterprise is then free to determine the composition of its output,
its methods of production, and the scale of its output and employment, but
it is not always free from a measure of influence over its decisions exerted
by the Commune. It may purchase its materials freely, except that many
materials are still subject to import restrictions. It may sell its products at
the best prices it can obtain, save for certain commodities which are
subject to price ceilings or other more flexible controls over prices, and a
few on which there are export controls. It may borrow from banks and
investment funds and may hold money on deposit with banks; but, until
recently, borrowing from or lending to other enterprises was not permitted, with the important exception of short-term trade credit. In 1961,
however, certain basic regulations were introduced to permit and facilitate
lending between enterprises.

The enterprise in the socialized sector has to hand over a considerable
portion of its income to the public authorities, and its disposal of what
remains is, in part, determined by legal regulations. Regulation and taxa-

---

[1] Apart from footnotes 2 and 5, this article is based on the situation as at the end
of March 1962.

tion, however, are so applied as to retain, as far as possible, a pecuniary incentive to efficient operation.

The receipts of the enterprise, after payment of working costs, excluding wages but including interest on loans and credits, are subject to compulsory deductions for (1) depreciation of fixed assets, (2) a tax known as "interest" on fixed and working capital owned by the enterprise, (3) miscellaneous taxes and membership fees, and (4) turnover taxes. What is left of the receipts of the enterprise after these deductions is known as its income and is subject to a profits tax, or "contribution," as it is called. Until recently, the rate at which this tax was levied was higher, the higher the net income of the enterprise relative to a hypothetical wage and salary bill, calculated on the basis of minimum wage rates. This progressive tax was considered to give enterprises too little incentive to increase productivity; and in the 1961 tax reform, it was replaced by a flat rate tax, amounting in most industries to 15 per cent. However, some progressivity—though less than that prevailing formerly—has been retained for the time being through the imposition of the temporary excess profits tax referred to below.

The net income of the enterprise, after payment of the above "contribution," is allocated between (1) personal incomes of the workers and (2) the business funds of the enterprise, to be used, for the most part, in the financing of new investment. When making this allocation, the enterprise has to observe certain rules: (a) the payment of minimum wages takes priority over other expenditures; (b) a reserve fund has to be established by the enterprise and a contribution has to be made to the reserve fund established by the Commune, to guarantee to workers of the enterprise and of the Commune, respectively, the payment of minimum wages; and (c) out of any increases in income, not more should, in theory at least, be assigned to increased personal incomes than may be held to arise from increased productivity or business efficiency.

The amounts allocated to the personal incomes of workers and to the business funds of the enterprise are subject to further taxation: of the amount allocated to wages, the enterprise has to pay 15 per cent to the communal budgets and 24 per cent to the Social Insurance Fund; of the amount added to the business funds of the enterprise, it has to contribute 20 per cent to the communal investment funds and 4 per cent to the communal housing fund. Moreover, if, during any year, an enterprise realizes enough income to allocate to its own funds, after payment of taxes and wages, an amount representing more than 6 per cent of its assets, it is considered as having made an excess profit, and 25 per cent of the excess has to be paid to the federal budget.

Each of the capital funds of the enterprise—the depreciation fund, the reserve fund, and the investment fund—is kept in a special bank account, subject to its own special set of regulations and separate from the ordinary giro account or working balance of the enterprise.

In general, enterprises in the socialized sector are very heavily taxed. If the present tax system had been in operation in 1959, 28 per cent of the net value added of enterprises would have been allotted to take-home pay, 20 per cent to personal income taxes and social insurance, 41 per cent to business taxes and other compulsory payments to government budgets and social funds, and 11 per cent to funds owned by the enterprise. The amount thus distributed is arrived at after allocation, to the depreciation fund, of 11 per cent of gross value added.

Despite the weight of taxation, the combined effect of the various regulations governing the distribution of the income of socialized enterprises is such that enterprises retain a real incentive to increase productivity and to economize in the use of materials.

Yugoslav firms are enrolled in compulsory associations or Chambers, which foster research and high productivity, and generally serve as an intermediary between the enterprise and the State. Though generally lacking in mandatory powers, they sometimes organize agreements fixing maximum buying prices for raw materials. Enterprises are also allowed to form business associations with power to make contracts and to organize joint production, marketing and purchasing, etc. There are certain safeguards, whose efficiency is difficult to gauge, against combination in restraint of trade.

The socialized enterprise can expand its capital stock by investment out of its own resources or by borrowing from from one or another of the social (public) investment funds. In the latter event, it usually has to put up part of the money from its own funds and often has to obtain a guarantee from the Commune. It pays a somewhat higher rate of interest on such loans than the capital tax payable on that part of the capital against which no loan is outstanding.

Finally, the socialized enterprise may be wound up by the local authority if it fails to meet its financial obligations, including taxes and wages on the minimum scale prescribed by law.

Agriculture and handicrafts are carried on for the most part by enterprises in which the means of production are privately owned. In agriculture, some 90 per cent of the land under systematic cultivation is owned by independent peasant proprietors, who number over 2.6 million. The remaining 10 per cent of the land is under public ownership. Half of it is cultivated by about 560 economic organizations operating, as in other branches of the economy, under workers' management. The other half is cultivated partly by collective farms of the general Eastern European type (Peasant Workers' Cooperatives) which, until 1953—before provision was made for every peasant to leave the cooperatives—played an important part in Yugoslav agriculture; and partly by cooperatives of a looser type which are designed to play an increasingly important role vis-à-vis the independent peasant farmers. The latter type of cooperative provides productivity-enhancing services for the private farmers with a view to gaining their confidence and their voluntary cooperation in expanding the socialist system of production in agriculture.

Private ownership of agricultural land in Yugoslavia is practically confined to those who cultivate it, and even cultivators are not allowed to own or rent more than 10 hectares (i.e., some 25 acres) or, in some exceptional cases, 15 hectares. Subject to these limitations (which do not apply to socialized and collective farms), land can be bought and sold, bequeathed and rented. Peasant proprietors may acquire other means of production freely, but lack of resources and exclusion from the price subsidies granted to socialized farms and cooperatives practically preclude them from acquiring any heavy or modern farm equipment. Private peasants run their farms as they wish, buy materials, and sell their products freely. They can borrow from the cooperative savings banks organized under the Agricultural Bank; but for long-term capital expansion they are dependent on their savings, since practically all the money invested in agriculture by the social investment funds goes to socialized farms and to agriculture cooperatives.

The economic role of the private farms is considerably less important, relative to that of the socialized and collective farms, than their respective acreages would suggest. They are small and ill equipped. While the socialized and collective farms and cooperative societies are well provided with tractors and other farm machinery, less than half the private holdings possess a plough, and less than 40 per cent a horse or other draft animal. The socialized and collective farms, under the guidance of agricultural experts, also apply more modern methods than do the private farms. Moreover, private farms are small—averaging, as they do, only some 4.6 hectares, against 670 hectares for the average socialized farm and 350 hectares for the average collective farm. As a result, crop yields per acre are about twice as high on socialized and collective farms as on private farms. Moreover, private farms, with low per capita productivity, produce mainly for home consumption, while the socialized and collective farms produce almost entirely for the market.

The role of the agricultural cooperatives is interesting and important. Membership is voluntary. Their financial resources are provided partly by the members and partly by the State. They provide many services, for payment, to both members and nonmembers. Thus, they purchase and market farm products; they sort and process such products; they procure and sell producer and consumer goods to farmers; they manufacture building materials, furniture, footwear, etc., for the village population; they accept savings deposits and provide short-term and long-term credit; they hire out tractors and farm machinery; and, recently, they have taken to organizing farm production on modern lines for peasant farmers on a profit-sharing basis. Some of the profits earned by such cooperatives are distributed to members, but most of them are retained to expand the resources of the cooperatives.

The Yugoslav authorities appear to be pinning their hopes for an improvement in the efficiency of Yugoslav agriculture partly on a growth of the socialized sector and partly on the work of these cooperatives with the independent peasants. It seems, however, that the voluntary cooperation of peasant farmers with the agricultural cooperatives has recently experienced some setbacks. A number of cooperatives, encouraged by the authorities to take up loans for the purchase of additional agricultural machinery, may have incurred excessive credit obligations and are not now in a position fully to service their loans. For the time being, these financial difficulties create a climate between independent peasant farmers and cooperatives that is not conducive to closer cooperation. Thus, in their effort to increase productivity in agriculture, the authorities, at present, emphasize the expansion of the socialized sector in agriculture.

WAGE AND PRICE FORMATION

In the enterprises of the socialized sector—as distinct from public institutions, such as hospitals, banks, etc.—workers are paid essentially by a share in the profits, and the wage has largely lost its function as a price of labor. This statement calls for certain qualifications, however. In the first place, there are minimum wages, set by the State. These are uniform throughout the country, but differentiated according to numerous groups of enterprises and categories of workers. An enterprise may not pay less than the minimum wage, and some—a few—unprofitable enterprises cannot afford to pay more. In most instances, however, minimum wages are far below the incomes actually received by workers.

The enterprise establishes its own scale of wages based on the prospective profits of the enterprise and on the desired allocation of these profits between personal incomes and the funds of the enterprise. These wages are influenced, however, though to a diminishing extent, by the trade unions and by the Producers Council of the local Commune. The trade unions, having no need to bargain for higher wages—since the enterprise itself is managed by its workers—try to minimize discrepancies in wage scales where these are not justified by differences in productive efficiency. Over and above the regular wage scales, quarterly or annual bonuses may be given in order to raise the total personal incomes of the workers to the desired proportion of gross profits. Attempts are made by the Communes to ensure that any abnormally high profits attributable to factors other than high personal efficiency are ploughed back into the enterprise rather than distributed as current earnings. If profits prove not to be high enough to cover the wages already paid, the deficit will be met either out of the reserves or other available resources of the enterprise or by short-term financing from the communal reserve fund.

While for the workers of the enterprise as a group the level of wages is largely governed by the level of profits, wage scales retain considerable importance in determining the relative wages of different types of workers and, through piece-rate systems, in providing the workers individually with an incentive to produce. To an increasing extent, however, the attempt is being made to provide this incentive by paying workers in particular units of the enterprise on the basis of the profits accountable to these units.[2]

Prices in Yugoslavia, for the most part, are freely determined by demand and supply on the domestic market, but the supplies and prices are very much influenced not only by domestic turnover and sales taxes but also by instruments of foreign trade policy, such as custom duties, export subsidies, and export restrictions.

Foreign trade (the average of imports and exports) is equivalent to some 18 per cent of Yugoslavia's social product, and the freedom with which, and terms on which, goods can be exported and imported have a great influence on the structure of relative prices on the domestic market. As a result of measures taken late in 1961 and early in 1962, the multiple exchange rate system with its so-called settlement rate (Din 632 per U.S. dollar) and its numerous "coefficients"—which had resulted in effective exchange rates running from 80 per cent to 250 per cent of the settlement rate—has been replaced by a system with a uniform exchange rate (Din 750 per U.S. dollar), supplemented, however, by subsidies amounting to 10 per cent, 22 per cent, and 32 per cent on various types of exports, and by substantial customs duties on manufactured imports. Moreover, despite a liberalization of imports in 1961, more than 70 per cent of imports are still subject to some form of quantitative restriction. The discrepancy between the prices of various foreign trade goods on the world market and their prices on Yugoslavia's domestic market has been considerably lessened by the shift from multiple exchange rates to import duties *cum* export subsidies and by the relaxation of import restrictions. Nevertheless, domestic prices of agricultural products (especially essential foods), fuel, and raw materials, and, to a lesser extent, semifinished products are still relatively low, while those of manufactured consumer goods, exportable capital goods, and luxury foodstuffs are still relatively high, compared with those prevailing in most western industrial countries. As a result, the production of industrial goods is still favored over that of agricultural and forestry products. The consequential diversion of income from agriculture, which is lightly taxed, to industry and trade, which is heavily taxed, has in the past made it easier to skim off a high proportion of national income in taxation and hence to attain that high level of public saving and investment which is largely responsible for the pace of industrialization. The same factors, however, bear some responsibility for the relatively lagging devel-

---

[2] In April 1962, the Federal Government issued an order setting out the principles and methods to be applied by enterprises when distributing their incomes, and also established by lot special committees for assisting and supervising workers' councils in the distribution of enterprise incomes.

opment of agriculture. The price distortions involved have also had a bad effect, misdirecting not only current production but also new investment, whether financed by enterprises or by social funds.

In their efforts progressively to remove these distortions in the price structure, the Yugoslav authorities have adopted the price pattern prevailing in the economies of Yugoslavia's convertible currency trading partners as the main standard by which to guide their price policies. In the course of the coming years, most prices on the domestic market are to be brought gradually into alignment with this price pattern, by means of appropriate investment and import policies, and above all by the planned gradual elimination of export subsidies and import restrictions. In this way, the authorities will attempt to correct the misleading price incentives to consumption, production, and investment, still embedded in the foreign exchange system.

Though prices, in general, are formed rather freely on the domestic markets, those of some goods and services are subject to varying degrees of regulation. Thus, the prices of a few goods and services (sugar, tobacco manufactures, and electric current) are fixed by the federal authorities. Federal price ceilings are still applied to materials in short supply, mainly domestically produced: crude oil and its derivatives, coke, steel products, copper, lead, zinc, aluminum, cement, some basic chemical raw materials, pulp, cellulose, kraft paper and bags, newsprint, artificial fibers, raw hides, wool, fodder of industrial origin, and pharmaceuticals. Altogether, goods still subject to ceilings comprise about 25 per cent of total domestic output of raw materials and semimanufactures. Price ceilings are also set locally for house rents and for utilities, such as public transport. Attempts, not always completely successful, are made to adjust ceiling prices to changes in production costs and in world market prices.

In addition to these definite measures of price fixing and price limitation, a looser system of advance notice and control of price changes is applied to important sectors of the consumer goods trades, comprising less than half of total consumption. This control is exercised at the retail level by the Communes, at the wholesale level by the Republics, and at the production level by the federal authorities. Enterprises are required to give the authorities one month's notice of intended increases in prices, together with a justification in terms of production costs, i.e., costs of materials, amortization at prescribed rates, labor costs, and "normal" income over and above labor costs—all these being calculated on the basis of the utilization of the plant to full capacity. Only a very small proportion of requests for price increases have been questioned by the federal authorities, and such questioning has often been accompanied by other governmental intervention, designed to reduce production costs. However, the facts that justification is required for price increases, and that permission can in the last resort be refused, must exercise a stablizing influence on prices. The range of goods subject to advance notice and control of price changes is being steadily reduced.

The general effect of these measures of price control is to keep house rents and the prices of public utility services, essential consumer goods, and raw materials lower than would otherwise result from the structure of production and consumption and the present foreign exchange and foreign trade system. Except as applied to monopolies and public utilities, price control is not regarded as a permanent feature of the Yugoslav economy, but rather as a temporary expedient to deal with the maladjustments and inflationary tendencies associated with the change-over to a more decontrolled type of economy. Not only has the range of goods covered by the various types of controls been gradually reduced, but scarcities have been relieved by raising certain controlled prices, for instance, house rents and tariffs on electricity.

In Yugoslavia, as in many other countries, the authorities guarantee minimum support prices on certain farm products, to be implemented, if necessary, by government purchase. Support prices are set for cereal, wine, beans, and quality livestock. The purpose of the support guarantees is to give the farmer a sense of security. In practice, market prices have always been above support levels, and since the 1961 foreign exchange reform they have shown a further substantial rise.

The absence of rigid wage costs inherent in the profit-sharing system of Yugoslavia, together with a spirit of competitiveness between the different enterprises, should make product prices more flexible than in other countries. If this were so it would be possible, by controlling the supply of money and the level of investment, to maintain the stability of the general price level, and also to bring about changes in relative prices—e.g., the changes in the relative prices of agricultural and industrial goods implicit in the recent trade and exchange reform—without detriment to the growth of output. It does not seem, however, that this potentiality has yet been fully realized. The workers expect to see their real wages grow *pari passu* with increases in productivity, or in relation to those of other workers, even when—owing, e.g. to bad harvests or to changes in relative prices of the type mentioned above—these aims may not be compatible with full employment. To achieve these aims, the enterprises may keep industrial prices from falling, or even raise them when the market situation does not warrant it. There will then be strong pressure on the banking system to expand credit so as to maintain production near to capacity. Unless this pressure is resisted, a sort of cost-induced inflationary pressure may develop; if it is resisted, those responsible for pricing in enterprises will probably come to realize the need for flexibility in the face of market situations.

FISCAL SYSTEM

The fiscal system in Yugoslavia exercises an important influence on the rate of saving, on the distribution of income, and on the incentives to invest in different branches of production.

The total amount of taxes, including those accruing to the social investment loan funds and other social funds (but excluding social security contributions, loan interest, and compulsory depreciation allowances), may be estimated at about one third of social product as calculated in Yugoslavia, and about the same proportion of national income as calculated according to western definitions.[3] An important tax reform was introduced early in 1961 which, though designed to leave the over-all tax yield unchanged, had a marked effect on the structure of the fiscal revenue. The structure of taxation before and after the reform was as follows:[4]

	Former Fiscal System (Per cent of total fiscal revenue)	New Fiscal System (Per cent of total fiscal revenue)
Capital tax	18	24
Turnover tax	24	28
Profits tax	31	18
Wage bill tax	11	13
Other local taxes	11	12
Tax on income earned outside the socialized sector	5	5
	100	100

Tax rates differentiate considerably between industries and between the socialized and the private sectors of the economy. The capital tax ("interest"), which is confined to the socialized sector, is nominally 6 per cent of the capital of the enterprise; but since lower rates are allowed to industries where profits are low and to those which it is desired to encourage, the average rate is only 4 per cent. Agriculture, both private and socialized, pays no capital tax. Turnover and sales taxes are applied partly for the purpose of absorbing profits considered to be abnormal, and they vary widely between industries. All essential foodstuffs (except salt and sugar), electric power, fuel, steel, and rolling stock are exempt from these taxes. A federal turnover tax, applied to more than 50 per cent of the goods produced, averages between 10 and 15 per cent, but the rate is generally higher for rubber manufactures, paper, and chemicals; for some consumer goods (large automobiles), it is as high as 65 per cent. Though an attempt is made to confine this tax to a single stage of production, there are cases—in textiles and metals—where it is levied at several stages. In addition, a federal turnover tax of ½ per cent was introduced in 1961 on all sales by economic enterprises.[5] The tendency over recent years has been

---

[3] Gross national product according to western definitions may be as much as 120 per cent, and national income as much as 105 per cent, of social product according to Yugoslav definitions which, being constructed on Marxist lines, exclude many services.

[4] These proportions are derived from a national application of the relevant tax rates to 1959 data.

[5] In April 1962 the tax was increased from ½ per cent to 1 per cent.

for turnover taxes on raw materials and semifinished goods to decline, and for those on finished goods to increase. Communal taxes on retail sales average between 3 and 5 per cent.

Profits and wage taxes also differentiate between sectors and between industries, though less so than in former years. Thus, the profits tax is confined to enterprises in the socialized sector; and even within that sector, it applies less severely to certain industries, and not at all to agriculture. Mining enterprises pay a special tax, which was introduced in 1961. This, however, does not represent a discrimination against mining as such, but is an attempt to tax away the greater part (80 per cent) of the rent element in the income of individual mining enterprises. The excess profits tax, by its very nature, bears more heavily on some industries than on others, and, like turnover taxes, is partly intended to reduce differences in the rate of profits earned in different economic branches. The tax on wages is uniform, at 15 per cent, throughout most socialized enterprises, but is less both for socialized agriculture and for private enterprise. There is also a surtax on personal incomes, which does not apply to agricultural producers.

Private farmers are taxed relatively lightly. While about one half of the gross income of socialized enterprises goes to pay taxes other than social insurance, the farmer pays a tax averging 16 to 17 per cent of the cadastral (conventionally computed) income, which is currently somewhat below the actual income of his farm.

It will be seen that these tax differentiations tend to offset in part the effects of the price policies, discussed in the previous section, on the incomes of different economic branches. Alternatively, it may be said that these price policies divert income into those sectors and industries where high differential rates of tax can be applied. The latter aspect is the more important where the price spread between industry and agriculture is concerned, but the former is the more important for the price spread between industries producing more essential, as against those producing less essential, goods.

The revenues from taxation are distributed among the budgets of the Federation, Republics, Districts, and Communes, the social investment loan funds, and special social funds. Roughly 60 per cent of the revenues accrue to the budgets and 40 per cent to the various social funds; of the latter, the social investment loan funds, which finance general economic investment, receive by far the biggest share. The special social funds are set aside for projects of a specifically "social" character, such as housing, the promotion of agriculture and forestry, water supply, roads, the training of personnel, etc. There is also a social security fund supported by social insurance contributions.

The federal budget receives the lion's share (60 per cent) of total budgetary receipts, including the receipts of government agencies, establishments, and firms, as well as tax revenues. The communes receive close to 20 per cent, and the remainder is fairly equally divided between Republics and Districts.

The expenditure side of Yugoslav budgets calls for no great comment, except to say that, over the last three years, about half of the federal budget was spent on defense, about 5 per cent on subsidizing the budgets of the Republics (which in turn pass on part of what they receive to Districts and Communes), and some 15 per cent on subsidizing the economy, especially agriculture, in various ways. Expenditure on export assistance, which in 1961 constituted almost 10 per cent of budgetary expenditure, should gradually disappear.

In general, the principle of budget balance is maintained. Under regulations introduced in 1961, banks are forbidden to extend credit to governments of Republics, Districts, and Communes. In an emergency, these governments may draw on reserve funds accumulated for this purpose. The Federation also plans to spend less than it receives, and though in the course of the year the Federal Government may borrow up to a certain amount, which has to be repaid before the end of the same year, its accounts on a cash basis have recently been in balance or surplus.

FINANCING OF INVESTMENT

The level of saving and investment in Yugoslavia is extremely high. Net investment in 1961 amounted to some 35 per cent of the social product; close to 6 per cent was financed from abroad, leaving some 29 per cent to be covered by domestic saving. If investment and saving were expressed in proportion to net national income on western definitions, the percentages would be rather similar. Social welfare investment, private construction, and administrative investment amount to some 9 per cent of the social product, leaving some 26 per cent for directly productive investment. Of this, on average, 90 per cent may represent investment in the socialized sector.

The share of private investment in directly productive investment depends largely on the year's agricultural output. Given their rather stable level of consumption requirements, private peasant farmers allocate to investment much of the additional income accruing to them in good years, thus raising their share in total investment. Even in agriculture's record year 1959, however, the share of private investment did not exceed 14 per cent.

The very high rate of saving is achieved partly through collective saving out of taxation and partly through saving of a more voluntary character by socialized enterprises and private farmers. Most investment finance is provided in the form of loans, but the need to repay the loans over a rather short period is a factor tending to augment the amounts saved by enterprises and local authorities.

In earlier postwar years, practically all investment was financed from taxation, and investible funds were provided directly by the authorities, largely in grants. By now, a considerable degree of decentralization has taken place. Nevertheless, investment policy remains the principal instrument of central planning in Yugoslavia.

The use of budgetary allocations is confined to the financing of investment in the fields of health, education, welfare, etc.—about 3 per cent of total investment. Much the greater part of the public financing of investment is done through social investment funds, at the levels of Federation, Republics, Districts, and Communes, by the investment funds of state institutions, and by a variety of specialized local funds, notably the housing funds. The investment funds of public institutions finance their own investment needs. The other funds, however, lend money for investment by enterprises and cooperatives. Only exceptionally do the social investment funds now provide money to investors on a grant basis—mainly for railways, roads, ports, and airports. The general investment fund subsidizes, to a certain extent, the investment funds of particularly underdeveloped Republics and regions, but the latter funds are used to make loans, rather than grants, to the ultimate investors. The social investment funds are administered by banks: the funds of the Federation and Republics, by the Investment and Agricultural Banks; and those of Districts and Communes by the Communal and Agricultural Banks. This mode of administration has the advantage, compared with budgetary allocations, of maintaining greater continuity of operation and of facilitating closer financial scrutiny of projects.

Another factor making for decentralization is the increasing importance of self-financing by enterprises through compulsory amortization funds and voluntary investment funds. These now account for some 30 per cent of gross investment financed by the social sector.

Despite these developments, the central authorities retain a considerable control over the pattern of investment. The general (i.e., federal) investment fund and the Republics' investment loan funds, all of which are managed by the Investment Bank (and to a lesser extent by the Agricultural Bank), provide, in combination, about 70 per cent of the resources used for investment lending; over 60 per cent is financed by the general investment fund alone, from resources that are derived from the proceeds of the capital tax, from a share in the profits tax, and from borrowing abroad, etc., as well as from repayment on earlier loans. Through the policy of requiring that the borrowing enterprises or local authorities put up a share of the finance for any investment project, the Investment Bank can control a very large part of the investments in the country. An additional instrument in the hands of the Investment Bank is its almost exclusive right to authorize the allocation of foreign exchange for imports of capital goods.

The usual technique for distributing investment funds is for the Investment Bank to publish statements at intervals regarding the purposes for which loans will be available, and to invite bids from investors, i.e., from local authorities so far as the setting up of new enterprises is concerned. Bids are then scrutinized, and an allocation of funds is made. All aspects of the operation receive the fullest publicity.

In inviting bids and in deciding how much is to be allocated to different branches of the economy, the Investment Bank is guided by the central investment program outlined in the Social Plan. Here a variety of criteria seem to be applied. Some account is taken of profitability, but this is a rather vague concept under Yugoslav conditions and considerable use is made of an alternative market criterion—the ratio of the value of additional output to that of the new investment. However, the existence of price distortions in the economy, and the fact that much investment is produc- tive only indirectly, make it impossible to rely entirely on market criteria in the planning of investment. Sometimes the need for additional capacity (i.e., for generating electric power) is calculated directly in physical terms. A preference is given to activities likely to improve the balance of payments. A general influence encouraging investment in certain branches of activity in preference to others is provided by the regulations prescrib- ing the minimum extent to which investors are required to participate in the financing of projects assisted by the general investment fund. The minimum participation is negligible in the field of power and fuel; in building it varies between 10 per cent and 30 per cent, in agriculture between 10 per cent and 40 per cent, in transport between 20 per cent and 50 per cent, and in industry between 20 per cent and 80 per cent.

Before providing investment finance for any individual project, the Investment Bank has to ensure that the income arising from the project will be sufficient to cover the interest charge on the loan, the cost of repaying the loan over a certain maximum period, and the capital tax on that part of the additional capital against which no loan is outstanding. Interest rates run mostly from 2 to 6 per cent; and though they vary somewhat according to the economic activity in question, they are so low in relation to the potential profitability of capital in Yugoslavia that they have little or no effect on the distribution of investment. More important are the federal regulations regarding the maximum periods within which investment loans have to be repaid. These naturally vary widely according to the nature of the investment (e.g., 30 years in the steel industry, 20 years in shipbuilding), but the average repayment period in industry is about 8 years.

As a rule, however, there are more projects that can meet these tests than can be financed by the available resources, and the Bank has to scrutinize projects. In doing so, it applies criteria similar to those pre- viously discussed, but with more emphasis on financial criteria. The bor- rowing enterprise has to provide detailed information about the cost, construction period, and probable yield of the investment, the balance of payments effects, etc., as well as information about its own solvency. Sometimes a loan is forthcoming only if the local authority is prepared to provide a guarantee. Ability on the part of the investor to repay the loan within less than the maximum period, or to participate with its own funds to more than the minimum extent required, are favorable factors.

Local investment funds have more liberty than the general investment fund in respect of interest rates and terms of lending. In 1961, however, these local funds were subjected to a federal tax of 6 per cent on the outstanding amount of loans granted by them, and they must therefore charge relatively high interest rates to their borrowers. In part, the local investment funds cover the investment needs of smaller enterprises, and in part they help the larger enterprises to obtain loans from the general investment fund by providing part of the investor's share in the total cost of the investment.

Any miscalculation regarding the cost or construction period of the investment is at the expense of the investing firm or authority, which is obliged in this connection to make a guarantee deposit with the Investment Bank.

Of all social investment funds and other special funds, only the general investment fund is allowed to borrow from the banking system, and this only for the purpose of meeting seasonal deficits.

A variety of regulations exists regarding the extent to which investment funds of enterprises and local authorities can be spent within a given period, and regarding the extent to which they must be spent on working capital. Since the main importance of these regulations lies in their impact on the monetary situation, they are considered in the following section.

MONETARY SYSTEM

The banking system in Yugoslavia—from which may be excluded the activities of certain banks as administrators of the social investment funds—consists of the National Bank, a few specialized banks, the banks of the Republics, and a large number of communal banks and savings banks. It is dominated by the National Bank, which accounts for about 20 per cent of the assets and over 60 per cent of the liabilities of the system. Before April 1961, when the National Bank transferred all outstanding credit to enterprises to the communal banks, the National Bank's share in the assets of the system was more than twice as large as it is now. The National Bank now grants credit, as a rule, only to the Federal Government, to the general investment fund, to the specialized banks, and to the Republics' banks. In addition the National Bank, through its many offices, handles the bank accounts of all enterprises as an agent for the communal banks and in this way keeps a check on all transactions between enterprises.

The specialized banks—the Foreign Trade Bank, the Agricultural Bank, and the Investment Bank—derive most of their resources from the National Bank and extend credits to their respective sectors. In exceptional cases, these credits are granted directly to enterprises but, as a rule, they are channeled through the banks of the Republics and the communal banks. The banks of the Republics serve as intermediaries between the National Bank and specialized banks, on the one hand, and the communal banks, on the other, and coordinate the credit operations of the latter in their respective territories.

Each of the (about 840) Communes is entitled to establish its own communal bank, which may accept deposits from, or extend credits to, all enterprises and institutions in its territory. All enterprises and institutions in the Commune stand as guarantors for the communal bank and are represented on its board. Where the resources of individual Communes are too limited to enable separate banks to operate on a sound basis, a number of them may combine to support a single bank. There are also cooperative savings banks, which provide credit and banking services for agricultural cooperatives and the larger farms.

All these banks, except the specialized banks and those of the Republics, are obliged to keep with the National Bank reserve deposits, the amount of which depends on the nature of the liability; these reserve requirements can be altered within limits at the discretion of the National Bank. At least equally important, however, for the control of the central bank over the rest of the system, is the fact that the National Bank is in a strong creditor position vis-à-vis most of the other banks.

The banking system has three main functions: (1) to maintain internal financial stability; (2) to provide the economy with an adequate, and appropriately distributed, supply of working capital; and (3) to watch over the transactions of autonomous enterprises and local authorities, to ensure that they observe all legal regulations.

The last-mentioned function, one commonly performed by banks in strictly planned economies, requires the canalization through the banking system, under the close supervision of the National Bank, of all business and governmental payments, other than those to and from consumers, farmers, and craftsmen. The system of financial control also finds expression in the creation of a multiplicity of special purpose bank accounts, the credits and debits to which are subject to regulations that alter quite substantially from time to time. The existence of so many different kinds of accounts makes it difficult either to measure the supply of money or liquidity, or to estimate the degree of credit expansion or contraction that may be required to produce a desired effect on the degree of demand pressure in the economy.

The principal forms of money and near-money are as follows: (1) currency, which serves as the means of payment for the population and the nonsocialized sector of the economy; (2) savings accounts of the population, which can be cashed on demand; (3) sight deposits of enterprises, governments, government agencies, social insurance institutions, and other public institutions, which can be used only for current transactions; (4) sight deposits of social investment funds, which can be used for investment lending but to a certain extent only for specific types of investment; (5) sight deposits of enterprises, which they can use to pay for investments in connection with their own operations;[6] (6) reserve funds of banks, enterprises, and governments; (7) temporarily blocked deposits of amortization funds and investment funds of enterprises; and (8) temporarily blocked deposits of social investment funds.

The second objective of the banking system, that of financing working capital investment, if interpreted in the sense that the banks are solely responsible for satisfying all demands for working capital funds, is, strictly speaking, inconsistent with the first objective of preserving internal financial stability. This was found to be the case in practice in the earlier postwar years, when Yugoslavia experienced a good deal of inflationary pressure as a result of the widespread conviction that the provision of working capital was a job for the banks alone.

This conflict of purpose has not yet been completely resolved, but its resolution has been sought along two main lines: (1) by so restricting the use of various types of bank balances as to promote an accumulation of inactive balances to offset part of the expansion of bank credit; and (2) by diverting an increasing proportion of the investment resources of enterprises and social funds to the financing of working capital.

The former approach was the first to be tried. It is now being gradually abandoned in favor of the second. There remain, however, the following restrictions: (1) social investment funds other than the general investment fund may spend during the current year only money that has been acquired in respect of previous years, while current receipts including repayments of former loans may be used only to finance working capital; (2) similarly, enterprises' expenditures on fixed capital out of their own freely disposable investment funds can be made only from income earned in previous years;[7] (3) depreciation funds of enterprises accumulate in blocked accounts for three months before being released;[8] (4) enterprises, institutions, and governments at all levels have reserve funds from which expenditures can be made only in certain emergencies, e.g., in the event of business losses, to permit the payment of minimum wages.

In order to increase the share of working capital investment provided by enterprises and investment funds (the second approach, stated above,

---

[6] In accordance with new regulations on enterprise funds, these deposits are gradually being transferred to the regular sight deposits of enterprises (item 3).

[7] In 1961, 40 per cent of the current income of enterprises, after payment of taxes and wages, was blocked until 1962. The remaining 60 per cent of current net income had to be used by enterprises to finance working capital.

[8] Prior to 1961, a large—though diminishing—proportion of depreciation funds were held in blocked accounts. Most of these were wiped out in 1961 in a single bookkeeping operation.

toward resolving the conflict of purpose), local investment funds are obliged to devote 35 per cent of their expenditures to financing the working capital of enterprises, and enterprises themselves can obtain access to new bank credits only if they are prepared to finance a substantial portion of the total sum required out of their own resources. The general investment fund also uses part of its resources to finance working capital investment. When new enterprises are set up, or the capacity of existing enterprises is increased, the total capital provided, whether by the social investment funds or by enterprises out of their own resources, must be sufficient to finance not only the fixed capital but also the initial working capital or its permanent addition. The banks cannot be called upon to provide this sort of credit.

The above-mentioned regulations and policies may be regarded as methods of limiting and controlling the demand for bank credit for working capital purposes. Increasing reliance, however, is now placed on the credit policy of the banks themselves—a more flexible instrument than any general obligations imposed on enterprises. As already mentioned, by making an appropriate degree of self-financing a condition of bank assistance, pressure is exercised on enterprises as well as on other borrowers (such as local governments and individual farmers) to reduce their demand for bank credit. As a result of the banking reform of 1961, the interest rates charged by banks for loans to enterprises have been increased and now run upward of 8 per cent. However, this probably still leaves the banks under the necessity of exercising considerable selectivity in dealing with credit applications.

Though laws enacted in 1961 envisage the use of commercial bills and Treasury bills, there is as yet no operative money market in Yugoslavia, and the amount of credit extended between firms, other than the supplier's credit, is rather limited. Therefore, the banks play a particularly important role in the distribution of working capital between enterprises and branches of economic activity, though they are beginning to share their responsibility in this respect with the local investment funds. In performing this function, the banks test individual credit applications by some of the same criteria as are employed by the Investment Bank for investment loan applications. Thus, they scrutinize the feasibility and marketability of the expansion of output for which the additional working capital is required, the solvency of the borrower, and his willingness to meet an appropriate share of the cost of the additional output out of his own funds. As with investment loans, the local authority may be required to guarantee the solvency of the borrower.

The recent devolution of the commercial banking function from the National Bank to the communal banks should greatly strengthen the hand of the former in controlling the total expansion of credit and of the money supply if only by imposing a series of buffers—the communal banks, the banks of the Republics, and the specialized banks—between the National

Bank and the insistence of the ultimate demanders of credit. As we have seen, the existence of variable reserve requirements for banks, and the strong creditor position of the National Bank vis-à-vis the other banks, should make it possible effectively to control the supply of credit, though the system is still at an experimental stage. A further safeguard lies in the limitations, enacted in the annual credit plan, on the amounts of credit that can be granted by the National Bank itself to the several specialized banks and to the banks of the Republics. These credit ceilings can be altered only by legislation.

While the reduction of relative price distortions in the Yugoslav economy over the last two years has been associated with appreciable increases in the general cost of living, monetary and fiscal policy has been sufficiently firm to maintain a fair degree of internal financial stability, despite a very high rate of investment and economic growth. In this, Yugoslavia has been assisted by substantial amounts of grants and credits from abroad.

The Soviet Union: Central Planning

The Soviet Union is the outstanding historical and contemporary example of central planning and has served as a model for central planning in the rest of the Communist world. A large, complex, dynamic economy under totalitarian control, it provides a striking illustration of the nature and problems of comprehensive and detailed physical planning in response to the preferences of the political authorities.

Nevertheless, the Soviet economy is not a pure case of socialist central planning. Although public ownership and enterprise are paramount, there is an important private sector in agriculture. Although planners' preferences are supreme, household preferences influence the composition and relative prices of consumer goods output. And although detailed planning and administrative commands in physical terms are the principal means of resource allocation, markets and prices play a major role in allocating the labor force and distributing consumer goods. In these respects, the Soviet economy is a "mixed" economy, in which expediency has forced upon Marxist socialist doctrine a grudging and limited tolerance of private enterprise and the market.

The four selections that follow, drawn from the extensive literature on the Soviet economy, illuminate key facets of the Soviet economic system. The first analyzes the material supply system which is at the heart of Soviet central planning. The second examines the role of prices and markets in the Soviet economy. The next selection reviews Soviet agricultural policy and explains the position and significance of private peasant agriculture. The last article shows how the limitations of centralized physical planning in the individual Soviet-type economies also prevent the attainment of a rational pattern of international trade between them. Two other facets of the Soviet economy, the monetary and banking system and enterprise management, are examined in Selections No. 19 and No. 20 in Part IV.

Herbert S. Levine[1]

15. THE CENTRALIZED PLANNING OF SUPPLY IN SOVIET INDUSTRY*

At the heart of Soviet centralized physical planning is the supply system which allocates major material inputs to enterprises. (Other parts of the planning process are concerned with the investment program, the labor force, etc.) The task of the supply system is to achieve "balance," or consistency, by assuring that total supplies of these inputs just equal total uses and that each enterprise obtains just the amount of inputs needed for its planned output. The principal tool of supply planning is the material balance, which compares the expected sources and uses of hundreds of important producer goods.

As the following article explains, Soviet planning has been unable to achieve consistency in supply plans, to say nothing of efficiency or optimality in resource allocation. The author examines the organization of the supply system and the use of material balances in the planning process. He then analyzes the various shortcomings of Soviet supply planning. He concludes with a discussion of the possible contribution of input-output and electronic computers to the improvement of Soviet planning, pointing out how they could lead to basic changes in its character.

[1] This is part of a study [done] as a doctoral dissertation in the Department of Economics, Harvard University. I am happy to acknowledge my indebtedness to Professor Abram Bergson for his advice and guidance, and the Russian Research Center and Ford Foundation for the assistance they have given me. I am also indebted to Profs. Alexander Gerschenkron, Robert Dorfman, and John M. Montias. I wish especially to thank the numerous Soviet economists who were kind and helpful to me on a trip I took to the Soviet Union during May and June 1959.

* Reprinted, with permission, from *Comparisons of the United States and Soviet*

INTRODUCTION

SUPERFICALLY, Soviet industrial supply methods do not appear to be much different from our own. A firm "buys" the input materials it requires, in most cases directly from the producer. Payment is made by transfers in bank accounts. Terms of the sale are stipulated in commercial contracts, and both buyer and seller are protected by the courts against violations, by the other party, of these contracts.

The similarities, however, end abruptly. First, the atmosphere in which the Soviet supply system operates is different from the one normally prevailing in the United States. The Soviet economy since its early days has been marked by a chronic sellers' market; i.e., the situation where demand is consistently pressing upon supply. This has been one of the major factors contributing toward the many negative characteristics of the supply system, which have been so well documented in both Russian and American writings. These writings center on the frequent inability of the system to satisfy the basic commandments of any supply system; namely, to get materials to consuming enterprises in the required quantity, of the required quality and at the required time, in the cheapest way possible. And they discuss what Soviet firms have had to do to counteract these deficiencies: padded orders, excess inventories, staffs of "expediters," vertical integration, etc.

A second and more fundamental dissimilarity is the centralized nature of the planning and control of supply in the Soviet Union. The Soviet firm does not buy its major input materials on an open market where the ability to pay the price asked is the only requirement for acquisition of the material. Major materials in the Soviet Union are centrally allocated even though on the operating level of the firm material transfers are accompanied by money payments. In order to acquire these major materials, a Soviet firm not only has to have the money, but it also has to have an authorization, in the form of a fund, from the government.[2]

Many of the operating characteristics of the Soviet supply system have already been well described in the works of Professors Berliner and Granick.[3] In this paper I would like to focus on the planning of this supply system—the major element of dissimilarity between the Soviet and Ameri-

Economies (Papers Submitted by Panelists Appearing before the Subcommittee on Economic Statistics, Joint Economic Committee, 86th Cong., 1st sess.) (Washington, D.C.: U.S. Government Printing Office, 1959), Part I, pp. 151–75. Herbert S. Levine is Associate Professor of Economics at the University of Pennsylvania.

[2] In the American economy, also, something more than the mere ability to pay is sometimes required for the acquisition of certain materials. But we are here thinking of the capitalist process in its more generalized form, i.e., as an "ideal type," in the Weberian sense.

[3] J. S. Berliner, *Factory and Manager in the USSR* (Cambridge, Mass.: Harvard University Press, 1957); and David Granick, "An Organizational Model of Soviet Industrial Planning," *Journal of Political Economy*, Vol. 67, No. 2 (April, 1959).

can supply systems. The planning of supply is differentiated from economic planning in general in that the fundamental question of the allocation of economic resources is not one of the primary problems. Supply planning begins from a set of given production targets, and its primary problem is to achieve balance in the plan, i.e., to assure that if a certain number of tons of steel output is planned, then the necessary amounts of all the input materials into steel are also planned. It is this vitally important problem of achieving balance in the plan which will form the core of this paper: how is it done, how effectively is it done and what changes and improvements are in sight.

The operational plan in the Soviet Union is not the long-term plan, the 5- or 7-year plan, but the short-term plan, the annual plan. This paper will concentrate, therefore, on the problems of constructing the annual plan. The periods both before and after the recent reorganization of industrial administration will be covered. This is done because, first, as an aid in analyzing Soviet economic growth, both the present and the prereorganization systems are relevant; second, in order to understand and evaluate the reorganization, it is necessary to know what preceded it; and third, many of the essential features of the planning system have not changed, but they stand out more clearly in the prereorganization system than they do in the present system, which has by no means achieved any final form as yet. The coverage of the paper will be limited to the planning of supply within the industrial sector of the Soviet economy only.

The paper begins with a short description of the organizations involved in supply planning, as a sort of playbill to enable the reader to identify the performers. This is followed by a discussion of how the annual supply plan is constructed with special emphasis on the balancing methodology employed. Then comes a section on the major weaknesses of supply planning and the possibilities of correcting some of them through the use of modern mathematical methods and high-speed electronic computers. The paper ends with some brief conclusions. This is a lot of territory to cover within the delimited confines of this paper. As a result, many points have been brushed over quickly, often too quickly. For this, I apologize.

Those who are familiar with American handling of materials control problems during the war will see certain similarities in the description of Russian planning methods which follows.[4]

I. ORGANIZATIONS IN SUPPLY PLANNING

The basic impact of the reorganization of 1957 was to change the administration of Soviet industry from vertical, branch lines to horizontal, geographic lines. Prior to the reorganization, there were normally between 20 and 40 economic ministries (such as the Ministry of Ferrous

[4] D. Novick, M. L. Anshen, and W. C. Truppner, *Wartime Production Controls* (New York: Columbia University Press, 1949).

Metallurgy), which administered firms throughout the country classified as being within a given sector. Now almost all of the ministries have been abolished and in their place there are more than 100 sovnarkhozy (councils of the national economy) each of which administers the firms lying within its economic-administrative region (a geographic area). The administration of the supply system has in a similar manner been changed from ministerial lines to regional lines.

At the top of the supply hierarchy, both before and after the reorganization, stands Gosplan S.S.S.R. (the State Planning Committee of the Council of Ministers of the U.S.S.R.). This organization, since the end of World War II, has had a checkered career. At the end of the war, it was a "permanent commission" of the U.S.S.R. Council of People's Commissars (now Council of Ministers) responsible for the working out of long- and short-term plans, including the annual supply plan. Its primary mission, however, was not the initiating and formulating of major objectives, but the assuring of the feasibility and consistency of a plan, and the prevention and eradication of disproportions within the economy. Among its various departments, Gosplan had a set of branch departments and a set of summary departments (svodnye otdely) which were organized more or less parallel to the existing ministries. The former were concerned with the output and the latter with the distribution of the products which came under the planning jurisdiction of Gosplan. Soon after the war, control over supply planning was taken away from Gosplan, when in 1947, Gossnab (the State Committee of the U.S.S.R. Council of Ministers for the Supply of Materials to the National Economy) was formed. Gossnab took on the function of constructing the annual supply plan. In 1951, the planning of the distribution of consumers' goods was split off from Gossnab with the formation of Gosprodsnab (the State Committee of the U.S.S.R. Council of Ministers for the Supply of Food and Manufactured Consumer Goods). But in 1953, Gossnab and Gosprodsnab were put back into Gosplan and the top organizational level of supply planning returned to what it was 5 years earlier. However, this situation did not last very long. In 1955, not only supply planning was split off from Gosplan, but the entire function of short-term planning when a separate planning organ, Gosekonomkomissiia (the State Planning Commission of the U.S.S.R. Council of Ministers for the Current Planning of the National Economy) was formed. This arrangement lasted for 2 years. In 1957, under the reorganization of industrial management, current planning and, with it, supply planning were put back into Gosplan.

Even this short description of the repeated organizational changes at the top planning level is sufficient to give the flavor of the postwar developments. Change has been the rule rather than the exception. There are several explanations for this, but one which is hard to avoid is that the political authorities have not been too happy with the organization of planning and within this of supply planning at the top level.

Before the reorganization, the hierarchy of supply planning below the top level ran as follows. Attached to the ministry, there was the glavsnab (main administration of supply) and the glavsbyt (main administration of sales). In those cases where there were glavki (branch main administrations) between the ministry and a group of subordinate enterprises, each glavk had a supply department. Finally, at the lowest level, there was the supply department of the enterprise.

The reorganization led to a number of changes in the organizations involved in supply planning. The planning hierarchy is, of course, different. The various levels now are: Gosplan S.S.S.R., republican gosplan, sovnarkhoz,* enterprise. At the top level, Gosplan acquired the former ministerial glavsbyty. Recently these were consolidated, reduced in number to between 10 and 14, and renamed main administrations for inter-republican deliveries. The gosplan of each union republic has increased in size and importance. The gosplan of the R.S.F.S.R. acquired the glavsnaby of the former ministries and combined main administrations for supply and sales have been formed in every republican gosplan (one main administration for supply and sales for each broad category of product). Main supply and sales administrations have also been formed at the sovnarkhozy. In addition, the sovnarkhoz has a number of branch departments and each one of these branch departments has a supply section which is active and important in the planning of supply for the firms within that branch and subordinate to that sovnarkhoz. At the bottom level, remaining unchanged by the reorganization, are the supply departments of the individual enterprises.

II. CONSTRUCTION OF THE SUPPLY PLAN

THE SUPPLY PLAN AND WHAT IT COVERS

The planning of industrial supply is related more to short-term planning than to long term. There is no supply plan as such in the 5- or 7-year plan. But the annual plan for the development of the national economy contains, in addition to sections on targets for industrial output, agricultural output, capital construction, introduction of new technology, labor force, etc., a plan for the material-technical supply of the national economy. The main elements of this supply plan are (1) an introductory resolution of the U.S.S.R Council of Ministers, which confirms the plan and contains its basic objectives, including some direct tasks to the individual ministries (now to the republics) for the economizing of materials; (2) material balances compiled for all centrally allocated means of production; (3) distribution plans for each centrally allocated material, by user ministries (now by user republics); (4) norms for the input of materials, including fuels and electricity, in production and construction, and tasks for the lowering of these norms.

---

* Editor's note: Regional economic council.

The annual supply plan, confirmed by the U.S.S.R. Council of Ministers, does not cover the distribution of all materials used by industry, but only a selected group of them. Until recently, input materials were classified into three, sometimes four categories. First, there were the "funded" commodities. These were the commodities whose distribution was set in the state supply plan. The term "funded" meant they were products which could only be obtained if the consuming unit had a fund or an allotment for their acquisition. In other words, they were products centrally allotted by the Government. These included the most important producers' goods in the economy: ferrous and nonferrous metals, fuels, chemicals, etc. Also included were machinery and equipment, and in addition, the major materials used by the consumers' goods industries.[5] They were classified in varying degrees of specificity, but rarely as fine as an input material specification has to be at the level of actual use in production. For example, in 1946, there were 70 different classifications of "funded" rolled ferrous metal products, but the metallurgical industry produced several thousand different shapes, sizes, and qualities. The number of "funded" commodities did not remain constant. It grew after the war, reaching a peak of 1,600 at the height of the centralization period just before the death of Stalin. In the early decentralization moves of 1953–54 they were reduced to about 800, and in 1958 they were reported to number 760.

The second category was "centrally planned" commodities. The distribution of these goods was planned by the main administrations of sales of the producing ministries. They were either goods of lesser importance than the "funded" or they had a more restricted group of consumers. Also classified as "centrally planned" were those commodities whose distribution was planned by the republican gosplany.

The third category was "decentrally planned" commodities. The distribution of these was controlled by local governmental organs and by the local offices of the main administrations of sales of the producing ministries.

A fourth category was sometimes added: "decentralized and self procurement." This included those products a firm could procure by itself, such as sand, rocks, some types of lumber, etc.

After the reorganization, the classification into "funded" and "centrally planned" commodities lost much of its rationale. The main administrations of sales of the former ministries which distributed the "centrally planned" commodities were now part of Gosplan S.S.S.R. Therefore, Gosplan (or at least sections of it) was distributing both the 760 "funded" commodities and the approximately 5,000 "centrally planned" commodities. In addition, while the main administrations of sales at Gosplan were planning the

---

[5] Classification as a "funded" commodity depended also on the degree of centralization of its production. In addition, I was told, in a personal interview with a Soviet economist, that the number of "funded" commodities in any 1 year was affected by how many Gosplan felt it could handle.

distribution of "centrally planned" commodities, the republics were planning the output levels of these commodities. The old classification system was clearly an anachronism. Soon the announcement came that "beginning in 1959, the notorious division of output into 'planned' and 'funded' will be abolished."[6]

Under the new classification system, Gosplan will plan the distribution of and issue fondy* for the acquisition of those products which are the most important for the national economy, those which are in the most serious short supply and those which are produced and used in several republics. These commodities include almost all of the former "funded" and some of the former "centrally planned" commodities. Estimates of the number to be planned by Gosplan vary from 800 to 1,500.

The republics will plan the distribution of the commodities of lesser importance and those commodities produced either wholly or largely within one republic. The individual sovnarkhozy will distribute those commodities of least importance and those commodities which are produced wholly within a single sovnarkhoz.

Our major interest, in this paper, is the centralized planning of supply. Therefore, we will concentrate on the planning of the supply of those products which are under the jurisdiction of Gosplan S.S.S.R. and which appear in the annual state supply plan: formerly the "funded" commodities and presently those commodities in the first of the new three categories.

CHRONOLOGY OF PLAN CONSTRUCTION

In this section, we will outline the sequence of plan construction. The supply plan for the forthcoming year (the planned year) is constructed during the current year (the planning year). The process is roughly one wherein general instructions flow down the planning hierarchy followed by a counterflow of fill-in information and suggestions from the bottom. This is followed by coordination at the top and the issuance of a fairly detailed plan. In the final stage the plan flows down again and is put into the thorough detail necessary for operational purposes. The formal chronology which I have set out below is a generalized view of the process. In reality, the stages are not always clear cut and practice often varies from one industry to another. The prereorganization system is described first and then some of the changes introduced by the reorganization are discussed.

The first stage of the planning process is a statistical analysis of the base

---

[6] The use of the word "notorious" might reflect the Soviet proclivity for kicking fallen horses, but it also might be a reflection of some of the problems resulting from the classification system even before the reorganization, such as lack of coordination between the distribution of "funded" and "centrally planned" commodities.

* Editor's note: Funds or allotments for acquisition of goods.

period. This is finished in the first half of the planning year. It includes a thorough statistical investigation of the previous year (that is 2 years before the planned year), preliminary data on the first 6 months of the planning year and some estimated data for the second 6 months of the planning year. The purpose of this statistical work is primarily to aid in the construction of the control figures (stage two) by uncovering temporary "bottlenecks" which should be concentrated upon in the planned year and by uncovering possible supplementary sources of increased output.

The second stage is the drawing up of the control figures. These are preliminary notes on the forthcoming economic plan. They are a set of aggregate output targets for a dozen or so of the most important commodity groups. They also contain some major investment targets. Their purpose is to serve as guideposts to the lower economic units in the construction of the annual plan. The control figures are worked out in Gosplan by the industrial and the summary departments, use being made of material balances to attain equality between the supply and demand for each of the commodity groups covered. According to the Soviet literature, these preliminary targets are based first of all on the economic-political tasks set by the party and the government, which in turn are determined by "the given stage of Socialist construction."[7] They are also set in relation to the long-term plan then in force, relying heavily on the results of the statistical investigations carried out in the first stage. The control figures are worked out in June and early July, and are confirmed by the Council of Ministers.

The third stage is the key stage. It is the one in which the plan comes up the hierarchy, is coordinated on a national scale at the top, is confirmed by the government and becomes a law directing the operating units in the economy. Actually, this stage begins before the completion of the second stage. It appears that all the levels—ministries, glavki and enterprises—start to work on their plans prior to the publication of the control figures. Sometime in May, Gosplan sends out forms for the ordering of materials. These orders are called zaiavki. (See Chart No. 1.) They contain data on materials required by the enterprise during the planned year, i.e., the year to come, and also data on materials used during the current year and the past year. The materials required are calculated by the "direct method": output targets are multiplied by a set of input norms (from this product, above-norm stocks are subtracted). Since work on the zaiavki begins before the release of the control figures, the enterprise puts together a set of tentative output targets, based on the enterprise's experience during the

---

[7] This is the phrase repeatedly used. In Western terms it means "planners' preferences." The planners look over the current stage of development and they (rather than the consumers) determine the major directions the economy will take in the coming year. (In this sense "planners" means the political leaders, rather than the people at Gosplan.)

CHART 1
ZAIAVKA

For (Group of Materials) Needed by the Enterprise in 1960

#	Designation			
1	Number			
2	Designation of Materials			
3	Unit of Measurement			
4	Stocks on Jan. 1st			1958
5	Delivered			1958
6	Used			1958
7	Stocks on Jan. 1st			1959
8	Confirmed		Fond	1959
9	Including changes		Fond	1959
10	Expected for year		Delivered	1959
11	Actual deliveries in first six months		Delivered	1959
12	Expected for year		Used	1959
13	Actually used in first six months		Used	1959
14	Actual stocks on July 1, 1959			
15	Expected stocks on Jan. 1, 1960			
16	For output sold			Requirements in 1960
17	Total	For maintenance		Requirements in 1960
18	For capital repairs	For maintenance		Requirements in 1960
19	Quantity	Temporary stocks		Requirements in 1960
20	In "days' needs"	Temporary stocks		Requirements in 1960
21	TOTAL			
22	Use of expected stocks			Sources covering 1960 needs
23	Mobilization of internal resources			Sources covering 1960 needs
24	Requested fondy			Sources covering 1960 needs
25	I		By Quarter	Sources covering 1960 needs
26	II		By Quarter	Sources covering 1960 needs
27	III		By Quarter	Sources covering 1960 needs
28	IV		By Quarter	Sources covering 1960 needs

This is a typical form of a zaiavka. It is illustrative of the documentation which constitutes the "paper pyramid" involved in centralized Soviet planning.

past year and the first part of the current year, and what directions it expects the forthcoming plan to take. Once the control figures are released (end of June–beginning of July) and are broken down by the ministry and the glavk, the enterprise has a clearer idea of what its production targets will be, and it is able to introduce the necessary corrections in the plan calculations it has been making.

In addition to output targets, in order to complete the zaiavki, the firm has to know how much of each input it will need per unit of output. This information is supplied by the input norms. The question, by whom and how these norms are set, is an extremely complicated one. For one thing, it depends upon the period. In some periods there were many norms inspected and confirmed by the highest planning organ. For example, in preparing the supply plan for 1949, Gossnab inspected more than 1,800 material input norms, and this grew as the drive toward centralization increased until for the 1952 plan it was above 7,500. But then in the early decentralization moves of 1953–54, the ministries were given greatly increased power over norm setting and only the "most important norms" were to be inspected by the top planning organ. The importance of the input material being normed, thus, is another contributing factor. The most important norms are established in the annual supply plan as obligatory direct tasks (adresnye zadaniia). These are set either as an average for a branch, or, in the case of the most important firms in the country, by specific firm and by specific item produced. In addition, the plan lists a number of targets for the general decrease in norms by industrial branch. The main mass of norms, however, are not listed in the plan, but are used for calculation purposes during the process of constructing the national economic plan. Some of these are confirmed directly at the enterprise and some at the glavk or ministry. Again there was much variation from year to year.[8]

The principle underlying the working out of input norms is that they must aid in the constant struggle to increase economic output by forcing the spread of technical progress and the economizing of material resources. To accomplish this, they must embody the achievements of the leading firms, but they must also be attainable by the average firm. The concept of an "average-progressive norm," which is a norm somewhere between the average and the best, was created to meet this need.[9] Norms are worked out originally by the firm and, depending upon the level at which they are confirmed, are inspected by technical bureaus up the bureaucratic line. As we will see below, norms are frequently changed by

---

[8] In 1952, at the height of centralization there were 2,230 norms established by Gossnab and the ministries for the use of rolled ferrous metal products, which covered 69 per cent of its total use in the economy, and 1,145 centrally established norms for the use of lumber products, which covered 97 per cent of their use.

[9] There are a number of different methods of calculating an average progressive norm. One is by the "analytical method," wherein the achievements of the leading firms are thoroughly analyzed and a realistic norm set as close to these achievements

higher organs during the construction of the annual economic plan.

With its estimates of output targets and input norms, the enterprise fills out its zaiavki and sends these orders along with supporting documents up to the glavk. Thus begins what is in many ways a political process, something akin to our collective bargaining. The glavk checks the estimates and requests of the enterprise and tries to remove some of the slack the enterprise has put in. The "padding of orders" is one of the most common methods used by the Soviet firm to increase its chances of fulfilling its output plan, under the existing strains of tight plans and supply unreliability. In its negotiations with the glavk, the firm tries to defend the estimates and requests it has made. But since the glavk has administrative power over the firm, it can force its opinion to prevail (although a firm can appeal to the ministry).[10] The glavk then combines the zaiavki of the firms subordinate to it and sends the combined zaiavki up to the main administration of supply of the ministry. Here the bargaining process is repeated. The ministry then sends its aggregated plan and zaiavki up to Gosplan S.S.S.R. Usually this was to be done before September 1, or at the latest September 15. The discussions which ensue between a ministry and the corresponding industrial department of Gosplan are a real analog of collective bargaining, for neither has administrative power over the other. In fact, there are at times unresolved disagreements which have to be settled by the Council of Ministers.[11]

During the period of September and early October, Gosplan is engaged in the crucial work of attempting to balance the supply and demand for each of the centrally allocated commodities. It does this by means of the material balances (this process will be discussed in some detail in the following section). Actually Gosplan, like the ministries and glavki, starts its work before the draft plans come up from below. In this way it has a forecast of what the material balances will be like when the ministries' plans do come up, and it is, therefore, prepared for the ensuing discussions. Gosplan sends a balanced draft of the plan to the Council of Ministers before the end of October. The plan is discussed by the Council of Ministers and, if necessary, certain changes are made. The plan is then confirmed.

Stage 4, the final stage in the construction of the plan, is the bringing down of the plan to the enterprise and its transformation into detailed operational form. The final plan, the fondy for the centrally allocated

---

as possible. For more than 20 years this has been the only acceptable method and yet it would appear that in practice the more formal "statistical method" is still widely used. Under this method an average progressive norm is often just the average of all the above-average input relationships achieved in production.

[10] The cutting away of fat is not carried to the limit because the plans of the glavki and of the ministries are (presumably) a summation of the plans of the enterprises, and thus their fulfillment depends upon the enterprises's ability to fulfill its own plan.

[11] It is also thought that the Central Committee of the Communist Party plays an important role in the settling of some of these disagreements.

commodities and the delivery orders for these commodities are sent to the ministries. The main administration of supply divides the fondy and the centrally established input norms among the subordinate glavki and the main administration of sales divides the delivery orders for the "funded" commodities produced by the ministry. The glavki in turn divide these among the enterprises.

A fund received by an enterprise entitles it to a certain amount of the "funded" commodity. But the "funded" commodity is defined in airily gross terms and thus the enterprise must specify exactly what shape, grade, and size it requires. The firm constructs a complete, specified list of the materials it needs within the limits of the fondy allotted to it and sends this list up to the glavk. The glavk checks the lists it receives, combines them, and sends the combined, specified lists to the ministry. There, the main administration of supply combines the lists it receives and sends the specified orders to the main administrations of sales of the appropriate producing ministries. This is to be done 1 to 1½ months before the beginning of the planned year.[12] The main administration of sales checks to see if the orders are within the limits of the fondy, and then it assigns specific orders to specific producing firms. Meanwhile, the aggregate delivery orders, which were sent down, have also been distributed to the glavki and the enterprises, so that the enterprises have already begun to work out their production and shipment schedules before receiving the specified orders from their main administration of sales.

As was the case with other stages, the fourth stage really begins before the end of the third. When Gosplan sends its draft of the plan to the Council of Ministers, it sends excerpts to each ministry so that the ministry can begin the arduous and labor-intensive job of specification and assignment of delivery orders. Then, when the plan is confirmed, the changes made by the Council of Ministers are incorporated by the ministries, glavki and enterprises into the work they have done up to that time.

The planning process proper[13] concludes with the signing of contracts between producing units and consuming units, in which delivery schedules and other delivery details are stipulated.

Since the reorganization, the essential nature of the planning process has not changed, but some of its features have. The hierarchical line is now different: Gosplan S.S.S.R., republican gosplan, sovnarkhoz, enterprise.

The chronology also is somewhat different. Stage 2, the construction of the control figures, was omitted, but is now being reintroduced in altered form. Stage 3 now begins at the enterprise. No control figures containing

---

[12] The specified orders cover only a 3-month period and thus the specification process is repeated before each quarter.

[13] The other part of the planning process is the changing of the plan during the course of the year as the need for changes becomes apparent. Russian economists repeatedly claim this is an important part of the planning process, and indeed when one reads of the tremendous number of changes introduced during the year, it is hard to disagree. But a discussion of this falls outside of the restricted scope of this paper.

output targets are issued, but rather each enterprise is to work out its own output targets on the basis of the yearly breakdowns of the 7-year plan. These yearly breakdowns have been worked out in much more detail and thus are more operational than were the yearly breakdowns of long-term plans in the past. As the middle and end years of the 7-year plan approach, the enterprise is expected to make corrections in these yearly breakdowns to take account of the accumulated divergences between experience and plan. The zaiavki are sent up to the sovnarkhoz, are reviewed, debated, and are combined and sent up to the republican gosplan. Here the bargaining process is repeated and then, for each centrally allocated product, the planned supply (including "imports" from other republics) and the planned demand (including "exports" to other republics) are balanced. For this purpose, regional material balances are used. A new procedure will be added starting in 1960. In order to give the gosplan of a union-republic some idea of how much of a given material it can expect to receive in the planned year, Gosplan S.S.S.R. will, at the beginning of June, issue a set of preliminary limits for the supply of somewhere between 50 to 200 of the most important input materials. The gosplan of the republic is to send its output plan and zaiavki up to Gosplan by August 1. Gosplan then has until September 15 to work out a balanced all-union output and supply plan. The basic method is still the use of material balances. Fondy (now confirmed by Gosplan itself) are allocated to the republics; the republics distribute them among the sovnarkhozy; and the sovnarkhozy to the enterprises. The specified orders go up the line: sovnarkhoz, republican gosplan, Gosplan. This is supposed to be done 1½ to 2 months before the beginning of the planned year. In Gosplan S.S.S.R., the main administrations for interrepublican deliveries, which grew out of the main administrations of sales of the ministries, assign specified orders directly to individual producing enterprises. And the process again ends with the signing of delivery contracts between suppliers and users.

Summarizing the results of the reorganization, the following stand out as important new features of the process of supply planning: (1) the more detailed yearly subdivisions of the 7-year plan, which serve as a starting point for the planning process in place of the control figures which were formerly worked out each year by Gosplan; (2) the increased importance of the republican gosplany and of regional balancing; (3) also the increased importance of Gosplan S.S.S.R. with the addition to its staff of the former main administrations of sales of the ministries, now renamed, main administrations for inter-republican deliveries (this, however, may not be a permanent feature).

MATERIAL BALANCES

The key element in the planning of industrial supply is the material balance. Every Soviet writer on the subject pays homage to it:

In the Socialist economy, the planned connection between the production and consumption of different types of products is guaranteed. Both the production and consumption of materials, are determined by means of the material balances, which are an integral component of the plan for the supply of the national economy.

By means of the material balances, the material needs of the national economy are determined, means for increasing the material resources of the economy are uncovered and the necessary proportionality in the growth of individual branches of the national economy in accordance with the demands of the law of the planned (proportional) development of the national economy is established.

The material balances permit the planning organs to work out measures for the mobilization of production reserves, for the overcoming of "bottlenecks" in the development of individual branches and to uncover supplementary resources.

A material balance is essentially a balance sheet of the supply and demand for a given product. At the Gosplan level a separate material balance is made out for each of the centrally allocated commodities

CHART 2
MATERIAL BALANCE *
Product X

Sources	Distribution
1. Production	1. Production-operation needs
a) By major producing Ministries (now by Republics)	a) By major user Ministries (now by Republics)
2. Imports	2. Construction
3. Other sources	a) By major users
4. Stocks at suppliers, at beginning of period	3. Market fund
a) By major supplier Ministries (now by Republics)	4. Export
	5. Increase of state reserves
	6. Increase of reserves of Council of Ministers
	7. Stocks at suppliers, at end of period
	a) By major supplier Ministries (now by Republics)

*This is a composite form. The categories often differ from product to product.

(formerly the "funded" commodities.)[14] On the left side of the balance, are listed all the sources of the product and on the right side, its uses. (See Chart No. 2.) Most of these categories are self-explanatory. On the sources side, the most important category is "Production." With most commodities it is often as high as 95 per cent of the total supply. "Imports" is usually insignificant. "Other sources" is of varying importance. In some ferrous metals, for example, scrap metal ("other sources") is an important element of supply. "Stocks" includes only those at suppliers. This is done because they are the only stocks capable of being distributed.[15] Stocks at users (if they are above normed levels) are taken into account by being

---

[14] Material balances, in modified form, are also used by lower planning organs.

[15] Actually, the positive difference between stocks at suppliers at the beginning and end of the year is what comprises a source of distributable supply. A negative difference denotes an added demand for the product.

subtracted from requirements when the zaiavki of an enterprise are made up.

The major categories on the distribution side are "production-operation needs" (which includes maintenance requirements) and "construction." The "market fund" denotes that part of the output of the product which is distributed more or less without further processing to satisfy the consumption needs of the people. The two "reserves" are quite different from each other. The "state reserve" is a permanent one, built up as a protection against national disasters, natural or manmade. The "reserve of the Council of Ministers" is an operational reserve to be dispensed during the course of the years to firms which are overfulfilling their output targets and thus are in need of additional input materials, and to firms which did not get supplies which were allotted to them, because of supply failures.[16] The production categories on the sources and distribution sides, before the reorganization, were broken down by producing and consuming ministries.[17] They are now broken down by republics.

The material balances are used at two stages of Gosplan's work. First, they are used to assure consistency in the control figures (now the preliminary supply limits), and second, they are used in constructing the final draft of the annual economic plan. At the control figures stage, Gosplan uses its own estimates of sources and distribution, but in the final draft stage, the information which comes up from below is used. We will concentrate here on the final draft stage.

The crucial problem in material balance technology is how are the planned sources and distribution brought into balance when at first there is an imbalance?[18] Usually, the direction of an imbalance is that the demand for a product is greater than the originally planned supplies.[19] The procedure appears to be that the industrial departments of Gosplan (which are organized along product lines) work on the sources of each product, while the summary departments work on the distribution. The two work closely together in trying to achieve a balance, keeping each other constantly informed of the adjustments each makes. What steps do they take when it is found that the demand for a product is greater than the planned supply?[20]

---

[16] The output targets of producers are set higher than the originally planned deliveries they have to make. This difference is what makes up the "reserves of the Council of Ministers." During the year the firms will receive orders telling them where to send this additional output.

[17] In most cases, there were a number of different ministries producing a given product.

[18] A subsidiary problem is: how is a change in the output target of one product reflected in the changes of other products?

[19] This can be logically deduced from the practice of padding orders by lower administrative organs.

[20] This is one of those clouded areas of administrative action, where a person would really have to be involved in the actual work before he could clearly analyze the method employed. The following "analysis" is based on personal interviews with Soviet economists and a number of written sources.

The basic principle, it is claimed, is that a plan is not brought down to a "bottleneck," i.e., an output target of one branch is not reduced because of a "bottleneck" in the supply to it of a deficit commodity. This, one author states, would be the easiest way, but is sheer opportunism.[21]

What is done is that on the one hand the corresponding industrial department attempts to increase the supply of the deficit commodity. It sees if stocks at suppliers can be cut (further). Also, planned imports, in a few cases, may be increased. But the major effort is to increase current production. This is to be accomplished within the planned capacity, by better or more intensive use of equipment. Sometimes the planned introduction of new capacity may be speeded up so that more of the year is operated within the greater capacity.

At the same time that the industrial department is working on increasing the supply of the deficit commodity, the summary department is working on decreasing the demand for this commodity. The basic principle is to accomplish this without decreasing the output targets of the users of the deficit material. The method employed is to increase efficiency in the use of this material, to economize, to rationalize, to spread the advanced experience of the leading firms. In other words, pressure is applied to decrease (further) the input norms.[22] Another method is the substitution of nondeficit materials for the deficit. These are always described as "fully substitutable" substitutes.[23] Throughout the balancing process, the priority principle is at work. Whenever possible, it is the sectors of secondary importance (usually the consumer oriented sectors) which have their allocations cut or are called upon to use substitutes. The emphasis is on guaranteeing the supply of the high priority sectors.

When a summary department makes changes which reduce the flow of the deficit commodity to other commodity sectors, it notifies the corresponding industrial departments. And when an industrial department increases the output of the deficit commodity in such a way as to call for an increase in required supplies, then it, in most cases, contacts the relevant summary departments.

To the extent that an imbalance is corrected by an increase in the output of a deficit commodity which is the type of increase that calls for an increase in the output of the materials used in its production, something similar to an iterative solution of the balancing problem might be envisaged. By an iterative solution, I mean one where the increase in the

---

[21] The phrase "deficit product" is used here to mean a product for which demand is greater than planned supply, during the process of plan construction.

[22] In a personal interview with a Soviet economist, the economist said that input norms could be decreased in two ways. One, he illustrated by tightening up his belt; the other was the method of increasing efficiency. He said they preferred to use the second method.

[23] It has also been suggested that the reserves of the Council of Ministers are originally set higher than required, so that, at the balancing stage, when the demand is greater than the supply, these reserves can be cut without any damage. But in a personal interview with a Soviet economist, it was strongly denied that such a method was used.

output of one commodity is followed by the increase in the output of all the inputs into that commodity, followed by the increase in the output of all the inputs into the inputs and so on down the line, all the time use being made of the set of input norms. Mathematically, an infinite number of such steps will yield a perfectly consistent set of material balances. But since the steps near the end become very small, the process may be stopped far short of infinity and an acceptably accurate solution derived.

It is frequently thought that the iterative approach is the basic method used by Soviet planners to achieve consistency in their plans. I do not think that this theory is correct. In order to see why, let us first look at the dimensions of the problem. How many steps, how many iterations would Gosplan have to perform in order to get a reasonably accurate approximation to a balanced plan? The number of iterations necessary, or in other words, the rate of convergence of the approximation procedure, depends on the structure of the economy—roughly speaking, on the degree of interrelatedness of the economy. The more interrelated an economy, the greater the number of iterations necessary. Unfortunately, data on the structure of the Soviet economy, in the detail necessary to give a precise answer to the question, are not available. But on the basis of *very crude* calculations, it might be said that somewhere between 6 and 13 iterations would be required. It is inconceivable that Gosplan, under the conditions which prevailed, could have performed that number of iterations. First of all, Gosplan does not handle the problem in the formal way usually assumed in discussing iterative methods. It does not put together, into one list, all the imbalances which appear at the first approximation, and then in an organized way apply the entire set of input norms to these imbalances. Rather, each product is handled by a separate section (indeed, by two separate sections), which keeps communicating its moves to the other sections. There does not appear to be any set order of communication such as first section A makes its changes, then section B, etc.; all sections work simultaneously. Secondly, in the postwar period, Gosplan was trying to balance an extremely large number of material balances, ranging between the current 760 and a high of 1,600. The problem of working changes through that many different balances is a formidable one for any bureaucracy. Thirdly, all this was and is done without the aid of electronic computers. The method of material balances, in the form in which it exists, is not amenable to computer technology.

But we need not rely solely on deductive reasoning in this matter. In a recent book, the director of the Economic Research Institute of Gosplan stated, that it was rare for even three or four iterations to be performed in tracing the effects of a correction in an output target:

Because of the great labor intensity of the calculation of changes in the material balances and the insufficiency of time for the completion of such work in practice sometimes only those balances which are linked by first order relationships are changed. As regards relationships of the second order, and especially of the third and fourth order, changes in the balances are made only in those cases where the changes are conspicuous (zametnyi).[24]

This statement points out the additional fact that Gosplan's calculation of indirect effects is not uniform; it is limited to "conspicuous" changes. Another facet of the nonuniform approach is that a change need not be passed on in the increased output even of all direct inputs, but can be balanced out by decreases on the demand side of any of these inputs. These nonuniformities in handling the problem make it difficult to "count iterations" or to see an iterative process clearly.

I believe that more important in Gosplan's balancing methodology than iteration procedures is the use of techniques which avoid second-round effects. This is certainly true when changes are made on the distribution side of the material balance of a deficit commodity. Pressure is put on users of the deficit commodity to economize its use by producing more efficiently. The supply of the deficit input material is cut without any change in the output target of the product which uses it. In this way the original rebalancing change does not reverberate through the entire system of material balances; it has no second-round effects. It is less clear to what extent avoidance of second-round effects is important in the making of changes on the sources side. When stocks are reduced, there are no second-round effects, and when imports are increased there are little if any second-round effects. But when a production target is increased in an effort to close a balance, is this always passed on to other sectors in increased orders for input materials? I have heard and read contradictory answers to this question. I think the safest thing to say is that usually increased supplies are ordered, but at times, increased output targets of the deficit commodity are to be met by more efficient production methods without additional supplies, thus avoiding second-round effects.

If the analysis offered here is correct, then we are led to the following hypothesis about the balancing methodology used by Soviet planners. By relying heavily on balancing methods which avoid second-round effects, through pressure on input norms, Gosplan contributes to the further tightening of the plan. That is to say, the very planning methodology used by Gosplan (the material balances and the ways in which they are balanced) itself adds an additional tightening to the plan as the balances in the final draft are hammered out at the top planning level.

Weaknesses of Supply Planning

In this section, we will discuss the problems connected specifically with the planning of supply, not supply problems in general (see "Introduc-

---

[24] If there are "n" centrally allocated commodities, then to calculate the direct inputs into a single output change, you need "n" multiplications (ignoring zeros). But to calculate the inputs into the inputs, you need "n^2" multiplications and for each succeeding iteration, you need "n^2" multiplications. Since $760^2 = 577,600$ and $1600^2 = 2,560,000$, it is no wonder that Gosplan, operating without electronic computers, has had to limit itself to only "conspicuous" relationships.

tion"). First the major planning problems as they existed before the reorganization will be described, and then one or two of the possible effects of the reorganization will be indicated.

Unrealistic Balances. The first question which arises is: How good are the balances worked out in the national economic plan? Are they realistic balances, or are they to some extent mere "paper balances"? From speaking with Soviet economists, one gets the impression that most economists are quite proud of their method of material balances despite some admitted shortcomings. I am sure their feelings were accurately represented by a Polish economist who told me: "The method of material balances is a primitive method, but it works." On the other hand, the Soviet economy is constantly beset by shortages. Are these shortages, these "imbalances," caused by faulty, unrealistic balancing of plans on the part of Gosplan, or are they caused by other factors operating in the Soviet economy? (See below.) A number of recent official pronouncements and analyses by Soviet economists lead one to believe that unrealistic balances are, at least, partly to blame. Khrushchev, at the 20th Party Congress, claimed that sometimes imbalances arise which are caused not only by failures to meet the established plans, but also by the fact that the plans themselves are deficient. The resolution of the December 1956 Plenum of the Communist Party stated that the top planning organs do not base their plans on the "real possibilities" of supplying the required materials to meet the established output targets. This leads to "excess tightness in the fulfillment of plans." In the book by the director of Gosplan's Economic Research Institute, mentioned earlier, he claims that the balancing methodology used, its lack of a sufficient number of full iterations, leads to the accumulation of "a number of errors in various parts of the plan, which under certain conditions manifest themselves, giving rise to certain imbalances and tensions in various material resources."

Thus there is some evidence that at times the balances achieved by Gosplan do contain elements of "paper consistency." This results, in large measure, from Gosplan's inability, in the material balances method, to cover enough of the indirect effects of a change in an output target, and its consequent reliance on pressure methods, which although having positive aspects from the point of view of forcing economic growth, at times introduce unrealistic relationships in the balances.

Lateness. A major problem of planning concerns the frequent failure of the planning organs to complete the annual supply plan before the beginning of the planned year. The Soviet literature is full of complaints about final plans not coming down to the enterprise until January, February, or March, and sometimes even later. This failure to complete the plan on time is not too difficult to understand when one thinks of what a tremendously involved job it is for a bureaucracy first to work up a balanced supply plan for an entire economy in a great number of aggregated indicators and then for subordinate levels to disaggregate the plan into the necessary operational detail. This problem was made even more difficult by the discontinuous nature of the annual plans before the reorganization: ". . . the planning system that developed was such that the annual plans broke off at the end of the calendar year and therefore had to be drawn up every year from scratch, as it were."

Some of the methods adopted by Soviet planners to cope with this time problem are of interest. One is what might be called the "correction principle." In order to speed up the planning process, planning organs usually begin their own work before receiving information from the previous planning stage. When they do receive the information, they then make the necessary corrections in their preliminary estimates.[25] As we have seen, work on the zaiavki began before Gosplan released the control figures and then when the control figures came out, the zaiavki were corrected. Also the specification process began before the confirmation of the plan by the Council of Ministers, and then the changes it made were incorporated by correcting the specified orders. A second speedup method sometimes used was to begin the construction of the zaiavki and the working out of the input norms not at the enterprise, but at the glavk or even the ministry. A third method was the practice of issuing "advance fondy." In order to allow an enterprise to operate during the first quarter in the absence of a supply plan, it was allotted "advance fondy" usually in the amount of 23 to 25 per cent of its previous year's total allotment.

Lack of Coordination. There is often a lack of coordination between the supply plan of an enterprise and its output and financial plans. This is partly a result of poor planning originally, but probably it is more a result of the constant changes introduced in plans both before and after they are confirmed. Changes are frequently made in one set of plans (say, output) without the necessary changes being made in the other set (say, supply).

Specification. One of the weakest parts of the entire planning process is the stage wherein the plan is brought down to the level of the enterprise and is put into operational form—the stage where the aggregate allotments are turned into contracts for specific goods. Remember, the system was: The fondy were distributed by the ministry to the glavk and by the glavk to the enterprise. The enterprise worked up a list of specified requirements within the limits of the fondy. The specified orders came up the hierarchy of the user ministry and a combined specified order was sent to the main administration of sales of each corresponding producer ministry. This ministerial main administration of sales then sent out specified production and delivery orders to the producing firms. The weaknesses of this process lay primarily within three major categories: excessive centralization, the administrative objectives of sales administrations, and the time factor.

(i) Excessive centralization: The sales administration of the ministry

---

[25] This correction process is not limited to the period of the construction of the plan, but continues during the year, while the plan is in operation.

assigned detailed orders directly to the producing firms. The frequent enormity of this job is indicated by the fact that every year the metals main administration of sales issued about 500,000 specified production and delivery orders. This excessive centralization frequently led to the lack of coordination between different plans mentioned in the previous section. Producing firms were often given delivery assignments greater than their planned outputs. The rational geographic distribution of orders was not sufficiently studied, resulting in excessively long transportation hauls. Contract details which should have been set in negotiations between producer and consumer firms were actually set by the producing ministry sales administration and the consuming ministry supply administration. This meant that the real needs of consuming firms and the real production capabilities and specialties of producing firms were often not adequately perceived. It also meant that the efforts to inculcate cost minimization at the enterprise level were weakened, because the enterprise was deprived of the power to decide what materials to use.

(ii) Administrative objectives of sales administration: The sales administrations were concerned with the problems of the producing units rather than with those of the consuming units. Their objective, in the last stage of plan construction, was to achieve an efficient loading of the productive capacities of the firms within their own ministry. As a result of this one-sided concern, consuming firms often ended up with an irrational array of suppliers. Frequently, a firm was to be supplied by a large number of suppliers rather than having its orders concentrated in a few. In fact, as specifications were made out for each quarter, suppliers sometimes were changed from one quarter to the next. These factors gave rise to serious scheduling and coordination problems. Another weakness was that the sales administrations did not put enough pressure on producing firms to adapt their detailed output assortments to the specific needs of the consuming firms, thus leading to imbalances in the detailed supplies and demands. The supply administrations of the consuming ministries were forced to accede to these imbalances because of their inferior power in the prevailing sellers' market. Finally, the aim of spreading technical progress was weakened because the sales administrations had little motivation to force the production of new and more economical (in use) types of materials.

(iii) Time factors: A firm was supposed to make out its specified input requirements 2 to 3 months before the beginning of the planned year, at a time when it did not know its detailed output plan. This created a number of difficulties in matching specific inputs and outputs. Due to the nature and timing of their planning process, Russian planners were forced to compress the planning of essentially successive problems into one time period. This was one of the factors which led to the great numbers of revisions in the plan while it was in operation.

All that has been said, here, about the weaknesses of supply planning should not be understood to imply that they were the sole cause of the general unreliability of the supply system. For there are two other major causal factors. One is the overall practice of tight planning; the other is the poor operation of supply organs. The supply plan could be perfectly constructed, perfectly balanced, but if the overall economic plan were very tight (marginal stocks of materials, tight construction schedules, little slack anywhere), then a few failures to meet some individual targets would create significant supply difficulties throughout the system. Also plans could be moderately slack and well constructed, but if the supply bureaucracy operated in an inefficient manner, then supply difficulties would result. All three factors are important causes of supply deficiencies.

One of the primary aims of the reorganization was to improve the operation of the supply system and, along with this, the planning of supply.[26] It is still too early to evaluate the effects of the reorganization on supply planning, but some comments can be made. The changed role of the long-term plan, with its more detailed, operational yearly subdivisions, will probably help to speed up the planning process and to provide needed continuity in the annual plans. On the other hand, specification procedures do not seem to have improved at all. And it is hard to judge what effects the reorganization will have on the vital problem of achieving balances in the plan—the prime function of the maetrial balances method.

But a new possibility now looms on the horizon, one which might have a profound effect on this balancing methodology. It is the possibility of adapting modern mathematical methods and computer technology to the planning of the supply system.

MATHEMATICAL METHODS AND ELECTRONIC COMPUTERS

Limitations of space do not permit a full discussion of the possible use by Soviet planners of mathematical methods. But let me here just briefly outline what the Russians are saying and what they are doing about the possible use of one of these methods.

Input-Output (I-O) is a mathematical method, which analyzes the interrelationships existing in an economy.[27] Its great advantage over the

---

[26] The prime concern of the reorganization in the supply field was with the deficiencies in the operation of the system, rather than, necessarily, with the planning of it. The major operational deficiencies, which resulted primarily from the absence of cross-ministerial coordination, according to the Soviet sources, were retardation of specialization and subcontracting for components; supply mainly within ministerial channels and thus often irrationally long transportation hauls; failure to develop diversified firms producing a range of byproducts from the given inputs; and duplication of staffs and organizations.

[27] In the I-O method, the output of each sector is divided into flows to each other producing sector and also to final demands (consumption, investment, government, and foreign trade). Starting from the intersector flows, a set of direct input coefficients is derived (direct input of one product per unit output of another product). Then by solving a set of equations, the direct and indirect input coefficients per unit of final output are found. These tell us, for example, not only how much coal is directly required to produce one automobile for final use, but how much coal is

material balances method is that it puts the technical intersector relationships among economic sectors into one unified scheme and allows them to be expressed mathematically in a very convenient and useful form— useful in the sense that vast numbers of equations can easily be handled through the use of electronic computers.[28] Soviet planners, by means of I-O techniques and electronic computers, after they had put together a realistic set of input norms, could rapidly construct a completely balanced output and supply plan.

Since 1956, Russian economists have been discussing the possibilities of adapting I-O techniques to their balancing methodology. Perhaps the first question which comes to mind is why were they so late. Professor Leontief's first book on I-O was published in 1941 and serious work on I-O problems began in the West soon after World War II. Among the reasons for the Russians' delay, I think, one can include bureaucratic inertia and opposition, low level of the necessary mathematical skills among economists, and the relative unavailability to economists of computers until recent years. But as important as any of these, is the fact that the use of mathematical methods in economics was, up to a few years ago, considered to be anti-Marxist. However, now I-O (also linear programming) has been separated from other econometric methods, and is considered not to be "negated by the Marxist theory of political economy." In addition, in an attempt to add further legitimacy, it is now claimed, but not proved, that since Professor Leontief was born and educated in Russia, his ideas were developed on the basis of early Russian experiments with national economic balances. Yet the charge of unorthodoxy is still a potent weapon, and the supporters of I-O, it would appear, still have to tread carefully.[29]

The Soviet discussion of I-O has both its negative and positive camps. Members of both camps almost always begin with the statement that I-O cannot be used for prediction purposes in the capitalist economy, because the capitalist economy is completely unpredictable. Although some do say that it could be used for more limited problems, such as mobilization. The rest of the criticisms are not too different from those

needed for the steel which goes into the automobile and so on. Thus, the direct and indirect input coefficient of coal per automobile tells us that if we increase the output for final use of automobiles by one unit how much more coal will be required throughout the economy to support this change in output. In other words, with these total cost coefficients, if we have an estimate of final demand (be it forecast or plan), we can determine the total output of each sector required for the production of this final bill of goods. I-O makes use of electronic computers to solve, rapidly, large system of equations. Its development is associated with the name of Prof. Wassily Leontief of Harvard University.

[28] One weakness of the material balances is that they are similar to the rows of an I-O table, while the important technical relationships in an economy are to be found in the columns.

[29] It is a sobering irony that the U.S. Government's I-O program was discontinued in 1953 because of allegations that in some way it was a socialist scheme and a threat to private enterprise. (See *Business Week*, August 29, 1953, p. 26.)

one hears in the West: assumption of constant coefficients, no substitution, no restraints, staticness, exclusion of capital equipment. It is common for a critic to end his article with an admission that I-O can perhaps play a small, restricted role in Soviet economics.

The supporters of I-O argue that it is a tool which could be used to utmost advantage in Soviet planning. It would assure a well-balanced plan. Through the use of total cost coefficients, the total effects of a change in any one output target could be calculated, and thus the necessary changes in all other outputs could be made. And what is of extreme importance, all the required calculations could be done rapidly on electronic computers. One writer emphasized this point by showing that in the calculation of the total cost coefficients for a 44 sector I-O model (remember, at one point, Gosplan had to balance 1,600 "sectors") 2,500,000 arithmetic operations were necessary. Yet an electronic computer was able to complete this task within 8 hours. Another advantage is that, after a balanced plan is derived, the calculation of the actual supply plan, i.e., the actual material flows from one sector to another, would be a simple matter—merely a multiplication of direct input coefficients times the levels of output of the corresponding products. Besides these basic points, supporters argue that changes during the operation of a short-term or long-term plan could more efficiently be made with the aid of total cost coefficients. The spreading of technical progress could be aided by using planned direct input coefficients rather than statistically derived ones as the basic data for I-O calculations. Under the new organization of industry, regional I-O balances could be made. On another level, I-O could be used for working out internally consistent prices. And finally, it could be used for some purely statistical purposes such as the calculation of certain economic proportions, comparisons of the labor and materials intensities of different products and certain statistical comparisons with the West.

If Russian planners were to adopt I-O methodology as it is practiced in the West, then among the many changes in planning techniques this would involve, there would be one of fundamental importance. This is the narrowing of the scope of politically determined basic plan goals from total outputs to final outputs (i.e., outputs for final uses: consumption, investment, etc.). In Western I-O practice, one starts with a given set of final demands and by means of a set of direct and indirect input coefficients, one solves for the levels of total outputs. Soviet planners, in the material balances method, start from a set of total output goals, which basically are determined by the political authorities in the society. That is the political authorities set targets, which include not only the amount of a product going to final uses, but also the amount which is needed within the economy to produce other products.

Are Soviet economists advocating such a change? According to a number of leading economists, including the very highly placed Academician V. S. Nemchinov, they are not. They intend to retain total outputs as the starting data for plan construction.[30] The primary use of I-O, according to these economists, will be to work out a number of different balanced variants of the plan. They say that the material balances method enables them to work out only one balanced variant of the plan, but with I-O they will be able to work out many from which they will choose the "best."[31] In addition, they claim that the material balances approach will remain the dominant one and that I-O techniques will only be an auxiliary planning mechanism.

There are, however, a few Soviet economists who do favor planning from a set of final outputs:

. . . the starting point of planning must be the final bill of goods [investment and consumption]. It is not sufficient to produce much steel or cement, lumber, or cotton. The aim is to produce a sufficient amount of machines, buildings, furniture, cloth, etc.

Another possibility is a mixed model, where some total output targets and some final outputs are given, and the remaining total outputs and final outputs are derived by solving the set of equations.

Only time will tell how far Russian planning will go into I-O techniques, but it does appear probable that in the beginning at least, its use will be restricted to the calculation of a number of plan variants and the use of total cost coefficients to calculate the total effects of any change in the plan.

As regards actual experimentation, there have been reports so far of four models worked out, including 9, 15, 17, and 44 order systems. These are all pilot models. For a system to have any operational significance it would have to be of the order of 500–1,000 sectors. There is also an experiment now in progress on a regional I-O study involving a single economic region (the Mordovskoi region). This is based on the method used in a U.S. study of the state of Utah.[32]

The new Laboratory for the Use of Statistics and Mathematical Methods in Economics, headed by Academician Nemchinov and the famous mathematician, L. V. Kantorovich, and possessing a staff of about 20, is working on I-O problems, mainly on problems of adapting statistical data

[30] The Soviet approach to the total output of steel and the total output of electricity as objectives in themselves is in part determined by the symbolic significance of these basic indexes as indicators of successful economic growth. But it is also a recognition of the fact that a high rate of growth of these basic industrial commodities is perhaps a safer assurance of economic growth than planning from a final bill of goods would be when foresight, knowledge, and techniques are still imperfect.

[31] One of the problems involved here is, of course, how do you choose the "best." But this is a problem of a different order. A choice out of many is still better than no choice at all.

[32] For a description of the Utah study see Moore and Petersen, "Regional Analysis: An Interindustry Model of Utah," *Review of Economics and Statistics*, November, 1955.

to computer use.[33] It is scheduled to operate, in the near future, at the computing center which is being erected in Novosibirsk. In addition, there are people working on I-O in the Economic Research Institute of Gosplan and in the Institute for Electronic Control Machines of the Academy of Sciences.

Thus Soviet economists are beginning to take notice of I-O and the possibilities of applying it to problems of planning. I-O in the Soviet Union has come a far way from the days when it was almost taboo to discuss it or work on it. Yet, on the other hand, it has by no means swept the field.[34] Much of the struggle still lies ahead. One bit of evidence of this is the extreme sensitivity, which supporters of I-O still retain, to questions of its origin and orthodoxy.

III. CONCLUSIONS

The general nature of Soviet supply planning can perhaps be best described as a combination of the central planning of aggregate categories with the successive setting of details down through the planning hierarchy and the application of constant pressure from the center to tighten production methods and to economize materials. This is not a picture of finely calculated balances, but is a combination whose aim is to contribute to economic growth.

One of the important operating criteria in the Soviet economy is the priority principle. The possible negative effects on economic growth of imbalances in supply plans are lessened because there are low priority buffer sectors to absorb the shocks of these imbalances. The operation of the priority principle also lessens the negative effects of the interaction of imperfect supply planning, overall tight planning and a not overly efficient supply bureaucracy.

Even though overall tight planning prevails, it should not be thought that the Soviet economy is everywhere so taut that the slightest failure in any one place will cause the whole economy to burst. Some operational leeway does exist. There are usually some unemployed or underemployed labor and materials to be found, which can be pressed into service when the need arises. This leeway is, in large measure, a result of the "informal activities" of the Soviet firm.

---

[33] This is a major problem. There have been numerous complaints that Soviet statistics are not adequate for use in I-O work. The main criticism is that they do not clearly show the technical relationships between sectors. Nemchinov's apparent suggestion that some I-O research be treated as classified work, in the same way as atomic energy and rocket research, has been interpreted as an attempt to gain access to detailed statistical data.

[34] In a personal interview with a Soviet economist, the economist complained that they could not get proper statistics for I-O work. When questioned on this, he said the data could be made available, but it would cost money to collect and process it and their problem now was to convince the higher-ups that I-O was a worthwhile project so that they could get the necessary budgetary allocations. He was told that this was a problem we could understand.

As an economy grows more developed, the number of interrelationships within it becomes larger. This intensifies the problems of supply planning. At the same time, however, the radical changes in the structure of the economy diminish, and thus supply relationships become more stable. This lessens the problems of supply planning. Yet it would appear that in recent years the increasing interrelationships have caused the Russians to become increasingly concerned with the deficiencies of their supply system.

One of the more promising means for counteracting these deficiencies is through the adoption of input-output techniques. The original flush of enthusiasm in the West for I-O may have diminished somewhat, and there are many perhaps who now feel that not too much should be expected of it. However, these criticisms apply to its use in the West. It should be kept in mind that under the type of economic organization that exists in the Soviet Union today, they have to plan their supply system. Thus, the appropriate question for them is not whether I-O is an ideal method, but whether it is better than the method Soviet planners use now—material balances. As far as assuring balance in the plan and speeding up the process of plan construction, there is no doubt of the superiority of I-O techniques. Yet the material balances method does have a significant organizational advantage. It allows for contact between planners and administrators and thus allows for the operation of certain pressure levers during the construction of the plan. What should perhaps be expected, therefore, is that the Russians will adopt I-O techniques in such a way as to combine it with these positive features of the material balances method.

If I-O techniques are adopted and thus the planning process speeded up, more time would be left for the troublesome specification stage. This would help, but an effective solution to the specification problem depends fundamentally on the creation of direct and stable relations between producers and users. It also depends on a diminution in the tightness of plans so as to lessen the degree of seller's market and make the market power of buyers more equal to that of sellers.

This discussion has concentrated on centralized supply planning methods. It is theoretically possible, of course, for more decentralized methods to be used, ones that would give lower level units more freedom to make their own economic decisions. However, the efficacy of any meaningful decentralization would depend upon the significant improvement of the Soviet price system, which up to now has been incapable of playing an effective role in the Soviet industrial supply system.

Morris Bornstein[1]

16. THE SOVIET PRICE SYSTEM*

Although relying primarily on centralized planning and administrative orders in physical terms to achieve their goals, Soviet planners also make considerable use of prices and markets. Prices are used in the Soviet economy to control and evaluate managerial performance, to allocate resources, and to distribute national and personal income. However, for a number of reasons, Soviet planners face serious difficulties in integrating physical and value instruments into mutually consistent, mutually reinforcing tools of economic control.

The following article analyzes the functions, characteristics, and weaknesses of the Soviet price system. It examines in turn the three major types of Soviet prices—industrial wholesale prices, agricultural procurement prices, and retail prices—explaining the conceptual and administrative problems involved in each. It concludes by evaluating the rationality of the Soviet price system according to several different criteria.

IN THE Soviet Union, as in all modern, complex economies, prices play an important part in the guidance of economic activity. However, their role in the Soviet economy is different both from their role in a capitalist market economy and from their role in a socialist market economy of the

[1] The author is grateful to the Ford Foundation and the Joint Committee on Slavic Studies of the SSRC and ACLS for grants in support of research on which this paper is based. He also wishes to thank the Soviet economists who granted him interviews during a visit to the Soviet Union.

* Reprinted, with the permission of the American Economic Association, from *American Economic Review*, Vol. LII, No. 1 (March, 1962), pp. 64–99.

Lange-Taylor-Lerner type. In the Soviet economy (and in the Soviet-type economies of Eastern Europe and Communist China), prices are not an autonomous force determining production, resource allocation, and consumption. Instead, prices are manipulated by the central authorities as one of various instruments intended to accomplish their planned goals.

This paper is an analysis of the role of prices in the Soviet planned economy. Following a summary view of the various functions of prices in the Soviet economy, Sections I–III deal with three major subsystems in the Soviet price system: industrial wholesale prices, agricultural procurement prices, and retail prices.[2] In Section IV some general conclusions are presented. The operation of the Soviet economy (in regard to those aspects pertinent to the subject of this paper) may be characterized as follows:

1. The bill of goods is determined by a central authority, although in some cases in terms of categories, of varying breadth, the specific composition of which is determined by individual enterprises.

2. To secure this bill of goods, the central authority allocates resources primarily in physical terms, without the use of scarcity prices, by estimating production requirements on the basis of technological coefficients and by using physical balances to equate sources and uses of intermediate and final products.

3. The central authority specifies, ordinarily in physical terms but usually also in value terms, maximum inputs and minimum outputs for each enterprise, although enterprises may have some role in determining input and output mixes.

4. There is freedom of occupational choice, and money-wage differences constitute the principal mechanism for distributing the labor force.

5. Consumer choice exists, with households free to determine the distribution of their money incomes between consumption and saving and free to buy whatever goods and services they desire in view of prevailing prices and available quantities.[3]

6. As a result of the importance of economic growth in the political authority's preference scale, the central authority emphasizes investment at the expense of consumption, stresses maximum output rather than optimum utilization of resources, and not only fully commits but tends to overcommit the resources of the economy and of each enterprise.

Within this framework, the functions of the price system may be classified under three very broad headings: (1) control and evaluation, (2) allocation, and (3) income distribution.

---

[2] Other parts of the price system, not analyzed in this paper, are wages, transportation rates, and foreign trade prices.

[3] Some limited degree of consumer sovereignty also exists, to the extent to which the central authority responds to evidence, revealed by the exercise of consumer choice, that consumers would prefer a different output-mix from that allocated to consumption purposes by the central authority.

CONTROL AND EVALUATION

Prices are used by the central planners to secure compliance by enterprise managers with the plans elaborated by the former and to evaluate the performance of the managers in the execution of their assigned tasks. Although resource allocation is determined by the planners largely in physical terms, it is necessary for them to express complex input and output targets for the enterprise in value terms in order to have a common denominator for physically dissimilar units of raw materials, labor, and capital goods. Thus the enterprise plan contains not only physical targets, but also value targets, such as those for value of output, cost, use of working capital, tax payments, and profits. To control and evaluate the use of inputs and the production of outputs by enterprises in physical terms alone would be extremely difficult, if not impossible. The use of value targets, moreover, enables the financial authorities (the Ministry of Finance and the banking system) to participate in enforcing enterprise adherence to, and execution of, plan targets.[4]

For control and evaluation purposes, it is convenient to have prices which are stable over long periods of time and are based on the weighted average cost of the industry. The former facilitates intertemporal comparisons of output and cost, while the latter provides an "objective" standard with which the costs of a given enterprise may be compared.

ALLOCATION

Because of the predominance of physical allocation, rather than allocation through the price system, the allocative function of prices is less important in the Soviet economy than the control and evaluation function. However, prices do influence the allocation of resources, and thus the pattern of production, in several ways. Four categories of participants in the economic process are involved: the central planning authorities, the managers of state enterprises, households in their capacity as suppliers of labor, and collective farms.

1. The Soviet planners (in *Gosplan*, the State Planning Committee, and in the planning organs of the ministries and regional economic councils) receive from the government (i.e., the leadership of the Communist Party) a number of broad targets, such as the size and distribution of the national product, as well as some specific targets, such as the level of military expenditures, foreign economic commitments, and physical targets for steel, coal, machine-tools, etc. The planners then deduce a pattern of output to attain these targets, primarily by the use of various "physical" tools, such as technical coefficients, material balances, and, more recently, some linear programming and input-output techniques. Prices influence

---

[4] Their role is strengthened by the Soviet policy of planning enterprise finances so that revenues exceed expenses by a narrow margin and by the requirement that enterprise funds be kept in the banking system, which supervises their expenditure.

their decisions regarding the pattern of output and the allocation of resources only to a limited extent, in the following ways:

a) Macroeconomic balances in value terms, such as national product and intersectoral accounts and capital-output ratios, are calculated and used to supplement, to a limited degree, the basic physical planning tools. To date, however, these value calculations appear to have been used primarily for an accounting function of measuring the results of physical planning decisions, rather than themselves serving as the basis for important production and resource allocation decisions.[5] But Soviet planners appear to be moving toward a greater and more positive role for aggregate value planning, as a result of the advocacy of this approach by a number of prominent Soviet economists, the growing acceptance in the USSR of mathematical methods in economics, and the progress of Soviet computer technology.

b) Prices may have some influence on the selection of technological coefficients for physical planning. Certainly, there are alternative production functions for many goods, and in the course of successive iterations in the balancing process, the technological matrix may be adjusted through the substitution of more abundant for scarcer materials. It has been suggested that relative pricing of substitutes, especially those involving "deficit" commodities is intended to guide the planners at least as much as the managers of state enterprises. To the extent to which this occurs, higher relative prices direct scarcer commodities to "more important" uses (i.e., those outputs higher on the planners' priority scale, which are not necessarily those outputs which themselves have higher relative prices).

c) The planners (including here the "project makers" or design engineers) make allocation decisions involving value calculations. These include decisions regarding alternative variants of a given-output investment project and the assessment of the benefits of modernization or innovation. Both of these involve a choice among alternatives on the basis of a value comparison of heterogeneous inputs (and the latter of outputs as well) and of the present and the future.

2. Prices also perform a limited allocative function at the enterprise level, because managers exercise a narrow range of choice and are guided in these choices by prices. It is impossible for the central authorities to specify in complete detail the inputs and outputs of each enterprise. The central authorities usually specify output targets in aggregate (or only slightly disaggregated) physical and value terms—for example, the principal categories of output in tons and the total value of output in rubles—giving the enterprise manager the responsibility to select the types, models, qualities, sizes, etc. Likewise in regard to inputs, the manager is

---

[5] Foreign-trade planning is an important exception requiring some value planning. Even if trade is not based on a comparison of domestic and foreign price ratios, value comparisons in foreign currencies are needed for balance-of-payments reasons. Thus, foreign-trade planning may be done in physical terms (by material balances and technological coefficients) subject to a specified balance-of-payments constraint.

told the amounts of the principal materials, the equipment, and the number of workers in each labor classification that he is authorized to use to achieve (and, if possible, surpass) his plan targets. Within these limits, the manager exercises discretion in deciding how to use the resources at his disposal to fulfill the enterprise plan, or, if it cannot be fulfilled in all respects, which parts to fulfill at the expense of which others. The pertinent prices influence his decisions regarding alternative outputs and inputs.

3. In the Soviet economy, prices affect both the total supply of labor and its distribution. Participation in the labor force is not compulsory. Rather, the state relies on low real wages, resulting from the relationship of money wages and consumer prices, to evoke a high participation rate. Wage differences, in turn, are the principal means of securing the distribution of the labor force (by skill, industry, enterprise, and geographical location) which the planners desire.[6] The wage structure is not a guide to the planners in their decisions regarding resource allocation, but rather an instrument for executing these decisions, i.e., for securing the allocation of labor planned in physical terms. Yet the wage structure allocates labor in the narrow sense that relative prices, rather than physical commands, are used to direct labor to the places assigned in the plan.

4. In the collective farm sector, the central authorities have used prices, along with delivery quotas, to influence the allocation of resources to certain crops and products in preference to others.[7]

To perform these allocation functions, scarcity prices, not merely accounting prices, are required. Only scarcity prices will lead planners to allocate resources efficiently and encourage enterprise and collective farm managers to produce the "best" (according to planners' preferences) assortment of goods in the most economical manner. Likewise, because wages are supposed to equate labor supply (by households) and demand (of enterprises, according to planners' targets), they also should be scarcity prices.

INCOME DISTRIBUTION

In the Soviet economy, the basis of income distribution is the "socialist" principle of unequal monetary compensation according to labor services rendered, rather than the "communist" principle of distribution according

---

[6] At the present time, qualifications to this simplified statement include (1) forced labor, (2) determination of the skills of the labor force through control of the educational system, (3) assignment of new graduates of technical schools and universities to their first jobs, and (4) such restrictions on mobility as the housing shortage. However, the much more stringent restrictions on freedom of occupational choice of the Stalin era have been eliminated.

[7] In addition, prices have been used (along with delivery quotas) to stimulate total output, but the aim in this case has been primarily to increase the productivity of given resources engaged in agriculture, by increasing real compensation and thus incentives.

to need; and the promise of unequal monetary compensation is the basis of production incentives.

The price system thus determines in the first instance the distribution of money income. The distribution of real income, in turn, is achieved primarily by the sale of goods and services to households exercising free choice in the expenditure of their (unequal) money incomes. However, in an effort to make the distribution of real income less unequal than the distribution of money income, the Soviet government fixes low prices for mass consumption goods and high prices for luxury goods by means of differentiated turnover taxes.[8]

Prices thus are called upon to perform several important functions in the Soviet economy. The remainder of this paper is devoted to an appraisal of how well Soviet prices perform their assigned tasks. For this purpose, the Soviet price system is divided into several distinguishable but interrelated subsystems: industrial wholesale prices, agricultural procurement prices, and retail prices.

I. INDUSTRIAL WHOLESALE PRICES

The term industrial wholesale prices is here applied to the prices at which goods are transferred or evaluated within the state sector of the Soviet economy. The term covers prices of producers' goods, including raw materials, semifabricates, and machinery, as well as manufactured consumers' goods. It excludes prices at which agricultural products are obtained by the state from collective farms but includes prices at which procurement agencies sell agricultural products to state enterprises for processing or to trade organizations for retail sale without further processing. It also excludes foreign trade prices, although it includes the prices at which foreign trade organizations buy from and sell to Soviet enterprises.

TYPES OF INDUSTRIAL WHOLESALE PRICES

The following are the principal types of Soviet industrial wholesale prices:

1. *Enterprise Wholesale Price.* This is the price at which a producing enterprise sells its product to other state enterprises. It excludes turnover tax on the product but includes any turnover tax previously paid by the enterprise on materials going into the product. If the enterprise is responsible for delivery of the product, this price covers transportation cost.

2. *Industry Wholesale Price.* This is the price paid by the state-enterprise buyer and includes, in addition to the enterprise wholesale

---

[8] The distribution of real income is also less unequal than the distribution of money income because of (1) the allocation of housing and (2) the informal rationing of queues and empty shelves when retail prices are fixed below the market-clearing level.

price, the following: (*a*) the turnover tax, if any, on the product; (*b*) the mark-up of the industry sales organization, if the product is sold by a central sales organization rather than by the individual enterprise itself;[9] and (*c*) transportation charges, if these are borne by the sales organization rather than the buyer. If there are no turnover taxes on the product and the product is sold by the enterprise itself, rather than by a central sales organization, the enterprise wholesale price is also the industry wholesale price.

3. *Settlement Price.*   In some industries where production costs diverge widely, notably in petroleum extraction, individual enterprises or groups of enterprises receive different prices, rather than a single, uniform enterprise wholesale price. In this case, the industry sales organization buys from the enterprise at its individual settlement price and sells to customers at the industry wholesale price.

4. *Price of "Own Procurement."*   This is the price paid by enterprises, especially small state enterprises under local control and producers' co-operatives, for scrap and for raw materials, particularly construction materials, obtained from collective farms.

5. *Local Wholesale Price.*   This is the price at which a product made from "own procurements" of raw materials is sold by such enterprises.

Of these five categories of prices, the first three are the most important, applying to the overwhelming bulk of Soviet industrial production, and are fixed by the national or regional authorities. The last two, of lesser importance, are fixed by the local authorities.

Functions of Industrial Wholesale Prices

Three principal functions of Soviet industrial wholesale prices may be distinguished: (1) assistance to the planners in the elaboration of the plan, (2) guidance for managerial choice among inputs and outputs, and (3) control and evaluation of managerial performance.

1. Soviet planners calculate many value aggregates, including those for output, cost, wages, sales, and the national accounts. Industrial wholesale prices, along with agricultural procurement, retail, and foreign-trade prices, are necessarily used in these calculations. For example, enterprise wholesale prices are used to calculate value of output and labor productivity targets for individual enterprises and groups of enterprises. Industry wholesale prices—at which goods are transferred within the state sector— are used in the calculation of costs, sales revenue, profits, and the contribution of the industrial sector to the national product. Both current and constant prices are used, depending upon the purpose of the calculation. Industry wholesale prices, together with planned wage rates and transportation charges, are used in the derivation of "estimate prices," at which construction cost estimates are prepared.

---

[9] For example, the centralized sales scheme is used in the metallurgical, petroleum, and cement industries, while chemical and machine-building enterprises sell their products themselves.

As a rule, industrial wholesale prices are used by the planners without any adjustment. However, there is an exception in the case of investment-project planners, whose task is to choose among alternative technological variants of a given-output project (e.g., a thermal or hydro-electric power station of a given capacity). In comparing operating costs against initial construction costs, they have sometimes used various "coefficients of scarcity" to correct for what they regarded as unduly low industry wholesale prices, which, in their opinion, inadequately reflected the scarcity of various raw materials. Because little has been published regarding these adjustments, it is not possible to estimate how widely they are used or how great are the adjustments made to the established industry whole-sale prices. In the absence of information on these questions, it is assumed in this paper that the planners in general use the established industrial wholesale prices.

Although industrial wholesale prices are indispensable in the elaboration of output, cost, sales, and profit targets, these value calculations fulfill primarily an accounting function rather than serving as the basis for allocation decisions.

2. The allocative effect of industrial wholesale prices is felt primarily in the guidance of managerial choice among alternative outputs and inputs. The enterprise plan specifies total output and its main component categories (the "assortment plan"), but the enterprise manager usually exercises some choice regarding the detailed composition of these categories, i.e., the types, grades, sizes, and qualities. He also has some discretion regarding his input-mix for a given output, although this discretion is sharply limited both by the technical possibilities for altering his production functions and by the physical allocation of many materials and the earmarking of expense categories by the central authorities.

In regard to outputs, the structure of industrial wholesale prices is supposed to induce managers to fulfill the assortment plan, in the first instance, and, within the limits of the assortment plan to stress scarcer in preference to less scarce items and higher quality in preference to lower quality items. Similarly, in regard to inputs, the structure of wholesale prices (and freight rates) is supposed (1) to encourage the use of less scarce in preference to scarcer varieties of raw materials (e.g., ferrous rather than nonferrous metals); (2) to economize transportation by making local materials and fuels "cheaper" to users than materials and fuels from distant sources; (3) to carry out a given fuel balance policy (favoring the use of coal and natural gas, in preference to petroleum); and (4) to promote mechanization, by encouraging the use of larger rather than smaller machines and the adoption of new models.

3. Finally, in the control and evaluation of managerial performance, industrial wholesale prices are used (along with other prices, such as wage rates, transportation rates, and, in the case of retail trade enterprises, state retail prices) in measuring the degree of fulfillment of plan targets. They are similarly used in comparing the performance of the enterprise, in

regard to output, cost, and profit, with the performance of other enterprises and with its own performance in earlier accounting periods.

"Good" or "successful" managerial performance is nominally measured in terms of the degree of fulfillment of the enterprise plan, but the latter, in turn, is composed of a number of targets or indicators, including those for output, cost, and profit. However, the structure of rewards for good, and penalties for bad, managerial performance specified by the central authority establishes a clear hierarchy in which the "quantitative" total output target ranks above such "qualitative" targets as those for the composition of output (the "assortment plan"), profit, and unit cost. In making such choices as are available to him in his circumscribed area of decision-making, the enterprise manager endeavors to achieve those plan targets which are accorded more importance in the evaluation of his performance by higher echelons, at the expense of those regarded by them as less important.[10]

This distinction is significant in the analysis of Soviet industrial prices because output (total and assortment) may be measured in different (relative) prices than cost and profit. (Output is also often measured in physical units.) Output is evaluated at constant enterprise wholesale index prices of some base period or date, because intertemporal comparison of the growth of output is of prime interest. Cost and profit are measured in current prices at which goods are transferred, including materials costs at industry wholesale prices and sales revenue at enterprise wholesale prices. These constant prices may be identical with current transfer prices at some point in time, such as the beginning of a long-term plan period, but they tend to diverge in level and structure as the two evolve separately.[11]

Output targets and input authorizations are also specified in physical terms, such as linear meters of cloth, tons of weight, surface area, etc. These give rise to what Grossman has called physical quasi-prices, measuring the terms of exchange between alternative products either in fulfilling the output target, or as input costs. Clearly, the relative importance of

---

[10] For example, the assortment plan may be sacrificed in favor of the gross value of output plan by producing more of the higher-priced and less of the lower-priced items in the enterprise's production schedule. Likewise, the relatively more material-intensive items may be produced at the expense of the less material-intensive, since the former contribute more, for a given amount of labor involved in their processing, to the final value of output. Similarly, the assortment plan may be sacrificed in favor of the profit plan by producing more of the items with higher unit profits and less of those with lower unit profits. Targets for cost reduction may be met not by increasing efficiency in the use of inputs but by decreasing quality. To enforce closer adherence to the assortment plan limited experiments have been undertaken to measure value of output on a value-added (i.e. wages or wages and profits) basis, rather than in terms of gross value of output. Also bonuses for fulfillment and over-fulfillment of output plans have been made contingent, at least in some industries, on the fulfillment of cost reduction plans.

[11] This divergence may be substantial, as during the 25-year period that 1926/27 prices were used for output calculations despite many changes in current transfer prices, or relatively modest, as during the period beginning in 1956 during which transfer prices of July 1, 1955 have been used as constant prices for output calculations and there has been no general change in transfer prices.

different products as measured in these physical units is likely to differ from their relative importance as measured by their relative prices either in the constant index price structure or in the current transfer price structure. Thus, a third price structure may be distinguished.

Because different enterprise plan targets or authorizations are specified in different prices, the relative importance of the different kinds of prices depends on the relative importance of the targets expressed in them. Because output targets are of primary importance, constant index money prices and physical quasi-prices tend to influence managerial decisions more than current transfer prices. As between the first two types of prices, both of which may be used in the measurement of output, their relative importance differs from industry to industry, depending upon the extent to which total output targets may conveniently be expressed in physical units.

FORMATION OF INDUSTRIAL WHOLESALE PRICES

Soviet enterprise wholesale prices are composed of two principal parts: planned average branch cost of production (*sebestoimost'*) and a profit mark-up.

The Soviet cost concept of *sebestoimost'* has no exact equivalent in Western cost accounting. It includes direct and indirect labor, including wages, salaries, and social insurance payments; basic and auxiliary materials, including fuel and power; depreciation (but not depletion) allowances; and various overhead expenses, such as those for postage, business travel, and expenditures for workers' housing and for workers' education.

Although in some instances differential rent and short-term interest payments for working capital are included in *sebestoimost'*, both rent and interest on capital are ordinarily omitted. As a result, Soviet cost accounting practices, in comparison with the results that would be obtained if Western accounting practices were used, result in lower total nominal costs and in different relative costs as among products and industries.[12] For convenience, *sebestoimost'* is hereafter rendered in this paper as "cost of production" or "production cost."

The cost figure used as a basis for enterprise wholesale prices (and, in turn, industry wholesale prices) is the planned average cost of production of the enterprises producing the product. However, the figure is not simply a weighted average of planned costs of all producers, but, rather, excludes some of the highest cost producers. The Soviet literature on the subject reveals some dispute about how "progressive" (i.e., how ambitious) the cost target should be. Some writers advocate a cost target based on the performance of "leading" enterprises, while others favor a more modest target which takes into account the capabilities of all enterprises in the corresponding branch of industry.

---

[12] The shares of the principal components of the *sebestoimost'* for aggregate Soviet industrial production in 1959 were as follows (in per cent): basic materials, 63.9; auxiliary materials, 4.8; fuel, 3.6; power, 1.7; labor, 19.3; and others, 3.2.

The other component of enterprise wholesale prices, in addition to planned average branch production cost, is a profit mark-up intended to provide a "normal" profit, for the branch as a whole, of about 5 per cent. Profit in the Soviet economy is not intended to allocate resources among alternative uses, but rather to provide a source of net income or accumulation to the state, to serve as an instrument of financial control, and to promote the "businesslike" operation of Soviet enterprises.

A major part of the profits of Soviet enterprises is paid to the state budget as profits tax, while the remainder is retained by the enterprise for the expansion of its fixed and working capital and for the payment of bonuses and the construction of housing, nurseries, and recreational facilities for the workers of the enterprise. In addition to the use of its own retained profits, the enterprise's expansion may be financed through budget grants representing the redistribution of profits tax and other tax collections. Periodic payments of profits tax liabilities, based on planned profits (which are in turn based on planned sales and costs), furnish a basis for supervision and control of enterprise operations by the financial authorities.

For both the accumulation and control purposes, the turnover tax also can be, and is, used. Soviet writers stress that profits and the turnover tax are both forms of "net income" to the state, and that both are needed, since each has its own special function. That is, although their economic nature—as a vehicle for monetary accumulation—is the same, they perform different roles in economic organization and administration. Profit is considered a tool of control designed to measure (one facet of) managerial performance. But it is convenient to have a supplementary form of accumulation which provides net income to the state without at the same time constituting enterprise income. Thus, in the case of consumer goods production, a high rate of accumulation can be achieved through the turnover tax without involving an abnormally high rate of profit for producing or trading enterprises.

Underlying this conception of the nature and role of profit is the notion that efficient operation of enterprises is promoted by a rather modest level of profit and is discouraged by either above-normal profits or below-normal profits or planned losses. It is asserted that unduly high profits fail to spur managers to reduce costs. Likewise planned losses and subsidies discourage managers from striving for lower costs and lead them to depend on outside assistance in the form of budget grants, rather than to maintain the financial independence that goes with "sound" operation. On the other hand, a pricing policy that keeps most enterprises in the industry near the margin of profitability is believed to promote efficiency, at the same time that it provides, through profits tax liabilities, a vehicle for control over enterprise operations by the financial authorities.[13]

---

[13] In Soviet parlance, this is the pricing policy which is consistent with *khozra-schet* ("business calculation") operation of enterprises, the characteristics of which are (1) the exchange of goods on the basis of state supply plans and contracts;

There are two principal reasons why enterprise wholesale prices have in various cases exceeded the level necessary to cover cost and provide a small profit. One arises simply from the infrequency with which prices are revised. The last general revision of industrial wholesale prices occurred on July 1, 1955, and the preceding one on January 1, 1952. The next revision is apparently scheduled for 1962.* During the interval between price revisions, reductions in costs lead to profits much in excess of 5 per cent in industries, such as machine-building, characterized by rapid changes in productivity. Second, above-average profits occur in the case of "deficit" or scarce commodities which are assigned relatively high prices, compared to the prices of substitutes, to discourage their use. However, this use of industrial wholesale prices as an allocation device—i.e., as a partial rationer of commodities—has been confined to a comparatively small number of basic industrial goods, notably nonferrous metals such as copper, tin, and lead, quality steels, and refined petroleum products.

Much of the Soviet literature on price formation is concerned with the conflict arising between the belief that a "normal" profit promotes efficiency and the fact that average-cost pricing inevitably means above-normal profits for lower-than-average-cost producers and below-normal profits (or losses) for higher-than-average-cost producers. Wide variations in unit costs of production exist, for example, in the extractive, metallurgical, machine-building, textile, footwear, and sugar-refining industries, due to differences in natural conditions of production, distance from sources of raw materials and fuels, technology, degree of specialization of production, and regional wage rates. To cope with the resulting differences in costs, two main approaches are used. In the metallurgical, chemical, and light industries, uniform enterprise wholesale prices are widely used, and the resulting variation in profitability, ranging from planned losses to high profits, is met through intradepartmental redistributions of funds to the enterprises in the former category from those in the latter.[14] On the other hand, some industries use settlement prices, which are different for each enterprise (as in sugar-refining) or group of enterprises (as in petroleum extraction).

In both cases, however, the objective is to secure a single buying price

---

(2) covering all of the enterprise's current (i.e., noncapital) expenditures from its own revenues; (3) direct dependence of the financial status of the enterprise on the effective use of its resources, i.e., on the successful fulfillment of the various targets of the enterprise plan; (4) control of enterprise activity through the control of its financial resources by budget and credit controls; (5) "material self-interest" of the employees of the enterprise in its financial results; and (6) personal and individual responsibility of the enterprise director for the use of state resources in accordance with the plan.

* Editor's note: The introduction of the new industrial wholesale prices was postponed until 1965.

[14] Under the functional form of economic organization in effect up to mid-1957, these involved redistribution of profits within a ministry. Under the territorial form in effect since then, funds are transferred among enterprises within a regional economic council.

for buyers of the product, in order to make their costs (in regard to raw materials and fuels), and thus their performance, more comparable. The widespread use of delivered prices (in some cases, differentiated according to geographical zones) is also directed toward this end. In addition, it places the demand for transport services with the seller, who is likely, under the prevailing conditions of a "sellers' market," to be less wasteful of them than the buyer.

The industry wholesale price for a good may differ from the enterprise wholesale price because of the turnover tax, as well as because of the sales mark-up and transportation charges. Before the 1949 price reform, the turnover tax was levied at very low rates (usually .5–1 per cent) on various producer goods to give the financial authorities an additional instrument of supervision and control. Since the 1949 reform, it has not been levied on producer goods except in the case of petroleum products, natural gas, and electric power, where the tax (rather than a higher profit mark-up) is used to secure the desired relative price structure for alternative sources of energy—i.e., to raise the prices of these sources relative to the price of coal.

On the other hand, in the case of some manufactured consumer goods, such as textiles, the turnover tax has been levied since 1939, and particularly since 1949, in a way intended to use the enterprise wholesale price structure to promote the fulfillment of the enterprise's assortment plan. On most manufactured consumer goods, the tax is levied as a specific ruble amount, permitting the existence of two distinct price structures—one for the state retail prices at which these goods are finally sold to households and the other for the enterprise wholesale prices received by producers. The difference between the two prices consists of turnover tax and mark-ups for the industry's central sales organization and for the wholesale and retail trade network. Thus the relative prices of two goods in the state retail price structure need not be, and usually are not, the same as their relative prices in the enterprise wholesale price structure. In the former, relative prices are set to manipulate consumption—essentially to adjust sales to supply. In the latter, prices are set with the aim of providing equal profitability for alternative varieties of output and thereby eliminating the incentive to achieve the gross value of output target by "violating" the assortment plan. If the tax were levied not as a specific ruble amount but as a uniform percentage of the final retail or wholesale price, the effect would be to apply the state retail relative price structure to the output of the producing enterprise. Under this price structure, certain varieties of output would be more profitable to produce than others, and the enterprise would attempt to produce more of the more profitable varieties and less of the less profitable varieties than called for in its assortment plan, since by doing so it would have to use less rubles of inputs to produce a given 100 rubles of output.[15]

---

[15] The tax is still levied as a percentage of the retail price in the case of many

EVALUATION OF INDUSTRIAL WHOLESALE PRICES

Soviet industrial wholesale prices clearly are not scarcity prices, inasmuch as they are fixed on the basis of average labor costs and neglect scarcity and demand. Supply and demand relationships are largely ignored in price determination (again, with some exceptions), and surpluses and shortages rarely lead to changes in these prices. How satisfactory are such prices for the performance of the three functions distinguished above?

1. Such accounting prices clearly do not offer sound guidance to the planning authorities in the choice among alternatives regarding production and investment, since they do not accurately measure the marginal costs of alternative inputs or the marginal values of alternative outputs. By omitting land and capital charges, these prices lead to the undervaluation of raw materials and equipment relative to labor in cost calculations and to the excessive use of the former relative to the latter. Recognition of these defects of industrial wholesale prices no doubt explains in part the unwillingness of Soviet planners to use them as the basis for resource allocation decisions and their reliance, instead, on physical planning techniques. Yet the preference for physical planning and the suspicion of prices as a proper device for socialist resource allocation have surely contributed to the Soviet failure to devise industrial wholesale prices which would more closely reflect scarcity.

The consequence of the reliance on physical planning, however, is that the resulting plans are not based on the precise evaluation of the terms on which alternatives are offered which a system of scarcity prices would provide. Hence, the plans do not achieve the optimum use of resources for the attainment of the goals set. (Also, the regime itself does not know with comparable precision the opportunity costs of alternative decisions facing it.) However, in the absence of scarcity prices, there may well be no loss, and indeed there may be some gain, in rationality by using physical planning techniques in preference to value calculations involving nonscarcity prices. Given the present industrial wholesale prices, Soviet planners may be wise not to rely on value planning.

2. Because Soviet industrial wholesale prices do not reflect relative scarcities of goods and factors of production, they likewise are not desirable guides for the choices among alternative inputs and outputs which enterprise managers are authorized to make (or which they make without authorization in the course of achieving some plan targets at the expense of others). However, precisely because the central authorities lack confidence that industrial wholesale prices will lead enterprises to achieve the results they desire of them, they limit severely, by commands and direc-

goods, particularly those whose assortment is considered relatively narrow (such as light bulbs, radios, and clocks) on the ground that in these cases the administrative advantage of not having to fix individual turnover tax amounts outweighs the disadvantage arising from the enterprise's incentive to deviate from the assortment plan.

tives in physical terms, the range of choices which enterprise managers can make on the basis of these prices.

3. The principal function of industrial wholesale prices is the control and evaluation of enterprise performance in the fulfillment of plans determined by the central authorities principally through physical planning. For this purpose, prices of the (merely) accounting type are satisfactory, and the lack of scarcity prices is not necessarily disadvantageous. Accounting prices do provide a supplementary method of verifying adherence to physical plans, and average-cost pricing facilitates comparison of the performance of the individual enterprise with that of the industry as a whole. The absence of an interest charge on fixed capital, although a serious deficiency in so far as allocation of capital is concerned, is not important for the control and evaluation of the enterprise, because capital as such (as distinct from specific capital goods) is not among the inputs which are entrusted to the manager and whose use by him in accordance with the enterprise plan is to be enforced and evaluated with the aid of the price system. Thus, although they fail to reflect relative scarcities, industrial wholesale prices can nevertheless perform their control and evaluation function reasonably well.

The unsuitability of industrial wholesale prices for allocative purposes restrains any inclination on the part of planners to shift toward value, rather than physical, planning. It also is a barrier to any substantial decentralization of decision-making to the enterprise level under which enterprise managers would determine their inputs and outputs on the basis of value calculations of cost, revenue, and profit. Either or both of these changes in Soviet economic planning would require a system of scarcity prices, reflecting both supply and demand (according to planners' preferences), upon which the central authorities could rely to secure the resource allocation and bill of goods which they desire.

II. AGRICULTURAL PROCUREMENT PRICES

Agricultural procurement prices here refer to the prices at which agricultural producers sell to state procurement agencies. Collective farm market prices, at which agricultural producers sell to households, are analyzed in the section on retail prices. Most of the discussion in this section concerns the agricultural procurement prices paid to collective farms, since the prices paid to state farms are essentially similar to the industrial wholesale prices analyzed in the preceding section.

State Farm Procurement Prices

State farm delivery prices (*sdatochnye tseny sovkhozov*) are essentially different in nature from the agricultural procurement prices paid to collective farms. In the case of state farms, the delivery price is a "transfer" price which performs only a nominal "accounting" function. In the case of collective farms, agricultural procurement prices directly and strongly influence the volume and composition of output.

State farms are "factories in the field" with a *khozraschet* status (see fn. 13) similar to that of state enterprises in industry, transportation, etc. Their employees receive money wages on a piece-rate basis, and they calculate cost of production (*sebestoimost'*) in essentially the same way as other state enterprises. Accordingly, their delivery prices are supposed to be comparable to enterprise wholesale prices in industry, covering cost of production (as reckoned in Soviet state enterprises) plus a small profit mark-up. Like other state enterprises, they are subject to profits taxes, on the one hand, and are entitled to receive budget grants, normally only for the expansion of fixed and working capital, on the other.

In practice, however, state farm delivery prices have usually been fixed very close to the corresponding state purchase prices for collective farms. These prices have not been high enough to cover state farm operating costs, and as a result state farms have long shown large operating losses (both "planned" and "unplanned") which were met by operating subsidies from the budget. Thus, the pricing of state farm deliveries has not in fact followed the operating-cost-plus-profit criterion generally applied since 1949 to industrial wholesale prices. Apparently the Soviet government has been reluctant to fix state farm prices "out of line" with collective farm prices. Since state farm costs (and thus, prices) are supposed to serve as a model and target for collective farms, state farm prices could hardly be fixed above the prevailing collective farm procurement prices!

Because state farm costs are reimbursed by the combination of delivery prices and subsidies, the failure of prices to cover costs does not restrain output. In contrast, in the case of collective farms, which do not receive subsidies, prices are the sole source of compensation for production expenses and productive effort. Because collective farmers do not receive fixed money wages but are instead residual claimants to the net income of the collective farms (after precedent claims for material production expenses, taxes, investment, etc., have been satisfied), the level of procurement prices has a direct effect upon their incentives and thus their productivity and output.[16]

COLLECTIVE FARM PROCUREMENT PRICES

1. *Objectives.* In setting agricultural procurement prices for collective farms, the Soviet government has pursued two conflicting objectives:

---

[16] Since 1958 a small minority of collective farms has shifted to a wage basis, that is, full monthly payments at fixed rates for specific tasks or norms of production. Even under these circumstances, the level of procurement prices determines the level of wages which can be paid.

(1) to fix the terms of trade for the collective farm peasantry so as to make it bear a large share of the burden of industrialization, and (2) to provide incentives to produce.

In the first case, the state has determined the terms of trade and real income of the peasantry through the relationship between agricultural procurement prices paid to the collective farms, on the one hand, and prices paid by the collective farms for material inputs and prices paid by collective farmers for consumer goods, on the other.[17] Because the collective farm peasantry would not voluntarily deliver at the terms of trade imposed by the state the quantities desired by the state—i.e., would not voluntarily pay the tax in kind levied by the state—a system of delivery quotas has been necessary to enforce these terms of trade. In addition to meeting the quotas fixed for deliveries at obligatory delivery prices, the collective farms were expected to fulfill "plans" for additional procurements at state purchase prices. Although the latter were higher than the obligatory delivery prices, they were still below collective farm market prices, and hence sales at state purchase prices were in most cases not voluntary but compulsory. In the case of raw material crops, the possibility of collective farm market sales does not exist.

In this light, the turnover tax on agricultural commodities, which accounts for the bulk of the difference between the procurement price paid to collective farms and the retail price charged final consumers, may be thought of as being borne in part by producers in the form of lower procurement prices and in part by consumers in the form of higher resale prices.

The Soviets have long justified procurement prices "below the value" of the commodity on the ground that this is the means by which the state is compensated for expenditures on behalf of the collective farm peasantry for irrigation, conservation, electrification, agricultural research, education and health measures, etc. This view in effect interprets that part of the turnover tax borne by the collective peasantry as a charge for specific services rendered to production, together with a contribution to the financing of general welfare expenditures benefiting the peasantry. Another interpretation is that at least part of the turnover tax represents a payment by the collective farms for the use of their land. Although all land in the Soviet Union has been nationalized, it is used by producers without an explicit charge. Soviet writers acknowledge that the state seeks to capture at least part of the differential rent arising from differences in fertility, location, and extent of mechanization through a number of devices. These include regional variations in procurement prices, in obligatory delivery quotas, and (up to 1958) in rates for payments in kind for

---

[17] As one Soviet writer puts it: "In other words, purchase prices, besides their direct functional role as an instrument of accounts between the producers of agricultural products and the state, acquire significance as one of the important mechanisms of distribution of the national income between town and country."

machine-tractor station (MTS) services, as well as direct taxes on collective farm income. The low level of procurement prices (high rate of turnover taxation borne by the collective farm peasantry) thus represents in part a rent charge by the state as owner of the land and in part a tax imposed by the state to finance its expenditures, both those directly affecting collective farms and those of more general effect.

The second objective of agricultural procurement prices is, through their general level, to furnish incentives to collective farm peasants to produce agricultural output in general; and through their relative price structure, to furnish incentives to produce certain agricultural products in preference to others. It is evident that this second objective, which would be furthered by higher procurement prices, conflicts with the first one of collecting a tax in kind through low procurement prices. It constitutes an alternative approach to agricultural procurement, stressing price incentives rather than coercive quota demands as the means of securing food and agricultural raw materials from the peasantry.

Allowance for collective farm market sales results in a significant improvement in the peasantry's terms of trade and real income and a marked increase in its incentive to produce, because collective farm market prices have been much higher than state procurement prices and because collective farm market sales represent an important share of total marketings, especially for individual peasant households. This is no doubt one of the reasons why the collective farm market has been tolerated by the Soviet state, despite its ideological incongruity. At the same time, it must be assumed that in fixing state agricultural procurement prices some allowance has been made, if only in an approximate and crude way, for the supplementation by collective farm market sales of the low prices paid on deliveries to the state. Cotton growers who could not sell part of their output on the collective farm market had to be compensated fully through state procurement prices, whereas grain and livestock producers were expected to augment their earnings from sales to state procurement agencies by sales, at higher prices, on the collective farm market.

The interrelationships here are complex, however. While collective farm market prices have no doubt influenced state procurement prices, the converse is also true. The state policy in regard to the prices and quantities of agricultural procurements affects both the supply offered on the collective farm market and the demand on the collective farm market of urban consumers unable to satisfy their requirements at state stores from the state's agricultural procurements. State agricultural procurement prices have been fixed after taking into account the prospects for collective farm market sales and the extent to which *average* realized prices (for food products) would therefore exceed state procurement prices.

2. *Price Policy since 1953.* One of the first steps taken by Stalin's successors in 1953 was to embark on a broad program to increase agricultural output, involving changes in planning and administration, delivery

requirements, taxes, investment, and prices. The changes in agricultural procurement price policy included a large increase in the general level of prices, a revision in the relative price structure in favor of food crops, efforts to calculate costs and to relate prices to costs, and the unification of multiple prices into single procurement prices for each crop.

In 1953, obligatory delivery and above-quota purchase prices were increased sharply for most food products. In some cases, such as vegetables and potatoes, average realized prices were also raised by reductions in obligatory delivery quotas, which released more of the crop for sale at the higher state purchase and collective farm market prices. The 1953 revisions, however, clearly were the result of hasty rule-of-thumb calculations.

The next round of price increases, in 1956, represented the initial response to the cost studies begun in 1955. Most procurement prices were increased again. In some cases the differential between the basic and the higher incentive price for a product was narrowed. For example, sugar beet base prices were raised roughly fourfold while the maximum premium price was reduced from 400 to 150 per cent of base. In the case of potatoes, the obligatory delivery price was increased by about 150 per cent and the above-quota purchase price by only 50 per cent.

The major change in agricultural procurement prices occurred in 1958 in connection with the decision to abolish the MTS's and turn their machinery over to the collective farms. Multiple pricing was eliminated, and a new single state purchase price was fixed for each product. The new prices are supposed to be incentive prices adequate to cover average costs of production, including a reasonable compensation for collective farm labor, and to provide for "accumulation" (i.e., collective farm investment in fixed and working capital).

The general constraint upon the 1958 price increase, as stated by Khrushchev, was that the total bill to the state for procurements from collective farms was not to increase—that is, that the new procurement bill was not to exceed the previous bill for deliveries plus the bill for MTS operations and investment. The desired level of turnover tax collections, out of the difference between agricultural procurement prices and state retail prices, also imposes a limit on the general level of agricultural procurement prices. Procurement price increases since 1953, in the face of reductions in retail prices in 1953 and 1954 and general stability in retail prices since then, have required reductions in the turnover tax rates on flour, meat, and sugar, and the elimination of turnover taxes on butter, potatoes, vegetables, and some meat products. Moreover, as a result of the 1958 procurement price increases, retail prices on vegetables were raised 10 per cent and on potatoes 8 per cent. Further agricultural procurement price increases thus would conflict with the present Soviet policy of maintaining a stable state retail price level.

The 1958 prices purported to cover average costs[18] of production and to provide for accumulation. A comparison of these prices with average collective farm costs in 1953–56 shows that they substantially exceed production costs of sugar beets, cotton, flax, and wool; slightly exceed production costs of grain, potatoes, and vegetables; and fall notably short of covering production costs of beef, pork, and milk. The "average costs" considered in fixing these prices are thus not the actual average costs of the immediately preceding years but rather appear to be anticipated feasible costs in the (near?) future in regions from which quota deliveries are required. These are lower than average collective farm costs in the past for two reasons. First, quota deliveries have been eliminated or greatly reduced in exceptionally high-cost areas, and second, cost reductions are expected from the transfer of the MTS machinery to the collective farms.

The prices fixed in 1958 are described as both "stable" and "flexible." They are expected to remain basically unchanged for some time, but annual adjustments up or down will be made for exceptionally bad or good harvests, in order to keep the size of the total procurement bill approximately constant. Thus, a number of prices were reduced for the bountiful 1958 harvest, while potato prices were raised for the 1959 crop. Prices will therefore tend to vary from year to year directly with cost, instead of inversely as under the former multiple price system.

The 1958 prices are also supposed to promote a rational pattern of regional specialization in agricultural production. Before 1958, regional differences received only token recognition. Although there was some regional variation in delivery quotas, MTS rates, and prices, the basic principle nevertheless was that every farm, regardless of natural conditions, should deliver some amounts of each of the basic food crops—grain, potatoes, vegetables, meat, and milk. Since the prices for these crops failed to cover cost, this principle was in effect a method of requiring all farms to bear part of the burden of the tax in kind. The general principle underlying the regional differentiation of the 1958 prices appears to be that price should be higher in the higher-cost regions, but that the margin of "profit" above cost should be higher in the lower-cost regions. This policy endeavors to secure a continued and perhaps expanded flow of output from the higher-cost regions while providing the greatest incentives (and means) for expansion of output to the lower-cost regions. It is hoped that future growth of output in the latter will eventually make it possible to curtail procurements from high-cost regions and thereby to reduce average costs and hence procurement prices.

An appraisal of agricultural procurement price policy since 1953 thus

---

[18] Some Soviet economists proposed basing prices not on average cost but on cost on marginal land—a suggestion rejected on the ground that it would remove the pressure for cost reductions imposed by average-cost pricing.

shows clearly a shift to a policy of providing incentives to expand agricultural output. The over-all level of agricultural procurement prices was sharply increased after 1952, while prices of manufactured producer and consumer goods bought by collective farms and individual peasants were reduced, as a result of general reductions in wholesale prices of producer goods in 1955 and in retail prices in 1953 and 1954.[19] Although precise calculations of the terms of trade cannot be made from available data, it is clear that they have improved substantially as a result of these price trends.

What is perhaps even more significant is that an effort is now made to set prices on the basis of, or at least with some recognition of, costs.[20] However, a comparison of relative prices and relative costs shows that technical crops still enjoy a favored position compared to food crops and that price still fails to cover cost for meat and milk production. The latter reflects the Soviet government's unwillingness, for internal political reasons, to raise retail prices on these products. The inadequacy of meat and milk prices—together with the still rather low prices for grain, needed for livestock feed—also helps to explain the failure of Soviet agriculture to achieve meat and milk targets during the first few years of the seven-year plan (1959–65). Thus, although the 1958 prices do represent a significant advance in the use of price incentives, the principle has not been fully applied to livestock producers.

Another objective of the price revisions of 1953–1958 was to reduce the marked inequality in income distribution within the collective farm sector. Due to these revisions, the income of food crop producers improved relative to that of technical crop producers, the disparity in income between the more and the less efficient farms was diminished, and—as a result of these two developments—regional differences in incomes were reduced.

Finally, the increase in collective farm money income has made possible both a large increase in money payments for collective work and a limited shift, on a minority of farms, from residual payments for labor-days to regular monthly wage payments at specified rates. The shift to wages, as part of the program of incentives, will surely tend to increase labor productivity on collective tasks.[21] It appears that, with a policy of "stable"

---

[19] Furthermore, since 1958, the collective farms have been permitted to buy at wholesale prices various goods previously sold to them at retail prices, such as motor vehicles, fuel, and hardware.

[20] In addition, price relationships in pre-Revolutionary Russia and price relationships abroad are also reported to be considered in fixing relative prices. "In the process of working out drafts of the new purchase prices, there was submitted to the corresponding government commissions much statistical material about average current procurement-purchase prices for individual products of agriculture relative to each other, and also relative to prices prevailing in 1913 and prevailing in foreign countries at the present time."

[21] In the opinion of N. Nimitz, "Soviet Agricultural Prices and Costs," in *Comparisons of the United States and Soviet Economies* (Joint Economic Committee,

agricultural procurement prices, primary reliance will be placed on increases in productivity and reductions in costs from this and other sources (such as the control by the collective farm chairman of the machinery used on the farm) to secure yield increases. Nevertheless, the increased attention of Soviet price-planners to the relationship of prices and costs suggests that further revisions in agricultural procurement prices may be made, subject to constraints imposed by retail price policy, to stimulate the production of lagging crops.*

III. RETAIL PRICES

There are two principal types of retail prices at which goods are sold to households in the Soviet Union: state retail prices and collective farm market prices.

STATE RETAIL PRICES

The state retail price is charged by state retail stores, consumer cooperative stores, and state and cooperative establishments providing services, such as restaurants, dry-cleaning shops, theaters, etc.[22] The consumer cooperatives, which operate primarily in rural areas, are closely supervised by the state, which determines their number, size, location, staff, etc.; allocates goods to them; and establishes sales plans for them. Of total state, cooperative, and urban[23] collective farm market sales in 1959, the respective percentage shares of the three types were 66.0, 29.3, and 4.7.

1. *Objectives.* State retail prices supposedly are fixed with the aim of clearing the market both in aggregate terms and for each commodity. In aggregate terms, the objective is to set the general level of state retail prices so that the total retail sales at that price level will absorb the money income which the population is expected to spend at state retail outlets.

86th Cong., 1st sess.) (Washington, D.C.: U.S. Government Printing Office, 1959), Part I, p. 275: "The significance of this trend for labor productivity can hardly be overestimated. Under a wage system using piece rates, the relation between individual effort and reward is direct and certain. When payments are shares in an uncertain total, the individual incentive to intensify effort is negligible."

* Editor's note: In 1962, procurement prices for livestock products were raised 35 per cent, and the corresponding retail prices were increased 30 per cent.

[22] Health and education services are, with minor exceptions, provided without charge. Although a price (rent) is charged in the case of housing, it is only a token charge which is recognized not to cover "cost" and which is not intended to equate supply and demand and clear the market. This explains why housing and associated services (electricity, gas, etc.) constitute only 4–5 per cent of the budgets of worker families. For a discussion of the multiple state retail price system used in connection with rationing from 1929 to 1936 and during the Second World War, see A. Baykov, *The Development of the Soviet Economic System* (New York: The Macmillan Co., 1947), pp. 236–39 and 251–52; and N. Voznesensky, *The Economy of the U.S.S.R. during World War II* (Washington, D.C.: Public Affairs Press, 1948).

[23] Statistics on rural collective farm market sales are not included in published Soviet trade statistics.

For individual goods, the objective is to fix the price of each at a level which equates planned supply and expected demand.

Soviet planners are reported to fix the general level of state retail prices by comparing two planning "balances," the balance of money incomes and expenditures of the population and the balance of sources and uses of consumer goods and services. The former includes the various sources of money income (wages, pensions, money incomes of collective farmers, etc.) and its disposition (among expenditures on goods and services, direct taxes, bond subscriptions, deposits in savings banks, etc.). The latter compares the several sources of supply of consumer goods (current production, various types of inventories, and imports) and the distribution of this supply (sales to the population, inventories, the armed forces and other state agencies, and exports). From these balances, the planners determine the price level at which planned supplies must be sold to absorb the amounts which households are expected to desire to spend on retail purchases.

The general level of retail prices depends upon both tax and wage policies. The Soviet government relies primarily on price-increasing taxes—namely, the turnover and profits taxes—to finance investment, defense, and social services. As a result, the general retail price level is higher than it would be if direct taxes were used to a greater extent. Planned increases in private consumption can be distributed among households by reducing retail prices or by increasing money incomes (or by a combination of the two). The first method distributes the increase in consumption among the population as a whole (although all consumers may not benefit to the same degree because of differences in the extent to which individual prices are reduced, differences in money incomes, differences in consumption patterns, etc.). The second method, however, is potentially much more selective and discriminatory. With stable retail prices, money wages of different segments of the population can be increased by different degrees (and at different times) to provide selective incentives for increased productivity and for occupational and geographical shifts. Since the Second World War, both methods have been used in turn in the USSR. From 1948 through 1954, retail prices were reduced each spring. Since 1954, the state retail price level has been kept relatively stable, while the money incomes of particular segments of the population have been raised by increases in agricultural procurement prices, pensions, minimum wages, and the wages of selected occupations (e.g., coal miners).

Under planners' sovereignty in the USSR, the basic mechanism of adjustment to a disequilibrium in the market for a particular good is to adjust demand to supply, in contrast to the adjustment of supply to demand which characterizes the response to consumers' sovereignty. The latter kind of adjustment occurs in the USSR only to a limited extent when, in response to evidence in the form of shortages or surpluses at the prevailing prices, planners modify the composition (types, models, etc.) of the output of the various kinds of consumer goods which can be produced with the resources which they have allocated to those lines of production.

In addition to the fundamental objective of clearing the market, retail prices on individual commodities are also set with other objectives, some of which tend to conflict with the basic objective. One such additional objective, arising from administrative considerations, is to keep prices unchanged (except for authorized seasonal variations) for long periods of time. It is obvious that this goal conflicts with the aim of balancing demand with supply.

Another objective is to make the distribution of real income less unequal than the distribution of money income, by fixing lower prices for mass consumption goods (e.g., basic foodstuffs) which predominate in the budgets of lower-income groups, and higher prices for goods (e.g., consumer durables and luxury foodstuffs) which are relatively more important in the budgets of higher-income groups.[24] In pursuit of this objective, prices of basic food products have deliberately been set and maintained below the equilibrium level, as persistent shortages attest. Thus, the informal rationing of queues and empty shelves helps to modify the distribution of real income from the initial distribution of money income.

Relative prices are also used to pursue other objectives of social policy. Low prices are set on books, to promote indoctrination and education, and on children's apparel, to aid large families, while high prices are intended to curb the consumption of vodka. In order to discourage home or handicraft production, relatively low prices are set on finished goods, such as baked bread and sewn articles, and relatively high prices on component materials, such as flour and cloth.

The turnover tax, which provides 40–45 per cent of total budget revenue, is the principal device used by the planners to secure the desired level and structure of retail prices. The principal components in the state retail price of a commodity are (1) the enterprise wholesale price (or the agricultural procurement price plus the mark-up of the procurement agency), (2) the turnover tax, (3) the wholesale trade margin, and (4) the retail trade margin. In addition, there are transportation charges. The several margins are intended to cover expenses and provide a profit at the respective stages. The shares of enterprise wholesale prices, turnover taxes, and the two trade margins in the total value of state retail sales in recent years may be estimated, respectively, at approximately 50, 40, and 10 per cent. Their relative importance in the prices of individual goods differs markedly, however, precisely because of the use of the turnover tax to fix the retail price at the desired level. The sum of the enterprise wholesale price and the trade margins provides a floor below which the retail price

[24] Thus the turnover taxes responsible for the relatively higher prices of the latter goods are in effect progressive.

should not be set but does not determine what the retail price should be. Instead, given the objective of equating demand with supply (or an alternative objective), the appropriate retail price is obtained by levying a turnover tax of the necessary amount.

The turnover tax serves as a cushion which separates the retail prices paid by households and the wholesale prices received by producing enterprises in industry and agriculture. It permits the planners to alter consumer prices without altering producer prices correspondingly, and vice versa. Thus, retail price reductions need not be accompanied by wholesale price reductions, but may be made at the expense of the turnover tax. The turnover tax separates not only the levels but also the structures of producer and consumer prices, since the different rates of taxation on different goods cause their relative retail prices to differ from their relative wholesale prices.

2. *Evaluation.* How successfully do state retail prices perform their basic functions of absorbing household money income and of equating demand and supply of individual goods? Certainly, the theoretical principle that these prices should be market-clearing scarcity prices rather than prices based only on cost (as in the case of industrial wholesale prices) is sound. Likewise, the principle that prices should adjust demand to supply, rather than the converse, is consistent with the Soviet concept of planners' sovereignty. Hence the question becomes: How faithfully in practice have Soviet planners implemented these principles? They could not reasonably be expected to achieve equilibrium in the markets for all commodities at every point in time—a feat not attained in free-enterprise economies either. To do this would require almost continuous adjustment of prices, which is not feasible under the highly centralized administration of the Soviet economy. Instead, a more reasonable objective would be to achieve an approximate equilibrium for most goods over a planning period of, say, a year or three or six months. Small disequilibria, between periodic price adjustments, could be met by the depletion or accumulation of inventories (except in the case of services).

However, this is not the approach which Soviet planners have taken. The persistence of shortages (and the unofficial rationing of empty shelves) of many, perhaps most, consumer goods for long periods after the abolition of rationing in 1947[25] indicates that the general level of retail prices (i.e., turnover taxation) has been too low relative to the level of wages and other money incomes. The result has been repressed inflation, except to the extent to which the excess purchasing power in the state retail trade sector has found an outlet in the collective farm market. Instead of rationing by a physical allocation system or by the price system,

---

[25] Evidence of widespread and persistent shortages at prevailing prices is provided by the Soviet press. See C. D. Campbell and R. D. Campbell, "Soviet Price Reductions for Consumer Goods, 1948–1954," *American Economic Review*, Vol. XLV, No. 4 (September, 1955), pp. 609–25, and almost any issue of the *Current Digest of the Soviet Press.*

insufficient supplies (at the prevailing prices) have been rationed through such inefficient mechanisms as the queue and influence with shop personnel.

Why has the Soviet government preferred repressed inflation and such rationing mechanisms to an equilibrium price level? One explanation offered by Soviet writers is that shortages stimulate labor productivity because they show that supplies and production are not adequate. This argument is not convincing, however, since high prices would indicate the need for increasing output of consumer goods just as effectively as shop shortages. Another reason might be the desire to minimize inventories, which is achieved by low prices which cause shortages to be typical of Soviet retail trade.

Perhaps the most likely explanation is related to the income distribution objectives discussed above. Just as formal rationing was used in the 1930's and 1940's to assure supplies of food, clothing and other basic consumer goods to lower-income groups, so in the 1950's informal rationing devices have been relied upon to enable them to obtain goods which they would be unable to buy at equilibrium prices. Higher-income groups able to pay the higher prices on the collective farm market can thereby avoid the frustration of queues and empty shelves, at least in so far as many food products are concerned. The Soviet leaders evidently prefer this method of rationing, as a means to secure what they regard as a more equitable distribution of scarce goods, to formal rationing, which they apparently consider inappropriate in peacetime, and to a major revision of the distribution of money income, which would have serious implications for incentives. Of course, it could also be argued that shortages were regarded by the Soviet leaders and planners as temporary, and that they expected the supply of goods to "grow up" to the price level in the course of a comparatively few years. It is true that the importance of this informal rationing mechanism has declined since 1954, as supplies of consumer goods have increased, largely as a result of the increase in agricultural production, while the general level of retail prices has remained stable and the wages of lower-income groups have been raised, both in absolute terms and in relation to those of higher-income groups.

The shortages which result from retail prices below the equilibrium level also conceal errors in relative prices which would be evident if the general retail price level were closer to equilibrium. Relative prices become significant only when they correspond to choices which are actually available to consumers. However, when the value of goods offered for sale does approach equality with the intended expenditure of the population, both shortages and surpluses are likely to occur because of errors in relative pricing. The existence of such shortages and surpluses in turn prevents the attainment of general equilibrium, since, under Soviet conditions, prices (or production) are not promptly altered to eliminate disequilibria.

It is not surprising that errors should occur in the fixing of relative prices. One source of error is inaccurate estimates of expected supplies. Supply estimates based on ambitious production targets in agriculture and light industry are likely to prove overly optimistic. In addition, as already noted, the assortment plan for the composition of output is often sacrificed by enterprise managers in order to achieve the gross output and profit targets. This in turn reflects the divorce, by the differentiated turnover tax, of the structure of enterprise wholesale prices from the structure of retail prices: the scarcest goods are not always those which contribute most to the gross value of output or those which are the most profitable to produce.

A second source of error is in the inaccurate estimates of demand. It is true that for many years information has been collected about family budgets, the structure of retail sales, and price movements on the collective-farm market. However, demand analysis is as yet a relatively undeveloped branch of Soviet economic science. This reflects the emphasis of Soviet planners on goals other than consumer satisfaction, and the below-equilibrium pricing and widespread shortages of basic consumer goods in the past. Under such conditions, it was not considered important to estimate elasticities of demand with precision.

There have been comparatively few adjustments of relative prices, chiefly involving consumer durables, since 1954, although Soviet writers have criticized the price reductions of 1948–54 as too "automatic" and "mechanical," because they involved uniform percentage reductions for broad categories of goods, without sufficient regard for the relative scarcities of goods or for prices of substitute and complementary goods. It is possible that the limited decentralization in 1957 of the responsibility for setting retail prices may lead to more flexible state retail prices, at least for the goods whose prices are no longer fixed centrally.[26]

However, there are several factors which tend to make many frequent price adjustments unlikely. One is the administrative cost of making such changes under a highly centralized system of economic administration. Another is the impact of retail price changes on the distribution of real income, which the Soviet leaders regard as a political question of primary importance: changes in the prices of bread, meat, and other basic consumer goods are the result of high-level political decisions, not merely of comparisons of expected supply and demand at the technicians' level. Finally, it is through retail prices that the chief source of Soviet budget

---

[26] Before March 1957, the goods whose prices were fixed by the central authorities in Moscow accounted for more than 90 per cent of total state and cooperative retail trade, while the authorities at the union republic and lower levels fixed the prices on the remainder. In March 1957, the latter were given responsibility for setting prices on a larger list of goods, accounting for about 45 per cent of total sales. However, the central authorities in Moscow retain responsibility for fixing the prices of such important goods as bread, meat, fish, butter, textile cloth, footwear, knit goods, tobacco, vodka, and most durables. The union republic and lower authorities set prices for sausage and confectionery articles, eggs, milk, sewn goods, furniture, toys, and nonalcoholic beverages.

revenue, the turnover tax, is collected. Changes in retail prices therefore involve fluctuations and uncertainty in tax collections.

COLLECTIVE-FARM MARKET PRICES

The collective-farm market price of a good is determined by supply and demand in the individual collective-farm markets, varying from market to market and from day to day in the same market. There are about 8,000 collective-farm markets, approximately half of them in towns of various sizes and half in rural areas. The markets occupy designated trading areas and are equipped with a varying number of stalls, benches, tables, storage bins, meat and milk control points, etc. Sellers are charged a small daily fee for the right to offer their wares. Half a million peasants are reported to participate in the markets daily.[27]

Although urban collective-farm market sales were only 4.7 per cent of total state, cooperative, and urban collective-farm market sales in 1959, their importance in Soviet retail trade is greater than this relationship suggests. First, collective-farm market trade consists almost exclusively of food products, while these account for only 45 per cent of state and cooperative trade. Thus, the share of urban collective-farm market trade in total food sales of these three marketing channels was 7.9 per cent in 1959. Second, the collective-farm market deals in a narrower range of food products than state and cooperative outlets. In relation to total trade of the three channels in the same food goods, the collective-farm market share in 1959 was 14.7 per cent. Finally, it would be desirable to compare the urban collective-farm market figure directly with the amount of *urban* state and cooperative trade in the same goods. Data are not available for this comparison for the Soviet Union as a whole. However, a special survey of 25 large cities in 1958 showed that the collective-farm market share in such a comparison was less than 20 per cent in 7 cities, between 20 and 30 per cent in 5, between 30 and 40 per cent in 8, and over 40 per cent in 5 cities. In the last group were the important cities of Odessa, Tbilisi, Rostov-on-Don, Baku, and Tashkent.

Although collective-farm market prices are set by supply and demand, both supply and demand are strongly influenced by the state. The demand depends on the extent to which the state retail-trade network is able, with available quantities at the established prices, to satisfy the effective demand of households—i.e., on the excess purchasing power remaining after household expenditures in the state retail trade sector. The supply offered by agricultural producers (collective farms, collective and state farm peasants, and urban workers with garden plots) depends on the size of the deliveries which they are required to make to state procurement agencies and the prices offered by these agencies.

---

[27] For a discussion of the collective-farm market, with particular reference to trends in government policy toward it, see J. T. Whitman, "The Kolkhoz Market," *Soviet Studies,* Vol. VII, No. 4 (April, 1956), pp. 384–408.

Despite its ideological heterodoxy, the collective-farm market performs several useful functions in the Soviet economic system. On the one hand, it provides an outlet through which some inflationary pressure can escape. Although excess demand cannot drive up state retail prices, it can and does raise collective-farm market prices to a market-clearing level. On the other hand, as noted in Section II, the prospect of sales in the collective-farm market at prices above those offered by state agricultural procurement agencies provides an additional and important incentive to agricultural producers to expand output and marketings.

Both of these effects are considered by Soviet planners in fixing the levels and structures of state retail prices and of agricultural procurement prices. The levels of both kinds of prices are lower than they would be in the absence of a collective-farm market to absorb some of the effects of low state retail prices and to offer peasants additional incentives. Likewise, the structure of state retail prices takes into account the availability of certain goods (e.g., raw food products but not clothing) in the collective-farm market, while the structure of agricultural procurement prices takes into account the possibilities for selling certain goods (e.g., meat and vegetables but not cotton) in the collective-farm market. Finally, as a result of the transfer of purchasing power from urban workers to peasants through collective-farm market sales, the structure of demand in the state and cooperative retail trade network is altered, since the goods bought by the two groups differ.

The difference between the collective-farm market price level and the state retail price level has been declining in recent years. A sample for 101 large cities shows that, for major food products sold in the collective-farm market, prices were 31 per cent above the state retail price level in 1959, compared to 45 per cent above in 1956.[28] The large difference between the two price levels clearly reflects the substantial extent of below-equilibrium pricing in state retail stores, although in part it also reflects a premium paid for the better quality and freshness of products in the collective-farm market. The decline in the difference between the two price levels over this period appears to be due primarily to the increased availability of goods in state stores and a corresponding easing of demand in the collective-farm market, leading to a smaller quantity of goods being sold at lower prices there. Differences between collective-farm market and state retail prices (aside from those due to differences in quality, ease of making purchases, etc.) will disappear only when state retail prices are

---

[28] These relationships do not in themselves provide a reliable indicator of the extent of repressed inflation, however, because they do not take into account the volume of sales in each trade channel and because some of the excess purchasing power of households after state retail purchases is involuntarily saved rather than spent on the collective farm market. On the first point, see F. D. Holzman, "Soviet Inflationary Pressures, 1928–1957: Causes and Cures," *Quarterly Journal of Economics,* Vol LXXIV, No. 2 (May, 1960), pp. 167–88.

fixed at equilibrium levels, as a result of increases in state retail prices or in supplies relative to household money incomes. Until then, the collective-farm market may be expected to continue to perform its useful, if ideologically unorthodox, functions.

The state's recognition of this is indicated by its promotion of the commission-trade form of collective-farm market trade. Since 1953, consumer cooperatives have carried on a form of collective-farm market trade in which they act as agents for collective farms and farmers, selling their surpluses for them in the collective-farm market for a commission of about 10 per cent.[29] In 1959 these commission sales constituted one-fifth of total collective-farm market sales.

The commission-trade price of a good is set by the consumer cooperatives on the basis of the prevailing collective-farm market price but always substantially (on the average, 17 per cent) below it. However, commission prices on the average have exceeded the state retail prices for the same goods by about 10 per cent. The objectives of the commission trade appear to be to exert pressure on the level of collective-farm market prices and to reduce the amount of time and effort which collective farmers devote to marketing, rather than producing, agricultural output.

IV. CONCLUSIONS

What can be concluded from the preceding analysis about the rationality of the Soviet price system? This depends on the concept of "rational prices." At least three concepts can be distinguished:

1. According to Mises, Hayek, and others, rational prices are those determined by consumer sovereignty in a competitive free-enterprise market economy. It is clear that by this criterion Soviet prices are not rational.

2. Another concept of rational prices is that they are scarcity prices, i.e., prices which equate supply and demand. Under socialism, such prices could be determined in a decentralized manner by the interplay of the supply and demand of socialist firms and households, or they could be determined in a centralized way by the planners. In the latter case, the pertinent demands might correspond to either consumers' or planners' preferences. The planners might strive for *consumer satisfaction*, as distinct from consumer sovereignty, or they might wholly or partly substitute their preferences for those of consumers. In both cases, equilibrium prices would be relied upon to allocate scarce resources to achieve the ends posited by the ruling preferences. However, while prices can be set to equate supply with demand according to planners' preferences, these preferences cannot themselves be based on an independent calculation of

---

[29] A somewhat similar arrangement existed from November 1946 to August 1949.

opportunity costs, as reflected in independently determined scarcity prices, since the scarcity prices in use are themselves fixed on the basis of planners' preferences. Instead, the planners' preferences must be formulated on the basis of other economic and political considerations.[30]

By the test of market-clearing prices, Soviet state retail prices are rational at least in principle if not completely in practice, and collective-farm market prices surely are rational. However, agricultural procurement and industrial wholesale prices are not rational, in view of the planners' reliance on delivery quotas in connection with the former and physical allocations in connection with the latter.

3. A third concept of rational prices is that they are prices which perform effectively whatever functions are assigned to them. These functions may include some or all of the following: allocation of resources, provision of incentives, control of enterprise managers, distribution of income, and the implementation of various social policies. For some of these functions, for example control of managerial behavior, rational prices may not need to be scarcity prices. On the other hand, scarcity prices may be used to implement decisions which are not based on scarcity prices, for example, when market-clearing retail prices are used to distribute consumer goods produced as a result of physical planning. Thus, one part of the price system may consist of scarcity prices and another not. Yet both kinds of prices (and the system as a whole) will be rational as long as each set of prices accomplishes whatever the planners desire of it. Ward has called such prices "rational realization prices."[31]

How rational are Soviet prices according to this concept, which is essentially that of the Soviet planners themselves? Although industrial wholesale prices are not scarcity prices, they still perform reasonably well their major function of control and evaluation of plan fulfillment. However, because they are not scarcity prices they are not appropriate for even the limited use made of them in resource-allocation decisions by planners and enterprise managers. Hence, according to this concept of rationality, industrial wholesale prices are irrational. Nor can agricultural procurement prices be judged rational by this standard, since they have not evoked the desired supply of agricultural output nor successfully allocated resources among crops within agriculture. Not until 1958 was an effort

---

[30] This problem has been identified as the "dilemma" of central planning by Eucken, Montias, and Balassa in their respective studies of the Nazi German, Polish, and Hungarian economies. See W. Eucken, "On the Theory of the Centrally Administered Economy: An Analysis of the German Experiment," *Economica*, New Series, Vol. XV, Nos. 58 and 59 (May and August, 1948), pp. 79–100, 173–93; J. M. Montias, "Price-Setting Problems in the Polish Economy," *Journal of Political Economy*, Vol. LXV, No. 6 (December, 1957), pp. 486–505; and B. A. Balassa, *The Hungarian Experience in Economic Planning* (New Haven: Yale University Press, 1959).

[31] B. Ward, "The Planners' Choice Variables," in *Value and Plan*, ed. G. Grossman (Berkeley: University of California Press, 1960), p. 140.

made to relate agricultural procurement prices to costs, and this relationship is still very imperfect.

It is more difficult to assess the rationality of state retail prices. They are in general still (though since 1954 progressively less) below the equilibrium level at which they are supposed to be set. In some cases, for example basic foodstuffs, this appears to be the result of the pursuit of another objective—a deliberate policy of underpricing to affect the distribution of real income. However, a similar justification does not appear to apply in the case of luxury consumer durables, some of which, such as automobiles, are underpriced, while others, such as cameras and watches, are overpriced. Hence, state retail prices cannot be considered completely rational either.

The irrationality of Soviet agricultural procurement prices and state retail prices has been reduced somewhat by price revisions in the past few years. Reform of the price system, especially industrial wholesale prices, has been the subject of intensive discussion among Soviet economists since 1956. The reappraisal of Soviet prices results from the search of the Soviet leaders for ways to increase the efficiency with which available resources are used. The pressure for greater efficiency comes from many sources, including the increasing complexity of choice in a growing and diversifying economy; the higher priority for consumption, formerly the residual sector which absorbed the effects of planning errors; and the effort to devise a sensible pattern of specialization and trade within the Soviet bloc on the basis of comparative costs.

The proposals for reform in industrial wholesale prices range from suggestions for modest changes in the relative prices of selected substitute raw materials to sweeping proposals that the planners use shadow prices which incorporate charges for nonlabor factors and which reflect relative scarcities. It will therefore be of great interest to see how far the general revision of industrial wholesale prices to be undertaken in 1961–62 goes toward fixing scarcity prices on the basis of which value planning can be assigned a major role in the direction of the Soviet economy.*

---

* Editor's note: Although many individual prices were changed in this price revision, the basic principles and character of the Soviet industrial price system were not altered and are still as depicted in this article.

Lazar Volin

17. AGRICULTURAL POLICY OF THE SOVIET UNION *

Soviet agriculture is not fully socialized, unlike the industrial sector, in which state ownership is complete. Instead, there are three types of enterprise in Soviet agriculture: (1) the state farm, operated like a state industrial enterprise; (2) the collective farm, nominally an autonomous producers' cooperative but in reality closely supervised by the state; and (3) the private plot ("household allotment") farming of individual peasant families.

The reasons for this ideologically heterodox arrangement and the efforts of the state to control collective and private agriculture are analyzed in the following article by Lazar Volin. He explains the nature, importance, and problems of each type of agricultural organization, emphasizing the roles of incentives and investment in expanding agricultural output. Despite various agricultural reforms since the death of Stalin, agriculture remains a serious problem for the Soviet leadership.

INTRODUCTION

THE PROBLEM of agricultural policy has long been in the foreground as a vital national issue in Soviet as in Czarist Russia. Following official revelation of weaknesses in Soviet agriculture after Stalin's death in 1953,

* Reprinted, with permission, from *Comparisons of the United States and Soviet Economies* (Papers Submitted by Panelists Appearing before the Subcommittee on Economic Statistics, Joint Economic Committee, 86th Cong., 1st sess.) (Washington, D.C.: U.S. Government Printing Office, 1959), Part I, pp. 285–314. Lazar Volin is Chief of the East European Analysis Branch, Economic Research Service, United States Department of Agriculture.

310

agricultural policy aiming to remedy them has become the subject of many official decrees, lengthy reports, and speeches of Soviet leaders and officials. Prime Minister N. S. Khrushchev seldom fails to touch on agriculture in his numerous speeches and has made it one of his main preoccupations. The rapid industrial growth that began at the end of the past century and that was accelerated during the last 30 years, has not appreciably diminished the prominent role of agricultural policy. Even though the Soviet Union has lost its predominantly agrarian character, close to half of the population still depends on agriculture for a livelihood. The expanding food and fiber needs of the growing population and the strains and stresses of agrarian collectivization have combined to keep agriculture in the public eye.

1. CONTRASTING OBJECTIVES OF AGRICULTURAL POLICY IN THE SOVIET UNION AND THE UNITED STATES

Agricultural policy, to be sure, has been a major problem in the United States as in Russia. But there the similarity ends. Actually the root causes and objectives of the agricultural problems and policies of the United States and the Soviet Union are diametrically opposite.

The United States, because of rapid technological development, has been steadily preoccupied with the problem of farm surpluses and excess capacity in agriculture, except during World War II and the years immediately thereafter, when maximum farm output was essential. Control of farm surpluses and other aspects of farm relief, therefore, have been the principal concern of U.S. policy.

The Soviet Union, on the other hand, has long been bedeviled by agricultural underproduction and agrarian overpopulation. Accordingly, not farm relief, but a rapid expansion of agricultural production in the face of considerable climatic obstacles, to feed and clothe growing numbers and a reduction of the agricultural population has been the central objective of Soviet policy. In pursuit of that objective, considerable emphasis has been laid on modern technological development in Soviet agriculture, particularly on mechanization of farming, for which the United States has served as a model. Tractors and combines, for instance, were largely imported from the United States in the early 1930's until new Soviet factories could be built with the help of American engineering skill. However, expansion of agricultural production in the Soviet Union has been firmly bound up with another and, as it often proved, conflicting objective; namely, an all-embracing state control of agriculture. That led to the forced collectivization in the 1930's of small peasant farming, the horrors of which are only too well known.

In the collectivization process, the economic welfare of the Soviet farm population was sacrificed and subordinated to the ideological and economic objectives of the ruling Communist Party. Among these, a rapid and lopsided industrialization with an overriding emphasis on heavy industry acquired the highest priority. For Stalin was set on building socialism in a country where, ironically, it could not have been expected to develop according to the strict Marxian tenets, precisely because Russia was not an advanced industrial country. Accordingly, agriculture was forced to make a heavy contribution of farm products, little being given in return by the government to the collectivized peasantry. And, of course, the overpopulated and often starving Russian villages supplied in the 1930's most of the large labor force required by industrial expansion and inefficient factories. But a part of this increased manpower was labor of liquidated "kulaks" (the more prosperous small peasant farmers) and others forced off the land. The "colonial" role of agriculture was practically acknowledged by Stalin, when he said 30 years ago that agriculture provides the Soviet state, bent on industrialization, with "something like a tribute." [1] This idea strongly colored the Kremlin's attitude toward agriculture for many years, especially during the Stalin era.

In the United States, by way of contrast, agricultural policy has been aimed at protecting the independent family farm enterprise, based on private ownership of land and capital, from the adverse effects of depression, surpluses, and other economic maladjustments. This has been done through programs for "stabilizing, supporting, and protecting farm income and prices" [2] for reducing farm costs, and conserving soil resources. While there has been considerable divergence of opinion about the effectiveness and desirability of some of these programs, nevertheless, there has been widespread public agreement concerning the desirability of maintaining and improving the standard of living of the farm people and of protecting it and the family farm enterprise as far as possible, against the vicissitudes of the elements and sweeping economic changes.

Another striking operational difference between agricultural policies of the Soviet Union and most non-Communist countries, including the United States, pertains to foreign trade. It is the field in which Government intervention on behalf of agriculture had early come on the scene and become especially active with the onset of the great depression. Tariffs, import quotas, and other forms of import restrictions to protect domestic producers from excessive imports and export subsidies and other export aids to help dispose of surpluses have become common practices of an active agricultural policy. (We are not concerned here with the merits or desirability of many of these devices, but merely with the hard facts of their existence.) In the Soviet Union, however, all foreign trading operations, exports as well as imports, are in the hands of the Government, which exercises a complete monopoly of foreign trade. There is no need, consequently, for the various restrictive and promotional devices em-

---

[1] J. V. Stalin's *Collected Works* (Russian), Vol. 12, pp. 49–51.
[2] Sec. 2, Charter, Commodity Credit Corporation, 1933.

ployed in foreign trade policies of other nations. Those in authority decide how much and when and where to export or import farm products.

2. COLLECTIVE AND STATE FARMS

In aiming at the expansion of agricultural production and, at the same time, at the establishment of a tight state control, Soviet agricultural policy was in a large measure devoted to making Russian agriculture conform to the Marxist-Leninist-Stalinist image. The transformation usually meant loss of efficiency, which became a problem in itself. It is still a problem of the Kremlin.

It was to the small family peasant farming that the weight of this collectivization policy was applied—and it was a crushing weight. Remember that small family peasant farming in Russia was important even before the revolution, when two-thirds of the private farmland in European Russia was owned by peasants who also leased a considerable proportion of the remainder. After the revolution and division of the larger land properties, small peasant farming became preponderant in the Soviet Union. (The collective sector, which came into being early in the Soviet regime, was insignificant.) Agriculture largely retained its individualistic character for a longer period than other branches of Soviet economic life, thanks to Lenin's new economic policy, or NEP, which replaced the regime of war communism in 1921. But toward the end of the 1920's this breathing spell came to an end, and it was the turn of agriculture to be ruthlessly collectivized. Thus the historic Russian trend toward small peasant agriculture, which began with the emancipation of peasants from serfdom in March 1861, was reversed by Soviet policy.

In developing agriculture along new collectivist lines, the Communist rulers were guided by the Marxist orthodox doctrine of the absolute superiority of large-scale production in agriculture as in industry. Lenin added to this doctrine the enthusiasm for that American invention, the tractor, as a vehicle for collectivist transformation of small peasant agriculture. As far back as 1918 he thought that if the Russian peasants were given 100,000 tractors and supplies needed to operate them, they would plump for communism, which he recognized was a mere fantasy in those days.[3] Stalin combined this ideological heritage with his notion of "building socialism in one country" through vigorous industrialization at the expense, initially at any rate, of agriculture. Resistance of peasants to such squeezing tactics of the Soviet state was only an additional argument from the Communist standpoint for speedy collectivization. For it is much easier, as experience proved, to make government-controlled collectives deliver grain and other required produce to the state at low fixed prices than to force a small individual farmer to do so. The latter is likely, under

---

[3] Lenin's *Works*, Vol. 29, ed. 4, p. 190.

such conditions, to produce less, to consume more, in short to become more self-sufficient and turn away from commercial production.

This tough Soviet agrarian policy, which began in the late 1920's, was softened somewhat from time to time by concessions to the peasants in order to win their cooperation. Nevertheless, there has never been any tampering with the basic principles of agrarian collectivism. Except for a brief period at the very beginning of the collectivization campaign in 1930, there has been no move toward decollectivization in the Soviet Union—not even after Stalin's death as in other countries of the Soviet bloc, notably in Poland. It is, therefore, symptomatic that Khrushchev recently selected Poland as the place to make a speech extolling agrarian collectivism.

Two collectivist types of farm enterprise have emerged in the Soviet Union. One is the collective farm proper, commonly known as kolkhoz or artel (plural kolkhozy). The other type is the state farm or sovkhoz (plural sovkhozy). These units have often been described and only a few words need to be said here. The state farms are owned outright and managed by the state and are usually larger in size and more specialized than collective farms. The collective farm represents in theory a self-governing producer's cooperative consisting of the pooled holdings of the formerly independent small peasant farmers. The self-governing character of the collectives, however, has become a fiction. They are in reality subject to tight state control and their formally elected managers are actually selected and removed at will by Communist authorities.

What principally distinguishes the two kinds of farms is the position of the workers. On state farms, workers are paid wages as in Soviet factories. On collective farms, the rank and file members, both men and women, work in the fields and in livestock centers under the direction of managers and supervisors just as they do on state farms. But, as a rule, they are not paid wages. They are residual sharers in the income of the collectives, after the state secures its share and provision is made for current production expenses and captial outlays. Thus, the workers have neither the certainty of income from their work on collective farms, which other Soviet workers possess, nor the control of farm operations exercised by independent farmers (although, like the latter, collective farmers must bear the risks of weather, pests, and plant and animal diseases). Collective farmers are not covered by the national social security system as farmers are in the United States. Collectives are supposed to have their own individual pension funds.

The payments to collective farmers vary with their skill and the amount of work performed. The greater the skill required, the larger the remuneration. A cumbersome system of payment has developed, based on so-called workday units, in which the performance of specified tasks or norms is measured and which serve as a basis for distribution at the end of the year of cash, grain, and other products. These are prorated to the total number of "workday" units earned per year by membership, so that each "workday" unit is credited with the same amount of cash, grain, etc. But the number of "workday" units and consequently the earnings of individual workers vary.

The uncertainty, the irregularity, the long waiting and confusion engendered by this complicated system has led recently to efforts to simplify it and make payments more regularly, by means of so-called advances. There is also a tendency to substitute cash payments for the multiple distribution of various types of produce and cash, and dispense with the workday units. It was found that, in addition to its cumbersomeness, the workday system does not encourage reduction of labor expenditures and costs, since the greater the number of workdays earned by an individual or a group of workers the greater the payments.

To a considerable extent, the improvement in the methods of payment, however, depends upon the improved economic position and the larger incomes of collectives. As was stated by the official report on the fulfillment of the economic plan for the first half of 1959: "As a result of increased cash receipts from the sale of agricultural products to the state, the number of collectives making money advances to their members increased considerably . . ."

To complete the picture of a collective farm, it must be pointed out that the peasant families have continued to live in their rather primitive dwellings, grouped in farm villages, as they did before collectivization. Even those peasant families in the western regions of the U.S.S.R., who lived on separate farmsteads (so-called khutors) similar to those in the United States, were, for the most part, forced by the Soviet Government to move into villages. Thus, collective farms, just as state farms, are essentially units of production. Consumption is of peripheral importance, and is left to the peasant household, except for the maintenance of such public welfare and educational institutions, as clubhouses, hospitals, schools, etc. It is true that Khrushchev has urged increased concentration by collectives on various forms of public consumption rather than continue argumenting the earnings of their members. He stressed especially such institutions as canteens, children's nurseries, school dormitories, etc., which tend to release woman labor that could be used in farm production. While some progress along these lines may be anticipated, for the present there is no question of any basic changes in the fundamental character of collective farms.

There is a question, however, whether the coexistence of collective and state farms, so unlike in many respects, will continue, or whether collectives will be supplanted by state farms. For, ideologically, the state farm has always been considered a superior type of economic organization, or in Soviet parlance, a higher type of "Socialist property" than the so-called kolkhoz-cooperative property; though recently this theoretical distinction has been officially deemphasized. According to official slogans, state farms were supposed to serve as a model for the less advanced collective farming and, by inference, at any rate, could be considered the future Communist ideal goal of the institutional structure of Soviet agriculture. There was a wide gap, however, between theory and practice. State farming expanded considerably in the early 1930's when many giant farms were created, and then came a reversal. The unsatisfactory production results led to official condemnation of the giantism, subdivision of the huge units was ordered, and deflation of the state farm sector took place through transfer of land to the collective farm sector. In 1940 less than 10 per cent of the total sown area was in state farms.

The limited role of state farming continued until the beginning of the Khrushchev program of expansion on uncultivated land beyond the Volga and Urals in 1954. In this area large mechanized state farms already were well established and, when the decision was again made to increase the grain area, several hundred new state farms were organized and many of the existing ones were enlarged. In the process, however, there was also a considerable absorption of collective farms. For instance, in the Kazakh Republic, where much of the expansion of the sown area on the so-called new lands took place, 833 collectives were merged into 188 state farms in 1957.

Conversion of collectives into state farms, however, was not confined to the "new lands" regions of the eastern U.S.S.R., but spread to a number of other regions; among these were, for instance, the irrigated cotton-growing regions in Soviet Central Asia and areas in the former war zone, where collective farming disintegrated during the occupation and remained weak despite postwar rehabilitation. The need of new capital investment by the state has been, apparently, an important criterion in determining whether to convert collectives into state farms. As a result of the process of expansion on new lands and absorption of collectives, the share of state farms increased from 12 per cent of the sown area in 1953, to more than one-fourth of the expanded acreage in 1957.

Another recent development also indicates greater reliance by the Soviet Government on state farms. It is the designation of a number of state farms, first near Moscow and subsequently near other large cities to specialize in growing cheaply potatoes and vegetables so as to lower their cost to the city consumer. Should this experiment prove successful it would operate to the disadvantage of those collectives which derive an important share of their income from selling potatoes and vegetables at high prices on the free market in the cities.

There are also other reasons why the revived dynamism of the state farming sector may portend a serious threat to collective farming. One is the considerably increased size of collective farms as a result of mergers and their acquisition of farm machinery from machine-tractor stations to be discussed in other sections. This further diminishes the difference between the two types of farming. Second is the revelation, by Khrushchev himself, of considerably lower labor productivity in collectives than on the state farms.

Khrushchev's figures show that both state and collective farms in the U.S.S.R. have much higher labor requirements per unit of product than U.S. farms, but collective farms have the highest of all, exceeding considerably even the state farm. Assuming similarity in the method of collecting these statistics on collective and state farms, some of the variations may be accounted for by differences in geographical location, in the quality of the labor force (age and sex distribution), in capital equipment or perhaps in some other aspect of a sampling process. It is possible, too, that the system of regular wage payments on state farms, for which the authorities are responsible, as compared with the sharing principle in collectives, tends to induce a greater economy of labor on state farms. Since the Government is not responsible for the payment of labor in collectives, it could tolerate this inefficiency, so long as it was not required to raise the fixed low prices for farm products and there was an abundance of manpower in the villages. But the latter condition no longer prevails since the war. Also the Government raised agricultural prices during recent years. However, it aims at lowering such prices eventually in order to reduce the consumers' cost of living. If collectives are not to be economically injured by lower prices, increased efficiency and greater labor productivity are essential. Awareness of this need, and consciousness of a growing relative shortage of manpower, probably explains Khrushchev's emphasis on increased labor productivity even to the point of publishing comparisons with the United States, which are highly unfavorable to Soviet agriculture.

3. FARM GIANTISM

Farm giantism has become a distinctive trait of Soviet agricultural organization. The cult of bigness, a feature of Soviet policy, has its ideological roots, as was pointed out earlier, in the orthodox Marxist doctrine of economic concentration, which stresses the similarity, as far as large-scale methods of production are concerned, between agriculture and manufacturing. This doctrine, which makes no distinction between the large and the optimum size of an enterprise, was further reinforced by the unbounded enthusiasm of Lenin and his disciples for farm mechanization, modeled on the American pattern. It was one of the motivating forces in the collectivization of small peasant agriculture and establishment of huge state farms.

As already indicated, this cult of bigness miscarried in the case of huge state farms in the early 1930's and corrective steps were taken. As for collective farms, it was also found, in the mid-1930's, that a number of units in the southern and eastern regions were too large for efficiency and subdivision was not uncommon. On the other hand, a "voluntary" merger of the usually small collective farms in the northern and north central regions was "recommended" by the decree of December 19, 1925, "Concerning the Economic and Organizational Strengthening of the Kolkhozy of the Non-Black Soil Area." In some regions then, before the war the average size of the collective farms was increasing; in other regions it was decreasing. In the country as a whole, however, the number of collective farms was slowly decreasing (after it reached a peak of 245,400 in 1935) to about 237,000 in 1940.

After collectivization in the annexed western regions after the war, the number of collectives in the U.S.S.R. increased to 252,000 at the beginning of 1950. In that year, however, a far-reaching change in the number and size of the collectives began. A mass campaign for merger and enlargement of farms was inaugurated, which resembled in its speed and relentlessness, and in the revival of gigantomania, the original mass collectivization drive of the early 1930's. This time, however, the pressure was exerted not on individual peasant farmers to join a collective, but on kolkhozy to merge "voluntarily" into super-collectives. The merger drive which Stalin initiated in 1950, was spearheaded by no other person than N. S. Khrushchev, then one of Stalin's lieutenants, who was just transferred from the Ukraine to Moscow. Khurshchev remains a dedicated believer in mergers on the ground of efficiency and economy, such as reduction of administrative expenses, etc. A decree of the Council of Ministers of the U.S.S.R. of June 7, 1950, No. 2427, which was not published at the time in the daily Soviet press or in other sources available to western students of Soviet affairs, gave a formal blessing to the merger drive, which was then already in full swing.

The mergers, ostensibly undertaken to increase farm efficiency, were not confined to small collectives or to specific geographic areas. Already-large collectives were also merged and the drive extended to regions with most diverse national and economic conditions. Collectives with a large expanse of level farm land were merged with those whose terrain was criss-crossed by marshes, lakes, bushland and forests and, consequently, had small fields. Neither sparsely nor densely settled regions escaped the merger drive. Several collectives, whose members lived in one village, were merged with collectives whose members lived in several scattered villages. In such cases, the peasants who became members of the new enlarged collectives continued, for the most part, to live in their separate villages which were connected, as a rule, by very poor roads, which often become no more than mud tracks in the early spring and fall. However, Khrushchev's idea of speedy resettlement of villages into so-called agro-towns, proposed by him in the spring of 1951, was quickly jettisoned by the Kremlin and has never been revived in its original form, even after its author came into power.

The irrationality of at least some farm mergers in the northern part of the country was acknowledged by an official report dealing with the Vologda Province:

In a number of districts the enlargment of the collective farms was made without taking into account the natural economic and other peculiarities. . . . Many collectives consist of 25 to 30 and more inhabited points which are not only separated from each other by 5 to 7 kilometers, but often are also cut off by natural obstacles—lakes and rivers.

Even Khrushchev cautiously hinted in June 1955 at the desirability of breaking up some large units resulting from recent farm amalgamation in the Baltic Republics.

After only one year of the merger drive, the number of collectives decreased by more than one-half, from 252,000 at the beginning of 1950 to 121,000 at the end of that year. By the end of 1953, there were only a little more than 91,000 collectives. Since 1954, a new factor—the absorption of collectives by state farms mentioned above—enters the picture. However, since the total figure of collectives absorbed by state farms has not been released, it is impossible to segregate the effects of such absorption from that of the mergers of farms into larger collectives. The liquidation of machine-tractor stations as machine operating units in 1958, which will be discussed later, probably also contributed to the mergers. It is significant that as late as the fall of 1958, Khrushchev urged the "model" collective in his native village, Kalinovka, with a tillable area of 3,200 acres, to merge with a neighboring collective, as he did not consider it sufficiently large. At any rate, as a result of the two processes, mergers of collectives and their absorption by state farms, the total number of collective farms decreased to about 60,000 by July 1959 or to less than one-fourth of the number at the beginning of the present decade.

The merger process resulted, of course, in a considerable enlargement of collectives. In terms of sown area per farm, the average size of the collective increased nearly 3½ times, compared with the prewar period, and the average number of families per farm trebled. Collectives, however, vary considerably in size from region to region. Thus, in 1956, in the northwestern region of European Russia, for instance, 64 per cent of all collectives had a sown area of 500 hectares and under (1,236 acres and under); whereas, in northern Caucasus, 23 per cent of collectives and in western Siberia, only 5 per cent had acreages that large. On the other hand, no farms of more than 5,000 hectares (12,355 acres) were in the north-western region, but more than one-third of the collectives in northern Caucasus, and nearly one-fourth in western Siberia had acreages of 5,000 hectares and over.

The large size of Soviet farms is particularly striking in comparison with U.S. units. Although farm size in the United States in recent years has been trending upward, paralleling the growth in farm efficiency, yet only slightly over 2 per cent of commercial farms in 1954 (not all the farms enumerated by the census, which includes a number of smaller units) had 500 acres or more of cropland harvested; many others had much less.

Yet collective farms despite their enlargement continued to be much smaller than state farms. The latter also have become enlarged and in 1957 had on the average an area of more than 20,000 acres under crops per farm as compared with about 2,800 acres in 1940. While a considerable number of new state farms were organized in recent years, some of the smaller farms were merged and others were transferred to various institutions or liquidated and a few were subdivided. The net result was first, a decrease in the number of state farms from 4,988 at the beginning of 1951 to 4,742 at the beginning of 1953, and subsequently an upward trend, which brought the number of farms to 5,905 at the beginning of 1958.

The huge size of collective and state farms has made it necessary to decentralize operations into more manageable units. The workers in collectives are organized into brigades, consisting of 40 to 60 workers, headed by a brigadier or a foreman. Each brigade is assigned to a unit of cropland or to a livestock center. Still smaller units, called zveno or squads are formed and these workers cultivate the more intensive crops such as sugar beets and cotton. State farms also are subdivided into branches (otdelenie), each of which is a farm unit by itself.

The team of U.S. Department of Agriculture economists which visited the Soviet Union in the summer of 1958 states in its report that they—

inquired about the availability of studies analyzing the relation between the size of the farm unit and its efficiency, with a view to determining the optimum size in different regions. We were told that such information was not available at the present time, although apparently some studies of this type are under way. We gained the impression that in striving for bigness, per se, farm efficiency was actually neglected. Even with brigade subdivisions, much time is consumed in going to and from places of work. Although Soviet agricultural authorities stress increasing efficiencies associated with larger sizes of operations in discussing desirable sizes of farms, their thinking is in terms of very large units by U.S. standards. They did state, however, that some of their largest farms, up to 150,000 hectares (about 375,000 acres), are considered to be too large. The present sizes probably are influenced by the greater ease of centralized management and control than by economies associated with size of operation. Large farms mean fewer units of contact for state direction of planning and operation; also fewer managers will be needed to translate the overall plans into specific operations.[4]

In addition to the fact that it facilitates central control over collective farming, the Soviet predilection for farm giantism may perhaps be also explained by its tendency to widen the gulf between the rank and file peasant membership and the management of the big collective, now mostly in the hands of outsiders. This gap is useful in the context of Soviet rule for it tends to enhance the driving power of management over labor.

4. MACHINE-TRACTOR STATIONS: THEIR RISE AND FALL

The merger process was also extended to another type of farm unit, which was the handiwork of Soviet policy—the state machine-tractor stations or MTS. These were the special units into which tractors, com-

---

[4] *Economic Aspects of Soviet Agriculture. Report of a Technical Study Group* (Agricultural Research Service, U.S. Department of Agriculture, 1959), pp. 12–13.

bines, and other large machinery operating on collective farms were grouped, together with facilities for repairing machinery and operating and supervising personnel. For a long time, in fact, the collectives were not allowed to own such machinery. While originally the idea of MTS was associated with the advantages of pooling power and machinery for joint cultivation by small peasant farmers, too poor to own tractors individually, it was adopted since the early stages of collectivization as an important instrument of state ascendancy and control over collective agriculture.

It should be borne in mind that the very fact of a catastrophic reduction in the number of horses early in the collectivization greatly enhanced the importance of the tractor, which was thrown, so to speak, into the breach on the draft power front. It can, in fact, be truly said that the tractor in the Soviet Union did not displace the horse, as in the United States, but replaced it in an emergency. Thus, he who controlled the tractor—the new source of farm power—controlled agriculture. This helps to explain why the Soviet Government, which was anxious to extend a tight control over the amorphous structure of the peasant collective farming, was clinging to the possession of tractors and other farm machinery. Since MTS were paid for their services to the collectives in kind, they have also become significant revenue producers (in terms of farm products) to the state.

There was at first no change in the pivotal role of the MTS after Stalin. On the contrary, one of the first steps of the post-Stalin regime in the agrarian sphere was, in various ways, to still further enhance the supervisory powers and the importance of the MTS, as, for instance, by transferring collective farm personnel, seasonally employed by MTS, to their permanent staff. However, the advantage of pooling tractors and machinery in a central unit, like MTS, was offset, sometimes seriously, by dual management of farm operations by the managers of the MTS and of the collectives. Khrushchev described this situation as having "two bosses on the land." There was often a conflict of interest between the management of the MTS and the collective. The former was interested primarily in performing those operations, like plowing, which brought the greatest financial returns, often at the expense of other necessary operations, like mowing hay. There were cases when plowing done by the MTS was superflous or even harmful. Difficulties also often developed regarding the timeliness of MTS farm operations, which is so important in agriculture, especially in Russian agriculture with its short season. It was complained, on the other hand, that collectives tended to rely too much on the MTS for even the simplest type of work, such as carting feedstuff for livestock, which could have been done by farm horses.

The decreased number and the increased size of the collectives, as a result of the merger campaign, made the existence of separate MTS seem less essential even from the Soviet point of view. There were anomalous cases where one MTS serviced a single collective farm. At any rate, an abrupt about-face by the regime ended this dichotomy in the collective farm system. On January 22, 1958, following some limited public discussion, Khrushchev proposed that MTS were to sell most of the machinery, except highly specialized equipment, to collective farms and, thus, be divested of the vital farm operating functions. They were to be converted into mere service and supply centers, so-called repair-technical stations or RTS. This radical reform was formally approved by the Supreme Soviet of the U.S.S.R. on March 31, 1958, and was rapidly carried out. By July 1959, 94 per cent of collectives bought farm machinery from the MTS on cash or credit. The magnitude of this transaction can be gaged from the fact that by July 1, 1959, there were purchased 512,000 tractors, 221,000 grain combines, and a large quantity of other machinery. In addition, collectives purchased also 100,000 new tractors, more than 25,000 grain combines and other new machinery. The total cost of the machinery purchased was 21.7 billion rubles, of which 17.2 billion rubles is the cost of the machinery acquired from the MTS. These expenditures may be compared with a total cash income of all collectives of around 95 billion rubles in 1956 and 1957 and a record of 130 billion in 1958.

The liquidation or, as it is officially termed, reorganization of MTS encountered, judging from what Khrushchev said, some ideological opposition within the Communist ranks. It was apparently based on objection to the downgrading of what was regarded by the official Communist line as a higher type of property—the "state" property of the MTS to the lower level of so-called cooperative-kolkhoz property. It may be surmised that this opposition found support or was inspired by Stalin's adamant stand against liquidation of MTS, which was proposed during his lifetime by some economists. Khrushchev tried to meet this ideological opposition by arguments which minimized the distinction formerly made by Soviet theoreticians between the two types of property. But in the main, in abandoning Stalin's legacy regarding MTS, Khrushchev was guided, to judge from his own utterances, less by ideological than by pragmatic considerations.

First of all, reorganization of MTS eliminated dual farm management. Second, considerable strengthening of the party apparatus in the countryside during the past five years made it feasible to dispense with the control function of the MTS. Third, the importance of MTS had diminished as an instrument of state acquisition of farm products. Fourth, the leadership calculated that increased prices and incomes and anticipated economies from more efficient management made it possible for the collectives to afford to purchase, maintain, and operate the MTS machinery. Indeed, its purchase may be also desirable from the Soviet point of view as a proper channel for investment of part of their increased income by collectives. For otherwise, the opportunity for productive capital investment by collectives is restricted if acquisition of machinery is barred, as it largely had been heretofore. The alternative to capital investment is, of course, a further increase of peasant earnings. But if this is not to be inflationary, it would necessitate a considerably faster pace for the Soviet consumers' goods industry and more efficient distribution of such goods in rural areas. There are, therefore, some implications in the sale of machinery by MTS to collectives of deflationary or disinflationary character.

While the transition which the virtual merging of MTS with collectives involved seemed to be rapid, the very considerable readjustment necessary was not always smooth, and it posed new problems. Among the various problems of adjustment, are those of adequate repair facilities and relations with the repair-technical stations, of supplying farms adequately with proper machinery, and especially with spare parts. A case, for instance, was reported in the Soviet press when, because of the impossibility of finding a wheel for a tractor, a new tractor had to be purchased. Repair technical stations were accused of selling defective machinery to collectives and not being helpful with repairs. But the elimination of "two bosses on the land" should make it possible to pinpoint managerial responsibility. This should, in the long run, contribute to farm efficiency, though the problem of finding suitable managers of collectives has, apparently, also not been solved.

5. HOUSEHOLD ALLOTMENT FARMING

While the dichotomy of the MTS and the collective farms was eliminated by Khrushchev's 1958 reform, another dichotomy remains; namely, the coexistence side by side of the large collective farm enterprise and the small household allotment farming (priusadebnoe khozyaistvo). The collectivist Leviathan has not swallowed as yet the individualist dwarf.

At first, a few words about the nature of the allotment farming. Peasant households in collectives as well as workers' families on state farms and some others are allotted small plots of land on which they grow potatoes, vegetables, sunflower seed, and other crops. These plots are allotted to a whole family and not to an individual member of the collective. This seems to be a survival of the old Russian institution of family property, though the plot, of course, is not legally owned by the peasant family; it is merely set aside for the family's use at the discretion of the collective. Furthermore, all adult members of the household must do a certain amount of labor on collective farms or work in state enterprises to obtain the household allotment. The peasant households are also permitted to own a small number of livestock and an unlimited number of poultry. They can sell their produce direct to the consumers on the free, so-called kolkhoz market in the cities, but they cannot use middlemen.

Household allotment farms accounted for only 3 per cent of the sown area in 1956 but for a much larger proportion of the livestock population, including almost half of all the cows. Such allotments were originally conceived as a subsistence, "an acre and a cow" farming, merely auxiliary to the collectives' farm economy at a time when they were not considered strong enough to take care fully of their members' needs. As so often happens, "the tail began to wag the dog." The household allotments not only helped greatly to feed the collectivized peasant population, but they frequently became the chief, or the only, sources of the peasants' cash earnings through sale at higher prices (not the low government fixed prices) on the free kolkhoz market.

How important the free market was as a source of peasants' cash earnings during the Stalin era can be gathered from the fact that, for some years, at any rate, the volume of sales on the kolkhoz market, mostly by members of the collectives, exceeded total cash income of collectives. This "acre and a cow" farming, however, is important, not only for the economic welfare and morale of the peasants, but also for the food supply of the nonfarm population, especially the supply of livestock products—products sold not only through the kolkhoz market, but also through government controlled outlets. Even in 1957, when the share of allotment holdings in state acquisitions of agricultural products was considerably less than formerly, they accounted for 19 per cent of meat deliveries, 16 per cent of milk and 11 per cent of wool.

Yet the household allotment became a thorn in the Kremlin's side, since it competed with the collective farm economy for the labor and loyalty of the peasants. The official view, therefore, has been that, as the collective farming becomes stronger and better able to satisfy the needs of its members and of the nation, the importance of household allotment farming should decline and eventually wither away. But, like the Soviet doctrine of the withering of the state—it is still in the future. Accordingly, the Soviet policy toward this kind of farming has been ambivalent, now restrictive, now relaxed—then again restrictive.

As during a short period in the mid-1930's under Stalin, so in 1953 after the late dictator, the "thaw" in agrarian policy began with a more encouraging or tolerant attitude toward allotment holdings. The cumbersome money tax on allotment holdings was simplified and taxes reduced in the fall of 1953. Acquisition of cows by peasant households was facilitated. Compulsory deliveries of farm products to the Government were first reduced and since January 1958 were entirely abandoned.

This new liberal phase again did not last long. In 1956, legislation was passed ostensibly for the purpose of permitting collectives to set up their charters without modeling them on the general model charter of 1935. The really consequential provisions of this law were to enable each collective to set its own minimum of labor, the size of the household allotments and the number of privately owned livestock. This was accompanied by a declaration favoring indirectly but not prescribing a reduction of the size of the plots. Subsequently there have been cases of reduction of plots, some apparently for purposes of equalization of such holdings between different families. But this has not assumed so far a mass character.

However, the government attitude toward private ownership of livestock, the most valuable component of household allotment farming, has become more restrictive in recent years, as was foreshadowed by Khrushchev in 1953 at the outset of the new post-Stalin course of agrarian policy. Khrushchev has been advocating during the last few years the sale of cattle by members to the collectives. He "recommended" to the peasants of his native Kalinovka to sell their cows to the model kolkhoz, and the "recommendation" was acted upon. But such liquidation is to be gradual with no definite time limit placed, depending upon when collectives are ready for the transition. Steps taken by authorities in some districts to hasten the process by pressuring the peasants were strongly rebuked. A much sterner attitude, however, has been adopted by the Government toward private ownership of livestock by workers on state farms and by nonfarm population, which is marked for elimination.

To sum up: household allotment farming is again being deflated. But, so deeply rooted is it in the rural fabric of the U.S.S.R., that it would be premature to conclude that its doom is near at hand.

6. GOVERNMENT PROCUREMENTS OF FARM PRODUCTS

Acquisition of farm products by the state is a fundamental problem of Soviet economics and politics. It runs like a red thread throughout the whole of Soviet history. It was at the root of both Lenin's new economic policy of 1921 and of Stalin's rural collectivization a decade later. It helped to kindle bitter intraparty strife in the 1920's and was a basic presupposition of the industrialization program under the 5-year plans. It is through Government procurements and prices paid for them that economic incentives and disincentives to the farmers largely operate.

The procurement system, however, was characterized, with respect to the same commodity, by a considerable diversity of methods or types of delivery and by a corresponding multiplicity of prices. Basic to all were the compulsory delivery quotas, calculated as so much grain, potatoes, meat, etc., per unit of tillable or total land. The lowest fixed price was usually paid for this type of procurement. Next, there was the so-called contracting method used for industrial and intensive crops like cotton, sugar beets, etc. Though essentially similar to compulsory deliveries, this method involved a graduated price scale, depending upon the quantities delivered, and also provided an opportunity for the farmers to buy some commodities at concession prices. Then there were the extra-or-above-quota purchases by the state for which considerably higher prices were paid after 1953 than for the compulsory deliveries. In recent years the extra-quota purchases became increasingly important while lower priced compulsory deliveries declined. Finally, there were payments in kind for the work of machine-tractor stations, which, of course, are now being eliminated with the dissolution of the MTS.

The reform of 1958 unified the different types of procurements into a single system of state purchases. Compulsory deliveries as such were nominally abolished, but the new system retains quotas per unit of land which collectives are supposed to meet. Instead of multiple prices, single prices are now fixed by the state for each commodity within a region. Although price stability is one of the aims of the reform, provision is made for raising or lowering of prices to cope with sharp fluctuations in output; thus, some recognition is given to the law of supply and demand. Another important change is the abolition of the variable premium prices for larger deliveries used for some crops like cotton, under the so-called contract system, on a considerable scale. A sample study of three groups of cotton growing collectives in 1956 showed that the differential in the average price per unit of cotton between the highest and the lowest was 40 per cent and between the highest and the middle group 20 per cent.

These changes simplified the cumbersome procurement and price system. There can exist now only two prices for a commodity in each locality, a Government price and a free market price if a commodity is traded on the limited private market. This is still a far cry from a rational price system, the lack of which, as many western economists pointed out, greatly handicaps economic calculations and planning decisions in the Soviet Union. But the reform takes at least a small step towards such a goal.

The abolition of premium price payments, no doubt, hits collectives growing such crops as cotton, sugar beets, hemp, and others which received preferential price treatment. So much was openly admitted by Khrushchev, who contended that the more productive collectives should obtain higher income, not from price differentials but by lowering of production costs and increasing output. In any event the average prices paid by the state to such collectives will be lower and so will probably the gross money income. This may have an adverse effect upon the output of certain crops in these usually more productive farms, which may or may not be compensated by increased production of other farms. In general, the new prices appear to have been tailored to benefit the average or less prosperous collective farms. The guiding principle was stated by Khrushchev in 1958 as follows: "Although the total expenditures of the state for the purchase of agricultural products will remain approximately at the same level as last year, they will be distributed more fairly among the collective farms, thanks to the new prices."[5] Khrushchev indicated further that the total procurement expenditures include also the expenses formerly incurred by the state for the machine-tractor stations which are now borne by the collectives themselves.

As a matter of fact, the stated objective of Soviet price policy in the

---

[5] *Pravada*, June 21, 1958.

years to come is that of achieving lower prices, concomitant with a reduction of the production costs. This brings up a new important facet of the procurement policy, namely the projected concentration of procurements in areas of most economical production, instead of requiring every region from the Baltic to the Pacific and from the Arctic to the Black Sea to deliver identical products like grain, for instance. This move is linked with what appears to be now more than a mere academic concern (as it had long been) with regional agricultural specialization. And regional specialization is to be based on production cost studies. This cost consciousness is itself a new phenomenon in the management of Soviet agriculture, heretofore preoccupied almost exclusively with fulfillment of physical targets. Khrushchev himself reflected the new cost consciousness when he said in his December 15, 1958, report: "It is impossible to carry on farming without a thorough analysis of the cost of commodities being produced, and without control by means of the ruble."[6]

7. ECONOMIC INCENTIVES AND FARM LABOR

Soviet policy in the agrarian as in other fields has always been a combination of coercion, indoctrination, and economic incentives. However, the proportions vary from time to time. There has been, for example, a special emphasis on economic incentives whenever a critical or difficult agricultural situation arose and appeasement of the peasantry was considered essential. It is only necessary to recall Lenin's celebrated NEP in 1921, which supplanted the harsh regime of war communism, with its requisitions of peasants' produce. Again, in the mid-1930's, Stalin relaxed his iron grip somewhat to secure a recovery of agriculture from the ravages of the initial collectivization drive.

But relaxation always was a short-lived luxury. Khrushchev himself showed in his famous "secret" de-Stalinization speech at the 20th Communist Party Congress, in February 1956, how harsh and unrealistic Stalin's policy toward the peasantry became in its latter stage. For instance, he proposed raising taxes on collective farms and their members by 40 billion rubles, when they received, in 1952, for instance, altogether only 26 billion rubles for the large quantity of products acquired by the state. This helps to explain the unsatisfactory agricultural production situation, particularly in the livestock sector, which Stalin's heirs inherited.

The contrast between agriculture and industry was especially glaring. According to Khrushchev, agricultural production in 1952 was only 10 per cent higher than in 1940, when industrial production was more than twice as high.[7] Even the 10 per cent increase may have been optimistic. During the Stalin era crop production estimates, especially the important grain

---

[6] *Ibid.*, December 16, 1958.

[7] *Ibid.*, September 15, 1953.

figures, were inflated by the use of the so-called biological estimates which grossly exaggerated the picture. These were estimates of crops standing in the field prior to the harvest, which did not reflect the officially admitted large harvesting losses and, in general, lent themselves to manipulation. They were not comparable with crop figures for other countries, or, indeed, with Russian figures prior to the 1930's. Such a statistical malpractice brought down, after Stalin's death, even the official Soviet wrath. Malenkov, for instance, declared in August 1953 that: "it should not be forgotten that our country, our collective farms can prosper with a crop gathered in the barn and not with a crop standing in the field."[8] Khrushchev in December 1958 spoke even more harshly about biological estimates, which he called eyewash (ochkovtiratel'stvo), accusing Malenkov himself of indulging in their use during Stalin's lifetime.[9] Incidentally, the U.S. Department of Agriculture and other agencies of the U.S. Government, as well as a number of other western specialists, were long critical of these inflated biological figures and stressed the need of considerable downward adjustment if they were to be used at all.

When it came to livestock figures, even Soviet official figures showed that cattle numbers at the beginning of 1953 were considerably below the precollectivization figures in 1928. No secret was made of the fact that livestock was greatly underfed. This, notwithstanding the much publicized official policy to increase the output of livestock products and improve the monotonous starchy diet of the Russian people.

To remedy the difficult agricultural situation and increase production of food and feed, Stalin's heirs once more put in the forefront of their blueprint of agricultural policy, in 1953, increased economic incentives to stimulate the interest and cooperation of the peasants in expansion of production. Thus, with Stalin's exit, the big stick was again to be accompanied by a somewhat larger carrot.

Turning to the question of implementation, of economic incentives programs, it should be borne in mind that the collective farm system of payment for labor, described in an earlier section, was designed precisely to provide economic incentives to producers. For this reason equality of income, usually associated with socialism, has been rejected by the Communist rulers of Russia. They do not consider it applicable to the present economic stage of development of the U.S.S.R., which they call Socialist, as distinguished from a future, full-fledged Communist society. On the contrary, variation in earnings among members of collectives to provide incentives to workers has always been encouraged. In fact, the very method of payment, based on workday units, is patterned on a kind of incentive piecework wage. Attempts of collectives to introduce some sort of a uniform daily wage in terms of workday units have always been strongly disapproved by the authorities.

---

[8] *Ibid.*, August 9, 1953.
[9] *Ibid.*, December 16, 1958.

That is also why rural communes, in which not only production but also consumption is socialized on egalitarian lines, have been proscribed by the Soviets. There were, to be sure, some communes organized in the U.S.S.R. in the 1920's and during the initial collectivization drive in 1930, but they were converted to the present artel form of collective farming. It is significant, in view of the recent Red Chinese experiment with communes, that Khrsuhchev attacked this type of agrarian collectivism in his speech in a Polish collective in July 1959.

Although the principle of economic incentives was thus recognized during the Stalin era, incentives failed to produce desired results because incomes of the collectives were very low, largely due to the low fixed prices paid by the Government, as admitted later by Khrushchev, for the heavy quotas of grain and many other farm products which they were obligated to deliver. This resulted in very small earnings of the peasants from their labor on many collective farms. The effect was to make peasants less willing and less efficient workers and to encourage them to concentrate on their household allotment farming.

It is true that the delivery quotas of farm products were legally fixed quantities, which were not supposed to be increased, in order that the farmers should be interested in maximizing output. In practice, however, increased output often led to increased exactions. If some collectives in a district could not meet their quotas, other farms, which had already delivered theirs, were frequently called upon to supply additional quantities so that the plan for the district should be completed. Khrushchev called this pruning of the more prosperous or efficient collectives. The disincentive effect of such exactions on the peasantry needs no elaborations and was reflected in the unsatisfactory agricultural situation during the Stalin regime described above.

The post-Stalin leadership adopted a policy of substantially raising the very low prices paid by the Government for farm products. Thus, in 1953 prices of livestock and poultry products were increased more than $5\frac{1}{2}$ times; milk and butter 2 times; potatoes by $2\frac{1}{2}$ times; and vegetables, on the average, by 25 to 40 per cent. Prices of grain and other products also were raised later. As a result of the increased prices and larger quantities acquired, the payments of the Government to collective farms and small household allotment holders more than trebled between 1952 and 1957. The total cash income of collectives more than doubled between 1952 and 1956–57, increasing from 43 billion to 95 billion rubles. This in turn made possible cash payments to peasants in many collectives in which such distribution had formerly been negligible. The cash payments, in fact, more than trebled between 1952 and 1956, increasing from 12 billion to 42 billion rubles.

Yet, even the greatly increased volume of cash distributed in 1956 represents only an average cash income of something over 2,100 rubles per peasant family on the collective farms, a sum roughly equivalent to about $200 at a realistic rate of exchange. In 1952 the average was as little as 623 rubles, equivalent, with higher prices, to less than $60 per peasant household. Moreover, since distribution of cash in some areas of intense crop production (such as cotton, sugar beets, etc.) are considerably above the average rate, many peasant families in the less prosperous collectives received much less than the average. However, it is well to remember that cash distribution by collectives is not the only major source of peasants' money income. As was pointed out earlier, the anomaly persists of the small household allotments, playing not just the theoretically assigned minor role of a mere subsistence-farming appendage, but actually rivaling and often outstripping collective economy as a significant source of peasants' income. In this connection, as was pointed out earlier, sales on the free market in the cities are very important. However, receipts from private sales have become smaller in recent years and they no longer overshadow cash income from collective farms, though the situation varies widely from region to region and from farm to farm.

Much less information is available concerning what is still the most important component of peasants' income from the collective farms—payments in kind. Without such information it is impossible to adequately assess the changed economic position of the peasantry. However, since in-kind payments are mostly in grain, and there were several large harvests in recent years, it can be assumed that more grain was distributed.

What of the effect of the post-Stalin policies of increased economic incentives on labor input? While helpful statistics on this point are by no means abundant, we do have some clue, however imperfect, from the reported total number of workday units earned annually by peasants in collectives. Between 1952 and 1956 the total number of workday units increased by 26 per cent. Incidentally, the figure for 1952 was still below prewar, but in 1956 it was 19 per cent above. This improvement reflects both a larger number of workers and a greater contribution per worker. The latter is shown roughly by the claimed increase of the average number of workday units per able-bodied worker—from 295 in 1953 to 335 in 1957, or 14 per cent. The increased contribution per worker, however, does not signify anything like a corresponding rise in the efficiency of labor. For workday units do not measure uniformly labor input in different collectives. Moreover, Soviet sources often criticize the so-called waste of workdays, meaning simply the wasteful, inefficient employment of farm labor. Attention has already been called to Khrushchev's striking statistical comparison between labor requirements per unit of product in the United States and the U.S.S.R., thus confirming firsthand observations of western specialists regarding low labor productivity in Soviet agriculture.

Raising of labor productivity in agriculture has been a major concern of Khrushchev's administration. Considerable attention in this connection has been given to improved training of farm labor through the establishment of short-term courses and of special schools. Drives were also organized to return to the farms skilled workers who migrated to cities and to bring farm specialists closer to grassroots.

In 1954, a drive began to recruit several hundred thousand young men and women for agricultural development in the eastern virgin lands region. Since then, each summer additional thousands have been sent to those areas on temporary assignments. Their services, however, have not always been effectively utilized. There have been also many stories in the Soviet press of hardship suffered by the newcomers in those regions due to the housing shortages and other causes. Finally there must be mentioned the annual or perennial mobilizations of students and other city dwellers to assist in harvesting crops. However, Khrushchev, for some time, has been highly critical of this practice and called for its elimination.

8. CAPITAL INVESTMENT IN AGRICULTURE; FERTILIZER PROGRAM

Agricultural production in the Soviet Union has been handicapped by a shortage of capital, as well as by climatic obstacles, and inefficient labor and management under the regimented system of a highly centralized agrarian collectivism.

For a long time agriculture served as an important source of capital accumulation for financing the Soviet industrial program. Reference has already been made to Stalin's statement in the late 1920's that agriculture contributed "something like a tribute" to the Soviet state. In addition, Russian agriculture suffered heavy capital losses during the all-out collectivization in the 1930's; as Jasny puts it:[10]

Instead of increasing by one-third, as planned, the investment in means of production in agriculture declined by considerably more, perhaps as much as one-half, during the first plan period, chiefly by livestock destruction in the collectivization drive. This decline was not fully made up until 1938.

During the post-Stalin period, however, belated recognition has been given to the capital needs of agriculture itself. Government capital investment in agriculture in 1956 was officially estimated (in July 1, 1955, prices) at 21 billion rubles, compared with a total of 63 billion during the preceding 5 years, and 25 billion during 1946–50. The collectives also were spurred to increase their own capital accumulation out of increased income. Their officially estimated capital investments more than doubled between 1952 and 1957, increasing from less than 10 billion to more than 23 billion rubles. The so-called indivisible funds, representing the capital assets of collectives, were estimated at 63 billion rubles at the end of 1952 and at 102 billion at the end of 1957, a rise of more than 60 per cent. Parenthetically, it may be noted that sizable collective farm investments acted as a brake on the rise of the peasant earnings. In addition to using

---

[10] *Socialized Agriculture of the U.S.S.R.*, p. 61.

their own resources for capital investment, there were also available to collectives increased long-term state credits in recent years. Whatever the faults or biases the above figures may have they are believed to be indicative of the trend.

Despite the marked improvement of the capital position of Russian agriculture during the post-Stalin era, the investment is still inadequate to use land and labor effectively. From this inadequacy stems, for instance, the imbalance in mechanization. Some operations, such as cutting the grain, are highly mechanized, while others, such as cleaning and drying of grain, are still to a large extent carried out inefficiently by hand labor.

Again Khrushchev stated in his June 29, 1959, speech that shortage of tractors hampered fall plowing in the new lands regions and consequently increased the load of fieldwork during the short spring season and affected adversely crop yields. As a matter of fact, Soviet farms have fewer tractors than the United States, even though the latter has a crop area of about 150 million acres less than the Soviet Union. At the beginning of 1957 there were 892,000 tractors on farms in the Soviet Union compared with 4,975,000 in the United States.

Another example of a shortage of capital investment in agriculture is the paucity of irrigation development in the extensive subhumid zone plagued by frequent devastating droughts and low crop yields. It is doubtless because of the need of considerable capital investment that Stalin's large program of irrigation in the subhimid regions of the European U.S.S.R. was deflated by his successors, though it would have paid off in stable and higher yields.

Still another type of deficiency in capital investment in Soviet agriculture is a qualitative one. It is characterized by wastefulness and decreased economic, and sometimes even physical, effectiveness of some forms of capital investment. There has been, for instance, a tendency in some collectives to build far too elaborate and costly shelters for livestock—so-called cow palaces. Then there were the tractors, produced uniformly much larger in size than needed in many regions. But this particular "gigantomania" is being corrected at present.

The utilization of capital equipment has also been often inefficient. The Soviet press, for instance, has been complaining year in year out about the idleness of tractors during the busy season because of poor repair work, shortage of spare parts, etc.

A field in which considerable investment of capital would be beneficial to agriculture is highways. As the report of the economists of the U.S. Department of Agriculture points out:[11]

The lack of all-weather roads in much of the country no doubt explains in part the separation of cream for butter production on most farms rather than

---

[11] *Economic Aspects of Soviet Agriculture. Report of a Technical Study Group* (Agricultural Research Service, U.S. Department of Agriculture, 1959) p. 32.

the marketing of whole milk. The inadequate transportation system also probably hinders the development of such agricultural crops as fruits and vegetables. The relatively few trucks and automobiles (631,000 trucks and very few automobiles on farms in 1957, compared with nearly 3 million trucks and over 4 million automobiles on U.S. farms) makes for cultural as well as economic isolation for the rural villages and their inhabitants.

A new government program, which, if successful, is destined to have a significant effect on Soviet agricultural production is that of greatly stepped up output of commercial fertilizer. The importance of this program is accentuated by the fact that, following a large expansion of crop acreage during the years 1954–57, the new 7-year plan, 1959–65, relies for the achievement of its high farm output targets primarily on an increase of per acre yields. Certainly increased use of commercial fertilizer, especially in the humid regions, would contribute to this objective.

The gross supply of commercial fertilizer available to Soviet agriculture increased between 1953 and 1957 by nearly 60 per cent. But, on a plant nutrient basis of 2.7 million short tons, the 1957 supply was still only 40 per cent of fertilizer consumption in the United States. Actually, commerical fertilizer in the Soviet Union so far has been used only in the growing of the most valuable crops, like cotton and sugar beets.

The 1957–59 plan calls for nearly trebling of the fertilizer supply. Whether this high goal will be achieved or not, it is reasonable to expect that a considerable increase of commercial fertilizer supply will take place during the next few years.

There is, however, great room for improvement in the handling, quality, and application of fertilizers. The Soviet press has been replete with complaints about the failure of collective farms to move fertilizer from warehouses. Even worse is the practice of dumping fertilizer in the open, near the railroad station, and allowing it to deteriorate. The U.S. soil and water use exchange group, which visited the Soviet Union in the summer of 1958, comments in its report:

The physical quality of mineral fertilizers in the U.S.S.R. is poor by our standards. The use of unmixed goods results in high expenditures of time on farms in handling, mixing, and application.

Fertilizer-application methods generally are crude, and there seems to be a lack of precision fertilizer-application machinery. On the other hand, airplanes are used extensively for broadcasting solid fertilizers, and the anhydrous ammonia applicators appear to be comparable to ours.

Decisions supplant extension education in obtaining widespread adoption of fertilizer practices on farms. This insures rapid adoption of practices but magnifies errors of judgment and prolongs poor practices that otherwise would soon be discontinued.

It should also be borne in mind that, while the use of commercial fertilizer has been increasing, Soviet authorities were seriously concerned in recent years about a decline, or inadequate use, of manure in the northern and central regions of the U.S.S.R. with their podzolic soils. The very low yields of grains and other crops in the podzolic soil area were attributed largely to the unsatisfactory manure situation.

9. PLANNING AND MANAGEMENT

Not only in the case of state farms, machine-tractor stations, and repair-technical stations, but also with respect to collective peasant agriculture, the Soviet Government has largely taken over the function of planning and management, which formerly devolved on decisions of numerous independent farmers. The Government now makes many decisions on crops to be planted and livestock raised; assembling of seed; sowing and harvesting practices; supply and use of farm machinery; manure, and commercial fertilizer; crop rotation; capital investment; proper care of livestock; provision of adequate fodder; and other details of farming with which the Government formerly did not concern itself directly.

During the Stalin era, agircultural planning and direction were highly centralized. Plans and targets for many details of farm operations were laid down for different regions in Moscow and on their basis goals were established by local authorities for each collective farm. By 1955, however, the Kremlin finally became convinced that detailed rigid planning of agriculture from the top stifled initiative on the farm and was detrimental to efficiency. Khrushchev and other Soviet spokesmen now severly criticized the old planning methods. One practice particularly aroused their ire; namely the widespread adoption of a crop rotations scheme in which perennial grasses played an important part. This crop rotation was recommended primarily as a soil improving practice, by a soil scientist named Williams who came to exercise a great deal of influence with the Communist Party leadership during the Stalin regime. It was adopted, not only in humid regions for which it was suitable and where it had been, in fact, long practiced, but also in subhumid regions where it only aggravated the difficult animal feed supply problem by displacement of other forage crops.

This incident highlights a striking peculiarity of Soviet agricultural policymaking and planning—the wholesale introduction by decree of innovations. It makes possible such accomplishments as expansion of the crop acreage in the course of four years by 90 million acres and rapid consolidation of the numerous noncontiguous strips of land into large fields adopted for modern power farming. But such planning from above also often leads to costly mistakes; sometimes, because the practice or measure introduced is based on unsound or obsolete principles and often, because of indiscriminate, general application of practices, suitable under certain conditions, but not under others. Since open criticism of principles is taboo in the U.S.S.R., once a certain line of policy is officially laid down, it often takes considerable time before such mistakes are corrected by an official reversal. Such was the case with crop rotation. A more recent example of indiscriminate application is the so-called double stage or windrowing method of grain harvesting, taken over from North America, which speeds the cutting of grain. It is very useful in regions with a short harvest season, like Siberia, often characterized at such times by inclement weather. But in the U.S.S.R. again all regions are urged to adopt this practice; those in which it is essential and those in which it is not necessary.

A good example of pushing a practice, which in the United States is considered largely obsolete, is checkrowing of crops. And for an illustration of the introduction of unsound pseudoscientific practices we must turn to the activity of the notorious opponent of Mendelian genetics and, for a time, under Stalin, a virtual dictator of Soviet biological and agricultural sciences, Lysenko. Although Lysenko's influence on research in biological and agricultural sciences declined considerably after Stalin's death, his star apparently is rising again. The Soviet Botanical Journal, which had vigorously criticized Lysenko and his methods, was curbed and had to change its tone.

Khrushchev's dissatisfaction with highly centralized agricultural planning led to a move toward its decentralization. The decree of March 9, 1955, assigned responsibility for detailed production planning of crops and livestock to collective farms themselves. Central planning was to be confined to the setting of the delivery quotas for farm products and the volume of work to be performed by the MTS. With the liquidation of the latter, this task now also devolves on the collectives. However, the 1955 decree has given to local authorities (including then the MTS) certain responsibilities in farm planning supervision with the result that these agencies often usurped the planning functions of collectives.

National goals, or drives, like the corn growing drive or the campaign to "overtake the United States in per capita milk and meat output" often result also in intervention by authorities with collectives. It is inconceivable, for instance, that a collective in a cotton growing region could shift to raising other crops at the expense of cotton. Again a collective would probably have to give a very good reason for not growing corn (maize) in view of the strong advocacy of that crop by Khrushchev. In planning its livestock production the management of a collective is expected to set high targets of output per 100 hectares of land. For milk and all meat it is tillable land, meadows and pastures; but for pork a special target must be set per 100 hectares of tillable land only. The goal for the output of eggs is per 100 hectares of the sown area of all grain.

It should also be remembered that for most agricultural products there exist two sets of prices: those fixed by the Government at which it buys farm products, and the usually higher free market prices. (Cotton is an example of a commodity for which there is no free market price since the whole output has to be sold to the Government.) Thus the managers of collectives are confronted by a multiplicity of yardsticks and pressures which makes proper planning difficult.

The pivotal role of the collective farm manager (chairman) and his assistants in the success of collectives, or lack of it, has been long recognized by the Soviet Government. The importance of the managerial function has been enhanced with the enlargement of the farm enterprise. But finding efficient and reliable managers poses a problem which the regime, apparently, has not been able to solve to its satisfaction, despite several campaigns to shift qualified and reliable party personnel and specialists from the cities to the farms, and notwithstanding the large number of agricultural specialists trained by colleges and vocational schools. In his speech at a meeting of the central committee of the Communist Party on June 29, 1959, Khrushchev again complained that party organs in a number of places, despite their large personnel—

cannot select good chairmen [managers] for the backward collectives. The result is as the proverb has it: "With 7 nurses in attendance—the child still manages to lose an eye." And what does it mean to select a good chairman of a collective, good brigadiers [foremen]? It means success to the enterprise. . . . Why is it that collective and state farms do not organize their work as well as factory personnel? Because some collectives have been headed by poor chairmen for long stretches at a time; some have brought as many as three collectives to ruin and are looking toward a fourth. . . . And the party organizations put up but a weak fight against such an evil. . . .

On the other side, there had been complaints of frequent turnover and irresponsible removal of managers of collective farms. The managerial problem apparently continues to be a serious one.

10. THE BATTLE FOR GRAIN; WHEAT AND CORN

Special Government programs, aiming at increasing the output of important commodities, have been characteristic of Soviet agricultural policy, both during the Stalin and post-Stalin periods. Such programs consist, as a rule, of a varying combination of increased economic incentives, higher targets for supply to collective and state farms of machinery, fertilizer, etc., and direct orders to local authorities and to collective and state farms, prescribing production targets and improvements in farm practices and management. Two of such programs, initiated by Khrushchev, have been of far-reaching significance; namely, the expansion of small-grain production, principally of wheat, and an increase in corn growing. Together they constitute the latest phase in the "battle for grain" which the Soviet regime has waged throughout its history.

The importance of grain in the Russian economy cannot be exaggerated. It predominates in the caloric intake of the population, which is growing at the rate of over 3 million a year. Increasing quantities of grain are also needed as livestock feed, to assure the large increases in output of dairy products and meat called for by the Government.

Grain production during the postwar period, however, failed to keep pace with increased requirements. During the Stalin era this was obscured from public view, as was pointed out earlier, by the misleading huge "biological" estimates of the crops standing in the fields and not stored in the barn. A considerably larger production, of course, was desired by the Stalin administration (of which Khrushchev was an important member). It was one of the goals of the last Stalin 5-year plan, 1950–55. The total grain area, however, during the years 1951–53 of 263 to 265 million acres was below the prewar area of 273 million acres (1940), though the wheat acreage was above prewar and trending upward. Thus the steeply increased grain production target for 1955 was to be accomplished predominantly through increased yields per acre. The increase was expected to result from a combination of measures for a putative improvement of agricultural technique, such as soil-improving rotation with perennial grasses mentioned above, tree shelterbelts, irrigation of 15 million acres in the subhumid regions of European U.S.S.R., the whole array known as the great Stalin plan for reconstruction of nature.

The post-Stalin administration largely abandoned, or deflated, the great Stalin plan for reconstruction of nature, some aspects of which, like the universal crop-rotation scheme with grasses, appeared questionable, while others, like the irrigation program, were considered too costly. Under Khrushchev's leadership, the Kremlin returned to the traditional Russian pattern of increasing agricultural production extensively by expanding acreage. To pursue this the Soviet Government turned eastward, where there were still considerable tracts of long uncultivated, or virgin, lands.

Acreage extension, paralleling settlement of these eastern regions—which are to Russia what the West was to the United States in the last century—has been proceeding since the 1890's. But never before has the extension occurred at so rapid a rate. In the three years, 1954–56, 90 million acres were plowed up with the aid of tractor power and added to the Soviet crop area, mainly the spring wheat area. This acreage is almost equal to the combined arable land of France, Western Germany, and the United Kingdom—an achievement which should not be underestimated. However, most of this new acreage is in a zone of unfavorable climatic conditions. It is characterized by severe winters, a short growing season accompanied all too often by devastating droughts, and frequently a rainy and cold harvesting season. It is, therefore, a zone of hazardous agriculture, suited mainly to spring crops and characterized by sharply fluctuating yields. This is shown by data for Kazakhstan, one of the main areas where the new development took place.

Even with low average yields, the multiplier of the large additional acreage is bound to result in a substantial increase of production, though one may be skeptical whether it is low-cost production as the Soviets claim. Since the eastern regions are relatively sparsely settled there is proportionately more grain available in good years above local requirements than in the older, more densely populated regions. This factor, and the prevalence of large state farms, facilitates the task of Government collections. Again, the extension of the acreage in the east provides a kind of insurance against mediocre crops in other regions of the country, as illustrated by the situation in 1959, when a considerable part of the new lands area was not affected by a drought or affected less seriously than most of the other important agricultural regions.

On the other side of the ledger is the fact of further considerable extension of Soviet agriculture into the precarious climatic zone of marginal or submarginal land. It is well recognized in Soviet agricultural circles that, in order to prevent dust bowl conditions and disastrous crop failures, a part of the acreage in these new lands regions, perhaps a fifth or more should be annually rotated as summer fallow, a practice which has been little followed so far. To replace this acreage, additional new land must be brought under cultivation if the cropped acreage is to be maintained. Thus the maintenance of the acreage at its present level presents a problem. But so long as the huge wheat acreage is maintained, with correspondingly large harvests, especially in years of good weather, Soviet wheat exports pose the threat of increased competition on the world markets.

The program for corn expansion is aimed directly at remedying the shortage of feed, which had been largely responsible for the weakness of the Soviet livestock sector. Khrushchev saw in corn a panacea for the unsatisfactory feed situation and he began to push strongly for a huge expansion of the corn acreage. In this he was admittedly influenced by the example of successful cultivation of corn as a major fodder crop in the United States.

Prior to 1955, corn acreage in the Soviet Union was small, varying between 9 and 12 million acres. By contrast there were planted 20 to 26 million acres of barley and 38 to 40 million acres of oats. Yields of corn per acre were about 14 to 17 bushels, or less than half of those in the United States. Climatic conditions in the Soviet Union do not favor corn growing beyond a limited southern area. In the rest of the country it is either too cold or too dry for successful corn culture. Nevertheless, the Khrushchev program in 1955 set a goal of not less than 70 million acres under corn by 1960, or nearly a sevenfold increase compared with 1954. It was realized that this would involve considerable extension of corn cultivation into regions where the growing season was too short for the grain to mature. Consequently, a much larger proportion of corn was to be used as silage in the Soviet Union than in the United States.

This crash program was undertaken in the face of climatic obstacles and without adequate preparation, without proper varieties, machinery, fertilizer, and significant incentives to the farmers. It met only with limited success. It is true that the corn acreage increased from less than 11 million acres in 1954 to 59 million in 1956. But this was, so far, the high water mark and during the two succeeding years less than 50 million acres were planted to corn. This is still a fivefold increase and corn is now grown in many regions where it had not been known before. But Khrushchev himself was scornful of the results in 1958, a generally good crop year, with respect to more than half of this acreage, from which corn was either harvested for silage before the ears were formed (30 per cent of acreage) or was reported as having been used for green forage (29 per cent of acreage). The latter is a euphemism, according to Khrushchev, for "the lost corn crop." Yet Khrushchev's enthusiasm for corn as "the queen of the fields" has remained unabated, despite some cautionary remarks, which he makes from time to time. Incidentally, he strongly recommended corn growing to Polish farmers during his visit to Poland in the summer of 1959. However, the excessive concentration on corn has probably increased the Soviet feed supply to a lesser degree than it might have been with a more balanced program.

SUMMARY AND CONCLUSIONS

1. Agricultural policy has been a prominent question in the Soviet Union as it was in Czarist Russia. It has emerged at every critical juncture in the history of the country. The recent transition from the Stalin to the Khrushchev regime has been no exception.

Agriculture, with close to half the people depending upon it for a livelihood, continues to be a more important sector of Soviet national economy than it is in the more industrialized countries of the West—and this despite the industrial growth of the Soviet Union.

2. The Soviet Union, notwithstanding its huge crop acreage, has been bedeviled by agricultural underdevelopment, by the failure of its agriculture to meet increasing food and fiber requirements of a growing population that is becoming increasingly urbanized. Therefore, the principal objective of the Soviet Government has been expansion of agricultural production. A sharp upsurge in farm products output has become, for political and physical reasons, extremely urgent for the post-Stalin regime, which cannot afford to proceed at Stalin's pedestrian pace. Hence the flood of official reports, speeches, and decrees spotlighting the agricultural problem. This preoccupation of the Soviet Government with increased production sharply contrasts with the concern of the United States with farm surpluses and farm relief.

3. Climate is more of a limiting factor in agricultural production in the Soviet Union than in the United States. More important is the fact that other basic and closely related objectives of Soviet policy clashed with expansion of production, namely: (a) the centrally controlled collectivization, ruthlessly forced in the 1930's on the small peasant family farming,

which emerged victorious after the revolution, and (*b*) the acquisition by the Soviet state at a low cost to itself of large quantities of farm products, which left little incentive to the collectivized peasantry to work as diligently on the large collective farms as on their own little kitchen garden plots.

4. Solely from the standpoint of production, central direction and planning of collective agriculture permit the marshaling of all available resources to achieve a specific goal on a large scale. This has resulted both in improvements and in costly mistakes—and both often made with little regard to economy and efficiency. The impossibility of public criticism of a policy once it has been officially adopted and, often, inadequate critical discussion before it is adopted—coupled with reliance on pseudoscience of the Lysenko type, which promises spectacular "pie in the sky" results— make prevention or correction of such mistakes more difficult.

5. An early example of improvement was the consolidation into large fields, adopted for power farming, of the numerous noncontiguous strips. These strips, into which small holdings were formerly divided, meant waste of land (for boundaries) and of labor. The plowing up and adding to the crop area of 90 million acres of virgin land within a period of four years (1954–57) is a more recent accomplishment; and it is a significant accomplishment even though much of this land must be considered marginal or even submarginal from a climatic standpoint.

Among the examples of costly mistakes committed by central authorities are: The great loss of livestock during the initial all-out collectivization drive; the indiscriminate adoption of many farm practices such as the universal use of perennial grasses in crop rotation without regard to regional differences; the equally indiscriminate adoption of certain types of farm equipment such as large tractors; the shift of crops into areas climatically or otherwise unsuitable for their production, such as the abortive extension of cotton growing from the irrigated regions of Soviet central Asia and Transcaucasia into the more northern dry farming regions of the Ukraine and north Caucasus; or the present extension of corn cultivation into regions in which it is either too cold or too dry for a successful corn culture. Yet another manifestation of large scale policy errors is the persistent "giantism" which, despite recognition of mistakes committed in the early 1930's, led to the creation again in the 1950's of huge unwieldy farm units through widespread mergers of collectives and growth of state farms.

6. The effort of the Khrushchev regime to remedy weakness on the agricultural front is being done without deviation from the basic principles of agrarian collectivism. In fact, the grip of state and party rule over collective agriculture has been tightened, although a shift of authority from Moscow to the republics, provinces (oblasts), and districts (raions) and some decentralization of the rigid, highly centralized planning of

Stalin's days has taken place. However, decentralization is not permitted to interfere with national goals which are deemed of critical importance, such as the expansion of corn growing to bolster the lagging feed supply, the expansion of the crop acreage on the virgin lands east of the Volga and the Urals and the campaign to overtake the United States in per capita production of dairy products and meat.

7. The most important reform of the institutional structure of collective farming during the post-Stalin period was the liquidation of machine tractor stations and sale of the machines to the collective farms. This move, stanchly opposed by Stalin during his lifetime, was made by the Khrushchev administration primarily to eliminate virtual dual management of collective farm operations or, as Khrushchev put it, the existence of "two bosses on the land."

8. The reform, undertaken to increase farm efficiency, tends to enhance the position of collectives, considerably enlarged by mergers, in the Soviet agrarian institutional scheme. Nevertheless, the rapid expansion of state farming, which now accounts for more than a fourth of the crop area instead of 12 per cent in 1953, may point to the eventual takeover of collectives. State farms had already absorbed many collectives and ideologically they have always been considered a superior type of economic organization, though this is at present officially minimized. How long the coexistence of two organizational types of Soviet agriculture will continue may depend largely upon whether the Soviet Government extends to collective farms the regular wage system now prevailing on state farms—a system which is similar to that in Soviet factories. The peasants or collective farms are residual sharers in the income after the state secures its share and current production expenses and capital outlays are met.

9. Although there has been no decollectivization recently in the Soviet Union such as took place, for instance, in Poland and Yugoslavia, limited concessions were made to peasants within the framework of Soviet agrarian collectivism. There was tax relief for the small allotment holdings of the peasants' and workers' families which play such an important part in their income and in the national food supply, especially in animal products. Because this small "acre and a cow" type of farming competes with the collective farm economy for the labor and loyalty of the peasants, as well as for ideological reasons, the Stalin regime came to look upon it with a jaundiced eye and behaved accordingly. But the attitude of Stalin's successors, after the initial spurt of liberalism, also has been ambivalent— now relaxed, now restricted.

10. In general, Soviet policy toward peasants has always consisted of a combination of force, indoctrination, and economic incentives but the proportion varied from time to time. During the Stalin regime force predominated. After Stalin, Soviet policy shifted to a greater emphasis on economic incentives. The very low prices paid by the Government for the

farm products which the collectives had to deliver were raised considerably. The whole system of deliveries was reorganized and simplified. Larger incomes of collectives as a result of higher prices and larger output permitted increased and often more regular distribution to peasants. But the stimulating effect of increased agricultural prices is to some extent lost when there is only a limited supply of consumer goods for farmers to buy because of the imbalance in Soviet industrialization. For the underemphasis of production of consumers goods has not been sufficiently redressed.

In any event, the visiting team of U.S. Department of Agriculture economists pointed out in its report: [12]

The system of collective and state-operated farms is not likely to provide production incentives for farm people that are equal to the incentives on family farms in this country. In other words, it may be difficult to substitute for the "magic of ownership which turns sand into gold." Also, the struggles incidental to establishment of collective farming may have left scars that will impede development of adequate production incentives.

11. The lagging capital investment in agriculture and inputs of agricultural machinery, commercial fertilizers and construction were increased. But capital investment is still inadequate to make possible an effective use of labor and land. Measures were also taken to increase or retain skilled labor on farms and to bring agricultural specialists nearer to grass roots. However, the problem of finding suitable managers for the large collective farms apparently has not been solved to the satisfaction of the government despite the large number trained and graduated from the agricultural colleges and vocational schools. Low labor productivity in agriculture, especially compared with the United States, has been giving considerable concern to the government which seems to lay increasing stress on cost reduction, economy of operation and greater incentive for individual effort in both work performance and management.

12. The changes in agricultural policy which have taken place during the post-Stalin period have had, for the most part, a beneficial effect on production. But some aspects, such as the persistent predilection for farm giantism and corn expansion on so large a scale, seem questionable. In the long run, even the program of expansion on the new lands in the eastern regions may prove unsound under the climatic conditions prevailing in those areas. During recent years, however, acreage expansion has been a highly important, if not the most important, factor next to the weather in the rapid expansion of production. However, recent Soviet figures on grain, meat and milk outputs seem overoptimistic. Further progress in increasing farm output may be expected. But, inasmuch as the government plan (1959–65) relies primarily on improvement of yields rather than on increased crop acreage to achieve its targets of large farm out-

---

[12] *Economic Aspects of Soviet Agriculture*, p. 54.

put, the progress may be at a slower rate. For experience indicates that the Soviet system of centrally planned collective agriculture has been generally more successful in increasing acreage than in improvement of yields and most successful in extracting large quantities of farm products which the Soviet State requires.

Nicolas Spulber

18. THE SOVIET-BLOC FOREIGN
TRADE SYSTEM*

*How does a centrally planned economy like that
of the Soviet Union decide which goods it is
economically advantageous to export and import?
The twin handicaps of irrational internal price
structures and arbitrary foreign exchange rates
have prevented planners in the Soviet Union and
other Soviet-type economies from making precise calculations of comparative advantage as a
basis for foreign trade. Decisions to export and
import are therefore made largely in physical
terms as part of the physical planning process.
The resulting trade—both between Communist
and non-Communist countries and among the
Communist countries themselves—takes place at
world market prices (or negotiated prices based
on them).*

*In this article, Nicolas Spulber analyzes the
principal characteristics and problems of the
Soviet-bloc foreign trade system. He discusses
the organization and conduct of foreign trade
and the nature of the prices and exchange rates
used. He then explains the limited success of efforts to achieve bloc-wide coordination of investment, production, and trade.*

FOREIGN trade is a state monopoly in each of the countries of the Soviet
bloc. The sphere of this monopoly encompasses not only all the export and
import operations, which must be concentrated in the hands of state-

* Reprinted, with the permission of the author and publisher, from *Law and Con-
temporary Problems,* Vol. XXIV, No. 3 (Summer, 1959), pp. 420–34. This issue of
Law and Contemporary Problems, published by the Duke University School of Law,
Durham, North Carolina, is Part II of a symposium on state trading. Copyright ©,
1959, by Duke University. Nicolas Spulber is Professor of Economics at Indiana
University.

chartered or designated agencies, but extends, moreover, to all the economic relations between each of these countries and the rest of the world, including their international accounts and credits. The international accounts and the other economic or noneconomic relations with other countries are handled on the basis of an organic component of the monopoly of foreign trade, the monopoly of foreign exchange.

The stated tasks of the monopoly of foreign trade are: to ward off capitalist economic penetration, to provide "maximum assistance" to domestic capital formation, and to facilitate the eventual "coordination" of the economic plans of the bloc countries. The development of foreign trade in each country is dependent on the overall economic plan: it is the latter which commands the dynamics of imports, which, in turn, determine the dynamics of exports. The government decides the volume, value, structure, and direction of its trade; thus, the monopoly offers maximum "protection" to the national economy. Tariffs, the key factor in the foreign trade of the nonbloc economies, play only a secondary role in the bloc countries.

The present article proposes to examine both the structure and the operation of the monopolies of foreign trade in the countries of the Soviet bloc, focusing in turn on: (1) organization of these monopolies; (2) their operation within and outside the bloc; (3) prices and rates of exchange; (4) extent and limitation of bloc-wide attempts toward coordination of trade and output. A final section summarizes the discussion and suggests some conclusions.

I

In each bloc country, the foreign trade system is headed by the ministry of foreign trade. The ministry plans all the relevant elements concerning the foreign transactions, in function of the domestic output plan, of various policy considerations, and of the existing commitments. It prepares and participates in the negotiation of foreign trade agreements, and controls and directs the organizations entering in the field of trade.

Both in the Soviet Union and in the Soviet-bloc countries, where the Soviet organizational set-up has been more or less faithfully copied, the ministry is organized into two types of sections or departments—"functional" and "operational." The usual functional departments are planning, foreign exchange and finance, contracts, bookkeeping and auditing, arbitration, personnel, and capital construction. The usual operational departments and/or administrations are import, export, tariffs, transport, and international forwarding. In various bloc countries, some of the functional or operational departments are split into two sections—one concerned with the relations with the bloc, the other with the nonbloc countries.

The key planning department prepares the draft-plan in close contact with the state planning commission, which transmits it to the state-chartered foreign trade corporations. The draft is constructed within the directives of the state planning commission by taking into account the basic proportions planned by it for the economy as a whole, the existing commercial commitments, the import requirements, and the foreign exchange available. The draft specifies the volume, prices and transport cost, structure, and direction of the foreign trade. The importing and exporting corporations draft, in turn, their specific plans on the basis of the physical balances (output and its allocations in physical terms) submitted to them by the producing organizations and their selling and purchasing departments. The corporations of foreign trade suggest, fit in, or complete modifications of the basic blueprint, which they present to the planning department of the ministry. The coordinated, yearly, or long-term (five–seven years) plan can then be established by the ministry and submitted for final approval to the council of ministries.

Among the other functional departments which have been mentioned above, the foreign exchange and finance department, which keeps in close contact with the state bank, concerns itself with balance-of-payments problems. The administrative-economic department prepares the budget of the ministry and plans and surveys the expenditure of the foreign trade organs. The contracts department studies market trends abroad, prepares the projects for interstate negotiations, and drafts instructions for the foreign trade organizations concerning the carrying out of contracts after their signature. The accounting and auditing department checks and controls the financial accounts of the ministry and its organs.

Schematically, the departments for import and export are subdivided into sections for planning and finance, and into operational sections corresponding to the basic industrial branches (metallurgy, chemicals, textile, leather, food and agricultural products, etc.). Each of the sections is, in turn, subdivided by commodities, and in the case of a key commodity, also by countries. This is the case in Poland, for example, for coal, in Rumania for oil, and so on. In some countries, a special department for capital goods—distinct from the departments of imports and exports—concerns itself with the import of capital goods. In Poland, for instance, the main subsections of this department are fully-equipped plants, power equipment, machines, railroad and vehicles, ships and shipping equipment, and agricultural machinery. The other operational departments concern themselves, as their names indicate, with the policies and economics of tariffs, transport, and forwarding, and are each subdivided into sections for planning, finance, accounting, personnel, etc.

The ministry conducts its domestic activities through foreign trade commissioners and through the monopolistic corporations. The commissioners are members of the regional or republican central bodies. They supervise the facilities connected with foreign trade, propose measures for trade expansion, and survey the application of the instructions and regulations of the ministry. The monopolistic corporations are "governmental agencies operating under special status." They are state-owned organizations placed on a "commercial basis." That means that each is an independent legal entity, organized, as stated, under a separate charter which specifies its endowment by the state for the pursuit of its assigned business. Each organization is expected to produce planned or above-plan profits, in agreement with scheduled costs and planned profit margins, in carrying out the tasks assigned by the plan and in transacting purchases and sales at the prices established by the government. The state does not guarantee their obligations, since they are independent legal entities. The relation with the production enterprises is that of customer and supplier, regulated by special contracts. Once the over-all economic plan is approved, these contracts are concluded, within the framework of the plan, by the corporations and the selling or purchasing organizations of the economic ministries or of the trusts and "combines," specifying prices and terms of delivery.

Each of the importing, exporting, or forwarding (transport and expedition) corporations has, in turn, its functional and operational offices following the pattern indicated for the ministry of foreign trade. Basically, the importing and exporting corporations specialize according to the main industrial branches and their needs, while their offices specialize, in turn, in one type of commodity. Thus, the main importing corporations are established in each bloc country for capital goods, basic raw materials, metals, and goods of mass-consumption (household appliances, textiles, food, etc.). The main exporting corporations are diversified according to the principal exports which the country has to offer. In the case of the Soviet Union, the export corporations handle notably grain (Eksportkhleb), coal (Soiuzugleeksport), oil (Soiuznefteksport), lumber (Eksportles), fibers (Eksportlen), as well as machines, equipment, and finished articles (Tekhnoeksport). In Czechoslovakia, for instance, the accent is on diversification in the export of fully-equipped plants (Technoexport), heavy machinery and equipment (Strojexport), precision engineering (Kovo), etc., and results in a sharper specialization in these fields. However, in Bulgaria, the corporations specializing in the sale of various agricultural produce tend to be more diversified. By and large, there are some twenty corporations in each of the countries of the bloc.[1] In most of these countries, a selling organization of the cooperatives is also authorized to enter the field of foreign trade, along with the state corporations.

In each country, a chamber of commerce, which is not directly included in the system of the ministry of foreign trade, assists the foreign

---

[1] Up to 1949–50, Yugoslavia had the same organizational pattern in this field. Since then, trade has been carried out by some 500 economic agencies organized as joint-stock companies by the state-owned producing enterprises. The Government controls trade via the fixation of quotas, prohibition of exporting or importing given goods, issue of licenses, and so on. Foreign currencies are sold through the Central Foreign Currency Fund and the currency clearing houses; discriminatory rates are established according to beneficiaries and the nature of goods imported or exported.

customers in all matters connected with trade, sends delegations abroad, arranges the participation in foreign-trade fairs, obtains patents for its citizens, and so on. To it are also attached arbitration commissions.

The ministry of foreign trade carries on its operations abroad through trade delegations (in Russian, called *torgovye predstavitel'stva*—in short, *torgpredstva*). The *torgpredstva*, as these delegations are known in all the bloc countries, are treated as state delegations and enjoy full diplomatic immunity within the bloc, since foreign trade is considered by these countries to be a state function. The *torgpredstva* control the commercial activity carried on abroad by their national foreign trade corporations and insure that it conforms to the national laws of the foreign trade monopoly, grant the documents needed for the agreed commercial operations, and also study the general business trends in each country with respect to trade possibilities. In some countries, including the United States, where the *torgpredstva* are not accepted as state delegations, the Soviet Union and its various satellites maintain commercial agencies directly subordinated to their respective ministries of foreign trade.

II

The existence of a group of Soviet-type economies has led to the appearance of a special foreign trade market distinct from the rest of the world market—namely, the bloc or intraplanned-economies market. The interstate commercial treaties concluded between these countries are based on agreements of "friendship and mutual aid," and have both a political and commercial aim. The stated political aim is to help the signatory countries to "construct a communist society in the USSR and a socialist society in the popular democracies," while the commercial aim is to provide a well-defined framework for their commercial agreements. The commercial treaties include the provisions for most-favored-nation treatment with respect to physical and juridical persons of a signatory power finding themselves in the territory of the other country, export and import operations, transport of freight or passengers, and custom duties. They contain further provisions concerning arbitrage competence, exchange of specialists, organization of trade fairs, and other points of secondary importance.

Trade agreements for a determined period of one, two, or five years are signed by the governments of the bloc countries, within the general framework defined by their commercial treaties. The trade agreements state the value of the envisaged trade turnover in rubles and specify that the prices of the goods will be "fixed on the basis of world prices." An adjoining quota list indicates in quantity or value terms the broad categories of the commodities to be exchanged. The long-term trade agreements are meant to insure the basic minimum supplies needed for the outputs scheduled by the so-called "perspective" plans. The yearly agreements are meant to adjust more concretely the flows of trade to the precise needs of the yearly "operational" plan. Upon the signature of the agreement, the state banks of the two signatory countries open to each other noninterest-bearing credit accounts for the specified amount of the trade turnover. For the implementation of this trade, contracts are then negotiated and eventually concluded between the appropriate foreign trade corporations of the two countries. These contracts finally specify the quality, assortment, agreed price, date, and place of delivery of each item.

Let us now follow a whole foreign trade operation as it is carried out in practice within the bloc. On the basis of the plan, contracts are concluded between the exporting corporations and the appropriate domestic organizations selling commodities earmarked for export. The prices paid by the exporting corporations are the factory price f.o.b., not including the famous turnover tax (a sales tax with varying levels, according to the item to which it is applied). For certain scarce commodities, a special purchase authorization may also be needed. Payment to the producer is done via the so-called "acceptance" form—*i.e.*, acceptance by the purchasing exporting corporation of the documents indicating that the goods have been sent to it by the producer. The commodity is forwarded by the exporting agency to the foreign importing agency via the appropriate channels. The settlement is made through the system of so-called "incasso with direct payment." The export organization is paid by its central bank, from the account of the buyer, upon receipt of the export documents. The bank then sends the documents to the central bank of the importing country, which, in turn, immediately credits the account of the exporter, and then presents the documents for collection of payments to the importing organization. In case of refusal of the buyer to accept the goods, the banks rapidly notify one another and adjust their accounts accordingly.

With the nonbloc countries, trade agreements are concluded in the same way, but the values involved are expressed in the currency of the nonbloc partner, in dollars or in rubles. These are, again, bilateral agreements, with accounts carried in clearing, just as in the case of the trade within the bloc. The balance of such accounts can be covered either by gold or foreign exchange, or by the shipment of additional commodities, as is also done within the bloc. In countries with which no clearing accounts are established, the payments are made through the foreign accounts kept by the central banks with various foreign banks. Whatever the case, the trade settlements with nonbloc countries are done via the usual letter of credit (and not through the incasso form). The exporter receives his payment from a specially agreed bank at the presentation, under specified conditions, of the export documents.

Some triangular arrangements involving one nonbloc and two bloc countries have been established on the initiative of the Soviet Union. Under one arrangement, specific Finnish exports to the Soviet Union were offset by given Polish exports to Finland, in exchange for Soviet exports to Poland. In another case, Burmese exports to the Soviet Union were offset by Czechoslovak exports to Burma, counterbalancing Soviet exports to Czechoslovakia.

Up to June 1957, the "clearing ruble" has played only the role of a bookkeeping unit of account. Since June 1957, the State Bank of the Soviet Union has started to act as a clearing house for intrabloc multilateral compensations. Given the fact that the bulk of the bloc trade continues to flow on the basis of bilateral agreements and through bilateral channels, the amount multilaterally compensable has remained, in all likelihood, rather small. This amount is built up by purchases above the minimums provided for by the bilateral agreements, purchases of various consumers' goods, and perhaps by various obligations arising from services.[2] Though the planners of each country might be inclined to retain the manageable system of bilateral agreements which guarantees them the supply of a given structure and volume of imports required by their output plans, it is possible that in the future, some triangular or quadrangular arrangements would be devised, especially for raw materials, which occupy a decisive place in intrabloc trade. Thus, for instance, Soviet iron ore exports to Rumania might be offset by Rumanian oil exports to Poland, counterbalancing in part Polish coal exports to the Soviet Union. Again, such arrangements might also provide, but still in limited margins, multilaterally compensable balances. In any case, since multilateral compensation means that each bloc country would stand ready to sell goods against clearing rubles, and since the case might arise in which some countries would build net export or import surpluses with the whole bloc (over and above their regular bilateral agreements), some limits must be set to the amount of clearing rubles which each country would be supposed to accept. This kind of arrangement, similar to the one which prevailed in the defunct European Payments Union, appears even more compelling in the bloc, given the planning of both output and foreign trade and the scarcity, by definition, of exportable commodities over and above plan. A supplementary, and probably also necessary, clause might be required to provide for the conversion into gold of some of the balances built in clearing rubles.

All these various elements—the necessity of insuring planned supplies, and hence the preference for bilateral arrangements, the scarcity of exportable goods over and above plan, the necessity of limiting the amounts of freely convertible clearing rubles, and the need of providing for the conversion of the latter into gold up to a certain amount—will, along with other factors, continue to keep the multilateral compensation within narrow margins.

---

[2] All the bloc countries have introduced, since 1957, varying premiums on the official rate of exchange in connection with payments for services. These rates now diverge significantly from the rates prevailing in trade.

III

As already stated, the bloc importer or exporter pays or receives payment for the respective goods from his central bank. Payments are made in the domestic currency—rubles in Russia, zlotys in Poland, korunas in Czechoslovakia, and so on—at the prevailing rate of exchange. In each bloc country, all gold and foreign exchange is concentrated in the hands of the central bank, and all foreign accounts are carried out exclusively through that bank. Each bloc government defines the gold content of its domestic currency, so that each bloc currency can be expressed in terms of any other bloc (or nonbloc) currency. However, no foreign currency, be it of bloc or nonbloc countries, circulates within these countries, and it is strictly prohibited to take the domestic currency abroad. It is officially stated that the rate of exchange of these domestic currencies is established in a planned fashion. Actually, the rate is fixed at an arbitrary level, since neither changes in the domestic wholesale and retail prices nor changes in the world prices of the goods exported or imported by these countries affect this planned rate of exchange.

Since domestic prices are looked upon as an element which can and must be extensively manipulated in all possible ways in order to meet various planned objectives, prices reflect only in part the underlying endowment of factors. As a rule, capital goods are furnished to the economy at various below-cost levels in order to keep the general price level down, while consumers' goods are charged with varying levels of turnover tax. Since the rate of exchange is also established at an arbitrary plateau, the planner of foreign trade is handicapped in trying to ascertain the efficiency of the foreign trade system as a whole, though he might be able to relate in a crude manner the profitability of one transaction to that of another. Each bloc country uses a different method in this field, though all these methods are qualified by their users themselves as being extremely deficient.[3]

---

[3] To illustrate the point, let us look more closely at one of these somewhat complicated methods of computing the profitability of foreign trade. In Hungary, the foreign trade enterprises use in the case of export operations a so-called "coefficient of foreign exchange," and in the case of import operations a so-called "coefficient of domestic realization." In the computation of both coefficients, the elements involved are the domestic and foreign prices paid and obtained and the official rate of exchange. Assume that the rate of exchange is 1 dollar for 6 forints, and 1 ruble for 1.5 forints. Assume further that a given commodity is purchased by the exporting enterprise at 1400 forints and sold for 200 dollars—*i.e.*, 1200 forints at the official rate of exchange. The coefficient of foreign exchange is taken to be the ratio of the domestic price to the price obtained, computed at the official rate—*i.e.*, $1400 \div 1200 = 1.16$. The coefficient is then 16% above parity. If the commodity is sold for 250 dollars, the coefficient is .93 ($1400 \div 1500$)—*i.e.*, 7% below parity. The lower the coefficient, the more profitable a transaction is presumed to be. In the case of imports, if a commodity is purchased for 200 rubles and resold for 360 forints, the ruble has been "obtained" at the rate of 1.8 forints. This figure is called the "domestic rate of real-

Generally, each foreign trade organization has an established "profit norm"—*i.e.*, a mark-up ranging from one to fifty per cent of the domestic wholesale price of the item traded. For an imported good, the mark-up is computed on the basis of the domestic wholesale price at which the good is sold to an industry. The mark-up on exported goods is calculated on the interior wholesale price, excluding the turnover tax, at which a good is usually sold by a domestic producer to a wholesale organization. If the price of the commodity sold abroad is, at the official rate of exchange, below the domestic price, including the profit of the exporting organization, the difference is covered by a subsidy from the budget. In order to obtain a particularly sought-after import, the ministry of foreign trade might enjoin the trading agencies to sell some exports at a price below cost. However, the trading agencies will generally try to sell at a profit.

Following a rule against price discrimination agreed upon in 1951, each bloc country will charge any bloc partner the same price for the same commodity, except for differences in transport cost. No assurance exists, however, of complete uniformity of prices for goods exported by more than one country in the bloc. A tendency in this direction exists through the mobility of buyers and sellers. As already stated, the prices at which the goods are traded in the bloc are based on "world prices." We do not know, however, whether these prices are prevailing in New York, London, or Bombay, in the same market for all commodities, or in different markets for different commodities. In establishing the price of a given commodity, the bloc partners "take into account the price of that commodity prevailing on the capitalist market in usual conditions of supply and demand." This presumably means that the world prices are purged of short-term fluctuations, though it is not at all clear how the bloc partners can ascertain the "usual conditions of supply and demand" in the "capitalist markets." The agreed export prices are then kept unchanged "for at least one year and for the overwhelming majority of commodities for a series of years." Hence, it is possible that at various times, the price constellation in intrabloc trade should diverge in some respects from the price constellation in the world market, even though the former constellation is patterned on the latter.

The utilization of the world price pattern creates many misgivings for Marxian economists, since according to Marx, any developed country is always in the position of exploiting a less-developed one. In Marxian terms, "an advanced country is enabled to sell its goods above their value even

ization." Since at the official rate of 1.5 forints, the 200 rubles equal only 300 forints, the coefficient of domestic realization is 1.20 ($360 \div 300 = 1.20$), or 20% above parity. If the domestic sale price is 279, the coefficient of domestic realization is .93, or 7% below parity. This time, the operation is presumably considered to be unprofitable. Obviously, since all the magnitudes involved—domestic price of an exported commodity, domestic price of an imported commodity, and rate of exchange—are distorted in various ways, these calculations at best allow a comparison between two foreign trade transactions of a closely related nature, but can hardly serve as an indicator of what is actually occurring in the foreign trade as a whole.

when it sells them cheaper than the competing countries,"[4] while a less-developed country "may offer more materialized labor in goods than it receives, and yet it may receive in return commodities cheaper than it may produce them."[5] Since 1948, the theory of an implicitly unequal exchange (more materialized labor of the underdeveloped area against less labor of the highly developed country) has been heavily stressed by the Yugoslav Communists in order to suggest that unequal relations might also arise among socialist states. Though the Yugoslavs have been expelled from the bloc and branded as "revisionists," the question of the utilization of the world price pattern within the orbit is still high on the agenda of the bloc economists. At various bloc conferences concerning these problems, the Czechoslovak and East German economists were decidedly in favor of the further utilization of the world price pattern, while the Hungarians and Rumanians seemed to agree to this solution only with numerous reservations. Thus, the Czechoslovak economist Vladmir Kaigl noted that it would not be "feasible to build a separate price-system completely severed from the existing world prices" and suggested that the gulf between the developed and the nondeveloped areas be bridged "by other means than an effort to deviate from world prices." The Rumanian economist Iosif Angel affirmed that the application of world prices to bloc trade "leads to effects harmful to the economy of industrially less developed countries." However, no one has indicated precisely how these harmful effects could be avoided by the manipulation of prices in foreign trade.

It is interesting to note that in 1951, the Russians were suggesting that the bloc countries were ready to set up their own intrabloc price system different in amount and ratios from the price system prevailing in the world markets. Nothing significant came out of these early claims, except the correction of world-market prices of short-run fluctuations. Furthermore, up to now, no one has proposed the adoption of the Soviet price pattern itself in intrabloc transactions. Such an adoption would make the ruble figuring in the intrabloc transactions convertible, within the limits of the trade agreements, into goods at the delivery prices prevailing in the Soviet Union. But the Soviet price pattern is so distorted that presumably neither the Soviet Union nor the satellites would be able to know who would benefit, and in what amount, from any foreign transaction.

IV

In order to provide for economic cooperation and coordination at the level of both trade and output planning within the bloc, a Council for Economic Mutual Assistance (CEMA) was formed in January 1949 by

---

[4] Karl Marx, *Capital* (Untermann transl. 1909), Vol. 3, p. 278.

[5] The paradox is presumed to arise from the fact that "capitals invested in foreign trade come in competition with commodities produced in other countries with lesser facilities of production." *Ibid.*, p. 279.

the Soviet Union and the East-Central European countries: East Germany, Poland, Czechoslovakia, Hungary, Rumania, Bulgaria, and Albania. Neither Communist China nor the Asian satellites (Outer Mongolia, North Korea, and North Vietnam) are members of CEMA. Communist China, however, sends an observer to its deliberations.*

CEMA has advisory and consultative functions. It makes recommendations, but lacks executive authority to enforce them. It has no fixed headquarters and meets roughly once a year in the capital of a different member country. At its sessions, CEMA examines the recommendations of its expert commissions, now some thirty-odd in number and of a permanent character since 1956, each of which has now its headquarters in the country best suited for its specific work. Thus, the Soviet Union is host to CEMA's heavy metallurgy commission, Czechoslovakia to the machinery-construction commission, East Germany to the chemical commission, Poland to the coal commission, Rumania to the oil and natural gas commission, Bulgaria to the agricultural commission, etc. In each commission sit permanent representatives of the ministries and planning authorities concerned in the member countries.

During the first years of CEMA's activity, which coincided with the first plans of development of the East-Central European countries—i.e., from 1949 to 1953—the essential method of coordination used in the bloc was the establishment of long-term trade agreements designed to guarantee the minimum supplies of basic materials needed for the carrying out of the independently-drawn national output plans. Most of these long-term trade agreements were concluded between 1950 and 1952, and CEMA was more or less instrumental in their preparation. During the same period, technical and scientific cooperation started to develop in the bloc through interchange of technical documentation, technical consultation, exchange of experts, training of technicians and workmen, and the like.

After the death of Stalin, the question of developing the "socialist division of labor" received increased attention from numerous bloc quarters. During the short period of the so-called "new course" (1953–55), economic coordination was envisaged not only at the level of trade as during the preceding period, but also at the level of output. Thus, the activities of CEMA were to increase in depth and facilitate as much as possible the dovetailing of the second long-term development plans of the East European countries, scheduled to start in January 1956, at the same time as the Sixth Five-Year Plan of the Soviet Union. While these plans were still in the initial stage of implementation, the upheavals in Hungary and in Poland in the fall of that same year threw them out of gear and forced substantial changes in the basic design. The Soviet Union itself stopped short of the completion of its Sixth Five-Year Plan and shifted to a new Seven-Year-Plan for the period 1959–65. The objectives of CEMA

---

* Editor's note: As a result of the Sino-Soviet split, Communist China no longer sends an observer to CEMA meetings and Albania is no longer an active member of CEMA. Mongolia has become a member of CEMA.

were then proclaimed to be not only to help in the coordination of the new output plans for 1961–65, the third long-term plan period in East Europe, but also to examine and suggest appropriate means for fitting together the plans for raw materials, fuel and power, capital construction, and transportation for the whole fifteen-year period extending from 1961 to 1975.

Within this broad framework, what has CEMA actually accomplished? While there has been much talk about the socialist division of labor, various factors have either prevented this division from occurring or have at best rendered it highly haphazard. The intrabloc division of labor has progressed little, because each of the countries of the bloc has attempted to build the same structure of production as that of the Soviet Union. Each has conceived and continues to conceive its industrialization as a process in which the national heavy (or producers' goods) industries must develop at a faster rate than the consumers' goods industries, regardless of the impact this policy may have on the standard of living. Each country has held dogmatically to the Marxian schema of "enlarged reproduction," positing that certain branches must develop faster than others, whatever the underlying endowments of factors might be. However, since 1955, it has been conceded in all these countries that each need not develop *all* the branches of the heavy industry, and that cooperation is necessary and possible without changing in any way the basic tenets of enlarged reproduction within each economy.

But at this point, various other key factors enter into play against any systematic division of labor. One of these factors is the impossibility of establishing some meaningful relation between the distorted interior prices and the international prices, a question which we have examined above in part three. Another factor is the inbuilt tendency of each plant, industry, sector, region, or country in the area to insure its supplies and thus accumulate stocks or even produce spare parts or any other goods in order to break the bottlenecks which would prevent the achievement of the main economic goal—namely, the fulfillment and even overfulfillment of the output plan. Self-sufficiency becomes a virtue within a planning system whose basic emphasis is on the fulfillment of given physical-output targets.

Another obvious factor which has operated against division of labor is the special role of the Soviet Union, given its size, economic potential, and political influence and its understandable reluctance to agree to any scheme which would imply a weakening of its control over its own output plan or a sharing of its investible resources ("accumulations") according to the bloc-wide endowments of factors. Hence, the lack of executive powers of CEMA and the necessity of achieving each specific division of labor via a bilateral or at best a triangular arrangement.

As a result of all these elements, the division of labor at the level of output ultimately presents a somewhat haphazard pattern, since it is shaped by political and technical-engineering factors, and not by cost and price considerations. It is stated now that by 1960, thanks to the help of CEMA, specialization will involve ninety types of machines, twenty-seven metallurgical products, twenty-five chemical products, and so on. Each of the permanent commissions of experts examines laboriously each type of product, taking into account each plant available, and recommends a specific technical-engineering apportionment among the members. The experts propose, CEMA recommends, and the various countries involved implement, if they so decide, the recommendations made via bilateral agreements. Thus, in certain cases, given plants in a given country are earmarked to produce for the whole bloc. For example, the Zemag Works in Zeitz, East Germany, manufactures agglutination machinery (for coal briquets, sawdust, ores, etc.), the Thälman Works in Magdebourg produces large cement factories, and the Förderbrücken Gerätebau in Leuchlammer manufactures coal-stripping and removing machinery. In some cases, outputs of given specifications (e.g., trucks of five or ten tons) will be produced in this or that country, viz. Hungary and Czechoslovakia. In other cases, cooperation consists in the establishment of a joint company in which one country furnishes the raw materials, the other the industrial facilities to exploit them, viz. the Hungarian-Rumanian company Romagchim for joint exploitation of the Rumanian natural gas.

This laborious bloc-wide technical-engineering apportionment, however, can be either obstructed or rendered of doubtful value if two important countries develop suddenly a very broad framework of bilateral cooperation. Thus, the Soviet-Czechoslovak economic relations were suddenly organized on the basis of extensive cooperation in a group of key industries following a bilateral agreement announced on January 29, 1957.[6] It is difficult to know exactly in what measure such agreements complete or cancel the bloc-wide apportionments already suggested by CEMA commissions. However, it is certain that future bloc-wide apportionments will have to be adjusted to the agreement already reached bilaterally by two of the most important members of the bloc.

The transition from the attempted coordination at the level of trade, which characterized the period up to 1953, to attempted coordination at the level of output, which started from 1955 onward, has had rather limited results to date. The output plans continue on parallel lines, and the planners reluctantly envisage any broad intrabloc division of labor. If, as far as trade is concerned, each bloc country affirms that it always stands ready to buy from a bloc member rather than from a nonbloc country, even if the bloc country's prices are slightly higher and the time of delivery somewhat longer, the inbuilt autarchic tendency of each planned economy plays strongly against systematic cooperation in the current period, just as in the preceding one. The East European planner will accept willingly credits, technical assistance, or scientific cooperation, but

---

[6] See "Economies Joined by Soviet, Czechs," N.Y. Times, Jan. 30, 1957, p. 14, col. 4.

will try to keep his domestic plan, as much as feasible, on an all-round basis and under his rigid control.

V

1. The monopoly of foreign trade has proven to be, for each Soviet-type economy, an important political-defensive and offensive tool. As far as defensive purposes are concerned, the monopoly has insured maximum protection against capitalist competition and maximum assistance to the national plan, since it has made the imports from nonbloc sources dependent on the plan needs and has tailored the exports to meet the needs of payments arising from the given imports.

2. As an instrument of political attack and offensive, the monopoly has insured the possibility, especially for the Soviet Union, of shifting rapidly from one market to another, of adjusting purchases and sales to political considerations, and of maximizing the impact of its operation, especially when the international market is in distress. In fact, the more unsettled the world market is, the more effective the monopoly appears as an instrument of commercial warfare. Furthermore, the more delicate the balance of power in the so-called noncommitted countries, the more powerful looms the capacity of the Soviet Union to adjust its trade to its political objectives. It is interesting to note that in periods of international tension, there is always talk of counteracting the Soviet monopoly of foreign trade by creating a similar foreign trade monopoly either on a national or an international scale. However, such a move is extremely difficult to fit within the framework of free-enterprise economies, and no concrete steps have thus far been taken in this direction.[7]

---

[7] Mr. James Reston recently stated that a high official of the United States Government has declared the following: "We have been discussing quietly inside our own government for six months the need to establish an overseas trade monopoly to compete with the Soviet monopoly on equal terms, but this is so foreign to our normal way of doing business that we have not mentioned it in public." N.Y. Times, Dec. 2, 1958, p. 17, cols. 3–5. Writing again on this problem a week later, Mr. Reston added that "men high in this Government" argue that "the United States may have to go to a radical system of state trading overseas, or even to combined state trading with the other free countries in order to counter Moscow's capacity to trade where it likes, at any prices it likes, for political advantage." Ibid., Dec. 7, 1958, p. E8, col. 4.

Let me note that these are not radical new ideas—though they may become radical new policies. G. Caillaux stated in 1931 in the French Senate that the only way of meeting the danger arising from the Soviet foreign trade monopoly was "to meet the adversary with his own arms." Caillaux suggested that France should decide "that nothing be sold or bought from the Soviets but through the intermediary of an Office whose task would be to watch that there will be balance between purchases and sales. . . . The same Office," added Caillaux, "purchasing directly for our importers, would sell them the acquired products at the prices prevailing on our market." The idea was soon taken over by Loucheur who suggested that the proposed solution be enlarged and that an International Office of Trade with the Soviet Union be formed. The Office would purchase from the Russians and "apportion the goods among the participating countries following a given scale based on their needs."

3. The pursuit of industrialization in East Europe and the organization of these economies on the Soviet model (centralized planning and monopoly of foreign trade) have encouraged, to a degree, development of intrabloc trade. Deliberate industrialization has facilitated the import of raw materials from the Soviet Union and the export toward the Soviet market of manufactured goods. Trade has further increased, thanks to the deliberate choice made by the various trading agencies involved, in favor of the intrabloc market instead of the extrabloc markets. But on the other hand, the attempt to develop each economy on an all-round basis and the manipulation by each of their own domestic prices has rendered the attempts toward a broad division of labor more implausible. The division of labor has been a hit-and-miss proposition in which, as stated, technology and engineering are supposed to provide answers which distorted costs and prices cannot give.

4. Given conclusion three above, can we conclude that "the less the degree of dependence of a national economy in its ordinary operations on trade with other countries, the less, *caeteris paribus*, will be the difficulties of setting up and operating a comprehensive national economic plan"?[8] This assertion is certainly true in general. It is easier to set up a domestic all-round plan by reducing foreign trade to a minimum. But on the other hand, Soviet-type planning, with its deliberate priorities and branch emphasis, creates enormous imbalances in the economy. These imbalances create, in turn, a serious need for trade. Certain imports are rapidly needed in order to break various bottlenecks, and exports are needed as an outlet for certain surpluses (even such surpluses as obsolete military equipment). Thus, the intrabloc market can and does play the role of a cushion for the imbalances of the plan of the most important economy of the bloc, that of the Soviet Union.

5. The Soviet-bloc economies indicate that the intrabloc trade is "a new type of trade" in which the partners enjoy "full equality," in contrast with the relations prevailing in the capitalist world markets. The facts adduced to prove these assertions are either of a very limited import or are completely irrelevant. It is stated, for instance, that (*a*) equality arises because the clearing operations are carried simultaneously by the appropriate organisms of *both* partners, and not only by one of the two partners; (*b*) equality is insured by the fact that "the law of value does not operate anarchically," but that it is kept under control, and prices are established on the basis of "mutual interest and voluntary understanding." Evidently, the fact that both partners keep the record of their operations is rather a simple procedure of double-checking than a sign of equality. As far as prices are concerned, the fact that they are kept stable or not is irrelevant to the question of equality and mutual interest. Actually, the procedure of omitting prices in the basic trade agreements and of leaving them to be

---

[8] Jacob Viner, "The Influence of National Economic Planning on Commercial Policy," in *International Trade and Economic Development* (1952), p. 85.

decided afterwards in the contracts concluded by the export and import agencies often places the weaker country at the complete mercy of the stronger partner. It is characteristic that in the trade with nonbloc countries, the question of the prices set by the Soviet agencies has always been one of the sore points of the trade with the Soviet Union. These prices have quite often proven higher than the international prices for goods of lower quality, with the result that many countries have had serious difficulties in implementing the trade agreement.

PART IV

Selected Aspects of Economic Systems

Rather than analyzing or illustrating particular economic systems, as in Parts II and III respectively, the selections that follow compare different economic systems from several standpoints. The first contrasts the importance and functions of the monetary and banking system in regulated capitalism, market socialism, and socialist central planning. The next article compares enterprise management in the United States and Soviet economies. The following three selections are concerned with the crucial question of the best economic system for the development of an underdeveloped country. The last article investigates the proposition that different economic systems are "converging," that is, becoming more alike.

Banking

The nature and functions of money and banking differ significantly in capitalist, market socialist, and centrally planned economies. These differences correspond to, and illustrate, the differences among these economic systems in the degree of centralization or decentralization of decision making and in the use of physical planning or markets and prices in resource allocation.

Depending on the economic system, the task of the monetary authorities may be regarded as monetary management, monetary direction, or monetary supervision. In a capitalist market economy, the central bank attempts to manage the level of private economic activity through its influence on the level of commercial bank reserves. In market socialism, the government's direction of the economy through the banking system determines not only the total amount of money and credit but also the distribution of investment funds among branches of the economy and specific enterprises. In a centrally administered economy, finally, monetary planning is subordinated to physical planning, and the banking system's assignment is to finance and supervise (that is, enforce) detailed enterprise plans for the production and distribution of goods. These differences in the role of the banking system in capitalism, market socialism, and central planning are analyzed and illustrated in the following selection.

Egon Neuberger[1]

19. THE ROLE OF CENTRAL BANKING UNDER VARIOUS ECONOMIC SYSTEMS *

Egon Neuberger analyzes money and banking in various economic systems from the standpoint of the central bank. He compares the objectives, functions, and instruments of central banking in free enterprise capitalism, "semi-planned" market socialism, and central planning—as illustrated respectively by the United States, Yugoslavia, and the Soviet Union. He concludes that while central banking plays an important role in all three economic systems, it is most influential in Yugoslav market socialism.

CENTRAL banking literature is usually limited to the discussion of the role of central banks within a relatively narrow institutional framework. It discusses the development of the mother of central banks—the Bank of England—from its origin in 1694 until the present, as well as the development of its offspring, the central banks in free enterprise economies most

[1] This paper is a modified version of a paper presented in Professor John H. Williams' seminar on international financial problems. The author wishes to express thanks to Professor John H. Williams who has given him encouragement and inspiration and to Mr. Herbert S. Levine who has helped him develop parts of this paper and has reviewed the whole paper critically. Any remaining weaknesses are the responsibility of the author. The author also wishes to acknowledge the assistance extended to him by the Ford Foundation and the Center for International Studies, Massachusetts Institute of Technology.

* Reprinted, with the permission of the author and publisher, from *Public Policy*, Vol. VIII (Cambridge, Mass.: Harvard University Graduate School of Public Administration, 1958), pp. 227–54. Copyright 1958 by the President and Fellows of Harvard College. Egon Neuberger is an economist on the staff of the RAND Corporation.

of which were established at the end of the nineteenth and beginning of the twentieth century. The literature tends to discuss central banking largely within the context of central banking traditions developed in recent decades. The logic of this arrangement is that banks not following these traditions are not to be admitted to the club, even though as Sayers has pointed out, these traditions "had in fact no claim to veneration as long established ways that had survived many changes of circumstance and been tried in many fires."[2] This paper attempts to treat central banking from a broader point of view, discussing the role of central banks under various economic systems.

The aim of the paper is modest. It analyzes some aspects of the role of central banking within the theoretical models of three economic systems and in countries whose economic systems approximate these models. The difference in objectives, functions, and instruments of central banks in the various systems are emphasized. No attempt is made to analyze all aspects of these economic systems or to compare their efficiency in fulfilling the goals of the societies in which they function.

Before proceeding to the discussion of central banking in different institutional contexts it is necessary to touch on two points: (1) how to define central banking for our purposes, and (2) how to differentiate between the three economic systems under discussion, i.e. free enterprise, central planning, and semi-planning.

WHAT IS A CENTRAL BANK?

There is no one definition of what constitutes a central bank. The most common and simplest definition is one given by Hawtrey: "A central bank is a banker's bank."[3] He further defines it as one whose essential characteristic is its role of lender of last resort.[4]

Not all authorities agree with this definition or with his stress on the role of lender of last resort. For our purposes, the more important consideration is the fact that Hawtrey definitely limits the concept of a central bank to one specific institutional setting. The *sine qua non* for the existence of a central bank is a banking system consisting of independent commercial banks, thus limiting it to free enterprise systems.

We will use a definition broad enough to cover "central banks" in many different institutional environments. A modified version of the definition given by de Kock will serve this purpose.

A central bank is an institution which constitutes the apex of the monetary and banking structure of the country and which performs certain specific functions in the interest of the economy as a whole.[5]

---

[2] R. S. Sayers (ed.), *Banking in the British Commonwealth* (Oxford, 1952), p. xii.

[3] G. Hawtrey, *The Art of Central Banking* (London, 1933), p. 116.

[4] *Ibid.*

[5] M. H. de Kock, *Central Banking* (3d ed., London, 1954), p. 22.

The necessary condition is that the institution must be willing and able to be the main executor of government policies in the monetary field. If there exist commercial banks in the system, its main role is to control their actions in line with government policy; if there are no commercial banks, its role is to implement government policies directly.

CRITERIA FOR DIFFERENTIATING ECONOMIC SYSTEMS

The problem of differentiating between various economic systems according to the degree of control exercised by the central authorities is much more difficult than the problem of defining a central bank. While we have surveyed much of the literature on the subject, no widely acceptable scheme appears to exist. In this case, the alleged motto of the Cambridge economists "It is easier to think it up than to look it up," appears to have some advantage.

The following scheme has been worked out to help us understand the differences between the three economic systems to be discussed in this paper.

Planning is considered as the conscious control of economic activity to achieve some given goal or set of goals. The type of planning, i.e., central planning, semi-planning, and free enterprise, is defined in terms of the degree of control, which measures the extent to which the central authority takes decision-making powers away from primary economic units.[6]

The degree of control is a multivariate function depending upon the scope and intensity of control and the types of instruments used.

The scope of control may be measured by two criteria:

1. The number and relative importance of the primary economic units directly and significantly affected by the controls.
2. The number and relative importance of the activities of the primary economic units directly and significantly affected by the controls. In this context, the control over investment activity is probably the most important single activity to be considered.

The intensity of control may be differentiated as follows:

1. Complete control over the decision-making power of the primary economic units. No freedom of choice is given to these units.
2. Partial control over the decision-making power of the primary economic units. (a) Substitution of planners' rules of behavior[7] for those of the primary economic units; the primary economic units can then maximize their objectives[8]

---

[6] We define a primary economic unit as the smallest unit in the economy which makes economic decisions. For purposes of production it would be the firm, for consumption the individual or the family unit, for the sale of a factor of production the unit owning or controlling the factor, i.e., the worker, landlord, or owner of capital, etc.

[7] We define rules of behavior as the criteria to be followed by the primary economic units, e.g., profit maximization, fulfillment of plans, etc.

[8] The objectives may correspond to the rules of behavior, e.g., profit maximi-

within the limits imposed by the planners' rules of behavior. (*b*) Retention by primary economic units of their own rules of behavior, with control exerted through the manipulation of instruments discussed below.

The instruments that can be used are:

1. Physical allocation of factors of production and commodities.
2. Price controls: (*a*) Direct, i.e., setting of fixed prices; (*b*) indirect, i.e., influencing the level of prices through taxes, subsidies, etc.
3. Controls over the allocation of purchasing power: (*a*) Direct allocation, i.e., credit rationing; (*b*) indirect allocation, i.e., using rates of interest.

The controls can also be differentiated by the degree of their selectivity:

1. Selective controls over specific objects of control.[9]
2. General controls over aggregates.

A glance at the criteria we propose makes it clear that no purpose would be served in trying to find the numerical value for the multivariate function defining the degree of control. All the scheme can do is to tell us what particular aspects of a system we must study in order to determine the degree of control in the system. The classification of a system as free enterprise, central planning, or semi-planning necessarily involves a value judgment. Any mechanical method of classification would be worse than useless.

The pure models of free enterprise and central planning are easy to determine from the scheme. The former would involve no controls of any type by the central authority over any of the primary economic units. The latter would involve control over the decision-making power of all primary economic units with respect to all their economic activities. The instruments used would be physical allocation or possible direct price controls over specific goods and factors. When the pure models are spelled out, it immediately becomes clear that no such systems actually exist. Therefore, rather than pursue our analysis in terms of the pure models, we shall use examples of real systems which approximate these extremes.

A semi-planned system, as its name implies, combines planning with free enterprise. Thus, the power to make certain decisions is taken away from the primary economic units, while other decisions are still within their discretion. There is an infinite number of such combinations none of which can be termed "the model of semi-planning." In the section on semi-planning, we shall define one specific model and shall describe the objectives, functions and instruments of a central bank in this model.

---

zation, or they may differ, e.g., maximization of prestige of entrepreneur, the "easy life," etc.

[9] We define objects of control as the factor of production and commodity, the price of a factor or commodity, or the amount of purchasing power over which control is exercised.

FREE ENTERPRISE ECONOMIES

The pure model of free enterprise describes a system in which the government plays no active part in the economic life of the country. This would be the case if there were a general consensus that the government was powerless to interfere with the operation of the economic system as guided by the market mechanism or that such interference was undesirable. As Polanyi states it:

A belief in spontaneous progress must make us blind to the role of government in economic life. This role consists often in altering the rate of change, speeding it up or slowing it down as the case may be; if we believe that rate to be unalterable—or even worse, if we deem it a sacrilege to interfere with it— then of course, no room is left for intervention.[10]

In the pure model of free enterprise, there would be no room for a central bank performing any active functions. The most that an institution of that type would be permitted to do is issue currency in response to the demand for it.[11] If we ignore the pure model of free enterprise which has never existed, we could describe free enterprise systems as those in which the primary economic units retain most of the decision-making powers and in which there are free markets to exercise this freedom. This describes the situation in most of the countries of Western Europe, the United States and some other areas in the nineteenth and twentieth centuries. In these countries there is not a complete absence of controls; for example, general aggregative controls over purchasing power or as they are more commonly called, indirect monetary controls, are compatible with a large degree of freedom of decision-making for primary economic units.

OBJECTIVES OF CENTRAL BANKS

The objectives of central banks are generally those of the community in which they operate and these are discussed in this paper. At times, managers of central banks have attempted to stress objectives other than those favored by the community as a whole, e.g., price stability, rather than full employment in the 1930's. These cases are exceptional and the attempts have not been successful in the long run.

Exchange Rate Stability. During the nineteenth century and for about the first three decades of the twentieth century the dominant objective of central banks was to maintain stability of the country's exchange rates as required by the operation of the international gold standard. The ultimate purpose of this action was the protection of the integrity of the country's

---

[10] Karl Polanyi, *The Great Transformation* (New York, 1944), p. 37.

[11] Throughout this paper we are discussing only central bank policy and ignoring government fiscal policies. It is done merely to facilitate the task of exposition.

monetary unit. The system was operated under the assumption that domestic prices and wages were flexible, so that equilibrium could always be restored by methods of inflation and deflation without affecting employment, except in the very short run.

Other objectives of central banks in this period were to prevent financial panic by acting as lenders of last resort and to provide an elastic money supply. These objectives are less limited than the maintenance of convertibility of the currency into gold and the stability of exchange rates. The prevention of panics and the provision of a medium of exchange in sufficient quantities to facilitate transactions are important functions in any system where barter is not the sole basis of exchange. For this reason, it is not necessary to discuss them in this section.

The provision of an elastic money supply is the only one of these objectives specifically mentioned in the Federal Reserve Act of 1913. In the preamble to the Act the following aims of the newly formed Federal Reserve System were listed: (1) provide elastic currency, (2) afford means for rediscounting commercial paper, (3) provide more effective supervision of the banking system, and (4) other purposes.[12]

In addition to following the rules of the gold standard, the central bank philosophy also included an adherence to the "real bills" doctrine. It was believed that if both of these were followed, central bank operation would become automatic and would lead to optimum monetary conditions without the need of any discretionary measures on the part of central bank managers.[13]

Price and Output Stability. The Great Depression brought great changes in this field as in many others. Gone was the confidence in the gold standard and the efficacy of automatic monetary management. Maintenance of stable exchange rates became subordinated to attempts at stabilization of domestic price levels and levels of output and employment. More than that, gone was the confidence in the ability of the central bank, and monetary policy generally, to cope with the problems posed by the depression.

Full Employment. Although the policy of stabilization of prices and output aimed at a stabilization at as high a level of employment as possible, the maintenance of full employment gradually developed as an independent and in some cases superior aim of monetary policy. This tendency became very apparent with the British and Commonwealth White Papers on Employment and the Full Employment Act of 1946 in the United States.

[12] *Federal Reserve Act of 1913 with Amendments and Laws Relating to Banking,* comp. E. A. Lewis (Washington, D.C.: U.S. Government Printing Office, 1948), p. 1. The provision of a means for rediscounting commercial paper could be interpreted as being aimed at preventing financial panics or as being part of the effort to provide an elastic monetary supply.

[13] Federal Reserve Bank of Philadelphia, *40 Years of the Federal Reserve Act* (Philadelphia, no date), p. 6.

Economic Growth. At the time that the goal of full employment gained in importance in the economically advanced countries, another goal came to the fore in the underdeveloped countries; namely, the goal of rapid economic growth. There was a change in emphasis from regarding the central bank as solely a guardian of stability in exchange rates and domestic prices to regarding it as one of the prime movers in the drive for economic development. But even when the central bank was made an engine of growth, its specific function within the governmental apparatus was still to maintain price stability, even as it helped other agencies in promoting growth.

FUNCTIONS OF CENTRAL BANKS

The usual functions of central banks in free enterprise economies fall into three categories:

1. The provision of a medium of exchange to facilitate transactions: (*a*) issue of currency; (*b*) provision of a clearing mechanism for inter-bank transactions; (*c*) granting of accommodation, in the form of rediscounts or collateral advances, and the general acceptance of the responsibility of lender of last resort; (*d*) direct credit grants to non-bank customers in areas where the banking system is not sufficiently developed.
2. The performance of general banking and agency services for the State.
3. The control of economic activity in accordance with the objectives discussed above: (*a*) regulation of the money supply: (1) regulation of currency issue and (2) regulation of credit; (*b*) regulation of foreign exchange transactions.

The functions in the first two major categories are not of very great interest for our purposes at this stage, as they concern relatively technical problems of banking. The interesting problems arise in determining how the functions in the third category, i.e. the control of economic activity, are applied to achieve the various objectives of monetary policy at different times and under different institutional systems.

As far as regulation of currency issue is concerned, most central banks, at the present time, are the sole issuers of currency and are able to control the total amount of currency in circulation. This control is not sufficient to maintain the proper amount of money in the economy. This is determined by two factors in addition to the currency issue: the volume of credit extended and the distribution of the currency between the public and the commercial banks. Thus, the central banks must combine control over currency issue and over credit extensions to achieve control over the money supply. Credit control is generally an overall type of control over the total level of credit, and only in exceptional circumstances do central banks in free enterprise countries use selective credit controls.

The scope of foreign exchange regulations varies widely among different free enterprise countries, ranging all the way from the mere provision of banking facilities by the central bank to very specific controls over types of transactions, types of commodities, the destination or origin of commodities, etc.

It should also be noted that central banks do not always perform all of the functions listed above. In some cases special agencies are set up to handle specific functions, e.g., exchange stabilization funds to handle foreign exchange.

INSTRUMENTS OF CENTRAL BANKS

In free enterprise economies commercial banks are the main sources of new credit creation. To perform the credit control function, central banks must try to control the activity of commercial banks. Four main instruments are used for this purpose: the discount rate, open market operations, control of reserve ratios, and moral suasion. In underdeveloped countries where the capital market is underdeveloped, central banks use various types of controls over reserves of commercial banks and other special instruments to compensate for the relative ineffectiveness of the discount rate and open market operations.[14]

The orthodox central bank action was to use the discount rate and to make the changes in discount rates effective by means of open market operations. Under the gold standard rules, whenever there was a deficit in the balance of payments which threatened the stability of the exchange rate, the central bank would raise the discount rate and sell securities on the open market. This was expected to have two effects: to cause a net inflow of funds from abroad to earn the higher interest rates and to raise the cost and reduce the availability of funds at home, thereby bringing on a deflation. With lower prices and lower national income, exports were expected to increase and imports to fall, thus correcting the balance of payments disequilibrium. If there was a surplus in the balance of payments, the bank would lower the discount rate and buy on the open market, and the mechanism would work in the opposite direction. As Keynes pointed out, this policy may work well in the short run and in the long run, but in between there is a very painful readjustment period until factors of production move and prices change.

We shall see that the extraordinary efficacy of bank-rate for effecting the above is due to the fact that it produces two reactions, . . . both in the right direction—one of them quick in action but not so durable, the other slow in action but calculated to establish gradually a new long period equilibrium. Thus bank-rate is both an expedient and a solution. It supplies both the temporary pick-me-up and the permanent cure—provided we ignore the *malaise* which may intervene between the pick-me-up and the cure.[15]

When the objectives of central banks shifted from exchange rate stability to price and output stability and then to maintenance of full employ-

---

[14] Cf. A. I. Bloomfield, "Monetary Policy in Underdeveloped Countries," *Public Policy: Yearbook of the Graduate School of Public Administration*, Vol. VII (Cambridge, 1956), pp. 232–74.

[15] J. M. Keynes, *A Treatise on Money* (New York, 1930), Vol. I, p. 214.

ment, the traditional instruments did not prove as effective. There was general agreement that central banks were unable to cure a depression since they could not force banks to make loans, but could only provide the banks with sufficient reserves to make them liquid. In addition, the existence of a liquidity trap or a very low elasticity of the investment demand schedule could frustrate any attempt by a central bank to cure a depression by monetary means. There is not as general a consensus regarding the effectiveness of monetary policy in combatting an inflation. However, it is beyond the scope of this paper to enter into this controversy.

If the major objective is to promote economic growth, the traditional central banking instruments are even less satisfactory. The likelihood of the existence of a low price elasticity of supply and a low interest elasticity of the investment demand schedule will cause an increase in money and a fall in rates of interest, even if that fall takes place, to result merely in increases in prices of domestic goods and in the demand for imported goods.

The contributions a central bank can make to economic growth in free enterprise countries are: (1) to improve the system of financial intermediaries in order to assure that savings are channeled to productive investments, (2) to provide direct loans in areas where private commercial banks do not find it profitable to operate, e.g., agriculture, (3) to attempt to conduct its policy of controlling credit in such a way as to permit the maximum amount of growth without causing runaway inflation or unmanageable balance of payments difficulties.

As we will see below, a central bank in centrally planned and semi-planned economies uses different instruments and is in a position to make more direct contributions to economic growth.

CENTRALLY PLANNED ECONOMIES

The pure model of central planning describes a system where the central authority takes all the decision-making powers away from the primary economic units. The central planning board determines the allocation of factors of production and commodities down to the last detail.

If the central authorities used the most extreme type of control, i.e., physical allocations of all factors of production and all finished products, there would be no need for any market mechanism or for money as a medium of exchange. In this case, no central bank would exist or if it existed it would be an anachronism with no functions.[16]

Theoretically, the central authorities could achieve the same results by setting the prices of all factors and commodities and by altering the prices until the desired allocations are reached. In this case, there would be a

---

[16] Even in this case, monetary calculations could be used for purposes of accounting and financial control. See discussion of *khozraschet* and "control by the ruble" below.

COMPARATIVE ECONOMIC SYSTEMS

market in operation and money would be required. Therefore, some institution would have to be created to issue and control money, i.e., a central bank. In this system, the role of the central bank would be to control the total volume of money (currency and deposits), so that given the velocity of circulation or the desire of the enterprises and households to hold cash balances, the amount of money is just sufficient to cover the payment for the goods produced. In other words, the central bank would have to control money in such a way as not to interfere with the price system set up by the planning board.

The Soviet system uses a mixture of physical allocations and price controls, with the former being the more important. In the areas where the price mechanism operates money is essential. Even where the allocation is performed by physical controls, money is used for purposes of accounting and financial control. Economic enterprises must buy most of their inputs and sell their outputs; transactions between enterprises are covered by transfers of deposit money in the accounts at the bank.

In addition to the use of deposit money for inter-enterprise payments, money serves another important function in the Soviet system. Maurice Dobb argues that the main reason for using money in the USSR is the need for using money wage differentials as the most efficient method of allocating labor. Wages in kind would not perform this function as efficiently due to variations in individual tastes which would have the result that the same wage in kind would have a different value to individual workers. And the absence of freedom of choice in spending would seriously diminish the strength of the incentive which a wage income offered.[17] Translating this into technical terminology, Dobb is saying that consumer utility from a given income is maximized at the point of tangency between the price line and the indifference curve; the only way that this can be achieved in practice is by permitting consumer free choice.[18]

Soviet writers mention both of these reasons for the use of money in the Soviet economy, However, they stress a third reason—the continued operation of the free price mechanism (the "law of value" in Soviet terminology) in the collective farm markets requires the existence of money.

The previous discussion has indicated that the objectives of central banks in free enterprise economies have evolved with the stage of develop-

---

[17] Maurice Dobb, *Soviet Economic Development since 1917* (New York, 1948), pp. 351–52.

[18] It is essential to differentiate between consumer free choice and consumer sovereignty. The former merely involves permitting the consumer to maximize his utility by choosing freely among the various commodities at the prices ruling in the market (even if these prices are determined by the planning board). The latter is a much more basic concept involving the orientation of all production to follow the wishes of the consumers as manifested on the market. Cf. A. Bergson, "Socialist Economics," *A Survey of Contemporary Economics*, ed. Howard S. Ellis (Philadelphia, 1948), p. 423.

ment of the economies, with the specific problems facing them, and the ideological climate. In the discussion of centrally planned economies we will use the example of the USSR to illustrate this type of system. This choice then leads us to discuss the objectives, functions and instruments of central banks as they exist in this case. If we took some other examples of centrally planned economies, e.g., the Nazi economy, we would certainly find different objectives and some differences in the functions and instruments.

OBJECTIVES OF CENTRAL BANKS

It is no easy matter to determine the objectives of the rulers of the USSR. It is clear that there is no one single objective. We might tentatively list the following objectives as probably motivating the Soviet rulers: (1) Political power of the regime, (2) military power of the country, (3) rapid growth of the economy, (4) advancement of "socialism" at home and abroad, and (5) increasing the welfare of the population. It is clear that certain policies will promote all or most of these objectives, while others may promote some objectives at the expense of others.

One of the objectives—the maintenance of a rapid rate of growth of the economy—is also one of the major methods used to satisfy the other objectives. At the risk of oversimplifying, we might say that the goal of Soviet economic policy is to promote a rapid rate of growth.

In free enterprise economies, this objective is pursued by means of government assistance to the private sector through monetary, fiscal and other policies. In the Soviet economy, it is pursued by means of a comprehensive economic plan which determines both the rate of capital formation and the allocation of resources. Since the allocation is not done entirely by physical controls, especially in the labor and consumer goods markets, money plays an important role. So does the State Bank of the USSR (Gosbank).

The objective of the Gosbank is to assist in assuring the smooth functioning of the plan, thus promoting the goal of rapid economic growth. It implements this objective by acting at two levels: (1) Directly in support of the plan by its control function, the so-called "control by the ruble,"[19] and (2) indirectly by means of assuring a smoothly functioning monetary system and the maintenance of stable prices.

The objectives of central banks in free enterprise economies, other than the objectives of economic growth and price stability, have never played any part in the activities of the Gosbank. The link between domestic prices and international prices was broken and the correction of any imbalance in the Soviet balance of payments was the function of the monopoly of foreign trade and not the central bank. Thus, exchange rate

---

[19] The meaning of this term and a description of the methods used in achieving this control are discussed below.

stability could not be a prime objective of the Gosbank. The rapid, forced development of the Soviet economy has put pressure on all resources and there was never any worry about unemployment due to insufficiency of effective demand.

FUNCTIONS OF CENTRAL BANKS

In our discussion of the objectives of central banks in centrally planned economies we have already broached their most important functions: "control by the ruble" and maintenance of price stability.

In comparing the functions of the Gosbank with those of central banks in free enterprise economies, it becomes clear that they are as similar as the different institutional frameworks permit. This is not surprising as the Soviets used existing ideas on the organization and functions of central banks as their model and modified them as needed.

The Gosbank performs some of the functions in all 3 categories:

1. It performs the function of providing a medium of exchange through the issue of currency, the provision of a clearing mechanism for transfers between enterprises, and the opening of deposit accounts for enterprises by means of credits. It does not grant accommodation in the form of rediscounts to commercial banks and does not have the role of lender of last resort; this is due simply to the fact that there are no commercial banks in the Soviet Union.[20]

2. The Gosbank performs general banking and agency services for the state. It acts as virtually the sole fiscal agent for all levels of government.

3. As in the case of free enterprise economies, it is the functions of the third category, those involving control over economic activity, that are of the greatest interest.

In the USSR, as in most other countries, at the present time, the central bank is the sole issuer of currency, and in this respect there is no significant difference between the two types of systems. In the case of credit regulation, however, the institutional differences reappear. While central banks in free enterprise economies maintain overall, general types of controls over credit extension by commercial banks, the Gosbank itself is the source of virtually all short term credit. In this case, it is not a question of monetary management, but rather one of monetary planning. However, the Gosbank does not determine the volume and direction of credit, but must follow the dictates of the general economic plan which is drafted by the State Planning Commission (Gosplan) under the guidance of directives from the top political hierarchy. One might even argue that despite the more direct nature of Gosbank's control over credit creation, it has less independent power than central banks in free enterprise countries.

The Gosbank has vested in it the exclusive right to deal in foreign

---

[20] It should be noted that the Gosbank is actually a network of banks consisting of the main office in Moscow and branches all over the USSR. The relations between the main office and the branches have some of the earmarks of the relation of a central bank and commercial banks, but the differences are much more important. The branches have little autonomy and must follow the directives issued in Moscow.

exchange. As mentioned above, the maintenance of stable exchange rates or the avoidance of balance of payments deficits are not objectives of the Gosbank. As a result, the foreign exchange regulation function is merely a technical task and not truly a control function.

In addition to these three control functions which correspond to similar functions in free enterprise economies, the Gosbank has one other very important function which has no counterpart in non-planned economies. This is the function of controlling the fulfillment of the financial and production plans of economic enterprises, the so-called "control by the ruble." The control by the ruble consists of several elements. The bank supervises the activities of the enterprises with regard to plan fulfillment. It enforces the application of economic accounting (*Khozraschet*) by the enterprises.[21] It also attempts to speed up the turnover of working capital by limiting working capital credits as much as possible without hurting plan fulfillment.

The significance of the control functions, as opposed to other functions of the Gosbank is stressed by Soviet authorities, e.g., "The basic function of Soviet credit is in the planned use of the resources of the socialist economy and in the speeding up of the tempo of the enlarged socialist production." Western authorities agree with this emphasis on the control function of the Gosbank; as one writer states: "In the Soviet framework, the control functions of the banks at least equal in importance the strictly monetary and financial functions."[22]

INSTRUMENTS OF CENTRAL BANKS

Instruments used by central banks in centrally planned economies are significantly different from those used in free enterprise economies. In free enterprise economies the major instruments are those employed to implement the credit control function of the central bank. Since the commercial banks and other financial intermediaries are the principal sources of credit, the central bank must approach its function indirectly by using its instruments to try to limit the credit creation of these organizations. The institutional situation in the centrally planned economies differs from this in two important aspects: (1) there are no commercial banks—the central bank itself is the major source of credit creation; and (2) there exists a central plan and the central bank is charged with assisting in the control over its execution.

These two differences make it clear that the nature of central bank instruments under central planning belongs to an entirely different cate-

---

[21] *Khozraschet* implies that each enterprise is supposed to operate in such a way as to cover all its costs and its planned profits from the sale of its outputs at prices fixed by the planning board. Any enterprise which does not manage to do this will find it more difficult to receive credits from the Gosbank and will be subject to much closer scrutiny by the bank.

[22] Gregory Grossman, "Union of Soviet Socialist Republics," *Banking Systems*, ed. B. H. Beckhart (New York, 1954), p. 759.

gory from those in free enterprise economies. The absence of commercial banks and the consequent concentration of all short-term lending activities in the Gosbank make the comparison between the Gosbank and, say, the Federal Reserve System meaningless in this respect. A better comparison could be made between the Gosbank and the "one big bank" model used by some economists, e.g., Sir Dennis Robertson.[23]

The instruments of the Gosbank connected with the control of credit are: the credit plan and the cash plan. The credit plan is based on the credit and financial plans of the economic enterprises and government institutions and not on the credit plan of the bank. Each enterprise submits a credit plan based on the provisions of the general economic plan. These plans are reviewed within the Gosbank and move up within its organization to the Economic Planning Administration of the Gosbank where all the credit plans are combined into the credit plan of the Gosbank. Once approved by the Council of Ministers, the quarterly plans become operational.[24] The fact that all wage payments in the USSR are made in cash gives the cash plan an independent significance. The control of the volume of currency emission provides a check on the amount of money appearing on the market for consumers' goods. In the case of the cash plan, the monthly plans are operational. The balance between inflow and outflow of currency is made up by issuing or withdrawing notes; this is regulated by the emission order given by the Gosbank's Emission Administration.[25] The Gosbank has little latitude for influencing the course of economic developments; it has to follow the dictates of the general economic plan. The key question that is not answered in any of the literature on the subject is the degree of influence the Gosbank exerts in the drawing up of the general plans. From the available information one might venture a guess that this influence is not very great; the planning of real magnitudes appears to have definite priority over financial planning. It is beyond the scope of this paper to discuss the role and success of the Gosbank in supporting the general plan through its not always successful efforts at maintaining price stability.[26]

The instruments of the Gosbank used in fulfilling its function of controlling the fulfillment of plans by enterprises—control by the ruble—differ no less from traditional instruments of central banking than do the credit and cash plans. The major instruments are: control over the utilization of current accounts of enterprises and the granting or withholding of loans for working capital, the so-called "credit sanction." In addition to the Gosbank, the Soviet banking system consists of four

---

[23] Dennis H. Robertson, *Money* (London, 1951), p. 86.

[24] Alexander Baykov, *The Development of the Soviet Economic System* (Cambridge, 1947), pp. 412–13.

[25] *Ibid.*, pp. 413–14.

[26] For an excellent discussion of this subject see R. P. Powell, "Soviet Monetary Policy" (unpublished Ph.D. dissertation, University of California, 1952).

specialized investment banks, each serving one sector of the economy; these banks also participate in applying control by the ruble. Their instruments are: preliminary control over projects submitted for approval and current control over the expenditure of the funds.

Control by the ruble relies mainly on a comparison of realized with planned expenditures on production. Its purpose is to avoid waste of materials through unauthorized use or poor plan fulfillment, and the bank is one of several agencies keeping a check on the performance of enterprises. According to Soviet authorities, bank control is considered very effective.

The possibility of control by the ruble arises from the fact that the granting of a credit is made directly dependent on the fulfilment of planned tasks, on the basis of which the need for the borrowed funds is established. On the other hand, the ability to repay the borrowed funds is assured by the fulfilment of the quantitative and qualitative indices of the plan, which strengthens the significance of credit for purposes of control. Therefore, bank credit is a very effective means of control by the ruble over the activity of economic organs.

Throughout the years, innumerable regulations have been issued to strengthen the control by the ruble. Among them are the following: (1) working capital funds of enterprises are kept at a sufficiently low level to force them to depend on borrowing from the bank; (2) all but the smallest transactions of enterprises must be made through their accounts at the bank; (3) enterprises are forbidden to lend to each other; (4) the bank can refuse to extend a credit approved in the credit plan if it discovers any irregularities, etc. However, a study of Soviet economic history, especially the highly inflationary period of the 1930s, throws some doubt on the effectiveness of Soviet financial controls.[27]

SEMI-PLANNED ECONOMIES

There is no one model of a semi-planned economy. For the purpose of analyzing the role of the central bank in semi-planning, we will define one specific model in which the central bank plays an important role. This "pure model of semi-planning" has the following characteristics: (1) Planners' goals are dominant, i.e., there is no consumer sovereignty. (2) The planning board leaves the maximum amount of decision-making power, compatible with the fulfillment of its goals, to the primary economic units. (3) It concentrates its controls on investment decisions which are the significant dynamic element in the economy; it decides on the rate of investment and on the allocation of investment funds between the broad sectors of the economy.[28] (4) Within these sectors the allocation is performed through indirect monetary controls, i.e., by the price of investment funds rather than direct allocations. (5) The economic enterprises

---

[27] Powell, op. cit., especially pp. 306–14.

[28] E.g., heavy industry, light industry, agriculture, transportation, etc.

are free to make all the decisions regarding the quality, size, etc., of the product, the scale of output, the factor proportions, etc. (6) No physical allocations or price controls are used; prices of goods and factors are formed on free markets; the only controls in the economy are controls over purchasing power. (7) Households are free to purchase consumer goods on the market and they can influence supplies and prices of goods within the limits imposed by the planning board's control over the volume of investment in consumers goods industries. (8) The central bank is the only bank in the economy.

It is clear from this brief description of the model that the central bank would play a crucial role. It would retain all its traditional functions, including the control over the aggregate volume of purchasing power with the purpose of avoiding inflation or deflation. It would not perform the control function performed by the Gosbank through its control by the ruble since enterprises would not be given specific plans to fulfill. It would, however, be given the very important function of investment funds allocation within the broad framework set by the planning board. The specialized banks in the USSR perform a similar function, but they merely allocate the funds according to the over-all plan issued to them by the planning board. This plan specifies the exact amount of funds to be given to each enterprise, leaving no discretion to the banks. Their only power is to withhold the funds if they feel the enterprise is not acting according to the rules. In our model, the central bank would have a much more difficult job. It would have to develop methods of allocating the funds which would result in optimum allocation within the limits set by the planning board's decision on the rate of investment and the allocation between the broad sectors of the economy.

It might be pointed out that the above model is an extremely simplified and idealized version of the Yugoslav "new economic system" introduced in the years following the break with the USSR in 1948. Simplified in the sense that only the most general principles of this system have been included, idealized in the sense that it implies much less control than actually exists in the Yugoslav system.

OBJECTIVES OF CENTRAL BANKS

The model helps us in analyzing the functions and instruments that can be used by a central bank, but it cannot supply us with the objectives motivating the managers of the bank. For this purpose we must deal with a specific country; we took the example of the USSR for centrally planned economies and will take Yugoslavia for semi-planned economies. In order to simplify the discussion, we might again accept the achievement and maintenance of a rapid rate of growth of the economy as the major objective in Yugoslavia, as we did in the case of the USSR.[29]

---

[29] For example, the Governor of the National Bank, Vojin Guzina, told the author in an interview on March 19, 1957, that he considered the attainment of maximum

But, even having accepted the similarily of economic goals as a working hypothesis, there is still a considerable difference between the specific objectives of the Gosbank in the USSR and the National Bank in Yugoslavia. Although the National Bank also tries to assist in assuring the smooth functioning of the plan, the Yugoslav plan is so much less comprehensive that the functions performed in achieving this objective are very different in the two countries. The objective of maintaining domestic price stability is more important in Yugoslavia. Prices are generally not fixed by fiat, but determined in the market.[30] In addition, prices perform a more important allocating function than in the USSR. Similarly, the objective of maintaining exchange rate stability is present in Yugoslavia; the link between domestic and foreign price levels exists, even though it is made very tenuous through a complicated system of exchange controls. Even the problem of maintenance of full employment cannot be ignored in the Yugoslav case as is possible in the Soviet case. The mere listing of the objectives of the National Bank of Yugoslavia indicates that it has more in common in this respect with central banks in free enterprise countries than with the Gosbank in the USSR.

FUNCTIONS OF CENTRAL BANKS

There is very little difference between the National Bank of Yugoslavia[31] and the Gosbank with regard to the functions in the first two categories, i.e., providing a medium of exchange and acting as agent to the government. The similarity is due mainly to the absence of private commercial banks in both systems. If it were not for this fact, both of them would be similar to central banks in free enterprise economies with respect to these functions.

---

economic growth without strong inflationary pressures as the major goal of the Yugoslav central bank. It should be noted that in the yearly social plans, where the economic policies of the Yugoslav Government are set forth, other objectives are stressed, e.g., in the 1956 plan it was economic stability, and in the 1957 plan it was improvement in the standard of living. It could be argued persuasively that these objectives are subsidiary ones and are stressed at particular periods when it becomes apparent that inflationary pressures or lack of incentives are becoming brakes on economic growth.

[30] The statement that prices in Yugoslavia are determined in the market is an oversimplification, but it is beyond the scope of this paper to enter into the process of price formation in Yugoslavia.

[31] Recently, the monopoly of the National Bank has been gradually broken and new banks have been created. The creation of the Investment Bank deprives the National Bank of its function of investment allocation. The creation of the Foreign Trade Bank and local communal banks means that the National Bank is no longer the sole source of short-term credit. It is not clear how far this process, now in progress, will go. If it goes far enough, the National Bank might become a central bank in the traditional sense of being only a banker's bank. There is nothing in the nature of the Yugoslav system or the spirit of the model of the semi-planned economy which would make such a shift irrational. It would not be rational, however, to introduce such a change into the Soviet system. In this paper, the role of the National Bank is discussed only in the period when it had the monopoly on all banking business and operated through a network of branches subordinated to the central office.

In the third category—the functions of control over the economy—the National Bank differs greatly from central banks in both free enterprise and centrally planned countries. In both of these types of economies, monetary policy does *not* try to devote itself to the allocation of resources. The job is done by the market mechanism in free enterprise systems and by physical allocations and/or price controls in centrally planned systems. The central bank supplies the medium of exchange to facilitate transactions and attempts to prevent price changes which would interfere with the allocations mechanism. As long as other allocating devices perform satisfactorily, the bank acts only in an ancillary capacity.

The situation is radically different in Yugoslavia. The credit function of the National Bank is extremely important and influences the economy at two levels: control of the overall price level and control of the allocation of investment funds.[32] The function of allocating investment funds is not an entirely new one for central banks; central banks in many countries influence the direction in which credit moves, and in some cases set up special agencies for the express purpose of channeling investment funds in the desired directions. But in the Yugoslav case this function is explicitly recognized and made one of the cornerstones of the whole system of economic controls. In our model we have eliminated all the other weapons of control in order to make it stand out in bold relief. The investment allocation function is certainly of the greatest theoretical interest as it differs most from central banking in other types of economic systems. In discussing the actual Yugoslav case, however, it is essential to point out that Yugoslav economic leaders themselves view the control over the total volume of credit as the crucial problem. From their point of view, the function of the central bank is assuring the smooth growth of the economy without inflation is of greater significance than the proper allocation of investment funds. The two functions are not independent of each other; if the control of inflation is unsuccesful the allocation of investment will be distorted in any system where prices serve an allocating function.

Another function of the central bank, which is unique in Yugoslavia, is the performance of *drustvena evidencija* (there is no good English term to describe this; the closest equivalent would be "social accounting"). This function is based on the maintenance of special accounts at the bank for all the important transactions of each enterprise; all changes that take place in the current account of the enterprise are entered here.

The purposes served by these accounts are: (1) to provide the bank and governmental organs with up to date information on the operation of each enterprise and groups of enterprises; (2) to enable the bank to control the utilization of the current account by the enterprise, e.g., to prevent the enterprise from withdrawing more currency to pay the wage bill than the earnings of the enterprise justify; and (3) to check on the fulfillment of

---

[32] The function of supplying short-term working capital credits to economic enterprises will not be discussed in this paper in order to concentrate on the more interesting function of investment credit allocation.

tax and other obligations of enterprises to the state. The last purpose is probably the most important in a system where the government control instruments are predominantly monetary and fiscal.

Other control functions of the National Bank in Yugoslavia include the control over the issuance of currency and over foreign exchange transactions. In the field of foreign exchange control, the National Bank has much broader powers than the Gosbank, and this function is much more important. The monopoly of foreign trade has been abolished in Yugoslavia, and this has increased the National Bank's responsibility for stability of exchange rates and balance in Yugoslav foreign accounts.

INSTRUMENTS OF CENTRAL BANKS

The instruments of a central bank in our model of a semi-planned economy differ considerably from those used by central banks in the other two models. The basic cause for these differences is the difference in the scope of economic planning in the various systems which determines the control functions of the central banks. A less important difference is the absence of commercial banks in the models of central planning and semi-planning.

A free enterprise banking system consisting of a central bank and private commercial banks requires monetary management by the central bank. The other two systems, where the central bank performs the commercial banking functions in addition to its other functions, requires monetary planning. Monetary planning in the semi-planned economy is much less intensive than in the centrally planned economy due to the less pervasive nature of the national economic plan. In our model of the semi-planned economy the national plan would include only the following elements: the total amount of investment, the amount of other non-consumption items, the tax structure, the allocation of investments by broad sectors of the economy, the degree of imbalance permitted in the balance of payments,[33] and the permissible changes in the price level. Under such a system, there would be no room for a cash or credit plan, such as exists in the USSR. Since the national plan does not include the production targets for each enterprise, it is not necessary to have a credit plan specifying the amount of credit to be given to each enterprise. What is needed instead is a decision on the total amount of credit to be extended to all enterprises; this is a function of the expected changes in total production, prices and the velocity of circulation of money. In the Yugoslav case, the credit plan was replaced by a credit balance when the "new economic system" was introduced in 1952. However, the credit balance was made operational only in 1957, when it was for the first time included in the social plan. The credit balance is supposed to plan total credits, total currency issue, and total deposits. The cash plan was used in the years 1945 to 1952 as one of the main instruments for regulating currency circulation

---

[33] To be covered by foreign loans, foreign aid, drawing down of foreign exchange reserves, etc.

and the equilibrium between the stock of money and the stock of goods. With the relaxation of planning in 1952, the cash plan became merely orientational, and was finally abolished as of January 1, 1956. The cash balance constitutes the currency aspect of the credit balance and is not used as an independent tool.

In the model of semi-planning the investment allocation between broad sectors of the economy, e.g., agriculture, light industry, heavy industry, etc., is determined by the planning board. The decisions can be based on any one of a number of investment criteria, but would certainly be based on some long range program of economic development. In central planning, the planning board also determines the allocation within the sectors.[34] In semi-planning the allocation within the sectors is performed by the central bank by means of investment credits. The rationale of this system is that the allocation between the broad sectors assures that the planners' priorities are met in a general way, while the allocation within sectors assures a minimum of misallocation. This is in a true sense a compromise between central planning and the rule of the market.

Several instruments could be used by the central bank to allocate credits within each sector: (1) It could list all the applicants for investment credits on the basis of some priority scheme. This would mean that the central bank is merely taking over the function of the planning board, but using the same type of administrative procedures. This method would not be in the spirit of the model of semi-planning. (2) It could grant credits to the firms with the best credit ratings. This would be sound banking procedure, but would not be in line with the objective of rapid economic growth. (3) It could grant credits to the firms who offer the most favorable terms, e.g., the highest rate of interest and the shortest repayment terms. If firms are profit maximizers and offer a rate corresponding to their marginal efficiency of investment, this would result in an efficient allocation of resources. However, even in this case there would be problems of the lack of knowledge of both the future generally and of possible external economies by the firms. The choice between this type of allocation and that performed in central planning involves the balancing of the greater knowledge of aggregative changes possessed by the planning board versus the greater knowledge of specific operations in each firm possessed by the managers of the firm.

There would be still other possible methods, but the ones listed above give a sufficient indication of the type of criteria that might be used. The actual method used in Yugoslavia for the share of investment funds allocated by the National Bank is a credit auction.[35] Auctions are held

---

[34] In the Soviet case, some freedom of decision is delegated to the ministries or lower organs; the planning board is not expected to make all the very specific decisions.

[35] No statistics are available on the share of total investments in Yugoslavia which are allocated through the auction system. The author has estimated that the auctions

periodically and enterprises falling within a given sector place bids offering a given rate of interest and repayment term. The documentation must be approved by expert committees and by local government organs for technical and economic soundness. The bank reviews the enterprise's financial stability, as well as checking independently on the technical and economic soundness of the project. The bids which pass this screening are then listed in descending order according to the height of the rate of interest offered and the shortness of the repayment term. The rate of interest is used as the primary criterion, and only when two applications offer the same rate of interest is the repayment term considered. The bank then goes down the list until all the funds allocated to this sector are used up. The rate of interest offered by the marginal firm becomes the rate paid by all firms receiving funds in this auction.[36] This method is similar to the procedure mentioned above where credits are granted to those firms offering the most favorable terms. The major difference is that the bank does not use price discrimination, but charges every firm the marginal rate of interest. The disadvantage of this method is that firms are tempted to offer very high rates of interest to be sure of getting the credits, knowing that only the marginal rate will have to be paid. The danger is that this could lead to a very high marginal rate if many firms played this game, and this actually happened. Another problem facing an attempt to combine allocation of investments by plan among sectors and by auction within sectors is the possibility that the funds allocated to a sector will not be taken up by enterprises in that sector. This happened in the case of an auction for credits for the mechanization of construction work, where credit applications totalled less than 50 per cent of the amount allocated for the purpose. In addition, the firm needs some idea of the rate of interest it will have to pay in order to make rational decisions on the capital intensity of the planned project. The auction system does not provide this knowledge. The auction method of allocation of investment credits, which resembles the methods used by some countries to allocate foreign exchange, has considerable theoretical interest and deserves further analysis.*

SUMMARY

The brief discussion in this paper has served to point up the differences and the similarities between the roles of central banks in various economic

---

account for between 10 and 35 per cent of total net investments, with a likelihood that the proportion is nearer to the lower limit. See Egon Neuberger, "Central Banking in Semi-Planned Economies—Yugoslav Case" (unpublished Ph.D. dissertation, Harvard University, 1957), pp. 187–93.

[36] After a year and a half of experience, the sole reliance on these two criteria was abandoned and many additional criteria were added. See Neuberger, op. cit., pp. 203–4.

* Editor's note: See Egon Neuberger, "The Yugoslav Investment Auctions," Quarterly Journal of Economics, Vol. LXXIII, No. 1 (February, 1959), pp. 88–115.

systems. The objectives of central bank action do not depend on the model of planning that exists in any country. They depend on the goals of those groups in the country that formulate national policies, and on the specific role of the central bank in the execution of these policies. We found that the major objective of central banks in the three systems may not differ substantially. This is particularly true if we compare the USSR and Yugoslavia to the underdeveloped free enterprise countries; in all three the major goal is economic growth with a minimum of inflation. The differences are more significant when other objectives, e.g., maintenance of full employment, exchange rate stability, etc. are considered. In this case, the objectives of the Yugoslav National Bank are closer to those of free enterprise countries than to the Gosbank.

There are three categories of functions performed by the central banks in all systems: (1) provision of a medium of exchange, (2) performance of banking services for the government, and (3) control of economic activity. The three systems discussed in this paper do not differ significantly with respect to the first two functions; their major differences are confined to the third category. Here the differences stem mainly from the variation in the degree of control exercised by the central authorities over the decision-making power of the primary economic units. The differences in the organization of the banking system of the country, e.g., the degree of monopoly of the central bank, contribute to the differences in the control function.

The same factors affecting the functions of the central bank also affect its instruments. All three systems use very different types of instruments, and even within each system there are great variations.

The central bank has no important role in the pure models of free enterprise or central planning. It does play an important role in countries which approximate the pure models. Despite the important role of the Gosbank in controlling plan fulfillment, it can be said that central banks in free enterprise economies play a more significant role. In the pure model of semi-planning or the Yugoslav system which approximates it, the central bank plays an even more important role than in the other systems. In addition to the function of controlling the over-all level of credit and money it also has the function of allocating investment funds. It is fair to say that our pure model of semi-planning gives the central bank more importance than any system that has ever existed.

Management

In every economic system, enterprise management has important functions of planning, coordination, administration, control, and supervision. However, the scope and character of these functions—management's responsibilities and powers—vary with the nature of the economic system.

In a capitalist market economy, management is free to adjust both outputs and inputs in pursuit of profits. In Lange's theoretical model of market socialism, managers are instructed to choose input combinations and output levels which lead to the most economical production of the socially optimum output, regardless of whether profits or losses result. In Yugoslav market socialism, however, enterprises follow the capitalist approach of adjusting outputs and inputs in pursuit of profit. In contrast, in a centrally administered economy, management's task is to fulfill the detailed plan fixed for the enterprise by the central authorities. Managers are expected to produce the scheduled output with the authorized inputs. The profit resulting from the sale of output is of subordinate importance. Thus, both management's assignment and its freedom to accomplish it vary with the economic system in which it operates. At the same time, it is interesting to note that essentially the same incentives—job security, promotion, and, especially, salary and bonuses—motivate management in all of these economic systems.

The following selection, comparing managerial incentives and decision making in the U.S. and Soviet economies, illustrates these points.

Joseph S. Berliner

20. MANAGERIAL INCENTIVES AND DECISION MAKING: A COMPARISON OF THE UNITED STATES AND THE SOVIET UNION*

Berliner points out the major differences and similarities between the U.S. and Soviet economies in managerial incentives and decision making. Since American managers operate in a much different economic environment, their problems and therefore their practices differ from those of Soviet managers. But in those aspects of economic life in which the two economies are somewhat alike, American and Soviet managers behave in much the same way.

The assignments, powers, and problems of enterprise managers differ notably in the two economies. In the U.S. firm, profit is the main criterion of managerial performance. The Soviet manager, on the other hand, is expected to achieve (or surpass) a number of plan targets— for output, cost, labor productivity, etc.—which are sometimes mutually exclusive. In the sellers' market of the Soviet economy, managers are much more concerned with the acquisition of inputs than with the disposition of output. The opposite is true in the U.S. economy, where the biggest problem of management under normal conditions is marketing, rather than purchasing. Thus, the energy spent by the Soviet firm on

* Reprinted, with permission, from *Comparisons of the United States and Soviet Economies* (Papers Submitted by Panelists Appearing before the Subcommittee on Economic Statistics, Joint Economic Committee, 86th Cong., 1st sess.) (Washington, D.C.: U.S. Government Printing Office, 1959), Part I, pp. 349–76. Joseph S. Berliner is Professor of Economics at Brandeis University.

obtaining materials is devoted by the American firm to selling and advertising.

At the same time, the two economies rely on essentially similar incentives to motivate managers toward whatever is defined as good performance. In both economies there are conflicts of interest between the owners of the enterprise and the hired professional managers who run it. And in both countries managers may engage in various illegal or evasive practices when they believe their interests conflict with existing laws and regulations.

THE REWARDS in income and prestige in the United States and Soviet economies are such that a larger proportion of the best young people in the U.S.S.R. turn to careers in heavy industry, science, and higher education, whereas in the United States a larger proportion of the best talent flows into such fields as heavy or light (consumer goods) industry, finance, commerce and trade, law, medicine, etc. Higher education, particularly technical, is more of a prerequisite for the attainment of a top business career in the Soviet Union than in the United States.

The principal managerial incentive in Soviet industry is the bonus paid for overfulfillment of plan targets. The incentive system is successful in the sense that it elicits a high level of managerial effort and performance. But it has the unintended consequence of causing managers to engage in a wide variety of practices that are contrary to the interests of the state. Managers systematically conceal their true production capacity from the planners, produce unplanned types of products, and falsify the volume and quality of production. In the procurement of materials and supplies they tend to order larger quantities than they need, hoard scarce materials, and employ unauthorized special agents who use influence and gifts to ease management's procurement problems. The incentive system causes managers to shy away from innovations that upset the smooth working of the firm.

Since American managers operate in a different economic environment, their problems and therefore their practices differ from those of Soviet managers. But in those aspects of economic life in which the U.S. economy approximates the operating conditions of the Soviet economy, American managers develop forms of behavior similar to those of Soviet managers. The separation of management and ownership characteristic of the modern corporation leads to conflicts of interest between managers and stockholder-owners, and management's pursuit of its own interest leads to activities similar to those of the Soviet manager striving to defend his interests against those of the owner-state. The spread of legislation constricting the freedom of operation of the American firm leads to the evasion of laws and regulations characteristic of the Soviet economy, though on a larger scale there. Finally, under wartime conditions the burgeoning of Government controls and the dominant role of the Government as customer alters the operating conditions of the U.S. economy in such ways that it closely approximates some of the normal operating conditions of the Soviet economy. The change is accompanied by black-market operations, hoarding, quality deterioration, and the use of influence, practices which are normal in the peacetime Soviet economy.

1. MANAGERIAL INCENTIVES AND RECRUITMENT

The most important decision a manager has to make is made before he ever becomes a manager; namely, the decision to prepare for a managerial career. The factors influencing this decision are of vital importance for our industrial society. Imagine the consequences if no one aspired to become a manager, or if young people chose management only as a last resort, or if other careers were so attractive that management got only the last pickings of each year's crop of youngsters. It might therefore be appropriate to begin with some reflections on the incentives that the United States and the U.S.S.R. offer their young people to choose a managerial career rather than some other.

The factors motivating young people to choose one or another occupation are probably not vastly different in the two countries. Family tradition is often decisive; many a youngster chooses a career simply because he wishes to be like his father (or mother). Special talents such as those of the artist, or early conceived deep interests, like the boy who must be a scientist, account for the career choices of some others. But most teenagers have no clear idea of what they would like to be. It is with respect to these youths that it is most interesting to speculate upon the incentive-pulls that the two systems offer for the choice of one career or another.

EDUCATION AND CAREER CHOICE

The role of higher education in career choice is different in the two nations. Higher education is very much more of a prerequisite for the prestigeful and high income occupations in the U.S.S.R. than in the United States. To be sure, the person with a high school education or less has an increasingly difficult time entering the managerial ladder of the large American corporation. But in such fields as trade, commerce, construction and in small business in general, the opportunities are still vast for a financially successful career. College, and education in general, is not of decisive importance. And the brute fact is that a college diploma can always be obtained somewhere in the United States, with very little effort or ability, by just about anyone who can pay the tuition and write a semiliterate paragraph. Those who don't aspire to a managerial position or who fail to make the grade can, as workingmen, nevertheless enjoy a standard of living that is the envy of the world. The point is that the young American who is not inclined toward academic work need not feel that he is out of the competition for our society's best rewards.

This is not true in the U.S.S.R. A number of conversations with young Soviet people have convinced me that to be a "worker" is something devoutly to be shunned by most young people who have reached the high school level. There are at least two reasons for this attitude, which seems so anomalous in a "worker's state." The first is the enormously high prestige that Russian (and European) culture has always placed upon the "intelligent," the learned man, the man who works with his mind instead of his hands. The Soviet regime has striven hard to make manual labor respectable, and it undoubtedly has succeeded in endowing the worker with a social position relatively much higher than before the revolution. But the young person who has reached the educational level at which he can choose between being a worker or an "intelligent" would, other things being equal, choose the latter without question.

Other things are not equal, however. In particular, the income possibilities of a worker are far smaller than those of a college graduate, and this is the second reason for the desperate, and sometimes pathetic, drive for a higher education. Of course, a person must have reached the high school level before he can even begin to think about choosing between the career of a worker or an "intelligent." The steady annual expansion in the high school population has had the effect of presenting ever-increasing numbers of young people with the choice, and few of them would freely choose to be workers. If the expansion of the school population had continued, giving more and more young people the opportunity to avoid being workers, it would have raised serious problems for the recruitment of the labor force. The radical reform of the educational system by Khrushchev was undoubtedly motivated, in part, by the wish to avoid that problem.

Thus, the undesirability of a career as a worker has intensified the desire for higher education. Add to this the fact that there is no private enterprise, no small business in which a man could pull himself out of a worker's status and reach a position of prestige and income comparable to the self-made American businessman. I do not wish to state that the door is completely closed. By dint of hard work, ability, and certain other qualities, a Soviet citizen without the college diploma can from time to time rise to an important position in some economic hierarchy. But his chances are about as good as those of an equivalent person in a progressive American corporation. And the young person evaluating the importance of higher education understands this.

Finally, the Russian teenager who decides he has to get a college diploma has very few easy ways out. He can't buy his way into college, as the American student can if he has the money. There are no private colleges that can set whatever standards they wish. To be sure there are instances of bribery or influence, but they are certainly the exception. If the Soviet student wants a college diploma very badly, he has to work hard to gain admission and to be graduated. The very intensity of the drive for education, and the competition of many applicants for the limited number of admissions, permits the high schools and colleges to maintain high standards of performance. Moreover the colleges are financially independent of student tuitions: not only are there no tuitions but most of the students earn stipends. The consequence is that the typical Soviet student works harder and has to meet higher standards of performance than the typical American student. The standards are different in the two countries, of course, because of differences in the philosophy of education. But there is no doubt that study is a much more serious business for the young Soviet student than for the American.

One final note on education and incentives. The quality of the managerial (and technical) manpower of a nation depends on the proportion of the population comprising the pool from which the managers are drawn. That is, if half the population were for some reason excluded from the pool, the quality of the managers would be lower than if the whole population comprised the pool. Both nations suffer in this respect from the fact that rural educational facilities are poorer than urban, which reduces the pool of the potential college group. Since the Soviet rural population is larger percentagewise than that of the United States, and since their rural educational facilities are probably relatively worse than ours, they suffer more than we from this loss. But there are other ways in which our pool is curtailed more than the Soviet. First is the fact that the private cost of education keeps a substantial portion of our talented young people in the lower income groups out of college. I admit that this fact puzzles me. With our network of free State universities and with a fairly abundant scholarship program, I don't fully understand why any competent student who really desired it could not get a college education. It is my impression, however, that systematic studies generally show that we are losing an unfortunate number of young people to higher education for financial reasons. If this is so, we are worse off than the Soviets in this respect, for their education is absolutely free, and most students of any merit earn stipends besides. Lower income young Soviet people may nevertheless be unable to go off to college if the family needs their earnings. A young Soviet woman told me, in reply to my question, that this was why she never went on to college. She is not a very good illustration of my point, however, for she went on to say that she really wasn't very smart anyhow.

The second group that is largely lost from America's pool of potential managerial manpower is the Negro and some other racial minorities. It may well be that the proportion of college graduates among some of the

Soviet national minorities is smaller than for the Slavic nationalities; I have seen no data on this. But I would doubt that their loss from racial discrimination is as large as ours.

The third and largest group lost from our pool comprises exactly half our population—the female half. Sex discrimination certainly exists in the Soviet economy, probably more in management than in science and technology. But undoubtedly the female population enlarges the pool of technical and managerial manpower much more in the U.S.S.R. than in the United States. The difference in the role of women in the two countries must, I think, enter into the balance I am trying to strike, but it is not a subject on which I would recommend that your committee consider writing corrective legislation. For one thing it is not perfectly clear which way sex discrimination works in the United States. Women discriminate against working about as much as jobs discriminate against women.

Let me summarize briefly this discussion of the relationship of education to career choice. Education, and particularly higher education, is more important in the U.S.S.R. than in the United States as the gateway to a prestigeful and highly remunerative career. Competition is keener for higher education, the cost of education to the individual is less, and the standards of admission and performance are higher in the U.S.S.R. Both nations lose part of the potential pool of managerial talent, the U.S.S.R. because of its large rural population, the United States because of financial burdens and racial and sex discrimination.

COMPETITION AMONG CAREERS

How does a managerial career compare with the attractiveness of other careers in the two nations? The young American not dedicated to some particular field, but motivated by a roughly equal desire for prestige and money, might select some field such as law, medicine, business, or engineering. He would decidedly not go into education or science. An equivalent young Soviet person would make a somewhat different choice. He would certainly not select law, which has been assigned a most humble role in Soviet society. Nor would he select medicine, for while the prestige is high, the income is low. On the other hand, higher education or science would be an excellent choice. The very title of "Professor" or "Scientific worker" would assure him one of the highest places of honor in the society. And an outstanding career in either of those fields would assure him an income ranking in the upper 10 per cent or perhaps even 5 per cent (data are hard to come by) of the population. The difference in the economic and social position of the scientist and teacher in the two countries is of fundamental importance in the matter of career recruitment.

The American who decides to choose a career in the business world has a much wider range of choice than his Soviet counterpart. A great variety of fields offer roughly equivalent rewards in prestige and incomes: advertising, accounting, finance, commerce, trade, sales, light manufacturing, heavy industry. Of all these fields, it is only the latter that would exert a great pull on the young Soviet person. For 40 years the Government and party have hammered home the central role of heavy industry, children are instilled with an admiration of technology, and heavy industry has been endowed with an aura of glamour that exceeds even our American fascination with technology. The ideological cards are stacked, in varying degree, against all other branches of the economy. In keeping with the ideology, the prestige and income possibilities in heavy industry are decidedly greater than in the other branches.

Not only will the student be attracted to heavy industry, but he is likely to choose engineering as his path of entry into whatever branch of heavy industry he selects. He would be attracted to engineering for the educational reasons discussed above. Engineering is, moreover, the most direct line of approach to a managerial career.

The Soviet engineering graduate will find his first job opportunities rather different from those of his American counterpart. If he is at the top of his class, the best offers will come from the research institutes, with top starting salaries and opportunities for graduate work. The poorer students will find lower paying jobs in industry. In the United States the situation is quite the reverse. The most successful students will be snapped up by recruiters from the large corporations, with the best starting salary offers. Some of the top students will, to be sure, spurn the attractive job offers and go on to further graduate work, but I suspect that many of those who go immediately into graduate work are the men who didn't get the good job offers. To be sure, many of the top American students who join the corporations are put immediately into research and development, but as many of them will be working on new passenger car or dishwasher design as will be working on electronic development and automation technique. The Soviet researcher is more likely to be working on the latter than the former.

The young Soviet engineer who goes into industry starts at the bottom of the managerial ladder, as chief of a production shop, or the design or maintenance departments of the enterprise. As new job opportunities develop, he faces the choice of continuing in direct production or taking one of the staff jobs in the enterprise, such as the planning department. If he stays in production proper, his career path may lead to chief engineer of an enterprise or to one of the higher economic agencies. If he moves into staff work, his career may lead to the directorship of an enterprise or of one of the higher organs. Either career leads to the pinnacle of Soviet management.

The paths that are least likely to lead to top management are finance or sales. I would guess the proportion of top management in the United States who started in such fields as finance and sales is much larger than in the U.S.S.R. There are no "colleges of business administration" in the Soviet

Union. The ambitious youngster who wants to work for the top of the Soviet business world studies engineering, not personnel and marketing.

Summarizing, industry in the United States has to compete with a wide variety of other branches of economic activity for its share of the best potential managerial talent. In the U.S.S.R. the values and the rewards are concentrated in relatively fewer fields, and industry is far more attractive than most others. Science and higher education, which scarcely compete with industry in the United States, are strong competitors of industry in the U.S.S.R. Among the various branches of industry, in the United States the light and consumer goods industries compete very effectively for both managerial and engineering talent. In the U.S.S.R. light and consumer goods industries are much less attractive than heavy industry. And finally the nature of industrial recruitment is such that technical education is much more important as part of the training of a would-be manager in the U.S.S.R. than in the United States.

My conclusion is that heavy industry, science and higher education attract, by and large, a better and more competent crop of young people in the U.S.S.R. than in the United States. Moreover, the competition for education is keener in the U.S.S.R., so that they get a more rigorously trained (trained in different ways, to be sure) corps of managerial, engineering, scientific and university personnel. On the other hand, such branches of the economy as sales, advertising, finance, trade and commerce, light industry, and law attract a much more competent group of people in the United States than in the U.S.S.R. Most of the outstanding people in these fields in the United States would, if they were Soviet citizens, have enjoyed successful careers in heavy industry, science, technology, or higher education. There is, after all, nothing startling in this conclusion. It is but another way of saying that each society gets what it pays for.

2. MANAGERIAL INCENTIVES AND DECISION MAKING

MATERIAL INCENTIVES

The incentives that attract people into management are not necessarily the same incentives that motivate managers to do their jobs and do them well. What are the goals of the manager? What are the considerations that impel him to make one decision rather than the other?

The moving force of our economic system is the pursuit of private gain. The worker chooses the higher paying job, the businessman accepts the more profitable contract, the investor buys the higher interest security. The usual exceptions must of course be made; the laws must be obeyed, public opinion may sometimes require that one decision be made rather than another, people make wrong decisions, a short-run loss may be accepted for a longer term gain. But by and large—"other things being equal," as the economist likes to say—it is private gain that determines economic decision.

The Soviets have at various times experimented with other forms of incentive, for it did not at first seem quite appropriate that a Socialist economy should stress private gain. But practicality won out over dogma, and private gain has for the last 25 years been the keystone of the managerial incentive system. To be sure, we still find references to various social incentives such as Communist enthusiasm. But we are also reminded that while enthusiasm is well and good, communism, as Lenin used to say, must be built "not directly on enthusiasm but with the aid of enthusiasm born out of the great revolution; [communism must be built] on private interest, on personal incentive, on businesslike accounting." Moreover, the incentive of private gain will be with us for a long time. According to the eminent labor economist E. Manevich, it will not disappear until the day of general overabundance arrives, until the differences between country and city are eliminated, and until the differences between mental and manual labor vanish. We are safe in saying that for the next several decades at least, private gain will be the central economic inventive in both economic systems.

The form that material incentives take is of some importance. For the American businessman it is clearly profit. If you ask why did he take on this contract rather than that, why did he order this machine rather than that, why did he ship by truck rather than train, the answer would normally be, "because it's cheaper that way," or what comes to the same thing, "because he would make more money that way."

For the private businessman managing his own business, profit is clearly the guide to his actions. But most American business is not managed in this way. The men who actually run the firm are salaried managers, hired by the stockholders' representative body, the board of directors. The profit of the business does not belong to the manager but to the stockholder-owners. The fact is that the private interest of the manager need not necessarily coincide with that of the stockholder. In order to bring the manager's private interest into closer coincidence with that of the owners, most corporations have instituted some kind of bonus system, on the assumption that if the manager has a direct stake in the profit of the enterprise, his decisions are more likely to be those that will earn more profit.

In fashioning an incentive system for its managers, the Soviet Government faced a problem similar to that of the American corporation. For all Soviet enterprises are run by salaried managers. If the Soviet manager's income consisted solely of his salary, it was conceivable that his private interest would not coincide at all points with the interest of the Government. Accordingly a considerable variety of supplementary bonuses are available to the managerial staff. The bonuses are designed to motivate managers to make those decisions that the Government considers to be in its own interest.

The amount of income earned in the form of bonuses is substantial. In 1947, the last year for which detailed data are available to me, the managerial personnel of the iron and steel industry earned bonuses averaging 51.4 per cent of their basic income. In the food industry at the low end, the percentage was 21 per cent.[1] Since these are averages, many individual managers earned considerably more than this. Bonuses of this magnitude must be a potent incentive indeed.

But incentive for what? This is surely the crucial question. For we can readily imagine an incentive which was extremely successful in motivating action, but action of an undesirable kind. The test of an incentive is therefore not only its motivating power, but the extent to which it leads to the desired kind of decision.

Before proceeding to the relationship of incentives to decision making, let me clarify the sense in which I use the term incentive. By incentive I mean that consideration which explains why one decision was made rather than another. If a young person decides to find employment in the electrical machinery industry rather than in the furniture industry, the difference in basic salaries in the two industries may well have been the decisive consideration. In this case salary is the effective incentive. But once in the job, the salary does not vary according to whether one operating decision is made rather than another. When the manager decides to put one order into production ahead of another, or to substitute one material for another, it is not his salary he is thinking about. It is usually the size of the month's bonus that will depend on the decision taken. It is in this sense that the bonus is the principal incentive in the operational decisions of the Soviet enterprise.

PRODUCTION DECISIONS

Two generations ago people debated the question of whether a Socialist economy could possibly work. History removed that question from the agenda. The last generation changed the question to whether the Soviet economy could work at all efficiently. That question has also been answered. These hearings would not otherwise be taking place. My discussion takes for granted that the Soviet economy is reasonably efficient, and that the question at issue is how efficient.

There is little doubt that the system of managerial incentives, broadly viewed, has created a corps of managers dedicated to their work and responsive to the production demands made upon them. Like their American counterparts, they are deeply involved in their work, they worry about production quotas, they demand results from their labor force. As

---

[1] Documentation and further discussion of this argument may be found in the author's *Factory and Manager in the U.S.S.R.* (Cambridge, Mass.: Harvard University Press, 1957).

hired managers, they are aware that if their performance is not satisfactory, there are always other persons spoiling for a chance at their jobs. I have no way of knowing whether the intensity of managerial life is greater in the U.S.S.R. than in the United States; in both countries there are variations from industry to industry. But there are two reasons why industrial life probably proceeds at a faster tempo in the U.S.S.R than here. The first is that the absence of free trade unions makes it difficult for workers to resist pressure for intense operation. The second is that industry is under constant exhortation from Government and party for ever-increasing levels of production.

But the question as indicated above is not whether management is motivated to work hard. It is rather whether the incentive system motivates them to do what the state wishes them to do; whether, in other words, they get as much mileage out of their effort as they might get.

One of the most interesting conclusions of the study of Soviet managerial incentives is that the bonus system is directly responsible for motivating management to make a variety of decisions contrary to the intent and the interests of the state. The decisions to be described go far back in the history of the Soviet economy, and have resisted countless efforts by the Government to eliminate them. Most of them have survived the great organizational changes in industrial organization of the past several years. They are clearly deeply rooted in the soil of Soviet economic organization.

First, consider the matter of the reporting of information. In a planned economy it is vital that the central planners have as accurate information as possible about the productive capacity of enterprises. The bonus system, however, acts as a prevailing motivation for managers to understate their real production capacity. The reason is that the most important of the bonuses available to managers depends on the extent to which the production target of the enterprise is overfulfilled. If the manager honestly reports his full production capacity, and if for some reason something goes wrong in the course of the month, then he and his staff will lose that month's bonus. It is safer therefore to report a smaller capacity than really exists, in order that the production target will be kept low enough to allow for emergencies. The Russians call this "insurance" or "security." The consequence is that the planners can never be sure that their plans are based on accurrate figures. The Government is aware of the problem: "This is fully understandable," writes a Soviet economist, "because the lower the plan, the greater the opportunity to fulfill and overfulfill it. . . ."

Because the higher state agencies cannot trust management's reporting of its productive capacity, various techniques have been fashioned for setting targets high enough to force the firms to operate as close as possible to capacity. One of these techniques is the arbitrary increase of targets over last year's production. As a prominent state planning commission economist put it, "they take as the base magnitude the level of production achieved during the preceding period and raise it by some percentage or other." Sometimes this technique helps flush out the manager's "hidden reserves," but in other cases the arbitrary increase in targets leads to impossibly high tasks. Indeed, the spirit of planning is reflected in the systematic use of high targets as a device for keeping managers working at as fast a tempo as possible. In the past targets have been set so high (deliberately, one suspects) that one-third of all enterprises failed to fulfill their annual plans. There is some evidence that in the last year or two this policy of deliberate overplanning has been modified, and we are told that in the first half of 1958 only 19 per cent of all enterprises failed to fulfill their plans. This still represents one out of five enterprises, and indicates that the high level of plan targets remains a dominant fact of life for the Soviet manager. The intense pace of plant operation has its distinct advantage from the state's point of view: it elicits from management a high level of effort that might not be forthcoming if the plans were set at a more modest level. But the price paid by the state is the manager's effort to defend his enterprise by concealing his full capacity.

When the target has been set, the manager's bonus depends on the success with which he fulfills it. Most of the firm's production does indeed follow the lines laid down in the plan. But when the end of the month rolls around and, as often happens, production is far short of meeting the month's target, then managers turn to a host of time-tested techniques of meeting—or seeming to meet—the targets. In certain types of production, such as metals, the target is expressed in tons; in such cases the manager might order his shops to curtail the production of relatively lightweight products (special and quality metals) and to throw more men and materials into the production of the heavier products. In textile production we read that the practice of setting targets in "running meters" (that is, in measures of length, without regard to width) causes managers to overproduce narrow-width cloth and underproduce broad-width. In firms with a considerable variety of products, the production targets are expressed in value units—so many millions of rubles of production. In such cases managers tend to overproduce those products that have high fixed prices (all prices are fixed): they may deliberately use more expensive materials in order to drive up the value of production. These are some of an endless variety of ways in which managers "violate the planned assortment of production"—to use the official expression of disapproval.

How widespread are these practices? We really don't know. From time to time individual managers are publicly excoriated for such practices, and figures are published to show how widely the planned assortment of production had been departed from. But these may well be extreme cases, and it would be unwise to generalize from them. Occasionally, however, the results of special studies are published, and they give us some idea of the magnitude of the problem. The State planning commission recently released the results of a survey of the production practices of 63 enterprises. Of the total production by these enterprises in excess of the plan targets, only 43 per cent consisted of the basic products normally produced by them; 26.5 per cent consisted of "products not included in the plan when it was originally confirmed," 20 per cent consisted of "other production," and 7 per cent consisted not of finished products but of an increase in semifabricated parts and goods-in-process. While these data are not precisely in the form in which we would want them, they do provide a good indication of managers' tendency to produce those products that are best from their own enterprises' point of view, rather than those products that the State would most wish to have produced.

Two other consequences of the bonus system (and the pressure of high targets) should be noted. One is the simple falsification of reported production. "Thus, for example," we read in a Soviet article, "if the plan is fulfilled 99 per cent, the managerial and engineering personnel receive no bonus. But if the enterprise fulfills the plan 100 per cent, they receive bonuses of from 15 to 37 per cent of their salary." Quite a lot of money hinges on that last percentage of production, and it is no wonder that management may succumb to the temptation to "fudge" the report a bit in order to earn the bonus. Again, the techniques of covering up for falsely reported production are myriad. To cite only one, production is "borrowed" from next month. That is, production that is expected to occur next month is reported as having been produced this month. If things go well next month, the "borrowed" output is "repaid"; if not the manager may get into trouble.

More serious than falsification, however, is the deterioration of the quality of production. The poor quality of much of Soviet consumer goods production is well known. In other types of production the danger of detection is greater, and quality standards are less readily violated. But the explanation of management's tendency to shave on quality is the same: the high production targets are so often not attainable, and the manager wants to keep his job. Much of the quality shaving is of a kind that is not easily detected: fewer stitches in the garment, fewer screws in the piece, greener lumber in the building, more impurities in the metal. But if the pressure is keen enough, more extreme forms of quality deterioration will be adopted.

Summarizing, the bonus system is an effective device for eliciting a high level of managerial effort, but in the context of excessively high production targets, it induces management to make certain types of decisions that are contrary to the intent of the State. The production of unplanned products, the concealment of production capacity, the falsification of reports and the deterioration of quality are the unintended consequences of the system of managerial incentives.

PROCUREMENT DECISIONS

The high level of production targets is but half the problem facing the Soviet manager. The other half is the perpetual shortage of materials and supplies. In order to get the greatest possible production from the available stocks of materials and supplies, the State employs a variety of devices to minimize the use of materials in production and inventory. Undoubtedly these devices have served to control wasteful use of resources, and they have also helped channel the flow of resources in the direction most desired by the State. But they have been self-defeating to some extent for they have forced managers to make certain kinds of decisions which frustrate the intent of the State.

The core of the matter is that managers simply don't trust the planning system to provide them with the supplies and materials they need in the right quantity and quality, and at the right time. The recent decentralization of industrial organization may have improved matters somewhat, but the evidence we have indicates that supply problems are still the most troublesome feature of managerial life. Moreover, the reasons are similar to those we used to read about before decentralization. For all important materials the manager must still obtain an allocation order from his home office (usually the Council of the National Economy of his district), which must in turn get the allocation order from the republican or all-union planning commission.

Thus, we still read of the "existing complicated system of obtaining allocation orders, under which every enterprise must submit detailed requisitions to Moscow a long time before the new planning quarter is to begin." Because plans are not always finally set at the time the planning period is to begin, enterprises sometimes start with "advance allocations," that is, temporary allotments of resources designed to keep them operating until the final allocation orders are available. Decentralization of the economy was supposed to have made it easier for neighboring enterprises to sell to each other without having to go through Moscow. But central purchasing agencies still exist, and agencies anywhere must find something to do. Thus the Chief Purchasing and Marketing Administrations located in the republic capitals (Moscow, for example) still insist on being the middleman in purchase and sale contracts between enterprises, even when the latter are located in the same outlying city (such as Sverdlovsk). Perhaps even more serious than the complex supply planning system is the large percentage of enterprises that regularly fail to fulfill their plans, or fulfill them by producing the wrong products or substandard products. Since the production of these enterprises constitutes the planned supplies of other enterprises, the supplies of the latter are delayed or simply not available. Perhaps enough has been said to explain why "managers of enterprises did not have confidence in the possibility of getting their materials on time and having them delivered to the factory by the supply depot's trucks."

What does the manager do to make sure he gets his supplies? Just as he "secures" his production plan by attempting to conceal the existence of some production capacity, so he "secures" the flow of supplies in various ways. He overorders, in the hope that if he doesn't get all he ordered, he may at least get as much as he needs. He also orders excessively large amounts of some supplies in order to be able to buy directly from the producer, instead of having to go through the maze of jobbing depots. A survey of 15 Moscow enterprises showed a 10.4 per cent overordering of metals for just this reason. Sometimes management's boldest efforts to obtain supplies are unsuccessful: ". . . over 300,000 construction workers undergo work stoppages daily because of the absence of materials at the workplace." In other cases their padded requisitions are accepted and they receive more than they need of some materials. The consequence is the piling up of hoards of supplies of all kinds, one of the most enduring problems of Soviet industrial organization. The Government has waged a longstanding war against hoarding. One of the weapons by which it attempts to hold hoarding within bounds is through the use of quotas of working capital; that is, for its annual production program the enterprise is allowed to keep on hand at any one time no more than so many tons of coal, so many board feet of lumber, so many rubles worth of inventory. These quotas must be negotiated between enterprise and government, and the enterprise's interest demands that they be set as high as possible. The mutual attempt at outguessing the other leads to a familiar bureaucratic game: ". . . enterprises try to 'justify' and obtain as large quotas of working capital as possible. The financial agencies, aware of this, strive on the other hand to reduce the quotas of working capital." This kind of planning is hardly calculated to lead to the establishment of the optimal quotas. It is more likely that some quotas will be too large and some too small.

The most interesting of the techniques used by managers to "secure" their supply of materials is the employment of special supply expediters called tolkachi, or "pushers." The table of organization does not provide for this occupation, yet so great is the need that firms manage somehow to employ these people. The chief job of the expediter is to make sure that his enterprise gets the materials it needs and when it needs them. Accordingly he spends most of his time on the road, visiting his enterprise's suppliers, handing out little gifts here and there to assure that his orders are well-handled,[2] picking up supplies of one kind or another that his firm may be able to use or trade for other goods. Much of their activity is associated with the black market, that is, obtaining materials for which no allocation order has been issued. This may be done either by wrangling an allocation order out of a reluctant government official by one means or another, or persuading an approachable enterprise official to sell him the things he needs without an allocation order.

Some tolkachi take up permanent residence in the city in which the chief suppliers are located, and only occasionally return to their home

---

[2] The gifts are not always very little. An expediter sent out recently to get tires for his trucking firm, was given 62,000 rubles in cash for the trip. He spent 42,000 rubles for gifts. He is now in prison. *Izvestiia*, April 4, 1959, p. 2.

firms for consultations. To keep the record clean, they are carried on the books as "senior buyer," or "supply agent." If they are known to be particularly adept at their jobs, they may be asked by other firms to represent them. Nothing is known of their incomes, but there is no doubt that they earn many times their base pay. And they fully earn it, both because of the vital nature of their work, and because the risks they take make them vulnerable to prosecution.

How widespread is the use of these expediters? Again, we catch only occasional hints of their prevalence. The most recent outburst against them reports that the number of tolkachi who annually visit the typical large enterprise runs into the thousands, and their expenses into hundreds of thousands of rubles. These, however, are only the reported expenses. More often than not their expenses are not reported as such but are concealed under such rubrics as "exchange of technical information," or "contract negotiations." Our latest informant, who is a senior investigator for the state control commission of the U.S.S.R., is of the opinion that despite continued official criticisms of the use of expediters, their number has actually been increasing. One of the reasons he adduces is interesting. In 1956, along with a wave of measures designed to give more freedom to plant managers, an order was issued relieving managers of the need to report in detail on all minor expenditures. Travel expenditures were among the items exempted. The measure had the unintended effect of encouraging the increased use of expediters.

The economic effect of the use of expediters is difficult to assess. There is no doubt that they are of vital importance to individual enterprises, but from the national point of view much of their activity involves merely the transfer to one fortunate enterprise of resources that otherwise would have gone to another. Since the higher priority enterprises have less need for expediters, the chances are that the net effect of their activity is to cause more resources to flow to lower priority enterprises at the expense of higher priority ones. On the credit side, however, their wide knowledge of sources of supply, of who has what to sell, is of some importance, and they do arrange for the movement of supplies that otherwise would have lain idle in one plant while another had need for it. In short the expediter possesses a certain kind of knowledge that may be as important to economic organization as the knowledge of the engineer or the machinist. The planning system is able to direct the bulk of the nation's resources with reasonable effectiveness, but substantial quantities of materials and equipment elude the main stream of planning. How to get these resources back into the system is a problem that has exercised Soviet economists for a long time.[3]

In summary, the incentives that motivate managers to strive for the

---

[3] Recently there have been numerous suggestions that enterprises and economic regions publish catalogs of the commodities they produce and the surplus materials and equipment they would like to sell. The expediters are rather like walking catalogs.

fulfillment of their production targets are the same incentives that motivate them to evade the regulations of the planning system. Because of the
tightness of the supply system, which is deliberately engineered by the
state, managers are compelled to defend their enterprises' position by
overordering supplies, by hoarding materials and equipment, and by employing expediters whose function it is to keep the enterprise supplied
with materials at all costs, legal or otherwise. The very planning system
that serves to channel most of the nation's resources in directions desired
by the state, serves also to misdirect a substantial volume of resources
toward uses that are contrary to the wishes of the state.

INVESTMENT DECISIONS

If one were to ask what feature of the Soviet economic system accounts
most of all for the rapid rate of growth, the answer would undoubtedly be
the high rate of capital formation. The question at issue is whether it is
as high as it might be, other things being equal. An examination of the
system of managerial incentives will provide part, though by no means all,
of the answer to this central question.

Management has a direct interest in obtaining new capital. It adds to
productive capacity, and it is good for the record to show steady increases
in production. Moreover fixed capital is provided to the enterprise as a free
grant by the state, with no interest charge. The problem, therefore, has
not been one of inducing management to accept more machines; it has
rather been one of dissuading management from ordering too many
machines. Far back in Soviet economic history one can find expressions of
the problem similar to that recently uttered by Khrushchev in connection
with the dissolution of the agricultural machine-tractor stations:

> The machine-tractor stations accept any machine whether they need it or
> not. They don't grow flax, but they take flax-growing equipment. They don't
> grow cabbage, but they take cabbage-planting machines. Consequently many
> machines are not used for years and hundreds of millions of rubles worth of
> state resources are frozen.

The reason enterprises accept any piece of equipment they can get their
hands on is similar to that discussed above in connection with materials
hoarding. One can never tell when he may need just that kind of machine
and not be able to obtain it. If one has a chance to get it now, order it by
all means. It may come in handy some day for trading in return for
something one might be able to use more readily. And above all, there is no
charge for holding the equipment; there is no interest payment, and if the
machine is not used there is no depreciation charge either. Hence there is
everything to gain and nothing to lose by holding on to as much machinery and equipment as one can obtain.

How to induce managers to take a less cavalier view of capital has been
a longstanding concern of economists. They look with some nostalgia at

the effectiveness of the profit motive under capitalism in this respect. An eminent Soviet economist put it this way recently:

> In order to increase his profit as much as possible, the capitalist strives to use his equipment to the fullest extent possible, and in no case will he buy a machine that he doesn't need at the moment, since every surplus machine slows down the turnover of his capital and reduces his profit. For the same reason he strives to keep his inventories down to the very minimum and to market his finished products as quickly as possible.

Recent economic literature contains a number of suggestions of ways in which Soviet managers might be induced to order only that amount of capital needed for production purposes. One of the more interesting is a proposal advanced by the author quoted above. He suggests that profit be calculated not as a ratio to total production cost (as has always been done), but as a ratio to value of invested capital. In this way the enterprise with too much idle capital will show a lower rate of profit, and profit is one of the principal indicators of overall performance. The suggestion is interesting because it proposes that return on capital be used as a criterion of performance, a rather "bourgeois" notion. It should not, however, be thought that the proposal envisages reliance on the "profit motive" as we know it. Profit is an important indicator of the efficiency of plant operation, but the firm does not "own" its profit, although it shares in the profit in a minor way. As a personal incentive, profit is relatively unimportant in Soviet industry, certainly by comparison with the bonus.

If the incentive system motivates managers to overorder and hoard equipment, the situation is quite the reverse with respect to technological innovation. Concern over managerial resistance to innovation is of long standing, but it has come to the fore in recent years in connection with increased emphasis on automation and modernization of plant and equipment. The reasons for managers' tendency to drag their feet in introducing new products or production techniques are well understood by Soviet economists:

> The explanation is, first of all, that the introduction of new technology involves certain risks and requires a considerable expenditure of time; secondly, after new technology has been introduced, more difficult plan targets are set and consequently there is less opportunity for fulfilling them and receiving bonuses.

When a manager has a well-running plant, when the workers have learned their jobs and have become experienced in using the existing equipment, he is reluctant to upset the cart by trying something new. A new production line means trouble. Production bugs have to be eliminated, workers have to be retrained, time is lost, and spoilage is high. The chances are that plans will be underfulfilled and the precious bonuses lost, particularly in view of the tendency for plan targets to be raised to the rated capacity of the new equipment. It is courting disaster to try new things. If the old machines are wearing out, it is safer to repair or even rebuild them rather than introduce the more complicated new models. Outlays on the rebuilding of old machines often exceed the price of a new modern machine.

There is another reason why managers shy away from innovation. Even if the potential gains from new technology are great, it usually takes a number of years before they are realized. But it is Soviet policy to shift managers around from plant to plant every few years. Therefore managers have a strictly short-run point of view. Why take on all the headaches of introducing a new line when one is not likely to be around to enjoy whatever benefits may eventually accrue? Capital investment policy is by its very nature a matter of long-term planning, and therefore does not commend itself to the short-run horizon of management.

How does the state combat managerial resistance to innovation? One technique is direct pressure. Pressure exerted on and by their own superiors explains much of the innovation that does occur. Enterprise managers may drag their feet for a long time, but when the direct order comes down that the new automatic line must be installed in the next 6 months, it is eventually acted upon. Pressure is also exerted through the Communist Party; if the party officials in the enterprise are under direct orders from Moscow that automation must be accelerated, they are in a position to force the manager to move faster than he otherwise might. Such pressures are important, although it must be noted in passing that both the manager's bosses and the local party people often try to shield the enterprise from such pressures. They are as dependent for their careers upon successful plan fulfillment as are the plant managers themselves.

Direct orders from above are one way of getting management to innovate. But innovation would proceed more rapidly if managers could be made to wish to innovate, instead of waiting until they are forced into it. The literature of the past few years is full of suggestions on how this can be accomplished. It is suggested, for example, that attractively high prices be set on new machines, in order to stimulate the producers of those machines to put them into production more rapidly. While this measure might ease the financial strain on the innovating firm, it will not remove the risk that the production plan may be sacrificed. And production is much more vital to the success of the enterprise than finance.

More to the point are the suggestions that the bonus system be employed as an incentive for innovation. Soviet economists seem to have enormous confidence in bonuses as a device for getting management to wish to do what the State wishes them to do. But how to adapt the bonus system to this purpose is more difficult. In the course of years a variety of special bonuses have been introduced for one purpose or another, in addition to the major bonus that comes from fulfillment of the production plan. There are special bonuses available for economizing certain critical materials, for reducing the volume of goods in process, for conserving fuel, for increasing labor productivity, for keeping the plant clean, for

reducing the volume of spoilage, for operating the plant without stop-pages, for winning Socialist competitions, and many others.[4]

This dilution of the bonus system may actually weaken its power as an incentive. If the special bonuses are small, they will not be very effective. If they are large they may detract effort from what is, after all, the main objective of the state: fulfillment of the production plan. For it is interest-ing to note the evidence that the relative size of the bonus for this or that special purpose often determines the manager's decision to concentrate on this or that objective. There are two types of innovation: relatively small measures such as organizational improvements or inexpensive alterations, and the more dramatic large-scale changes in production techniques. The former are included in the overall enterprise plan each year, under the name of the plan of organizational and technical measures (Orgtekhplan). It happens that there are certain bonuses available for the design and introduction of the large-scale innovations, but none for the fulfillment of the Orgtekhplan. The consequence is that research and managerial person-nel concentrate on the large items, and pay little attention to the small ones, even though the latter could result in great savings with relatively little cost and effort. Thus the very potency of the bonus as an incentive militates against its use for too many special purposes which may compete with each other.

To conclude this discussion, the unreliability of the supply system and the absence of a charge for the use of capital motivate management to order more fixed capital than they need and to hoard machines and equipment. This tendency deflects a certain amount of currently pro-duced capital goods from being put directly into production in their best uses. On the other hand, the incentive system discourages management from taking the risks associated with innovation. Direct orders from above lead to a substantial volume of innovation, and in many cases management may consider certain forms of innovation to be to their interest. The provision of special bonuses for innovation, if they were large enough to compete with the production plan bonus, might help provide an incentive for innovation, and much of the current discussion in the Soviet Union seems to point to this as the next phase.

3. SOME COMPARATIVE OBSERVATIONS

The preceding section has shown that Soviet managers are motivated to make a variety of decisions that are contrary to the interest of the state. Since the state's interest is paramount in the Soviet scheme of things, we may properly conclude that the incentive and decision-making system is "relatively inefficient," or "less than perfectly efficient." Let me caution

---

[4] Not all these types of bonus are available to the director himself, but they are available to different groups of managerial personnel.

the reader once more against inferring from this that Soviet managers do not do a good job. They do. There is no doubt that their system works well. If I have chosen to concentrate on the "pathology" of Soviet management, the purpose was not to create the impression of ineffectiveness, but to illuminate the gap that every economy shows between the actual and the ideal.

A comparison of Soviet and American management will help drive the point home. No one doubts that American management does a good job. But it would be fatuous to allege that it operates with perfect efficiency. An exploration of the inevitable gap between the actual and the ideal in the case of American management will help to place the corresponding gap in the U.S.S.R. in proper perspective.

A comparison of Soviet and American management is difficult for a curious reason; namely, we don't know enough about the more intimate aspects of American managerial practice. A moment's thought will make the reason clear. The American firm is a private enterprise in the full sense of the word. Its internal affairs are no one's business but its own. No one has the right to pry except with special cause. To be sure, the laws of the land have, over the years, required enterprises to disclose more and more of their private affairs to public and governmental perusal. But large sectors of the enterprise's internal operations are protected from the eyes of curious outsiders.

One of the most striking differences in the conduct of American and Soviet management is precisely in this matter of privacy. The Soviet enterprise is a public enterprise in the fullest sense of the word. It has no right to conceal its operations from any officially recognized agent of the state. And a great range of such agents have been deliberately endowed by the state with the obligation of keeping close watch on management and disclosing any irregularities or sources of inefficiency that come to their attention. These agents include the "home office" of the firm (the regional economic council, or formerly the ministry), the state bank, the local governmental body, the central government's State Control Commission, the Finance Department (the tax collector), the local Communist Party boss and his staff, the party secretary of the enterprise itself, and indeed just about anyone in the enterprise who enjoys the extracurricular activity of attending meetings to discuss the affairs of the enterprise (the aktiv).

If we can imagine an American business executive suddenly placed in charge of a Soviet firm, it is this public character of the enterprise which above all would drive him to distraction. It means that any government official can at any time demand to examine any aspect of the firm's operations he wishes to, that at any time he can be called on the carpet by the local party boss to explain a charge made by an irate customer, that any member of his staff (perhaps bucking for his job) can write a letter to *Pravda* exposing him for having made an irregular deal on some supplies, that any scatterbrained worker who wants to "get his picture in the papers" can rise at a public meeting that the director is obliged to attend, and compel the director to explain why he hasn't yet installed the new assembly line. The point is that the result of this authorized prying often finds its way into the published Soviet economic and political literature, which gives us an insight into the more intimate operations of the Soviet firm that we cannot have in the case of the American firm. But in view of this committee's expressed interest in comparisons of the United States and Soviet economies, I have attempted certain comparisons below which appear to be highly suggestive.

Managers and Owners

The original form of modern business organization was the small firm in which the owner was also the manager. The owner-manager was responsible to no one but himself for his business decisions, and his interest as manager could not conflict with his interest as owner. The development of the modern giant corporation, however, had led to that separation of management and ownership first elaborated in the work of Berle and Means.[5] Under the new conditions the private interests of the hired managers (and the controlling group) need no longer coincide at all points with the interests of the stockholder-owners. This is precisely the relationship between the hired Soviet manager and the owner-state.

Berle and Means concluded from their study that "the controlling group, even if they own a large block of stock, can serve their own pockets better by profiting at the expense of the company than by making profits for it."[6] This is precisely what Soviet managers do when they produce unplanned commodities that are advantageous to their firms but not to the State, when they overorder and hoard commodities, and when they resist innovation. Because of the differences between the two economic systems, we should expect that the precise forms that the owner-manager conflict takes would be different in the U.S.S.R. and the United States. In the United States they are to be found in such decisions as the awarding of subcontracts, the accounting of profit in such way as to benefit the claims of the controlling group, the awarding of bonuses and other benefits to management, and in dividend payment policy. As in the Soviet enterprise, the accountant is of crucial importance in handling the books of the enterprise in such way as make the best possible case for the manager; it is he, for example, who figures out the best way to distract the state's attention from the large expenditures on tolkachi. The accounting techniques are, of course, different in the United States; they involve "the charging or the failure to deduct depreciation; charging to capital expenses which properly should be charged against income ac-

---

[5] Adolph A. Berle, Jr., and Gardiner C. Means, *The Modern Corporation and Private Property* (New York: The Macmillan Co., 1945).

[6] *Ibid.*, p. 122.

count; including nonrecurrent profits as income though their real place is in surplus; and the creation of 'hidden reserves.' "[7]

A major difference between the Soviet firm and the American firm is that in the last analysis profit remains the criterion of managerial performance in the latter, whereas the Soviet manager is evaluated by a number of criteria that are sometimes mutually exclusive. Both systems have attempted to bring managerial interests into harmony with owner interests by some sort of profit-sharing system. In the Soviet case, it is clear that profit plays a very minor role, compared with bonuses, as a managerial incentive. In the United States the manager shares directly in profit to a very limited extent, and often follows other goals in his decisions. "The executive not infrequently tends to look upon the stockholders as outsiders whose complaints and demand for dividends are necessary evils . . ." concluded one American student of management.[8] In like fashion the Soviet manager often begins to feel like the "boss" and resents the intrusion into "his" affairs of the state, which after all is the owner. I have described above some of the ways in which the Soviet manager promotes the interest of "his" enterprise by means contrary to the interests of the owner-state. In the American corporation the forms are somewhat different. ". . . profits are reinvested in the business for the sake of bigness and to protect the company, and the interests of the stockholders may be given second place to the business leader's conception of what is best for the firm itself." Executives manifest a "general unwillingness to liquidate unsuccessful enterprises" and thus put themselves out of jobs, however consistent liquidation might be with the interests of the stockholders.[9] The dramatic growth of corporate self-financing in recent years has strengthened the power of management to expand their own enterprises without having to go through the "test of the marketplace" for capital.

It was observed earlier that the desire for "security" and for what the Russians call a "quiet life" motivates a wide variety of managerial decisions such as concealing production capacity and resisting technological innovation that might rock the boat. Students of American management have also noted the change from the adventurous business tycoons of earlier days to a more professionalized managerial climate in which "greater emphasis is placed on education, training, and a scientific approach, and less on rugged, venturesome, and frequently heedless individualism. The desire for security seems to have increased, and the concomitant of a growing emphasis on security is a diminishing desire for adventure for its own sake."[10] There is indeed a remarkable parallel to this development in the change in the character of Soviet managers. There would have been a

[7] *Ibid.*, pp. 202–3, 335.

[8] Robert A. Gordon, *Business Leadership in the Large Corporation* (Washington, D.C.: The Brookings Institution, 1945), p. 309.

[9] *Ibid.*, p. 309.

[10] *Ibid.*, p. 311.

great affinity between the industrial empire builders of 19th century America and the Soviet directors of the first two decades of the Soviet regime. Those directors were often men of little education who came out of the romantic conflict of revolution, who dreamed great dreams of building an industrial nation and who created an ethos of bold plans and adventurous undertakings. The old Commissar of Heavy Industry, Sergei Ordzhonikidze, would have understood the spirit of the ironmonger, Andrew Carnegie, and the man who built the great ZIL automotive works (now named after him) had the drives and the dreams of the bicycle mechanic, Henry Ford.

Time, and Stalin's purges, removed most of those oldtimers and their place has now been taken by Soviet-educated young men born not of revolution but of bureaucracy. Organizations seem to develop "organization men" types, whether the organization happens to be communist or capitalist. An American reporter visiting with a group of Communist intellectuals reports that one of them had badgered him with questions about David Riesman's book, *The Lonely Crowd.* "The Communist had read Riesman's book and had been fascinated by it—not, he said, because of its application to life in the United States but because of what he maintained was its extraordinary relevance to the present conditions of life in the Soviet Union."[11] It is not, on reflection, very surprising that the job of running an industrial bureaucracy should place a common stamp on men of otherwise different backgrounds. The same would probably apply to the running of a large city or a large university.

MANAGERS AND THE LAWS

We have found that the Soviet manager is often compelled to evade regulations or even break laws. Part of the explanation is simply that there are so many laws. If a Chicago manufacturer fails to ship an order to a New York firm, and ships it instead to another Chicago firm, he has nothing to fear but the ire of the New York firm. But if a Kiev manufacturer fails to ship an order to a Moscow firm and ships it instead to another Kiev firm, he has injured a state enterprise and is subject to administrative action, a fine, or even criminal prosecution. If an American firm sells a substandard generator, he may lose money or his business. But if a Soviet firm sells a substandard generator, the director may go to prison. Thus, even if Soviet managers acted exactly as American managers do, we should expect to find more illegal or evasive activity in the Soviet Union than in the United States.

With the growing complexity of our society, more and more legislation is enacted to protect the public from potential abuses. With the growth of such legislation, managers find their activities more and more circumscribed by laws and regulations. The Soviet manager apparently treats such legislation rather lightly when it conflicts with the interests of his

---

[11] *The New Yorker*, April 6, 1955, p. 52.

firm (and his career and pocketbook). How does American management react when confronted by a spreading web of restrictive legislation?

It is not easy to find out very much about American managerial practice in this respect. Unlike the Soviet press, which throws its pages open to reports of the irregular activities of managers in order to warn others, the American press is likely to shy away from this kind of reporting. Moreover the private nature of American business keeps this sort of activity from coming to light as easily as it might in Soviet industry. Nor is it the sort of thing that businessmen are inclined to talk about very readily. If it is true that a businessman would more readily be interviewed on his private sex life than on his private business activity, then we should require the late Dr. Kinsey to help provide the answers to the extent of unlawful or quasi-lawful business activity.

Prof. E. H. Sutherland, the eminent American criminologist and sociologist, made a bold attempt to investigate the phenomenon he refers to as "white collar crime." His study is based on the decisions of a limited number of courts and administrative commissions against the 70 largest industrial-type corporations in the country. In the period 1935 to 1944 these 70 corporations were convicted 585 times for such practices as restraint of trade, misrepresentation in advertising, patent and copyright infringements, unfair labor practices, granting of rebates, and a few others.[12] The average was 8.5 convictions per corporation. These data provide some idea of the extensiveness of such practices but they clearly understate the magnitude for a variety of technical reasons. Sutherland's conclusion is that "a great deal of scattered and unorganized material indicates that white collar crimes are very prevalent."[13]

The point I wish to make is that when American management finds itself in a position approximating that of Soviet management they tend to react in ways similar to those of their Soviet counterparts. Sutherland's unique study notes many aspects of American managerial practice that are astonishingly similar to those one might find in the literature on Soviet management. "These crimes are not discreet and inadvertent violations of technical regulations. They are deliberate and have a relatively consistent unity."[14] It is in precisely this way that the Soviet manager deliberately misappropriates earmarked funds or decides to shave on the quality of production. There is evidence that the Soviet manager, aware of the fact that "everybody does it" and that the investigating agencies have restricted budgets, counts on the law of averages (and his own superior shrewdness) to get away with it. So a member of the Federal Trade Commission wrote that "about the only thing that keeps a businessman off the wrong end of a Federal indictment or administrative agency's complaint is the fact that, under the hit-or-miss methods of prosecution, the

---

[12] Edwin H. Sutherland, *White Collar Crime* (New York: Dryden, 1949), p. 26.

[13] *Ibid.,* p. 10.

[14] *Ibid.,* p. 217.

law of averages hasn't made him a partner to a suit," and "Samuel Insull is reported to have remarked during his trial that he had only done what all other businessmen were doing."[15]

Similarities in managerial practice are paralleled by similarities in attitude to such violations, and toward the administrative agencies enforcing the laws and regulations. The Soviet manager does not think it is "wrong" to use influence to obtain materials unlawfully, or to fudge his reports to the Government. Success is the important thing, and if you are successful you can get away with all sorts of violations. There is evidence that the Soviet manager feels contemptuous of government planners and of party hacks who try to tell him how to run his business but who themselves had "never met a payroll." Sutherland's picture of American management's attitudes contains strains of the same kind.

> The businessman who violates the laws which are designed to regulate business does not customarily lose status among his business associates. Although a few members of the industry may think less of him, others admire him. . . . Businessmen customarily regard government personnel as politicians and bureaucrats, and the persons authorized to investigate business practices as "snoopers."[16]

In the first section of this paper, it was pointed out that a managerial career carries a great deal of prestige in the Soviet Union and attracts a large number of the better students. These youngsters have been raised in Soviet schools and have absorbed the incessant propaganda of the Communist regime. Many of them enter industry as green novices fresh from school, filled with high ideals about building the socialist fatherland and working for the common welfare. One wonders about the process by which the naive, idealistic young Komsomol member is transformed into the hard-headed manager who knows all the angles for survival in the Soviet business world. Numerous incidents such as the following provide a key to the answer. A young Soviet chemist had been assigned to the quality control department of his enterprise. He was quite pleased with himself when his test showed that a sample of production, which had previously been declared acceptable by his laboratory chief, turned out to contain an excess of phosphorus. He reported the "error" and expected to get a bonus for it. Instead, his boss obtained a new sample, gave it to an outside chemist for analysis, and submitted a report showing that the batch of production was acceptable after all. The young chemist protested, was transferred to another shop, and was finally fired on trumped-up charges.

What happens to such young people? Some never quite get the point and remain ordinary engineers in the plants. Others learn to adapt themselves after a few buffetings and when they decide to play the game according to the real ground-rules, begin to rise in the managerial hierarchy.

---

[15] *Ibid.*, p. 218.

[16] *Ibid.*, p. 220.

It is interesting to note that Sutherland's interviews with American businessmen turned up accounts rather similar to that narrated above. His explanation of the process by which the naive American youngster is initiated into the business of selling used cars, settling insurance claims, covering up irregularities in clients' accounts—indeed, toning down the results of chemical analysis—helps explain the process of transformation of the young Komsomol member:

> In many cases he is ordered by the manager to do things which he regards as unethical or illegal, while in other cases he learns from others who have the same rank as his own how they make a success. He learns specific techniques of violating the law, together with definitions of situations in which those techniques may be used. Also he developes a general ideology. This ideology grows in part out of the specific practices and is in the nature of generalization from concrete experiences, but in part it is transmitted as a generalization by phrases such as "we are not in business for our health," "business is business," and "no business was ever built on the beatitudes." These generalizations . . . assist the neophyte in business to accept the illegal practices and provide rationalizations for them.[17]

Summarizing, the economic world in which the Soviet manager operates compels him to engage in a variety of illegal or evasive practices. Since the Soviet business world is enmeshed in a much greater web of laws and regulations than the American, the Soviet manager finds his interest in conflict with the laws and regulations more often than his American counterpart. But when American managers' interests conflict with the laws, they too are prepared to take the chance of violating them. Both American and Soviet managers justify their actions by an attitude of contempt for governmental controls and investigating personnel, and by a hardheaded view that "business is business" and "everybody does it." Young people in both systems who wish to achieve managerial prominence have to learn to play the game according to the rules, or disqualify themselves from the tough competition for the top.

MANAGERS AND OVERFULL EMPLOYMENT

Many of the peculiarities of Soviet management spring from the fact that the economic system works under conditions of perpetual overfull employment. By "overfull" employment I mean a condition in which there are not merely as many jobs as employables (as under full employment), but the demand for labor far exceeds the available supply. The same applies to other factors of production: materials, equipment, and commodities in general are demanded in far greater volume than the current rates of production. The ability of the Soviet Government to maintain, through the planning system, a condition of permanent overfull employment is one of the greatest economic assets of the regime. We err when we interpret evidence of shortages in the Soviet economy as signs of

---

[17] *Ibid.*, p. 240.

economic weakness; they are rather indications that the economic engine is racing with the throttle wide open.

But just as an engine does not work at its maximum efficiency when it is working at its maxiumum capacity, so the Soviet economy pays a certain price for the advantages of overfull employment. It is the perpetual shortages of supplies that account in large measure for the losses due to overordering and hoarding. The hunger for goods by both firms and consumers encourages the deterioration of quality. The "sea of ink" associated with materials allocations, price fixing, priorities, and all the rigamarole of a controlled economy nurtures the spread of the tolkach and the use of influence for personal gain.

The normally functioning American economy does not confront our managers with this kind of problem. Hoarding makes no sense when materials are in adequate supply. Competition and consumer resistance force the quality of production up to standard. The role of influence is narrowly circumscribed when the bureaucratic machinery of Government controls is removed. The biggest problem of American managers under normal conditions is marketing, not purchasing. The energy spent by the Soviet firm on obtaining materials is spent by the American firm on selling and advertising.

Thus, the major differences between the practice of American and Soviet management are to be ascribed to the differences in the economic environment. The interesting question is, How do American managers behave when placed in an environment that approximates that of the Soviet manager? The obvious test case is war. During World War II the national emergency forced us into a state of overfull employment. Along with this came the total immersion of Government into economic life, with a great burgeoning of materials allocation, price fixing, cost-plus contracting, and a prevailing shortage of supplies.

It is interesting to note that the rate of growth of production during the war rose to levels rivaling the current rates of Soviet economic growth. The implication of this fact is important; it means that there is no magic in the Soviet economic system. Our economy could grow as rapidly as the Soviet economy does if our people would consent to being pushed around as totally as the Soviet people are.

But like the Soviet economy, we paid for our high rate of production in various forms of waste. One of the first consequences of the introduction of materials controls was the rise of the black market. The only full-scale study of the black market, to my knowledge, confirmed what many people felt to be the case at the time:

> During the war at least a million cases of black market violations were dealt with by the Government. Illegal profits ran into billions of dollars. Business interests and Government vied with one another in estimating the seriousness of the black market; business estimates, curiously, often being higher than those of the Government. Such extensive conniving in the black market in illegal prices

and rationed commodities took place among so many businessmen, ordinary criminals, and even the average citizen that serious questions might be raised as to the moral fiber of the American people.[18]

To understand the position of the Soviet manager, we must realize that the American black market flourished at a time when the Nation was fighting for its life and public indignation acted as a restraint. But if the economic controls that led to violations could not be justified by a national emergency, they would be thought of as just irritating obstacles, as so many hurdles that the resourceful manager must overcome as part of the risks of the game. There is good evidence that the Soviet manager takes just this amoral attitude toward economic controls, and it is therefore quite understandable that the evasion of controls would be more widespread.

The high quality of American production in normal times is a byword in international markets. But the effect on the economy of shortages was similar to that in the Soviet economy. One of the techniques used by Soviet managers is to represent lower quality merchandise as of higher quality, and to sell it at the higher price. In the United States during the war—

upgrading was one of the most difficult violations to detect, particularly where no professional investigator was available who could appraise the grade or where there were no State or Federal grades stamped on the commodity.[19]

The reports of Government investigators read like some of the indignant letters of complaint we read in the Soviet press; men's shorts made of cheesecloth, water-resistant baby's pants which permit a third of a glass of water to leak through after one laundering—

if you pick up a board by both ends without breaking it in the middle, it's No. 1 Select—

testified an American businessman.[20]

One of the features of Soviet managerial life which helps protect the manager is the feeling of "mutual support" among various officials whose fortunes depend on the success of the enterprise. The Communist Party secretary doesn't report the manipulations of a successful director because the party benefits from the success of the enterprise; the people in the "home office" (the Ministry or the Council of the National Economy) are reluctant to fire a director who violates the laws in order to get the materials his plant needs, for while the next director may be more lawabiding, he may not succeed in fulfilling his plan. This tendency to maintain a solid front against authority is a source of great irritation to the Government, which periodically inveighs against it but has not been able to

---

[18] Marshall B. Clinard, *The Black Market* (New York: Rinehart & Co., Inc., 1952), p. vii.

[19] *Ibid.*, p. 224.

[20] *Ibid.*, p. 45.

eradicate it. A similar sense of common front prevailed among groups of businessmen.

Nothing better illustrates the degree of organization and consensus among businessmen than their reluctance to testify against each other. . . . Some businessmen felt that the trade would disapprove of behavior that might undermine the solid front against the Government as well as interfere with supplies.[21]

One of the major differences in the position of management in the two countries is the nature of the penalty for failure. Under ordinary conditions the unsuccessful manager loses his job. But the Soviet manager faces many more situations in which the action necessary to get the job done carries with it the threat of criminal action. Indeed, whenever the Soviet Government has found some managerial practice too damaging to its interests and too intractable to the normal sanctions, it has turned to the criminal courts. Immediately after the death of Stalin the punishment for economic transgressions was relaxed, but the new regime has not been able to continue operating without the courts. One of the severest economic problems following the decentralization of industry was the tendency toward "localism": that is, each economic region tended to favor the plants in its "own" region, and would discriminate against plants in other regions. When all exhortation failed, the Government had to turn to the law. Today, a manager who fails to honor the orders of plants outside his own region is subject to "administrative action, fines, or even criminal punishment."

Financial penalties, such as fines, have rarely proved successful as restraints on Soviet managerial behavior. American managers seem to have reacted the same way to the fines imposed for black-market violations. "They don't hurt anybody." "It just comes out of profits, like a tax." "They make so much money on the black market they can afford to pay steep fines." But imprisonment was another matter. "Jail is the only way; nobody wants to go to jail." "A jail sentence is dishonorable; it jeopardizes the reputation." This would not be quite the same in the case of the Soviet manager. At least during Stalin's lifetime some of the best people served their time in jail, and it definitely did not destroy their reputation among their neighbors; although the neighbors might be wary of associating with them. One has the impression that large numbers of Soviet managers feel the chances are fair that some day they will do their stretch, hopefully for a minor transgression.

The wartime economy of shortages injects the government into business life not only as an agency of control but also as the largest customer of many firms. In the Soviet case we have noted the importance of the tolkach, the expediter, the peddler of influence. We might note in passing that the economic system of Nazi Germany, in which government had also assumed a dominant role, also gave rise to this chap. The Germans

---

[21] *Ibid.*, pp. 306–7.

called him the "contact man." As described by an American student of the
German economy:

To influence the powerful agencies of control, however, he [the German
businessman] has good use for what might suitably be called a private relations
department. Under the Nazi system of control of business by an absolute government, the contact man, or graft, or both, take the place of the public relations executive.

The contact man is primarily a political figure. His job is to pull wires. He
knows the influential members of the all-pervading Nazi Party in a position to
bring pressure successfully to bear upon the men in charge of controlling
agencies. . . . Two types of contact man are known to be used: one is an independent agent whom the businessman hires, or attempts to hire, whenever
necessary; the other is carried on the payroll of the business in a more or less
permanent capacity.[22]

The words might well have been written about the Soviet economy. In
that sector of the U.S. economy in which Government plays a dominant
role as customer, the symbols of the mink coat or Dixon-Yates, depending
upon one's political persuasion, come to mind. "Washington," wrote
Senator Paul Douglas, "is indeed full of lawyers and 'representatives'
whose primary commodity is 'influence.' "[23] The techniques of the American influence-peddler differ little from those of his colleagues in the Soviet
or Nazi economy. Gifts and quid pro quo favors are standard among
Soviet tolkachi. Another way in which Soviet enterprises manage to exert
influence is to have one of "their" men placed in other organizations that
can be of use, rather like the unusually high employability in industry of
retired military personnel. During the war the problem was particularly
acute because of our Government's desperate need for skilled managerial
personnel, many of whom were on loan from corporations with which the
Government placed contracts. But the use of influence is not confined to
Government-business relations, as Senator Douglas pointed out in his
critical defense of the ethics of Government personnel:

As a matter of fact, the abuses which have been exposed and properly de-
nounced in the field of Government are quite widespread practices in private
business. Thus the "padding" of expense accounts is so common that they are
often referred to as "swindle sheets." Purchasing agents and buyers frequently
exact toll from those who seek to sell them, and their Christmas presents and
other perquisites appreciably increase their income. Business managers and directors think nothing of awarding contracts, insurance, and underwriting privileges on the basis of friendship and relationship rather than the quality and
prices of the goods and services supplied. All this is taken as a matter of course
in private business, although it obviously increases costs and intercepts gains
which should go to stockholders and consumers.[24]

---

[22] L. Hamburger, *How Nazi Germany Has Controlled Business* (Washington, D.C.:
The Brookings Institution, 1943), pp. 94–95.

[23] Paul H. Douglas, *Ethics in Government* (Cambridge, Mass.: Harvard University
Press, 1952), p. 56.

[24] *Ibid.*, p. 25.

While gifts, payoffs, and bribery play their role in the Soviet scheme of things, the subtler and much more pervasive technique of influence is known as "blat." To have good blat with someone means that one has an "in"; one can always count on him for a favor because of friendship or family ties or some other relationship of confidence. Blat may be used to obtain everything from a new apartment to a carload of coal. The prominent British observer, Edward Crankshaw, has called blat the most significant word in contemporary Russia.[25] The way in which the American equivalent of blat is cultivated is described in one final quotation from Senator Douglas:

Today the corruption of public officials by private interests takes a more subtle form. The enticer does not generally pay money directly to the public representative. He tries instead by a series of favors to put the public official under such feeling of personal obligation that the latter gradually loses his sense of mission to the public and comes to feel that his first loyalties are to his private benefactors and patrons. What happens is a gradual shifting of a man's loyalties from the community to those who have been doing him favors. His final decisions are, therefore, made in response to private friendships and loyalties rather than to the public good.[26]

Summarizing, many of the differences between Soviet and United States managerial behavior spring from differences in the economic climate in which they operate. The stress on quality and appearance, the drive for innovation and technological development, and the interest in cost reduction reflect the force of competition and the buyer's market. Such similarities as have been observed in managerial behavior, spring from features of the economic environment that are common to the two systems, such as large-scale organization and the intrusion of Government into the economy. Under wartime conditions our economy takes on more of the features of normal Soviet economic life, and the consequence is that our managers adopt more of the normal practices of Soviet management.

---

[25] *New York Times Magazine*, June 3, 1951, p. 35.

[26] Douglas, *op. cit.*, p. 44.

Economic Development

There is no single economic system best for the economic development of every underdeveloped country. One would hardly expect the same economic system to be equally appropriate for feudal, peasant, and proletarian societies; more or less industrialized economies; heavily and thinly populated areas; tropical and temperate regions; etc. Nor can a country simply adopt a particular economic system in operation elsewhere. Instead, each underdeveloped nation must choose—from economic theory and the experience of other economies—the combination of economic institutions and instruments best suited to its stage of development, resource endowment, cultural and social traditions, and development objectives.

The study of comparative economic systems helps in this choice by showing the features, advantages, and disadvantages of various economic systems in theory and in practice. The three selections which follow analyze different economic systems as engines of economic development. They suggest combinations of government and private activity, of centralization and decentralization, and of planning and market forces which can promote economic development. The first emphasizes the role of the state in economic growth. The next presents the case for the market as a vehicle for economic development. The last shows how government planning and private decision making can work together for economic development.

Alexander Eckstein

21. INDIVIDUALISM AND THE ROLE OF
THE STATE IN ECONOMIC GROWTH*

*In this essay Alexander Eckstein analyzes the
circumstances in which the state may be expected
to play an important role in economic development. He then examines the activities in which
the state is likely to engage and their effect upon
individual choice and decentralized decision
making in economic life.*

I

Economic growth can be viewed as a broadening of the range of alternatives open to society. Clearly, technological and resource constraints are
likely to be so compelling and overriding in primitive or underdeveloped
economies as to leave comparatively little scope for the exercise of
choice—either individual or social. On the other hand, the situation is quite
different—at least in degree—at more advanced stages of economic development. At these stages, one of the principal manifestations of this broadening in the range of alternatives is precisely the greater opportunity to
exercise choice over the form in which choices in the economy become
institutionalized. This, in turn, requires a delineation of the spheres of
public vs. private choice and a determination of the relative weight of each
sphere.

One of the aspects of individualism, and possibly the one most relevant
for our purposes, is the scope for individual choice and decentralized
decision making in the economic sphere. In a preponderantly free enterprise market economy the institutionalization of these ingredients of individualism is more or less automatically assured. This does not, however,
mean that this sytsem necessarily assures equal scope for the exercise of
choice on the part of all individuals in the economic system, or that it

* Reprinted from *Economic Development and Cultural Change*, Vol. VI, No. 2
(January, 1958), pp. 81–87, by permission of The University of Chicago Press.
Copyright 1961 by The University of Chicago Press. Alexander Eckstein is Professor
of Economics at The University of Michigan.

provides a greater scope for individual choice than an alternative system might. In contrast to preponderantly free enterprise market systems, in economies in which the public sector looms quite large, the scope for individual choice and decision making may be more a function of the political rather than the economic system. Thus the mechanism through which economic policy is formulated and the role of the ballot box in economic policy formulation become major conditioning factors.

In essence, what this suggests is that there is a potentially positive correlation between individualism and economic development. The extent to which this potential is translated into reality will depend upon the role played by individual choice and initiative in resource allocation, regardless of whether the choices and decisions are in fact arrived at primarily within the confines of the economic or political process. With this context in mind, let us attempt to spell out some of the factors and variables that are likely to condition the role the state may be expected or forced to play in the process of economic growth and its impact upon the position of the individual.

II

In analyzing the role of the state in the process of economic growth, the following elements may be considered as essential:

1. *The hierarchy of objectives, goals, and ends of economic development*— This necessarily involves an examination of both the qualitative and quantitative aspects, that is, the character, range, and variety of the ends sought as well as the level to be attained. The interplay of these dimensions of content, range, and level will be one of the principal factors defining the ambitiousness of the particular economic development program. In respect to content, several broad categories of objectives or motivations may be cited, for instance, those revolving around nationalism and those related to a striving for rising standards of living. In a sense, these might be considered as ultimate ends which need to be, and are in fact, broken down into a series of derived and possibly more concrete goals. Thus, at the stage when these objectives are disaggregated and sorted out as to the ranges and levels involved, they inevitably tend to become competitive rather than complementary entities in the sense that under *ceteris paribus* assumptions, the wider the range, the lower will have to be the level, and *vice versa*.

2. *The time horizon in economic development*—This entails a definition of the rate at which the goals are to be attained. In a sense, it is but another aspect of the hierarchy of objectives, since rapid or leisurely growth may be an explicitly stated end in and of itself.

3. *The means available* for attaining—at the desired rate—the content, range, and level of ends explicitly or implicitly formulated. Here one would have to consider such variables as resource and factor endowments and the state of the arts prevailing in the particular economy.

4. *The structure and character of institutions: social, economic, and political*—This is possibly the most complex of all the categories listed here.

The considerations most relevant for our purposes revolve around the rigidity of the institutional framework, its capacity to generate, absorb, and adapt itself to economic change and to the disruptive forces of industrialization. This would mean investigating factors such as the prevailing value system, class structure, social mobility, contractual and legal arrangements, degree and character of urbanization, land tenure system, degree of commercialization and monetization, character and structure of state organization, structure of political power, etc. However, analysis of these variables is greatly complicated by virtue of the fact that some of them are rather intangible, while their particular chemical mix—that is, the nature of combinations and interaction between the different institutional factors—and the reaction produced may be quite unpredictable. In effect, it is much easier to provide *ex post facto* rationalizations or explanations as to why and in what ways certain types of institutional structure were more conductive to industrialization than others, than to assess *ex ante* the height and the tensile strength of institutional barriers and their resistance to economic development.

5. *The relative backwardness of the economy*—From an economic point of view, relative backwardness—and the emphasis should be on relative—involves certain advantages and disadvantages. The disadvantages lie principally in the field of foreign trade, while the so called "advantages of backwardness" may be found in the realm of technology. Thus industrially advanced countries enjoy certain competitive advantages in world markets, and particularly in the markets of the underdeveloped areas themselves. This in and of itself can under certain conditions become a major handicap in the industrialization of backward countries. On the other hand, as Professor Gerschenkron has pointed out, one of the essential ingredients of relative backwardness is a gap in the levels of technology used and applied. Therefore the backward country can reap large potential gains by importing advanced technology from abroad and thus, in effect, make a technological leap from comparatively primitive to highly advanced levels.

At this point another aspect of relative backwardness may be usefully introduced, namely the gap in material welfare or standards of living, and the gap in national power produced by differences in levels of industrialization. All three of these gaps—in consumption, technology, and power—could be viewed as different aspects of a "demonstration effect" through which the gulf between a potential and actual state is forcefully brought home. Characteristically, it is in this shape that the pressure for industrialization of backward countries is manifested. Once the disequilibrating and innovating forces of modernization, industrialization, and urbanization have been introduced on an appreciable scale,[1] one could say that, *ceteris paribus*, the greater the relative backwardness, the more acute will tend to be the "tension" arising from this chasm between the potential and the actual, and thus the greater will be the pressure for industrialization.

Given the five categories of elements and variables considered above, we are now in a position to state our hypothesis concerning the conditions

---

[1] This scale effect is, of course, both crucial and indeterminate, in the sense that what will be the operationally significant range will inevitably vary from country to country, depending upon size, institutional framework, etc.

under which the state will tend to play a greater or lesser role in the process of economic growth. On this basis then one could say that:

a) The greater the range of ends and the higher the level of attainment sought;

b) the shorter the time horizon within which the ends are to be attained, that is, the more rapid the rate of economic growth desired;

c) the more unfavorable the factor and resource endowments;

d) the greater the institutional barriers to economic change and industrialization; and

e) the more backward the economy in relative terms

the greater will tend to be the urge, push, and pressure for massive state intervention and initiative in the process of industrialization, and at the same time, the greater will be the need for such intervention if a breakthrough, rather than a breakdown, is to be attained.

III

Assuming that the state is compelled to make a major commitment on behalf of industrialization, what types of measures may the state be expected to adopt and what effect may these have upon the position of the individual, or more specifically, upon the individual choice and decentralized decision making in the economic sphere? From this point of view, a sharp distinction needs to be made between the elements and the degree of state power applied in the process of economic growth.

In analyzing the qualitative aspects of state intervention affecting the economic sphere, one could perhaps distinguish between five categories of action: provision of social overhead, provision of economic overhead, application of direct and indirect levers and controls, government operation of enterprises extending beyond the overhead sectors, and central planning.

Provision of social overhead might entail maintenance of law and order in the society; provision and enforcement of legal and contractual obligations; supply of educational, health, and social welfare facilities; assumption of military and defense functions, etc. In effect, these are categories of action which to the extent that they are provided at all, are usually furnished by public rather than private agencies.

Provision of economic overhead may involve the institution of central banking and of monetary and fiscal facilities, the development of a highway and railroad network and of other public utilities.

Application of direct or indirect levers and controls may be based on a wide variety of measures, such as introduction of tariffs, railroad rate discrimination, tax privileges and other types of subsidies, rationing of goods and of credit, price controls, etc.

Government operation of enterprises extending beyond the overhead sectors may range from management of some industries, or a few firms in different industries, to public ownership of all means of production.

Central planning may involve more or less total concentration of economic decision making in the hands of a national planning board.

Admittedly, this fivefold classification is arbitrary, and the line of demarcation between the different categories is quite blurred. Yet, in terms of their effect upon the exercise of individual choice and initiative, they present qualitatively rather significant differences. Thus, most of the items in the first two categories belong to what, in industrializing societies at least, are usually considered as the minimal and essential functions of a state. In contrast, centralized and comprehensive planning combined with total government operation of the economy may be regarded as maximum functions. One of the key questions that needs to be posed in this context is which one, or which combination, of categories will the state use to promote economic development? Whichever means it uses, how massively, to what degree, and with what intensity will it apply its power to the provision of these different categories? Moreover, how will particular kinds and degrees of state intervention affect factor supply, particularly the supply of capital and entrepreneurship?

It may turn out that the more massively and rapidly the state provides what can be considered its minimum functions, the less may be the pressure or the need for it to provide the maximum functions. Therefore, the reliance upon maxima may in effect be a function of past and current failure to provide the minima. In these terms, then, one could say that a necessary precondition for the broadening of opportunities for the exercise of individual choice, individual initiative, and the growth of individual values in underdeveloped countries, launched on a development program, is a high degree and rapid application of state power for the supply of social and economic overhead, combined with partial controls and planning as circumstances may demand them.

Theoretically one could, of course, visualize a system in which amidst public ownership of the means of production, national planning, and resource allocation was—within wide limits—based upon the operation of free consumer choice and consumer autonomy. Realistically, however, it would be extremely difficult to build sufficient checks and balances into such a Lange-like model to prevent it from slipping into a totalitarian mold. On the other hand, this is much less true in the case of partial planning and partial government operation of enterprises, which in many situations is needed to reinforce the provision of social and economic overheads, if comprehensive government planning and management is to be avoided.

The failure of the state in the minimum fields tends to be more or less directly reflected in capital formation and the growth of entrepreneurship. Thus, in many traditional societies, accumulations of merchant and other forms of capital tend to be dissipated because of: (*a*) the absence of adequate and contractual arrangements to protect these holdings from the more or less arbitrary ravages of officialdom, and (b) the failure of the state to institute a social security system, so that old age assistance, poor relief, and similar functions must be privately assumed through the family and kinship system. At the same time, condition (a) tends to reinforce the economic risks of various types of business and industrial investments. Moreover, the same condition further encourages the flow of capital into land investment, which in an environment of acute population pressure and agrarian value orientation, represents one of the safest and most profitable forms of holding. However, from the standpoint of the economy, this is merely a transfer payment, ultimately representing a leakage of investment into consumption. In effect, then, this is a milieu in which the state—through sins of commission and omission—tends to undercut actual and potential sources of capital accumulation, while at the same time making its contribution to the narrowing of business opportunities. Under these conditions the scarcities of entrepreneurial and technical talent tend to be further intensified through the neglect of education facilities. Moreover, to the extent that some education is provided, its orientation is frequently inhospitable to the growth of scientific and technical knowledge.

Viewed in these terms, perhaps one of the most important contributions the pre-industrial European city made to the industrialization of the continent was that it provided a legally and more or less militarily protected haven for the accumulation and conservation of capital, and for its investment in fields that were eminently productive from a point of view of economic development.

Amidst such circumstances, the formidable barriers to modernization and industrialization are likely to be perpetuated, while economic, social, and political tensions mount under the impact of innovating influences ushered in—as a rule—through foreign contact. Unless some means are found for alleviating these tensions through a process of change and adaptation, the potentially explosive forces in society may be expected to burst forth, sweeping away the old order, capturing the state, and using it as a total and far-reaching instrument for mounting an industrial revolution.

On this basis, one could argue that if India, for instance, wishes to avoid a totalitarian path to industrialization, her current plans and efforts do not provide for enough, rather than for too much, state intervention. Thus the large gap in the financial resources available for the implementation of the Second Five Year Plan may be a symptom of the inability and the reluctance of the Indian state to mobilize the means adequate for the implementation of the ends sought. But, even more fundamentally, perhaps, the inadequacy of the government efforts to spread adult education—both basic and technical education—rapidly, may be an important factor in inhibiting the attainment of certain economic objectives, while at the same time it serves to reinforce the great gulf between the small elite and the rural masses—a factor representing marked potential dangers in the political realm.

To sum up this phase of my argument, it may perhaps be useful to attempt to work with the concept of an "optimum level and pattern of state intervention" parallelling other optima—e.g., the optimum propensity to consume—incorporated in different types of economic and social science models. For our present purposes, this optimum would have to be defined in relation to two broad sets of objectives, i.e., striving for rising standards of living combined with an increase and/or preservation of the scope for the exercise of individual choice and initiative. The definition would also have to take account of the specific circumstances in each case, particularly in relation to the qualitative and quantitative aspects of state intervention, and to the variables listed in Section II above.

IV

We have discussed thus far the role the state may need to play in the process of economic growth without any reference to the character of the state and its capacity to perform the tasks required of it. Historically, however, particularly in the underdeveloped countries, the state—and the social structure on which it was based—was one of the very agencies hampering economic development. The same conditions that create the need for massive state intervention, in one form or another, also tend to breed a type of state which is singularly unequipped to intervene effectively on behalf of economic development. That is, economic backwardness is usually associated with political and other forms of backwardness.

Thus in China, for instance, the state has played a passive to actively negative role *vis-à-vis* the economy. The very concept of economic change and economic dynamism was alien to such a society with the nexus between economic growth and national power and/or welfare only very dimly understood, if perceived at all. The function of the economy was a largely static one, being charged with the primary task of supporting the ruling elite. Therefore, the state assumed very few responsibilities in the economy, beyond assuring that it would provide a stable, continuing, and adequate source of revenue for the imperial household and the gentry-bureaucracy.

The continuing failure of the traditional Chinese state to respond to the challenge of modernization, the institutional rigidities permeating the traditional social structure, the incapacity and unwillingness of the ruling classes to come to terms with change, their inability to understand the character of the innovating influences and to follow a policy of enlightened self-interest, have all served to retard the process of industrialization for so long that cumulative tensions of such explosive proportions were generated that they could no longer be contained, while at the same time perhaps nothing short of such an explosive force could have broken the shackles of the old order and swept away the barriers to economic growth. The violent eruption of the Chinese economy into what seems to bear the earmarks of an industrial revolution under totalitarian control can thus be viewed as an illustration of a resort to maximum solutions in the face of repeated and continued failure of the old state to perform and furnish the minimal functions referred to in the preceding section.

This course of development contrasts sharply with that experienced in Japan, where the breakdown of the old order accelerated by innovating influences produced a realignment of elites. The new elite, which bore some continuity with the old, then set out very deliberately to use the state as an instrument for modernization and industrialization. In doing this, the state from the outset paid major attention to developing rapidly the social and economic overhead sectors and to provide a general framework within which all types of enterprises, private and public, large and small, would grow. The state in effect conceived its role as initiator and promoter of the development process, leaving much of the execution to private enterprise.

While this is not intended to suggest that the Japanese experience can necessarily be duplicated in other countries, and in different circumstances, it is worthwhile to note that the state was able to perform this kind of a role amidst conditions which *ex ante* would have seemed exceptionally unfavorable. Not only were factor and resource endowments poor—in many respects poorer, perhaps not only absolutely but relatively, than those of some major underdeveloped areas today—but institutional barriers were formidable too.

However, an analysis of the conditions under which the state would or would not be *capable* of performing the functions required of it would be beyond the scope of this paper. Rather, I have tried to confine myself more specifically to a spelling out of the conditions under which and the ways in which the state may be *required* to assume a large role in initiating and promoting economic development without jeopardizing the growth of opportunities for the exercise of individual choice and initiative in the economic sphere.

Harry G. Johnson

22. PLANNING AND THE MARKET IN ECONOMIC DEVELOPMENT*

In this article Harry G. Johnson discusses the use of the market mechanism as an instrument of economic development. He suggests several reasons why the role of the market has frequently been neglected in economic development theory and policy. Johnson examines the functions of the market and its advantages and disadvantages in the context of economic development. He concludes that the market is a relatively cheap and efficient instrument despite its shortcomings. He therefore recommends that government development planning improve and strengthen the market system.

ECONOMIC development is a field of study in which economists have only recently begun to specialize, and in which consequently there is as yet no settled body of economic doctrine. I must therefore begin with the warning that what I am about to present is not the agreed view of a representative group of economists, but rather my own opinions. Though I have drawn on the literature of development and of economic theory in forming these opinions, I cannot say that the results constitute an authoritative statement of the present position of economics.

The fundamental causes of economic growth are not a subject with which economists have dealt much in the past, and they are not a subject with which economists can claim to be qualified by training and technique to deal now. My subject is not, however, the causes of economic development, but planning and the market in economic development; this involves the theory of markets, and on that subject economists by profession have a

* Reprinted, with the permission of the author and publisher, from *Pakistan Economic Journal*, Vol. VIII, No. 2 (June, 1958), pp. 44–55. Harry G. Johnson is Professor of Economics at the University of Chicago.

great deal to say. Indeed, from the time of Adam Smith, the theory of markets has been the core of economics as a social science.

It is true that the full ramifications of the market as an instrument of social and economic organization were not appreciated from the start by the classical economists. The English classical economists understood the functions of commodity markets; but they did not link the theory of distribution to the pricing process. The integration of the theory of factor prices with the theory of commodity markets was left to J. B. Say, and later Walras and Marshall, to work out. But the relation between the market and economic development lay at the center of the foundations laid by Adam Smith. Smith was concerned with economic development, and at the heart of his work was the market, determining the extent of specialization and division of labor and the limits to increasing productivity.

In recent times, there has been a retreat both in economic theory and in economic policy from the nineteenth-century ideal of the unfettered market as a principle of economic organization. But the economic pros and cons of this retreat have been fully debated, and the economist consequently has a great deal to say about the relative merits of the market as contrasted with other methods of economic organization, and the circumstances appropriate to each.

The subject of planning and the market in economic development is, therefore, one which falls definitely within the field of the economist. Before I go on to discuss it, I must define more precisely what I mean by it. "Planning and the market" may be interpreted in two different ways. First, it may refer to the contrast between direction of the economy by Government and the policy of *laissez-faire*. This is not my subject, though in a wider philosophical and historical context it offers much to discuss. For example, though *laissez-faire* and direction are often regarded as opposites, if one looks to the history of economic development one finds (as Professor Easterbrook has shown[1]) that economic development is almost invariably a process in which planning and direction on the one hand and freedom of enterprise on the other play their part, and are mixed. There is almost no case in which economic development has been entirely planned or entirely unplanned. The usual pattern is one of some framework of control by Government, within which the entrepreneur provides his services—a mixture of bureaucracy and enterprise, in which bureaucracy takes care of the major risks of development and enterprise faces and overcomes the minor ones. Another relevant point that Easterbrook makes is that an economy which succeeds in finding a formula for

---

[1] Professor Easterbrook's analysis was presented in the Marshall Lectures at Cambridge University in the spring of 1956. Unfortunately these lectures have not been published, but some of the ideas are available in W. T. Easterbrook, "Long Period Comparative Study: Some Historical Cases," *Journal of Economic History*, Vol. XVII, No. 4 (December, 1957), pp. 571–95.

growth tends to repeat that pattern after it has become inappropriate. For example, Britain has gone on trying to work the internationally-orientated pattern of her nineteenth-century development; Russia has been very successful in developing heavy industry but has not yet solved the problem of agriculture.

The alternative interpretation takes planning, in the sense of a general direction of the economy, as an established principle, and considers the market as an alternative to other and more direct means of detailed control. Given the general framework of economic planning, there is still a choice between two alternative methods of looking after the details. One is by direct detailed planning by a central authority, the other is by leaving the working out of details as far as possible to the operation of the market. (There is a third alternative, in which the Government is itself the entrepreneur and investor, which I shall consider later.)

This alternative interpretation is the one I shall be using: I shall discuss the question of the market mechanism as against detailed planning as an instrument of economic development. I should like to make it clear from the start that I am going to make a strong case for the market, as the preferable instrument of economic development, on two main grounds. The first is that the achievement of the desired results by control methods is likely to be especially difficult and inefficient in an underdeveloped economy; at this point I should like to remind you that a large part of Adam Smith's argument for *laissez-faire* was the inefficiency and corruption he saw in the Governments of his time. The second is that the remedies for the main fault which can be found with the use of the market mechanism, its undesirable social effects, are luxuries which underdeveloped countries cannot afford to indulge in if they are really serious about attaining a high rate of development. In particular, there is likely to be a conflict between rapid growth and an equitable distribution of income; and a poor country anxious to develop would probably be well advised not to worry too much about the distribution of income.

I am going to make a fairly strong case for the market, because the market figures relatively little in the literature of economic development, and the theoretical analysis which economics has developed in relation to markets is often overlooked or disregarded. Before getting down to business on the subject of markets, I should like to explore a little the question why, in the theory and policy of "economic development," so little scope is usually allowed to the operation of market forces. There have been, I think, three main groups of factors at work.

In the first place, there seems to be in human societies a set of social and psychological factors favoring intervention in the market. In this connection it is important to remember that the free market as commonly understood is essentially a characteristic of the nineteenth century—before then, and since, the common feature of economic organization has been intervention in the market. What are these factors? One of them, I believe, is the impatience of idealists and would-be reformers with the working of the market, and their desire to take direct action to improve things, according to their criteria of improvement: this attitude reflects the intellectual arrogance typical of reformers. The attitude is reinforced by the fact that the defects of market organization seem obvious to anyone, or can be made to seem so, whereas the socio-economic functions of the market are obscure and difficult to appreciate. The discovery of these functions was indeed the great achievement of the classical economists, and constitutes the only claim that economics has to the status of a science. The obscurity of the market's functions makes it easy, also, to confuse opposition to unattractive features of the free enterprise system which express themselves through the market, such as inequality of income and wealth, with opposition to the market as a mechanism of organization.

Opposition to and dislike of the market for the reasons I have just discussed is frequently allied with a positive belief in the desirability of Government intervention in the market, and a faith in the disinterestedness and effectiveness of such intervention. Belief in the desirability of Government intervention in the western world is associated with the spread of socialist ideas, and in its modern form can be traced back to Benthamite utilitarianism; elsewhere, it can probably be associated with the nature of the State as the dispenser of justice in primitive economies. Belief in the efficiency and disinterestedness of Governmental intervention is associated with the growth of the modern career civil service, with its standards of incorruptibility, particularly in Britain and countries influenced by the British example. (This explains why the belief is less prevalent in the United States than in other English speaking countries.) It is, in my opinion, an important question for underdeveloped countries whether their civil services are of the caliber required to administer the kinds of social and economic programs adopted in the advanced economies.

Opposition to the market as a means of economic organization is also inherent in the characteristics of an established and functioning civil service. One of these characteristics, a corollary of the standards of administrative efficiency and "public service," is a natural propensity to regulate. A good civil service, or a bad one, is rarely prepared to decide that non-intervention is the best policy; and to the bureaucratic mind the functioning of the price system as a regulator appears mere disorder and chaos. Another characteristic is an antipathy towards entrepreneurship; the entrepreneur is an agent of change, and as such disturbs the orderliness of the economy and makes it more difficult to regulate. This is not, of course, a universally valid generalization: civil services have, at times, played important entrepreneurial roles themselves, though usually under the pressure of political events. One special feature of the generally anti-entrepreneurial attitude of civil servants, noted by P. T. Bauer in his studies of West African trade,[2] is specially relevant to underdeveloped economies. This is the antipathy of the British-trained type of civil servant, literate and "responsible," to the semi-literate and socially unacceptable type of individual who possesses the knack of making money by trading—the small-scale entrepreneur on whose activities economic development from a low level may well depend.

These characteristics of civil services are important in considering the uses and limitations of control methods in economic development. The economist, or any other intelligent man, can easily think up ways in which market processes could be improved on by means of controls, assuming that he administers them himself and has infinite time in which to do so. But would the conclusion in favor of controls be the same if it were accepted that their administration had to be entrusted to a "responsible" civil servant of the British type, let alone a civil service with a less ingrained tradition of honesty and disinterestedness?

A third factor antithetical to the market has been the character of modern economics itself, as applied to economic planning. Modern economics has been strongly influenced by the theoretical revolutions of the 1930's, which were inimical to competition and the market. On the one hand, both the theory of monopolistic competition and the new welfare economics have been excessively concerned with criticisms of the efficiency of the market mechanism, criticisms formulated from a static viewpoint not obviously relevant to growth problems. On the other hand, the Keynesian revolution fostered aggregative thinking to the neglect of older ideas of substitutability in production and consumption (which in turn have receded into the limbo of mathematical economics); and the habit of aggregative thinking has to some extent been reinforced by the modern emphasis on statistical verification which has necessarily postulated simplicity of economic relationships.

In addition to these theoretical developments, development economics has been strongly influenced by the nature of the major problems with which economics was concerned before it turned to "development," namely mass unemployment and war finance, which inculcated the habit of thinking about economic structure as given, and of applying other criteria than consumers' choice. Two features of war-time economic planning are frequently overlooked in the attempt to carry over its concepts and techniques to peacetime planning. In the first place, the battery of controls applied in war-time rested very heavily on a strong appeal to patriotism. The application of similar techniques might be possible in an underdeveloped country which could mobilize and concentrate all the instruments of communication and propaganda on the single aim of devel-

---

[2] P. T. Bauer, *West African Trade: A Study of Competition, Oligopoly and Monopoly in a Changing Economy* (Cambridge: Cambridge University Press, 1954), especially chaps. 11, 12, pp. 145–71.

opment; but the capacity of most countries to do this is doubtful, especially as development presents no single dramatic objective comparable to victory. Secondly, in spite of the propaganda and the patriotic appeal, war-time economic policy in most countries ran into serious difficulties with the resurgence of the market in the form of black markets of various kinds, shop shortages, incentive problems, and so on.

I have been discussing various reasons why thinking about economic development has been inimical to, or neglectful of, market considerations. I now want to recapitulate briefly the various economic functions of the market and the price system as a method of economic organization. I shall be brief, as the argument is a familiar one.

In the first place, the market rations supplies of consumer goods among consumers; this rationing is governed by the willingness of consumers to pay, and provided the distribution of income is acceptable it is a socially efficient process. Secondly, the market directs the allocation of production between commodities, according to the criterion of maximum profit, which, on the same assumption, corresponds to social usefulness. Thirdly, the market allocates the different factors of production among their various uses, according to the criterion of maximizing their incomes. Fourthly, it governs the relative quantities of specific types of labor and capital equipment made available. Fifthly, it distributes income between the factors of production and therefore between individuals. Thus it solves all the economic problems of allocation of scarce means between alternative ends.

These are static functions; but the market also serves in various ways to provide incentives to economic growth. Thus the availability of goods through the market stimulates the consumer to seek to increase his income; and access to the market provides an opportunity for inventors of new goods and technical improvements to profit from their exploitation. Moreover, the market serves particularly to provide an incentive to the accumulation of capital of all kinds: first to the accumulation of personal capital in the form of trained skill, since such skill earns a higher reward; and second to the accumulation of material capital, since such capital earns an income.

The argument, then, is that a properly functioning market system would tend to stimulate both economic efficiency and economic growth. And it is important to note that the market does this automatically, while it requires no big administrative apparatus, no central decision making, and very little policing other than the provision of a legal system for the enforcement of contracts.

All this sounds very impressive; but it is clearly not the whole of the story. What, then, are the objections to the market, how serious are they, and what should be done about them in the context of economic development? I shall discuss these questions in some detail. But first I shall state briefly the central theme of my discussion. It is that in many cases the objections to the market can be overcome by reforming specific markets, so as to bring them closer to the ideal type of market; and that to overcome other objections to the market may be very expensive and may not prove to be worthwhile—in other words, the defects of the market mechanism may on balance be more tolerable than they look at first sight.

Now, what are the objections to the market? They can, I think, be classified into two main types. One type of objection is that the market does not perform its functions properly. The other type of objection is that the results produced by the functioning of the market are undesirable in themselves.

I begin with the first type of objection, that the market does not perform its function properly. Here it is useful to draw a distinction between two quite different sorts of cases—those in which the market operates imperfectly, and those in which a perfectly functioning market would not produce the best results.

Imperfect operation of the market in an underdeveloped country may be attributable to ignorance, in the sense of lack of familiarity with market mechanisms and of awareness of relevant information, or to the prevalence of other modes of behavior than the rational maximization of returns from effort. In the first case, the appropriate Governmental policy would seem to me to be, not to assume from the market the responsibility for allocative decisions, but to disseminate the knowledge and information required to make the market work efficiently and provide the education required to use it. The second case implies a more fundamental obstacle, not only to the use of the market but also to economic development itself, and suggests that successful economic development requires a basic change in social psychology. To my mind, it raises a serious question of fact. Is it really true that people in underdeveloped countries are strangers to the idea of maximizing gains? The idea that they are is very common in the literature and policy-making of economic development; one of its manifestations is the implicit assumption that both supplies and demands are completely price-inelastic. I am very sceptical about this, partly because of Bauer's work and partly because at least some of the actions of Governments in underdeveloped areas presuppose that even the poorest producers are susceptible to price incentives. I personally do not think one is justified in assuming as a general proposition that ignorance and illiteracy necessarily imply that men are not interested in making money. If it is true, there will be serious difficulties in the way of economic development; but again, the appropriate Governmental policy would seem to be to educate the people in the practice of rational economic behavior.

Even if the market functions perfectly, it will not produce the best possible results by its own criteria if there is a difference between social and private benefit or cost. This type of case may be particularly relevant to economic development; it includes the case of increasing returns to scale, and can be extended to include the possibility that technical progress or capital accumulation tend to proceed more rapidly in industry than in agriculture. But it raises an immediate question of fact—whether divergences between social and private benefit or cost are numerous and important or not. This is an important question, but one on which we do not know very much for certain. The theory of increasing returns is logically intriguing, but the influence of increasing returns still has to be disentangled from that of technical progress in historical growth. Again, it is a fact that few advanced countries are not industrial; but this by itself does not establish the wisdom of a policy of forced industrialization in an underdeveloped country. Aside from the question of fact, the existence of divergences between social and private returns does not necessarily indicate a need for the Government to replace the market mechanism; instead, the operation of the market can be perfected by the use of appropriate taxes and subsidies to offset any divergences between social and private returns.

I now turn to the second type of objection to the market, the point of which is not that the market does not work in the way it should, but that the results produced are undesirable in themselves. Here, I think, there are two major objections to the market. The first is that the income distribution produced by the market is unjust and socially undesirable. The distribution of income through the market depends on the wealth and talents of different individuals, and on their individual skill in seeing a profitable opportunity of employing their money or labor. If they make a wise or lucky choice, they may obtain a much higher income. The objection is that this method of determining the distribution of income is not just. But if you attempt to intervene in the distribution of income, you immediately encounter the problem that such intervention interferes with the efficiency of the market system. If people are not allowed to enjoy the income they could obtain by their decisions, their decisions in turn will be affected, and the efficiency of the system will be impaired. There is, therefore, a conflict between economic efficiency and social justice. The extent and importance of this conflict is likely to vary according to the state of economic development. The more advanced a country is, the more likely are its citizens to have consciences about the distribution of income, and to accept the high taxation necessary to correct it without disastrously altering their behavior; and on the other hand, the higher the level of income reached, the less serious will be any slowing down of the rate of growth brought about by redistribution policies. An advanced country can afford to sacrifice some growth for the sake of social justice. But the cost of greater equality may be great to any economy at a low level of economic development that wishes to grow rapidly, particularly as it is evident that historically the great bursts of economic growth have been associated with the prospect and the result of big windfall gains; it would therefore seem unwise for a country anxious to enjoy rapid growth to insist too strongly on policies aimed at ensuring economic quality and a just income distribution. I should add that the problem may not be in fact as serious as I have made it out to be, since in the course of time rapid growth tends in various ways to promote a more equal distribution of wealth.

At this point I should like to digress on a special aspect of the conflict between the market principle and considerations of social justice, which appears in some underdeveloped countries, the conflict created by opposition on moral grounds to the payment and receipt of interest. Now the view that interest is a bad thing is economically nonsensical (unless it is merely a terminological dispute) until the economy has reached a stage at which no more capital can usefully be employed. I am not here referring to the administrative difficulties of removing interest from the economy, but to the economic principle involved. The problem of underdeveloped countries centers around the scarcity of capital. If capital is scare, there should be both an incentive to the accumulation of it by saving, and a device for rationing supplies of it among alternative uses. These are the functions of interest. If you "abolish interest" in the sense of forcing interest to be called by some other name, as was the practice in the Middle Ages, the result will merely be inconvenience; but if you abolish interest in the economic sense, the result will be the loss of the economic services performed by interest. On the one hand, the amount of private saving will be reduced and its allocation to investment distorted by the restriction of investment to activities over which the saver has personal control. On the other hand, insofar as there is a pool of investment funds (created, say, by taxation or monetary expansion, or made available by foreign aid), some method will have to be found for rationing it out among competing claims if it is to be used efficiently. This problem has in fact arisen in Russia, where the engineers and planners who assess investment projects have had to work out concepts which amount to the rate of interest, to fill the gap created by the refusal of Marxian dogma to recognize that capital has a scarcity value and is productive.

The same sort of argument makes it seem undesirable for the Governments of underdeveloped countries to use their monetary policy to favor themselves with low rates of interest. Governments now often enjoy the privilege of paying a rate of interest of $2\frac{1}{2}$ or 3 per cent; this encourages them to think, and to plan, as if capital were easily available. There seems no reason why Governments should enjoy low rates of interest when capital is scarce; on the contrary, it promotes wasteful investment and also, for reasons explained below, tends in the long run to promote inequality of income distribution.

I have been discussing the objection to the results of the market system on the grounds that it produces an undesirable distribution of income. A second objection of the same sort is that the free market will not produce as high a rate of growth as is desirable. I think there is a strong case for this objection, because people's actions in regard to saving and investment depend very much on their guesses about the future. Now people are likely to know their own current requirements better than the Government. But the requirements of the future have to be looked at not from the individual or family point of view or that of the nation as a collection of individuals, but from the point of view of the ongoing society. The needs of society in the future, many economists agree, tend to be underprovided for by the free market.

Even if the conclusion that state action is desirable to raise the rate of growth is accepted, this conclusion nevertheless does not carry with it a number of corollaries which are often attached to it. In particular, it does not necessarily imply that the state ought to undertake development saving and investment itself. Private enterprise may be more efficient than the Government in constructing and operating enterprises, so that the best policy may be to stimulate private enterprise by tax concessions, subsidies, and the provision of cheap credit. Similarly, it may be preferable to stimulate private saving by offering high interest rates, rather than by forcing savings into the hands of the state by taxation or inflation. One argument against a policy of low interest rates and forced saving is that it may in the long run contribute to the inequality of income distribution. The reason is that the poor or small savers are mainly confined to low-yielding fixed-interest investments, directly or indirectly in Government debt, because these are safe and easily available, whereas the larger savers can invest their money in higher-yielding stocks and shares or directly in profitable enterprises. There is, therefore, an opportunity here for Government both to stimulate saving for development and to improve the distribution of income.

There is another reason for being wary of the proposition that the state should undertake development investment itself—the danger that if the Government undertakes investment itself, especially if its administrators are not too clear on their objectives, the result will be the creation of vested industrial interests inimical to further development, and resistant to technical change.

To summarize the foregoing argument from the point of view of development policy, it seems to me that much of development planning could usefully be devoted to the improvement and strengthening of the market system. This does not imply the acceptance of all the results of *laissez-faire*, especially with respect to the rate of growth; but there are reasons for thinking that too much emphasis on a fair or ethical distribution of income can be an obstacle to rapid growth.

The argument I have presented has been concerned mainly with one side of the case for the market. The other side concerns the costs and difficulties of controls, in terms of the manpower costs of the administration they require, and their effects in creating profit opportunities which bring windfall gains to some members of the community and create incentives to evasion which in turn require policing of the controls. I have touched on that side of the argument sufficiently frequently to make it unnecessary to elaborate on it further.

Instead, I shall comment briefly on international markets in relation to economic development, since so far I have been implicitly concerned with internal markets. Economic development planning inevitably has a strong autarkic bias, by reason both of its motivation and of the limitation of the scope of control to the national economy. Nevertheless, international trade can play an important part in stimulating and facilitating the development process. Access to foreign markets for exports can permit an economy with a limited domestic market to exploit economies of scale, and the potentiality of such exports can serve as a powerful attraction for foreign capital and enterprise. Similarly, the capacity to import provided by exports can give a developing economy immediate access to the products of advanced technology, without obliging it to go through the long and perhaps costly process of developing domestic production facilities. Economic nationalism and excessive fear of the risks of international trade, by fostering aversion to exploiting the advantages of the international market, can therefore retard economic development unnecessarily.

One further comment on the international aspects of the market and economic development seems to me worth making. Discussion of the international side of development has been mostly concerned with commodity trade and commercial policy. But in fact one of the most important ways in which the world market system is imperfect is with respect to the international mobility of capital and labor. The problem of international capital movements has received a fair amount of attention, labor mobility and immobility much less. Now, the process of economic development in the past, especially in the nineteenth century, was characterized by vast movements, not only of capital, but also of labor, about the world. The mass movement of labor between countries has now been more or less shut off by the growth of nationalism. I believe it is important to recognize this restriction on international competition, and its implications for programs of economic development. It means—looking at the world economy as a whole—that the solution to the problem of maximizing world output cannot be approached directly, by bringing labor, capital, technology, and natural resources together at the most efficient location; instead, the other productive factors have to be brought to the labor. To a large extent, "the economic development of underdeveloped countries" is a second-best policy,[3] in which gifts of capital and technical training by advanced to underdeveloped countries are a compensation for the unwillingness of the former to consider the alternative way of improving the labor to resources

---

[3] See J. E. Meade, *The Theory of International Economic Policy*, Volume II: *Trade and Welfare* (London: Oxford University Press, 1955), and R. G. Lipsey and Kelvin Lancaster, "The General Theory of Second Best," *Review of Economic Studies*, Vol. XXIV, No. 1 (1956–57), pp. 11–33.

ratio, movement of the labor to the resources. The fact that development is a second-best policy in this respect may impose severe limitations on its efficiency and rapidity.

To conclude, I have been concerned with the role of the market in economic development; and I have aimed at stressing the economic functions of the market, in automatically taking decisions about various kinds of allocations of economic resources, and the place in economic development programs of improvements in market organization and methods. I have been advocating, not a policy of *laissez-faire*, but recognition of the market as an administrative instrument that is relatively cheap to operate and may therefore be efficient in spite of objectionable features of its operations. The general assumption on which I have been arguing is that economic development is a process of co-operation between the state and private enterprise, and that the problem is to devise the best possible mixture.

Gerhard Colm and Theodore Geiger

23. PUBLIC PLANNING AND PRIVATE DECISION MAKING IN ECONOMIC AND SOCIAL DEVELOPMENT*

The authors show that every development plan —even in a highly centralized economy—involves some combination of direct implementation through government action, and indirect implementation through government guidance of the actions of individual decision makers. The success of the development effort therefore depends on the country's ability to work out a coordinated relationship between government and private plans and activities. The authors discuss the nature of the planning process in less developed countries and the appropriate roles for the government and private sectors in an economic development program. They then explain the various techniques for harmonizing public planning and private decision making with each other and with the goals of the national development effort.

REGARDLESS of its name, every modern form of economic system combines some measure of public planning with some latitude for private decision making. Even in the freest of market economies, the government's own expenditures are planned in accordance with annual requirements and with the anticipated longer-range needs for those services considered

* Reprinted, with permission, from *Organization, Planning, and Programming for Economic Development* (United States Papers Prepared for the United Nations Conference on the Application of Science and Technology for the Benefit of the Less Developed Areas) (Washington, D.C.: U.S. Government Printing Office, 1962), pp. 15–27. Gerhard Colm is Chief Economist and Theodore Geiger is Chief of International Studies of the National Planning Association.

appropriate for it to provide, and many large private enterprises plan their investment and market development programs for five or ten years ahead. Even in the most centralized socialist economies, the planning and administering authorities must take into account the probable responses of individuals and of local institutions to central government directives regarding production, consumption, saving, and investment. Hence, the task of harmonizing public and private decision making confronts every modern economic system, though in different forms and in different degrees.

The less developed countries of Latin America, Asia, and Africa are in the process of working out reconciliations of public and private decision-making which are relevant to the character of their economies, consistent with their social values, and more or less effective in achieving their chosen goals. The variation is very wide, ranging from such countries as Mexico, Brazil, and Argentina, in which private decision making in the free market plays the major role, to countries like Niger and Chad, in which the modern sector of the economy consists of a few government-owned or foreign-owned enterprises of various kinds. In consequence, it is impossible to discuss public and private decision making in a way which is equally valid for all less developed countries. While our aim is to present some guidelines and suggestions, the analysis which follows is necessarily cast in the form of a generalized discussion of the subject and is not to be construed as descriptive of any particular country.

FUNCTIONS OF GOVERNMENT PLANNING AND PRIVATE DECISION MAKING IN LESS DEVELOPED COUNTRIES

To a greater or lesser degree, the countries of Latin America, Asia and Africa are faced with common difficulties in seeking to accelerate their economic and social advancement. Among the problems relevant to the subject of this paper are: (a) the inadequacy of the existing infrastructure (transportation and communication, energy, and power facilities, etc.) and social capital (education, health, and housing facilities, etc.), (b) the shortage of investment capital, (c) the limited supply of managerial and technical skills, (d) the inadequate incentives and institutions for stimulating productive investment and increasing productivity, and (e) the heavy dependence upon foreign trade and external aid for obtaining the capital funds and the capital goods required for economic and social development. In such circumstances, governments have had to assume responsibility for discharging three types of functions in order to insure that economic and social development would actually occur in their countries.

The first function is that of national development planning. Broadly speaking, this function consists of defining the goals of the national development effort, estimating and mobilizing the necessary domestic and foreign resources of money and skills, and allocating or guiding them to those specific uses which seem likely to make the greatest contributions to achieving the national goals. This function may be carried out by explicit preparation of a long-range national development plan, as has been done in India and Pakistan, and is now beginning in several Latin American countries. Or, it may be done implicitly and unsystematically, as was customary in many less developed countries until recently. Today, most countries have recognized that, to be effective, national development planning must be carried on in a deliberate and systematic way.

The second function of government in economic and social development is to initiate those investments and manage those activities which comprise the public sector of the economy. In every economic system, there are certain essential services which only governments can perform (national defense, maintenance of law and order, etc.). In addition, there are certain types of investments which are so large or so pervasive in their importance to the economy as a whole that it is necessary or desirable for the government to undertake them. These generally include certain kinds of infrastructural and social overhead capital.

However, the public sector may cover a much broader range of economic activities either by deliberate preference, as in socialist countries, or because there are no practical or acceptable alternative ways of conducting them. For example, in some less developed countries, significant accumulations of capital exist in private hands, but these are often not invested in ways which directly and immediately contribute to economic growth. Traditional habits or present uncertainties may cause such private funds to flow into real estate, commodity transactions, money-lending, and other activities promising quick or large returns, which may eventually result in luxury consumption or investment abroad, usually in Western Europe or the United States. In other countries, there is no private capital or private sector of the economy in the modern sense of the term. In default of government initiative, too few private entrepreneurs would come forward to take advantage of such economic opportunities as may exist. Hence, for a variety of different reasons, the governments of many less developed countries not only invest in essential services and infrastructure but also establish and operate, at least initially, some or all of the new economic activities that are envisaged under the national development plan.

The third function of government in economic and social development is to stimulate, guide, and assist private initiative and activities so that they contribute to achievement of the national development goals. Virtually all the less developed countries are explicitly or implicitly committed to a significant measure of private economic decision-making as an essential complement to the economic functions of the central government. This results not only from deliberate choosing of the social values served by decentralized, nongovernmental decision making in economic life. Paradoxically, it is necessitated by the same scarcities of capital and skills as have impelled governments to assume the national development planning function and the entrepreneurial and managerial functions comprised in the public sector of the economy. In most less developed countries, neither the governments nor the ruling political parties possess the trained supervisory personnel, the technical skills, and the funds necessary to replace all significant privately conducted activities by central planning and government operation of the economy. Determination of the output and consumption of certain types of activities and products—especially those in services and consumer goods industries—seem to defy the detailed directives of central planners. Moreover, there are always potential sources of capital, talents, and initiative that are unavailable to governments, particularly when they operate by compulsion, but which can be stimulated to manifest themselves voluntarily by appropriate incentives and encouragements. The less developed a country, the less it can afford to neglect the potential resources that could be activated only voluntarily and in decentralized, nongovernmental forms.

In addition, the more numerous and detailed the entrepreneurial and managerial decisions that have to be made by the central government authorities, the slower, more cumbersome, and less flexible the operation of the economy becomes. Most less developed countries have found that the market mechanism is a much less wasteful way of making many kinds of economic decisions and for getting many kinds of economic tasks accomplished. A system of centralized direction of production, investment, and consumption is also susceptible to political pressures and the ponderous inflexibility of bureaucratic control. Some of the socialist countries have recognized this deficiency of a large, centralized public sector, and have tried to solve their problems by decentralizing many economic decisions and activities, and providing market-type incentives and pressures for guiding them. Yugoslavia is the leading example of such a country.

Also, many less developed countries have concluded that there are substantial benefits to be derived from attracting responsible private investment from the more developed countries. Continuing, well-conducted enterprises established by foreign companies and businessmen in less developed countries significantly increase the amount of capital available for productive investment; disseminate much needed managerial and technical skills among the local population; and create opportunities for—and often provide financial and technical assistance to—indigenous enterprises to get started as suppliers of the materials, components, and services required for their own operations.

There is a wide variety of different ways by which the government carries out its third function of stimulating and channelling private economic initiative and activity. (See section on "Government Policies in Support of Private Investment.") Thus, it is able to select the particular combination of policy measures that seems best adapted to achieving national development goals in socially acceptable ways.

The question, then, which each less developed country must answer for itself is which economic decisions and activities can best be undertaken by the government and which by private institutions and individuals. This choice is sometimes deliberate, but more often it grows out of the historical background and existing socio-political structure of the country.

THE PARTICIPANTS IN PUBLIC PLANNING AND PRIVATE DECISION MAKING

In order to clarify the interplay between public planning and private decision making, the actors or participants have to be defined.

IN THE PUBLIC SECTOR

Though we usually speak of the government, it must be remembered that the term covers a multitude of ministries, departments, and agencies, each engaged in planning its own activities. These include not only the several ministries or departments of the central government, but also those of provincial and local governments, as well as quasi-governmental agencies, such as social security funds, central banks, development banks and corporations, port authorities, railroad administrations, public utilities, highway commissions, government-owned and managed manufacturing enterprises, and so on. The planning of each of these governmental institutions has a greater or lesser effect on consumers, workers, and private enterprises. Each of these units of government is interested in specific policies and often subject to pressures from various groups in the population.

The multitude of activities and effects of the various parts and levels of government can themselves be planned only if there is some central planning agency which coordinates and directs planning for the government as a whole. Such a body is, in effect, responsible for the national development plan, as distinct from the different sectoral, functional, and regional programs, which deal in greater detail with the separable parts of the national economy.

The central planning agency has different locations in various countries. In some, it is located under the jurisdiction of one of the ministries (economics or finance); in others, it is organized as a ministry of its own; and in still others, it is an agency under the jurisdiction of a planning council in the office of the country's Chief Executive. National development planning is not a separate activity isolated from the other functions of government. Like budget-making, it is intimately related to all functions. Therefore, it can be effectively carried out only if, regardless of the location of the planning agency, it has the full backing of the country's Chief Executive, who is responsible for all official policies. This dependence on the highest governmental authority is best symbolized when the national development planning function is performed by an agency in the office of the Chief Executive, or the Prime Minister, and when he is directly involved in the planning process as head of a planning council.

Generally, the sectoral and functional programs contained in the national development plan can best be prepared and implemented in a decentralized manner by the individual ministries, departments, and agencies concerned. However, in some less developed countries with a scarcity of government planning personnel, the central agency may have to take on the additional functions of guiding the programing activities and training the programing personnel of the individual governmental and quasi-governmental agencies of the central administration and of provincial and local authorities.

In the Private Sector

While the participants in the public sector can be readily identified as units of the central and local governments, there is no simple way of defining the many different kinds of non-governmental enterprises and activities that play significant roles in national development efforts. A definition by enumeration will be clearer than a definition by characterization.

In some less developed countries, non-governmental activities in commerce and industry may take the form of corporate enterprises similar to the business corporations of the United States and Western Europe. In many other less developed countries, the most important commercial, industrial, and financial activities in the private sector are individual and family proprietorships, like those that predominated in the highly industrialized nations at earlier stages of their development. However, in most parts of Africa, Asia, and Latin America, the numerically largest portion of private economic activity is in agriculture and takes the form of large estates and of small peasant farms, the latter producing either cash crops, or subsistence crops, or a mixture of both.

In recent years, other forms of non-governmental economic activity have been established in less developed countries and have been assuming increasing importance. These include producers and marketing cooperatives, predominantly in agriculture; credit unions and other types of cooperative saving and lending institutions; productive enterprises financed or managed by trade unions, political parties, kinship groups, etc.; and similar institutions. In addition, there are various kinds of local community projects and village organizations. Though many of them may be officially sponsored or government financed, their operations largely depend upon the voluntary initiative and labor of their members, and they may be properly classified as part of the private sector.

Less numerous, but economically more significant, are various forms of joint government/private ventures, involving the participation of local entrepreneurs, and often of foreign companies, which contribute capital and managerial and technical "know-how." When, as is most often the case, the private participants in such joint enterprises are responsible for management, these activities, too, may be considered part of the private sector.

These many and diverse forms of private economic activity play different roles in the national development effort through people's decisions regarding what and when they will produce, consume, save, and invest. In the traditional forms of private economic activity (e.g., peasant farming, latifundia, moneylending, shopkeeping, etc.) these decisions tend to be based upon short-run calculations and on the assumption of static economic conditions, not of dynamic growth. Indeed, by definition, the less developed and more traditionalist a country, the more private economic activities will be of a subsistence nature in agriculture and characterized by a static outlook in commerce, banking, and industry. If these traditionalist and static enterprises are to contribute more effectively to economic growth, their motivation and decision-making have to be reoriented toward the prospects for future expansion and growth. One essential element in bringing about such a dynamic transformation is to enlist the active participation of the numerous, smaller types of private enterprises in the national planning effort.

Generally, it is only the larger, more modern, and more productive private enterprises, including the subsidiaries of North American and West European companies, that are oriented toward longer-term growth expectations. Some follow the practice, increasingly prevalent in the developed countries, of undertaking their own long-range planning of investment and market development within the framework of the national development plan. Such private planning plays a most important role in ensuring that the private sector will make the fullest possible contribution to achieving the goals of the national development effort.

THE CHARACTER OF PLANNING IN LESS DEVELOPED COUNTRIES

The publication of a plan is merely one stage in national development planning. The process as a whole consists not only of preparing the plan, but also of debating and adopting it, implementing it, and then comparing actual performance with the plan and revising it periodically on the basis of experience.

A national development plan always should have a long-range perspective covering general goals for at least ten years ahead, and more details of specific objectives for an intermediate period of four or five years. It should be an operational tool, closely related to the annual government budget, particularly for the short-run period of the next year or two. Operational shorter-term and perspective longer-term planning should be in fluid interrelationship, particularly through the "feed-back" effect made possible by effective progress reporting and evaluation, and periodic revisions.

In an economy in which private decision making plays the major role, the national development plan establishes goals for social and economic development; determines the programs in the public sector; presents forecasts of agricultural, industrial, and commercial investments in the private sector; and estimates the international transactions needed to realize the objectives. These estimates of investments in the private sector and of international transactions are of a different character and significance from the detailed investment programs prepared for the public sector.

In the public sector, the government can determine the specific programs needed and can then direct the execution of these programs. However, even in the public sector, there is an important qualification. These programs are financed either by voluntary private savings and taxation, or by forced savings of various kinds, such as inflation, restriction of consumption, compulsory labor, etc. While the programs are determined in part on the basis of estimates of the productive facilities, manpower, and skills needed to achieve the national development objectives, the expected growth in turn is the most important factor determining the financial resources which will become available.

In the private sector there is the additional task of estimating the likelihood that private domestic and foreign decision makers will in fact engage in the activities postulated by the plan. In addition, it is important to know the amounts and kinds of consumption which would be compatible with the national development goals and with the public programs subject to government direction. For this purpose, the plan has to contain consistent relationships among investments in public undertakings (infrastructure); in social capital (education, health, housing); in directly productive enterprises (public and private); and among government and private savings, consumption, and the other major components of the national domestic and external accounts. For the private sector, the estimates have not only to be consistent with the public sector and with the plan as a whole; they must also be realistic—that is, they must represent realistic forecasts of consumer actions, personal and private institutional savings, etc.

The government can influence consumption by price, tax, wage, and other policies and by a number of other devices discussed in the next section. For the determination of these policies, the plan has to serve as a guide. Thus, the estimates of the sectors in the economy which are not under direct government control commonly consist of forecasts of actions of private decision-makers as they are likely to behave under the influence of government policies specifically designed to affect their behavior. The realism of the forecast depends in part on the degree of influence the government can and intends to exert over the behavior of the private sector.

The uncertainty is inevitably greater with regard to the estimates of international transactions embodied in the plan. A country that depends largely on exports of a few primary products traded on world markets can usually exert little influence on the prices and quantities of these exports.

Hence, this item in the plan will always be purely a forecast, and it must be treated as independently given data. In contrast, other variables in the plan are subject to a greater or lesser degree of direct or indirect control (e.g. imports), and can be so adjusted as to be compatible with the independent factors. Because forecasts of the more or less independent factors may turn out to be erroneous and because these factors themselves cannot be significantly influenced by government policies, it is always prudent to provide contingency measures for adjustment in the other, controllable sectors in case adverse developments occur; for example, if export earnings are less than expected.

In forecasting investments in the private sector, an important distinction needs to be made between what may be called "strategic" investments and "collateral" investments. The former relate to increases in capacity in key industries which are essential for the fulfillment of other parts of the plan. These private investments are often projected on the basis of actual negotiations between the planning agency and the private enterprises concerned. As to the collateral investments, they may be estimated on the basis of surveys of the intentions of private enterprises, taking into account the fact that new investment opportunities arise with expanding markets. Thus, the collateral investment decisions will generally be made automatically as the economy expands in the course of economic development. Inclusion of a projection of collateral investment in the plan is necessary in order to estimate the total demand for funds and the total increase in productive capacity which are likely to be forthcoming. These estimates are, however, less firm than those for the strategic investments and are subject to a considerable margin of error.

It has not been possible in the short space available to indicate more than a few of the many ways in which goal setting, program determination, forecasting, and choice of implementation policies interact with one another in the complex process of planning for economic and social development. The essential role which the forecasting, or projection, of the main components of the national accounts and balance of payments plays in the planning process is not always sufficiently recognized. Conversely, it is sometimes denied that any process which relies so heavily upon forecasting can legitimately be called planning. Those who hold this view maintain that national development planning is only possible if the government has, and is willing to use, the power of directly determining all significant decisions in the economy concerning production, consumption, saving, and investment.

Such a narrow definition of planning is neither accurate nor useful. It is not accurate because all national economic plans, even those of the most centralized and authoritarian socialist countries, contain an important element of forecasting the probable future behavior of individuals and organizations. The level and composition of consumer demand as specified in the plans of centralized socialist economies are essentially estimates of the likely behavior of consumers under certain conditions fixed by the government, rather than directives that will inevitably be obeyed, or which could be exactly enforced. The production goals fixed by central socialist planners, particularly in agriculture, contain a large measure of uncertainty—and to that extent are forecasts—because they are based upon assumptions about the effects on productivity not only of the weather and other natural phenomena but, more importantly, of the attitudes and motivations of farmers and other producers. The external transactions posited in the plans of socialist economies also contain a large element of forecasting. Their inability to control the behavior of world markets and of other governments is one reason why these countries strive to minimize their dependence upon imports—especially from noncommunist economies—despite the higher costs often involved in such autarkic policies.

Indeed, planners of all ideological persuasions have to recognize the fact that governments have only a limited capacity to influence or offset the effects of certain developments, such as a drop in the world prices of primary products, natural catastrophes, the initiative and conscientiousness of the individual citizen, and the variability of producer and consumer responses. Also, a country cannot enjoy the advantages of vigorous innovation and enterprise without giving the managers of private and public enterprises a high degree of freedom from bureaucratic regulations and political interference. However, no country pursuing a determined policy of social and economic development could expect that all required adjustments in the plan would be made only in the public sector. A successful economic and social development plan depends on the ability to work out a constructive relationship between government planning and private decision making, particularly with respect to strategic investments.

TECHNIQUES FOR HARMONIZING PUBLIC PLANNING AND PRIVATE DECISION MAKING

For each country, the major elements in its national development plan can be ranged from those which are most independent of control, such as foreign trade and the weather, to those which are susceptible of control by the government, such as public expenditure programs. In between, are the many factors in which private decision-making predominates but is subject to more or less influence by government policies. Thus, every plan implies some combination of direct implementation through government action, and indirect implementation through the guidance provided by government policies and by the planning process itself for the actions of private decision makers.

While public and private economic activities should be conducive to realization of the goals of the national development effort, they do not always have this character. In the public sector, governments may not make the necessary decisions or may not carry them out effectively, for a variety of political and social reasons. Similarly, the results of private decision making may not always contribute to economic and social advancement, and in some cases may be counter to it, again for a variety of reasons. Insofar as the causes are accessible to remedial action—and this is not always possible at any given stage of a country's political and social evolution—there is a variety of techniques for harmonizing public planning and private decision making with one another and with the goals of the national development effort.

THE ANNOUNCEMENT EFFECT OF THE PLAN

A national economic development plan will generally specify the amounts of investments in the different branches of industry in the private sector which are consistent with the other elements of the plan and are required for the increase in production posited as a goal for a future year. The problem is to maximize the probability that private decision makers will actually undertake the investments proposed in the plan.

A major factor working toward this result is what has been called the "announcement effect" of the plan. If the managers of private enterprises are convinced that the government is determined to execute the programs and actions required of it in the public sector and, hence, that there is a good chance that the development goals could be achieved, then the plan for the private sector represents not only what is required of private enterprises but also reveals the opportunities for expansion likely to occur in various industries. In effect, it becomes a matter of self-interest on the part of entrepreneurs to increase productive capacity in line with the opportunities highlighted in the plan. This result depends, of course, on the conviction that the plan is feasible and that the government and other private decision makers will play their respective roles. Success breeds success, and the "announcement effect" can be a continuing one rather than a one-time event.

It is particularly important for the success of the "announcement effect" that the investments be made which provide the transportation and energy facilities and other elements of infrastructure required for expansion of the private sector. Public educational and training programs, and housing for additions to the work force, are often required for labor mobility and industrial expansion. Confidence in the plan can also be strengthened if representatives of private enterprises are consulted in the planning process so that they have a sense of participation and have an opportunity to explain the kinds, locations, and timing of the infrastructure and social capital investments they believe are needed for the success of their own efforts. Such private participation in national development planning is discussed below.

GOVERNMENT POLICIES IN SUPPORT OF PRIVATE INVESTMENTS

Important as it can be, the announcement effect of the plan is not sufficient by itself to induce the required investments by the private sector.

Assuming that the reasons for the lag are not primarily deficiences in infrastructure or social capital, they are usually caused by a lack of capital available to the private sector; by absence of the required technology, skills, or manpower; or by attitudes and motivations which are not conducive to increased investment or increased productivity. There is a variety of government policies which can help to fill these gaps, and provide incentives and pressures for more productively oriented behavior by private individuals and organizations.

Fiscal and monetary policies of various kinds are important means by which governments can support the private sector. The government's budgetary policy has a major influence on the activities of the private sector through the size and timing of a surplus or deficit. Special tax benefits can be provided for stimulating productive investments, and differential rates may be used to discourage traditional kinds of investments which make little or no direct contribution to the national development goals. In providing such tax incentives, however, care must be taken to prevent possible misuse of them as tax "loopholes." Sometimes, the entire tax system needs to be reformed in order to ensure that all groups in the population contribute equitably to the national development effort.

Through its ability to influence long- and short-term interest rates, the government can ease the shortage of investment or operating capital available to the private sector from the commercial banks and other private lending institutions. More important in many less developed countries than interest rate policy are the ways in which the government exercises direct control over credit availability, investment licensing, construction permits, rationing of capital obtained as foreign aid, etc.

Governmental policies relating to prices and wages can help to maintain the profitability of efficient enterprises within a framework of reasonable price stability. In addition, price policies for public enterprises can be designed which will improve the performance and prospects of private enterprises. Import and foreign-exchange policies can help the private sector to obtain the quantities and kinds of capital goods, materials and components, and operating supplies which can only be purchased abroad; and they can also provide protection against foreign competition for "infant" industries.

Agricultural policy is particularly important in less developed countries, for the agricultural sector often provides the major source of domestic savings for investments in infrastructure, social capital, and new industries; of the foreign-exchange earnings needed to import capital goods; of labor for new factories and service trades; of food to feed the growing population of the towns; and perhaps also of some of the raw materials required for manufacturing. The capacity of the agricultural sector to fulfill these functions exercises a major influence on the development of industry and other new activities. Hence, it is generally necessary to undertake extensive and continuing programs of technical assistance and vocational training in the countryside; to provide adequate credit facilities for agricultural improvement; to encourage the development of producers' and marketing cooperatives and other new forms of cooperation among small farmers; to build farm-to-market roads, irrigation systems, and other installations; and to institute other measures required to increase agricultural productivity. In some countries, basic reform of the whole agrarian system is required before agriculture can begin to play its proper role in the national development effort.

Often, however, more direct measures of specific assistance to the private sector are needed. Development banks—sometimes operating through industrial development corporations—serve as important instruments for extending loans, and in some cases equity capital, to enterprises wishing to expand, or to new ventures which lack the financial resources required for investment in accordance with the plan. Government subsidies have also been used, either in the form of low-interest loans or of outright grants to cover the initial deficits of new enterprises, public and private. Whether institutionalized in development banks and corporations or administered by regular government agencies (e.g. ministries of finance or industry), such government loans and grants form an important link between the public planning process, on the one hand, and the decisions of private enterprises, on the other. Their effectiveness is increased when development banks and corporations provide not only funds but also managerial advice, particularly to new enterprises.

A major contribution to the development of the private sector is made by government policies and measures for mobilizing external resources of funds, commodities, and technical assistance, and making them available by various devices to private enterprises. These external resources may take the form of aid from international organizations and the governments of other countries, or they may be obtained through private foreign investment and the nonprofit activities of educational, research, and philanthropic institutions, trade unions, cooperative societies, and other voluntary private groups in the developed countries.

There is also a regulatory or restrictive group of government policies, in addition to the measures of positive stimulation and assistance just outlined. It may sometimes happen that enterprises will invest faster than envisaged in the plan in order to gain an advantage over competitors or for other reasons. This may be beneficial except where, as in countries with a basic shortage of capital, it may divert resources from higher priority purposes. In such cases, funds for financing "excess" expansion may have to be restricted.

Alternatively, it more often happens that, despite the government's incentives and subsidies, traditionally oriented enterprises—indigenous and foreign—may not invest in the expansion or modernization of their facilities, which may play a strategic role in achieving the objectives of the plan. In this case, new entrepreneurs may be encouraged by the government, or it may itself have to make and initially operate the investments which the private sector is unwilling or unable to undertake.

Other types of limitations on the freedom of action of the private sector imposed by governments include the regulation of the monopolistic and restrictive practices of private—and sometimes public—enterprises, the protection of labor and consumers, the maintenance of public health and safety, and the elimination of other activities and conditions considered socially undesirable.

Governments have to consider not only the impact of restrictive or compulsory measures on the specific enterprises that have provoked them but also the broader effects on attitudes and motivations in the private sector as a whole, as well as the implications for achievement of the national development plan. Since inconsistencies between the objectives of the plan and private decisions are bound to arise from time to time, it is essential that machinery be provided for resolving those conflicts that are of strategic importance in a manner which is just to the individual enterprises involved and is in the best interest of the national development effort as a whole.

In this brief space, it has been possible only to list the main kinds of policy instruments at the disposal of governments for stimulating the private sector to grow and to contribute as effectively as possible to the national development effort and for harmonizing private activities with those of public authorities. In many ways, this is the crucial portion of the strategy of economic and social development. Selecting the proper combination of policy measures and direct subsidy programs is an exceedingly difficult task in most less developed countries not only because of the scarcity of the required financial resources and administrative skills but, more fundamentally, because of social and political obstacles. As already explained, national economic projections or forecasts are most useful tools for helping governments to determine the particular combination of public policies and programs needed to assist the private sector to perform its functions more effectively. But, whether these policies and programs will actually be carried out depends upon the willingness and ability of the government to overcome the political and social resistances to change, the weaknesses in its administrative capabilities, the resentment of influential special interest groups, and sometimes even the apathy of the people themselves. However, all of these difficulties can be significantly eased to the extent to which the private sector and the people generally become voluntary participants and partners in the national development effort.

PRIVATE PLANNING AND PARTICIPATION IN PUBLIC PLANNING

The harmonization of public planning and private decision making is not a one-sided process involving only policy choices and actions by the government. It also requires appropriate measures by private decision makers.

In order to contribute most effectively to the national development effort, private enterprises need to engage in their own long-range planning, particularly of their investments in plant and equipment. It is desirable for large enterprises of all types to calculate the productive capacity, manpower, import, and financial resources they are likely to require during the planning period. These private plans should then be made available on a confidential basis to the government planning agency and revised periodically. This applies particularly to what we have called strategic investments in the private sector. Mention has already been made of the desirability of meetings between government planners and the managers of such strategic private enterprises. These negotiations are important not only to ensure consistency in the requirements of the public and private sectors but also to foster constructive attitudes on both sides and mutual understanding.

If the private sector is to make the greatest possible contribution to the national development effort, the many different kinds of private decision makers, large and small, have to be permitted and encouraged to participate actively in the public planning process so that they can acquire a sense of voluntary commitment to achieving the objectives of the national development plan. One method used in a number of countries is for the planning agency to establish advisory committees composed of representatives of industries, the farmers, the trade unions, and other significant private groups. In addition to such direct participation of the private sector in the planning process, each country will, of course, officially review and legally adopt its national development plan in accordance with its constitutional and political procedures.

Ultimately, the success of a national development plan depends upon the basic attitude toward it. To the extent that both public planners and private decision makers recognize that the planning process is a tool, not an end in itself, the task of harmonizing public planning and private decision making will be less difficult in practice and more fruitful in results. Successful fulfillment of this task will make a most important contribution to social and economic progress within a framework of democratically developing institutions.

Convergence of Economic Systems?

Are Western capitalist market economies and Communist centrally planned economies becoming more alike? Some economists believe this is so because of concurrent trends toward greater state intervention in the regulated capitalist economies and toward greater decentralization in the centrally planned economies. Others question whether these tendencies are marked enough to justify a conclusion as strong as "convergence." The following article presents a distinguished economist's appraisal of the evidence for convergence.

Jan Tinbergen

24. DO COMMUNIST AND FREE ECONOMIES SHOW A CONVERGING PATTERN?*

In this essay, Jan Tinbergen points out how changes in Communist centrally planned econo- mies and in Western capitalist market economies have tended to reduce the differences between them. However, he stresses, these differences are still very striking. Tinbergen discusses the im- portant problems currently facing each type of economy. He then indicates how the possible solutions to their respective problems may fur- ther narrow the differences between the two types of economies. He concludes by stating his belief that there is for each country an "opti- mum" economic system which combines ele- ments of capitalism and socialism and the market and planning.

It should be noted that some economists would disagree with certain aspects of Tinbergen's anal- ysis. For example, they would question the ac- curacy of some of the evidence he cites, such as the statement (2, vii) that Communist countries have given up the idea that each country should have its own heavy industry, and the implication (4, v) that workers effectively participate in en- terprise management in Communist centrally planned economies (a category which excludes Yugoslavia). They would also emphasize that, to the extent to which capitalist market and socialist centrally planned economies have been converg- ing, this movement has been and is likely to con- tinue to be slow and gradual, rather than rapid and dramatic.

* Reprinted from *Soviet Studies*, Vol. XII, No. 4 (April, 1961), pp. 333–41, with the permission of the author, the editors of *Soviet Studies*, and the publisher, Basil Blackwell & Mott, Ltd. Jan Tinbergen is Professor of Economics and De- velopment Planning at the Netherlands School of Economics.

1. We ARE witnessing today the coexistence of two radically different economic systems, the "communist" and the "free" economies (according to western terminology) or the "socialist" and "capitalist" systems (according to the eastern vocabulary). The various names given to them are far from precise. Perhaps the most imprecise thing about them is the suggestion that each of these systems represents something well-defined and hence invariant. Reality shows both to be in permanent change. Analysis of the nature of this change can prove quite fascinating. This essay proposes to show that the changes are in many respects converging movements. As will be seen, our essay is a very brief sketch only, trying to indicate a few main tendencies and not going into any detail, or, for that matter, into differences between the communist countries.

The main forces behind the changes may be brought under two broad headings. On the one hand each system is learning from experience and trying to overcome some of its own weaknesses. On the other hand the systems begin to influence each other more and more. While in the beginning the communist system was not taken seriously by the free system this has changed to a considerable extent. The communist system has been interested in some "capitalist" achievements from its very start. Now it is not so much imitating some of the western methods as learning economics from its own experience.

2. Some of the major changes which have occurred in the communist system since the Russian revolution will very briefly be summarized in this section:

(i) For a short while it was thought that specialized management was superfluous and that "the workers" could take care of this activity. It was soon learned that specialization is more efficient with regard to management. In fact, the traditional principle of resistance to specialization in all forms is becoming increasingly less prevalent.

(ii) For a short while an attempt was made to equalize incomes in a drastic way. The well-known consequences of such equalization by decree forced the regime to introduce a wage system which makes wages largely dependent on productivity. Strangely enough, this was then labelled "socialist wage policy."

(iii) For some time planning was done in terms of physical quantities and not in terms of money values. Gradually the use of money as a common denominator penetrated into the planning system and the significance of prices and costs was more and more recognized.

(iv) For a long time interest was considered an unnecessary concept as a consequence of the elimination of private ownership of capital goods. Gradually it was discovered that the elimination of interest as a form of private income does not mean that it should also be disregarded as a cost element.

(v) Rationing was abolished a few years after the Second World War and free consumer choice accepted as a proper institution. Gradually some more emphasis was given to consumption as the purpose of production.

(vi) Mathematical methods of planning, considered as "capitalist" for a long period, were recently recognized to be objective and helpful and are now widely discussed and applied.

(vii) A profound change is under way in the concepts of international trade, not only between communist countries but also between communist and free economies. The idea that each country should have its own heavy industry is no longer adhered to.

3. The so-called free economies have also undergone thorough changes, which will now be summed up.

(i) The public sector nowadays is considerably larger than it was in the nineteenth century. Especially in western Europe public utilities are publicly owned; railways and tramways, coal mines, steel works, insurance companies and banks are often in the public sector.

(ii) The amount of taxes levied in western economies, often in the neighborhood of one quarter of national income, means that taxes are among the important regulators of economic activity. In addition a considerable portion of the nation's savings is made in the public sector.

(iii) Free competition has been limited in many ways as a natural consequence of some technical forces (high fixed costs of production). It has also been voluntarily restricted by such movements as the drive for standardization.

(iv) Partly as a consequence of (iii) governments have limited the freedom of entrepreneurs by anti-trust laws.

(v) Access to education has been given gradually to an increasing portion of the population, often by providing education without charge. Moreover, education has been made compulsory up to a certain age.

(vi) Market forces have been eliminated or modified in some particularly unstable markets, especially in agriculture and in some cases even international commodity agreements have been concluded.

(vii) Planning has gradually been given an increasingly important role, both in big private enterprises and in the design of national economic policy.

(viii) Deliberate development policies have been in existence for a long time. In the nineteenth century already, transportation facilities were often created with public help. At present a whole range of measures, from tax facilities to government investments in infrastructure as well as in manufacturing industry proper, are applied to further the development of remote areas or poor regions.

(ix) Some forms of price and wage control as a direct means to prevent inflation have been used recently in a few "free" economies.

4. Several of the changes recorded above are in fact bringing the communist and the free economies closer together. This cannot be said,

however, to mean that the differences are already small. There are very large differences still. But the process has not stopped. Both types of economies are facing many problems. They will have to move further. In this section we try to give a picture of the most striking differences still in existence and in the subsequent sections of the most important problems to be solved in both types of economies.

(i) The most striking difference is, of course, the size of the public sector. It should not be forgotten, however, that the power of the private sector in western countries is not commensurate with its formal size. In many indirect ways western societies have reduced this power. For example, taxes take away almost half of the profits. Of the remainder, a large part is invested and only a small part paid out as dividends. Western as well as communist economies are to a large extent dominated by managers. In the west, shareholders are no longer powerful. Social legislation in many respects also restricts the freedom of action of private entrepreneurs. So do a number of regulations with regard to quality control, pollution of water and air, building activity, town and country planning and so on.

(ii) Another important difference is the degree of freedom in production decisions. Factory managers in the west have much more freedom in this respect than managers in communist countries where a still very large number of items is planned centrally.

(iii) Accordingly, there is a considerable difference in the degree of detail in which the future course of the economy is planned in communist countries and in "free" economies. This refers to production as well as, e.g., to foreign trade.

(iv) Prices are controlled centrally in the communist countries to a much higher degree than in western countries, where, as a rule, only a few agricultural prices are under direct control. Here again, however, western countries use more indirect means of influencing prices. Among these, competition is the main institutional means, but import duties and monetary policies and (in Holland) wage control and price control of some other items are supplementary instruments.

(v) Industrial democracy is very different in the two types of countries. In the west only some beginnings have been made with codetermination of workers or their organizations in some social issues. In the communist world workers are given opportunities to participate in the discussions about the economic plans of the enterprise and about the use of a portion of the enterprise surplus.

(vi) Education constitutes another subject in which there is still considerable difference. In the "free" countries a certain portion of the potential students of secondary and university training cannot receive the education they need for lack of financial means. The portion is declining, however, as a consequence of several types of financial help, which in some countries enable as much as half of the student body to carry on their studies.

(vii) The differences in the level of savings are recently less striking between such countries as the continental European countries and the communist countries than they were before. Savings of about 20% of national income are now no exception in these western countries; Japan is saving nearly 30%. The United States and the United Kingdom, however, save considerably less.[1]

(viii) Regarding the principles of the international division of labor and the priorities of investment projects the differences between east and west are rapidly disappearing.

5. Corresponding to these problems the communist countries may have to face the following issues:

(i) A major problem seems to be the question of whether or not a gain in efficiency will result from making a large number of small enterprises in essence "private" enterprises by some sort of lease or concession system. If one tries to imagine the volume of administration now usual, say, in shops, it must be a burden on general efficiency.

(ii) A second major problem seems to be whether or not more freedom in production decisions can be given to managers. With rising real incomes citizens of the communist countries will require a finer pattern of qualities and assortment which it is hardly possible to plan centrally. Those closest to the market can probably best judge the needs. There does not seem to be any danger of the central authorities losing control over general economic development as a consequence of granting this type of freedom for the individual manager.

(iii) One also wonders whether or not the number of items planned centrally should be diminished in order to relieve the central planning agencies of a heavy burden which appears to have relatively unimportant qualifications in terms of increments in national wellbeing produced. The same may well apply to international trade planning.

(iv) The next question communist countries might put to themselves relates to price fixing. What harm is there in permitting prices to move as a consequence of relative shortages or abundances and letting them contribute to restore equilibrium? Is not such a method in fact quicker than a mere adaptation in production programs or stocks? Prices will have to move anyhow as a consequence of technical progress and changes in crops. It remains an open question whether the changes should be permitted to individual sellers or only to central authorities. In other words, there seems to be a choice here where the answer is not so clear beforehand and where there is an element of discretion.

(v) A very fundamental question, going far beyond economic institu-

---

[1] One may comment that probably the U.S. and the U.K. are the most mature economies among the western countries. Interestingly enough, however, continental Europe used to have the same low savings rate as the U.K. and the U.S. for a long time, but after 1950 showed a remarkable increase.

tions, is of course the one about a possible widening of democracy in our sense. It is not within the scope of this essay to make any speculations on this important subject.

6. Certainly the "free" economies also have to face questions.

(i) Has the public sector the correct size? In the United States important commentators have made the point that it is too small in that country and that recently some public tasks have been neglected.

Even if in European countries the question does not seem to be a controversial issue, the related question of how further to restrict the privileges of some forms of private income or capital still is one under discussion. There is an interesting argument about the possibility of restricting consumption financed out of capital gains, introduced by Nicholas Kaldor's book on an expenditure tax. Possible restrictions on the income paid to directors are discussed and the case for higher inheritance taxes has not been decided upon. The impression of a certain stagnation in the reforms in this field is due not so much to general satisfaction about the present state of affairs as it is to the fact that progressive political parties are re-thinking their programs.

(ii) There is not much debate in western countries about restricting the freedom of decisions of managers about their production programs. Rather there is an increasing interest on the side of management for general economic forecasts and market analysis to help them in their decisions.

(iii) Accordingly the case for some more planning is a living issue in the west. One government after the other feels it has to do something in this field. The most recent example is Belgium, with a possibility for Germany to follow. In Asian countries planning is generally accepted; only the methods differ. The borderline European and Asian country, Turkey, has just established a planning agency. Latin American countries are one after the other engaging in some planning. There is a wide variation in the degree of detail planned and the time has come to discuss in a more precise way which degree of detail is the most appropriate. The outcome of such a discussion may also have its value for the communist countries.

(iv) Price formation is an issue of discussion in the west mainly when the general price level is at stake: should not governments have more instruments to counteract inflationary price rises, especially of the cost-push type? The existing situation is unsatisfactory. The use of only monetary and financial means contains the danger of creating unemployment before the price level goes down. Wage control as an indirect means of controlling prices is not accepted. International integration in order to strengthen competition may give some help in small countries, but does not solve the problem for larger countries. It may therefore be that after all some new form of price setting is necessary.

(v) There is a continued pressure in western countries to facilitate the access to education for larger groups of the population. Some of the proposals are going into the direction of the communist solution, namely to pay a wage to the student. Other proposals are more traditional.

(vi) Industrial democracy is an unsolved question too. The attempts so far made in Western Europe differ from country to country. None is very satisfactory.

7. The picture given shows that communist as well as "free" countries have to solve some problems and that there may be further tendencies to a converging movement. This is true particularly for the main question about the degree of decentralization in production decisions and planning. It is to some extent also true for the process of price formation. It is less clear with regard to the formal side of property, but a distinction between formal property and the real situation must be made. As already observed, both the income from property and the freedom of decision with regard to its use have been strongly reduced in the west and the process may continue.

It is interesting to add a more theoretical analysis to the factual description already attempted. What does economic science have to tell us about the probability of a further convergency of the organization patterns? It is evident that economic science can only tell us something about the subject in so far as economic forces will determine the movements. Clearly in the past other than economic forces have been at work. Nevertheless, would it be denied that economic considerations are important both to communists and, let us say, to Americans?

The chapter of economic science we may first consult is welfare economics. In principle, it tells us about the conditions which the optimum pattern of organization of society has to fulfill. Its contents have long been considered a defense of the free enterprise system, but wrongly so. It is true that welfare economics show that uniform prices (i.e., absence of price discrimination) are among the conditions for maximum welfare. But these can be established just as well by a system of government-controlled pricing as by competitive markets.

Another proposition of welfare economics is that prices should be equal to marginal costs. This statement implies that for the activities characterized by high fixed costs and technical surplus capacity private enterprise cannot be the system leading to maximum welfare, unless two-part pricing be applied for these activities.[2] Even in the case where all enterprises in these branches of activity would apply two-part pricing the question might arise whether or not a more efficient administration of this system could be obtained if these enterprises were combined. This combination, in turn, in order not to degenerate into a super-monopoly should be in

---

[2] J. Tinbergen, "The Theory of the Optimum Regime," *Selected Papers* (Amsterdam, 1959), p. 264.

public hands. Socialization may be the best solution therefore for all the activities concerned.

Similar remarks are valid with regard to activities showing external effects. It can be shown, on the basis of welfare economics, that activities of this kind should be carried out by integrated units; integrated, that is, with the producers or consumers whose wellbeing is affected by the external effects. Socialization may again be a solution.

In concrete terms, the most important activities falling under these two categories are about the same as those already socialized in Western European countries, namely public utilities, rail and air transportation, highway construction and education. Possibly also steel and coal should be added and perhaps other types of transportation.

A further subject relevant to welfare economics is taxes. Two principles are important: first, that there must be some form of income redistribution and second, that income tax is not the optimal way of doing so. The redistribution taxes should approach as much as possible the lump-sum type, i.e., the type not taxing marginal income. Wealth taxes are perhaps the nearest example we know today.

All this points to the desirability of some sort of a mixed system, as far as property is concerned, and to a tax system which may hit personal wealth more than it now does in the west. It also points in the direction of admitting more decentralization with regard to the activities showing constant or increasing costs, i.e., generally for industries where small units are justified, as the communist countries may discover in the future.

8. Reference to another chapter (or chapters) of economics may be needed, in order to answer the following questions. What element of truth is there in the contention sometimes made that there is no optimum in the middle, but rather a tendency for optima to be at the extremes?

This opinion is sometimes illustrated by the argument that "once you start to deviate from market price formation you have to regulate more and more until the whole economy is regulated." Is this illustration relevant to our subject and would it, in a general way, disprove the assumption of an optimum somewhere halfway? The alleged tendency to divergency rather than convergency can no doubt be observed in some cases of war economy regulations. If you start rationing and price control in some markets you will soon find it necessary to regulate other markets too. The argument does not necessarily apply to other types of intervention, however. An interesting example to the contrary can be found in business cycle policy. Here it is generally accepted that if you regulate the total flow of demand by appropriate instruments—e.g., financial and monetary policy—you may then leave most markets to themselves. You can, in addition, select a few markets showing characteristics of instability, which may be controlled without the necessity for controlling other markets.

Those to be controlled are the ones showing long production lags or a long life of the products.

In the same manner the ownership of the means of production is not characterized as such by a tendency to spread. In Western Europe there exists a public sector of a certain size which has maintained itself for years without making it necessary to expand it rapidly in order to preserve some equilibrium. If in the U.S.S.R. private business has virtually vanished it is because it was discriminated against on ideological grounds and, in the initial period, for reasons of political power.

In the case of planning a similar position can be maintained. Planning the main elements of the economy does not necessarily imply the need for detailed planning.

It cannot be argued therefore that there is an inherent tendency for economic regimes to move to the extremes. Our theoretical reconnaissance therefore seems to support rather than to undermine the views derived from observation. No doubt the optimum organization of the economy will differ from country to country and from period to period. It is also hardly conceivable that we will soon be able to indicate precisely where the optimum lies, or even to say whether "east and west" will actually "meet" in their attempts to find the "welfare summit."

9. This essay may be concluded with a few remarks about the "non-committed" countries, that is non-committed to one of the two economic systems at the extremes. Being underdeveloped countries at the same time, they still have a significant number of feudal elements. They are less subject to preconceived ideas about the economic system. If the state sector plays an important role in some of them it is because the necessary initiative was first taken in this rather than in the private sector (Turkey, India).

This group of countries is now facing some very urgent economic needs, partly as a consequence of increasing contacts with the outside world, partly because they have only recently become independent states. The most pressing need is the one for a higher level of production. Another need is to live under a system of stabler prices. Several secondary aims of policy can be derived from these primary ones, such as the full use of resources, an increase in investment levels and a diversification of their production pattern.

Because of the presence, in today's world, of the two major systems the underdeveloped countries are looking to both in order to learn from them. They are above all interested in rapid growth and less in such issues as parliamentary democracy, since they have hardly ever had it. The communist example impresses them greatly. Planning is in high esteem. State initiative does take up part of the tasks neglected by private initiative. The willingness to interfere with price formation is understandable since they are often depending on typical unstable markets. Conditions seem favorable in these countries to try to combine the best elements from communism and free enterprise. These countries therefore may become the experimental ground for economic regimes.

They may, as they sometimes do in technical matters, skip one phase in their development and at once aim at the best solution. They should try to. And we may follow with particular interest the pattern of society that is emerging.

This book may be kept

F